BUSINESS ETHICS

Principles and Practices

DANIEL ALBUQUERQUE

OXFORD

UNIVERSITY PRESS

OXFORD

UNIVERSITY PRESS

YMCA Library Building, Jai Singh Road, New Delhi 110001

Oxford University Press is a department of the University of Oxford.
It furthers the University's objective of excellence in research, scholarship,
and education by publishing worldwide in

Oxford   New York
Auckland   Cape Town   Dar es Salaam   Hong Kong   Karachi
Kuala Lumpur   Madrid   Melbourne   Mexico City   Nairobi
New Delhi   Shanghai   Taipei   Toronto

With offices in
Argentina   Austria   Brazil   Chile   Czech Republic   France   Greece
Guatemala   Hungary   Italy   Japan   Poland   Portugal   Singapore
South Korea   Switzerland   Thailand   Turkey   Ukraine   Vietnam

Oxford is a registered trade mark of Oxford University Press
in the UK and in certain other countries.

Published in India
by Oxford University Press

© Oxford University Press 2010

The moral rights of the author/s have been asserted.

Database right Oxford University Press (maker)

First published 2010

ISBN-13: 978-0-19-569964-7
ISBN-10: 0-19-569964-5

Typeset in Baskerville
by Le Studio Graphique, Gurgaon 122001
Printed in India by Chaman Enterprises, Delhi 110002
and published by Oxford University Press
YMCA Library Building, Jai Singh Road, New Delhi 110001

To
Maria Urban

Foreword

The issue of development of moral leadership for managers and organizations has acquired centre stage in social discussions and intellectual discourses. This has led to the search for a new model of human beings and organizations, beyond the economic dimension. This model has its basis in the sacro-socio-economic (spiritual, social, and economic) view of human beings, organizations, and society. As institutions, corporations have acquired dominance in the lives of people. Hence, there is an expectation that corporations should behave in an ethical manner. For this expectation to be met, a new corporate model based on the triad of profit, social responsibility, and good governance is needed. This triad should be rooted in the sacro-socio-economic view of 'business metaphysics', the underlying principles of business management.

Moral development of an individual implies moving beyond greed to goodness and to Godness. For the development of a 'good society' and 'good corporations', there is a need for moving beyond greed. Dr Daniel Albuquerque, in his path-breaking and thought-inspiring book, *Business Ethics: Principles and Practices*, has shown us this path.

Albuquerque opens his Preface with Kant's challenge, *Sapere Aude*, meaning dare to know. In the context of the book, the phrase means to be intelligent and wise. He implies that business managers—instead of being cynical and complaining about the futility of ethics— must take up the moral challenge of doing business ethically.

The author uses the principle of consciousness of Sri Aurobindo to make managers aware of the moral challenges of business in the contemporary world. He then offers a programme of ethical standards to meet the challenge that is spearheaded by the principle of duty and further adds six principles. Thus, the manager has a breastplate of seven principles to meet his challenges: duty, utility, means and ends, justice, prudence, conscience, and stewardship. The author clearly lays out a taxonomy of decision making for individual, team, and corporation and at social levels, which offers the manager/board of directors a decision-making tool in the most critical times.

The author also directly delves into the practical applications of the principles, policies, and practices in everyday management of the business areas, from manufacturing to marketing, from human resource management to advertising, and from the complex world of finance to workplaces. Concepts and related cases to illustrate complex moral relationships and dilemmas of everyday business management are dealt with deftly.

Today, as moral challenges are taken to a higher organizational level of corporate governance, which is taking precedence in the globalized business world, the burning issues of financial meltdown, market regulation, and insider trading are dealt hands-on with currently active cases in this book. The issue of corporate social responsibility is brought down to earth and would successfully bring a new consciousness among corporations and their internal and external policies.

The author also offers the challenges of the contemporary geopolitical world to human moral existence. He believes that businesses can work for the peace and prosperity of the peoples of the world. Environmental protection and sustainability are the survival issues of mankind. Arms trade, the biggest business in the world, and poverty, the worst of human moral degradations, are dealt with great sensitivity and poignancy. The values of democracy, peace, and non-discrimination of genders are issues that will never be solved, but the author has put them in a compelling moral perspective.

This book is an original contribution in the field of business ethics. The uniqueness of the book lies in the fresh insights from both Western and Eastern perspectives on ethics. The author has taken the omega-circle approach to the study of business ethics. This approach has roots in the *syadvad* (multiple perspectives) philosophy, wherein reality is viewed in many different ways to arrive at an integrative and balanced solution.

The book has five parts, and each part consists of four chapters. Both the book and the chapters are set to context with introductions. Apart from the main case study in each chapter, every concept is illustrated with a mini case. These are followed by a fund of questions that will spur even the most unwilling student to think about the subject. This methodology is quite unique and would help students and practitioners in internalization and practice of ideas. The chapter-end 'management mantras' are delightfully inspirational.

The organization of the book is a singular achievement for the author. This book is indeed an important contribution to business metaphysics as well as its practice in day-to-day managerial and organizational contexts. Business schools will find it extremely useful for a course on business ethics, as it fulfils admirably the criteria of syllabus on the subject and related themes such as corporate governance. Corporate managers would find a treasure trove of ideas to improve the ethical climate of their organizations. I wish all the students, executives, managers, and others an enchanting and rewarding experience.

Dr Subhash Sharma
Dean
Indian Business Academy (IBA)
Bangalore and Greater Noida

Preface

Two things fill the mind with ever-increasing admiration and awe, the oftener and more steadily we reflect on them: the starry heavens above and the moral law within.

—Immanuel Kant

Sapere Aude! Have courage to use your own reason. Thus challenged Immanuel Kant, the German philosopher, in his essay *On Enlightenment,* which led the human civilization to the 'Age of Reason'. It not only became a motto of universities and centres of learning, but also a slogan of the modern age. Knowledge enlightened mankind as never before, and science and technology were reaped as its fruits. The human sciences were developed to know human beings better, just as the physical sciences were developed to understand the laws of nature better. Knowledge increased our consciousness about ourselves and our behaviour in relationship to others. This body of knowledge or science is ethics. Ethics consists of knowledge derived from our moral experiences, from our right and wrong behaviour. Thus, while to gain knowledge and put it to use for human development became an admirable goal, knowing oneself became the greatest challenge.

Nothing can be taught! The challenge to know oneself was met by Sri Aurobindo, the modern sage of India who advocated the principle of consciousness, the force that underlies all that exists. It is a dynamic principle that embodies reason, the faculty of learning that is activated only if the person wills it to be so. Hence, he declared: 'Nothing can be taught, but everything can be learnt.' In other words, the power to know lies within us like a hidden treasure; only if we will to know, we will become conscious of it and discover it for ourselves.

ABOUT THE BOOK

This book has been written for postgraduate students of business management and business administration. Management executives on training, instructors, and students of development programmes will also benefit from this book.

This book deals with business ethics and embodies human reasoning with heightened consciousness about the contemporary world. To make informed decisions and develop moral leadership is the aim of this work. It is to be achieved through a thorough training by putting management students, trainees, or professionals on a project.

The global financial crisis of 2008 has clearly shown that business management is abjectly bereft of moral leadership. The emphasis in this book is on training and not teaching, on learning rather than being taught. The goal of training is to achieve moral consciousness and proficiency in professional duty. The armchair or classroom debate on whether ethics can be taught has gone on for too long, and must be immediately dispensed with if people have to repose their confidence in business again.

Pedagogy

The book offers a rich bouquet of information that includes 20 major cases, 90 mini cases, and 25 inspirational stories for students of business management.

All concepts discussed are analysed and are supported by mini cases within the chapter. Full length cases are provided at the end of each chapter to illustrate all the nuances dealt within.

In-depth questions aid to evaluate and help formulate one's own perspectives. The discussion questions are pedagogical guides to case analysis, moral reasoning, and drawing of conclusions.

Ethics development programme in each chapter provides the actual training in ethical practices. It includes sections on games and quizzes aimed at helping the student to develop the habit of practising ethics and inculcating morals-based judgment.

Each chapter concludes with an apt 'management mantra' that sums up the theme of that chapter.

CONTENTS AND STRUCTURE

This book is divided into five parts, consisting of four chapters each.

An overview of the contents is provided below.

Part I introduces the conceptual foundations and theories of ethics as applied to business management and setting up of moral standards, and a description of decision-making processes.

Chapter 1 deals with the meaning, definition, and scope of ethics as a discipline and its understanding in relationship to law. It also demonstrates learning of moral values in real-life business situations.

Chapter 2 provides a global perspective to the study of ethics by trying to understand Eastern and Western ethical practices to enable us to become knowledgeable and appreciate each other's cultural and social spheres. It tries to show that business may be conducted globally, responsibly, and in harmony despite cultural differences and clashes.

Chapter 3 caters to the study of the philosophy of business. The philosophies that rule the world and also rule businesses, such as socialism, capitalism, etc., give rise to several questions: What philosophies are relevant today and how to improve on them? From local to global, which business strategies succeed? How are people central to businesses? An attempt has been made to answer these and other questions in this chapter.

Chapter 4 provides an elaborate taxonomy of the processes of decision making from individual, team, corporate, and social levels. There are seven standards of moral reasoning:

duty, utility, means and ends, justice, prudence, conscience, and stewardship. Arguments forwarded from any one of these standards give typical sets of moral reasoning with conclusions. It also has a methodology to analyze any case. Hence, for all the technical solutions of moral reasoning or ethical judgments, one must refer to this chapter. It provides the litmus test, as it were.

Part II deals with the basic business disciplines of manufacturing, marketing, advertising, and finance and the application of ethical standards to them.

Chapter 5 presents the consumer as the ultimate stakeholder: Ours is a consumer-driven society where the manufacturer is the provider. The relationship between the former and the latter constitutes a unique ethical connection. This is expressed by the duties of the manufacturer and the rights of the consumer.

Chapter 6 deals with the market, which is the place where goods compete to attract and capture the consumer. Marketers employ strategies not only to sell the goods but also to keep the customers as loyal as possible. Problems arise in the adoption and application of such strategies. The fundamental question that we have dealt with here is: What are the marketer's imperatives?

Chapter 7 deals with the age of communication in which the marketer–consumer interaction takes place through the medium of advertising. In essence, advertisements are promises. The questions this chapter deals with are: How serious are these promises? Do businesses keep their promises?

Chapter 8 tackles ethics in the world of finance, where managing money is the core of any business, and mismanaging it is easy. If the history of mankind may be described as a history of war, then that of business may be described in terms of financial scams. In this chapter, both individual as well as institutional responsibilities are discussed.

Part III deals with ethics in the workplace. The workplace is where people come together with the purpose to work and earn their livelihoods. Workplace is a defining place of ethics, for here various relationships are formed. Each workplace develops its own ethos. How can managers be leaders of their teams? How can they exercise moral leadership? Questions such as these are discussed in this part. The moral leadership is possible only if it is practised in day-to-day and mundane matters.

Chapter 9 introduces the theory that workers are the most important link in the chain of modern economy which consists of resources, entrepreneurs, government, laws, capital, production, and society. The economy is thus worker centric and the worker is entitled to his/her rights and is obliged to perform duties.

Chapter 10 further propounds the theory that individuals, unlike the machines of production, are people who have intellect and will and must be treated with respect. Their privacy, consent, health, human dignity, and family concerns are paramount for the employer.

Chapter 11 introduces the concept of the contemporary worker, who is highly conscious about current issues, sensitive to injustice, mindful of conflicts, and knows where he/she stands vis-à-vis the employer. This chapter deals with abuse of power by the management, whistleblowing, conflict of interest, bribe, etc. The pivotal issue is about transparency in organizations.

Chapter 12 discusses various on-the-job problems. However lofty the ideals of an organization, its real test lies in how it solves the everyday problems of its employees. These problems range from discrimination based on caste, creed, and colour to gender and job reservations.

Part IV deals with the life of a corporation in a world that is analysed through various aspects, both local and global. Corporate social responsibility gets special treatment and the burning issues of financial meltdown, market regulation, and insider trading are dealt hands-on with currently active cases. The issue of corporate social responsibility is dealt with in a down-to-earth manner and would successfully bring a new consciousness among corporations, both to their internal as well as external policies. The moral challenges are taken to a higher organizational level of corporate governance, which is taking precedence in the globalized business world.

Chapter 13 explains that corporations are no longer an entity of curiosity but part and parcel of modern life. As legal entities in and of society they must work within the norms of society. Just as it is expected of an individual to be responsible for self, so too are corporations expected to behave responsibly and hence arises the need for corporate governance. This consists of self-regulation, and the corporation is expected to be a good member of society.

Chapter 14 deals with the institutionalization of corporate governance, which consists of creation of codes to adopt best practices in the interest of the shareholders and the society at large. It is expected of corporations to add value to the shareholders and not deprive them of their investments through mismanagement and misadventures.

Chapter 15 covers the concept of corporate social responsibility. Since the corporation depends for its existence on society, it owes a great deal to it. Not just good citizenship but leadership defines it. Corporations are increasingly conscious about this fact and are taking steps to assume morally binding leadership roles in society.

Chapter 16 explores the geopolitical world and examines how corporations have succeeded where nations have failed in crossing boundaries. However, there are serious questions about economic justice and the fate of the poor, who are the majority in the world. This chapter deals with the ethical dilemma of whether corporations should serve the poor or work for profit?

Part V deals with the contemporary challenges to business: the geopolitical world and human moral existence. Businesses can work for the peace and prosperity of the peoples of the world. Environmental protection and sustainability are the survival issues for mankind today. Arms trade is the biggest business in the world that destroys normal business, and poverty the worst of human moral degradations. Values of democracy, peace, and non-discrimination of genders are issues of compelling moral perspective. It is a world where managers get to demonstrate moral leadership.

Chapter 17 discusses the various challenges of environment. The environmental problems are serious and businesses bear major responsibility for the present state of affairs. However, they can take up the challenges and turn them into sustainable opportunities.

Chapter 18 tackles the problems of the cyber age. It is an age that seemed like only a fiction till some years ago. The benefits of technology have been felt all over the world. However, technological progress has raised issues such as privacy, data theft, intellectual property rights, etc., in its wake.

Chapter 19 raises the issue of global conflicts. To understand global business, one must be aware of the reality of conflict, militarization and terrorism, and how all of these are related to businesses and international relationships.

Chapter 20 broaches several unresolved problems that exist in our highly complex and differentiated world. These range from the basic problems of food, shelter, and clothing to human rights and animal rights. What solutions can businesses offer to alleviate human suffering and usher in progress? The answer lies in the moral leadership that corporations must show to face these challenges.

ACKNOWLEDGEMENTS

The intellectual capital investment of this book consists of

- Literature research from books, periodicals, newspapers and weeklies
- Electronic media, both the Internet as well as TV reportages
- Vast background of academic classes, seminars, discussions, conferences, and peer appraisals

All the authors and the resources used in any form have been duly acknowledged and documented. The references to electronic media, if not specifically mentioned, then to be taken as retrieved within the period of April 2008 to April 2009.

Special acknowledgements are due to the following agencies and people:

- Oxford University Press, Delhi, the publishers
- Goa Institute of Management, Ribander, Goa, for the use of the library
- Fr Romualdo De Souza S.J., founder and former director of Goa Institute of Management
- Mr P.F.X. de Lima, Director, Goa Institute of Management
- Dr Subhash Sharma, Dean, Indian Business Academy (IBA), Delhi/Bangalore for the Introduction and being a source of inspiration
- Dr Nikolaus Knoepffler and Dr Peter Kunzmann, World Ethics Center, University of Jena, Germany
- Dr Wilhelm Baumgartner and Late Dr Franz Wiedmann, University of Wuerzburg, Germany
- Mrs Freeda Meiselbach e Albuquerque, for being my sole and soul support

DISCLAIMER

I would like to state that

- Events, reports, places, persons, names, etc. are from the public domain. Thus, for instance, when names, figures, and sequence of events of existing persons in all cases are mentioned, they are from the public domain—print or electronic—which the public already knows and in no way should be interpreted as investigative or referred to as evidence of anything else other than making of an academic point of argument.

- The cases, anecdotes, incidences, etc. are utilized to illustrate a point in question. These have no intention whatsoever to judge, caste aspersions, or formulate an opinion against anyone in any other relation than to study and discuss for purely academic purposes.
- There are some fictitious anecdotes and events that have been referred to as such and no reference to places, persons, and events is intended.

CONCLUSION

The study of ethics, on the one hand, is an exciting quest into the innermost recesses of our behavioural tendencies expressed through our attitudes in relationship to others, and on the other hand, it is a challenging journey into the firmament of a multitudinous and complex social expanse. It is a venture in theory and practice, knowledge and its application. If business be considered an adventure, then its compass is ethics; it is the 'N' (North) on the compass that determines the direction one intends to take. I wish you a great and fruitful adventure, and would be grateful to receive your accounts of experiences and suggestions to improve the quality of this ethical compass. You may contact me at info@seatofwisdom.in.

DANIEL ALBUQUERQUE

To the Instructor

General Guidelines

The knowledge of business administration or management development programmes is best obtained by doing. This book advocates the project method through which it aims to develop moral leadership. The other methods, such as case-based study, classroom learning, self-study in distance learning, etc., are left to the discretion of educational establishments and their faculty or instructors.

Project-based Study

Project-based study is the recommended approach for this book because it directly and immediately results in training. Today, an increasing number of business schools of repute are adopting this method. It is also extremely useful for executives, since they usually have a running project at hand and would be able to integrate this method in their business ethics course.

   This book encourages the reader to practise the theories learnt by taking an active part in the various projects as suggested in the section Ethics Development Programme. A few guidelines on conducting and assessing projects are provided below:

1. Project may be individual or group in any area of preference.
2. It may be integrated with other ongoing projects. For instance, if there is a marketing project going on, then the problems and difficulties of ethical nature, such as relationships, communication, conflict situations, and above all, the decision-making backgrounds and processes, may be made part of the ethics subject.
3. Project workload may be 120 hours, on-project time.
4. The classroom workload may be 30 hours.
5. Evaluation may be (i) ongoing evaluation of the project by the instructor (40%), (ii) project report and its presentation in class (35%), and (iii) lectures/quizzes/ etc. (25%).

Case-based Classroom Study

The case-study method is basically a classroom teaching method. Its advantage is that it helps develop various nuances of a concept in the situation of a story. The student is able to grasp the significance of the application of a certain principle, the processes of decision making, its application, and the consequences. The disadvantage of this method is that the cases and illustrations are tailor-made for a pedagogical objective.

Each full-length case and the various mini cases throughout the book provide insight into various ethics-related issues. Evaluation may be carried out as follows:

1. Ongoing evaluation, particularly the quality of case discussion (30%)
2. Assignment and classroom presentation (50%)
3. Exam/quizzes, etc. (20%)

Game Method

The game method consists of adoption of one of the games as a mode of simulation of actual behaviour and decision making. It lays stress on the strategies adopted by the participants and the consequences derived and experienced. It involves intense experimentation on participants as individuals and groups.

As is instructed in the section Ethics Development Programme, there need to be highly trained instructors and other observers. Constant feedback and analysis is called for. A separate programme needs to be drawn to fix a customized timetable. The participants must be very well informed and must submit their commitment in writing. This is because there may occur several conflicts that cause psychological trauma in the participants. The administrators of the game must take sufficient care to estimate whether they have the wherewithal to deal with this method and will be morally and legally responsible for allowing the experiment.

Assessment must be through continuous observation and feedback on the following criteria:

- Stability of the participants
- Direction of the intended goal
- Quality of communication
- Quality of decisions
- Moral courage

The assessment will be in grades: A, B, or C. If the trend goes below C, the game must be terminated.

Self-Study

The greatest benefit of self-study is that it helps one to be flexible as to when and where to study; its demerit is that one may not study at all.

However, apart from it being recommended for students of distance learning, self-study is also be meant for those students who have to attend some optional courses for improving their general awareness, not necessarily having to go through a classroom evaluation.

Although the book may be read in any order, I suggest that students first read the introduction to each part. The chapter-end 'management mantras' should be read next, as these will get them interested in the topic. Then, subsequent to reading the part chapters, a group discussion on the related current issues and a reflection on the outcome, followed by a short write-up on the same, will be most beneficial.

DANIEL ALBUQUERQUE

Contents

PART THREE

Managers and Workplaces
Managing People in the Organization

The animal is satisfied with a modicum of necessity; the gods are content with their splendors. But man cannot rest permanently until he reaches some highest good. He is the greatest of living beings because he is the most discontented, because he feels most of the pressure of limitations. He alone, perhaps, is capable of being seized by the divine frenzy for a remote ideal.

—Sri Aurobindo

*karmaṇy evādhikāras te mā phaleṣu kadācana
mā karma-phala-hetur bhūr mā te saṅgo 'stv akarmaṇi*

You have a right to perform your prescribed duty, but you are not entitled to the fruits of action. Never consider yourself the cause of the results of your activities, and never be attached to not doing your duty.

—Srimad Bagavad Gita

Part One

Managers and Morals

Setting Ethical Standards

LEADING LIGHTS OF MORAL KNOWLEDGE

SRI AUROBINDO (1872–1950), the prophet of Indian freedom struggle, holistic thinker, educationist, and poet. Nothing can be taught, he held, but everything can be learnt. His synthesis of Eastern and Western thought gives free India an enlightened path. He advocated a harmonious society with diversity of culture. He set the industrious people of Japan as an example for Indians to emulate and create a new work ethic for the development of India.

IMMANUEL KANT (1724–1804), the German philosopher who gave to the world a new metaphysics, the theory of knowledge, and the most comprehensive understanding of moral theory. His advocacy of duty as the principle of moral obligation compares and synthesizes well with the concept of duty in the Gita. His clarion call, *sapere aude*, meaning dare to use reason and be wise, is a challenge to moral behaviour. He advocated the idea of world citizenship.

Setting Ethical Standards

Path to Moral Knowledge

Practical principles are propositions which contain a general determination of the will, having under it several practical rules. They are subjective, or maxims, when the condition is regarded by the subject as valid only for his own will, but are objective, or practical laws, when the condition is recognized as objective, that is, valid for the will of every rational being.

—Immanuel Kant

Physical science will not console me for the ignorance of morality in the time of affliction. But the science of ethics will always console me for the ignorance of the physical sciences.

—Blaise Pascal

ETHICS—THE SPIRIT OF THE TIMES

In his work entitled *The God Delusion*, the evolutionary theorist Richard Dawkins (2006) introduces the German word *zeitgeist* (*zeit*—time, *geist*—spirit), which means 'the spirit of the times'. The book illustrates the moral evolution of man in society. The need to develop a collective action to ensure the basic needs of survival, shelter, and food led to a social consensus on what values were acceptable and what were not. These were codified and adhered to by society. Families imbibed the practice of these codes in their members, which helped them live a harmonious social existence. Failure to live by these codes invited reprimand and even punitive action.

As times changed, so did the codes. There was a time when women were considered mere chattel or property of their husbands, to the extent that in India the wife forfeited her right to live when her husband died. She had to immolate herself on the funeral pyre of her husband. That practice, called *sati*, has now been abolished. If sati is carried out, the law charges the accomplices with murder. Slavery, child labour, and cruelty to animals, which were previously not considered as morally offensive, are now not only looked upon as morally wrong, but also carry severe legal penalties. This

goes to show that there is a moral evolution in society. Society is becoming morally more sensitive, rational, and caring than before.

Today's diverse and highly sophisticated world is populated with innumerable professions such as medicine, law, engineering, technology, and business. Society extends its codification specific to all professions, and business is no exception. Business has now become so diverse and complex that society is wary of business serving it in the best possible manner. Therefore, business ethics comes into play. Society expects business managers to be morally accountable for their actions. Previously, society considered business to be a profession that was conducted purely for profit. Today, society expects good governance, citizenship, and social responsibility from business corporations.

Genesis of Ethics

Society in the past, in its collective wisdom, formed rules and regulations, just as today's associations, clubs, political parties, and business corporations form constitutions with bylaws to govern their members. It developed its own ethos or culture, a sum total of its practices that formed into customs and became tradition. A scientific study of the above is called ethics, which studies not only the code but also its rationale. It seeks to know the underlying principles of human action in society. The study of ethics helps us understand our social nature better. It helps us solve the problems of conflict and form new ways and strategies to improve our social life.

MORAL NATURE

Moral status determines the place of an individual in society. Each individual claims a moral right within society. Born within the bounds of society, he/she may rightfully claim its membership and privileges and, in return, practise and promote all the customs (this is what moral literally implies) and traditions. Thus, actions are founded on the moral status that is conferred on an individual by society. All of his/her actions, therefore, must be reasonably explained within the confines of moral obligations. He/she not only has the moral right to be a member of society but also has an obligation that is morally binding towards it.

We have seen that society has a collective mind that reasons the moral codes its members must practise. At the same time, an individual who claims his/her moral rights is also able to submit to reason all his/her actions in accordance with the social codes of conduct. Moral development or moral reasoning is our subject matter in the four chapters of the first part of this book.

MORAL REASONING

The essence of moral reasoning consists of proceeding from a given general principle to analysing the morality or right or wrong of an individual human action. This kind of reasoning process, from the general to the particular, is called deductive logic. It is qualitative in nature and, hence, any relativization or quantification causes problems. However, students of ethics, who study the subject as a scientific discipline, cannot dismiss the relative and quantitative aspects in the analysis of their subject. The scientific process is according to an inductive logic that proceeds from individual instances to a general

law, or from particulars to a general principle. When we study ethics as a discipline, we use both the inductive and deductive ways of reasoning.

OBJECTIVES OF PART I

The objective of the first part of the book is to understand ethical concepts—the mental models of our moral experiences—and, from these building blocks, understand some of the existing ethical theories, such as utilitarianism and deontology, upon which certain business models or systems such as capitalism or socialism are built. The concepts, knowledge, and theories of these business models suggest that these are founded on a definite process of reasoning. The objective is to solve ethical problems that arise in the field of business management. Ethical problems are individual moral experiences that are pregnant with the relative aspects in human behaviour and are unique and diverse in their own ways. These bring to conformity the general principles of ethics in order to meet the standards that society has set for its individuals. For a successful attempt at ethical reasoning, we need deductive as well as inductive or qualitative and quantitative reasoning. Once the student is equipped with both these processes, he/she would be able to analyse in his/her managerial career the ethical choices to be made and the moral dilemmas to be faced intelligibly, justly, and prudently.

Consequently, Part I of the book elucidates the fundamental concepts of ethics, their development, and their goal. Chapter 1 deals with the concepts of ethics and morality and their scope. Chapter 2 consists of the development of morality within the given environments or cultures. Chapter 3 consists of the various perspectives that have developed due to the different systems of thought and their applications, and Chapter 4 brings us to the conclusion, given the background and systems of thought on how we think, reason, and decide on moral issues.

We gain moral knowledge through our own experiences of moral behaviour and that of others. These experiences generate in us a fund of ideas that we associate, mould, and form to shape our

---

Ethical Imperative

Scene I	Home	Parent to child	Don't argue, listen!
Scene II	Classroom	Teacher to pupil	Don't argue, understand!
Scene III	Barrack	Colonel to Lt Colonel	Don't argue, obey!
Scene IV	Shopfloor	Supervisor to worker	Don't argue, work!
Scene V	Office	Manager to assistant	Don't argue, answer!
Scene VI	Government office	Finance minister to under-secretary	Don't argue, comply!

Food for thought

Does morality mean blind obedience?
Is freedom against moral action?
What role does human reasoning play in the making of ethical choices?

Note: An adaptation of Kant's example from his essay *On Enlightenment* (1784) is presented here to bring home the point of moral imperatives. However, it is false to believe that Kant proposed blind obedience. His works symbolize human freedom.

---

lives. We make critical decisions through which we may turn our lives around and change ourselves and others as well. The decisions we make not only affect us, but if we are responsible for others, which as managers we are, then our decisions affect others too. Thus, moral decisions, irrespective of the profession, affect both the service providers as well as the clients.

CONCLUSION

We observe that in nature, things come into being, develop and grow, and find a natural end. We also observe that each of these beings live in an environment suitable to its nature. The social-ethical environment is to us what the water is to fish. It is our ethos and it makes us ethical. Thus, our social nature is ethical. Come then, let us explore our ethical environment, where business management has its place too.

The sentiment expressed by Blaise Pascal, at the mast of the opening page of this part, leads us to the inner nature of man. It behoves one to be conscious of one's acts within the living environment and to make wise choices. Pascal was a great intellectual and one of the pioneers of modern mathematics. It is most admirable to promote science and advance the cause of human development. The happiness that we seek comes from the values that we seek, which help us to achieve those scientific goals. Philosopher Immanuel Kant observes that the principles on which these values are based are 'valid for the will of every rational being'.

Ethics: Meaning, Definition, and Scope

There are no moral phenomena at all, but only a moral interpretation of phenomena.

—Friedrich Nietzsche

True ethics is Dharma, the right fulfillment and working of the higher nature, and right action should have right motive, should be its own justification and not go on the crutches of greed and fear.

—Sri Aurobindo

LEARNING OBJECTIVES

After studying this chapter, you will be able to

> Distinguish between ethics and morals
> Define business ethics within the confines of ethics
> Understand the nature of ethics as moral value
> Differentiate between law and ethics

INTRODUCTION

The study of ethics is a systematic science. Its scope encompasses all human relationships in a society. Ethical behaviour in business is an economic relationship with the people within a society. Hence, it is also called political economy. Business ethics deals with the study of the problems arising in the relationship between the field of business and its management. In this chapter, we will deal exclusively with the concept of ethics. A concept is a mental model or a mental construct. With the mental model of ethics, we can understand the various other concepts that go into its making. Once the complex structure of this model is ready, we can execute it just the way architectural engineers execute blueprints. The task of business ethics is to enable managers to execute these mental models consistently, contingent on business management situations. The consistency must be such that it becomes a universal principle or a point of reference for right or wrong business actions.

ETHICS AND MORALS

Let us first try to learn the key terms 'ethics' and 'morals'. Note the linguistic use of the terms—they seem as if they are in the plural form, just as 'economics' or 'politics', but we treat them as singular. Generally, ethics and morals are used as synonyms. There is nothing wrong in such a usage, for after all, the meanings of all words depend on their common usage. However, in formal study, we need to understand the meaning of the terms in a qualified way so as to make our subject of study precise and well defined.

Meaning

The terms 'ethics' and 'morals' are etymologically, that is, from their very roots or terms, different. The word moral(s) is derived from the Latin root *moralis*, which implies custom. In other words, it refers to a behaviour that is accepted or rejected due to an accepted social custom. The word ethics stems from the Greek word *ethike*, which attributes to a social environment, referred to as ethos or social milieu. This latter meaning embraces much more than mere custom. It refers to everything that is part and parcel of society and not just what is allowed or forbidden.

Another point of difference between the two refers to their usage in ordinary language. For instance, a lawyer defending an alleged rapist would accuse the victim as 'morally fallen' and not as 'ethically fallen'. On the other hand, a committee that is formed to probe the behaviour of the members of Parliament would be called 'ethics committee', not 'moral committee'. The meaning of the word is in its usage. Thus, both these terms have their unique characteristics.

Usage

However, the terms are intrinsically *not* different. Both of them refer to the same reality of human actions, which may be characterized as morally or ethically positive or negative as the case may be. It may be true that the terms (ethics and morals) sound different but they refer to the same social reality wherein a certain body of accepted norms forms a code of conduct in society. The actions of the members are described as 'moral' or 'ethical' depending on the linguistic nuances of the meaning in a particular case as well as on the conventional use of the terms. It is in the use of the words in a given context that the meaning becomes clear.

In academic usage, however, moral behaviour refers to a concrete behaviour such as showing respect to elders. Ethics, on the other hand, is used to mean a discipline or a systematic study of moral behaviour such as justice. People's behaviour in a society can be morally characterized in their day-to-day actions. It is in the classroom that we analyse the ethical significance of these actions.

These terms are generally interchanged with one and the same meaning, that is, to determine whether some human action is right or wrong. They deal with the application of a socially accepted code of conduct. This conduct may be termed as either moral conduct or ethical conduct.

EVOLUTION OF ETHICS

Social conduct has evolved along with the evolution of society. When your elders tell you 'Do not cheat', they are referring to a social code of conduct. Social conduct has developed in society over hundreds of years. The codes of conduct have been passed down from generation to generation, and there is a pattern to the evolution of such codes. Acceptable behaviour is promoted and elevated as a social value, and unacceptable behaviour is rejected and condemned. In ancient India, there was no moral problem with the custom of *sati*—immolating the wife on the funeral pyre of the deceased husband. But society has evolved humanely and has condemned the act as unacceptable and morally reprehensible.

The laws of a country are based on the customs or moral codes of its society. Penalties are prescribed for bad actions—actions that contradict the established laws. The laws are a measure against those people who cross the limits of the code of social conduct, and ensure that good citizens are protected from the negative consequences of the law-breakers.

The object of the social codes of conduct is to maintain, promote, and elevate harmonious relationships. 'Honour your parents' is one such code. It maintains a peaceful relationship between parents and children and promotes respect for each other in the family. Because of its salutary effects, it is considered as one of the fundamental values to be cultivated.

CLASSIFICATION OF ETHICS

To have a clear picture of the structure of the concept of ethics, the above discussion can be brought under three headings: normative ethics, applied ethics, and meta-ethics (see Fig. 1.1).

Normative ethics Norms or standards are also known as values or codes. Norms set clear guidelines for social interaction in a community. Normative ethics is a subject of study wherein students study moral standards. These moral standards can be applied

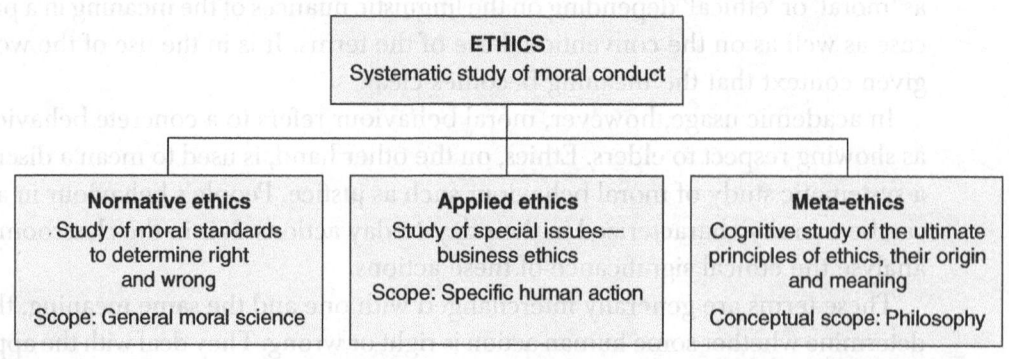

Fig. 1.1 Classification of ethics

to human actions to judge their moral character, that is, whether they are right or wrong. Examples of some of the moral standards are utility, duty, conscience, use of right means for right ends, justice, prudence, and stewardship. Just as there are several standards to measure distance, such as meter, yard, mile, etc., so also there are several standards to judge an action right or wrong. We shall study more about these standards in the chapters that follow.

Applied ethics Business ethics comes under the classification of applied ethics because it concerns itself with the special application of ethics to problems relating to a definite field of human relationships. Normative standards of moral judgment are applied by business managers to the business decisions they take. The ethical element is part and parcel of the integral process of decision making on a business management problem. Business ethics, therefore, deals with the application of normative standards to specific business experiences. The study of business ethics is as essential for a businessman as the study of professional norms for a medical practitioner. We expect a doctor to diagnose correctly so that the right medication is given. There are chances that he could diagnose a simple ailment but report it as a serious one in order to exploit the patient financially. Likewise, a client places trust on a businessman for a transaction and hopes that the latter does not deceive. Thus, applied ethics is strictly professional ethics.

Meta-ethics The Greek word *meta* stands for beyond. Thus, meta-ethics literally means beyond ethics, suggesting an in-depth study of the discipline. In other words, it is a scientific study of the concepts of ethics in itself. You may not find these concepts practical, because nowhere in the world will you find a perfect human being who is perfectly good, perfectly happy, perfectly duty-bound, and so on. These are abstract ideas that are considered as supra-standards, and are concepts that can be conceived as perfectly as perfection itself. We study these concepts as ultimate principles—principles such as good and evil, right and wrong. We study them just the way we study theoretical physics when dealing with the principles of gravitation, energy, or light. The character of these principles is universal in nature. For instance, if we handle 'duty' as an ethical principle, it would be applicable as a standard of ethical judgment in all the cases of duty. Hence, meta-ethics is a study of the general principles that govern right and wrong human actions.

APPLICATION

The relevance of ethics is in its application. Just as when we study the theory of relativity in physics, we ensure that the laws or principles of relativity are applied to the factors and elements being considered, so too in our study of ethics, the universal principles have to be applied to individual contexts and situations. We have to abandon the absolutism of universal principles. For instance, killing a man is wrong. But we approve the killing of the enemy in a war and the government honours the act with medals for bravery. This is due to the fact that such an act has served a higher principle, that is, the protection of countrymen. Ethics, in the practical sense, is also known as moral action and is an applied discipline that deals with a particular human action and also assesses to what extent it is compatible with the general principles.

BUSINESS ETHICS

Business ethics concerns itself with adhering to the social principles of the situations in which business takes place. The analysis of this definition leads us to the following discussion.

Business for Profit

It would seem that business ethics does not come within the confines of ethics. As Adam Smith (1779), the father of modern economics says: 'People of the same trade seldom come together, even for merriment and diversion, but the conversation ends in a conspiracy against the public, or in some contrivance to raise prices.' People find mechanisms to generate the highest possible returns when conducting business. No one holds it against a worker for demanding higher wages, or a landlord for increasing the rent. Their actions are not considered illegal or unethical. Profits are the just wages for invested capital and entrepreneurship. Hence, these should not be resented and should be left alone outside the boundaries of ethics. Business is for profit; the just reward for doing business lies in the excess returns received on the investment.

Inspiration: Parental Lesson

Origin of the moral world

'Your visit is enough for me to get well. Why bring a doctor and spend money on his fees?' This was the gentle rebuke of the aged father of A.P.J. Abdul Kalam, the father of Indian missile technology and the former President of India, whenever Kalam visited his house along with a doctor. When his father died at the age of 102, a heart-broken Kalam reflected: 'He was a plain and transparent man. My father pursued the supreme value—the Good.' His mother died soon after. He felt that he should have taken time off from his work and the preoccupation with technology to take care of his old parents. But when he visited a mosque, a quiet reflection there made it clear to him that his parents had, in fact, achieved their highest accomplishment, while he had still a long way to go. 'The next morning,' he writes, 'I was back at Thumba [the space centre situated in Kerala], physically exhausted, emotionally shattered, but determined to fulfil our ambition of flying an Indian rocket motor on foreign soil.'

Questions

1. Are parents, family, and others a good source of moral values?
2. Is ethics all about positive attitude?
3. What do you understand by good?

Source: A.P.J. Abdul Kalam with Arun Tiwari, *Wings of Fire*, pp. 85–86.

Again, as Goethe (1809) said: 'Everything which is properly business, we must carefully separate from life.' This is because business requires definite strategies; life must be led in freedom.

Business with Ethics

No matter how hard one tries, it is impossible to separate life from business. For a businessman, business is life. Mahatma Gandhi (1948) said, 'It is difficult but not impossible to conduct strictly honest business. What is true is that honesty is incompatible with amassing of large fortune.' The business world is an important part of society, as it is concerned with the livelihoods of people. Business activity too is subjected to the code of conduct without any exception. People expect businessmen to possess the same rationality as any other citizen. Therefore, there is no separate business ethics for businessmen, as ethics applies to all the activities of people. Consequently, we have to keep business within the bounds of ethics.

Character of Business

'There are two fools in every market: one asks too little, one asks too much,' so says a Russian proverb. Is there a concept called *balanced profit*? The business in a society reflects its character. Transparency International, in its corruption perception index, gives Finland, Denmark, and New Zealand the first place with 9.4 points. India is way down at 72, with just 3.5 points on a scale of 10. We may gloat over our cultural heritage and religious and ethical glories of the past, but we stand exposed before the world as a corrupt society. Corruption prevails in all walks of life, whether political, social, or economic. If we have to improve our business, we have to improve our business behaviour.

Professional Ethics

The aforementioned discussion may be understood through the following distinctions: ethics and business ethics. We have studied the distinction between normative and practical ethics and have established that business ethics comes under practical ethics and is applied to a particular activity.

Just as a society functions on the social codes of conduct and a country is governed by its constitution, a business is run on corporate codes. In other words, there is a professional code of conduct for any business. These codes keep evolving as other things around evolve and develop. Therefore, not only should business be defined within the confines of ethics, but it should be practised strictly under its own professional code of conduct. This distinction helps to orient the general principles of ethics and business to a particular activity. The principles, however, do not change. For instance, there is a manager who is doing very well in his career because he is both efficient and honest. To his neighbours and friends, he is not only a very successful businessman, but also a very good family man. To a question asked by a journalist on how he divided

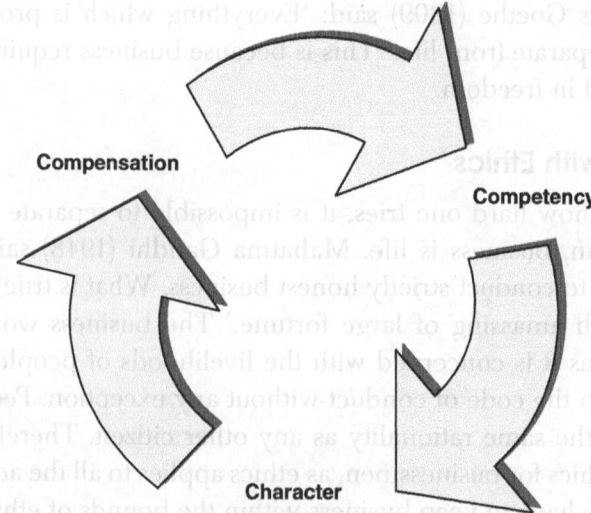

Fig. 1.2   Professional characteristics

his time between his family and business despite his busy schedule, he replied, 'Efficiently.' 'What is the secret of your success?' asked the journalist. He replied, 'Honesty.' The journalist looked inquiringly as if to say, 'Look, business and family are separate.' The businessman said, 'Both efficiency and honesty work equally well at work and at home.' The character of a true professional remains undivided, whether at work or at home. Our roles may change from time to time and from place to place, but the integrity of our character should be maintained.

Business ethics, thus, professionally adheres to a code of conduct that is in accordance with the normative principles. Further, it may be concretely stated that professionals bear the following marked characteristics: (i) competency of educational qualification, (ii) professional skills, and (iii) compensation (salary/remuneration, etc.). See Fig. 1.2.

NATURE OF ETHICS AS MORAL VALUE

Value-free Ethics

It would seem that business is an ethically neutral or value-free activity. In other words, the only value business is concerned with is the monetary value. It is not in the interest of business to mix ethical values. An ancient Arabic wisdom states, 'Live together like brothers and do business like strangers.' Business should be kept free from other social relationships and obligations. The only successful relationship that exists in business is that of a vendor and a customer.

It is also said that 'for the merchant, even honesty is a financial speculation.' Indeed, for a businessman every factor in the business is measured in terms of money. The volatility that we see in the stock market is a clear example of the speculative nature of business, which is directly proportional to the prevailing attitude of the people.

Running on Trust

Successful ethics implies successful business

Jamsetji Tata founded Tata Iron and Steel Company Ltd, popularly known by its acronym TISCO, in 1907. Now it is just Tata Steel. It is one of India's oldest companies. Today, it is India's largest and the sixth largest steel producer in the world. It produces 28 million tonnes of steel, employs 82,700 people, operates in 24 countries of four continents and has a commercial presence in over 50 countries. What is the secret of its corporate success?

Tata Steel is one of the few steel companies in the world that is economic value added (EVA) positive. It was ranked the World's Best Steel Maker for the third time by World Steel Dynamics in its annual listing in February 2006. Tata Steel has been conferred the Prime Minister of India's Trophy for the Best Integrated Steel Plant five times. Regarded globally as a benchmark in corporate social responsibility, Tata Steel's commitment to the community remains the bedrock of its hundred years of sustainability. Its mammoth social outreach programme covers the company-managed city of Jamshedpur and over eight hundred villages in and around its manufacturing and raw materials operations through uplift initiatives in the areas of income generation, health and medical care, education, sports, and relief.

It has been awarded Asia's Most Admired Knowledge Enterprise award in 2003 and 2004.

Questions

1. What is the fundamental moral value of Tata Steel?
2. Has ethics made any difference to the way of doing business?
3. What are the benefits to an ethics-based company?

Source: http://www.tatasteel.com/default.asp.

Further, Adam Smith observes that the baker bakes and distributes bread not because he possesses the virtue of charity, but because he wants to gratify his self-interest, which is to earn his livelihood. An employer rewards an employee for his productivity. Ethics is the last thing on the employer's mind when disbursing the bounty.

Human Relations

In the aforementioned argument, it appears that the more you negate the union of ethical values to business, the greater is the affirmation that it is not a value-free enterprise. All relationships are human relationships. Ethics is another name for human relationships. One may well distinguish the relationship between two siblings and two strangers with many good reasons. But what one is unable to do is to categorize one relationship (between siblings) as human and the other (between strangers) as non-human. It is, in fact, ridiculous to affirm that the relationship between a vendor and a customer is not a human relationship. Business relationship is indeed a type of human relationship.

Further, it is ethically not adverse to have self-interests involved. It becomes unethical when such an activity is an outright exploitation of one's personal interests. Being ethical and unethical is a part of human nature and, therefore, it is the subject of a systematic study called ethics.

Concept of Value-free Ethics

Nowadays, we are familiar with 'sugar-free' soft drinks, 'caffeine-free' coffee, and 'alcohol-free' beer. The concept of 'value-free' business ethics is quite appealing to businessmen. It appears as though it may be pursued devoid of all rules within a social vacuum. The concept of value-free ethics came to economics in a rather ironical fashion. Ludwig von Mises, known as the father of the Austrian School of Economics, proposed the pure theory of economics, stating that economic concepts are a priori, that is, they are not dependent on experience, but are purely virtual concepts. The concept of choice, for instance, is a pure concept. It is immaterial whether one chooses water or wine, but the concept in itself is free of such particular elements. Hence, choice is value-free (*wertfrei*). Applied to ethics, it would mean that we should be able to study the principles of this discipline, such as goodness, truth, justice, honour, etc. in their pure form.

It is obvious that such value-free ethics, when understood in the right sense, leads us to study meta-ethics or the fundamental principles of ethics as a pure science. However, if we are to apply an ethical standard to such a study, it would be called a pure study of values, not value-free ethics.

Ethics as a Principle

We have established that social evolution has developed definite principles of civic behaviour, which have attained the status of principles. By principle, we understand that something proceeds and depends on it for its cause. For instance, when you kick a football, force is the principle that propels it into motion and the ball remains in motion till the force lasts. In other words, the physical world functions strictly according to the laws of physics. It is expected that people also submit their behaviour, both in thoughts and in actions, to these principles. An action is valid as long as it reflects the principle, just as the speed of the moving ball depends on the force it receives.

All moral actions are directed towards their object, the good, which is the principle of all happiness. This is not only the sole purpose of our existence but our co-existence with others as well. We cannot be happy alone; we can only be happy together. The universal idea of the good is applied to individual instances. Individuals are good in their own particular way, and are good in so far as they share the essence of goodness. The universal good is a pure or general idea. It is formed through a process of abstraction of the essence from individuals or particulars (see Fig. 1.3).

Business Ethics as Professional Code

Business ethics is not a pure science but a professional practice, and society expects businessmen to abide by the principles of a civil society, just as it expects professionals from other areas such as medicine, bureaucracy, politics, and sports to do so. Thus, instead of a value-free business ethics, we have a value-loaded or value-based business practice.

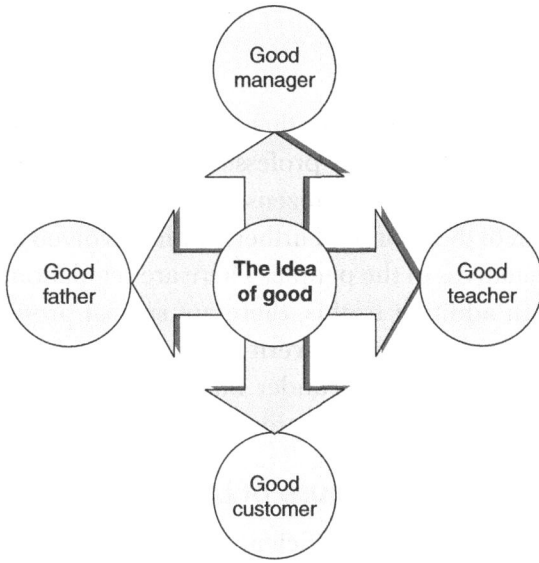

Fig. 1.3   Ethics as a principle

Commitment versus Competency

Goodbye Mr Chips

James Hamilton's *Goodbye Mr Chips*, a heart warming story of a simple school teacher, has become a classic in English literature and has inspired generations of professionals. Arthur Chipping was a simple school teacher at a boys' boarding school at Brookfield. He entered the school service as a young fresher and lived his entire life on the campus.

Chipping was not brilliant. He lacked the talent to teach. He was the butt of jokes for the pupils, as well as the teachers. The headmaster had to reprimand him for not being able to control his class and use his authority. Soon, Chipping earned the nickname Chips.

What redeemed him? He was quiet and shy, but dedicated to his work. Although it was quite hard for him, he performed his task with great dignity and perseverance. He spent all his time preparing for his classes. Nothing ever prevented him from his duty, neither sickness nor adversity. Indeed, even upon the death of his dear wife, he was in his class punctually, as always.

When he retired, he had nowhere to go. But then, the school authorities did not want him to go anywhere because he was not only a part and parcel of the school, but they felt that *he* was the school. He had become the identity of the school. During the war, when many teachers left school to join duty at the front, he returned to the classroom and the school functioned despite the war. His old students and colleagues fell in the war and it grieved him no end. Yet, he would stand before the school assembly every morning and take the roll call of the fallen soldiers to honour them. In his own quiet and simple way, he instilled bravery and dedication in the hearts of the young citizens of his country.

Questions

1. What makes a true professional, commitment or competency?
2. What kind of employee would you prefer, capable or loyal?
3. Do emotional attachment and professionalism go together?

Note: James Hamilton's, *Goodbye Mr Chips* was published in 1934 and first adapted for the screen in 1939. Free ebook available at http://gutenberg.net.au/plusfifty-a-m.html.

LAW VERSUS ETHICS

Adequacy of Law

There is a compelling argument that the law can regulate human behaviour, that the law is sufficient to regulate any professional discipline, and that ethics is not necessary. The law of the land is for the citizens, and the rights of every citizen are enshrined in the constitution of the country. Further, law has evolved through the legislative process of the representatives of the people. There are regulations for running institutions in a civil society. In addition to this, there are special provisions made for the business community through acts that govern all business transactions—whether of individual proprietors or of companies under business law or corporate law. These laws are exhaustive and may be applied precisely in case of disputes.

Ethics as the Principal Cause of Law

The proposition that law is sufficient and that ethics is unnecessary is equivalent to saying that cause is immaterial, but effect is everything. The fundamental assumption is that man is a social animal. Society, a community of people, is a system that functions according to its natural order or its environment, which is also called its ethos.

Just as every other human pursuit originates and grows within the bounds of a society, business also originates and grows in a society. Business is an honourable profession, just the way law, medicine, education, craftsmanship, engineering, and so forth are. Ethics is that civil fabric that holds society together for a common goal, that is, to achieve the common good. This is its essence. The common good is to be achieved through the pursuits or vocation that each and every individual in a society follows. The achievement of each and every member of a society adds to the greater good of the community. Ethics acts as an agent of approval and disapproval of the activities of its members.

Ineffectuality of Ethics

Murali, the manager of a hotel, signs a contract with Seema, a singer, to perform twice a week for the next two months. The rate per performance is Rs 2000. One day, Seema absents herself without proffering any reason. Murali cannot condone this behaviour that has caused him personal anguish and loss in his business. He wants to rescind the contract and demands compensation for the suffered loss.

Solution by law

There is a twofold remedy for Murali: (a) Under the Indian Contract Act (Section 75), Seema has clearly violated her contract. Her employer has the right to rescind her contract. (b) Under the same Act the manager is perfectly within his rights to claim the sustained financial loss.

Conclusion

Ethics is toothless. What would ethics do in such a case when the deed is perpetrated and the damage is done? Nothing at all! Thus, ethical values are just humble pleas for good behaviour, while the law has the power of enforcement behind it. The stipulated punishments are clear deterrents. Moral persuasion is a balm to the conscience that makes one feel good. The law, on the other hand, makes sure that justice is done to the victim and the perpetrator of the fraud or crime is suitably punished.

Business bashing

When business ethics is mentioned, it is assumed that its purpose is to chastise those who are doing business. So now, in the name of ethics, cumbersome laws and regulations have been enacted by the legislature and government machinery, codes by the corporations, directives by the chambers of commerce, recommendations by the non-governmental agencies, and edicts by the religious leaders. These regulations and several other norms now contribute to the burdens of the businessman. It is no wonder that many businessmen see these as the scourge of a businessman!

CONCLUSION

From the above debate, we are able to draw the following conclusions.

First, it is important to know the place a business and its management hold in society. Business is a part of society, and everyone has a stake in it. Hence, it cannot be allowed to do its own will, but it must do the will of the community where it originates and grows. If society dies, business goes down with it.

Second, business ethics guides its practice, as people expect it to be done. The objective of managerial decisions is to promote business and add to the shareholder's value without compromising the interests of any stakeholders in and of society. Practice of good business ethics makes the businessman a thorough professional.

Third, the law is meant for those who trespass on the rights of others. The purpose of the law is to protect the good from the bad. Hence, the law is for those who do evil, to deter them from their activity. The greater the sense of ethical sensibility in a society, the greater is the likelihood of achievement of the common good. Society makes laws through its legislative organs to suit definite regulatory needs. The laws are also repealed when they become obsolete. However, the ethical principle, the good, remains unchanged and the values of justice, equality, prudence, etc. that follow from it also remain unchanged.

Fourth, on the chapter mast we referred to two great philosophers: Frederick Nietzsche—the German philosopher of late 19th century—and Sri Aurobindo. Indeed, as the first one affirms, we do not find morality as a physical entity. We do not see it walking around. Morality is about norms or values that are set by society to be followed uniformly by its members. It is natural that it becomes a matter of debate, discussion, and disagreement as to what constitutes the right behaviour and how to distinguish it from the wrong one. Such a discourse among people on social behaviour leads to various interpretations. Hence, according to the philosopher, there is confusion about morals. We, however, feel that Nietzsche, in order to make this point, rejects the moral experience that we undergo everyday in our lives. Anything that we experience is a result of a thing or an event, both of which belong to the world of phenomenon, the former to the physical and the later to the social.

Sri Aurobindo, on the other hand, alludes to the entire complex moral tradition of India with just a single word, *dharma*. Dharma in Sanskrit implies duty. We often face

the problems of moral choices within society. For instance, we have to choose between leaving the family behind and looking for a job in the city, joining the army or looking after our old parents, cheating a bit in business or suffering loss. Here dharma, the traditional behavioural pattern that society has developed over hundreds of years, guides us in our actions. We are able to make ethical choices based on the precedents and thus discern our duty, which is, what we must choose and do.

Sex and Settlement

Downfall of a great manager

Infosys Technologies is a formidable name to contend with in any part of the IT world, not merely for its prowess as a leader in IT but also as a great corporation with an enviable ethics track record. But records so painstakingly created over a long period of time, with grit and determination, can tumble down with one bad example. As the new millennium approached and the business institutions were worried sick about the Y2K syndrome, Infosys was involved in an unlikely scandal—a sex scandal.

Phaneesh Murthy was one of the directors of Infosys and headed its operations in the US. After having worked for almost a decade in the US, Phaneesh was sued by Reka Maximovich, an employee of the company, on grounds of sexual harassment and unlawful termination of employment. The matter became too embarrassing for the company both abroad and at home. Phaneesh resolutely refuted the charges, but then resigned. The tipping point came when the company agreed to make an out of court settlement for $ 3 million. Battered by the law, the company learned its moral lessons and put in stricter codes of conduct for its employees.

Phaneesh, the brilliant professional from the reputed Indian Institute of Management (IIM), Ahmedabad, weathered the storm and got on with his life. He became

Contd

Box Contd

the CEO of iGate, which had acquired and merged with Quintant of Bangalore. A certain Jeniffer Griffith filed a suit for sexual harassment against him for a sum of $ 8 million, which again went for an out of court settlement, for a lesser amount.

Questions

1. Is it true that law is sufficient and ethics is not required?

2. Does being a competent professional ensure good ethics?
3. Is the company's ethics record a dependable intangible asset?
4. Is there a need to train professionals in ethical behaviour?

Source: http://timesofindia.indiatimes.com/articleshow/935032.cms and http://www.rediff.com/money/2003/jul/30igate.htm, accessed on 5 April 2008.

SUMMARY

- The terms 'morals' and 'ethics' are used synonymously.
- Ethics is a systematic discipline with basic assumptions and well-grounded theories.
- Business ethics is applied ethics, a system of professional ethics developed for business executives to help in decision making.
- We learn our basic ethical values from our parents, educational institutions, and society.
- Industrial establishments like the Tata Steel inspire business students in their profession to be responsible to society.
- The ethical principles are worth upholding even in extreme adversity.

KEY TERMS

Applied ethics   Application of ethical principles to a particular problem, e.g., business ethics.

Business ethics   Form of professional ethics.

Ethics   Academic discipline, also sometimes applied to individual actions.

Good   The object of ethics/morals.

Mental model   A construct of concepts; may be simple or complex.

Meta-ethics   Study of pure concepts or principles of ethics.

Morals   Human action that may be judged as good or bad, ethical or unethical.

Particular   Individual instance where a universal idea such as the good is applied.

Principle   A basic truth or law or assumption.

Professional ethics   Specific application of the principles to a particular, specialized occupation.

Universal   General mental model of a quality, abstracted from particulars, e.g., good.

CONCEPT REVIEW QUESTIONS

1. Why should ethics be defined?
2. What do we learn through the classification of ethics?
3. What is more important, ethics or law? Give reasons.
4. Why is the subject of ethics seen negatively in the context of business?
5. Can ethics be taught? Explain.

CRITICAL THINKING QUESTIONS

1. What is the meaning of learning a lesson from an incident?
2. What is the meaning of teaching a lesson when you are angry?
3. Describe a scenario where
   (i) All act ethically.

   (ii) All act unethically.

   (iii) More act ethically but some unethically.

4. How would you apply the concepts of 'relative' and 'absolute' to ethics?

FURTHER READING

Amartya Sen, *On Ethics and Economics*, Oxford, Basil Blackwell, 1987.

CASE STUDY

A Matter of Principle*

Important principles may and must be inflexible.

—Abraham Lincoln

Mid-December 2005 was a shocker to the working women of Bangalore, the IT capital of India. Pratibha Shrikrishnamurthy, an employee of the HP GlobalSoft, was raped and murdered allegedly by a driver of the pickup vehicle, who was on unauthorized duty.

There is blanket ban on night shifts for women in Karnataka. IT and ITES women employees are exempted from such shifts. It is mandatory for the concerned companies to provide a two-way transportation for its women employees, along with a security guard. The provision of the security guard had to be changed due to a representation given by the concerned women, about their anxiety that the security guard himself could be a security hazard. The notification in the official gazette accordingly changed the provision of a security guard to 'adequate security'. The companies were now responsible for providing security for their women employees, as they deemed fit.

On the fateful night of 13 December 2005, or rather in the early hours, Pratibha was picked up by a certain Shivkumar, supposedly a newly appointed driver. As per the company rules, she was supposed to cross-check with the 24 × 7 help desk of the company, whenever a new driver came to

pick her up. The victim, however, was taken in easily by the company procedure that Shivkumar followed, who promptly gave a blank call to her office on her mobile. The company now refuses to accept that Shivkumar was their authorized driver.

As per the law, the company gave the next of kin, Gowramma, the mother of the deceased employee, the usual statutory payments and further conferred on her a range of benefits on compassionate grounds—a onetime payment of Rs 11 lakh and a monthly annuity of Rs 15,000, for the rest of her life.

Som Mittal, the CEO of HP GlobalSoft, had to contend with the complaint by the labour department of not providing 'adequate security'. Under the Karnataka Shops and Commercial Establishment Act, Section 25 read with 30(1), Som Mittal had to pay Rs 1000 only as fine, for not providing 'adequate security'. Som Mittal refused to pay. It is two years since the case was registered, and Mittal is fighting it out in the Supreme Court of the country.

The motive for taking the petty matter of having to pay the fine of Rs 1000 to the highest court in the land, purportedly has huge consequences.

* *Source:* Various newspapers. It is an ongoing case and has not come to a conclusion.

Mittal is presently the president of Nasscom and would like to prove it as a test case for the corporates. His contention is that a CEO cannot be held criminally responsible for the said security lapse. Mittal feels that he has a strong and infallible case. But the Supreme Court has declined to go into the merits of the case. Consequently, Mittal has to go back to the Metropolitan Magistrate's Court in Bangalore and give a reason for not wanting to pay the fine and close the case. There is apparently a convincing clause in the Karnataka Shops and Commercial Establishment Act, Section 3, which states that 'nothing in this Act shall apply to (among others) a person occupying positions of management in any establishment.'

Mittal wants to prove that in the outrage of the aftermath of the rape and murder of his employee, the labour department went overdrive in implicating his role in the case as the CEO of the company.

Discussion Questions

1. Has this case anything to do with ethics?
2. What are the principles at stake?
3. Who are the primary stakeholders in this case and what is their relationship to each other vis-à-vis this case?

4. How are law and ethics related?
5. How worthwhile is it to salvage one's non-implication in a case in this manner?
6. How would you deal with the 'aftermath' or the 'public sympathy syndrome'?
7. Can you identify where the public sympathy syndrome affected the outcome of the case?
8. Does public opinion count in ethical judgment?
9. What would you do differently than Mr Mittal, the CEO?
10. How should corporations conduct themselves with government departments?

Going Further . . .

- Play act the case (try to get into the skin of the characters).
- Assume that you and your group are HP GlobalSoft employees. Discuss this case.
- Now, discuss the case as though you were the management team of HP Globalsoft.
- What will your stand be if you are a director in this company?

ETHICAL DEVELOPMENT PROGRAMME

I. Acquaint yourself with a company through visits. Communicate with the managers and employees and make a report on how well the company suits society.

II. Write a letter to a close relative and explain why you want to become a manager. State your ultimate goal in life.

III. Ethics Quiz

Manager's Everyday Ethical Judgment

This quiz consists of two parts: Part I is about the manager as a public person and Part II is about the manager as an individual. When you have completed the quiz, be honest with yourself and compare your attitudes as a manager and as an individual. If there are discrepancies, then you would be termed as a person with double standards.

If there is harmony, then you would be called a person of integrity.

Part I—Manager as a public person

1. You represent a company that supplies woollen cardigans. One of your best customers places a very large order. Your natural instinct would be to tell him to be more realistic, since the company's record of supplying adequate material is limited. You stop in your tracks because with such a bulk order your commission is going to soar. What would you do?
   - (a) You take the order because you think that there is no reason why the company cannot actually supply the stuff.
   - (b) You warn your customer about the problem and let him decide on a realistic volume of the order.

(c) You dissuade the customer and refuse to take the order because you do not want your longtime customer to suffer any undue business loss.

2. You are a junior manager, with a staff of twenty, in an IT firm. You are happy that your staff comes and reports practically everything to you, including the juicy gossips. There is this young lady who is an extrovert. She comes over to you and gives an eye-witness account of her colleague's romantic involvement with your senior manager. This opens your eyes to the deferential attitude your senior shows to her colleague, for there is some hush-hush information that the lady in question would be duly promoted. What would you do?

(a) Report the relationship to the higher authorities.

(b) Tell your informer to mind her own business, since this is a private affair.

(c) Tell your boss about the rumour of his affair with your office staff.

(d) Do nothing.

3. You are the general manager of a company. Your best friend's son is in your organization and is an upcoming middle manager. When he meets you, he tells you excitedly that he is going to buy a new apartment. He is confident that with the kind of money he is earning, he will be able to pay the loan in monthly installments. But you know from the board of directors that he is one of those who would have to be retrenched very soon. What would you do?

(a) You tell him about the retrenchment.

(b) You warn him not to go ahead with the apartment loan, since something unpleasant will take place, which you cannot disclose.

(c) Tell his senior manager to guide him, dissuade him.

(d) Do nothing.

4. You are on the board of directors of a company. At a board meeting, the CEO mentions an anonymous letter that was written by an employee about the irregularities in financial disclosures. He also informs the board that the matter was submitted to the external auditors of the company and they ruled that there was no truth in the allegations. The CEO moves to the next item on the agenda. What would you do?

(a) You are disturbed by what is going on. Yet, since the issue is resolved by the auditors, you let it pass.

(b) You decide to ask the CEO privately for more clarification.

(c) You intervene during the meeting and demand an explanation and even ask for a separate committee to be formed to investigate the issue.

(d) You take it upon yourself to employ another independent auditor.

5. You and your friend have just been placed in the same company after your MBA. Both of you have been assigned a project. Whenever you go to your friend's cabin, you find him surfing pornographic sites on his computer. What would you do?

(a) You say nothing.

(b) You join him and give him company.

(c) You tell him not to waste the company's time and your time, but concentrate on the project at hand.

(d) You tell the superiors.

Answers

The answers given here are typically not the only answers in ethics. They use simple common sense judgment. However, these are very close to the optimum balance.

1. (b) Communication, complete and transparent, is the key to relationship building. It also prevents misunderstandings.

2. (a) Reporting to the higher authorities may be a better choice if you would like to avoid any conflict in the future. This is because a senior is involved with a staffer. This could lead to a conflict when certain decisions would have to be taken. For instance, your senior asks you to fire a senior staffer instead of the lady involved. Further, there is a conflict of interest, because the senior has already informed his lady love quietly to move an

application to fill in the post that would be left vacant due to the dismissal.

3. (c) This is a catch 22 situation, where if you tell, you and your company are damned; if you don't, you and your friendship are damned. If you take recourse to the first two options, these may lead to a considerable loss to the company. Since the middle manager is likely to spread the news, there could be a big stir and everyone would stand to lose. His senior manager could shed more light on the situation of his job and workout a plan that would eventually save the middle manager. Thus, a concerted effort is recommended.

4. (c) The first option to let it pass is highly unethical for a board of directors. Yes, one may speak to the CEO later, but what good is it going to do to the company. Your duty, therefore, would be to use your right to intervene and demand inquiry. This action will save your company from the cunningness of its highest officer and institutionalize the value of accountability in the organization.

5. (c and d) Since you find that he is doing something wrong for himself morally and since you are his friend you could admonish him. However, you could be more practical by saying that this behaviour of his is coming in the way of your project and that it is unfair that you alone should bear the major burden of the work. If he continues in his habit then you have a duty to tell the superiors thus, not letting your friend's behaviour to ruin your project and your career.

Ratings

All five: Excellent; *Four*: Very good; *Three*: Satisfactory

Part II—Manager as an individual

1. You are financially sound. Your friend comes to you for some help. You do not want to jeopardise your friendship by declining to help, but at the same time you do not want to part with your money.

   (a) You direct him to another common friend who is known to have money.

   (b) You say that presently you do not have the money, but will do the needful as soon as possible (wishing that in the meantime he will solve his problem and not return).

   (c) You will tell the truth why you cannot part with the money.

2. You have a friend who has bought a new dress and wants to know your opinion. Frankly, you do not like it and you know that if she wears it, the entire class is going to ridicule her.

   (a) You say that it is unusual, thereby suppressing what others may say about it.

   (b) You ask her whether she could not find something else, thus putting a question mark on her choice.

   (c) You give her an honest opinion and tell her what you think of the dress, thereby suggesting that your opinion is independent of what your friendship consists of.

3. You are at a store where you have bought several articles. The billing assistant has missed a costly item.

   (a) You just pay the bill as it is and go.

   (b) You tell the billing assistant that an item has been omitted and correct the bill.

   (c) You tell yourself that the money not included in the bill will be given to a needy person.

4. You find a person lying on the road, unattended to by passersby, after being hit by a speeding vehicle.

   (a) You also pass by.

   (b) You feel guilty for not helping and later write a letter to the editor about the apathy of the people against their fellowmen.

   (c) You call the police and ambulance service and wait till they arrive.

5. You see that your colleague who is sitting next to you in a conference is busy on his computer surfing the Internet during the proceedings.

   (a) You ignore the matter.

   (b) You tell him to stop it and not distract other participants.

   (c) You join him by subtly encouraging him with your whispered comments and soft giggles.

Answers

1. (c) Telling the truth plainly earns respect. Circumvention makes one lose trust and costs friendship.

2. (c) Dress, fashion, etc. is a matter of opinion. By giving your opinion you are not only honest to yourself, you do not force others into it. Your friend will appreciate your sense of judgment.

3. (b) Anything other than paying up will result in stealing. Option (c) is quite tempting; but it is wrong to steal from one and give to another.

4. (c) If you want to prove to yourself your sense of morality, this is the one.

5.(b) The earlier you convey to him to stop, the better it is for everyone, including yourself.

Ratings

All five: Excellent; *Four*: Very good; *Three*: Satisfactory

Note: Make this quiz a personal charter and not another test to score better.

Management Mantra

The Interview

A company advertised for a job. Two men were selected for the interview. The first man opened the door and came in. His profile showed brilliant credentials. When the interview was over, he walked out through the door that he had left open. The following day, the second man was called in. He opened the door, stepped in, and shut the door behind him. His credentials were not very impressive but the employer gave him the job instead of giving it to the man who was better qualified. The reason being that the first man could not care less to close the door behind him. This showed that he was lazy and careless and lacked ethics or the customary courteousness. The second man, however, shut the door behind him. His actions demonstrated his awareness of what was going on around him. Moreover, he behaved ethically.

> MANTRA   *Priority is given to a conscientious person—somebody diligent and thorough, guided by own sense of ethics. Skills, on the other hand, can always be learnt on the job!*

Eastern and Western Ethical Thought and Business Practices

Morality is largely a matter of geography.

—Elbert Hubbard

A civilization must be judged by the manner in which all its principles, ideas, forms, ways of living and work to bring that harmony out, manage its rhythmic play and secure its continuance or the development of its motives. A civilization in pursuit of this aim may be predominantly material like modern European culture, predominantly mental and intellectual like the old Greco-Roman, or predominantly spiritual like the still persistent culture of India.

—Sri Aurobindo

LEARNING OBJECTIVES

After studying this chapter, you will be able to

> State the universal norms and tell if they are geographically limited by culture
> Determine whether Eastern values suit Western businesses
> Evaluate whether Indian values hinder business
> Understand *dharma* and its implications for business management

INTRODUCTION

The world of political economy may be divided into two kinds of people—global fans and local fanatics. Take the example of people migrating from the East to the West. Western governments are under pressure from two groups at home—the professional establishments who are running short of personnel want to have them, but the locals protest, since they feel that their jobs will be taken away. The world is a much traversed planet, and yet there are serious cultural differences among the nations. Sportsmen soon forget their sportsmanship and indulge in racial slur. Western businessmen look askance at the way their Eastern counterparts conduct business and cast doubts about the integrity of the deals to be signed. There are several trade barriers, taxes, and tariffs that hinder fair trade practices. The question we will deal with is, whether it is possible to have global business ethics practices in a multicultural world, much unified and yet divided.

UNIVERSAL NORMS AND GEOGRAPHICALLY DIFFERENT CULTURES

Cultural Values

Indeed, it would seem that the universal norms are confined to the geographical hemispheres, because culture shapes our values. Cultures are geographically diverse. The European culture is different from the Asian culture, whereas the African culture is different from both the European and Asian cultures. Cultures are confined to territories. Even the old civilizations of Egypt, Mesopotamia, China, and India were geographical pockets. Each of these cultural centres developed their own ethos, where the social relations that developed were typical to their environment.

Manners—Indicator of Values

Let us specify where the ethical values get translated into good manners or etiquette. If you go to a European wedding in a *kurta pyjama*, it may be construed as being rude. Chances are that you may be thrown out for not wearing a decent dress, and for having dared to come in straight from the bed, in night clothing. Likewise, when half-clad European tourists visit Indian temples with their shoes on, they hurt the religious sentiments of the Indians. There have been instances in business where Western products have exhibited the Eastern religious symbols of gods and goddesses on their footwear or undergarments, and this has led to angry protests that have cost many lives.

It is therefore wise to understand and respect the cross-cultural differences and conduct ourselves in an appropriate and friendly manner, rather than put up the false pretence of global business ethics.

One Humanity, Many Values

We can no more confine ourselves to geographical boundaries and remain isolated from the vagaries of cultural differences. The fundamental assumption of ethics in any region or culture is that human beings are endowed with the ability to be good. Man's basic nature is oriented to the good. The aim of every human action is good, although it may not end up as such, due to the complexities of relationships and the contexts in real-life situations.

For instance, *Casablanca*, the classic movie set in North Africa against the background of World War II, brings out the complexities of a relationship and the choices people have to make. Rick Blaine is the owner of a nightclub (a character essayed by Humphrey Bogart) who, for all the ironies of life, has to forego marrying his sweetheart Elsa (Ingrid Bergmann) in Paris. But it is even more ironical when Elsa walks into his club with her husband Victor Laszlo. Victor, a Resistance leader, is actually on the run from the Nazis. Elsa, who is still madly in love with Rick, is in a dilemma. She cannot make up her mind on whether to run with her fugitive husband, or stay back with Rick. She asks Rick to decide for her, since this dilemma is too hard for her to bear. She would do as he decides. It is a battle for Rick, too. He finally makes up his mind. He lies to Victor about his relationship with Elsa. He tells Elsa to go with her husband and so, Elsa and Victor leave. Indeed, it goes without saying that after this event both the characters may rue their decision. Stories such as these are not exceptional in real life, and are to be found irrespective of territorial boundaries. Noble decisions of personal sacrifice have enriched the lives of people beyond their boundaries. However, in this episode, this is not the only issue. Should one tell lies to save a marriage? Is telling lies a good thing?

Manners

Good manners and etiquettes, although very edifying, are not the essence of ethical behaviour. Whether one holds a fork in one's right hand or left hand is totally insignificant when compared to the value of telling the truth. Truth is appreciated beyond boundaries and all cultures have the same definition for the fundamental values such as truth, justice, love, and respect.

Universal versus Particular Values

The above example places before us a distinction in human behaviour—universal principles and their particular values. Problems arise when we universalize our particular values as universal principles. We are formed by particular instances and exclusive cultures and pursue definite interests. This is because our beliefs are influenced by our parents and elders, by the communities we belong to and the religions we follow, our definite political convictions, our professional rules, and personal ambitions. These are causes for dreadful disagreements and even wars. Thus, we should not be surprised that the values that we hold so dear collide and we lose faith in ourselves. That is why when people say that 'ethics is an oxymoron', they are not to be charged as cynics.

On the other hand, the principles of right and wrong are definitely universal, only if we can rise above our individual and treasured behaviour patterns. For instance, if honesty is our universal principle, then it translates into not to cheat, tell lies, or mislead. Through the practice of honesty, one's conscience is formed, which guides with simple 'dos' and 'don'ts' and the person turns habitually into a good person. One cannot hold a good person down, irrespective of the territorial boundaries and ideological chasms. Good leaders such as Mahatma Gandhi and Nelson Mandela have become the conscience of mankind beyond all geographical, racial, and cultural boundaries.

Nature of Values

From the above discussion, the first distinction that we must draw is between the formal and material aspects of ethics. To have a deeper understanding of moral concepts we must go from individual or *material* instances of behaviour to a general or *formal* concept. This process of thinking, from the particular to the general, is known as the *dialectic* or Socratic method. It enables us to question particular instances—the material aspect—and by the elimination of peripheral elements we arrive at the general concept—the formal aspect. We are then able to define them and apply them universally. For instance, how best do we arrive at the concept of justice? Is the death penalty given to a merchant for adulterating food that led to the death of some people considered as justice? Is letting off Nick Leeson, the derivatives manager whose actions saw the Barings Bank suffer total insolvency, justice? We feel outraged when corrupt corporations get away lightly for their misdeeds. For instance, McDonald's products are charged for causing obesity and Coca Cola's manufacturing units for environmental damage. It is true that none of the above instances serve as examples where justice is done. We see what justice is not, and through it what is meant by justice. The meaning of justice that we know is devoid of individual imperfections and therefore universal. The universal concept is an ideal, as it were, that the individual instances would like to come close to. A good man is one who comes as close as possible to this ideal, and the not-so-good one goes astray and moves farther away.

Theory and Practice

In ethics, we may do well to remember the gap between theory and practice. Just as studying music with notes, meter, tune, timing, etc. does not produce a musician without actually practising assiduously, so also, merely by learning the universal principles of ethics, one does not become a moral hero. Extraordinary people such as Mahatma Gandhi show that moral victory, through moral actions, is the greatest achievement worth having.

There are a great many professionals such as musicians, painters, medical personnel, and architects who have excelled in their field due to the highest possible standards that they have set for themselves. Have they really achieved perfection in its fullest sense? Definitely not. But they have reached a very high degree of perfection from which others can be inspired. No matter how great the practitioners of ethics are, they cannot arrive at an absolute perfection of their ideals, though they do come very close to them.

Business management is a field for practising ethical principles. We may not reach the zenith of the ideals, but all the same, without such lofty ideals the pursuit of perfection would be meaningless. It is by practice that some of our corporations have become leaders in good governance, employee care, and customer satisfaction. Their way of doing business has changed the lives of many people. Their presence has made a difference to the community.

SUITABILITY OF EASTERN VALUES TO WESTERN BUSINESS

Western Models

Eastern values will not be helpful for Western businesses because history proves that modern business management is a Western development and has been adopted successfully by the rest of the world. There are several fundamental value theories on which the Western business is based, such as utilitarianism. This theory professes a normative value defined as 'the greatest happiness of the greatest number', which is

---

Wisdom of Socrates

How to solve an ethics case?

Socrates met an acquaintance who said, 'Do you know what I just heard about your friend?' 'Hold on a minute,' Socrates replied. 'Before telling me anything, I'd like you to pass a little test. It's called the Triple Filter Test.' 'Triple filter?' 'That's right,' Socrates continued. 'Before you talk to me about my friend, it might be a good idea to take a moment and filter what you're going to say. That's why I call it the triple filter test. The first filter is Truth. Have you made absolutely sure that what you are about to tell me is true?' 'No,' the man said, 'actually, I just heard about it and...' 'All right,' said Socrates. 'So you don't really know if it's true or not. Now let's try the second filter, the filter of Goodness. Is what you are about to tell me about my friend something good?' 'No,

on the contrary...' 'So,' Socrates continued, 'you want to tell me something bad about him, but you're not certain it's true. You may still pass the test though, because there's one filter left—the filter of Usefulness. Is what you want to tell me about my friend going to be useful to me?' 'No, it is not.' 'Well,' concluded Socrates, 'if what you want to tell me is neither true nor good nor even useful, why do you want to tell it to me at all?'

Questions

1. Why is critical reasoning important to solve a case?
2. Why it is important to raise several questions before finding a solution?
3. What is the source of ethical solutions?

---

quite a democratic principle where both the self-interest of the individuals and the welfare of the greatest number of people are legitimately pursued.

Further, facts bear that Indians who migrated to the US have adopted the Western models such as market economy, competition, and self-actualization and have realized their wildest dreams of possessing wealth and prosperity. The same is happening in India now. American management education and business models have been brought into the country and in a very short time, India has made a giant leap in economic development. The ethical dimension is concretely fulfilled by the practice of corporate social responsibility, thus helping individuals and communities alike to participate with equity and dignity in economic prosperity.

Eastern Values

It is clear from the above argument that Eastern values are really successful when applied to Western business models. Why did expatriate Indians succeed so quickly, while indigenous businessmen took scores of years to succeed, irrespective of the best of business models? Why has India suddenly made a giant leap with Western business models but Indian ethos?

Utilitarianism is a value that seeks happiness in numbers, and sacrifices the legitimate and inviolable rights of those who are not a part of the greatest number. The business models of competition, market economy, and self-actualization suit it perfectly. The entire business machinery rolls mercilessly. Those who cannot stand it must succumb to it. Only the fittest will survive!

The entire Indian ethos revolves around the single value of *karuna* or compassion. It is that principle which unites people into a society in which the individual is brought up in a culture to care for the community, and the community makes it its responsibility to take care of the individual. This is the dual character of the Indian ethos, where both the individual and the community are two inseparable parts of one reality. This is also reflected in the Indian theology, where the *Atman* or the soul and the *Paramatman* or the Almighty God, although dual in their manifested nature, are actually one entity. Thus, the ethics of care stems from the depths of spirituality. Such a value suits both the East and the West.

Social Dilemma

It now becomes obvious that utilitarianism does present an ethical dilemma, when an individual's personal interest clashes with the social interest. A young man's personal duty may be to stay home and look after his ailing mother, but the larger interest for which he would be called upon to do his duty would be to join the army to defend the country.

On the other hand, it is a fact that the Indian cultural trappings were not business friendly. Indians have experienced the scourges of the caste system, the feudal mindset, and an undesirable attitude towards dignity of labour. It is the socialist revolution from the West that shook the foundations of the Indian society, more than any economic benefits from the colonial regime that introduced the Western business models and education.

Presently, a movement is sweeping across the world towards an integration of business models and social value systems. The concept of an integrated business is taking shape. Multinational companies are striving to see a common ground where both their employees and customers come to share one culture. American food chains in India have adapted to the Indian palate, but have successfully introduced their efficient and effective management practices.

Integrated Business

From the above discussion, we may deduce the fundamental aspirations in man for integration and unity. There are business values and business models. Business values are the guiding principles of business models.

What is the place of business values in a free-market economy? This is an obvious question that some suggest should preclude any value system because market forces will determine our actions. Such a laissez-faire attitude may actually do more harm than good. Without a legitimate regulation that bespeaks of the responsibility of every member of a society and all its civic bodies, there is going to be a political, economic, and social chaos.

Business is done with people; if business has to exist, then it must co-exist with people and should be beneficial to them. Business models work fairly within the context of values that maintain harmonious relationships, such as justice, fair means to attain set goals, prudence, and good citizenship.

Enable the Disabled

How to learn by doing

Gaurav Khatri, who is in his twenties, is a young and successful IT professional from Delhi. One day, as he was waiting at a traffic signal, he saw some youngsters teasing and ill-treating a blind boy. The youngsters were well-dressed and appeared to belong to good and respectable families. Khatri was shocked to observe such bad behaviour. He got out of his car and reprimanded the young goons, but they humiliated him in such a way that it horrified him. He resolved right then and there to do something about it and followed the blind boy. The boy lived in a welfare home. Khatri put his skills to work and developed speech-recognition software for the welfare home intranet facility. On his follow-up visit, Khatri was surprised and delighted to be welcomed with broad smiles. Khatri admits that a momentary episode at a traffic island, changed his perspective of life permanently.

Questions

1. Is being ethical a challenge?
2. What rewards do ethics offer?
3. How can we help to create a culture of ethics?

Source: Adapted from 'Geeks to the Grassroots', *Times of India*, 2 March 2008, p. 6.

The welfare of civil society is the goal of the government. It is within its rights to regulate business, as people mandate it. Business must submit itself to the will of the people, which is supreme.

DO INDIAN VALUES HINDER BUSINESS

Caste System

It would seem that Indian values are a hindrance to business practices. The image of the Indian businessman, whose caste in ancient India was known as *Vaisya*, has been a negative one. Manu, the lawgiver, spoke of businessmen as 'deceivers in open day light' and equated them to the *Sudras*, the lowest caste. The Indian society further battered their image. The trade name of *bania*, the businessman, became synonymous with that of a black-marketer, exploiter of the employees, shady dealer, and adulterator. In other words, the businessman was someone who was ready to sell his soul for profit. The image of the businessman in India is taking a beating even today when small investors are deceived in the stock market. Hence, there must be something in the Indian social fabric that makes business a stranger to the principles of ethics.

Negative Image

We often read about shipped cargo being rejected abroad for substandard quality. Recently, in the last quarter of 2008, Ranbaxy, the reputed pharmaceutical company, faced an embarrassing situation when the US banned some drugs that were exported by the company. The garment industry has also been at the receiving end. There is a persistent, negative image of Indians in general, and their businesses in particular, as being dishonest, corrupt, substandard, unprofessional, and having no value for time, which is so fundamental to business. It further shows that others cannot trust us—and trust is the cornerstone of business.

Understandably, one may defend Indian values by saying that there is nothing wrong with them; it is the people who do not practice it that are at fault. Yet, what is it in those values that is so difficult for some to practice, while others have no difficulty in abiding?

Augmentation of Values

The above argument is a confusion of categories, a case of mistaking material for virtual. There are social, cultural, and historical reasons for the deterioration of the Indian businessman's character; moral values are not the cause for its loss.

We have established earlier that expatriate Indians have succeeded in the West because they got opportunities and the business models of the West to function. These successful businessmen vouchsafe for the fact that the real secret of their success was the family values that they had imbibed in India. Opportunity and business models were both not created by our political economy. However, once the economic reforms started, the indigenous businessman took the initiative to adopt new business models in an environment of great opportunity. India has become the second fastest growing economy, globally. Today, the Indian corporate sector is keen on its social responsibility and has been investing in people's projects, and conducts its programmes efficiently. China is the only country that is ahead of India. However, it is to be noted that China had started its reforms about two decades before India did. We must also remember that both these countries have much of their ethical values in common.

One of the outstanding values that Indians possess is patience. The West considers it as procrastination and laziness. But with the right environment, this quality has borne fruits and Indians have become unstoppable globally. Spirituality is another unmistaken value of the Indians, which even the worst critics admit that Indians possess in abundance. Today, many Western companies acknowledge that spiritual anchoring gives purpose and direction to business.

Finally, let us review a contrast of values and businesses that are closer home. While industry and commerce are marching ahead, it is agriculture that is lagging behind. Is it because our farmers are low on moral values, or is it because of the faulty policies that our successive governments have been dishing out? Given the same opportunities and models of free-market enterprise as commerce and industry, our rural areas too will become the perfect examples of balanced development.

Thus, Indian values and Western business models are the right ingredients for a successful and value-based business management.

Clash of Cultures

The contemporary debate on the clash of cultures puts forth the challenges of the integration of cultures rather than their clashes. Conflicts originate when people's views differ. For instance, the value of honesty is not questioned but what constitutes honesty in a given instance is debated upon. Again, no one objects to clothing that is modest. Problems arise when a piece of clothing offends the sentiments of the people because it conflicts with their culture. In Turkey, the Islamic dress is forbidden in the Parliament House, to symbolize that it is a secular state. France has forbidden religious symbols like crosses, Islamic garments, and turbans in schools. It is mandatory for those riding two-wheelers to wear helmets. The Sikhs face a problem because they cannot wear one over their turbans. So, in the West, the Sikhs often have to fight for their religious right to wear the turban.

There are many reasonable ways to sort out these ambiguous situations. People can have peaceful discussions and hold dialogues and find suitable solutions to these conflicts. It is the uncompromising attitude rather than the ethical value that creates and sustains moral problems.

Values Withstand Challenges

From the above discussion we may draw the following conclusions. It is a fact that political and economic realities have brought people of different cultures together. Their coming together has made them realize that they are different. Conflicts arise when each group tries to dominate the rest. Political, regional, ethnic, and religious aspects get involved in a very complex way. The above conflicting situations challenge us to rethink our actions and not revise our values. The changed world needs to have a new attitude, not a new value.

Successful businesses have successful values. The Indian values are no exception.

PROGRESSIVE BUSINESS DHARMA

Values Are Static

It appears that it is not possible to have progressive business ethics because ethical values are static. Progressive means developing from small to large, or from simple to complex, just as in a biological process. But business ethics deals with the social behaviour of the people doing business. Business is a social activity of human interaction that involves economics. Definite standards are set. The integrity of the goods and services of the customers, as well as the employer–employee relationships, can be strictly and quantitatively maintained. There can be no discrepancy in the quantity of a kilogram of grain. If a doubt still prevails, it can be solved by referring to the standards of weights and measures.

Secondly, as the age old cliche goes, 'the business of business is business.' We have to avoid all ambiguous situations and ethical dilemmas. Many detractors of the above business dictum consider it a 'licence to kill', as it were. The dictum, however, simply states that business must be done the way it is meant to be done. One must follow the exact business rules which are laid down, just the way rules are laid down for any sport. One does not keep on changing the rules of the game as the game progresses. If

---

Doctor in the Dock

Is plagiarism not dishonesty?

The headline said it all: *Indian doctor in UK found guilty of dishonest plagiarism.*

Dr Raj Persaud is a brilliant and learned psychiatrist, who is gifted with equally great talents such as writing books and conducting radio shows on BBC Radio 4. He wrote a book called *From the Edge of the Couch*, wherein he plagiarized several scholarly papers from the field of psychology. He was found guilty before the General Medical Council. The Indian doctor admitted to having plagiarized some of his colleagues' works, but insisted that he was not dishonest. The Chairman of the Council, however, felt that copying the works of his colleagues and presenting them as his own thoughts was a dishonest act. The Council suspended him for three months.

Questions

1. Does the above case make the people in the UK think that all Indians are dishonest?
2. When a mistake is committed and is more than obvious, should one confound it by denying it?

Source: http://www.thaindian.com/newsportal/health/indian-doctor-in-uk-found-guilty-of-dishonest-plagiarism 10062225.html ANI 20 June 2008.

---

we allow this to happen in business, people will manipulate it to such an extent that the business will die.

Hence, it is important that the codes are already established in business ethics. Managers learn these codes as a part of their terms and conditions of employment in an organization. Entrepreneurs have their set of codes enshrined in the Companies Act, according to which, companies come into existence as artificial, moral persons before the law. Thus, business ethics cannot be progressive. If a business has to be successful, the business ethics it holds has to be static.

Values Are Dynamic

It is fallacious to assert that business ethics is static. On the contrary, the discipline is extremely dynamic in nature and allows progress in a world of heightened business interaction. In business ethics, we deal with the practical concepts of good behaviour. We study behaviour in a systematic way. In other words, we try to analyse our behaviour in a given situation. Knowledge is not static. It is the awareness or familiarity gained by experience. The data we deal with are the business practices—the real cases, where business decisions have led to beneficial or harmful results. We try to come to conclusions and determine the morality of the entire process through analysis. Business ethics is a process-oriented discipline.

Codes Based on Values

In the earlier argument about progressive thought in business ethics, professional codes have been proposed as an alternative. The progressive thought is not contrary to the codes. The codes have been deduced from the fundamental values to suit particular professions. While doing so, the quantifiable activity is a logical conclusion. A grocer has to conform to the standards of weights and measures, as it is a part of the professional code of conduct. It is deduced from the value of honesty. Thus, the antagonist who argues that business ethics is not progressive fails to see the progress made in detail.

The assertion that managers have to learn the codes of conduct from the terms and conditions of employment is true. It is also true that these codes lay down boundaries within which a business person conducts himself/herself. Just as in any sport that is extremely competitive, a sportsperson can excel depending on his/her competency in the field, so also in any business a good businessperson can excel because he/she strictly abides by its codes.

Business *Dharma*

We saw earlier that progressiveness is viewed variously—as a natural development as is exemplified in nature, or as to do with the intellectual understanding of a concept through analysis.

It appears as though the term 'dharma' has not been used on purpose in the above debate. The classical way to seek our aim in life or *purushartha*, is a fourfold pursuit. Wealth or *artha*, physical love or *kama*, righteousness or *dharma*, and spiritual liberation or *moksha* are the four pursuits of perfection of our lives. Dharma is, in fact, an all-pervading concept to these pursuits—the guide to goals, the regulator of actions, the principle of good character or *sucharita*, the source of virtue or *guna*. Whether it is the acquisition of wealth or the nurturing of physical love or the transcendental pursuit, each is exercised according to the dharma applicable to it. Thus, dharma is a comprehensive governing phenomenon that embodies the spiritual virtues, as well as the physical laws and codes.

If business ethics is understood under the concept of dharma, then most of the confusion between ethical values and the laws of the state, and the precepts of society and the codes of the corporate world, could be eliminated. In the Upanishads, dharma is clearly interpreted in terms of the virtues that should be practised. These are *ahimsa* (non-violence), *satya* (truth), *asteya* (non-stealing), *brahmacharya* (continence), *maitri* (friendship), *dharma* (professional duty), *karuna* (compassion), *dama* (self-control), and *saucha* (cleanliness).

Any individual, professional, corporation, or association can make one of the above values the focal point of their business. The rest of the values will fall in place automatically. Mahatma Gandhi made the first virtue, ahimsa, the central point of his leadership. We see how the rest of the values such as satya, brahmacharya, saucha etc. fell in line and aided the freedom movement.

When one adheres to one of the virtues, an apparently insolvable dilemma is resolved. For instance, Arjuna was in a dilemma about going to war against his own people. But his teacher and charioteer, Krishna, told him that it is the dharma of a soldier to put up a good fight and not to worry about the outcome. We expect soldiers

---

The World According to Huntington

Six reasons for clash of civilizations

(a) The basic reasons are history, language, culture, tradition, and religion. Relations formed on the basis of the above elements cause severe differences, which give rise to conflicts.

(b) As people are interacting with one another across the globe, they are becoming aware of the differences in geography, colour, and race. These disparities are giving rise to conflicts.

(c) Because of economic development, the identities defined by the nation–states has weakened, and the religions (read fundamentalists) have tried to revive their identities through a process of unsecularization, thereby causing conflicts.

(d) After having successfully exported its culture to the elite of the other countries, the West is going to face antagonism from the Russians, Hindus, Asians, Islamic nations, etc. Hence, conflicts will arise.

(e) In a world of melting political boundaries, choosing ethnic sides and proving what you are becomes foremost. You may hold dual citizenship but cannot follow two religious faiths. Thus, conflicts will occur.

(f) Trade blocs are being formed around the globe and there is a rise in economic regionalism. The common cultures in places like North America, Europe, Arab and Central Asian regions, and South East Asia enhance it. Conflicts, both on the macro and micro level, are inevitable.

Source: Samuel P. Huntington, *The Clash of Civilizations*, Council on Foreign Relations Inc. (1993).

---

to wield guns and not play the fiddle; we expect teachers to impart good education; we expect doctors to treat with care; we expect businessmen to conduct commerce with fairness to all the parties involved. Likewise, people expect that the business dharma is followed in business transactions.

Dharma—The Fundamental Principle

Dharma is the ultimate principle of all that is and that acts. It is not to be construed as a tenet of Hinduism because the concept is part and parcel of all the religions, communities, and regions of practically the whole of Asia. It refers primarily to the natural law that states that everything exists because of this principle. Social principles also have their basis in the natural order.

CONCLUSION

A few years ago, you would not sell *sarees* in Britain because there would be no one to wear them. Today, you can have a large store, with the very best of sarees, in central London because there is a handsome clientele of expatriate Indians and others from the sub-continent. The Indian food has also won the hearts of the people around the globe. So, it would seem that cultural barriers pose no problem. But now, think of having a pharmaceutical production unit in Saudi Arabia. You need to employ many locals, including women. The unit produces an assortment of contraceptive products. Islam does not permit contraception. Even if there is liberalization in the free-trade zones, problems will still arise because the local society will not allow anything that is against Islam.

McDonald's is the biggest food chain in the world. Beef is served in only those places where it is culturally accepted. In India, where vegetarian food is preferred, one finds ample varieties of it in their outlets. Business has to embrace the local culture, not vice-versa.

How to do business with people of different cultures and different values is a crucial question to be answered in the world of global economy that is growing smaller day by day. The basic ethical principles of truth, honesty, duty, and justice remain and are recognized as such in every culture. So also people experience love, generosity, and care irrespective of their race, religion, and nationality. Culture may be local, but ethics is universal. To respect other cultures and be sensitive to their customs is an important principle of business ethics.

SUMMARY

- There are normative principles that have universal applicability, such as truth, goodness, compassion, etc.
- Cultural expressions bring diversity to human behaviour.
- Great problems that include wars and genocides have been arising out of cultural differences.
- The value of humanity—one human family— is precious.
- Business has its ingenious ways to cross over the cultural differences.
- People all over the world easily adopt the successful Eastern and Western business models.
- The mix of Eastern values and Western business models has spelled success and have created new integrated models.
- Dharma is an all-pervading principle; its advantage is that it is based on natural order.

KEY TERMS

Artha   Wealth.

Culture   Beliefs, traditions, customs, laws, way of life of a community.

Dharma   Natural order, ethical values, regulations of a profession.

Guna   Virtue.

Habit   Formation of one's nature through repeated acts.

Kama   Physical love.

Laissez-faire   Liberal and let free to function as is the wont.

Moksha   Liberation.

Purushartha   Perfection of life's pursuit.

Sucharita   Cleanliness.

CONCEPT REVIEW QUESTIONS

1. Are ethical values people and place specific?
2. What values do the East and West have in common?
3. Do Indian values help Western businesses?
4. Would you recommend the Indian caste system as a tested organizational model?
5. What is your opinion about the cultural clashes in business?

CRITICAL THINKING QUESTIONS

1. Does cultural identity have a place in the business world?

2. Is culture a bondage?

3. Is it wrong if the ethical values are really subjective?

FURTHER READING

Subhash Sharma, *Management in New Age, Western Windows Eastern Doors* (2nd ed.) (1st ed. 1996), New Age International Publications, Delhi, 2006.

CASE STUDY

Tipping Point of Ethics on the Glazier

*The Parable of the Sadhu**

Part I

'The most exciting thing in the world is to climb the Everest' is an understatement. The adventure is par excellence. Ever since Tenzing and Hillary conquered the pinnacle of the world, a procession of sorts has followed them and it has become the ultimate destination of all adventurers, as well as tourists around the globe. Some people had unique experiences, a few had mystical experiences, while others faced some home truths like there was life beyond family and work. It gave a new meaning to their existence. It is no wonder that the Himalayas is considered the abode of gods and is seen as a place where our *rishis*, the holy men, attained enlightenment.

When Mr Bowen McCoy, the protagonist of this story, began trekking these mountains, enlightenment was the last thing on his mind. To the envy of his colleagues at Morgan Stanley and friends in the US, he was on a sabbatical, and that too, trekking the Himalayas!

McCoy came across abandoned people along the way. He thinks that this experience has organizational relevance to the fact that individuals and groups do or do not take up responsibility in the face of acute ethical dilemmas.

McCoy and his friend Stephen, who is an anthropologist, went on a six-day trekking programme. The

object was to arrive at Muklinath, an ancient pilgrimage centre, by crossing a pass over a crest at 18,000 feet.

They camped at 14,500 feet. Their companions were four people from New Zealand, two couples from Switzerland, and a Japanese group belonging to a hikers club in Japan. In the early hours of the morning, at 3.30 am, the New Zealanders marched ahead. McCoy and Stephen followed them later. The Swiss followed them after a while, and the Japanese rested in the camp.

It was day break and McCoy and his friend decided to rest for a while. They were at 15,000 feet. Shortly afterwards, they were stunned to see one of the New Zealanders coming towards them, carrying the body of a man who was barely clad and had no footwear. The New Zealander told them that he had done his part and would like to get back to his team, so that they could cross over the pass before it became too hot and the ice began to melt. He said that now it was their duty to do something for this man because the Sherpas and the porters were there to help them.

The wretched man was a *sadhu*, an ascetic, on his way back from a pilgrimage to Muklinath. He had probably strayed away from the usual path that others take. They dressed him up and made him comfortable. McCoy reasoned that since he

---

* Adapted from Bowen H. McCoy, 'The Parable of the Sadhu', *Corporate Ethics, Harvard Business Review*, September–October 1983. It won HBR's Ethics prize.

had problems with altitude, he must depart early so that he can make it to the summit. The Swiss left too. Stephen tried his best to help the sadhu, by asking the Japanese to lend their horse to take him to the base camp. They refused, but gave some food instead. He could not use the porters because the leader said that it would delay them and tire them and they would not be able to go across the pass. Stephen's pleas were finally answered when the porters helped him carry the sadhu to a sunny spot 500 feet below.

Stephen was the last man to reach the summit. McCoy ran to congratulate him. Stephen had this chilling retort,'How do you feel about contributing to the death of a fellowman?'

No one knows as to what happened to the sadhu. Only Stephen, who last saw him, could recollect that the sadhu was trying to ward off a dog of the Japanese party.

Part II

Please pause here and discuss your position. Take a moral stand.

Part III

The following is a summary of the discussion between McCoy and Stephen.

Stephen: What happened with the sadhu is an example of the breakdown of ethics between the individual and the corporation. As long as it suited them, they helped. When it became inconvenient, they passed the buck. No one was ready to take the ultimate responsibility.

McCoy: Everyone contributed as much as they could. Someone rescued and carried him down. Others clothed him, fed him, and put him in a comfortable place.

Stephen: It was a standard Western man's solution. Money, some food, some comfort, but not the solution to the fundamental problem!

McCoy: What more do you expect? Here we are from the US, Switzerland, Japan, and New Zealand—trying to fulfil our life's dream. The incident of the sadhu was unexpected. Given the circumstances, we have all done our best to help. Even the Sherpas, who helped as much as they could, did not want to risk their trip to the summit.

Stephen: What would the Sherpas do if the man were a well-dressed Nepali? What would the Japanese do if the man were a well-dressed Asian? What would you do if it were a Western woman?

McCoy: We fulfilled our responsibilities way beyond our limits. Did we have any other choice?

Stephen: Our choices were—firstly, the sadhu could have died in our care. Secondly, the sadhu could have recovered and walked down to the village that was a two-day descend. Thirdly, we could have carried the sadhu down to the village and made sure that he was taken care of well.

McCoy: The care that we took of him should to some extent satisfy the first two conditions. The third one is not called for. You cannot expect us to radically drop all that we yearned for, planned, and executed so meticulously just because of this unexpected incident!

Part IV

The following are a summary of McCoy's reflections:

1. We pass over moral life situations as they occur, only to regret them later. We realize how ambiguous the dilemma was and console ourselves by saying that we did whatever we could.

2. The instant decision to take care of a fellow human being in need could not be met because of the stress of the mountains and the objective of the summit. Is it not true that we have to take instant decisions as managers among other pressing things like acute stress and targets that have to be met?

3. What is the limit of our responsibility as individuals and as a company?

4. How do we recognize that there is a moral dilemma? Only Stephen could recognize it. Or is it that we deliberately fail to do so, by giving practical reasons, and pass the buck?

5. One of the problems in right decision making in the sadhu incident was that we were a disparate group from different parts of the world, with different cultural backgrounds, and there was no leader to take the initiative. Although Stephen tried, he did not get support from the rest.

6. The fundamental reason was that the incident took place most unexpectedly, in a context that no one could have predicted. There were no precedents to look for. No one distributed circulars with directives and no theories were discussed. Right action was needed and it did not come forth.

7. Some organizations have ingrained good values that matter. The managers are able to see the ambiguous dilemmas and contribute to the organizations more than profitability could. Companies with doubtful value systems are not able to cope with the stress, such as acquisitions and mergers. But managers who are morally strong do not have to resort to golden parachutes.

8. Business ethics is not a constraint. It is a great force. Managers cannot run away from problems; they are there to solve them.

9. Corporate culture is nothing but ethics at its heart. Managers who imbibe the mission of the company are a support to other individuals. In an organization, employees need to support each other and the organization must support each employee. Only then will the people grow and the company cultivate a moral culture.

10. All organizations have their stated lofty goals and they strive towards it as a team. But how many organizations are ready to drop their strategy suddenly on moral grounds? The people in the story helped the sadhu as much as was possible under the circumstances. But if they were to follow Stephen's moral directives, then they would not just have to change, but completely give up the lofty aim of reaching the mountain summit. What would have happened in case they did change their plans and help the sadhu as Stephen had wanted? May be this act of theirs could have opened vistas they could never have imagined! Is this the way a company stumbles upon a new path?

Part V: *Significance*

The parable of the sadhu is a metaphor for human relationships, leadership, moral initiative, ethical issues raised by the individual in the organization, cultural management, individual and collective responsibility within the organization, openness to new and unexpected situations, readiness to learn from experience, to see opportunities where others see only problems, and to act responsibly and resolutely in unexpected situations.

Discussion Questions

1. Why did McCoy and the other climbers make the decision they did about the sadhu?

2. What were the consequences of their decision?

3. Does the story help you to understand the decision-making process? Give reasons.

4. What is the ethical content of the story?

5. What were the situational factors affecting the decision of each character in the story?

6. Why did the sadhu's predicament challenge McCoy?

7. What were the stakes involved when the climbers decided to help the sadhu?

8. Why should McCoy have shouldered the responsibility?

9. How much was he in control of the situation? What choice did he have?

10. What power had McCoy over the rest of the group?

11. How much power does one need in order to influence the actions of a group?

12. To what extent are personal values, goals, situational factors, responsibility, and power common to managers?

13. Who or what are the 'sadhus' or the predicaments in your life that pressurize you to make a committed decision that changes the course of your life?

Going Further . . .

Conduct a workshop. Simulate morally ambiguous situations. Role play the incident. Compare similar situations where you studied or worked. Find examples in literature. Let each group discuss one point. Make presentations. Take resolutions.

ETHICAL DEVELOPMENT PROGRAMME

Management Training

Take a break for a couple of weeks from your usual occupation. Do something that you always wanted to, but could not. At the end of your undertaking, make an intense analysis of all your situations and decisions. How would you implement your experience in your present organization?

Interview

Dr Subhash Sharma is well known in the management education world, both in India and abroad.

Academic: Passing out of the famed portals of the Indian Institute of Management (IIM), Ahmedabad, he earned his doctoral degree (Ph.D) from the University of South California (USC), Los Angeles, US.

Distinctive Management Thinker: Publications: *Creation from Shunya* (1993), *Management in New Age: Western Windows Eastern Doors* (1996 & 2006), *Quantum Rope: Science, Mysticism and Management* (1999), *Arrows of Time: From the Black Holes to the Nirvana Point* (2001), *New Mantras in Corporate Corridors: From Ancient Roots to Global Roots* (2007), and scores of scientific papers.

Institution Builder: Women's Institute for Studies in Development Oriented Management (WISDOM), Banasthali, Rajasthan; Indian Institute of Plantation Management, Bangalore; Indian Business Academy (IBA), Bangalore and Greater Noida. The Indian School of Business (ISB), Hyderabad, has honoured him with the title of Wise Guru.

Question: Management in New Age. What do we understand by it?

Dr Sharma: Evolution of management discipline could be viewed in terms of the three eras or waves, namely, the scientific era starting with Taylor's scientific management approach, followed by a humanistic phase under the influence of Maslow, McGregor, etc., and now the new age with new issues of social and human concerns such as gender, environment, work–life balance, ethics, good governance, social responsibility, etc. These issues are leading us towards the third era or wave of the evolution of management thought, namely, the wave of spiritualism in management. Hence, Eastern thoughts with their spiritual heritage have started impacting the corporate world. Yoga and meditation entered the corporate world as stress management tools. Now more 'Indian doors' are opening through the broader idea of spiritual concerns. Thus, management in the new age implies a movement towards a holistic approach that is metaphorically represented by the title of my book, *Western Windows Eastern Doors (WWED)*.

Question: The new age in management is a result of the evolution of the three stages or waves, the third one being a holistic approach, where the Western and Eastern cultures interact and increasingly impact not just businesses, but also economics and governance. How deep do you think is such a convergence of cultures?

Dr Sharma: Interaction between the Western and Eastern cultures in the context of management started with the emergence of the 'Japanese Management', wherein a fit was discovered between Western technology and Japanese culture. Now the idea of 'Indian Management' is emerging, wherein a new fit is being discovered between Western management and Indian spirituality. This interaction is contributing to the emergence of the third wave of management, in the form of spirituality in management. Sooner or later, this will be recognized as the contribution of 'Eastern Doors' to the development of management thought. This convergence is currently at the emergence stage and in due course, it will become the new architecture for developing corporations in the context of sustainable development that would include 'Western Windows' and 'Eastern Doors'. In fact, a well-designed house needs both windows and doors—windows for looking outside and doors for entering inside. The holistic perspectives will lead us towards the WE (West + East) models of management, as the West without the East and the East without the West would remain incomplete, just as science without spirituality and spirituality without science remain incomplete. In my book *WWED*, I suggested that 'scientific temper should be tempered with spiritual intensity' and 'spiritual temper should be tempered with scientific curiosity'. Through such an approach, a deeper convergence will arise between the Western and Eastern cultures in the field of management and its related disciplines.

Question: I see a very clear convergence philosophy, a 'fit' that connects the Eastern spirituality with the Western science and the emergence or 'wave' thereof that evolves into a human activity such as management. Let us accept that it is possible for a meeting of minds on the questions of scientific management pursued with spiritual dynamism, or pursuit of ethical values. But what about the unifying of their hearts? (Heart is a metaphor for culture.) You speak about 'ethnocentricism' (Ch. 4) in your work. How would this help us to build new management models?

Dr Sharma: In addition to the meeting of minds, the unifying of hearts is also taking place in a subtle manner. Today, many transnational corporations are operating in various countries. Their managers are dealing with different cultures that are representing different expressions of the 'heart'. They incorporate such experiences in their management processes. For example, diversity management has emerged as a new theme because of such experiences. Earlier 'ethnocentric' biases were under correction. Now, they are leading to new theories, concepts, and models in management. Within the corporate world, we are coming across a new 'confluence of civilizations' or a new 'confluence of national cultures', as employees of transnationals come from different civilizations and cultural roots. This leads to a greater inter-weaving of various cultures. One can smell the Indian flavours in the Silicon Valley in San-Jose. In fact, there is a mingling of many such smells in the contemporary corporate world that are taking us away from the rigid ethnocentrisms of the past. It is being reflected in the new management practices that are being followed, such as diversity management and better sensitivity towards employees with diverse cultural needs.

Question: You observe a new cultural milieu emerging among the people or employees of transnational corporations, which helps them to alienate from the old ethnocentric mindset. In your

work you begin section 5 with a verse: *Man is a bundle of contradictions/a single model is mere simplification,/complexity is the crux of his nature,/he is really a strange creature.* Managers today are confronted by cultural contradictions. So, how would a global manager manage human relationships, which I feel is what ethics is all about?

Dr Sharma: There are several models of 'man' namely, the economic man driven by utility maximization and greed, man as a consumer, man as a social being driven by kinship, man as a politician being driven by power, man as a resource as in human resource development, man as a rebel and revolutionary, man as a rational being, man as an irrational and creative being, man as a spiritual being, etc. These models of human beings provide us with different perspectives and we find the manifestations of these various perspectives in different ways in the market, organizations, and society that is leading to several contradictions. Managers have to deal with these various manifestations of human beings. Hence, managing human relationships becomes critical to the success of any business, or for that matter, any human endeavour. In human relationships managers display dominance of lower self (ls), middle self (ms), or higher self (hs) that are represented by the *tamas*, *rajas*, or *sattava* qualities. To extend or reformulate Freud, behaviour can be analysed in terms of three levels namely, *id*, *ego*, and *eco*, with an equivalence to the *guna* theory. Ego driven managers tend to exclude others, while eco driven managers include others in their relationships and decision-making processes. You have rightly stated that ethics is all about relationships that are inclusive.

Question: I would like to pick up your term 'eco'. In your work you put forward what you call an 'Ecotarian View'. You would like to describe human relationships in this new perspective. Today business is global. It is in a way, the most important part of culture. How can we overcome our cultural and deep ingrained attitudes, come out of our own shells, as it were, and be open to other cultures? Would we then lose our own identity?

Dr Sharma: When we use the phrase 'Ecotarian', it implies 'concern for others'. Ecotarian not only implies concern for the environment but also implies concern for our fellow human beings. In contrast to the utilitarian world view, the ecotarian approach to human relationships implies respect and dignity for others, including their culture. Hence, it implies, being open to the viewpoints of others without losing one's own identity.

Question: We see that the Indian companies are acquiring multinationals, as well as, other smaller companies abroad. Some even say that India is sort of, reversing the role of the East India Company. I hope such a syndrome as East India Company does not raise its head again. What I mean to suggest is that acquisitions and mergers are fine on paper, but on the ground there is almost a clash of cultures. I suppose cultures go beyond mere businesslike good manners. How does one co-exist in a workplace with a globalized economy?

Dr Sharma: The metaphor of East India Company is not applicable to Indian companies, because acquisitions by Indian companies, are not a part of any design of colonialism. Further, acquisitions and mergers should be viewed in terms of mutual adjustments of cultures and not merely in terms of a clash of cultures. Mutual adjustments would create a path for confluence of cultures that I also refer to, as the 'wisdom path' that is arising out of interactions between the various cultures. This is also the '*sangam*' (*sang-mei-hum*: we are together) approach or confluence. In a globalized economy, the workplaces can become confluence points for the confluence of cultures and creation of 'confluence teams'.

Question: May I move from the workplace, towards the motivation to work? You state in a verse in your work (Ch. 14) '*He is modeled as a resource,— to be used, abused and misused.*' Would employees be motivated to work in a culturally diverse place? Would not a group of employees from a mono-culture, be more productive for a company, since there would be no cultural clash?

Dr Sharma: The modelling of a human being as a resource is a very limited view of human beings. It is an extension of the idea of a human being as a factor of production. This is an economized view, as well as a productivity-oriented view of man. Hence, it prefers a mono-culture so that man can be commanded and controlled easily. Now, a new view is required, wherein workplaces are places

of fulfilment. This is particularly needed in a knowledge economy as we are dealing with highly educated, knowledgable workers with diverse backgrounds and nationalities. Further, organizations have to think about the quality and excellence in addition to productivity. A culturally diverse workplace can create better conditions and better motivation for quality and excellence, as it recognizes the cultural dimension of human existence.

Question: In your work, you deal with what you term as 'migrant ethics and the spirit of achievement'. It is true that the migrants have a greater motivation to succeed than the original natives. The history of the world clearly shows the progress achieved by the migrants over thousands of years. In fact, all progress comes through these migrations. North America is the best example. What indeed is the migrant ethics?

Dr Sharma: Migrant ethics is represented by an inherent desire of human beings to succeed in a new space–time context. It incorporates the spirit of adventure and exploration. In specific migrant work ethics, three mantras are followed, namely, sincerity, integrity, and responsibility. This approach to work ethics leads to success, as the experience of North America shows. You have mentioned that the history of the world shows that all progress comes through the migrations that have taken place. If we extend this idea into the future, space explorations and the desire for future inter-planetary travel also represent the inherent and deep-rooted spirit of migrant ethics in human beings that leads to a spirit of achievement.

Question: This brings me to ask you the most important question emerging from your book that concerns my readers. The MBA model of decision making. I believe your approach to draw out the deep nuances of decision making from the *sankhya* philosophy is highly relevant. It intrigues me to ask you that how much irrationality is involved in decision making?

Dr Sharma: The MBA model draws our attention to interplay the *manas* (intuition), *buddhi* (intellect), and *ahamkar* (ego) in decision making. *Manas*-driven decisions are intuitive and creative, *buddhi*-driven decisions are rational and analytical, and *ahamkar*-driven decisions are irrational and ego based. In general, our empirical observations indicate that many managers tend to base their decisions on ahamkar. Recent feuds in some well-known family businesses are pointers to the same. However, effective managers and leaders transform their ahamkar into *aumkar* (spiritual synergy) and thereby, inspire others.

Question: It has been quite enlightening having this dialogue with you. I am grateful to you for this opportunity. My readers—management students, trainees, executives, and others—would be glad to receive a message from you.

Dr Sharma: Yes, it was indeed wonderful to have this dialogue with you. My message for your readers is drawn from the metaphor of the tree as a symbol of leadership. There are three types of leaders—the date-tree leaders (we are reminded of Kabir who said, 'What is the point of being great if greatness is like the date tree. People can't enjoy its shade or eat the fruit it bears.'), the banyan tree leaders (nothing grows under a banyan tree), and the *peepal* tree leaders (Buddha had his enlightenment under a *peepal* tree). *Peepal* tree leaders are

the leaders who enlighten others; they create more leaders. Today, we have a dominance of date tree and banyan tree leaders in society and the corporate world. We need to transform this situation. Hence, our educational institutions in general, and business schools in particular, should focus on developing *peepal* tree leaders. Such leaders would create a new awakening and create business organizations that are based on a new integration of market values (profit, competition, etc.), social values (justice, social equity, etc.), and spiritual values (love, compassion, etc.). This will take us towards a new vision of a balanced society wherein market, society, and spiritual development find a new balance that will lead us towards the next evolutionary step in the form of a 'sacro-civic' society.

Exercise

After a thorough study of this interview, write an essay as though you were a wise guru.

Make a charter for yourself and for your occupation.

Management Mantra

Danda or Dharma: The Ultimate Alternative!

The antinomy of dharma is *nirdharma*. Dharma is rewarded, but nirdharma is punished with a *danda!* The danda or the rod signifies the instrument of punishment, coercion, or force. The teachings of the *Puranas* declare, 'Danda moves the universe, piercing, cutting, wounding, maiming, afflicting, causing pain, causing consternation, and panic in the hearts of all. It is the danda and danda alone, irresistible and terror striking, that makes the earth prosper, that brings about morality and makes virtue possible.' The danda has been described as a hideous and black eunuch—with four fangs, four arms, eight legs, and numerous, huge, unblinking eyes—that stands erect and lashes out a forked tongue. Danda, in a word, is a merciless judge.

> MANTRA   *You may escape dharma, but there is no escape from the danda!*

Doctrines, Dogmas, and Business Management

Morality is not properly the doctrine of how we may make ourselves happy, but how we may make ourselves worthy of happiness.

—Emmanuel Kant

Commercialism is a modern sociological phenomenon; one might almost say that is the whole phenomenon of modern society.

—Sri Aurobindo

LEARNING OBJECTIVES

After studying this chapter, you will be able to

> State whether ethics is pragmatic
> Critically analyse the scourge of socialism
> Determine whether the social market economy is an alternative to communism
> Decide whether business has any viable philosophy

INTRODUCTION

When the stock market is in upswing, bullish, you ask your colleague, 'What do you think about it?' He tells you that there is confidence among the investors in the growing economy and that the market reaction is a sign of that confidence. Then you say, 'People are quite pragmatic, aren't they? They want to see value for their money through the greatest possible benefit [pragmatism].'

That evening on TV, you see a communist leader offering his views on the sudden spurt in the stock market: 'It means that the graph of the greed of the rich is rising higher! It has no significance for the poor. The only truth is that the poor will become poorer since they are not a part of the capitalistic system [socialism].'

A professor of economics makes a point in his lecture about the strong and rising stock market: 'There is a bullish trend in the market due to highly superfluous and totally ambiguous reasons. We are not able to clearly define the market position. However, on the social front, it is going to create problems. Large segments of our society will suffer due to the unpredictability of the markets. They are not part of the market and yet they become victims of it since factors such as inflation, price rise, etc. are going to affect them directly. The social sector of the country will suffer immensely. Hence, we must develop a system of inclusive capitalism [welfare or social market economy].'

The above espouse different theories of business and all of them have people-centric problems. It is important to determine the philosophy a business is going to adopt. If our basic business assumptions fail to have sound moral grounds, either of the theories will result in an economic disaster for the people. In this chapter, we shall examine the beliefs or assumptions or the theories behind the systems of business that the world has adopted, reformed as per times, and at times also discarded.

PRAGMATISM AND ETHICS

It is certain that these two concepts—pragmatism and ethics—are poles apart. To be pragmatic is to do things in the most convenient way possible. To seek immediate relief from sickness makes more sense than to prolong one's misery by adopting a sanctimonious attitude of divine intervention for the healing. So too in business, by adhering to some ideology or artificial regulation, one cannot conduct business. The market tells us what to do. The Sensex (Bombay Stock Exchange) lost over a thousand points on a single day in February 2008, causing a mayhem of sorts in financial terms to the investors. But the resilience of the market economy system is such that in the end, common sense prevails over market index. The investors evaluate their options and after making the appropriate corrections needed in the money market, their business continues as usual. Of course, the lessons learnt in the bargain are a source of knowledge for such future eventualities.

Understanding Pragmatism

The US is home to pragmatic philosophy. When we translate its metaphysics to the field of business, we have a market economy that is fundamentally based on the practical principle of the right to own private property. Private property is the supreme right of the modern man and it has two concrete consequences—production and distribution. Enterprise and freedom go hand in hand to create an economic philosophy called capitalism. Capitalism functions solely on the principles of demand and supply. These two principles are also called the forces of market economy. In other words, in a free-market economy there is no control over supply and demand. The forces depend on the exercise of free choice by the people. What the natural law is to the physical world, the law of supply and demand is to the political economy and business. This helps businesses to draw a distinction between business and ethics. It helps people keep away their value judgments and conduct business strictly as business.

Simply put, pragmatism is practical philosophy. It does away with the bondages of dogmas and unbending beliefs and traditions. For instance, interest on loans cannot be charged on religious grounds. An individual owns nothing but the state owns everything, as believed by communism. Economy must be strictly regulated to establish equality, as professed by socialists, because it even melts national and cultural boundaries. For instance, the stock market behaviour, for better or for worse, is a global phenomenon. As the sun rises in the East, the Japanese stock exchange comes alive and its trail ends after a full day at the New York Stock Exchange, where the ups and downs, gains and losses, joys and sorrows are shared.

Business firms are on firm footing when their objectives or achievable goals, which give a direction to their actions, are stated clearly. Suppose a company is in the business of providing industrial data. Its objective will be to collect facts through the best possible research and supply to its clients promptly. Quick response and high accuracy become the goal of the company. Performing these tasks well ensures customer satisfaction.

'We have to be practical.' This is the single mean that runs across the business world. 'Customer satisfaction' and 'value addition to the shareholders' are the twin shibboleths of the practical business world.

Pragmatism and Problem Solving

The object of a pragmatic approach in business is problem solving. The business world has interpreted the theory of knowledge on pragmatism for its own purposes, rather than to understand what pragmatism really stands for. Businesses face problems of various kinds on a daily basis. Employers in the manufacturing area face problems related to unskilled workforce, inadequate training, wages and disputes. Service industries such as telephone, transport, etc. face problems while dealing directly with their customers. Then, there are the more serious issues of misappropriation of funds, law suits, bribery, and the like. All these need a clear analysis of the particular situation and an appropriate solution. We cannot have generalized solutions that can be applied universally. Each case needs to be studied on its own merits and the desserts be fairly delivered.

More often than not, the term pragmatic is used to allow exceptions to a code of behaviour that is not easy to follow. Thus, it is considered practical to offer a bribe in order to get work done. It saves time and everyone is a winner. It is considered a smart move by an organization to fudge its accounts and evade tax. After all, the company thinks, it is practical to bolster its investments rather than to comply with and pay the taxes, which the government does not anyway spend for the benefit of the people. The company believes that it has acted wisely and has a clear conscience because it is going to spend this money well and its customers will benefit from it. Ethics in such cases is not practical.

Ethics Is Human Action

It is facile to argue and extricate ethics from a pragmatic approach to business. We must delve deeply into the concept of pragmatism to analyse its implications on business management. All philosophical pursuits, whether idealistic or empiricist, have a place for practical affairs. Immanuel Kant, who wrote the systematic treatise of ethics, *The Critique of Practical Reason* and *The Fundamental Principles of the Metaphysics of Morals*, established that ethics is a practical discipline. The 'moral law within' is established by the universally applicable axioms. These axioms are nothing but an expression of our common will; the only thing that is 'good in the world and beyond it is the goodwill'.

The concept of goodwill is not what we ordinarily understand in business terms as the favourable attitude created among customers towards our business. In pragmatic philosophy, goodwill is that which is desired of us, the minimum that is needed to make an action good. This requirement can be fulfilled by doing one's duty, that is, duty for duty's sake. The Gita too expounds the principle of duty by insisting that we fulfil our moral obligations by doing our duty without seeking fruits for our actions. When one does his/her duty for the sake of duty alone, all the moral dilemmas are resolved. Doing one's duty is the most pragmatic thing to do in the world.

Based on this and their own experiences in the US, two philosophers, C.S. Peirce and William James, made it their mission to seek practical meaning into these concepts. Peirce stated that '[i]n order to ascertain the meaning of an intellectual conception one should consider what practical consequences might conceivably result.' (Pierce 1878). William James, his colleague, who shaped the thought of American pragmatism by making individualism its mainstay, advocated that '[w]e have the right to believe at our own risk any hypothesis that is live enough to tempt our will' and that '[t]he pragmatic method tries to interpret each notion by tracing its respective practical consequences' (James 1896).

What becomes clear in the above conceptual analysis is that ethical values originate at our will—our desire to do something—and that action must be consistent with our thought on that action so as to derive its inner meaning. Sometimes, we rate the actions of others as thoughtless, or those that we cannot conceivably understand as having little practical value. It implies that those actions not having a meaning or a purpose that can be willed as 'good' cannot be approved. This shows that moral precepts are more than arbitrarily made up codes, because if actions have to be right they must be consistent with the concept of good. This is the essence of moral reasoning. Our actions would have to be intelligibly explainable. Those actions that can sustain such scrutiny would also comply with the fundamental moral principle—the will that is good.

Pragmatic Business Theory

The pragmatic business theory has two fundamental assumptions—first, the inalienable right to private property and second, the right of the individual. Private property is not merely the ownership of physical possessions and assets, but also such things as patents and copyrights. However, in a free-market system this becomes very complex and the entire society gets involved in cross-relationships. Entrepreneurship develops from individuals and family holdings to firms and companies, where the monies of a large number of stakeholders are involved. Furthermore, enterprises cross both physical and cultural boundaries and become multinational entities, thereby involving an even larger number of stakeholders. Firms have to cross over their stakeholders and reach out to indirect stakeholders too. With this, the responsibilities of enterprises are enlarged much more than the increase in shareholder value. This is the meaning of pragmatism. It is not business for business' sake; it is business with a definite common good.

What happens to profit in a pragmatic business? A private property or a private enterprise cannot sustain itself on charity. It has got to earn its money just as a landlord earns his rent and a worker earns his wages. The capital must draw profit. But in the pragmatic business paradigm, profit alone is not the end but a means to further create wealth. When we come across the richest people on the planet, such as Warren Buffet, Bill Gates, L.N. Mittal, Azim Premji, or the Ambani brothers, we notice that profit is the last thing on their minds. They are only concerned with ways to expand more, innovate more, and create situations for higher standards of living in society.

What is inside the mind of a successful entrepreneur? Mukesh Ambani of Reliance, one of the largest private companies in India, reveals what is on his mind. He says that the country faces huge social and infrastructural challenges. The government alone cannot handle it. As a business leader, he considers it his duty to form an effective partnership with the government and address the needs speedily and efficiently. Community building, healthcare, education, and other social areas are meant for such public–private partnerships. The objective is the well-being of society, which in turn fosters growth. Implementing such projects transforms both the business, as well as society.[1] Thus, pragmatic business is not an end in itself. Business is a means to achieve social ends.

Pragmatism and Capitalism

Pragmatism appears to be nothing but patent capitalism; private property and individualism are nothing but capitalism. In fact, pragmatism and capitalism are synonymous with each other.

We may answer any objection quite simply as follows. Pragmatism is a philosophical theory of creating a relationship by converting a concept into a reality, for a useful purpose. In other words, pragmatism implies doing something meaningful. What should we do to live meaningfully? We have to earn our livelihoods. We have to do business, and we do it by managing the resources that we possess and creating more resources out of them. That is how we translate pragmatism into capitalism. It is true that this translation has difficulties. Certain salient features of capitalism such as competition have lead to income inequalities, which in turn become social inequalities. These convert firms into oligopolies and, as a result, these firms face exploitation and alienation.

---

[1] *Outlook Business,* 26 January 2008, p. 48.

The ills of capitalism are very important to the study of ethics. They deal with the questions of justice. They go deeper into the principles of production and distribution. To study this angle of justice, we will turn to socialism.

Lost but not Found

Ashok Kumar is a manager in a nationalized bank in Bangalore city. As per the bank's policy, he was supposed to fulfil a term as a manager in a rural area. He was transferred to Gumla, a town in Jharkhand. The bank was situated on the outer periphery of the town. Kumar's Hindi was weak and he depended on the branch staff for office communication.

One afternoon, after the customer transactions were closed for the day, Kumar saw Sitaram, the cashier, go over to a couple of his colleagues. Sitaram looked desperate, and his colleagues seemed to sympathize with him. In between their conversation, they darted anxious looks at Kumar and shrugged their shoulders and, at other times, nodded their heads in hopelessness. Kumar sat quietly for a while, wondering if his intervention may be construed as an interference in their private matters. He had an eerie feeling that they were hatching a conspiracy against him because he was a stranger to this place and they were all locals. After a while, he saw that Sitaram's colleagues had convinced him to go over and speak to the manager.

As Sitaram came in, Kumar braced himself up and hurriedly showed him to a seat. Kumar noticed that Sitaram was terribly nervous and realized that he was not involved in a personal problem, but an official one. Kumar gave him a warm smile. Sitaram felt a bit better. Sitaram began explaining anxiously. He said that at the closing of the cash counter, he found that there was a shortage of Rs 4000. He revealed that a small incident took place, wherein he and a client exchanged some angry words due to the long wait at the cash counter. He then referred to an old woman who had come with a bank draft that was duly approved for cash payment. At the counter closing, when he found that the cash was short, he suddenly and clearly realized that the old woman had presented herself at the counter immediately after the angry client. Instead of giving her

ten notes of Rs 100, he had actually given her ten notes of Rs 500.

The manager was immensely relieved to note that it was not a matter of a clash of cultures! Yet, he was worried about the consequences of the discrepancy in the closing balance. The bank was not going to bear this loss. He ticked off one option. What next? Well, he called the rest of the staff into his cabin to discuss the case. They came up with several suggestions. Ultimately, Kumar decided to pick one of the suggestions. One of the staff knew the old woman because she was from his village. He volunteered to call her to the bank the next day.

The next day came and went, but the woman did not turn up as she had promised. Several days passed by and the matter grew serious, since the procedure remained incomplete. The manager decided to go to the old woman's house along with the cashier and the staff who belonged to her village. When they questioned her, the woman denied that she had received currency notes of Rs 500. She said that a draft for Rs 1000 was sent to her by her son, who was a labourer in Patna, and that she had received just that amount from the counter. She even showed them four notes of Rs 100 and said that she paid her dues of Rs 600 to the grocer.

Kumar had to do some hard thinking. It was simple to follow the rule book and ask the cashier to furnish the amount. But this was fraught with danger because the cashier was a highly respected and esteemed senior staff and no one would believe that he had swiped the money. This would set him against not only the bank staff, but the locals too. If they even got a whiff of the 'harassment by the outside manager', the entire town would pounce on him. Should he follow some accounting procedures to neutralize the amount? The auditors would find that out anyway in the next inspection. He could be pulled up and his clean record would be

Contd

blemished for life. Should he reimburse the amount and forget this as a bad dream? That would be too tame. His family and friends would deride him for it. Kumar wondered who had stolen the money, after all? He had an extremely uneasy feeling that this could be a conspiracy against him. How he wished that he was back in Bangalore, enjoying a meal with his family at his favourite Chinese restaurant!

Questions

1. How serious are the cultural differences within India?
2. What prejudices do people have against those from other states?
3. How difficult is it for the people of the North Indian states to do business with those of the South Indian states, and vice-versa?

Source: This is a true incident related to the author by one of his friends, though people and place names have been changed.

CRITICISM OF SOCIALISM

Karl Marx lived in a religiously dominant society that influenced economics, politics, and culture. He concluded that a refutation of religion would be a logical move to reform the contemporary state of affairs. In fact, it would lead to a social revolution, not reform. In other words, the society of his time needed a revolutionary change to establish a new order. It needed to move away from the clergy-centred ethos to a worker-centred one. Due to the Industrial Revolution, which was the phenomenon of his time, the worker was the primary constituent who defined society and was the most neglected one too. Thus was born modern socialism, which was based on the twin principles of 'work according to ability' and 'desserts according to needs'. The goal was to establish a just society with equality in distribution. The revolution that began during the early years of the twentieth century and spread around the globe started to decline towards the end of it. If we have to free ourselves from the failures of socialism, it is important to begin by its criticism.

Scourge of Socialism

Since the fall of the Soviet Union, the bastion of socialist communism, it would seem that socialism, after all, was not all that bad. The Chinese communism has revamped itself into a capitalist autocracy and has modernized itself economically to suit the contemporary needs of the people. It all began with Karl Marx's reflection on the predicament of the worker. For instance, a worker who works in a cotton mill has the task of machine maintenance. Both the man and machine develop problems. The man is sidelined and another is employed to take care of the machine. What happens to the sidelined worker? The worker is expendable, but not the machine. This is dehumanization. The worker is related to the product of labour, merely as an object. He is not only alienated from the fruit of his labour, but is eventually stripped off his dignity and alienated from himself too. Capitalism dehumanizes workers by only exploiting them for their work and not giving them their rights.

Capitalism, the machine of production, becomes concentrated with a few wealthy entrepreneurs. They manage all the economic resources to their advantage. They exploit the worker to the utmost. A vast number of workers contribute their skills in production without justly getting their returns. In the final analysis, the worker is not a part of his produce, either in name or in monetary gain. This may be illustrated with the plight of the construction workers in our cities. Since there is no work in their villages due to the uncertainties of agriculture, labourers throng to the cities, looking for work. They are mostly employed in the high-rise construction industry. They live in shanties provided by the builders. They work in unsafe conditions while their little children are left to play in the dirt and cement around the site. Once a building is constructed, big multinationals establish their offices in the building, or if it is a block of apartments, up-market folk move in to live there. The building is known by the name of the company that built it, and the engineers and managers enjoy the prestige and fortune. The labourers are shifted by their contractors to the next building site, where they live in another shanty. It is this sort of dehumanization, depravation, exploitation, and alienation that Marx and Engels decried in their work *The Communist Manifesto* (1848).

Socialism has been the greatest turning point in the history of mankind. People rejected capitalism on both counts—its principles of private property and individualism. Property belonged to all the people and hence to the state. For the first time in human history, individuals came to hold everything in common. People embodied themselves in the state to produce a totalitarian people's rule. Justice was for each, according to his needs—just and equal distributive justice. All will work as per their ability and all will receive as per their needs. This is the highest form of human association, the realization point of civilization.

Totalitarian Logic

The socialist order that was established by the communist system adhered to a crass form of distributive justice, where the fruits of labour had to be shared equally with the less able. As a result, the worker lost the initiative to give his/her best. In a crowd of proletarians, the worker lost his/her identity. He/she felt that he/she worked for an empty ideal. The worker lost motivation, since nothing belonged to him/her, to the extent that he/she as an individual belonged to the state. The worker lost all rights to property as well as self. The dictatorship of the proletariat degenerated into the oligarchy of the officials of the one-party system. The logic of totalitarianism controlled everything—religion, culture, food and clothing, entertainment, education, economy, policy, and politics. The control was total and absolute and it would not tolerate any division or difference, whether in thought or in deed. The actions of the very same worker, of whom and for whom the state existed, was suspected. The worker who once worked for the master and earned the daily bread in the communist state became an enemy of the state even if he/she thought differently. The capitalist who could not care less to control his thinking was not allowed to think freely by the communist state of which he was the essence. The collapse of the freedom to think and to own runs against the very nature of one's existence. Thus, the communist manifesto got divided within itself and embraced self-destruction.[2] The price that communism demanded and the number of people who paid with their lives are more than the number of people who lost their lives in the two world wars and the Nazi holocaust put together.

Indian Socialism

India is a perfect case study for social and economic disparities. Ironically, socialism was introduced in India in the early years of its independence and even after fifty years, more than 50 per cent of its population of over half a billion people live below the poverty line—that is, they earn less than Rs 50 a day. These were the very ingredients needed for communism to succeed. There should have been a bloody revolution at the grassroots level by the people. What went wrong with socialism in India?

India was not wholly spared from socialism. The socialist policies, such as planned economy with five-year outlays, a constitutional amendment making the nation officially a socialist state, agricultural and food subsidies, a mixed economy truncated by licenced businesses known as *licence raj*, large-scale government ownership known as public sector units, nationalized banks, and the likes, all failed. They failed for the same reasons that communism failed. In addition to this, the sentiments of the people to preserve personal freedoms, cultural autonomy, and the uniqueness of the Indian spirit did not allow communism to succeed fully. In some states of India, such as Kerala and West Bengal, communism prevailed but only as a party in a multiparty democracy.

Despite poverty, Indians rejected communism. They have been through exploitation by feudal lords and colonial masters. They have borne the brunt of the caste system and the ravages of poverty. There have been wars, invasions, and cultural upheavals. But the Indian ethos will not allow communism to take hold. The Indian ethos is easier to experience than to describe. The fabric of the Indian ethos is woven with strong threads of moral character or dharma. Individuals or a group of individuals, or even an era or epoch, may suffer from definite aberrations of the dharma, but in the heart of every Indian, there is an unshakable belief that dharma or the moral law always prevails.

Lessons from Socialism

The above discussion about the rise and fall of communism needs to be studied carefully. Socialism has taken various *avatars* and communism is only one of

---

[2] George Orwell's *Nineteen Eighty Four*, published in 1949, focuses on a repressive, totalitarian regime.

them. Even that differs from country to country. The following lessons may be taken note of.

(a) The first lesson that is to be learnt from socialism, which historically began with the French Revolution, is the realization to humanity that all are equal in human dignity, that the well-being of all is ensured by the right of liberty, and that there is a new social contract called fraternity that is different from the old one, as that of a master and a servant.

(b) The second lesson we learn from socialism is that no one individually, or as a group, has the right to the limited resources of the earth; these belong to all and in equal measure. Amassing of wealth by a few creates classes and this leads to conflicts. Society must come together to form a classless society.

(c) The third lesson to learn from socialism is that it is the worker, and not his master, who defines society. Work is a human resource exploited by the capitalist that robs the worker of his human dignity and alienates him in society. All must work according to their ability and must be satisfied to receive benefits as per their needs.

(d) The fourth lesson is the genesis of the state, which comes into existence due to the totalitarian will of the people. The state is supreme, and any dissent is tantamount to the basic social human contract of equality and brotherhood.

(e) The fifth lesson to learn from socialism is its failure to evoke liberty. Individual liberty became the victim of the socialist doctrine and hence, lost all humanity from its ideology. It served an illusory giant called the state, failing to recognize the individuals who made up the state. Stripping people of liberty and personal freedoms was to strip them off humanity and all its dignity and, therefore, identity. It is freedom that constitutes an individual as a person, not any kind of person such as a mere worker, but a moral person who is responsible for his own decisions and actions. A moral person constitutes one's identity before society, as well as legally before the established law of society. The denial of moral freedom denies one of personal identity and thereby, personal responsibility for one's actions.

Indeed, we cannot ignore socialism. It goes to prove howsoever negatively and at an immeasurable cost to human lives that the greatest moral that we have is liberty—the very essence of man's will.

Social Market Economy

Anglo–American Capitalism

The economy in the urbanized West, which developed after World War II, successfully proves a point that capitalism works. It produced the West German economic miracle—the *Sozialmarktwirtschaft* (discussed later). It raised France, England, Austria, and the Benelux countries from the ruins of war to the pinnacle of economic prosperity and a very high quality of life. The communist countries of Eastern Europe that were under

---

Patil in God's Own Country

Social justice or union thuggery?

Damodar Patil runs a successful interior decoration business in Mumbai. When he got a proposal for a job to be done in the newly built house of a well-known personality from Kerala, Patil readily accepted. He thought he could mix business with leisure in the state known as God's own country because of its natural beauty, vibrant culture, and traditional hospitality. Everything regarding the work was settled, the details chalked out, and the costs agreed upon and duly assigned. Patil's men arrived with the material in two trucks at the designated place in Kerala. As the men got ready to unload the truck, they realized that a small group of men had surrounded the trucks and had started yelling at the workers who were unloading. They could not understand what the men were saying because they did not know Malayalam. But they certainly knew that they had caused a problem. Curious onlookers gathered around and the crowd started to swell steadily.

Patil nervously surveyed the crowd for somebody educated, who could help him. Amid the confounding situation he mused, 'Well, Kerala has 100 per cent literacy!' Sure enough, a reasonable-looking man volunteered to help and told him in perfect English, though with a heavy local accent, that this was a local labour issue. Workers brought from outside would deprive the local workers of their rights. The loading or unloading, which was a part of the local labour, was their right and hence, they be compensated for loss of their rights. Perhaps reading Patil's mind, he added for good measure, that communism is a way of life in the state. Then he made a queer gesture, as if to say that Patil either put up with it or reload and go back!

Questions

1. Has communism in India compounded our economic problems?
2. What is the solution for a lucrative employment?
3. What are the labour problems that small businesses face in India?

Source: The circumstances of the case are true but have been adapted with necessary changes. Character names have been changed.

---

the erstwhile Soviet Union as also several other countries from around the world, from China to Latin America, also thrived, but only through the propaganda of prosperity rather than real prosperity. In the 1980s, China buried its socialist economy and adopted the capitalist model of economy. It survived, while the rest of the communist countries collapsed, and the Soviet Union vanished from the world map. Thus, history proves that capitalism works. It works because it has very strong inherent principles for wealth creation and growth, private property and the right of ownership. Thus, the capitalists distribute wealth, while the communists distribute poverty.

Another reason why capitalism works is that it respects individual freedom. The freedom of choice creates opportunities for entrepreneurs. From merely satisfying the needs of consumers, capitalism furthers consumer wants to the fulfilment of their higher order needs. They are able to enjoy comforts and further satisfy their social desires of status and achievement. Not only commerce, but also art, sports, entertainment, and leisure enrich lives.

The concept of Sozialmarktwirtschaft (social, market, economy)

After the two extreme doctrines of capitalism and communism, a form of socialism arose, as there was a need to overcome the evils of both these doctrines. While capitalism prospered in the developed Western countries and communism was pursued in many other parts of the world, the Western European countries took a middle path between the material socialism of the communists and laissez faire of the capitalists. Private property and ownership of capitalism was combined with the human worth of socialism to form a new doctrine, where both the state as well as the citizens became partners in the enterprise of society. This system had the free-market system of the capitalists, as well as the fundamental concerns of the citizens, such as education, health, and employment. The German political and social establishments formed the concept of *Sozialmarktwirtschaft* (*sozial*—social, *markt*—market, *wirtschaft*—economy). Some described this concept as capitalism with a human face, while others described it as socialism with a human face.

The problem in Germany was that the conservatives (professing capitalism) had less faith in such a doctrine, while the socialists could not reconcile with private enterprise. However, the growing pressures of the social responsibility of the government forced the political establishment to reform. Since the beginning of the 1980s, there followed a concerted effort at reforms such as healthcare, pension, education, and apprenticeship. Recently, firm steps have been taken in the field of environmental protection. German industry has been motivated to partner in the social cause. The trade unions have become partners in corporate governance. Presently, the grand coalition government in Berlin, consisting of both the conservatives as well as the socialists, goes to show that a people-centric national enterprise is desired. The ideological differences and the party dogmas and doctrines would have to succumb to the common good of the people.

Indian Model of Mixed Economy

The social market economy can be better understood from the Nehruvian point of view. Jawaharlal Nehru, a freedom fighter and the first Prime Minister of independent India, had articulated a socialism that avoided the pitfalls of communism and the mistakes of capitalism. He charted a course, a middle path as he described, where the best ideas of capitalism and socialism synthesized. Thus, Nehru strongly supported private property, ownership, and enterprise. He resented the concept of profit, but promoted the idea of social responsibility, which has become the mainstay of today's corporations, to be acceptable in society.

On the other hand, he believed strongly in planned economy by the state, which would have had complete control over policy and regulation. This had disastrous consequences in the post-Nehruvian era, when this aspect of control took hold of the political establishment. In the absence of a clear economic doctrine, the political economy of the country embraced the Soviet model of socialism, thus nationalizing banks, the aviation industry, food industry, etc. on its way. A burgeoning and blundering bureaucracy sealed the fate of an enterprising initiative and business leadership.

As the 1990s approached, communism collapsed and along with it, India's socialist model lost steam. India, unlike China, which was already nearly two decades into economic reform, was most ill-prepared and was forced into reform by the new and resurgent economic global phenomena.

It is close to two decades now and India is still a fledgling economy due to the slow pace of liberalization, political and ideological rivalries, and a burgeoning poverty-ridden populace that accounts for 60 per cent of the total population of 1.2 billion.

India would thus need a doctrine whose principles ensure quality of life for every citizen through complete economic freedom. For this purpose, corporations would have to be seen in a different light from those who are hungering for profits. Corporations, trade unions, not-for-profit organizations, and charitable and non-governmental organizations have to become citizens. Thus, the model of the government on one side and the rest on the other must cease. This is the synthesis of capitalism and socialism.

Doctrines and the Role of Business

From the above discussion, it becomes increasingly clear that business is a phenomenon that is heavily controlled by governments, irrespective of their subscription to any particular ideology. Today, business enterprise is the only occupation that significantly occupies people's mind. The prospect of better and fulfilled lives is more real in business enterprises than in dogmas and doctrines, and political ideologies.

Business has become a highly competitive activity of man. There is a need, therefore, to study it as a special discipline, just as other streams of natural or social sciences. Business integrates knowledge and skills from all sciences and professions. We have to look beyond the shibboleth 'the business of business is business.' There is a need to seek certain principles that sustain and promote business and put its purpose in the right context.

PHILOSOPHY OF BUSINESS

At times, if people mistake economics for business philosophy, they may be well forgiven because it is an important aspect of economics. We may safely say that business is the applied branch of economics, and business ethics is its applied philosophy. From Adam Smith to Peter Drucker, there has been a concerted effort to make business, with all its branches of production, distribution, and services, a subject of philosophical discipline.

Right Business Philosophy

Here, the word right, is to be understood doctrinally or ideologically, rather than ethically or morally. A rightist view is an outlook that one considers to be a phenomenon, strictly with one orientation and deprived of any deviation. Those who hold the rightist views are also called conservatives, because they follow their doctrine as purely as possible. Hence, they are also called purists. Fundamentalists is another term used for them because they assert their views vehemently. In the field of business also, there are rightists or conservatives who propagate strong views and believe that business has no motive other than profit.

It may seem that it is ill-advised to see more into a business than just business. Milton Friedman (1970) is a purist in so far as the business philosophy is concerned— 'business is for profit.' The ideas of social conscience and corporate social responsibility of corporations are the causes for corruption of the essence of business. Sticking responsibility on corporations for social causes is to run away from the task of business. This has been the doing of those reformists who would like to contravene capitalism and take it back to communism again.

Business executives owe their responsibility to their organization, even if that organization is a philanthropic one. It is for the promoters of a business to know why they are running a school or a hospital, but as far as the executive is concerned, his/her loyalty is to the employer and he/she has to be profitable in the way the employer wants.

Thus, responsibilities must be understood as attributed to real persons. Both the promoters and their employees may have several social and business responsibilities. But responsibility cannot be pinned on to an artificial person like a corporation. The only responsibility that the corporation has is that its shareholders' values increase. The shareholders, employees, or customers may spend their own money in whatever way they like, but that does not affect the corporation.

It is the business of the government to take responsibilities for its citizens. So it charges taxes from corporations, as well as individuals, and conducts beneficial programmes for the people. Corporations, on the other hand, have shareholders who, in their collective wisdom, appoint people to look after the affairs of their company and await results in terms of profits. The last thing that they desire is that their monies be channelled to philanthropies. Those who preach social responsibility are merely professing public hypocrisy by playing to the gallery.

Left Business Philosophy

At the opposite end of the spectrum of right business is the left business. It is a system of thought that thinks only in one aggregate—the state. Individuals are lost sight of in the woods of the state. Hence, private property, individual ambitions, and all that encourages profit are shelved. The state runs the business and the trade unions rule the roost. In the UK these people were called the labour, while in the US they were known as democrats, or to a large extent, in pejorative sense, as liberals. These people were supposed to tax corporate businesses and rich income holders and operate state-run welfare programmes for the people.

Poverty and Planning

What is the Planning Commission of India doing?

Montek Singh Ahluwalia[a] is one of the highly respected economists of India. Along with Manmohan Singh, the present prime minister of India, he was instrumental in the reform and liberalization of the Indian economy in the early 1900s. As the deputy chairman of the Planning Commission of India (the prime minister is the ex-officio chairman), he shoulders the responsibility of allocating large outlays of funds to the areas of development. From agriculture to heavy industry, from health and education to infrastructure, from minerals to public distribution system, it is a monumental undertaking. The commission makes plans for five years and calls the programme the five-year plan. Jawaharlal Nehru, the first prime minister of India, borrowed the idea of the five-year plan from the Soviet Union and introduced it in India in 1951. The current plan (2007–2012) is the eleventh since its inception.

Perhaps there is nothing wrong with the planning. Some of the achievements are stupendous, such as the irrigation plan, heavy industry, the green revolution in agriculture, science and technology, nuclear technology development, and space missions and defence technology.

However, the main goal of the commission, that is, poverty alleviation, is far from meeting the target. Transparency International India[b] has shown in its research that the so categorized below the poverty line (BPL) people, whose number runs into over three hundred million, have not benefited from any planning. On the contrary, they suffer under it. They suffer due to the corruption involved. Without bribe they do not get bank loans, healthcare, electricity, and even ration, the food from the public distribution system.

Some highlights

- There is a large gap in the perception of corruption and its actual experience.
- Thirty-five per cent of the BPL households pay bribes for the services they receive.

- The benefits of technology, such as computers, RTI Act, social audit, and e-governance have not trickled down to the BPL level.
- Two per cent of the BPL households are victims of influence peddling, particularly in the areas of land records, electricity connections, schooling, and housing.
- Two per cent of the BPL households do not use the PDS system.
- The bribe paid by the BPL households in 2007 stands at Rs 8830 million.
- The poorest BPL households paid Rs 2148 million as bribe for the services they received.

The Planning Commission is the government's contribution to the mixed economy. Many economists feel that mixed economy has been the bane of India's development. Further, it was worsened by the so-called *licence raj*, wherein private industries had to buy their licences to run their businesses. The regime of licencing has now been relaxed, although not fully eradicated. This system put India on the corruption map, since obtaining licences meant paying kickbacks to the bureaucrats.

It is believed that if India becomes a corruption-free nation, it will attain the living standards of the US in less than ten years.

Questions

1. Has not the policy of mixed economy encouraged a decadent culture of corruption?
2. Has mixed economy destroyed the ethical fabric of our society?
3. What measures can you suggest to eradicate corruption?
4. Can you expect a business to be honest when its business licence is obtained through corrupt practices?

[a] *Source:* http://planningcommission.nic.in/.

[b] TII—CMS *India Corruption Study 2007 with Focus on BPL Households*, National Report 2008, http://www.cmsindia.org/cms/highlights.pdf.

As the fall of communism was imminent, England, the cradle of capitalism, saw its golden age under the so-called Thatcherism years of the late 1970s and through the1980s, when Margaret Thatcher, the then Prime Minister, put into practice the kind of capitalism proposed by Milton Friedman. The same period saw in the US another practitioner of capitalism, of business for business' sake: Ronald Reagan. His name turned into an ideology, be it in politics or economics—*Reaganism* and *Reaganomics.*

Both communist socialism and Anglo-American capitalism had a sudden death syndrome and consequently ended within the years of the last millennium. They died of the same problem—both lacked the subject in their objectives. Capitalism had profit or money as its objective and could not care less for the people; communism had the state as its objective and people did not count.

The new labour in England and the liberated liberals in America tried to shape a new doctrine and a new world order. After several financial scams and losses in billions of dollars, people woke up to the idea of corporate governance in business, to care not only for the stockholders, but also all the stakeholders in society.

Philosophy of Business Not Business Philosophy

After the above discussions, it is important to make a basic distinction between the philosophy of business and business philosophy. We are quite familiar with the business philosophy of a company when it adopts a particular model for doing business. For instance, low-cost carriers or budget airlines is an air travel business model that has generated big business. There are some other very successful contemporary business models such as online auction, banking, travel, and hospitality services. There is also the model of direct home or door-to-door sales. It is the oldest model that thrives and has not lost its appeal.

On the other hand, the philosophy of business is a theory about business that discusses the fundamental principles of its existence and its actions. What constitutes business? What is its nature? How does it operate? Under what rules does it operate? Who are the people involved in business? What is their role in such an activity?

Philosophy is a discipline of thought. It is logic when we study the laws of thought; it is epistemology when we study the nature of knowledge; it is metaphysics when we study the principles underlying reality; it is ethics when we study the norms of life. Any subject when submitted to a systematic discipline of thought becomes its philosophy.

We have mentioned in this chapter why business must become a discipline of our study. There was a time when both business and the businessman had an adverse image in society. Both were tolerated as necessary evils in society. Today, economic activity plays a central role around the globe, and business and its management have grown in their own right to demand a discipline of their own. There are several theorists who have advanced the cause of business management studies. They espouse various philosophies to support their theories. Thus, Milton Friedman is a conservative who advocates unabashed American capitalism, whereas Peter Drucker is a moderate who advocates strong ethical values and management by objectives as the ideology.

Business activity has become very complex today and is conducted swiftly and instantly. This has thrown up several issues and problems related to stockholders, stakeholders, corporate governance, social responsibility, human resource, income discrimination, gender problems, intellectual property rights, affirmative action, and scores of other elements. All these need to be systematized through a definite method so that an ideal superstructure may be built.

The discipline of business consists of its laws of thought (business logic) and a critical thinking that will make its premises consistent and body of knowledge coherent (the theory of business knowledge). We would have to study the principles of how to conduct business (the theory of business ethics). The mast of this chapter has thoughts from two great philosophers—Immanuel Kant and Sri Aurobindo—who gave us systems of philosophy. It is indeed an age of commercialism that we have developed for ourselves. All our activities, including business activity, are directed with the objective of happiness. The philosophy of business is not yet a full-fledged science, but we must develop it so that we may become worthy of that happiness.

Peter Drucker, the Business Philosopher

System for running business

'Management is doing things right; leadership is doing the right things.' This is one of the most memorable and oft-quoted words of Peter Drucker (1919–2005). He was born in Austria, studied in Germany, and worked first as a journalist in Britain and then immigrated to the US and became its citizen in 1943. He taught at the New York University till 1971. He then went to Claremont University, California, where he developed the MBA programme. Over thirty works in management established him as the undisputable thinker of management discipline. Terms such as knowledge economy and knowledge worker are coined by him.

To begin with, his thoughts reflected on the method of scientific management propagated by Frederick Winslow Taylor, often dubiously referred to as the father of business management. It struck him that business elements can be analysed to improve efficiency. He advocated that it is a mistake to think that man is an economic animal. It is important to stress the communitarian aspect of man. The goal must be the progress of the community, wherein the needs of the individuals are met. He also thought that non-profit organizations are better suited in society towards attaining this goal. His

saying that 'there is no business ethics, there is just one ethics' is very famous. He, thereby, advocated a holistic approach to business. In other words, business is a part and parcel of society and it is established for the benefit of all. It is from this standpoint that today corporations are making social responsibility as their primary concern. To achieve this end of the well-being of the community, he advocated the concept of management by objectives. Today, this has become the article of faith for good corporate governance. Corporations have been able to set their priorities right. Profit is not the primary goal, but a goal to continued existence. The primary goal, however, is to serve the customer.

Questions

1. How much do customers matter in your business philosophy?
2. Is Peter Drucker's philosophy of business relevant?
3. Would it be in the Indian interest to adopt such a philosophy of business?

Laxmi Narayan Mittal's Business Philosophy

Steel tycoons business philosophy

'Reach for the stars but always keep one foot on the ground' was the best advice that L.N. Mittal received. It is at once ideal, as well as real. He says that ambition soars high and along with that the compulsions of achieving the goals. It then becomes difficult to practise integrity. It becomes difficult to stay in touch with reality. Success makes you fly and you cannot keep your feet

grounded. But reason it out—there is really no reason to lose sight of reality.

Questions

1. What do you understand by business ambition?
2. Is ambition a moral quality?
3. Does success define good business?

Source: India Today, 28 January 2008, p. 70.

SUMMARY

- Concepts or mental models to help structural thinking in business are important.
- There are different philosophies or sets of such models, depending on the economic, political, and cultural situations.
- Pragmatism appeals as a business model that is quickly able to relate to business problems and their resolution.
- One of the sub-structures of pragmatism is capitalism. It relates to individuals close to their nature of freedom and private ownership. It encourages private property and enterprise and ensures a good quality of life for the people.
- Capitalism, however, causes economic inequalities that lead to alienation of a class of people.

- Socialism overcomes the disadvantages of individualistic approach and takes responsibilities collectively.
- Communism has been the most expressive form of socialism and has helped to raise the awareness of the people around the world to their legitimate rights.
- Due to the lack of personal liberty and social freedoms, communism failed in its promise of social justice.
- Communism also failed economically for failing to understand human nature, which works on self-interest.
- The need of the hour is for a new philosophy, wherein both personal liberty and economic justice form the fundamental principles of a society. These principles ensure an egalitarian society. Business will reflect this philosophy.

KEY TERMS

Business model   Approach to do a business.

Capitalism   Free-market enterprise based on right to private property and individual freedom.

Communism   Highest form of socialism achieved in a classless society where state is supreme.

Distributive justice   Fairness in sharing the economic resources.

Doctrine   A teaching of consistent beliefs.

Dogma   A teaching consisting a tenet or belief.

Egalitarian   A state of equality and fairness without prejudice to race, gender, or status.

Equality   Impartial conduct, invariably related to justice and egalitarian society.

Fraternity   Brotherhood of man, value of worldwide humanity.

Government   A body of people managing the affairs of the people.

Human rights   Rights ensued from being human under the principle that all human beings are equal.

Ideology   A body of consistent ideas or beliefs.

Justice   To give one his/her due.

Leftist   To follow a collective ideology in its orthodox or pure fashion as struggle against exclusive groups.

Liberty   Right of freedom, personal autonomy, and independence.

Philosophy   The discipline of thought.

Pragmatism   Meaningful application of a concept to reality.

Private property   Right to ownership of economic resources: land, labour, and capital.

Rightist   To follow an ideology in its orthodox or pure fashion, safeguarding individual or group exclusivity.

Social market economy   A synthesis of the principles of social justice and free-market economy.

Socialism   The doctrine that follows the social principle of work according to ability and reward according to need.

Society   A group of people bound by culture.

CONCEPT REVIEW QUESTIONS

1. How helpful is pragmatism to business?
2. What are the principles of capitalism?
3. What are the advantages and disadvantages of socialism?
4. What failed communism—the people or the principles? Give examples.
5. What do you understand by philosophy?
6. Distinguish between philosophy of business and business philosophy.

CRITICAL THINKING QUESTIONS

1. What is an ideology and how does it affect business?
2. What does freedom of thought mean to you?
3. How can one overcome economic injustice?

FURTHER READING

John Rawls, *A Theory of Justice*, Harvard, MA: Harvard University Press, 1971.

CASE STUDY

Nandigram Massacre—Symbol of People's Resistance against Acquisition of Property

Nandigram—The Red Rag to the Marxist Communist Party of India

Nandigram makes headlines
Times of India, 15 March 2007

Nandigram turns blood red
KOLKATA: At least 11 people were killed in police firing at Nandigram, in east Midnapore, on Wednesday, as the administration moved in to take charge of an area that had virtually been marooned since 7 January 2007. The casualty, West Bengal's worst in 30 years of Left Front rule, left the state

stunned. Trinamool Congress estimates put the toll at 50. PWD minister, Kshiti Goswami of the RSP, a Left Front constituent, said 50 bodies were taken to hospital, but it was impossible to ascertain how many were actually dead.[a]

Geography of Nandigram

Nandigram is a village in the east Midnapore district of West Bengal. It is situated on the banks of the river Haldi. On the opposite bank lies the well-known industrial city of Haldia, which is under the administration of the Haldia Development Authority of the West Bengal State Government. Although

---

[a] *Times of India*, 15 March 2007.

it is in such proximity to an industrial city, the village is unaffected by development and is primitive in its living standards. The roads are rudimentary and the transport is archaic and hazardous. The only connection to the nearby Haldia city is by a ferry. There is no bridge over the river. The houses of the village are not clustered together. The nature of their landholdings and their lifestyles has made people build their houses far from each other. In the absence of a proper road network, people are forced to walk long distances.

Nandigram for SEZ

The Government of West Bengal deliberated that Haldia could be made an industrial hub if Nandigram, which was across the river, could be acquired for special economic zone (SEZ). The Government of India introduced the SEZ policy in April 2000, with the object of enhancing foreign investments to promote exports from the country. Accordingly, the policy furnished that the allotted SEZ would be deemed foreign territory for the purposes of trade operations, duties, and tariffs. The state government had the important role to facilitate and provide for the approved projects. The SEZs also have the advantages of income tax exemption for the first five years, permission for 100 per cent foreign direct investment, and hosts of other benefits. The projects may be established by private, public, or foreign firms or as a combination of their partnerships.

This was a fast-track development programme and the development-starved people of Nandigram would welcome it. Haldia Petrochemicals, as well as the Indian Oil Corporation, had already created over a lakh jobs. Now, if Nandigram too could be integrated into the project, an even greater opportunity for employment could be created.

Indonesia in Nandigram

To be very brief, the Government of West Bengal zeroed in on an Indonesian group called the Salim Group of Sudono Salim, who is a close associate of the late General Suharto, the ex-president of Indonesia. The Nandigram venture would be an equal partnership project, that is, a fifty-fifty partnership deal between the Salim Group and the West Bengal Industrial Development Corporation. The group wanted 35,000 acres of land. Apart from the chemical industrial setup, the group would also construct a 100 km-long and a 100 m-wide Eastern Link Expressway and a four-lane road bridge over the Haldi river, connecting Haldia city to Nandigram. Both the road and the bridge would be connected to National Highway 34.

Ground realities of Nandigram

Nandigram is a collection of villages. It is politically well organized under the Marxist Communist Party of India (CPI(M)), which is the leading faction in the Left Front government. Probodh Panda (CPI(M)) is the Member of the Parliament, representing the constituency. He had serious reservations about the acquisition of land. He had very valid reasons:

(a) The people are totally dependent upon the land.

(b) It is a multi-crop land.

(c) The total number of people to be affected by the acquisition is 40,000.

(d) Losing these landholdings would mean losing livelihoods.

Formation of BUPC

The divisions in the mind started reflecting on the ground. The like-minded people in the political spectrum shifted and public opinion started forming, and along with it originated the association called Bhumi Uchchhed Pratirodh Committee (Anti-Land Acquisition Committee). The resistance movement was started by the activists of the Trinamool Congress, breakaway activists from CPI(M) and Forward Bloc (faction in the Left Front government), Naxals and Maoists, and other party activists and individuals. The object was to use all possible means, to stop the government from acquiring the land of the people, and to save livelihoods. What people failed to comprehend was that a government that took pride in land reforms was now ready to take away land and the livelihoods of its people. Table 3.1 shows the chronology of the events at Nandigram.

SEZ

China

Deng Xiaoping, the supreme leader of China, said, 'As long as it catches mice it doesn't matter whether the cat is black or white,' thus justifying the deviation from the communist economic ideology. Deng had opened up the economy as the US warmed up to the Great Dragon. Deng saw what others did not see—the fall of communism. He cleverly mobilized political opinion for modernization as early as the 1970s and then continued vigorously in the 1980s in such a way that reforms could not be reversed. A special economic zone (SEZ) was created in a small village called Shenzhen, which for all practical purposes became a free-trade zone, free from all controls and taxes and tariffs. Shenzhen became a 10-million-strong ultra-modern city in less than two decades. By that time, China had progressively introduced modernization in the rest of the country, which turned to be an economic miracle of the millennium. Today, China is the power-house of the world's manufacturing industry.

India—Who 'sez' it is good?

India woke up from its stupor only in the year 2000 and followed several other developing countries like Brazil, Russia, the Philippines, Poland, Ukraine, etc., and the commerce ministry declared an SEZ policy. Over a thousand SEZs were declared practically in all the states. Some export-oriented units got the free tag immediately. Then began the uphill task, as the land had to be acquired from the farmers. They refused to part with their ancestral holdings, the only means of their livelihood. Also, the paltry compensation by the government was no incentive. The farmers are the largest vote-bank. Hence, it was natural that the issue got politicized, as every party tried to fight for the farmers' share of votes.

Economists feel that development through SEZs is merely a myth. Research clearly shows[a] that whatever reforms and liberalizations have taken place both in India and China are statistically more significant than whatever the SEZs could achieve through exports and FDIs. While simple people such as Indian farmers perceive that SEZs are nothing but a land-grab exercise, economists cannot make sense as to what is the actual role of SEZs in a liberalized and open economy, where the SEZs are a detriment to the level playing field for those who are outside of it.

[a] Leong, 2007.

Table 3.1 Nandigram chronology

Date	Event
3 January 2007	The chairman of the Haldia Development Authority puts up the notice for land acquisition. The first uprising—information received about the government's land acquisition; government officials and the local police station become the targets.
7 January 2007	The BUPC-Trinamool Congress combine clashes with CPI(M) cadres. Death toll: 6.
8 January 2007	BUPC and CPI(M) clash. CPI(M) supporters and families shift to makeshift camps at Khejuri. BUPC and supporters dig up roads, put up barricades, and keep the police away.
9 January 2007	Chief Minister (CM) announces visit to Nandigram. CM admits administrative failures to tackle situation.

Contd

Table 3.1 Contd

Date	Event
7 February 2007	Officer of the District Intelligence Branch (Sadhu Chatterjee) is assaulted. Officer goes missing.
10 February 2007	Missing officer's body found in Haldi river with multiple injuries.
11 February 2007	CM visits Heria, Nandigram. Promises not to acquire land. People do not trust. BUPC refuses to lift blockade of Nandigram.
14 March 2007	The massacre: 3000 police and armed groups of CPI(M) cadre against BUPC-mobilized 2000 men, women, and children. The encounter result: 14 dead (official), 50 (unofficial). Arson. Rape. 3000+ displaced. High Court, Kolkata, directs CBI to investigate and file report.
17 March 2007	CBI arrests 10 CPI(M) activists. CBI also seizes large cache of arms and ammunitions from them.
26 March 2007	CBI files report.
June–July 2007	Court hearing by division bench of Chief Justice S.S. Nijjar and Justice P.C. Ghosh.
3 September 2007	CM announces new chemical hub at the island of Nayachar, 30 km off Haldia.
25 October 2007	Recapture of Nandigram: Armed CPI(M) cadre marches in; police do not act. Just watch.
7 November 2007	25,000 villagers (more than half the population of Nandigram) leave homes and take shelter in villages for fear of being attacked by the CPI(M) cadre.
10 November 2007	CPI(M) cadre fires at the rally at Maheshpur in Nandigram. Result: 2 dead.
12 November 2007	Nandigram falls to CPI(M). National Human Rights Commission (NHRC) sends notice to the government demanding report.
13 November 2007	Five companies of Central Reserve Police Force (CRPF) arrive in Nandigram. CM Buddhadeb Bhattacharya justifies: 'The opposition was paid back in the same coin.'
16 November 2007	High Court, Kolkata, rules 14 March 2007 police firing as illegal.
18 November 2007	In *People's Democracy*, the CPI(M) mouthpiece, the CM denies that Nandigram is chosen for chemical hub; he affirms that Nayachar is the one for the purpose.
21 November 2007	A weeklong debate, acrimony, and condemnation follows in Parliament and the CPI(M) is totally isolated on the issue.
25 November 2007	CRPF unearths arms and ammunition and maoist literature.
6 December 2007	In Khejuri, in Nandigram, unidentified graves are found, with charred bones—victims of BUPC-CPI(M) clash.

Source: Indian Express and Times of India.

Party and the government stand

The party and the government reiterated repeatedly that 'The government has no intention to acquire land in Nandigram. It is the political designs of all the opposition parties, both at the state as well as at the centre, to cleanse Nandigram of the CPI(M). The events of Nandigram are unfortunate and the deaths are regrettable. The gains of land reforms will be upheld; industrialization will not be given up. The attempts to isolate the party will fail.'[c]

National and international reaction

The country was aghast at the state-sponsored violence and its condoning of its party cadre's belligerence. The media, both national as well as international, focused on the atrocities and individual cases of the dark night of 14 March 2007. The national press was unequivocal in its condemnation of the violence. The governor of West Bengal said it all when he described the violence as 'cold terror'. The accusations of CPI(M)'s fascism and intolerance were highlighted. Some even compared the episode to the Jallianwallah Bagh massacre, evocative of the notorious massacre under the British colonial rule. The political parties—Trinamool Congress and the BJP—called for protests and a *bandh*. Protests and solidarity resolutions were witnessed all across the country. There was pandemonium in the Parliament, demanding the dismissal of the state government. There followed a sympathy wave, and all kinds of celebrities, such as activists, writers, artists, cinema artists, and foreign personalities such as Ramsey Clarke, the former Attorney General of the United States of America, descended on Nandigram. Members of the National Human Rights Commission also took interest.

Business Reaction

The Government of West Bengal had earlier acquired 1000 acres for Tata Motors from Singur, in West Bengal, amidst a great deal of controversy. The people were opposed. There was a standoff. After much acrimony and several rounds of negotiations, the controversy had just calmed down. The businesses were wary about Singur, but since the Tatas, who for the first time in their existence, hit back at the business rivals, the conspiring confederates retreated and calmed down.

Nandigram was different. This was a heady political mix. The political battleground spilt blood. The businesses only kept a watchful eye and nothing more. The Indian business lost its voice completely. It signed over a dozen deals, worth well over one lakh crore rupees with the Government of West Bengal. The government needed to acquire at least 25,000 acres of land for the purpose. The government, this time around, did not want to take recourse to the Land Acquisition Act of 1894. It wanted to deal with the people with direct purchases. Needless to say, the government did not succeed in its attempts. Whether serious attempts were made is also doubtful. Various wordy terms such as 'land aggregation', etc., were utilized, but nothing was instrumentalized.

In the meantime, the businesses wanted to run their business as usual, currying favour with the political establishment. They were waiting for an opportune moment so that the government would acquire land for them. However, the businesses were in a shock when it was revealed in February–March of 2008 that the Government of Goa had approached the Central Government for scrapping its already approved SEZs through de-notification, and those which were being processed in the Directorate of Commerce not to be considered.

There is an undercurrent among the people against the SEZs. What are the state governments and the central government going to do? What are the businesses going to expect? These are the unanswered questions.

---

[c] Prakash Karat, 'What Really Happened in Nandigram', *Rediffnews*, http://search.rediff.com/dirsrch/default.asp, 23 March 2007.

Discussion Questions

1. Why do you think this case has anything to do with ethics?

2. What are the facts of the case? Are they neutral or partisan?

3. What would you do to find the real facts? What are the real facts in this case?

4. Who are the stakeholders and what stakes do they have in Nandigram?

5. What ethical principles are at stake in the Nandigram episode?

6. When it is a question of development of an entire village of 40,000 people, should the loss of a few lives make any difference?

7. What are the limits of human rights?

8. If the land acquisition is as per legal procedures, should we care for the sentiments of it being an ancestral property?

9. Was it not the duty of the people of Nandigram to obey the law?

10. If the project is beneficial in terms of general infrastructure, development, employment, industrialization, then why did the people of Nandigram oppose the project? Why do they want to be dependent on unpredictable agriculture and other uncertain factors?

11. Why do you think gross injustice was done to the people of Nandigram?

12. If the goal of the government was development, could it not have adopted some people-friendly means for the proposed chemical hub?

13. How can one manage a macro relationship among the government, a corporation, and the people?

14. Do you think the violence at Nandigram could have been avoided?

15. Do you think the politicians and police will have a clear conscience after the massacre at Nandigram?

16. How would you have managed the conflict (a) as the chief minister of the state, (b) as the village head of Nandigram, (c) as the chairman of the Haldia Development Authority, (d) as a CPI(M) party cadre, (e) as a school teacher of Nandigram, and (f) as a citizen of Nandigram?

17. What are the short-term and long-term decisions that could bring normalcy to Nandigram?

18. What is the modus operandi for the implementation of these decisions?

19. What lessons can the corporates learn from the Nandigram case?

20. What are the lessons learnt from the Nandigram episode by the government and politicians who manage the affairs of the people?

21. As the chairman of the Haldia Development Authority, how would you change this challenging situation as a turn-around in industrial enterprise and human relations?

22. As a manager or a management student, what lessons do you learn from the Nandigram incident?

Going Further . . .

- Integrate the discussion groups with the classes of business law, human resource management, corporate governance, managerial economics, organizational behaviour, and strategic management.

- Conduct a local seminar. Invite important people, industrialists, journalists, lawyers, bureaucrats and some local politicians and *panchayat* members.

- Simulate Nandigram.

ETHICAL DEVELOPMENT PROGRAMME

Management Training

Form a group and identify the closest SEZ in your area. Get acquainted with it. Investigate both the social and economic aspects. Position yourself as a mediator between the government machinery, the law, and the people.

Famous Doctrines and their Ethical and Economic Relevance

Do you have a doctrine, teaching, belief, or command of your own? What system of thought do you follow? What theory do you propose? What is the philosophy of your life? Are these questions relevant to a manager? As a manager, what would be your line of action? What reasons would you give to explain your decisions? Would you not need a system to explain what you do? What reasons can you proffer when there are no true reasons? How will you explain it? You ought to give a moral reason for your decisions and actions. You will find such reasoning in one system of thought or doctrine or the other.

A doctrine is a system of thought. We often describe it as being a theory or a formal structure to which we submit our world. By world we mean not the physical world but the virtual world, the world of ideas. Here, we will juxtapose a few doctrines to compare and contrast a few doctrines that have shaped our civilization, our way of life, culturally, economically, politically, or morally.

Absolutism versus *Relativism*

A doctrine that holds the truth is complete and total. It is a dogmatic and unyielding belief in what one holds to be true, objectively and universally. In ethics, it would mean that the standards of moral judgment are supreme and eternal. In terms of political economy, it would mean totalitarianism, where no dissent is possible. For instance, the doctrines of socialism or communism are absolutists in nature. It is opposed to 'relativism', a doctrine where the complex aspects of the truth are considered. The truth is relative, namely, it may vary from individual to individual and group to group. All knowledge is relative to our experiences and the conditions through which we experience it. In ethics, it would advocate the relative standards of judgments, thus making room for cultural, national, and other differences. In political economy, it would allow for plurality, economic, and social independence. Market economy is an example of relativism. There is a famous observation in Aristotle's work *Nicomachean Ethics*, which states that '[F]ire burns both in Hellas and in Persia; but men's ideas of right and wrong vary from place to place.'

Capitalism versus *Socialism*

This is a system of doctrine that holds private ownership as its fundamental principle. Ownership of property, production, and enterprise, or, in short, the right to capital is possessed by the individual and has been further endorsed in the constitution of the country. It is again augmented by individual freedom and respect for the law that protects the freedom of other individuals. Capitalism creates its own forces of political economy, which functions freely in society and helps to create a free-market economy. The ethical consequences of capitalism are that individuals are responsible for their actions. This obligation is further shared by corporations. Hence, corporate social responsibility is an avowed principle of capitalism.

Socialism is an antithesis of capitalism. It dismisses private property ownership and advocates collective ownership. While all must work as per their abilities, they must receive desserts as per their needs. It decries the exploitation of labour by the capitalists. Politically, it establishes the dictatorship of the proletariat. A nation is the wellspring of culture for its people. Thus, its political, economic, and cultural aspects are under the control of the state. Hence, it is also known as totalitarianism. What is right and what is wrong is determined by the state and one's moral existence is defined by one's submission to it.

Determinism versus *Doctrine of Free Will*

In day-to-day matters, when an event such as a stock market crash takes place, you would like to determine its cause. Cause determines the effect. Everything in the world is due to a cause. Since the effect follows the cause, the former is predetermined by the latter. In cultural terms and as an explanation to our moral actions, there is a widespread belief in India that not only our physical actions, but also our future, are predetermined. Some describe it as fatalism, while others say it is a *karmic* consequence. In short, according to determinism, human actions are not free. These are done under certain compulsions and forces, beyond the control of the agent. Psychology helps us to understand the problem better. It advocates that the cultural environment is responsible for our actions. Human actions are responses to the external stimuli. Hence, one cannot be blamed for one's wrong actions. This goes way beyond relativism, as it does not consider the perpetrator guilty of his/her actions.

Free will, on the other hand, advocates freedom of the will. The good will, according to Kant, determines our actions and is always free. This is the fundamental moral postulate that makes individuals responsible for their actions. Problems abound since causal arguments sound very convincing, but who can deny that we act in a certain way because of our prevailing circumstances? Could we not have changed our views to avoid the argument? Is it imperative to raise the prices of your products just because the rest of your competitors are doing it? You could change a business environment by your decision rather than let a business environment force you into a decision. Thus, the postulate of the free-will also confers freedom on its subjects. An action has moral character if it exhibits the freedom of the will.

Rationalism versus *Voluntarism*

Human beings are endowed with two important faculties—reason and will. Rationalism is a doctrine that advocates that only that which can be arrived at rationally is true. All that is verifiable is rational. Religious beliefs, habits, and prejudices are irrational. Our moral conduct must be rationally explainable. A moral tenet without sound reasoning is inadmissible. Profit is a rational objective of business and there is nothing immoral about it.

Voluntarism advocates the second faculty of the humans—the will as a principle of not only existence but also action. Thus, all that is real is nothing but the will. The world that we see around us is only a representation of the will, which is mostly illusion or *maya*. History, for instance, is nothing but the revelation of such a will. Psychology explains it better, since will is the only force within us that is emotional and drives us to act. There is a very large school of thought in business today, which considers that it is the emotional quotient that advocates the business decisions that are made. In ethics, it implies that the will alone is the supreme moral faculty, while the rest such as conscience and reason have no place. Kant concluded that besides the good will, there is nothing in this world or outside it that is good.

Guidance

The above is a mere cursory look at the opposing doctrines, theories, or ideologies that have shaped the civilization of man. Decisions will be made and the future will be shaped, depending on the system of thought that one follows. In management development programmes that are conducted for the executives, consultants and experts force their clients to chalk out their business philosophy, aims, goals, and mission without founding such practices on a system of thought.

Choose a system of thought that appeals to you and is in tune with your upbringing and culture. For instance, if you choose the doctrine of the Gita, then you will dwell upon the ethical value of duty as the standard for all your business decision making and activity. Do not merely say it so to yourself. You would do well to sit down, reflect, and write out a personal charter of ethics.

Management Mantra

Philosophy of Thinking for Yourself

A disciple once asked his Zen master as to what was the greatest teaching. The master replied, 'Buddha is your own mind.' The disciple was so profoundly impressed that he left the monastery and spent the next twenty years as a hermit in the solitude of the woods, deeply meditating on the truth that he had heard from the master. One day, he met another disciple of the same master. The hermit wanted to know what the master had told the other disciple about the greatest teaching. The disciple quoted the master as saying, 'Buddha is not your own mind.'

MANTRA *Make up your own mind.*

Decision Making: Moral Reasoning and Its Application

My dharma must be my karma, and my karma must be my dharma.

—DA

It is quite possible for a man to do business and make money and earn profits and yet be a spiritual man, practice yoga and have an inner life. The Gita is constantly justifying works as a means of spiritual salvation and enjoining a Yoga of Works as well as of Bhakti and Knowledge.

—Sri Aurobindo

LEARNING OBJECTIVES

After studying this chapter, you will be able to

> Understand decision making
> Describe the essence of decision making
> Define the decision-making process
> State the classifications of decision-making processes

INTRODUCTION

A manager is defined as a decision maker of the area he/she handles. A corporation too is known to make organizational decisions. Irrespective of whether the decision maker is an individual or an organization, decisions are important and without decisions nothing worthwhile is possible.

Reasoning precedes decision. A decision is arrived at after a rigorous thinking process. As in logic—the science of reasoning, wherein conclusions are arrived at after making deductions from the given principles or inductions from a hypotheses—so too in a decision-making process, one must submit to the laws of reason.

The definition of decision and the complexity of decision making are so enormous that distinguished philosophers fail in their efforts to clarify the meaning and apply it to the different categories of human thoughts and actions, relationships, times and circumstances, situations, levels of understanding, cultural backgrounds, languages, interpretations, professional areas, and laws.

Philosophers such as Immanuel Kant, whose teachings have been integrated in this book, have tried their best to explain conceptually, through the theories of the mind, the epistemological character of decision making and the nature of the practical judgments. Psychologists such as Lawrence Kohlberg have carefully and scientifically observed and researched human behaviour in terms of psychological development and the nature of decision making, and their bearing on the moral nature of man. The best minds in quantum studies, such as Roger Penrose, Shelby D. Hunt, and Scott J. Vitell, have tried to map the processes of the mind in decision making.

One may know all the theories, qualitative or quantitative, but that does not ensure one to be moral. Morality lies in its practice and not theory. In essence, a manager is an employee and it is important for him/her to know what his/her brief is. Theories are fine, but guidelines to clear actions are helpful for the manager in performing his/ her tasks. One does not expect the manager to sit down and rigorously go through the Hunt–Vitell theory of decision making or the Kantian morality in all its categories. The manager needs a clear code of conduct.

UNDERSTANDING DECISION MAKING

Decisions in Ordinary Life

In our day-to-day life, decision making is not as dramatic as the Shakespearean question of 'to be or not to be' because there is a ready choice of one thing or the other. Most of the time, we live our lives waiting to make another decision. In other words, most of the time we are in a state of indecision. You go shopping with sufficient cash, but then consider using your credit/debit card instead. This choice is equally disagreeable, so you go around spending a lot of time, weighing your options as to what to buy or what not to buy. More often than not, you end up buying nothing. Your spouse, who accompanies you, is angry because both of you could not agree on one thing! You stand to gain nothing because of your indecisiveness and also create a conflict.

Making simple choices in life is after all not as simple as one wishes it to be. Career choices are even more difficult. 'What would you like to become?' is a perennial question that the elders ask the young. The young are naturally irritated because they have 'not yet made up their mind' or just ward off the query by saying plaintively, 'I don't know.' So it becomes quite discouraging to know that the promising youngsters live in a serious state of indecision. Then, there are other serious social issues about marriage, how many children to have, whether or not to abort a female foetus, how to care for aging parents, whether to purchase an apartment or hire one or build one's own house, take a loan or not, what school to send the children to, how to earn, spend, and save money, and a myriad of other actions and situations that one needs to take decisions on to move ahead. But the decisions are not forthcoming, and experience shows that by the time the persons concerned are willing to take a decision, it is too late.

Decisions in Professional Life

If ordinary life presents us with almost insurmountable difficulties in decision making, the decisions to be taken in our professional life are even harder because professionally we are responsible to a vast number of people. If you are a lawyer, you will go through a great deal of indecisiveness before taking up a case because you are not certain whether you can make a strong case with the facts and evidences you have at your command. You also have doubts about your client's ability to pay. You may wonder about the case hearings and their timings, which may not suit your schedule. If you are a businessman and want to diversify, you will be confronted with pro and contra arguments by your family members, your partners, and friends. On one hand, the people close to you warn you about the risks of the business, but on the other hand, experienced business people in the desired field fill you with optimism. You being a business management graduate refer to all the right theories and they prove that your family and friends are right. Thus, you spend most of your precious business time in indecision. In doing so, you lose time. To your chagrin, those people whom your family and friends had considered as fools, and made you believe the same, have succeeded famously in their new enterprise; only you have been left behind. You feel disappointed, frustrated, and even insulted by your indecision. The biggest irony of this entire episode is that you are a graduate from a famous business school, whereas those who have thrived in their enterprise do not even know what a college looks like from the inside!

Organizational Decisions

In spite of the several problems and conflicts that exist within families and work places, these organizations may be considered as small and intimate enough for us to cope well with. We can convince our near and dear ones or our clients and customers about the decisions that we make and the consequences we bear and make them bear. But today, life is impossible without being a part of larger organizations. Whether one likes it or not, one is a member of his/her community, state, and country. Citizenship imposes rights and duties. Just a simple purchase of breakfast items such as bread, butter, milk, tea, coffee, and a newspaper makes you a valued customer of astonishingly large corporations, in whose sphere you are the bottom-line. All the decisions that they take have hundreds of crores of rupees at stake. You may look disdainfully at the newspaper that costs just Rs 3. But hundreds of reporters, innumerable advertisers, and a large number of employees have spent a whole night formatting and producing

---

Moral Argument

Moral reasoning is logical

- If an action violates the law, it is morally wrong.
- Child labour violates the law.
- Therefore, child labour is morally wrong.

the paper. They have had to take innumerable decisions and go through many hardships to lay the paper at your breakfast table. These people who are in business cannot afford to be indecisive. It is clear that if you want to do business and stay in business, you have to make decisions that you may or may not like. But if you choose not to decide, it is at your own peril.

A corporation, which literally implies a body, has a special decision-making body called the board, which consists of members called directors. The board of directors makes important policy decisions for the firm and the managers are responsible executives, who carry out these policies. Thus, while there is a general direction given by the board, the managers are responsible for their own areas of functioning and they need to take quick and effective decisions. Indecision will cause loss of time and money.

ESSENCE OF DECISION MAKING

What is Decision Making?

People love mathematics, quantum theories, and equations and think that if they can get hold of an equation, they could solve problems as scientifically and as precisely as theoretical physics. There is no harm in such scientific pursuits, and this should be truly recommended and encouraged. However, problems arise when we start to quantify even those things that are not the subject of quantification. Even psychologists and social scientists who make qualitative judgments get attracted to equations because they too want to solve the problems in their field scientifically and precisely and thus avoid personal risks and responsibilities. Decision making is a very specialized science today and predictions on possibilities, probabilities, and uncertainties are carried out in elaborate equations. Managers and students are very often led to arbitrate themselves to quantitative measures in decision making.

Decision making is purely a qualitative affair. Here, we deal with unquantifiable mental processes. While evolving both naturally and socially, human beings developed a special faculty called reason. It makes human beings, who are otherwise animals biologically, intelligent beings. On one hand, they have very strong likes and dislikes and would like to have all their wants and desires fulfilled, and the controller or the director or the manager of their desires is their will. On the other hand, in order to achieve what they want, they utilize their intelligence to gather as much information and knowledge as possible about what they want, and the controller or the director or the manager of these activities is called the intellect. Based on the information supplied by the intellect, the will makes the final decision. This inner decision, which is not yet actualized externally, is called intention or the motive of action.

Intention or Inner Decision

Intention is the mind of a person. Intention is what you make up your mind to do and have not yet done, but circumstances permitting you will materialize your intention. To make up your mind is another clear phrase that describes decision making.

Intention determines the morality of an action. This may be illustrated in the following way. You have found something very valuable in your neighbour's house and the only way you can have it is by stealing it. You decide to do it. You break into the house in the dead of the night, but there is a burglar in there already! Your activity of breaking in awakens the household. So now, you help your neighbour to nab the burglar! As a result of the changed circumstances and your smart posing, you become a good neighbour who has come to the rescue!

In your heart of hearts, you know that you are a robber who unwittingly became a good Samaritan, or someone who helps his neighbour. Your good qualities are praised in the entire neighbourhood and you become a role model in society. The news is in the dailies of the city you live in and you become popular. Yet, you know within yourself that you are not what others perceive you to be.

Intention is the core reality of morality. People who follow the principle of 'the means must justify the ends' often reveal their true self or intentions as they really are. The objectives and actions of those managers whose intentions are transparent are always consistent. If the organization realizes that the manager's intentions are good and clear, the consequences whether positive or negative will have little bearing. Clear intentions establish the conduct of a good leader.

Relationship of Intention, Action, Morality, and Law

From our discussion above, it should be clear that while intention is directly and irrevocably connected with morality, the law, at least to begin with, is directly related to action. A court of law judges the actions. For example, when the law investigates a murder case, the law tries to determine the intention or motive for which the murder was committed—whether it was a conspiracy, whether it was in a fit of anger, or whether the gun was fired accidentally. Thus, although the law begins by considering the action, it ends with finding out the intention of the deed so that a just sentence is passed.

Therefore, both legally and morally, intention determines the nature of an action. Intention is the essence of being human, a person who is made up of the will and the intellect. Without intention, there is no identifiable person. Intention is the identity of the person on to whom a definite responsibility may be fixed.

Anatomy of an Individual Decision Maker

Human beings, as objects in the world, share their existence with inanimate objects such as rocks, liquids, and gases and animate objects such as plants and animals. They are a higher being than both inanimate and other animate objects. However, unlike plants, animals not only live, but experience feelings too. But human beings, apart from the above characteristics, have a unique characteristic known as reason.

The aspect of reason defines humans. Humans are rational animals who make a distinction between thought and action. Thought is an instrument of pure reason that analyses the data supplied to it. Action, on the other hand, is two-fold. First, it has a special, internal ability that directs itself to the desired things known as the will. Once

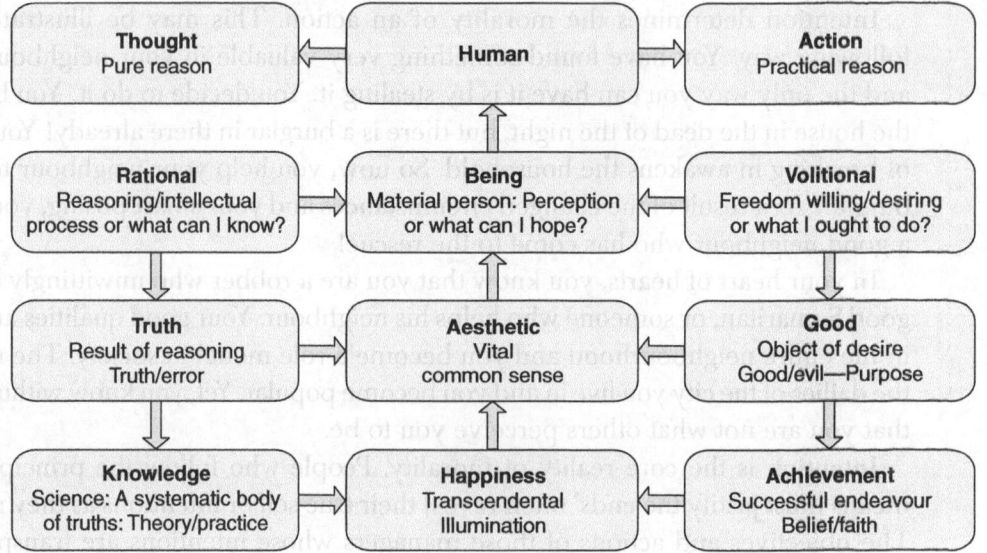

Fig. 4.1   Anatomy of an individual decision maker

the will is directed towards an object, it sends the same for a rational analysis to the intellect. Second, once the analysis is received from the intellect, it weighs its options and choices and makes a decision (see Fig. 4.1).

Rational and Volitional as Human

The data from the will is processed through the faculty of intellect and it offers rational choices of various degrees back to the will. The will then makes a choice, a volitional choice, and a choice that is deliberate and specific. Deliberation shows that the choice that is made has a definite purpose, whose object is good. Volitional choice further implies that the choice is voluntary or, in other words, one that is completely free. Thus, a human being by his/her rational nature has two important faculties—the will that ensures free choice and the intellect that is used by the will to make a choice. We separate these only academically, but in reality they are inseparably one in a human being.

Truth, Good, and Aesthetic Aspect

The proper object of our intellect is the truth; what is light to our eyes is truth to the intellect. The intellectual process gives us the truth. The process consists of following the laws of reason, which are also known as logic. Immanuel Kant called it critical reason or pure reason. The object of our volition or will is the good. This is why we say that the will is always good. Just as our reason seeks truth and nothing but the truth, so too our will seeks nothing but the good. The object of the will—that is, the good—and the object of the intellect—that is, the truth—are the determining factors in the constitution of a human act, that is, an effective decision. Thus, it is normal to hold that only adults with the capabilities of intellect and will, who are able to make a reasonable decision, are held responsible for their decision and action. For instance, the law of the land proposes to prosecute only those who have reached the stipulated legal age. Children or people with mental disabilities are considered as those who are unable to make responsible decisions because they are unable to make a rational and free choice.

Truth and good go hand-in-hand to make what is noble and excellent in human pursuit. We call such pursuits of refinement, civilization, and culture as the aesthetic aspect of human beings. These bring us to aims higher in life than the mere existence of animals and other animate and inanimate objects.

At this level, we, human beings, are expected to understand the truth and follow the pursuits of our will. This is the absolute minimum that every human being is capable of doing. Hence, this is what he/she ought to do and is called duty. This understanding of duty is known as deontological in nature, which is, deciding to do something because it is one's duty to do so. Immanuel Kant famously phrases it as 'duty for duty's sake'. This is also known as the moral imperative. Many misinterpret Kant to mean that it is cold rational morality. However, the Gita enlightens us with the same concept of duty as a moral directive that states, 'Seek to do your duty without aspiring for rewards.'

Knowledge, Achievement, and Happiness

A consistent body of truths that creates knowledge, and the pursuit of good, when working together, results in achievements. Thus, an individual who grows up learning and being educated can hope for happiness. This is far ahead of merely doing one's duty. Here, we would be guided by the ultimate objective that we want to achieve. Happiness is the ultimate goal in life. This is also known as the teleological pursuit.

Thus, both deontological and teleological aims are not contradictory but complementary. A habitual performance of duty forms in us a disciplined, moral person. When we have grown sufficiently in this manner, we attain virtues or good performances that become habitual. These lead us to even higher goals and, eventually, to the ultimate goal of seeking happiness.

In the anatomy of a human person, we have seen three different streams—the rational, the volitional, and the aesthetic. We may thus conclude the nature of an individual being in the famous triad *satyam* (truth—knowledge), *shivam* (will—creative), and *sundaram* (aesthetic—happiness).

Definition of Morality

The central purpose of our existence as human beings is to enrich our interests of intellect and will, thought and desire, and to strive towards their excellence and enrich ourselves with the ultimate goods of knowledge, beauty, and happiness. Morality is being true to ourselves, where we intelligently strive for what we desire. Morality, more specifically, is how we live and the choices that we make and these are both intelligent and good. The question, why to act morally, then becomes easier to answer. It is our nature to act morally. The degree of the excellence of our moral choices may differ due to the circumstances that we live in. But the fundamental intention, namely, the will to do, remains the good will. Hence, it behoves that the minimum morality will consist of doing our duty because our profession demands it. To do our duty is to be moral. This is the essence of professional behaviour. The professional codes of conduct are based on the principle of duty. Duty, and duty alone, constitutes a manager's morals.

Once the basic moral behaviour, that is, the level of duty is achieved, greater excellence may be achieved through the pursuit of the highest possible goals. This is expressed in the triad *sat* (knowledge), *chitta* (consciousness), and *ananda* (bliss).

Anatomy of Social/Group/Organization Decision Making

Basic assumptions of society

Down the centuries, there have been several theories about the origin of the human society. The most prominent of them are religious, social contract, and evolutionary. Some believe that human beings live in society because it has been planned by God in that manner. Those who propose the social contract theory observe that due to their basic needs like shelter, safety, and food, people came to an agreement to pool themselves together to achieve a common purpose. The evolutionary theorists carefully study the development of society through its various stages, which started from simple gatherings to complex political, economical, and culture-based societies. No matter what theories may one subscribe to, all have the following basic assumptions.

(a) The world has an order.
(b) Humans, who are a part of this world, can know this order and explain it rationally.
(c) People are social animals (Aristotle).
(d) Society is a group of people who have come together with a purpose.
(e) Society creates a rational order to achieve the purpose.
(f) Being a member of society, one has rights and carries out duties.
(g) There has been an evolution in the social groups. From being mere tribes and kingdoms, they have developed into nation-states and are striving for a global union of the people.
(h) People act socially, that is, in a collective manner.
(i) People express their will collectively to form governments, who are empowered to maintain law and order and use their power punitively against the erring.
(j) There are religious, political, cultural, and economic groups and organizations within society, with definite objectives.
(k) These groups and organizations enrich society through their achievements.
(l) These organizations have an intelligent order that is compatible with the mother organization, which is society.

Figure 4.2 illustrates the anatomy of social/group decision making.

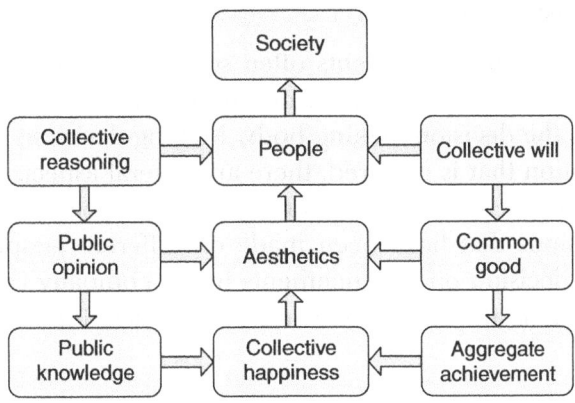

Fig. 4.2 Anatomy of social/group decision making

Society or organization and intelligent order

Just as an individual human being acts intelligently to attain definite goals, an organization also has well-spelt-out goals. Society or the organization lives in a collective consciousness. Initially, when the will is moved towards an object, there is a struggle to make a choice between the given options. If the decisions are not acceptable to all, there could be further struggle and conflict. If this is not resolved, then there would be a split.

Public opinion, common good, and progress

Since an organization has its own mind, over time it is able to generate a common opinion among many opinions. There is a debate as to what is the most acceptable common good. Once it is settled, progress can take place. Just as in the life of an individual, so too in the life of an organization, once the choice is made, progress can be achieved.

Common goal, achievement, and happiness

What a group or an organization can achieve is greater than what an individual can achieve. Doing things collectively is the intelligent way. The concerned groups and organizations spend time and energy on weighing the options and form a new course of action. The guiding principle in collective matters is the achievement of the common good that may be expressed, for instance, peace in times of war, standard of living in times of an economic upswing, alleviation of poverty in times of underdevelopment.

Moral Argument

Moral reasoning must be based on facts

- Causing harm to human life is wrong.
- Approximately 30 per cent of drugs sold by the chemists in India are spurious.

- Hence, the pharmaceutical product vendors share the blame for causing harm to the patients.

Decision-making body

Organizations and governments often select a group of individuals and give them powers to make recommendations on a particular subject. This special group of people is named as the decision-making body. Making decisions is not easy. Apart from all the information that is required, there are several aspects that need to be taken into consideration, such as the temperamental and emotional aspects, the consequences of the decisions that have been made on different people and their interests. For example, a decision on retrenchments in the company can lead to severe conflicts, since livelihoods are directly affected by such decisions.

DECISION-MAKING PROCESS

Cognitive Development Necessary for Decision Making

How much does the decision maker really know when making a decision is the most important factor in judging the value of a decision. The value of a decision depends on how intelligently the decision has been made. Decision-making needs information to sort out the choices. Further, it needs all the previous experience and knowledge and the ability to make certain predictions from the given degree of knowledge. Children are less likely to make mature decisions because their cognitive abilities are still underdeveloped. An educated person is likely to make better and clearer decisions than an uneducated one. The Swiss psychologist Jean Peaget (1923–1980) developed the four stages of cognitive development.

Table 4.1 shows us clearly that cognitive powers are developed as early as eleven years and that people of this age may realize the gravity of their actions. Yet, the law takes a lenient view until the age of eighteen to hold people fully responsible for their actions.

Individual and Organizational Development of Moral Decision Making

Individual human beings are subjects of growth such as biological growth, psychological development, cognitive development, education, and moral growth or social fitness.

Table 4.1   Stages of cognitive development

Stage	Approximate age	Characteristics
Sensory motor	Birth–2 years	Discovery of relationship between sensory and motor behaviour
Pre-operational	4–7 years	Use of symbols through objects, and beginning of the use of language
Concrete operations	7–11 years	Development of rational thinking, logical use of language and communication
Formal operations	11 years onwards	Development of abstract reasoning

We do not expect a small child to carry a heavy load because he/she is physically unable to carry it for sheer weight. Likewise, a young person who is a minor is unable to make decisions about marriage or business partnerships or attend to legal matters in the court. Moral decisions and actions also demand a certain development of the moral sense and maturity. It is sufficient for a child to know that telling lies and stealing from his/her parents' purse is wrong and these invite correction and punishment. On the other hand, if a manager tells lies and misleads the board of directors or siphons away large sums of money, it causes serious damages and the manager is held responsible for the grave misdeeds.

Pre-conventional Morality

Very often, managers and management students advocate the view that whatever morality they had to know has been taught to them by their parents and that they do not need any further lecturing on matters of morals. When we apply Lawrence Kohlberg's method of moral development, such people are developed in the lowest form of moral category, where mere social dos and don'ts are considered sufficient knowledge in ethics. This clearly shows the complete immaturity of these people. They would not like to progress or develop from their childhood state, when they were told exactly what to do, and they now feel that they know what is expected of them. Further, they work purely for their own interest and keep away from the coercive methods of the superiors. This is called puerile morality, or childish morality, wherein one satisfies self by claiming to know what is right and what is wrong.

It is the same with organizations. Just like individuals, if given the opportunity, organizations grow to maturity. These organizations are satisfied with puerile morality. They are satisfied when they feel that they have good top-down control and their system of rewards and punishments is clearly laid down. The employees too succumb to the pressure of their superiors. They perform to avoid negative appraisals and go to any extent to meet the targets. They have a child behaviour image, which consists of a reward in the form of an ice cream if the child behaves well or a rap on the knuckles if the child misbehaves!

Conventional Morality

When individuals grow into adults, they are expected to not only follow social conventions but also the law of the land. People are well-developed in their sense of citizenry and try to abide by the law. In other words, ignorance of the law is not presumed. Organizations come under the purview of the law and are treated by the latter as artificial persons who are responsible for their actions.

If organizations achieve the maturity of conventional morality, it implies that they value the principle of justice and apply the same standard for all, whether they are the principals, employees, or other stakeholders. Instead of playing the role of the parent or the boss or the cop, the leadership takes up guidance as the working philosophy. Team work is encouraged and rewarded. Collective responsibility is valued (see Table 4.2). Cooperation is the watchword for the employees in such organizations.

Table 4.2   Kohlberg's stages of moral development, adapted as suitable to organizations

Stage	Pre-conventional	Conventional	Post-conventional
Person	▪ Follow rules to avoid punishment ▪ Act in own interest ▪ Obey for the sake of obedience itself	▪ Follow the law ▪ Fulfil social obligations ▪ Be a good citizen	▪ Have knowledge of the fundamental moral principles ▪ Balance between individuals and groups ▪ Acknowledge diversity and encourage plurality ▪ Tolerate dissent
Leadership	▪ Autocratic ▪ Coercive ▪ Reward	▪ Guiding ▪ Encouraging ▪ Team	▪ Transformational ▪ Servant-leadership
Employee	▪ Task ▪ Meet target	▪ Work group ▪ Collaboration	▪ Empowerment

Post-conventional Morality

Not very long ago, we lived in a world where we used animals as our wont. But not any more, because people have realized that animals have life in them and also feel pain and satisfaction, life and death, and all that is associated with a life of the senses. Animal rights are now enshrined in our laws. Cruelty to animals is a punishable offence, and hunting of certain wild animals for game is as serious as homicide. These are the modern day developments in our moral treatments, which have been extended even to animals. Indian traditions treat animals with great kindness and give them the place of gods. As our moral sense develops, it includes more subjects into its fold.

There was a time when business organizations functioned on basic morality. There were hardly any rights for workers, and child labour was accepted as normal. Workers could be hired and fired any time. There was no concept of minimum wages or rules for working hours, safety and security, and health benefits. Today, organizations show greater responsibility towards society and its members. Thanks to the socialist revolution, the worker is the centre of an organization. Child labour is banned.

Organizations have also come a long way from the days of the pre-conventional stage of public behaviour. Today, top-down management is no longer popular. There is greater insistence on team work, collective leadership and empowerment, and, above all, service. This has happened due to a continuous and constant process of organizational thinking, which is a reflection of what is going on in society. Organizations are in constant dialogue with society, its institutions and individuals, and about professional behaviour. Society rightly demands an account of all the activities of organizations and the fulfilment of responsibilities.

This has been made possible because there is a constant debate in society, among the nations and the world as a whole, on what justice, common good, civic society, the means used to achieve ends, egalitarian society, and several other concepts are being developed and applied to on a large scale.

Management Morals

The above discussion may be distilled to one single proposition. All decisions are moral decisions. Wherever a decision proceeds through man's intellect and will or, in an organization, through the collective will of the corporation, with the intention of obtaining a good or achieving an object, it is a moral decision. In brief, a moral decision is that on which you can fix responsibility. Managers have to grow up and build up their moral propensities. The entire business of management is a complex web of decision making. Expertise in moral matters, therefore, is an imperative that managers cannot ignore. Unless managers reach a moral development of the post-conventional stage, it would be next to impossible to deliver decisions that are at least conventional, fair, and at par with the law of the land. Servant-leadership and empowerment are worthy goals to be achieved.

Choosing, Deciding, and Doing

Decision making consists of three concepts—choosing, deciding, and doing.

Choosing implies that there are options to choose from. You go into a shop to buy clothes. The variety of clothing offers you a large choice. You observe and examine the clothes for their quality, compliance to current fashion, their price, etc. You have not yet chosen but you are in the process of choosing.

Deciding implies that you have to make up your mind about the choices that are before you, but you also have to consider several other factors before you choose an option. You may feel that you should wait for a while until new stocks come in, or wait for the festive season discount, or you could run short of money, or the money in your purse is not yours but borrowed for something more important, such as paying the medical bills of your family.

Deciding involves reasoning. Let us apply our will and intellect or the method of reasoning. The choices are before you and you are in the process of choosing. This activity is being caused by your will, that is, you desire to buy something. Your will then wants an expert opinion, as it were, and that is when the intellect comes in and investigates the choices and passes the information by making a critical analysis of every choice. Decision is then made by the will, basing it on the deliberation supplied by the intellect. The decision will be good or bad, right or wrong, entirely depending on the help of the intellect.

Doing what you have decided completes the process of decision making. Doing may be defined as an operation or action by an agent. An agent is one who acts or operates. The act or decision may be distinguished as intrinsic action or extrinsic action. An intrinsic action is the final decision by the will, and the actual operation has not taken place yet. But as far as the agent is concerned, the decision has been made intentionally. The actualization of the decision is the external operation by the agent— the action is performed actually. It is like an engineer's blueprint (intentional) that is actually carried out in building a real structure of concrete and mortar (actual). The importance of an intrinsic decision is that it is primary and without it an external

Table 4.3   Choosing, deciding, and doing

Choosing	Deciding	Doing
Options or choices	Decision making	Carrying out the decision
Intellect	Will	Action
Intellectual process	Deliberation	Deed
No moral consequences of choices being right or wrong	Moral judgment undetermined by any of the choices, but made in complete freedom	Operationalization of the decision

<table>
<tr><td colspan="2" align="center">Moral Argument</td></tr>
<tr><td colspan="2">Moral reasoning should be based on accepted moral standards</td></tr>
<tr>
<td>
<ul>
<li>All human actions can be justified if done for the sake of duty.</li>
<li>A soldier is honoured for killing in war.</li>
<li>Is not killing another human being wrong?</li>
<li>Are not soldiers who kill people in battle wrong?</li>
</ul>
</td>
<td>
<ul>
<li>The soldier did not kill for a personal motive or interest.</li>
<li>Killing was not his aim; protecting the country was.</li>
<li>He did his duty by defending several more lives.</li>
</ul>
</td>
</tr>
</table>

structure could not have come into existence. The actualization is secondary to the nature of decision making. Hence, in moral matters, intention is judged as good or bad, and the will that decides is held responsible. What we have shown above is moral reasoning, which is also known as judgments of practical reason. Moral decisions arrived through rational processes, intellectual, and volitional operations are moral judgments (see Table 4.3 for a summary of these three concepts).

CLASSIFICATION OF DECISION MAKING

Very often, the science of decision making is lost amidst a plethora of theories. It is important, therefore, to classify the significant theories so that under a given subject we know exactly what type of decision-making theory to apply. Table 4.4 shows a classification that is easy to follow.

Decision-making theories are classified under normative and descriptive theories.

Normative model

A normative theory, as it clearly suggests, is founded on the basic assumptions, which in this case, we call axioms. An axiom is an assumed guiding principle or mean or maxim, which we accept as a norm or a standard to function for a purpose. 'Do unto others as you would have them do unto you' is considered as the golden mean in

Table 4.4 Classification of decision-making theories

	Individual decision	**Group decision**
Normative theory (Qualitative)	1. Classical economics 2. Statistical 3. Moral	1. Game 2. Welfare economics 3. Political
Descriptive theory (Quantitative)	1. Experimental 2. Learning 3. Surveys of voting behaviour	1. Social psychology 2. Political science

normative theory. Normative theory deals with ethical human behaviour. Classical economics, statistics, the science of classes and sets, politics, political economy, and the practice of game theory, whether considered for an individual or a group or a corporate behaviour, are all under the guidance of moral maxims. Normative theories are qualitative in nature because the nature of norms is transcendental. Transcendental refers to a priori propositions such that they do not need any empirical reference. These are the general ideas formed by our mind and applied to individual events. The intellectual process involved is deductive (see Table 4.5).

Brief Synopsis of Normative Principles

The term principle or standard is synonymous with value judgment or moral judgment. We have enumerated seven principles. There may be more or less of these standards, depending on how theories are expressed and delineated. One needs to adopt any one of the norms as one's guiding principle. The rest of the principles will adequately

Table 4.5 Standards of moral judgment

Case	Standard	Application
Public distribution system Essential food items distributed to the public through fair-price shops	Utility	Greatest possible benefit to the greatest number of poor and needy
Employment	Right/duty	Employer–employee relationship is maintained through well-defined rights and duties
Monopoly	Means and ends	Refrain from anti-trust violations
Wages	Justice	Payment of just wages
Acquisition of land for industrial use from farmers, which is the only source of their sustenance	Conscience	Corporate social responsibility to innovate and help the poverty stricken farmers
Chief executive	Prudence	Act responsibly
Industrial effluents	Stewardship	Setup technologies for purification to save environmental damage

express themselves without specific application. Mahatma Gandhi adopted the principle of 'the means should justify the ends', and all the other principles aligned with it naturally. Kant's all-encompassing maxim 'Act only according to that maxim by which you can at the same time will that it should become a universal law' is applicable universally, irrespective of situations and circumstances. This is the perfect moral direction one looks for when seeking guidance.

Utility or greatest happiness principle   This is also famously known as utilitarianism and it is equally popular among quantitative or descriptive ethicists and researchers in the social, economic, political, and psychological fields. It is a kind of democratic principle, wherein the good of many is sought. There are liberal and conservative applications of this principle. The liberals stress upon the inclusiveness of this principle, while the conservatives are more worried about the ones that are excluded. In other words, this is a principle that is inherently against its universalization. Finally, the difficulty lies in measuring the pleasure and pain of the people. In spite of the difficulty, this is a very useful and practical norm that people easily adopt as a universal principle. The discipline that studies this principle is known as utilitarianism.

Right/duty   'One man's right is another man's duty' explains the complementary nature of this principle. In a society, one's rights are automatically protected when the rights function as imperatives for others to uphold. This interdependent and interrelated principle ensures liberty, equality, and justice in society. It helps enumerate and enshrine these concretely in the constitution of the country and the law upholds the right of individuals and groups without favour or prejudice. The ethics of duty is known as deontology.

Means and ends   The means of our actions should justify our ends. We want to be happy. That is a worthy end to pursue. But we may not pursue this end by those means that are detrimental to the rights of others. Wanting to have money is not unworthy, but if it is to be acquired by stealing, then it is most unworthy and despisable. This principle also has another characteristic that is not very often spelt out, that is, human dignity is an end in itself and not a means. Kant's maxim 'Act so that you treat humanity, whether in your own person or in that of another, always as an end and never as a means' only emphasizes giving human beings the dignity of an end. This is the principle on which human rights are based.

Justice   The simplest definition of justice is to give what is one's due. In human interaction this simple principle assumes complex proportions, as every area demands justice. *Distributive justice* is how justly wealth is shared. This is the pillar of economic justice and is the root of socialist revolution. *Retributive justice* deals with the assignment of merited rewards or punishment. It involves the huge and complex process of judiciary and administration of impartial justice. *Compensatory justice* is to make up for the loss suffered. War victims may not get complete replacement, yet those who have inflicted affliction would be convicted and the victims will be compensated for. This deals with a healing and reparative process. *Caring justice* stems from the principle of compassion. It has come to the fore in the face of extreme gaps between the haves and the have-nots. *Virtue ethics* is a positive form of justice that is very often seen in its negative form as blind, impartial, and devoid of any feeling. The concept of justice is justifiable to every form of argument and it is no surprise that all actions, including the most sinister ones such as war, torture, and human slaughter, are able to attract justification. To avoid all the pitfalls follow the maxim: 'Do unto others as you would have them do unto you.'

Conscience   It consists of a purely subjective opinion about what is right or wrong and is, therefore, a technically weak principle. However, it is the most powerful and supremely emotional principle of morality. Leaders such as Martin Luther King Jr. and Nelson Mandela have been the voice of conscience that moved the world and changed it for the better. Conscience may or may not be well formed. The well-formed conscience is able to judge actions for their moral worth; the not well-formed conscience is unable to judge actions for their moral worth. A conscience, which always follows the golden mean, may be judged as well formed.

Prudence   Prudence is the management of affairs with commonsense. It may be understood in four ways. First, it is an ability to discipline oneself and govern one's own affairs in the most reasonable way. Second, it is the competence and wisdom to manage a task. Third, it is the skill and judgment of using resources. Fourth, it is the caution exercised and risk foreseen before arriving at and implementing any decision. All the above descriptions of prudence are not only descriptions of good management principles, but also of good morality. Decision making, risk management, practical use of reason, and self-discipline are what make one a good manager not only morally, but also professionally.

Stewardship   It is the role of a manager, beyond the call of employed duty, to take a keen interest and special responsibilities in the fulfillment of tasks. The concept of stewardship has been contemporarily developed to apply in a special way to the principals or the promoters of firms. It clarifies that ownership does not entitle one to misuse one's resources or the public funds in the money market. The driving force behind corporate governance is the principle of stewardship. Firms are creators and guardians of wealth. Stewardship also extends in a special way to the protection of environment. All are endowed with a special responsibility towards the well-being of our planet, the Earth. The principle finds its further expression in every consumer. Reckless consumerism is uncaring, while responsible consumerism, such as the use of bio-products, encourages not only small-scale farmers, but indigenous produce as well. Thus, stewardship nurtures the judicious use of limited resources and develops a sensitive social concern. Corporations have adopted this principle under corporate social responsibility (CSR).

Moral Maturity Meter

As against the quantitative standard discussed in the Hunt–Vitell model in the next section, here (see Table 4.6) we give a qualitative model to judge moral decision making.

Descriptive Model

Descriptive theories are empirical and proceed from hypotheses that need to be proved inductively. Market research is a very good example of such a theory. Descriptive theories about learning and research are based on experiments, surveys and opinion polls, and social and political researches. The fundamental pre-suppositions are yet to be proved and as per the research and tabulations of facts and figures, approximates are drawn. It is a quantitative exercise and no certainties are possible. Only probabilities and percentages are the ultimate result. Decisions will have to be taken based on these concrete but probable results. Since there is enough room for allowing mistakes, taking risks becomes easier.

In the area of moral behaviour, there are attempts made to descriptively find out ways of decision making. They bring together all the individual and social factors that create an environment for decision making. Given all the variables, what would be the outcome is the mission of such theories.

Figure 4.3 shows the most popular theory of decision making by Shelby D. Hunt and Scott J. Vitell. The theory is named after them as the Hunt–Vitell model.[1] A brief synopsis of the model is as follows. We must remember that the stages given below overlap during the process and time of decision making.

Table 4.6 Moral maturity meter

Individual	Organization	Moral maturity
Child	Autocratic: Top-down control	Pre-conventional
Adolescent	Coercive: Reward and punishment	Pre-conventional
Adult (a product of society)	Guiding	Conventional: Submission to law
Adult with educational maturity (law abiding)	Teamwork	Conventional: Respect to law
Adult with social consciousness (leader)	Transformational	Post-conventional: Seeking new dimensions
Adult with social consciousness and commitment (leader and philosopher)	Empowering	Post-conventional: Application of newfound principles and service through example

---

[1] The Hunt–Vitell model has been adapted with some visual changes. However, the interpretation is largely Kantian in nature.

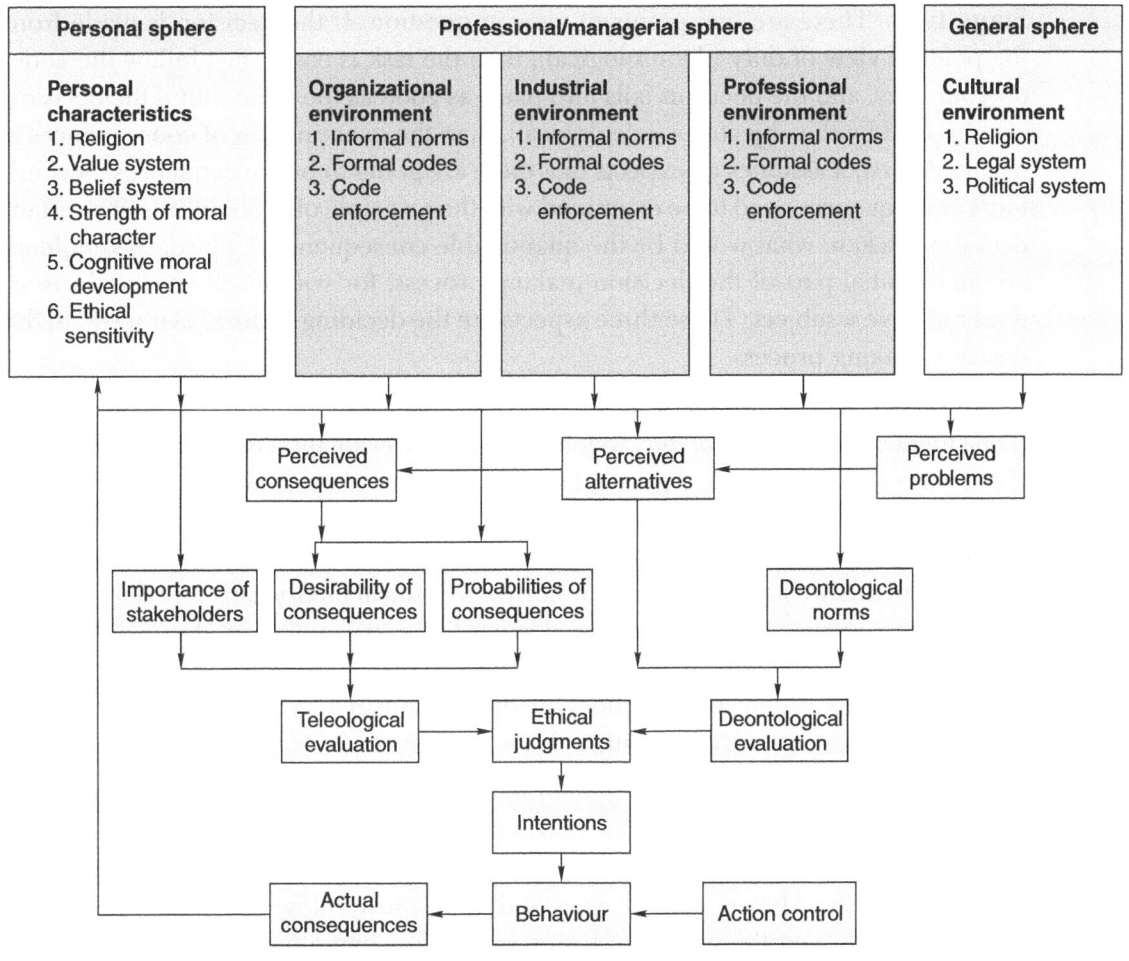

Fig. 4.3   Hunt–Vittel model of decision making

Source: Shelby D. Hunt and Scott J. Vittel, 'Why Do People's Ethical Judgements Differ', *In Business Ethics: New Challenges for Business Schools and Corporate Leaders* pp. 18–37; Robert A. Peterson and O.C. Ferrel (eds); Prentice Hall of India, New Delhi: 2005, p. 20.

General background   Society represents one ethics. Professional ethics is a part and parcel of society, of which business ethics is also a part. The general sphere of ethics, distinguished as personal and general, is shown in the two boxes in the extreme left and right corners. This is the general background in which ethical behaviour occurs.

Specific background   The three boxes in the centre represent the professional sphere through the specific areas of organizational, industrial, and professional environment, where appropriate codes have been derived from the general sphere and applied to the specific spheres.

Stage one   The problem is perceived, the alternatives are weighed, and the consequences are predicted.

Stage two   There are two points of view in question. If the decision is made from the point of view of duty (deontological), then the task is easy—just follow the code, do your duty, and the decision falls into place as good as the code. But if the decision is motivated by the objectives (teleological), then the examination of consequences is essential. First, it assumes or expects that there are going to be consequences. Second, these consequences need to be examined with the principle of probability—if a certain decision is taken, what would be the quantifiable consequences? Third, stakeholders are an essential part of the decision-making process, for without them, the decision does not have a subject. These three aspects are the deciding factors, as it were, in the decision-making process.

Stage three   The appraisal or evaluation of the decision-making process is two-fold. If one follows the principle of duty (deontological), the evaluation is a logical conclusion. If one follows the teleological principle, evaluation becomes difficult, as the reference to various consequences could pose problems. Dilemmas arise, conflict situations occur, and it is difficult to apply ethical standards without compromise. All the standards of judgment that we have shown in our normative ethical theory calls for relativization. Telling lies is wrong. But if a UN peacekeeper lies to the militia in Darfur, Africa, so that food convoys can pass through the barrier and reach thousands of hungry people, would it be right? When consequences are drawn, ethical dilemmas arise and decision making becomes not just risky, but is also a gamble.

Stage four   Ethical or moral judgment in the case of deontological application, as has been stated above, is logical. One makes the judgment, whatever the consequences. Judgments with teleological background would have to settle for relatively less rigorous ethical judgments. Hence, experts suggest that we must follow the weaker portion of any principle. Given the option of losing one's life when attacked, one may in self-defence kill the attacker.

Stage five   The background to the above stage and the point of the beginning of action is the intention. The central point of decision making, between the process of judgment and the beginning of the decided action, is the intention. It is the motive of duty and also the motive of consequences. It is the intention that will make an action good or bad, irrespective of the fact that it was based on the principles of duty or teleology.

Stage six   This stage consists of three important aspects—action control, behaviour or action, and the actual consequences. Once the mind is made up, the intention is fixed and the agent is still in control. The saying that 'you are the slave of a spoken word and of an unspoken word the master' applies here literally. As long as the intention is in the mind and the action is not taken, no consequences can be drawn. However, once the agent lets go of the intention, control over the action depends upon the situation where the action occurs, and the consequences can be barely controlled. That is why, when we make decisions and put them into practice, we hope for the desired consequences.

Responsibility of the person   It is the decisions that a person takes that determine the moral character of the person. Life's experiences enable people to judge fairly, whether the intentions are good or bad. This, of the course, depends upon the transparency of the person in letting known the motives. Whatever be the consequences, if it is proven that the intentions are good, the moral action will be judged as good.

Merit of the model   This model is realistic of the fact that human beings are limited in the power of both reason and action. Absolutism or the idealism of the norms is prudently measured and situations are taken into account. An action takes place in a social milieu, which is equally imperfect. The decision is made to fall back on the background from where the person comes, thus making full provision for the circumstances of the cause.

Chiasm of Managers' Decision Making

Here, we shall dissect the entire procedure of a manager's decision making. Decisions are criss-crossed with consequences (as seen in Fig. 4.4), as a relationship of the principles of cause and effect; and moral standards are juxtaposed against the areas. The chiasm is not a watertight compartment but is active in an endocrinal manner that makes it function like a single organism. Decision making is a dynamic process that defies quantification. The sum of all the variables involved in the decision-making processes, and their interactions, cannot be added up to show a logically inevitable or predictable decision. The dynamics of the decision-making process give us strong indications of a probable decision. No matter how minute our observations are and how rigorous our methods are, why we make the decisions that we make still remains highly speculative.

Decisions	Moral standards or codes of conduct
• Objective oriented • Value addition to stakeholders empowering • Value for customer's money • Compliance to law	• Utility • Right/duty • Means/ends • Justice • Conscience • Prudence • Stewardship
Areas	**Consequences**
• Manufacturing • Marketing • Advertising • Human resource • Workplace • Finance • Environment	• Shareholders • Employees • Customers • Suppliers • Community • Environment

Fig. 4.4   Chiasm of decision making

Moral Argument

Three imperatives of moral reasoning

(a) Act only according to that maxim by which you can act and at the same time will that it should become a universal law.

(b) Act as though the maxim of your actions where by your will to become a universal law of nature.

(c) Act so that you treat humanity, whether in your own person or in that of another, always as an end and never as a means.

SUMMARY

- Man is endowed with reason, which he uses as an instrument to build his world as an individual, as well as, a member of society. He performs several actions such as breathing, eating, sleeping, etc. These are merely physical actions and do not affect other persons. Actions of interpersonal relationships, such as giving and receiving, buying and selling, agreeing and disagreeing, helping and harming, honouring and dishonouring, stealing and not stealing, lying and telling the truth, deceiving or aiding all such actions, attract value judgments like good or bad, right or wrong, ethical or unethical, moral or immoral. Such judgments are arrived at through an analysis, which can be called moral reasoning. It is measured against the moral values or the ethical standards of judgment. All the judgments are to be applied impartially. Double standards are self-contradictory in ethics.

- All are not capable of making moral judgments. Little children are not able to act morally. Hence, no one charges them with guilt. As a person grows, it is assumed that the person also grows with a sense of moral sensitivity, whereby the person intuitively learns about the value of moral actions through the collective consciousness found in society.

- A moral action is obtained through a deliberate motive that is followed by an action. It involves adequate knowledge, the will, and the actual carrying out of action. The essence of the moral action lies in willing it, that is, it is a freely willed action and not a coerced one. A forced marriage is a null and void marriage, since it lacks the consent or the will of either one of the partners or both the partners.

- The moral imperative of duty—act only according to that maxim by which you can at the same time will that it should become a universal law—is the minimum requirement to be a moral person. All the other standards of moral judgment will make the person even more virtuous, as in the teachings of Socrates, where virtuous living is its own reward, and is the happiness that one seeks.

- The object of morality is good, the good that is determined by the good will, the very foundation of morality. The morality of an action depends on our will and not on the outcome of our action. The Gita admonishes us to only perform our duty and not seek the fruits of our actions, for these are out of our control. Only our will is in our control.

- A moral action is more qualitative than quantitative, more normative than descriptive, and more subjective than objective, but one can will that such an action is universally natural as well as personal.

KEY TERMS

Good All that we want, irrespective of everything else. When others argue about what is good for us, we employ our instrument of reason to cogently justify that what we want is really good.

Practical reason or *phronesis* According to Aristotle, *phronesis* is practical wisdom, the ability to make the right decision in difficult circumstances.

Reason An instrument. It has a mechanism, a system of functioning. The thoughts or concepts produced by our minds are the primary elements that are molded into propositions. These are further systematically arranged to produce cogent arguments. A body of cogent arguments forms a body of knowledge, which is characteristically quite systematic. That which is not cogent is not consistent and is rejected as not being proper knowledge.

Relativism In ethics, there are two main types of relativism. Descriptive ethical relativism claims that different people have different moral beliefs, but it takes no stand on whether those beliefs are valid or not. Normative ethical relativism claims that each culture's (or group's) beliefs are right within that culture, and that it is impossible to validly judge another culture's values from the outside.

Rights Entitlements to do something without interference from other people (negative rights) or entitlements that obligate others to do something positive to assist you (positive rights). Some rights (natural rights, human rights) belong to everyone by nature, or simply by virtue of being human. Some rights (legal rights) belong to people by virtue of their membership in a particular political state; other rights (moral rights) are based in the acceptance of a particular moral theory.

Utility (happiness/pleasure) The actions that promote happiness are considered morally right; ones contrary to happiness are wrong. Utilitarianism, the philosophy based on this principle, proposes greatest happiness for the greatest number of people.

Will is the faculty that directs our desires to what we want. Our will determines what we want. We always, without fail, want something good, even if it is not considered as such, by others.

CONCEPT REVIEW QUESTIONS

1. What is a moral act?
2. Who can act morally?
3. Why should one act morally?

CRITICAL THINKING QUESTIONS

1. Is it morally right to tell a lie in order to save a life?
2. What is the moral status of an incurably sick person who wants to commit suicide?
3. What is the moral value of a person who pays taxes to the government for fear of being penalized?
4. How would you judge the moral integrity of a person who promises to repay the loan he/she has taken, but does not intend to repay it?

FURTHER READING

Adam Smith, *A Theory of Moral Sentiments*, Oxford: Oxford University Press (1976).

CASE STUDY

Kohlberg's Research Case

Tracing Moral Development

The following short and simple case is historic. Lawrence Kohlberg utilized this case while interviewing about seventy people of different ages, and he came to discover the celebrated findings of the six stages of moral development.

The Case

Heinz is a poor man. His wife suffers from cancer and needs immediate medicine. The medicine is very costly and Heinz cannot afford it. The chemist is unwilling to lend it to him on credit. Heinz breaks open the store, steals the drug, and administers it to his wife.

Framework to analyse the case

(a) What are the facts or circumstances that constitute the case?

(b) Who are the people involved?

(c) What is/are the moral issue or issues that concern this case?

(d) Which is/are the moral principle or principles that are at stake?

(e) What argument can be put forward after taking into consideration the above four questions?

(f) Do the persons involved in this case pass the duty test?

(g) What kind of moral responsibility or accountability does each member in the case bear?

(h) What solutions would you provide to solve the problems that have risen from this case?

(i) What are the lessons that have you learnt from the case?

Table 4.7   Case analysis schema

Heads	Particulars	Remarks
Facts	Heinz steals medicine for his wife.	Focus on essential facts.
People	▪ Heinz, poor, cannot afford to buy medicine. ▪ Heinz's wife suffers from cancer, needs medicine. ▪ The chemist, businessman, may suffer loss by selling a costly drug on credit to a poor man who is unable to pay.	Examine the people involved and their relationship with each other.
Moral issues	*Heinz:* Stealing. *Chemist:* Refusal to help a genuinely, needy person.	Examine immediate moral concerns.
Principles	*Heinz:* Means and ends, justice. *Chemist:* Conscience, prudence.	Pin the case with just one or two principles.
Argument	Heinz, who is desperate to save his wife's life, finds stealing a lesser evil and is ready to bear the consequences if the law catches up with him. The chemist finds no legal obligation to help, since he has to run a business. His conscience does tell him that he should help, but his business sense tells him that if he is going to help the needy, he will end up losing in business.	Analyse from the general principle to arrive at the particular conclusion.
Duty test	▪ Has Heinz done his duty? It is natural that his duty is to aid his dying wife. But is it his duty to steal? ▪ Is it the chemist's duty to help by lending the drug on credit?	The duty test eliminates emotional or sentimental aspects from a rational judgment. This may seem unkind but it provides the ultimate test for a minimum requirement of a moral action.

Contd

Table 4.7 Contd

Heads	Particulars	Remarks
Accountability	■ Heinz has a compelling argument on compassionate grounds. However, the moral principle that 'ends do not justify the means', although harsh in this case, is yet quite valid. His action causes injustice to the chemist, who suffers a loss for no fault of his. ■ The chemist also has a good argument, which makes good business sense. However, if he were to listen to his conscience, his commonsense or prudence would have guided him to make an exception in this case. The good deed itself would also have won him a loyal customer for the future.	Do not accuse. Point out the outcome of the argument.
Application	■ The solution to the above problem is typically ethical. The attitude of the whole society is questioned and it demands moral responsibility towards the individuals. ■ Today, societies around the world have developed systems of medical insurance and care even for the poorest of the poor. However, all societies or countries do not have such systems due to poverty and the lack of means for such massive provisions. ■ An individual has a moral right to claim freedom from hunger, disease, and homelessness.	Suggest a solution that is compatible to the principle employed in the argument.
Lessons	■ Moral actions involve relationship with other people. If Heinz had not appeared on the scene, not only would the chemist have been spared the loss, but also the social stigma of being an insensitive person to the dire needs of a poor man. ■ A business organization has several lessons to learn from this case. It has the primary responsibility towards the welfare of all its employees, shareholders, customers, and society as a whole. ■ A corporation cannot shirk its responsibility by merely saying that its concern is to add value to its shareholders. It has the duty to consider its role as a good citizen to the people in the community. ■ A corporation needs to develop a caring conscience. In the above case, this directly applies to the state of pricing policies in the pharmaceutical firms today. ■ Managers within an organization are the people who take decisions on behalf of the organization. Hence, managers are morally responsible for the consequences of their decisions. ■ Managers who are directly responsible for the employees must take care to ensure their safety and security.	Although these are personal reflections, make them as following from the universal ethical principles.

Discussion Questions

(a) Does Heinz represent a large part of the Indian society?

(b) Is the unrelenting chemist a reflection of the Indian business community?

(c) Examine six different Indian companies that may fit into the six different moral stages of development.

Going Further . . .

Workshop: Divide the class into six groups, each representing a stage of moral development. Let each group simulate a company that reflects the moral stage of that organization.

Further Reading

Re-read Chapters 1–3, and analyse the case studies all over again with the above case scheme.

ETHICAL DEVELOPMENT PROGRAMME

Management Training

(a) Conduct a small research at your campus or workplace and test at what stage of moral development are the concerned people in.

(b) Analyse your company and find out at what stage of moral development it is in. (This could be a part of the summer project for MBA students.)

Management Game

A game, in general, is a structured and organized activity with definite objectives, rules and rewards or payoffs, and punishment for the infringement of rules. Although highly entertaining, games, sports, and athletics have become sophisticated disciplines today. The ethical content of these is defined as the spirit of the game.

In academic disciplines such as physical sciences like physics and mathematics or social sciences like economics and politics, game is a term used to refer to a situation of human interaction. It is an interesting and amusing educational tool, which also simulates real-life situations. It is a method of studying decision making by actually involving people into making decisions, where two or more individuals or groups interact and their choices influence each other. John von Neumann and Oskar Morgenstern published a work called *The Theory of Games and Economic Behaviour* in 1944. It has become a tool for studying the phenomenon of human response in physical, as well as social sciences and computers. The objective of the game is to discover the strategies people use when they face certain situations. The strategies are classified into equilibrium, defection, zero-sum game, and co-operation. Games such as centipede, hawk and

dove, prisoners dilemma, stag hunt, and several others are in vogue. The games give us a close glimpse of the complexities of relationships. In international politics, for instance, one can gauge the tensions of the arms race. In trade, the deception between free trade and protection; in business, the strategies of competition; in organizations, the relationship between the employer and employees (trade unions).

Try the following games.

A. Prisoners' Dilemma

This is a classic among games.

Game structure

A and B are taken into custody by the police. Since evidence is in want, the police hit upon a bright idea. They separate them and offer them a secret deal:

(a) If one testifies against the other and the other remains silent, the former goes free, and the latter receives a full ten-year term to serve in jail.

(b) If both remain silent, both get merely six months in jail.

(c) If both betray each other, each receives a five-year term.

Neither prisoner knows what the other is going to do (see Table 4.8).

To play this game, set up a situation. For instance, people may be divided into two groups. If it is a classroom situation, each group may be asked to form a company. If it is an organization, then divide people into groups. The monitoring authority will create conditions for competition by

Table 4.8 Prisoners' dilemma

	Prisoner B silent	Prisoner B betrays
Prisoner A silent	Six months in jail	A in jail for ten years
Prisoner A betrays	B in jail for ten years	A and B in jail for five years

setting up some terms and the payoff. The time limit will depend on the availability of time and the objectives to be achieved within a time frame. Further, you may take some tips from the popular reality TV shows to sharpen the focus or eliminate some people without the payoff.

B. Watch and Analyse

Watch a real-life team game like basket ball, volley ball, foot ball, etc. and analyse.

(a) Which of the players will suit your company and in what position?

(b) What qualities or attitudes of theirs were you impressed by?

(c) What were the conflicts that arose and how were they solved?

(d) What were the attitudes of the players at the referee's decisions?

(e) What strategy helped them to win the game?

(f) What was the ethical or unethical element in the strategy?

(g) What is the moral maturity of the individuals, as well as the teams?

(h) What went wrong for the losing side?

(i) What do you learn from the analysis?

Management Mantra

The Blind Man and the Woman

I once came across a beggar couple. The man was blind, but the woman could see. The woman led the man while they begged and the man collected the money and placed it in his little money bag. Later in the night, they sat in a corner of the railway platform. He took out the money bag and she helped him to sort out the coins. He felt the coins, counted the money, and set aside a certain amount of money to be kept in a different pocket. She had no say in the matter. He then ordered her to do some chores like fetch water, bring food from a vendor, etc.

This is the image of our intellect and will. The will is blind and is led by wishes and desires. It has no means to find out a method to get at them. The intellect on the other hand is quite skilful in observation and examination of the objects of the will. The intellect obeys the will unconditionally and has no say. The will is the decision maker.

> MANTRA *Where there is a will, the intellect finds a way.*

Part Two

Managers and Management Areas

Application of Ethical Standards to Business Disciplines

Application of Ethical Standards to Business Disciplines

The Way of Moral Action

Where marketers are liars,
And accountants cheat,
And advertisements are a big bluff,
There customers get a bad treat.[1]

—Subhash Sharma

If we stop thinking of the poor as victims or as a burden and start recognizing them as resilient and creative entrepreneurs and value-conscious customers, a whole new world of opportunity will open up.

—C.K. Prahalad

THE NEW WORLD ORDER

Modern business management developed in the post-World War II era, in the so-called free world, a term reserved for the developed countries of the world, where the philosophy of capitalism and the system of free-market economy prevailed. The socialist world, where the economy was controlled and regulated by state marketing, had limited relevance because free choice for the people was restricted as a policy. Underdeveloped countries were not in the marketing picture.

The world has now come a long way and is at crossroads in the first decade of the twenty-first century. While communism is committed to history, capitalism has hit a huge roadblock. People around the world who thought that the business model of the free world, which was based on capitalism, was closer to their dreams started adapting to this most successful system, when all of a sudden, the world of the protagonists of the great dream—which consisted of the developed Western countries, the club of the rich eight, the G-8—just collapsed. It melted down financially, and further, got locked in the morass of a bailout.

When businessmen say that the 'market is down', they mean that their faith in the market has failed. When they say 'credit crunch', they mean that the creditors have lost trust in them. When they say 'liquidity shortage', they mean that they are bankrupt due to greed. When they say 'closures', 'foreclosures', or 'retrenchment', they mean that greed and mismanagement have caused havoc. When they say 'financial meltdown', they mean that they have been irresponsible and have lived beyond their means.

The perspectives of business management in all work disciplines, starting from manufacturing to human resource management, and also from marketing and advertising to finance and international trade, have changed since the last century and after the financial meltdown in the new century. The diverse human society has grown into one global kinship and physical affinity.

---

[1] Subhash Sharma, a leading management thinker and well known for writing management rhymes, has penned these lines exclusively for this introduction to Part Two.

Mausoleum: The magnificent dwelling of two dead souls

This calls for an open, transparent, and ethically sound relationship. The building blocks of this relationship are trust and good governance. Translated into ethical language, it calls for those means to be adopted, to build and maintain this relationship, that justify the end.

MARKET IS A REPUBLIC

The Taj Mahal at Agra is the signature image of India. As a symbol of India, it transcends all historical, political, social, religious, and economic considerations. India is labelled, packed, and sold with the Taj, at its missions or embassies, during its festivals and tours, at its hospitality establishments, and through its consumables, durables, disposables, and all those goods that can be bought and sold within and outside the country. This marketing strategy wins a special place in the hearts and minds of the people. The Taj Mahal is a brand par excellence.

What the Taj is to the aesthetic sensibilities of the people of the world, a product is to the needs of the people. The needs of the people is the cornerstone of the market. Anything beyond that which is built on this cornerstone defines the quality of the well-being of the people. The better the edifice, the better is the well-being of the

people who live in it, and the greater the well-being of the people, the greater is the market. In order to build a good market, we need to manufacture the product, inform what we want to sell through advertisements, and then do the actual selling. However, all this needs money or finance. The four disciplines of manufacturing, marketing, advertising, and finance are the subject matter of the second part of this book.

Which discipline of business management comes first? Capital or money or finance, and its management, is literally the beginning and the end, or the aim of any business. We start a business with an investment of our capital resources. We produce or manufacture products and put them up for sale on the market. We inform the consumers about the product through advertisements in the media, and hope to recover our investment with profits. We then reinvest, diversify, innovate, produce higher quality goods and services, compete, and retrieve our returns. This cycle of the disciplines of business continues and the business grows.

The growth and sustainability of a business is what matters. Indeed, where does it grow and who sustains it? A business grows in the market that sustains it. Who forms the market? The people with needs or wants or desires form the market. We, the people, live in a market. We can borrow Abraham Lincoln's definition of democracy and say that the market is of the people, by the people, and for the people. Business thus grows

Hut: The humble dwelling of 700 million living souls

in a market ethos. Every product and service in the market creates its unique ethos. The clothes we wear, the food we eat, the houses we live in create an ethos, a culture or a philosophy of life. In short, ethics, the habits and the rules set by the people, governs the market. Any business discipline that falls short of this suffers setbacks. Business cannot survive against the will of the people. The market is democratic in nature.

NATURE OF THE INDIAN MARKET

Very close to the Taj, there lies the bustling city of Agra and its surrounding rural areas with a population of approximately two million. This is a miniature picture of the Indian economy in a city-village set up. The area is overpopulated and congested. The richest of the rich and the poorest of the poor live here. Industry and agriculture are the common occupations. Tanneries, foundries, and every imaginable polluting manufacturing units and sub-units can be found in this area. Very little that is sold here comes from branded companies and even if they do, most of them such as soft drinks, foodstuffs, and textiles are spurious. Most of the commerce concerns itself with what is popularly known as local products, which are not branded products. As in the rest of India, Agra also has unorganized industry and unorganized labour, which caters to a nearly staggering 90 per cent of the economy. This is a very humbling experience for the organized sectors that are brandishing their brands. Take for instance gems and jewellery, a traditional business dealing with gold, pearls, gems, and precious stones of all kinds. The famous brands such as Tanishq and Gili are not even a drop in the ocean. India is the largest gold market of the world, and yet, it is dominated by the unorganized sector. The largest sector, which is agriculture, employs over 60 per cent of the labour force of India, and is the largest unorganized sector on which India's economy depends. It would be fitting, therefore, to call India's so-called unorganized sector as the informal sector. For this, indeed, is the real India, where none of the classroom-learnt Western categories of exchange, commerce, and trade apply.

NEW PARADIGM FOR INDIAN MARKETING

It is high time that we used our knowledge resources to forge new paradigms of exchange to suit the Indian market. What kind of order or system can we discover in the ever-growing economy of the world? If the informal sector has spread so far and wide, it must have a good reason for its sheer acceptability among the masses.

In the following four chapters, we will see the problems arising out of the organized disciplines of business management and expose them to the prevailing situation in India. If Indian business has to mean something, it must have relevance to the lives of the people of India. Several econo-mists, such as Amartya Sen and C.K. Prahalad, have inferred that the Indian market is found to be at the bottom of the demographic pyramid, that is, the large base of the population consists of the poor. The poor are in majority. They form the largest market. Any marketing that is going to serve these people will not only find a rewarding business, but will also be serving the least favoured people of society. Doing business with them in an innovative way will not only bring profit to the companies, but it will also empower them to be partners in the business. There is no better ethical movement than the empowerment of the poor. This is a challenge that can be taken by any business, and it will be a victory for both the busi-nessman and the consumer. Consequently, the business disciplines of manufacturing, marketing, advertising, and finance will take on a new meaning.

ECONOMIC EMPOWERMENT OF THE POOR AS AN ETHICAL TOOL FOR PROFIT

The prognosis is that in a couple of decades, India is going to be one of the five consumer economies in the world if the economy continues to grow between 8 per cent and 10 per cent of the GDP. With the population over one billion and the size of the economy above $1 trillion, India is yet to become a beacon of light, as seven out of ten Indians are poor, which implies that out of every ten poor persons in the world, four or more are Indians. See Fig. P2.1.

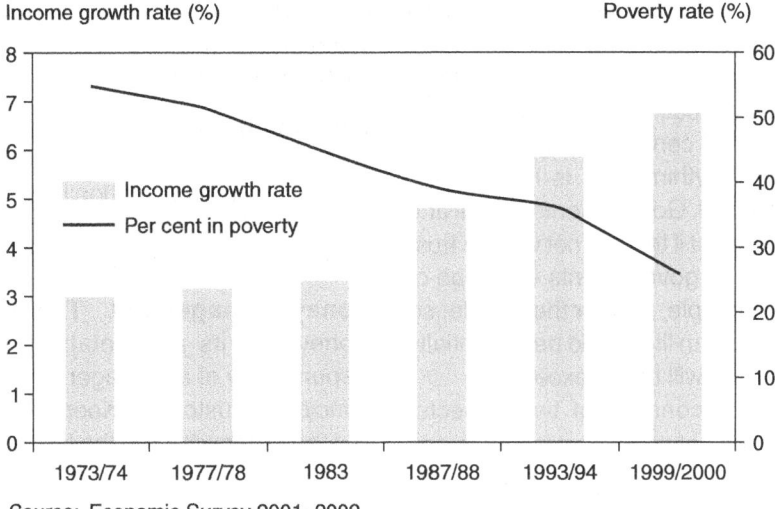

Source: Economic Survey 2001–2002.

Fig. P2.1   Income growth and poverty rates

This should be good news for the Indian marketers because a market of 700 million people yet remains untapped. This market is bigger than the markets of the developed countries of North America and Europe put together. Though business as usual will not work for such a fresh market that needs to be developed, it offers a chance for a paradigm shift, by enabling the economically backward to move towards prosperity and a good standard of living. If marketers with intelligent ideas could empower the poor masses of India, it would be an economic revolution of the social kind. One may call the new market paradigm an economically empowering marketing.

MARKETING PARADIGMS

Let us now discuss the existing marketing paradigms in India—social marketing and societal marketing.

For a long time, governments have adopted a paradigm that is known as social marketing. Social marketing consists of subsidized marketing for a cause. India's essential goods and services run on subsidies. Thus, from agriculture to family welfare, from public distribution to health, India is an enormous engine of social-welfare marketing. As the country progresses in its economic development, the subsidies are either reduced or restricted

to groups that are below the poverty line, or are cancelled in order to move to a normal, profit-oriented market system.

The societal marketing paradigm is advocated by the proponents of corporate governance. It has a wide field of application and has been defined under the heading of corporate social responsibility (CSR). To begin with, it was no different from social marketing. Companies, just like individuals, used to have some programmes in philanthropy, such as running free schools or dispensaries for the poor. However, under the CSR programmes, the concerns for the community became more focused and corporations projected themselves as good citizens. They started participating in some basic economic activities of the people, such as financial aid and technical support for agriculture, better market access to form products, promotion of self-help groups, and tried to initiate action that benefited all. In other words, they transferred their marketing philosophy of success to social living.

INTEGRAL MARKETING

We will introduce a new concept called integral marketing in this section. We have already discussed about the economic empowerment advocated by economists and business strategists.

We have also elucidated the concepts of social marketing, societal marketing, and corporate social responsibility. Yet, these do not provide us with a satisfactory approach to business management in the twenty-first century. It is going to be a people's century. Anything that is not people-centred will be rejected. Governments will fall and businesses will bite dust if they do not win the trust of the people. Just as governments would be of the people, by the people, and for the people, so too all spheres of human life would be essentially humanistic. Business will be no exception.

Integral business consists of two aspects. Firstly, the distinction between the promoters and shareholders and the people at large, which exists now, will disappear. Secondly, people will demand accountability. Corporate leaders would have to provide service leadership. Just as the government of the people is a public servant, so too the corporation is a public servant.

Marketing will show a vivid reflection of integral business. We may call it integral marketing. It consists of two aspects. First, marketers involve people directly in the business, thus eliminating middlemen. This is facilitated through the latest communication technology of the Internet, which can be accessed through computers and cellular mobiles. Second, based on the first aspect, consumers become partners in business.

Following are the essential principles of marketing.

Bottom-line   The customer is the *sine qua non* of business activity. Without the customer, there is no business and, far less, its management.
Principle   Utility: Patronize the customer. Do not victimize the customer.

Manufacturer   Entrepreneurship is a passionate pursuit. In the hustle and bustle of business activity, one may easily lose sight of the goal of manufacturing. The goal is the consumer.
Principle   Duty: Give value to consumers' money. The consumer must not feel cheated.

Integral marketing   Market is of the people, by the people, and for the people. Goods and services are the means of interaction. Marketing is a socio-economic relationship.

Principle   Means and ends: Maintain and safeguard the harmonious marketing relationship. Do not breach the trust.

True communication   Truth, goodness, and aesthetics are the Holy Trinity of advertising. With deception, communication breaks.
Principle   Conscience: Tell the truth about the product. Do not deceive.

Money management   The management of money and its accountability is the greatest responsibility of a manager.
Principle   Custodian: Keep the monies in order and the order will keep the firm going forever. Do not embezzle the resource of exchange.

Social responsibility   Not just a right to life and livelihood, but a right to a better standard of life is in the interest of both the businesses and the people. Managers bear social responsibility. The manager is a leader.
Principle   Justice: Fairness and justice in all dealings. Do not mislead.

Management   Business discipline is both a science and an art. The systems of management are scientific, but the relationships to be developed and maintained are an art of social science. The manager maintains a balance between economics and civics.
Principle   Commonsense: Make a necessary virtue out of commonsense. Do not deceive yourself.

OBJECTIVES OF PART II

In Part II, we will deal with four important areas of business management—manufacturing, marketing, advertising, and finance. As has been delineated above, we will focus on the new paradigm, integral marketing. We had discussed the various doctrines that influenced business in Chapter 3. We also examined whether social market economy is possible or not. In Chapters 5–8, we will prove that an integral market economy that empowers people is not only possible, but has already started working in some select cases. We will prove that these cases can also become profitable.

Gillette, the King's Razor

Gillette razors and blades are as common as the basic necessities of life. They are safe, cheap, and easy to use, and fulfil the basic necessity of shaving for millions and millions of people around the globe. It is unthinkable that our civilization got introduced to such a simple product as late as the beginning of the twentieth century. In 1903, in the first year of its production, the company sold fifty-one razors and 168 blades. The following year it sold over 90,000 razors and nearly 1,24,0000 blades.[a] (Fig. P2.2 shows the patent document.) Today, after a century, the numbers are in billions.

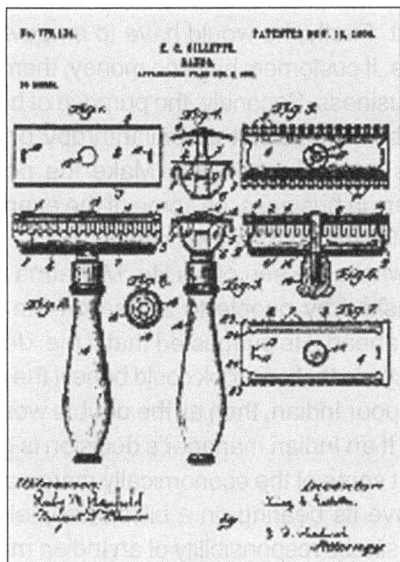

Fig. P2.2   Gillette's patent (1904)[b]

Source: http://eu.wikipedia.org/wiki/King_Camp_Gillette.

Gillette's management disciplines:

Excellent product For men who, unlike women, take little time to groom themselves, shaving is the quickest, vanity-free means of personal grooming. The Gillette product, which is easily available and disposable, is found to be in every man's kit that likes a clean shave.

Easy to use Gillette meets the needs of its customers without much fuss. Be it razors, blades, aftershaves, or shaving creams, the product is complete. Man has the wherewithal to groom himself efficiently.

Precision manufacturing Gillette has become synonymous with the sharpness and the smoothness of its safety blades. In India, the product caters to all the economic segments. Gillette Presto is very low-priced, thereby targeting the lower income group; Gillette Sensor Excel is targeted towards the middle-income group, while Gillette Mach 3 is for the up-market customers.

Sales and marketing Gillette is one of those highly efficient, fast moving consumer goods (FMCG) companies who have been able to penetrate the global market as only a few others have done. They have been able to forge partnerships, such as with Proctor and Gamble in India, and run an excellent supply chain logistics. It is good to remember that King Camp Gillette, the inventor of the blade, was a salesman.

Ideal advertising Although the company employs brand ambassadors from the world of sports, the focus of its advertisement has been the product itself. The company has in the past made some ads that have become classics. For instance, the baby with the shaving foam on its cheek and the Gillette razor in the hand exudes safety, rather than vulnerability.

Finance The company is known for its good financial management and global expansion. Gillette India Limited is one of the successful companies in India and has faired very well as a listed company. Under the leadership of Saroj K. Podar, it has been the leader in the men's grooming segment. In 2005, its net profit rose to Rs 6.87 billion, as compared to Rs 6.12 billion the previous year.[b]

Suitable social philosophy The founder, King Camp Gillette (1855–1935), was a social reformer at heart and had authored several books on building a harmonious society. However, it is his invention of the safety blade that made him famous. His social philosophy of benefiting society by whatever one does seems to have helped this useful product to become a globally necessary consumer product.

Gillette is a case of the best practices of all the business management disciplines working in harmony.

Contd

Box Contd

A good business does not trumpet its ethical values. Its ethics, is, however, very well demonstrated in the service culture of the company.

Questions

(a) What do these concepts convey to a business-man—need, want, or desire?

(b) What is the fundamental principle of doing business?

(c) How important is it to have harmony among the classical business management areas?

[a] *Source:* 'Products of the Century—Health and Grooming,' *Fortune.com*, 22 November 1999, http://www.fortune.com/fortune/1999/11/22/pro7.html.

[b] See http://business.mapsofindia.com/india-company/gillette-india.html.

CONCLUSION

There is a perception in society that businessman is a cheat and a business manager is a manipulator, exploiter, and a person without conscience. Although all our seven principles of business ethics are important in conducting the disciplines of management, prudence should be the leading one. Prudence is the seat of managerial decision making. It takes all the aspects into consideration and tries to make a wise decision, which is both fair and practical.

For the Indian business manager, there could never be a better and more prudent decision than the one that is taken with social consciousness. When more than 60 per cent of the people of our country live in poverty, a manager's task is well cut out. Firstly, he would have to empower customers. If customers have no money, there is very little business. Secondly, the purpose of business must be defined not as philanthropy or charity but as integral marketing. Make the poor your partners in business, as some of the examples in the following chapters will show.

Towards the end of his life, Mahatma Gandhi was asked by people to advise on the way to move ahead. He suggested that if the decisions and actions that one took could benefit the poorest of the poor Indian, then all the doubts would melt away. If an Indian manager's decision is going to benefit some of the economically marginalized, it will have its bearing on a billion people! This is the business responsibility of an Indian manager.

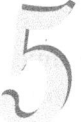

Manufacturing: Consumer, the Ultimate Stakeholder

The buyer needs a hundred eyes, the seller not one.[1]

—George Herbert

Two-wheelers—with the father driving, the elder child standing in front and the wife behind holding a baby—are very much the norm in this country. In that form two-wheelers are a relatively unsafe mode of transporting a family. The two-wheeler image is what got me thinking that we needed to create a safer form of transport.[2]

—Ratan N. Tata

LEARNING OBJECTIVES

After studying this chapter, you will be able to

> State the duties of manufacturers
> Understand the rights of consumers
> Define ethical consumption
> Differentiate between legal business and moral business

INTRODUCTION

The ethical orientation in this chapter is based on the twin principles of rights and duties, which along with the principle of utilitarianism becomes important, since the purpose of all businesses is the benefit of the customer. We will delineate the four themes mentioned in the learning objectives in the light of 'consumer, the ultimate stakeholder'.

Although the term 'manufacturing' stands for something produced by hands (the Latin words *manus*, meaning hand, and *facere*, meaning to make), today its meaning implies machine and technology-based industrial production. It is a process where raw materials are transformed into finished goods on a very large scale. Some finished goods such as steel, fabric, leather, chemicals, etc. are the raw materials that are used

---

[1] George Herbert, Jacula Prudentum (No. 390), 1651. See http://en.wikiquote.org/wiki/george_Herbert.

[2] Ratan Tata on motivation for the Nano car; see interview at http://tatanano.inservices.tatamotors.com.

to produce machines, planes, trains, clothes, shoes, medicines, and so forth. All the manufactured goods are produced with the purpose of selling them to consumers. Consumers are those who buy goods from the manufacturers through several middlemen such as distributors, dealers, and retailers.

Consumers characterize the modern world. Today, our society is a consumer society. Consumers dominate the world. Consumers demand and manufacturers work to supply and satisfy the demands. Manufacturers compete with one another to produce better goods and increase sales, as consumers seem to show an insatiable desire to consume. Marketers and advertisers sharpen the desires of the consumers to the extent that people buy goods and employ services that they do not even need. Needs are created, wants generated, and desires satisfied. This is consumerism. It is a belief that happiness lies in having more than what one already has—for instance, having a better and more magnificent house, or a bigger and better car, or more expensive clothes, or maybe eating food that is of a better quality and is more sumptuous. From being a nomad to becoming an agriculturist and later evolving as a craftsman, man has progressed to the industrial and technological stage. Life at this stage is highly complex. Society is based on the creation of wealth, the goods and services produced, and at the same time, society consumes what it produces. This is the economic life-cycle of man. Consumption determines production, while demand creates supply. The producer is at the service of the consumer, who in turn repays the former's services with money. The one who has the money is the stakeholder.

The shareholder concept in business management is simple. It is the stakeholder concept that is tricky. In its strict implication, a stakeholder is a bookmaker or bookie who accepts bets from the customers, who are called punters in the betting jargon, and holds that money, which is known as stake money, till the activity for which the betting has taken place is over and the dividend is declared. All activities with unpredictable end results attract betting, such as outcomes of sports, horse racing, elections, dice, cards, casino gambling, and even mundane things such as whether the next car that passes by has an even or odd registration number. To 'bet', 'wager', and 'gamble' or to 'take a risk' are the terms used in such cases. Since business too involves unpredictability and the businessman takes risks, and the stakes are dependent on an unforeseen and unpredictable customer who holds the dividends back until he/she buys and pays for it, the customer is considered to be the businessman's stakeholder. There are many products and services competing in the market for the customer's attention. What products will be accepted and what will be rejected, or who will win and who will lose, all depends on the vagaries of the customer.

In this chapter, we will delve into a fairly new concept known as consumer, who is the ultimate stakeholder. We have been brought up on some clichéd terms such as 'customer is king', 'customer satisfaction', 'what the customer wants', and several others that mean exactly what they may say. But when it is seen from the customer's point of view, the reality of the supremacy of the customer is a chimera. The above clichés are from the sellers' point of view, to position themselves as the custodian of the buyer's interest.

There are two subjects—seller and buyer. The buyer sees the seller as someone who can give value for money, whereas the seller sees the buyer as someone from whom money or profit can be made. It is value for money versus profit. It is a unique situation where two subjects have stakes in each other. Such interdependence of interests brings the subjects in close relationship. This relationship is based on the value of trust. While the seller builds the relationship through the quality of goods and the services offered, the buyer reciprocates it with loyalty, even pride. For instance, there is a family that has a tradition of buying cars from the same company over several generations, while there is another family whose faith in a particular bank is unshakable.

Business exists for the customer. Without the customer there is no business. In any business, the seller is the bettor, who has taken risks against all odds, to put out a product or service, by making a bet that there would be customers who would bite the bait, hold the stakes for the seller, and render returns on the investment. Thus, the customer is the ultimate stakeholder without whom business has no existence.

Indeed, the customer alone holds the stakes. The seller does everything possible—manufactures, supplies, distributes, advertises, markets, etc.—till the customer goes and buys it. The moment the customer releases the money, he/she ceases to be the customer; he/she has become an owner of the good or service. The so-called after-sales service and customer-care do play a role in building up a customer base for the future from the existing customers.

'Customer, the ultimate stakeholder', is the buyer of the goods or services that a seller has risked the knowledge, skill, and money to produce and sell, and hopes that the buyer will buy. Thus, the seller has stakes in the buyer and the buyer holds the stakes until the parting with money. It is noteworthy how the two values of faith and hope connect and work together. The seller expects faith from the customers, to trust the company and its products, while hoping that the customer will buy from him/her, and hence, risks money in the business.

The moral issues in a seller and customer relationship are very serious. The moral onus is always on the seller for the quality, quantity, safety, health, and service of the product vis-à-vis the customer. Also, the relationship of trust itself, that which guarantees business, is at stake. However, the operational moral principles at stake here are the rights of the customer and the duties of the manufacturer.

DUTIES OF THE MANUFACTURER

Product to Suit a Human Need

Levi's is as much a world phenomenon as Coca Cola and Xerox, where these brand names are synonymous with their products. But Levi's jeans have something more appealing than most other jeans sold in the world. They were meant for the labourers who worked in hard and difficult workplaces such as mines, railroads, and tunnels. These rugged pair of pants became the workman's symbol not only in the US, but all over the world. It is perhaps the only piece of clothing in the world whose value rises

Stakeholder Concept

Debunking the popular theory

The dictionary defines a stakeholder as a person who is entrusted with the stakes of the bettors. To be more specific, it is a person who takes care of the bets and returns the entrusted money with dividends to the winner. Derivatively, in business management, it is a figurative for the entrepreneur who has risked money in the enterprise and expects the customer to return it with profits. In other words, the entrepreneur has placed stakes on the customer. So, the customer is the stakeholder.

R. Edward Freeman[a] advocated the concept of a stakeholder in such a way that it completely reversed the roles and subsumed within it all those who had a stake in the business and also those who were presumed to have such stakes. Thus, entrepreneurs, shareholders, and employees became the obvious stakeholders. The base was further enlarged to include the social existence of entrepreneurship, which included government bodies, social organizations, trade unions,

even prospective employees, customers, and competitors who had no direct money at stake, but were a part of the society where such entrepreneurship existed.

After almost a decade of Freeman's advocacy of the concept, in 1995, T. Donaldson and L. Preston published a paper in the *Academy of Management Review*, examining 'The Stakeholder Theory of the Corporation: Concepts, Evidence and Implications', which helped develop a thought with an ethical perspective. The 1990s was the decade of the discovery of corporate governance, which was highlighted by corporate social responsibility. The stakeholder concept became a ready instrument to make all the parties concerned in business, that is, all those who had claims in the enterprise, to be described as stakeholders.

It should be remembered that the real stakeholder is the customer; the rest are claimants on the returns by the customer. In this sense, the customer is the ultimate stakeholder. See Fig. 5.1.

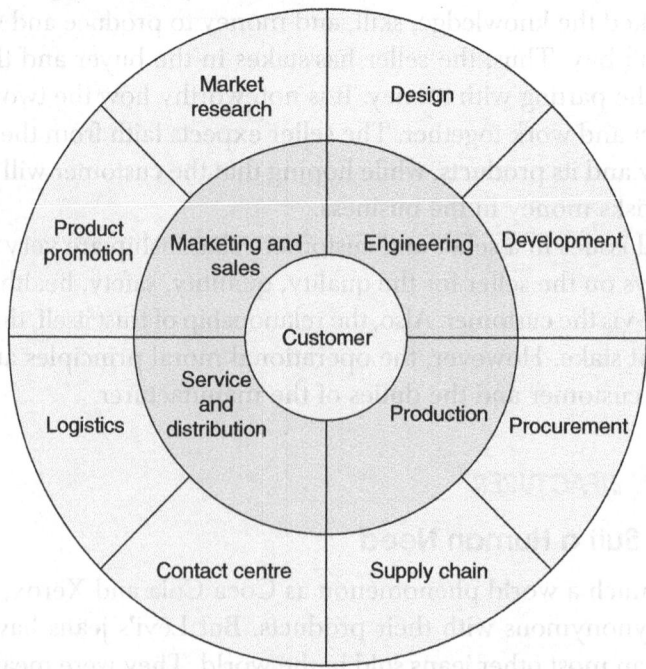

Fig. 5.1 Customer, the motive for business

[a] R.E. Freeman, *Strategic Management: A Stakeholder Approach*, Boston: Pitman, 1984.

the more it is worn, gets old, and even worn out. Jeans as serrated, unthreaded, stone washed, and in other scores of forms are higher end fashion statements.

Denim, the sturdy fabric, out of which jeans, jackets, and other apparels are made, was discovered as early as 300 A.D., in Nimes, France, and was known as *serge de Nimes*. Levi Strauss, a German *émigré*, founded a company in San Francisco in 1853 by the name Levi Strauss & Co. In 1872, a certain Jacob Davis wrote to Levi's company for the supply of work trousers, made preferably with a fabric that was reinforced with rivets at the seams, to withstand the vagaries of hard labour. Levi's jeans continues to thrive to date.

The moral question in manufacturing, marketing, and selling a product is to ask whether the product in question fulfills genuine human needs or not. Today, firms are blamed for creating a need, rather than recognizing a real need. Innumerable ads suggest that if you do not have the product that is being advertised, then you are out of sync with the fashionable world. They repeatedly and relentlessly stress upon its need such that it works on your subconscious and compels you to buy it. Detergents and cosmetics take a huge lead in creating a compulsion out of a basic human need, rather than supplying what is needed. Both these products are the most commonly used ones. People need them. But due to competition, a need is made into a compulsion in favour of a particular product, because it has something special that the other products do not have. Thus, the popular brand of shampoo that magically clears all dandruff is a compulsive need. The scientific truth is that whether one has dandruff or not depends on one's health. A soap or a shampoo or some clear water can only wash it away. It is the same with toothpastes. Though there is a need to clean one's teeth and mouth, the claim that only a particular brand of toothpaste can clean the mouth, whiten the teeth, and kill the germs is factually wrong. The claims made by hair oils and gels that they nourish the hair, help it to grow, strengthen it, prevent it from breaking, and so on are scientifically ridiculous, since hair is after all a dead substance.

Product Development

Product development may be distinguished in two ways, historical and technical. For instance, when we observe the development of the Ford car, from the first model to the latest one, we marvel at the sheer visual change that this product has undergone. We are also able to judge the enormous change in its technology when we lift the hood of one of the car and see the engine. On the contrary, we can see that the Ambassador car of Hindustan Motors has not developed much, either visibly or technically.

Technical development is most obvious in electronic and computing devices. The original computer scaled to a large building, but today's mobile phone offers a much more powerful computing capabilities. Similarly, all the modern gadgets and consumer goods win a market niche due to their so-called cutting-edge technology. Be it washing machines, cooking ranges, refrigerators, or air-conditioners, all have a technically proven, ultimate selling point that promise to be less energy consuming, more environmentally friendly, noise-free, or consuming less water.

Let us take a couple of examples from the service sector, such as banking and insurance. In India, there has been a revolution in these two fields. Till the end of the 1980s, these sectors were so staid and stiff that people wondered about the use of these two institutions. Banks were used to only deposit or withdraw money, and insurances were mandatory for vehicle owners and salaried people only. The common man was least affected by these government-run services.

In March 2008, Reliance Capital (Adhikari 2008) from the Reliance Group made an ominous announcement that it would enter the microfinance market. Reliance Capital is not a bank; it is specifically classified as a non-banking finance company (NBFC). The business plan was to supply money to microfinance institutions that in turn would serve their self-help groups (SHGs). Although microfinance to SHGs is not novel, the NBFCs entering this segment with clear social responsibilities are definitely new. Further, this new financial agency developed more attractive products for its customers. Some of the products especially developed and offered to the customers are credit cards, housing loans, loans for small and medium enterprises, demat services, both online and offline broking, mutual funds, and insurance services. Consequently, an NBFC would become a one-stop shop for all financial services, which could overshadow the traditional banking system. Since NBFCs are not banks, they are not bound by the stringent RBI regulations of cash reserve ratio, statutory cash reserve ratio, etc. They could spread very quickly into the rural areas of India by using direct customer services through their agents. The traditional banks are quite staid and tied, compared to the ease with which a basket of financial products are offered to the customer directly. Reliance Capital is already attending to over a hundred thousand customers a month. Other big companies such as Tata Capital, Birla Finance, and Bajaj Finance have also set foot into developing revolutionary financial products for the masses.

The morality of product development lies in the principle of duty towards the customer, where the customer could hope for an updated product that is qualitatively better than before. In a command economy, the interest of the customer is not the motivator for the producer. But in a free economy, the entrepreneur makes it a duty to be aware of it. The entrepreneur constantly thinks of ways to woo the customer, by marketing a better product and reaching out to a larger base.

Second, the principle of utility plays an important role. Technologically better and cheaper goods ensure a greater benefit to a larger number of people. The greater the number of customers, the lower the prices of a product or service. This allows the entrepreneur greater returns on investment, which further motivates to develop and innovate as per the needs of the customers and invest appreciable money in research and development.

Research and Development

Research is of two kinds, basic and applied. Basic research is a purely theoretical pursuit to understand the subject in question better and develop conceptual tools to enhance the knowledge. Applied research, also known as research and development (R&D), is where the theoretical knowledge is put to use. In an industry, highly sophisticated machineries are built to develop new products and test them. In a business, knowledge is accumulated for the development of products and services through market research. R&D becomes an imperative for the manufacturer, in order to supply products and services that are more developed, to stay ahead in the competitive market.

A mere 0.8 per cent of GDP spent by India does not speak much for R&D. However, companies are waking up to the need for R&D in order to become market leaders, as well as to give customers value-based products.

One of the leading firms in R&D is the Bangalore-based biopharmaceutical company Biocon. In early June 2008, Biocon launched a unique product in India called pre-filled syringe devices.[3] Erypro Safe and Nufil Safe are life-saving drugs that have been developed by the company for kidney and cancer patients, respectively. There have been several disadvantages in the use of conventional syringes, such as injuries, infections, and the tediousness of having to draw the drugs into the syringes each time the medicine is injected, given the working conditions of the medics and paramedics. The pre-filled syringes allow for neat and patient-friendly administrations of these costly drugs. The needle of the syringe has been further designed and qualitatively improved by increasing the needle sharpness from 3 to 5 bevels, thus reducing the pain suffered by the patient. The company has spent over Rs 20 crore in the R&D of these life-saving drugs.

The above is a good example of R&D. There are, however, morally controversial subjects being researched and developed. For instance, there are a wide range of genetically modified agricultural products, which include cotton, grains and pulses, and vegetables. People are scared to eat genetically modified foodstuffs because they have no knowledge of its effects on the body. Many experts fear that these may not only cause cancer, skin diseases, or affect the various organs of the body, but may also affect the very genes of our human organic composition.

Whether it is dissecting a frog in a college lab, or running tests on animals in the cosmetic industry, R&D has very serious moral issues to face. In recent years, organizations such as People for Ethical Treatment of Animals (PETA) have succeeded in sensitizing people to the fact that animals too have some basic moral rights. They must not be misused, caged, tormented, starved, displayed for the vicarious pleasure of people, or used in sports such as bull fights.

Innovation

Innovation may be best described as an improvement on invention. The microprocessor is an example par excellence. It is like the invention of the wheel. Just as the wheel

---

[3] *Business Standard*, 17 June 2008. For more details, see http://www.business-standard.com.

defined the industrial revolution, the microchip has revolutionized the contemporary world. From wrist watches to rockets, from small hand-held calculators to complex industrial robots, microchips are the basic components. Just as we cannot think of any technical apparatus without some kind of wheels attached to it, so also the efficient functioning and control of these latest inventions cannot be thought of without microchips. Along with microchips, laser technology and fibre optics have made modern technology incredibly advanced and an essential part of everyday life, at every turn. Whether it is the functioning of traffic lights on the road or being able to watch television at home, without the chip, the laser, and the fibre-optic, life that we enjoy would seem impossible.

Nowadays, manufacturers have good and inexpensive technology at their disposal. They only need to apply it to give value to their customers. ITC has an innovative programme for the farmers of rural India, called e-Chaupal. The company has built farming communities around computer-generated information in the villages through which farmers are able to determine the prices of their grains. Earlier, they used to go to the traditional market area called *mandi* and were forced to sell at unreasonably low prices to the agents and brokers. The information acquired through e-Chaupal has empowered farmers to do their own business and therefore eliminate the middlemen. Now, they sell their produce directly to the food processing companies or the large industrial retailers.

Hindustan Lever Limited (HLL) has an innovative marketing programme for its soap. The company has trained people in rural areas to maintain good personal hygiene by washing their hands regularly with soap. It has conducted workshops and demonstrations to teach them the benefits of washing their hands to avoid the intake of germs that cause diseases. It has also set up small businesses in villages, where soap, iodized salt, and the like can be bought to keep diseases at bay. We will study this marketing programme in detail in Chapter 6. So, where squalor and disease once marked a village, today thousands of villages have become less prone to diseases due to the various innovative programmes of the companies and have developed an army of small entrepreneurs. More of such innovative practices have brought solar lamps, affordable sachets of all consumables, mobiles, computers, education, transport, and entertainment to the villages. Thus, innovation, whether technological or in the field of marketing, has benefited a large number of people.

The above goes to show that when manufacturers and marketers are committed in their social duty and are focused on doing business, innovative ideas are generated and put into practice. The benefit to the customer gives satisfaction to the manufacturer and the marketer and they are able to motivate all those who are involved in the entire chain of business. Innovation helps to empower the customer. The customer's empowerment in turn generates even more business. Wealth is created in the process for all those concerned with the business, and the standards and the quality of living get a boost. In this way, innovation is able to generate a social change for the better.

Micro Magic

Two Krishnas and the global customer

C. Krishnarao Prahalad and M.S. Krishnan (2008) share more than Lord Krishna's name. They share ideas that can make sense to every individual across the globe. It is a twin idea—give value to the customer by allowing the customer to be a co-creator, that is, a partner in product innovation. In other words, we see a big change taking place in the consumer habits. If the consumer habits of the young are a signal to go by, then the websites that give personalized attention to their customers is only the beginning of a new customer revolution. Individuals are becoming important, and knowing their needs and doing something about them creates a new customer relationship, where the customer is going to make the product to suit self, and not vice-versa. For instance, the authors say that when one bought a car in the past, one bought that which was available and used it till he thought of buying a new one several years later. Today, technology allows the dealer to be interactive with the customer long after the car has been bought. The customer can reach out to the dealer in emergencies, with the help of the GPS installed in the car. For instance, when an accident takes place, or a sudden ailment or problem that the customer's child is suffering from gets aggravated while they are driving, the customer can seek the dealer's help through the GPS. Thus, there is the service provider who takes care of individual customers; the former has to marshal a slew of resources to serve a customer as an individual. The authors then coined a symbol to represent this new phenomenon. According to them, N=1 represents the single individual customer and R=G represents the resources mustered to customize the service, in order to provide the service to that single customer. The much dreamed about customized and personalized service is thus possible through the already existing technologies. It is now left to the creative and innovative managers to put together teams for such a business and add a customer as the most important variable in product development and marketing.

The moral value of the above idea is a very good one. The personalized service is going to bring in a big change in the individual attitude. It will generate a social concern within society and people will be more aware of other people's needs. A new social consciousness sharpens the moral values of not only the individuals, but also of society at large.

Questions

(a) What are the ethical implications of the basic assumption of the authors?

(b) How practical are the solutions of customization of products and services?

(c) How important is it to give value to the customer?

Source: C.K. Prahalad and M.S. Krishnan, *The New Age of Innovation*, Tata McGraw-Hill Publishing, 2008.

Product Safety

The history of mankind is closely related to the discovery of fire. From generating fire through friction by rubbing two pieces of flint together to the more complex ignition and combustion methods used nowadays, safety comes first. Making fire and preserving it was not only inconvenient but was also very hazardous. Till John Walker, a British pharmacist, invented the first match in 1827, fire was not so easily available at hand; but even then, it was still not safe. In 1844 Gustave E. Pasch, a Swedish chemist, invented the safety match as we know it today, and his compatriot John Lundstrom began to manufacture and supply it in large quantities. Sweden, the country of Alfred Nobel, who invented the dynamite, is still a market leader in the production of safety matches. Safety matches have taken all sorts of fancy forms now, such as book matches and water proof matches, and their logos and emblems adorn hospitality and entertainment establishments. The history and variety of safety matches is so vast that it is no surprise that it has become a leading hobby among collectors. The English elegantly call it a box of matches, but the Indians quite simply say match box or matches; they are actually known as safety matches.

Product safety is the supreme duty of the manufacturer. Failure to conform to safety standards results in harm to the customers. Today, the greatest concern of customers around the globe is whether the products they use are safe or not. The building materials used by builders has caused anxiety to millions of people. In India, researchers believe that at least 40 per cent of the drugs sold are spurious. Food grown in chemical fertilizers contain toxins. Electrical equipments and gadgets are dangerous, particularly for children. Computers and other ubiquitous gadgets that use chips contain deadly chemicals such as cadmium, lead, and mercury. Ever since the advent of mobile phones, controversies regarding their safe use have risen: from fears of the users being afflicted with cancers and tumours to their networks' undue interference with the functioning of other equipments inside an operation theatre or on an aircraft. The quality of baby foods or toys have been of great concern to all parents.

The moral dilemma becomes acute when certain products are inherently harmful either directly to individual customers or to society as a whole. Products that contain tobacco are inherently harmful. Cancer is considered to be directly related to the use of tobacco, not only through its direct use as in smoking, chewing, and ingesting, but also through its passive use. Similarly the consumption of alcohol is not only related to health problems but also to social problems.

Households have been economically destroyed because the families' breadwinners have become alcoholics and have squandered the family income. They have reduced their families to penury and children to lack of education and other amenities of life. Further, there are also products that can destroy not only nations but the entire humanity as well. Arms proliferation—its sale, its potential, and the real use to destroy—is morally unjustifiable. The greatest dilemma in the arms race is that while defence is legitimate and justifiable, preparation for war and killing is unjustifiable. Tobacco destroys health and leads to loss of money in healthcare, alcohol destroys health as

---

Facts about the Use of Tobacco

Smokers in the world: 1 billion	Deaths related to tobacco use: 5.4 million annually
Passive smokers: half of world's children.	Tobacco death toll in 20th century: 100 million, expected to rise ten times more in the twenty-first century
Concentration of smokers: in low- and middle-income countries	

Source: See Anuradha Mascarenhas, 'No Tobacco Day', in *Indian Express*, http://www.indianexpress.com/story/316793.html.

Over-the-Counter Death Dealing

Deadly trade in spurious drugs

You have been prescribed antibiotics by your physician and you buy them and ingest them as per the instructions, but there are no perceptible signs of improvement and your illness deteriorates. From allergies to life-threatening diseases people have become victims of spurious medicines. India in general, and North India in particular, is the victim of spurious drugs. Since medical doctors are scarce and people's refusal to consult physicians stems from prejudices and lack of money, the spurious drug industry is making merry. The situation is further worsened by the pharmacists who readily sell these products over-the-counter without the physicians' prescription whether they are in the know of its spurious nature or not.

According to World Health Organization (WHO), India produces 35 per cent of the world's spurious drugs. The magnitude of the problem is unabatedly on the rise.[a] Unlike other imitations and counterfeits such as shoes or appliances, medical products cannot be easily identified as fake due to the nature of packaging and inability to determine the quality.

Some of the counterfeits may be harmless, where mere distilled water or some harmless base such as coconut oil may be used. But this does not help the sick consumer. It causes delay and the delay in health matters may be even more dangerous than spuriousness.

Drug fraud consists of its contents being harmless and useless, being less potent, having toxic substances, or falsified expiry dates and following several other ingenious ways of manufacturing, packaging, including batch numbers, marketing, and advertising. It is a false and dangerous industry that eats into the funds and lives of the people. The most heinous act being that this is perpetuated by exploiting the consumer's ignorance and helplessness to detect any fraud.

Questions

(a) What technological innovations can the pharmaceutical industry introduce to combat the menace of spurious drugs?

(b) What legal recommendations do you propose to stop the menace of spurious drugs?

(c) How can consumers help to remedy the situation?

[a] See http://www.thehindu.com/thehindu/seta/2003/07/31/stories/2003073100190200.htm.

---

well as family economy and the social fabric, and arms race can destroy everything, including the human race. Compared to the above, it would seem that the safety match is perhaps the only invention that man has been able to make safe.

Moreover, the duties of the manufacturer lie in the rights of the customer. The ethical relationship between the manufacturer and the consumer is that of rights and duties. It is also the standard of ethical judgment. The rights of the customer naturally become the duties of the manufacturer.

CONSUMER RIGHTS

On 15 March 1989, India celebrated its first National Consumer's Day. Ever since, there has been a steady improvement in the consciousness of the growing number of customers about their rights. In 1962, the US had introduced the Consumer Rights Bill and on that occasion John F. Kennedy, the then President, had declared that if consumers were offered substandard products, or unsafe drugs because they were not able to make an informed choice, then the money spent by them was wasted, their health was lost, and the country's interest was damaged.[4] Consumer protection laws have been instituted in most of the developed countries.

Consumer Rights and the Law

India enacted the Consumer Protection Act (COPRA) in 1986 and enshrined the following six rights.

Safety The safety of the customer is paramount. Goods and services must ensure the safety and security of the consumer. Information of any hazard or risk must be documented and given to the customer.

Consumer safety means the right to be protected against the marketing of goods and services that are hazardous to life and property. The purchased goods and the services availed of should not only meet their immediate needs, but also fulfil long-term interests.

Before purchasing, consumers should insist on the quality of the products, as well as on the guarantee of the products and services. They should preferably purchase quality marked products such as ISI, AGMARK, etc.[5]

Information Advertising, labelling, and other information about the product or service has to be unambiguous and clear.

The right to information means the right to be informed about the quality, quantity, potency, purity, standard, and price of goods so as to protect the consumer against unfair trade practices.

The consumer should insist on getting all the information about the product or service before making a choice or a decision. This will enable the customer to act wisely and responsibly and also to desist from falling prey to high pressure selling techniques.[6]

Choice Commerce is done under free and fair trade. Monopolies and cartels are detrimental to price regulation and are against the law.

The right to choose means the right to be assured wherever possible of access to a variety of goods and services at competitive prices. In case of monopolies, one has the right to be assured of a satisfactory quality and service at a fair price. It also includes the right to basic goods and services. This is because unrestricted rights of the minority to choose can mean a denial for the majority of its fair share. This right can be better exercised in a competitive market, where a variety of goods are available at competitive prices.[7]

Representation The consumer is paramount and has the right to have his/her grievances heard. The Indian consumer courts, unlike the regular courts, provide speedy and free legal advice and deliver justice.

---

[4] See http://www.cuts-international.org.
[5] See http://fcamin.nic.in/Events/EventListing.asp?Section=Consumer%20Rights&ID_PK=18&ParentID=0.
[6] See http://fcamin.nic.in/Events/EventListing.asp?Section=Consumer%20Rights&ID_PK=18&ParentID=0.
[7] See http://fcamin.nic.in/Events/EventListing.asp?Section=Consumer%20Rights&ID_PK=18&ParentID=0.

The right to represent means that the consumers' interests will receive due consideration at the appropriate forums. It also includes the right to be represented in the various foras that have been formed to consider the consumer's welfare.

The consumers should form non-political and non-commercial consumer organizations, which can be given representation in various committees formed by the government and other bodies in matters relating to consumers.[8]

Redress   The consumer redress in the consumer courts is efficient and implemented immediately.

The right to a redress means the right to seek a redress against unfair trade practices or unscrupulous exploitation of consumers. It also includes the right to a fair settlement of the genuine grievances of the consumer.

Consumers must file a complaint of their genuine grievances. Many a times the complaints may be of small value but the impact on society as a whole may be very large. They can also take the help of consumer organizations in seeking redress of their grievances.[9]

Consumer education   Consumers have the right to demand transparency from manufacturers. The government and social welfare organizations have the responsibility to educate the consumers.

The right to consumer education means the right to acquire the knowledge and skill to be an informed consumer throughout life. The ignorance of consumers, particularly the rural consumers, is mainly responsible for their exploitation. They should know their rights and must exercise them. Only then can real consumer protection be achieved with success.

The law has been able to bring about a commendable change in judicial reforms to offer speedy justice within the limited period of 90–150 days through the establishment of the special consumer redressal courts. The shortcomings of the act consist of the exclusion of two important consumer rights—basic necessities and a healthy environment. These are also fundamental human rights. However, social organizations and non-governmental organizations have been able to exert pressure regarding these two issues.

The Centre for Consumer Action Research and Training (CART) has followed in the footsteps of Mahatma Gandhi and has organized a consumer boycott concerning the basic needs and health. CART also promotes the rights to opportunities. The government has innumerable schemes targeted at the people below the poverty line (BPL), but the targeted people very often do not get to avail the benefits of the scheme. Although the critics of the law have been quick to point out that COPRA has not been able to root out the malady of corruption and the rising prices, yet the Act has been a boon. Ever since the Right to Information Act 2008 has come, many of

---

[8] See http://fcamin.nic.in/Events/EventListing.asp?Section=Consumer%20Rights&ID_PK=18&ParentID=0.
[9] See http://fcamin.nic.in/Events/EventListing.asp?Section=Consumer%20Rights&ID_PK=18&ParentID=0.

the basic consumer problems have been given another strong legal arm to deal with the offenders.

INFORMED CONSUMER

The saying that 'the devil lies in the details' is absolutely true when it comes to the task of information given to the consumer. Booklets, manuals, instruction leaflets, and labels on the packing contain information. There are two kinds of information—product advertisement and statutory information. The statutory information is often in fine print and is merely to fulfil an obligation. This information should consist of contents, manufacture and expiry dates, risks, and several other aspects regarding the safe use of the product. The maximum retail price, the bar codes, etc. must be in the stipulated size and prominently displayed.

Problems in Accurate Information

In November 2003, the Federation of Medical and Sales Representatives Association of India (FMRAI) staged a demonstration before the Ministry of Health against the sale of spurious drugs. Earlier on in August, FMRAI declared the objectives of their action. The association wanted to highlight the menace of spurious drugs in India. They would organize street corner meetings in over 300 cities and towns, across the country, distribute leaflets, and instruct people. The association wanted to convey to the public that 40 per cent of the pharmaceutical market in India is under the clutches of black market and that the Ministry of Health had failed to address the problem of spurious drugs under the Drugs and Cosmetic Act 1940. More and more drugs under various names have been flooding the market, but the essential drugs such as for malaria, filaria, and TB have been neglected. Drugs such as Viagra, meant for erectile dysfunction, and anti-obesity pills are marketed by American companies. After a research, the Food and Drugs Administration Agency in the US came to the conclusion that 85 per cent of the so-called new drugs are merely variants of the existing ones.

CONSUMER POLITICS

The anti-India rhetoric against outsourcing by the developed countries in general, and the US in particular, has had an unnerving effect on the IT companies. India specializes in IT products and services. Political leaders from the outsourcing countries have found a pet issue to ensure jobs for their citizens and have accused India of depriving their citizens of jobs by offering IT services at a very low price.[10] During the American presidential election campaign of 2008, the political pitch against outsourcing reached a crescendo. China, which is known as the manufacturer of the world, bore the brunt

[10] See http://www.time.com/time/magazine/article/0,9171,1739309,00.html, accessed on 12 May 2008.

of Hillary Clinton when she said that if she became the president she would 'stand up to China and other non-market countries' (implying India) that 'subsidize their exports and put our manufacturers at a disadvantage'.[11] She proposed immediate and aggressive crackdown on such trade practices, which she felt were unfair. However, a group of Congressmen of the US House of Representatives visited the Indian IT centres. They found to their amazement and approval that the computers, other accessories, and even the air-conditioners belonged to American companies.

PROBLEMS OF POLITICS AND ECONOMICS

Our economic reality has become so complex that it crosses borders and businesses have become global, but political realities have not changed with the times. We have nation-states and tight borders, and national interests that transcend individual interests. This is called geo-politics. There are wars and conflicts over issues other than trade and commerce. In the 1980s, Japan became the manufacturing hub of the world and

---

Death Penalty for Adulterators

Greed for profits kills innocent

Parents stood outside a Chinese court in Shijiazhuang, China, with several protest placards, one of which read 'Sanlu Milk Powder give me back my child'. Sanlu made history for a wrong reason. It adulterated its milk products, which killed several children and hundreds of thousands of children became ill with long-term physical challenges.

When India witnesses heinous crimes such as gang rape, mutilation of limbs of innocent children, etc., the politicians talk about the need for the legislation of capital punishment for the offenders of such appalling crimes against humanity. In China, when the story of the melamine-tainted milk broke out—several children had died and over 3,00,000 children became very ill—the public demanded the execution of the executives of Sanlu dairy.

The trial began in early January 2009, and the case is still going on. The court is discovering horrendous facts. Sanlu executives, in order to buttress the low-quality milk, used melamine, a chemical that is used in plastics, whose high nitrogen levels mimicked protein in nutrition tests. The majority of users were children, who developed stones in their kidneys. The general manager and several other employees of the company are now firmly behind bars. The people expect that justice be done soon.

The justice system in China is quick and harsh. The accused have been sentenced to death. That the general manager of the Sanlu dairy is a woman and a mother further sharpens the irony of this terrible tragedy.[a]

Questions

(a) Why does an ethical issue such as the health of children become so accentuated?

(b) Is justice a matter of emotion or reason?

(c) How can managers be made aware of their basic ethical responsibilities?

[a] See Emma Graham-Harrison http://www.reuters.com/article/latestCrisis/idUSPEK294403.

---

[11] See http://www.time.com/time/magazine/article/0,9171,1739309,00.html, accessed on 12 May 2008.

the developed countries led a similar divisive politics. That did not stop Japan from its goals. In the 1990s, China became an export-oriented economy and despite political and economic pressures surged with its focused manufacturing. As the new millennium dawned, the Indian expertise and service industry took off. Indian companies acquired large companies from developed countries. Politics again played spoilsport. As a result, the economies of the developed countries became the victims of their own policies and politics, slipped into the debt trap, and got decimated in the financial meltdown of 2008. It clearly showed that despite the protectionism of the politicians, the consumers in those countries consumed, and they consumed way beyond their means. Lee Iacocca, once the chief of Chrysler, and regarded as the best management pundit, had advocated fair trade instead of free trade.

CONSUMER PRIVACY

Consumer privacy is a sensitive issue in our communication age, wherein every victim of its violation cries out for ethical behaviour. Privacy concerns are not merely in the fields of consumerism and health, but are also prominent in the workplace. Here, however, we are concerned with the protection of consumers' private information. Consumer privacy[12] is as old as the developed human consciousness. The famous Hippocratic oath taken by physicians on their graduation originated in ancient Greece to ensure the patient's privacy. All professions and trades involve seller or service provider and client relationship. Invariably there is some private information of the client that the seller or the service provider is privy to. This information is personal and as such is safeguarded by the law as well as society at large, as one that is to be protected to maintain customer confidentiality and safeguard personal information. Any trading or passing on of such information is in contravention of not only the law but against the conventions of society. Infringements on privacy may bring some short-term returns to commerce, but in the long run such strategies recoil and the trade secrets of the business concern may well be disclosed in public.

Consumer privacy in India, particularly after the boom in cellular phones, has become a serious problem. Take for instance the theft of cellular phones, whose cost is estimated at over Rs 500 crore annually. The loss of these phones implies not only the loss of money, but the loss of identities as well. The problem becomes compounded if the phone turns up in the wrong hands. Indian Cellular Association (ICA) has called for the creation of a central registry agency where a consumer or a service provider can register the International Mobile Equipment Identifier (IMEI).[13]

The manufacturers of the mobile sets are doing research and development to tackle the issue at the production level. The various features being engineered are mobile tracker, emergency SMS, and privacy lock, which allow the users to take care of their

---

[12] For a clear and comprehensive understanding, see http://www.consumerprivacyguide.org.
[13] See http://living.oneindia.in/insync/mobile-security-050207.html.

Consumer Dilemma

Behavioural targeting versus consumer privacy[a]

Are you conscious that you are being tracked or watched while you are surfing the net? The answer is in the negative, but this is a fact of the Internet age. Does this make you feel comfortable? Would you agree to people stealing your data? Would you mind if advertisers observe your surfing behaviour and accordingly target their ads at you? There is something that you would not like to reveal to your marketers, but you expose your supposed needs unawares. For, someone is watching you without your knowledge. It is as though someone was stalking you.

This sort of tracking and placing ads in the surfer's path is known as contextual targeting. Advertisers may have to spend money on tracking technology but the benefits of alluring the customers unconsciously are enormous. The moral problem lies in the fact that you are being exploited by an advertiser without your knowledge. The advertiser has exploited your behaviour. You have lost your right to privacy without your knowledge. Agencies around the world are urging their governments to bring in legislation to protect the consumers' privacy. This can be done by offering surfers a clear choice of track-on/track-off facilities. But marketers will not give up what they are after.

Questions

(a) Why privacy on the Internet is such a serious issue?

(b) Would not prohibition of tracking take away the marketer's legitimate right to study consumer behaviour?

[a] Harry Wang, *E-Commerce Times* part of the ECT News Network, at http://www.linuxinsider.com/story/63421.html, accessed on 17 June 2008.

---

mobiles and their personal safety. The mobile tracker, for instance, has two numbers pre-fed by the original user, which can be used to track the stolen mobile and give the necessary information to the police.

ETHICAL CONSUMPTION

Ratan is a car manufacturer. He employs thousands of workers and consumers, hundreds of goods and services as inputs to the production process, spare parts, and other supplies and the like. Ratan, the manufacturer, is a consumer as well. The raw materials, spare parts, and other services are produced by others, who in turn become consumers of what they need to produce. This dynamic process grows exponentially and becomes a very complex system of human interaction, where each individual is dependent on someone else, whether for production or consumption. Mankind has progressed from hunting-gathering to a complex consumer society.

We are a consumerist society. We orient all our education, skills, and training to advance production. We are in a state of constant exchange of goods and services. We, all the nations and people, are engaged in the production of wealth. We have set our goals of well-being in wealth. We, therefore, go through a cycle of production and consumption; every producer is also a consumer. Consequently, the ethics, that is, the economic behaviour of the people towards each other in a consumerist society, is not

---

Consumer Movement Wins Independence for the Country

Swadeshi

The first consumer awareness in our country was born out of the aspiration for independence from British colonial power. The British had total monopoly of the Indian market. Mahatma Gandhi pointed out that the economic power of the colonial rulers came from their exploitation of thirty crore Indians. The power of such a large mass of people could be used in a non-violent way, to subdue the foreign rulers. He urged the people to boycott British products. These products were made from raw materials produced in India (swadeshi). This was economic exploitation of traders and farmers in India. Gandhiji urged Indians to refuse to buy what the oppressors were selling, they could eventually win back the country.

Thus began the *swadeshi* movement with a two-pronged strategy. The first strategy was to refuse to buy the British goods. The second one was to turn every village into a self-sustaining engine of self-dependence for all the human needs. He advocated the production of *khadi* through spinning the humble *charkha*. It became a potent symbol of self-reliance, economic and political independence, and, above all, of moral strength.

'*Swadeshi* is a call to the consumer to be aware of the violence he is causing by supporting those industries that result in poverty and harm to workers and to humans and others', said Gandhiji. He walked to Dandi to make salt against the law of the times. That day *swadeshi* became a world movement, a symbol against political oppression and economic exploitation.

Questions
(a) Would *swadeshi* be considered as protectionist in the global economy?
(b) What are the moral implications of consumer boycott for political ends?
(c) What kind of moral justification is possible when vigilantes or the so-called cultural police forcefully shut down sales of some commodities or films or books?

---

linear as is often assumed, for instance, in the case of manufacturers, middlemen, and consumers. The ethical nature of a consumerist society is a dynamic and complex network of relations, since a producer is also a consumer, and vice-versa.

CLASSIFICATION OF UNETHICAL CONSUMER BEHAVIOUR

The basic assumption that we can arrive at from the previous discussion is that ethical manufacturing, marketing, advertising, and accounting cannot happen without equally ethical consumption. For instance, although consumers profess against environmental devastation, yet when it comes to buying, they may buy what damages the environment. We may classify five types of consumer delinquents (Chatzidakis et al. 2004).

Denial of responsibility The consumer buys a piece of machinery and handles it without knowing how to operate it and the machine has a breakdown. The consumer blames the dealers and others and denies any responsibility for the malfunctioning of the machine.

Denial of injury The consumer, due to recklessness while driving a car, or negligence by not taking care of injurious or poisonous substances, causes loss or damage, but denies outright that any serious damage was done because no one really got injured.

Denial of victim   The consumer defrauds a seller outright and justifies the act by saying that the seller deserved it because he/she had cheated the consumer many times before.

Condemning the condemners   A petty offence of the consumer is discovered, such as pilfering in a super bazaar or giving bribe for a certain service, and he/she turns offensive.

Appeal to higher ideal   The consumer, typically a gambler or a punter at the horserace who has begged, borrowed, and stolen money and cheated the system at these recreational places, justifies the action by saying that it was done to earn money for family.

The attitude and the frequency of such acts in society as a whole determine the general character of the consumers. It also calls for consumer awareness and education. Individuals would like to disown responsibility for their actions, and if this becomes endemic, manufacturers and marketers too would counter with more intricate unethical behaviour.

BUILDING ETHICAL CONSUMER COMMUNITIES

There are encouraging signs of consumer communities that go beyond consumer protection for legal matters. For instance, consumers are increasingly becoming aware of organic products. Although, initially these products may be costlier than the regular ones, preferring to buy organic products has encouraged bigger markets. These alternate markets are quickly becoming the standard ones due to the continued patronizing by consumers.

Motivation for Ethical Consumption

In ethical consumer communities, the motivation for consumption of organic products contextually originated from the issues of environmental protection. This immediately related to human health. Thus, consumers became aware of the contents of foodstuffs and the various processes of production, which made them refuse to use environmentally harmful products. Animal testing, emissions and effluents, toxins and gases, genetically modified foods, and goods produced through child labour worked as demotivators. Organically grown food, recycling, bio-degradable packaging, etc. became the rallying points of motivation. This in turn has motivated manufacturers to change their production, packaging and distribution methods, and use of technology.

Measuring Consumer Motivation

Motivation is nothing other than the core of ethical decision making. Sufficiently conscious buyers will make ethical choices, giving an impetus to the manufacturers and marketers, indicating their preferences. Thus, instead of imposing an ethical change and binding manufacturers and marketers to legal consequences, ethical consumers can bring a sea of change to the way business is conducted. From Table 5.1, we may safely conclude that consumers' motivation is related to their buying behaviour.

Table 5.1   Ranking for consumer motivation

Ethical issue	Exploitation of the third world	Animal testing factory farming	Damage to environment	Recycling	Genetically modified food
Exploitation of the third world	1.000	0.926	0.933	0876	0852
Animal testing factory farming	0.926	1.000	0.939	0.847	0.925
Damage to environment	0.933	0.939	1.000	0892	0879
Recycling	0.876	0.847	0.892	1.000	0.872
Genetically modified food	0.852	0.925	0.879	0.872	1.000

Note: Motive ranking—Spearman correlation coefficients (all significant at $p < 0.001$)

Source: Freestone & McGoldrick (2008).

About Stakes, Sweepstakes, and Odds

Punter's day out

If it is not the golf course that the business executive heads for on a weekend, then it has to be the race course. These places give an air of importance and status. The executive could learn a thing or two about business acumen at these elitist sports events. The language of horse racing is aptly adopted in business circles to describe certain concepts rather picturesquely. The stakeholder concept in business management owes its gratitude to horse racing. In fact, the sport is a perfect metaphor of conducting and managing business.

To bet and to win money is the purpose of horse racing. The one who bets is called the punter, who may bet on a horse for a win or place the horse of choice, say, second, behind the winner. This way of betting is known as betting each way. It is called a forecast, wherein either of the horses bet upon finish first and second.

The punter registers the bet with a bookmaker, who is popularly called a bookie. The bookies operate not only on the race course premises, but also at some other establishments, and have recently started operating online. For instance, you win a dividend of Rs 500 at the end of a race, where you had booked your bet for Rs 100. You have made Rs 400 on a stake of Rs 100. The bookie who holds your stake money is the stakeholder till the dividends are declared and disbursed. The ratio between the dividend and the stake money is known as the odds. The odds in the above example may be reckoned as 4 to 1.

According to the number of bets on the horses, the odds get shorter or longer. The punters always examine the trend of the odds before putting in their money. There is always a starting price, which is the declared official rate of the race course. The favourite horse is the one with the shortest odds, while the one with the longest odds is known as the outsider.

Sweepstake is such a common term in business, and many miss the origin of the term that comes from horse racing. It consists of the prize money that has its sources in race horse owner's fees, subscriptions, and a basket of several other sources that make a big prize for the first three winning horses; the owner of the horse that stands first takes the largest share. Derby at Epsom, UK, Kentucky in US, Irish Sweeps in Ireland, and Melbourne Cup in Australia have very large sums of money as sweepstakes.

LEGAL BUSINESS VERSUS MORAL BUSINESS

Prostitution is legal in several countries and yet, no society considers it morally right. Society considers sexual pleasure to be moral only in marriage. It is marriage that forms the foundation of society, allowing procreation of children in the protection of a family. Sex reserved for marriage ensures the continuance of a civilized society. Thus, all the social customs and the laws of the land encourage sex within the union of marriage.

Several products and services are produced and marketed legally but do not have moral sanction. Several religions consider the use of condoms and other contraceptive products as deviating from the moral path. The moral reasoning behind this is that the use of these products is in contravention of the natural law of procreation.

Mother of All Dilemmas

Virginity on sale

Prostitution may be described as the oldest profession, and yet, virginity has never been its essential feature. Things are changing in the Internet age of marketing. Natalie Dylan, 22, from San Diego, California, US put up her virginity for auction to the highest bidder. The bids went up from several thousands to millions. A thirty-nine-year-old Australian raised the stakes to $3.8 million. She has still not accepted the bid. What would then be the acceptable bid?[a]

A host of moral, religious, social, cultural, and business questions arise from the seller–buyer, manufacturer/marketer–consumer relationships. It is clear that on moral and religious grounds, selling one's virginity or letting oneself be traded as a prostitute is unconditionally wrong. However, purely moral grounds become a landmine of debate. Whose morals are we speaking about, after all? Do they not differ from culture to culture? In our times, cultures have become tolerant about sexual morality. Homosexuality is being legalized in several countries. Prostitution is legalized in more countries than homosexuality is. Even the morally conservative cultures make allowance for prostitution as a lesser evil.

From the point of view of business, ethical questions may be asked as to what can be commoditized and what ought not to be done. One understands donating one's organs for transplantation and saving lives of others as a virtue. But the selling of kidneys has hit the lowest mark in medical morality in India, where unsuspecting and uneducated labourers became the victims of greedy medical doctors. It is thus extremely difficult to decide when a body part is a commodity to be sold and when it is morally degrading and heinous.

In the virginity sale dilemma, the young lady admitted that she was born and brought up in an upright family, but selling her virginity did not constitute a dilemma to her. Millions of web pages, tons of reams of paper, and thousands of TV hours have not been able to solve this dilemma. How could one be a prostitute and still be morally upright? How could one go to a prostitute and not be morally responsible for encouraging the trade? How can the sale and purchase of virginity remain above moral approbation?

Questions

(a) Why does one's virginity on sale cause a debate?
(b) In the Indian culture when dowry is paid, is it not tacitly understood that the bride is a virgin?
(c) Could this not be a good business idea that you establish a company to auction body parts on the Internet?

[a] Elisabeth Landau, http://www.cnn.com/2009/LIVING/01/22/virginity.value/index.html.

Products such as alcohol, tobacco, and psychedelic drugs such as opium, hashish, and marijuana have legal sanctions, though restricted in some cases. However, these products are undesirable because they impact health and cause family and social problems. Alcohol abuse can cause family bankruptcies. Drugs are banned due to their harmful effects. Drug addicts are a burden on society. Finally, tobacco products such as cigarettes are legal, as their production is allowed. The government earns very high revenues, since these products are heavily taxed to discourage people from buying them. The moral argument against the use of tobacco products is that they are harmful and cause illness and death.

The Dilemma

The moral dilemma is, how does one do these legal businesses and yet remain morally upright? See Table 5.2 for some examples of moral dilemma in business.

Dealing with Punishment and Guilt

A trader used to supply rice, cereals, oil, and other groceries to the local school for its mid-day meal scheme. He used to adulterate and supply substandard provisions. On a fateful day, however, something went drastically wrong. Dozens of children were rushed to the local health centre for food poisoning. The ill-equipped health centre could not cope with the misery. The parents of the affected children bayed for the trader's blood and rushed to his house. As the infuriated mob barged into the house, they saw that the trader's wife and other relatives sitting around three corpses and mourning. The trader had committed suicide because his two children, who also went to the same school, had eaten the food and died. The tragedy shattered him. His

Table 5.2   Moral dilemma in business

Legally right	Morally wrong/doubtful
Webmaster in an adult industry, involves editing and uploading of sexually explicit data	▪ Against family and social values
Production manager in a cigarette factory	▪ Against your conscience, because cigarettes cause death. You would not like to be associated with a trade that causes innocent peoples' suffering and death
Soldier/bomber pilot/officer/in the military, involves in combat and gives orders to kill the enemy.	▪ Involves killing (of the enemy), someone who is not even known and has caused no personal harm. Arial bombing—causes loss of life and property ▪ Soldiers suffer from trauma and depression
Gynaecologist working in a hospital, performs abortions.	▪ Involves termination of foetus, the developing human being, against conscience, family, and social values
Criminal lawyer, legal counsel to a litigant	▪ Twisting facts to save the offender Against conscience and social values

sorrow and guilt knew no bounds. The incident is reflective of the hundreds of such tragedies in India.

Several states in India have mid-day meal schemes, which invariably end in misery for the children. The suppliers seem to have lost their conscience, even with regard to school-going children, and supply adulterated and substandard foodstuffs. Adulteration of foodstuffs and essential commodities is a criminal offence in India and is punishable with a prison term and penalty. The Food Adulteration Act 1954, under the Ministry of Food and Family Welfare is well in place, except that its implementation has caused problems. However, adulteration is so rampant that the ministry is unable to cope with it. Few get punished.

Punishment by the criminal justice system may ensure punishment for the guilty and retribution for the aggrieved. However, perpetrators of unethical deeds have to cope with their personal, psychological guilt. The consequences of guilt, particularly in business dealings and relationships, are severe because guilt is self-punishment.

SUMMARY

- Manufacturing is the starting point of consumption.
- Consumption is the motivation for manufacturing.
- The business area that lies between manufacturing and consumption sets off the marketer–consumer relationship.
- The utilitarian principle that highlights the consequences of one's action forms the core of ethical questions.
- The manufacturer's primary duty is the satisfaction and safety of the consumer.
- The consumer has a natural right to satisfaction for money's worth.
- Just as the manufacturer must be a responsible producer, so also the consumer must make fair choices.
- Manufacturers' greed may cause irreparable damage to consumers.
- Manufacturers have the supreme duty to follow the law of the land. Failure to do so invites punishment.
- For the manufacturer, the moral punishment of guilt, loss of reputation, and social rejection is much more severe than legal penalties and punishments.

KEY TERMS

Consumer A person who purchases goods and services.

Consumer as stakeholder The consumer is the one who holds what is of interest—money—for the manufacturer and the marketer.

Consumer forum A body of consumers with legal and statutory status to whom other consumers can go to discuss their problems.

Consumer privacy The consumers' personal data protection.

Duty of the consumer The consumer is responsible for his/her choices.

Duty of the manufacturer The products and services marketed are not detrimental to the consumer.

Ethical business Businesses or professions that are right/wrong in the eyes of society, custom, or moral reasoning.

Ethical consumer One who makes conscious moral decisions on the nature of the products or services before buying; one who buys only what is right to buy and refuses to buy what is wrong, e.g., products manufactured through child labour.

Greed   Excessive and inordinate desire to possess personal riches and comforts.

Guilt   Psychological feeling of one's offence; charging one with legal offence.

Informed consumer   A customer with adequate information before making a choice.

Legal business   Business matters that come under the purview of the law.

Manufacture   Goods and services produced to market.

Punishment   Award of due monetary penalty or corporeal detainment in prison, or both, for the offences committed against the law; moral punishments are imposed through social strictures, stigma, and ostracising the wrong doer.

Redress   Making amends or reparation for the wrong or harm done.

Stakeholder   One who has the responsibility to safeguard another's interests.

CONCEPT REVIEW QUESTIONS

1. Why is the consumer also known as a stakeholder?

2. What are the alternative descriptions of a manufacturer?

3. How can a manufacturer perform ethically without undermining the financial returns?

4. How can one find out what the consumers want?

5. How can ethical consumerism change business?

6. Discuss some of the salient features of consumerism.

CRITICAL THINKING QUESTIONS

1. How legitimate is the concept of stakeholders in business management?

2. How can you ethically relate production and consumption, and demand and supply, in a consumerist society?

3. Comment on ethical consumption as a moral choice.

4. Why is moral leadership important for entrepreneurs?

5. Discuss production ethics.

FURTHER READING

C.K. Prahalad and M.S. Krishnan, *The New Age of Innovation*, Tata McGraw-Hill Publishing, 2008.

CASE STUDY

The Giant Nano—Making History at Birth

The News

Shifting inflected forms, India's Nano benumbed the senses at the Geneva Motor Show, stealing the thunder at the super car exotica with consummate ease. The world's cheapest car from the Tata stable even got the top automakers agreeing that 'small' could, indeed, be 'big'.

—Financial Express (Airy 2008)

The Birth of an Idea

Victor Hugo's belief that no one can stop an idea, whose time has come, is true of the man at the helm of affairs at the Tatas, Ratan Naval Tata, the chairman of the group of companies whose name it emblazons. The idea originated when he reflected upon the misery of the people while commuting. He felt terrible when he saw a rickshaw puller in Kolkata. The safety hazards of an entire family consisting of a husband, a wife, two children, and a baby in the wife's lap riding on a two wheeler bothered him. So he contemplated and improvised a scooter with a safety bar that safeguarded against a fall. He tried to develop a four-wheeled transport with a scooter engine and worked on several such contraptions that only an engineer's mind could conceive. In his world of ideas, he finally settled for a safe, small, environmentally friendly, and what was to be the world's cheapest car.[a]

The idea got a sudden unexpected burst. In a strange way, the word was spoken, perhaps at an unguarded moment, yet spoken, and instead of going back on it with clarifications, he set it up as the goal to be achieved: 'It was never meant to be a Rs 1-lakh car; that happened by circumstance. I was interviewed by the *Financial Times* [British newspaper] at the Geneva Motor Show (2003) and I talked about this future product as a low-cost car. I was asked how much it would cost and I said about Rs 1 lakh. The next day the *Financial Times* had a headline to the effect that the Tatas are to produce a Rs 100,000 car. My immediate reaction was to issue a rebuttal, to clarify that that was not exactly what I had said. Then I thought, I did say it would be around that figure, so why don't we just take that as a target. When I came back our people were aghast, but we had our goal.'[b]

The Team

Ratan Tata did not make a secret of his idea; he spoke to many in the industry so that it could be made in partnership but there were no takers. He tried a regional tie-up with Singapore and Malaysia, but without success. One fine day in early 2003, soon after the famous promise at Geneva, there trooped into his Bombay House five engineers from the Pune plant. They showed him slides on cheap personal transport and were eager to know what the chairman had in mind. The chairman spoke his mind briefly and clearly. 'Make a real car that costs just marginally more than a two wheeler. Make me also part of the team', he added for good measure.

The chairman, the top five engineers, and another five hundred technicians made the Nano team. Except for the motivation generated by Tata, there was nothing else. There were no benchmarks; they would have to be set. There was no clear brief of specifications; it is something that was never

done before. The work started and along with it, frustration mounted as failures increased. But no one was to be blamed. The team moved with a singular purpose under the innovative leadership of Girish Wagh, a 35-year-old who had given the Tata's most successful utility vehicle, the Ace, as head of the small car project.

However, when something is to be created and not produced, one is at one's wit's end. The top leadership—Ratan Tata, the chairman himself and the managing director of Tata Motors, Ravi Kant—rallied around their engineers and technicians. One of the things the managing director did was to analyse the various products of the competitors, by taking them apart and making them realize why the customers go for the products of the competitors. Such close and objective self-examination sharpened their focus. What would the customer like and at what price?

The Product

A car as cheap as a good two wheeler is like the proverbial cake that you cannot have and eat too (Narayanan 2008). Yet, Narendra Kumar Jain, a highly respected engine engineer at the Tatas thought it was possible. For two years he scoured the globe for an engine—all sorts of engines, including two-wheeler engines, to fit the small car. Nothing fitted and nothing worked. So he started where all great things begin, on a clean sheet of paper, at the drawing board. Several designs showed up on his computer but nothing seemed

---

[a] Interview in *Economic Times*, 11 January 2008, Mumbai.

[b] See Ratan Tata's interview of 2007 at http://tatanano.inservices.tatamotors.com/.

to compute. Finally, through frustration and glimmers of hope, a couple of prototypes known as alfa and beta were selected. After a severe process of analysis and repetition, the chosen prototype was frozen. Thus, a new heart was created for a new car (Narayanan 2008).

All the rest of the functions of design and components too went through a severe time of test and rejection until perfection was achieved. Although it meant a new and unconventional turn to suppliers, yet all felt that they were all part of something significant in the making. In the process, thirty-five patents were filed, and for Tata Nano it is going to be more. Indeed, it was very significant and pathbreaking and new benchmarks were set, as many doyens of the industry said at its inauguration in New Delhi and at the motor show at Geneva. The specifications were

- Rear-mounted 624 cc engine with 34 bhp
- Four-door monocoque design
- Fuel efficiency 20 kpl
- Top speed 105 kmph
- Four-speed manual gear box
- The length stretching to 3.1 meters, and width to 1.5, giving the customer slightly more inner room than the Maruti 800
- Safety survival measure at 48 kmph with frontal crash
- Emission standards are Bharat III and Euro IV compliant[c]

The Philosophy

A car is what a customer would like to have. It is a dream for millions of Indians to own a car, just as they once wanted to have a telephone. In the absence of a modernized public transport, a comfortable personal transport is a luxury that can be only dreamed of in this country. Further, to own this dream at an affordable price is something a commoner cannot think of. Just the way a mobile phone can be found in every pocket, the Tata small car expects to find its way to the front yard of every house. Exactly a century ago, in 1908, Henry Ford thought of a car for every American, in the same

way. He realized his philosophy through two principles, that is, the division of labour and the assembly line. These two principles reduced cost, increased efficiency, and produced cars in large quantities. It also made it possible to pay the workers handsomely. Ford created wealth for America and made the Americans realize one of their big dreams of owning a private car.

Tata proposed two principles. The first was value to the customer and the second was empower a team to deliver that value. The enormous inventory of the car components had to be minimized to cut costs without minimizing the quality of technology. The engineering brains had to rise to the challenge of a new creation and design, and convince the suppliers to follow the new philosophy. In the arduous process of engineering a product to take the markets by storm, no one spoke of making money or asking what is going to be the profit when Rs 1900 crore had to be spent on the prototype. Wealth creation and making profits will take care of themselves if one firmly believes that all the stakes are with the customer.

The Public

Ever since the announcement, there was a palpable suspense in the country in general, and in the industry in particular. While the entire media, the experts, and the automotive industrial houses saw why it was impossible to make a car for just one lakh, the people of India had a quiet conviction that the Tatas could do it. This is the faith that the people of India have in this company. Tatas can deliver on their promise and give value to their money. A promise by the Tatas is an article of faith for the people of India. The people of India may not trust the very governments that they themselves have voted and elected, but there is no reason for them to doubt when the Tatas make a promise!

The Value

When a client buys the Tata Nano, he should feel that he has profited by the purchase. Such a realization is a turnaround in business philosophy. It is the entrepreneur's right to earn profits. The customer too will not only have got money's worth,

---

[c] See http://tatanano.inservices.tatamotors.com/.

Electric Vehicle

Silent revolution

In the parking lots of the malls in Bangalore, it is a common sight to see provisions made to recharge the car batteries of Reva, the electric car. Unlike Nano, Reva did not get much publicity, but the way it works is quietly making sense to the customers.

Electric vehicles (EVs) do not use fossil fuel, so there is no emission and pollution. Reva, if mass produced, could cost much less than what it costs now, a whopping Rs 3.5 lakh. But there is no encouragement from any quarters to promote the vehicle that could substantially help save the environment. In the past 8 years, only 2500 vehicles have been sold. If the Reva gets encouragement and could be produced to the proposed volume of the Nanos, which is 2.5 lakh cars a year, then Reva will definitely pose a serious competition to

Nano's price tag of Rs 1 lakh. In addition to this, Reva will cause no pollution, an invaluable environmental bonus and a gain in terms of carbon trading.

Developed countries give not only a subsidy (Fitter 2008) to the buyers of EVs, but also other benefits. In UK, benefits consist of tax exemption, free parking, and some areas are reserved only for EVs. Japan gives a direct subsidy of US$ 2600. Norway offers facilities just like the UK and 100 per cent duty exemption on imported EVs. France gives a direct subsidy of €2000 and privileges as in the UK. The US gives a direct subsidy of US$4,000 and benefits as in Europe. India, which is a subsidy paradise for all things great and small, has not yet given a thought to it!

Source: Pierre Mario Fitter, 'Reva Takes Charge', in *Business World*, 28 April 2008.

---

but this investment of Rs 1 lakh will win the customer returns in the form of an ownership of a car that was other wise unthinkable, providing ease and comfort of travel, personal satisfaction, as well as a new status in society.

Once the imagination of the customer is thus arrested, through the best practice of making the customer the stakeholder, the returns for the entrepreneur will come through the sheer scale of sales. It is believed that the launch of the Nano has generated a frenzy of publicity, which otherwise could have cost over Rs 500 crore. There is no guarantee that publicity would have captured the imagination of the entire world the way Nano did.

This only goes to show that the fundamental attitude of the entrepreneur to give the customer the very best, at a very low cost, is made transparent through the product.

The Ultimate Stakeholder

For whom is the car made? The answer to this question could be found at every stage of its making. Nano is a street car, a car for the man on the street. In other words, it is a common man's car. The media has already branded it as the people's car. Such

cars have become iconic. The very first Ford Model T in 1908 was a people's car. In 1938, Adolf Hitler, the German dictator, inaugrated the Volkswagen, which literally means people's wagon or vehicle, with the same state-owned company name. It is known by its model name Beetle (*Kaefa* in German) all over the world and is still very popular in South America. Since then, there has been no such people's car except, to some extent, the Maruti 800 of Maruti Udyog. But till recently, Maruti 800 was a car owned by the middle class only, and cost Rs 2 lakh, so it did not qualify as a people's car.

Nano's target customers are the masses of India who are mobile on two wheelers. The company is confident and conscious of its brand supremacy. There is no doubt that with the adequate volumes of production being delivered on time, the company is ensured of its returns on investment. The success or the failure of this product ultimately depends on the commitment of the customers, which is determined by the affordability of the customer. The affordability of the customer is well gauged. The fortunes of the Tata Motors are well ensured in the masses of the prospective Indian customers.

The Name

To conclude, a note on the name Nano. It is a term implying a billionth of a measure. It is at the same time a combining form. Thus, a nanosecond means one billionth of a second and a nanogram is a billionth of a gram.

Discussion Questions

1. What message does a customer get through the making of the Nano car?

2. The Nano proves the utilitarian principle. Discuss.

3. Can monetary values and moral values co-exist?

4. Do you agree to the fact that the customer is the ultimate stakeholder is a moral issue?

5. Enumerate a few best practices in the industry that uphold the moral values in the service of their customers.

6. What is the spirit of the Tatas that enables team building and empowerment?

7. How would it have affected the customers if the Nano project failed to keep the price tag at Rs 1 lakh?

8. Are best practices in the industry only basket cases?

9. Could the customer movements and associations help the industry to understand what the customer wants?

10. Are customers exploitative when they change their brand loyalties?

11. Irrespective of the adhered emission standards, producing fossil fuel cars and that too with such high volumes of 2,50,000 seems environmentally irresponsible in the twenty-first century. Comment.

Going Further . . .

Conduct a panel discussion involving some of the above questions. Involve the faculty of operations management, organizational behaviour, finance, human resources, market research, etc. Also invite a local Tata Motors dealer.

ETHICAL DEVELOPMENT PROGRAMME

Research on Commuters

Make a study of the plight of the commuters in your city or town. Make a plan to ease out the problems related to the traffic on the road, along with the concerned authorities, such as the department of transport. Your action will have far reaching consequences. You and your company/institute will be known for your good work. The commuters and the government will save large sums of money on fuels due to efficient traffic movement. There will be fewer frayed tempers, as is often seen in congested roads and traffic jams. It will promote social harmony.

Privacy Agreement

Draft a document for a privacy agreement.

All registered companies have a privacy agreement. Privacy agreements on the Internet have become commonplace. To download, use, or participate in any of the Internet software or other programmes, the customers have to agree to

certain terms and conditions, wherein the privacy terms are also spelt out. The customers are supposed to agree to terms and conditions by clicking on the button 'Agree' or 'Do not agree'.

Include some essential features like:

(a) Company profile

(b) Purpose and scope of business

(c) Privacy terms and conditions

(d) Indemnities

(e) Disclaimer

Consumer Protection Quiz

(Try to answer the following questions on your own after studying the Consumer Protection Act 1986.)

(a) You have filed a complaint against a medical practitioner for mishandling your case. But the said medical practitioner challenged you by saying that you could not sue him under the Consumer Protection Act (CPA).[14]

---

[14] Based on the problems and solutions in http://www.vakilno1.com/consumerprotect_qns.htm.

(b) You are a farmer who purchased seeds from a seller. The seeds were bad and did not germinate. The opposite party contended that you were not a consumer, since agriculture should be regarded as commercial.

(c) You applied for a bank loan and your application was rejected. Can you approach the CPA?

(d) You went to purchase a car that needed prior booking. You booked and the dealer gave you the date of delivery. In the meantime, the price of the car increased and the dealer demanded the extra money to be paid. Would you pay the extra money or go to the consumer court?

(e) You had applied for a UTI scheme that said that your money would grow twenty-one times in twenty-eight years. It did not happen. The UTI extended the period by another two years. How will the CPA rule this case?

(f) Your car driver got your car involved in an accident. The insurance company refused to honour your claims on the grounds that on their investigation, the driver did not possess a valid driving licence. What chances do you have in the consumer court?

(g) Your colleague had a grievance against the company that you both once worked for. But due to other engagements, he neglected to complain earlier on. Now, after four years, he has come to you for advice about going to the consumer court. How would you advise him?

(h) You bought a TV and you had problems with it. You took care to complain to your dealer and then further followed it up with the company, but the problem was not resolved. In the meantime, the stipulated period of two years elapsed. Does this mean now that the consumer court is irrelevant to your case?

(i) You purchase a bottle of Scotch whisky of a renowned label and find to your consternation that it is spurious. What remedy can you seek?

(j) You sent a letter by speed post through the Indian Postal Service, but it was not delivered by the postal staff. How is the postal employee responsible?

Answers

(These answers help only in a limited way. You would have to study the Consumer Protection Act 1986 in order to fully and cogently solve the problems.)

(a) The medical practitioner can be sued under the Consumer Protection Act 1986 for his or her professional negligence that resulted in physical and financial damages to the patient.

Section 2(d), in defining a consumer in Clause (ii), uses the expression 'hires and avails of'. The word hire means 'employ for wages or fees'.

Second, the words 'any service' in Section 2(d)(ii) in the Consumer Protection Act includes medical practitioners also.

Third, Section 2(o) of Consumer Protection Act, which defines service, exempts only two types of services, namely, 'service free of charge' and 'contract of personal service', which postulates a relationship between a master and a servant. A doctor, whose service is requisitioned for a patient, answers the clause 'contract of service' but never 'a contract of personal service'. Thus, a negligent medical professional can be brought under the Consumer Protection Act 1986.

(b) The Act says that the purchaser is the consumer and is entitled to a redress.

(c) The consumer court cannot judge an application for a loan that is based on various factors of credit that the concerned bank alone can decide. The CPA does not meddle with the discretion of the bank that seeks viability for its business.

(d) You must go to the consumer court. You are not responsible for either the price increase or for the delay.

(e) The CPA will rule it as 'deficiency in service' and will order for a redress of your grievance.

(f) The consumer court cannot grant you any relief. It will uphold the view of the insurance company. It was your duty to check your employee's driving licence when you hired him.

(g) It is too late. The CPA allows a period of two years only.

(h) It is correct that two years is the period of time allotted to file a complaint under the Act. The time begins when the cause for action arises (Section 24-A). However, the Consumer Forum does have the power of discretion to determine a cause of sufficient reason. The reasons must be convincing and the evidence, such as correspondence with the company, is important. However, merely the correspondence issue may not clinch the consumer court's conclusion in your favour.

(i) You have every right to file the complaint, but since you have already opened the bottle, there is no way to prove that the contents were the same before you opened the bottle. Since adulteration is a criminal offence it does attract provisions of the penal code, but again proving it beyond doubt in a court is very difficult for the very same reason as cited for the consumer court.

(j) Section 6 of the Indian Post Office Act 1878 provides that the government shall not incur any liability by reasons of loss, delay, undelivery, or damage to the postal article and that no postal officer shall incur any liability unless it is proved that the staff had acted fraudulently and wilfully and was negligent.

Management Mantra

The Wizard of Menlo Park

Imagine 1093 patents won by a single person from a single country, and thousands more granted by other countries. It is just unthinkable in the twenty-first century. Thomas Alva Edison (1847–1931) achieved this remarkable feat through the magic of his hard work. He was one of the greatest inventors, researchers, manufacturers, and businessmen ever known in history. He had very little formal education, but was endowed with an insatiable curiosity and a voracious appetite for science books. The businessman in him found expression as early as when he was just 12 years old. He sold newspapers, sweets, and sandwiches on trains. Three years later, he published his own weekly called the *Weekly Herald*. With the financial help that he received from the Western Union, where he worked as a telegraph operator, he built a technical lab in a rural surrounding, known as Menlo Park.

In this laboratory at Menlo Park, he began a life of intense research along with his colleagues, and invented practically all that without which life seems to be impossible today. His inventions include the fire alarm, cement mixer, cement products, electric bulb, and storage battery, all the infrastructure needed for large electricity generation and transmission, innovation of telephone phonograph, motion pictures, microphone, synthetic rubber, and hundreds more. However, his very first invention and his first patent, the voting machine, was never used. Though disappointed, Edison continued to invent. The stock market ticker tape was a great hit and brought him enormous fortune. The phonograph brought him the popular title 'The Wizard of Menlo Park', for it had a magical effect on the public, an unimaginable invention that one could not even dream of.

Edison was a keen businessman. He was the founder of many new approaches to business such as mass production, mass distribution, mass transportation, low pricing, and research and development. He had very little time for anything in life other than work. He was so possessed with his ideas and obsessed with his work that his family felt neglected. He has given a new meaning to the word genius. If we could follow Edison's philosophy strictly, we too could become Edison.

> EDISON'S MANTRA   *Genius is one per cent inspiration and 99 per cent perspiration.*

In the Marketplace

Marketing is a social and managerial process by which individuals and groups obtain what they want and need through creating, offering, and exchanging products of value with others.

—Philip Kotler

Unless you build relationships of trust with your customers, listen, learn, and respond to their changing needs, and empower your people to correct mistakes when they occur (not days or weeks after they have been measured), you will not establish an environment for long-lasting customer relationship.

—C.W. Pollard

LEARNING OBJECTIVES

After studying this chapter, you will be able to

> Determine product positioning and competing
> Define packaging, labelling, and launching
> Understand pricing and its consequences
> Know the brand management imperatives

INTRODUCTION

Remember the day you struck your first business deal? You were sitting across from your friend, who was waving a wonderful looking, bright big crayon. You knew at once that you wanted it. You were ready to do anything for it. Very soon, you were bargaining and haggling with him for the crayon in exchange for a pocketful of chocolates that you had. He would not budge; yet he would tempt you by showing a bit of that lovely crayon. You couldn't resist. You promised him that in addition to the chocolates you had, you would bring him some more the next day. He agreed. You got the crayon, but you did not bring him the promised chocolates the following day. Remember the fight that followed and the bruises you sustained and the problems that this incident brought to your teacher, parents, and the principal? You struck your first business deal at the tender age of four and created tricky ethical problems for your schoolmate, teacher, parents, and the principal!

You can create a market anywhere, even on a school bench, where goods and services are exchanged, bought, and sold. Indeed, today's market is as big as the globe itself. Most of it is very complex, such as the stock markets that function all over the globe, round the clock. Some deals are visible, some invisible. The market is so large and so complex that it is not comprehensible, predictable, or even remotely controllable. However, the marketplace, whether real or virtual, is intensely based on human relations, which are enormously complex and interlinked, unlike the one you created while sitting on your school bench.

Marketing, the buying and selling of goods and services, is the essence of business. It is a science that is based on not only great business risks, but also on a keen study of all the market factors. Only after market research can a product be positioned for sale in the market vis-à-vis the competitors' products. Further, to differenciate the product, it is made attractive by certain value additions, such as particular appearance and comparative product advantage. Great care is taken to decide the exact time of product launch, in order to meet the seasons, festivals, and other aspects affecting the buying of the product. Logistics such as supply and distribution are the real nitty-gritty of marketing. The bottom-line, of course, is the line where the customer first looks at the price. If that were right, the marketing manager could easily win the Nobel Prize, as it were. But there are a growing number of customers who may not look at the price line as much as they look at the brand of the product that they buy. Customers have become brand conscious and, consequently, may buy not just any tea but only Tata Tetley, or not just any car but the one from the BMW stable, or not just any spectacle but a Gucci!

Marketing is business in action. Ethics is its judge. When a product is introduced in the market, the entire business chain—from the manufacturer to the distributor, from the manager to the advertiser, and from the sales executive to the retailer—is accountable to the customer. What means are used to position, price, and advertise the product makes ethical reckoning. The main principle at stake in marketing is that of the means justifying the end.

Marketing morality may be analysed in three ways:

(a) Theoretically, through the seven principles of business that we have already espoused
(b) Consequentially, through the effects it is going to have on all the stakeholders, from the entrepreneurs to the customers, from the shareholders to the competitors, and from the employees to the society at large
(c) Practically, investigating the actual processes such as product positioning, packaging and launching, pricing and distributing, advertising and branding, etc.

Since we are dealing specifically with the discipline of marketing, we will follow the third method of examining the processes and assimilate the other two as the need arises.

PRODUCT POSITIONING AND COMPETING

To let your customers know what you sell is the essence of business. What means you employ to achieve your goal is the concern of business ethics. In a free market, there are already several competitors vying for the same market segment. Introducing another product into the same segment is very hard. Managers use certain strategies to position products. This can cause twofold problems—first vis-à-vis the competitors, second the customers.

Product Manager

It is the responsibility of the product manager to research, select, develop, place, and promote the company's product. The product manager would have to deal with all problems that arise from the customers. According to the mission of the company, he/she would have to carefully study the target market, the competitors, and the strategies to be adopted to place the products. The product manager's job is further subdivided. It is now common to have a product marketing manager who would be responsible for marketing strategies. The marketing strategy, the line of attack, so to speak, in aggressive marketing, is under the microscope for ethical issues. The ethical examination consists of the means used in these strategies to achieve the end, that is, the sale.

Finding Favourable Product Position

For an Indian product manager, a study of product management by Dabur India would be highly beneficial. It is a company that is completely indigenous and has developed and placed products in the market that have won accolades from the customers. It has won a place in the imagination of the people because it has re-discovered the ancient science of Ayurveda and has innovated it to give relevant and highly valued products to the Indian customer. Its authenticity has helped it to expand its business outside the country.

Dabur India[1] is a company that manufactures pharmaceutical, health care, skin care, hair care, oral care, and personal care products. It also has food products and juices. In November 2008, it acquired 72.5 per cent of Fem Care Pharma, a market leader in women's skin care products. With the acquisition of the new firm, the company hopes to have gained a favourable position in this growing market of personal care products. Dabur is a company that is growing at the rate of 40 per cent and has both reputation and financial prowess to position itself as the leader in the personal care segment. Dabur, with an international presence in South East Asia and South Africa, can bid for a strong performance in the region. Earlier, the company had bought Balsara, the well-known hygiene and home products company. Coupled with this

---

[1] See the press release at http://www.dabur.com, accessed on 26 November 2008.

experience and the well-managed system costs, Dabur is in a very good position to promote the products of the new company it has acquired.

Dabur had its humble beginnings when Dr S.K. Burman opened a small pharmacy in Calcutta (now Kolkata) in 1884. Presently, with its sprawling headquarters in Ghaziabad, the company has spread far and wide, even into the remote areas of the country. Products such as Dabur Chyawanprash, Vatika Hair Oil, Hajmola, and Real Active juices are household names. With its motto 'dedicated to the health and well-being of every household', it has captured a place in the hearts and minds of the people of India.

With its brand ambassadors, Amitabh Bachchan, the megastar of Hindi cinema, and Mahendra Singh Dhoni, the megastar of Indian cricket, it has made its products recognizable throughout the length and breadth of the country.

Competition to Affirm Leading Position

Dabur's competitors in the market are Baidyanath, Himalaya, Hamdard, Zandu, and several other Ayurveda-based companies.

The four Ps of marketing—product, price, place, and promotion—determine how a company is going to position its product in the market. As far as the product itself is concerned, positive values will secure a win over the desired market segment (see Fig. 6.1).

Following are some of the attributes required to position a product successfully among the competitors:

(a) Relative cost   (b) Availability
(c) Quality   (d) Service
(e) Performance   (f) Durability
(g) Name recognition

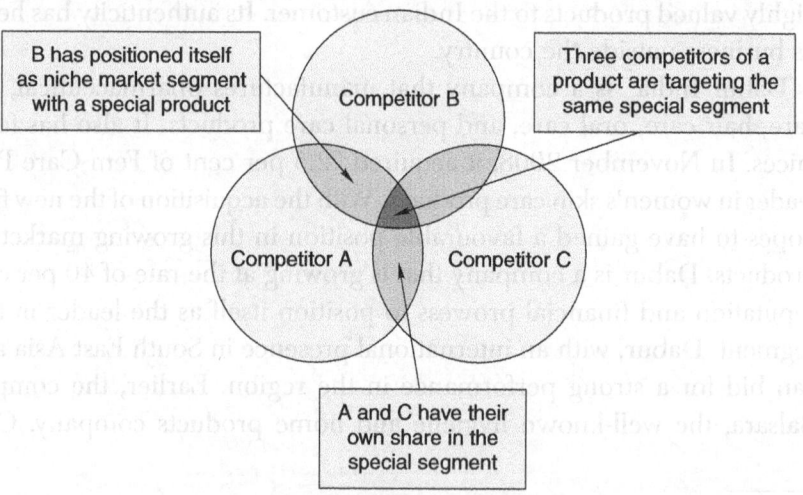

Fig. 6.1   Market segmentation

One can attribute all the above qualities to Dabur products. With its efficient supply chain management, it can score over other competitors in saving costs. Second, its market penetrability is very extensive and products are available not only in pharmacies but also in grocery stores. As far as customer satisfaction is concerned, it delivers very well. Its Dabur Honey is a sweet success. Adopting a child-friendly strategy by giving a booklet of *Pooh, the Honey Bear* with Dabur Honey has gone down very well with the little customers, making honey a healthy food product for children. Third, the scores for the three attributes of quality, service, and performance have been excellent. Finally, Dabur has earned a name for itself for supplying good and healthy products. With the acquisition of Fem Care Pharma, Dabur is now a well-established leader in India's skin bleach creams and soap market.[2]

Strategies of Competition

Dabur is no longer a challenger or a follower of its competitors; it is a leader. Since it has been a pioneer in the area of Ayurveda-based pharmaceuticals and health care products, it has a clear advantage as per Porter's generic strategies, vis-à-vis close competitors as well as followers. Whether it is cost management, product differentiation, or securing market segmentation, it has been able to surge ahead. Since 1884, the company has enjoyed phenomenal growth. It is listed both on the NSE and BSE and has crossed the $2 billion market cap in 2006.[3] In strategic terms of growth, it has been able to scale both horizontal as well as vertical integration. Its diversification strategy, particularly in the promotion of its juices, has become very popular with children, the youth, as well as others.

Product Differentiation

Dabur's competitors too have products such as chyawanprash and hair oils that are Ayurveda based. Dabur, however, has been able to differentiate its products in packaging and labelling and advertising. With its well-known brand ambassadors, the company has successfully built up credibility. Being in business for over a century, it has a loyal following. Thus, product differentiation, with few changes made, results in creating a special identity, which becomes the ultimate selling proposition (USP). Dabur's USP is that it is dedicated to health through Ayurveda, India's oldest natural science of medicine.

Packaging, Labelling, and Launching

Emperor Napoleon, during his extensive wars, developed a strategy to feed his army by making them live off the land. In other words, they had to cater for themselves in

---

[2] Corporate Roundup, *The Economic Times*, 12 January 2008.
[3] See 'Milestones' at http://www.dabur.com/en/about/company/milestones.asp.

Getting Noticed in the Market

Humour attracts

In the little town of Calangute in Goa, which is known for tourism, there are restaurants by cheek-a-jowl and the market is not only saturated, but there are too many restaurants chasing very few customers. In this situation, a small household turned their little house into a restaurant. It was brave enough to start this business, but it was too bold when the signboard read, 'Warm Bear Lousy Food'. It is amazing that the restaurant is doing a roaring business. The customer certainly understands the sense of humour and knows how to read the opposite of literal meaning. The marketer won not only the mind but also the heart of his customer, by establishing a unique, friendly, humorous, and cheerful relationship even before the customer stepped into the restaurant. Further, the restaurant adheres strictly to simple, local, staple food prepared by members of the household. Customers immediately recognize the authenticity of the food served. Tourists flock to it because of the specialty of the place and its people; the locals flock to it because the food is as good as home food. Thus, the restaurant is able to run both in the tourist season as well as off it.

Others are not so lucky. They try to position themselves in this congested market and jostle for the attention of foreign tourists with the old colonial names

of the Portuguese to suggest the affinity to the visitors and to create curiosity among the indigenous holiday makers. Thus, you find Aldea de Goa, Marina Dourada, A Lua, Senor Angelo, Casa Portuguesa, and many such names.

The above case is innocent at first sight. But there are several local factors that make the tourism business difficult. The business is limited only to the tourist season, from November to April. Licences and approvals, loans to be arranged, and supplies to be organized is only one part of the story. These small businesses have not only to contend with their competitors, but have also to fight the unorganized and unauthorized outlets. Conflicts are inevitable and then there are the police, the politicians, and also anti-social elements who enter the scene. It is a competition that is beyond market positioning. It is a fight to survive.

Questions

(a) What is the ethics of positioning a product?
(b) Is authenticity an ethical virtue or marketing strategy?
(c) How can one deal with conflicts involved in product positioning?

---

whichever town or village they found themselves in. However, this antagonized the locals, since they were forced to give away their food. In 1809, Napoleon hit upon an idea and incentivized it with an offer of 12,000 francs for the person who could preserve food for his army. A chef from Paris discovered that food packed in tin containers and sterilized by boiling could be preserved for a long time.[4]

Packaging

The saying that you cannot judge a book by its cover may be true, but it is the cover that entices a book lover to buy it. The adage 'the taste of the pudding is in its eating' is also true in spite of all the hype of colourful labels and attractive packs that the food products come with. Packaging products is big business. It involves vast scientific

---

[4] Kenneth R. Burger, *A Brief History of Packaging*, University of Florida; see http://edis.ifas.ufl.edu/pdffiles/AE/AE20600.pdf.

application and technology, since products are in all the forms of a substance, that is, solid, liquid, and gas. The packaging material could also be in a variety of substances such as metals, wood, glass, plastic, textile, synthetic materials, etc. Packaging is an art because the customer views the packing first and, the marketer's priority for the appearance of the product is very high. Package designing is a highly creative and technical activity. Lately, the aspect of environmentally friendly packaging has taken the centre stage. Mentioned below are some of the objectives of packaging and their ethical relevance.

Container   It is a physical necessity that most contents need a suitable container. Every product is packed so that it can be stored, transported, exhibited, and sold.
Ethics: That the packaging is appropriate and does not cause leakage or waste, or lead to chemical reactions such as often found in plastic or metal packing, or any other harm to the customer.

Physical protection   Packaging provides physical protection from shock, vibration, temperature, and compression.
Ethics: That the packaging is not haphazard, causing damage to the product and robbing the customer of an authentic product.

Barrier protection   To keep the product in its original condition, clean and fresh measures in packaging are taken so that it is free from moisture, oxidization, and other factors that can affect the product adversely. Vacuum packaging of foodstuffs, tamper-free packs, and closures for pharmaceutical products are obvious examples.
Ethics: That if extreme care is not taken, a product could pose a threat to the health, safety, and well-being of the customer.

Agglomeration   Small products such as sachets, stationary products like erasers, pencils, etc. are bulk packed.
Ethics: That the products in bulk pack do not miscount, thus causing loss to the stockist or the distributors.

Portion control   The immediate container of the product is a natural vessel for the quantity. Soaps are wrapped and liquids are bottled.
Ethics: Packaging has become deceptive—large packs are made to suggest greater quantity, intriguingly designed to unduly attract customers. Many supermarkets have now heeded the complaints and have made provisions to take back heavy packaging material.

Convenience   In distribution, the handling, storing, display, and sale packaging is most convenient.
Ethics: That some designers and packers may not lose sight of the purpose of packaging. There is an outcry by customers that packaging has become extravagant and has lost its practical purpose.

Ethical and Sustainable Packaging

Due to the high levels of environmental campaigning, there is an increased awareness for ethical and sustainable packaging. Even the small cities and towns of India now resent the use of plastic. Governments and local bodies and non-governmental agencies are working for environmentally friendly packaging by promoting bio-degradable materials for packaging. Figure 6.2 shows the factors that influence ethical and sustainable packaging. Factors that resist are indicated by outward-pointing arrows, and the ones that promote by inward-pointing arrows.

Negative factors such as time, cost, ability to market to consumers in the usual formats, and actual measurement of success adversely affect the ethical and sustainable practices. Sustainable packaging is developing into a standard format of packaging, mainly due to consumer consciousness, which is supported by the press, TV, and other opinion-shaping media. The availability of new and environmentally friendly materials, along with the positive outlook by manufacturers and retailers, has impacted the packaging industry in a positive way. Recycling, use of lightweight and efficient materials, and, above all, ensuring biodegradability have facilitated the cause of ethical packaging. More and more corporations are adopting the new culture of sustainability as their corporate social responsibility.

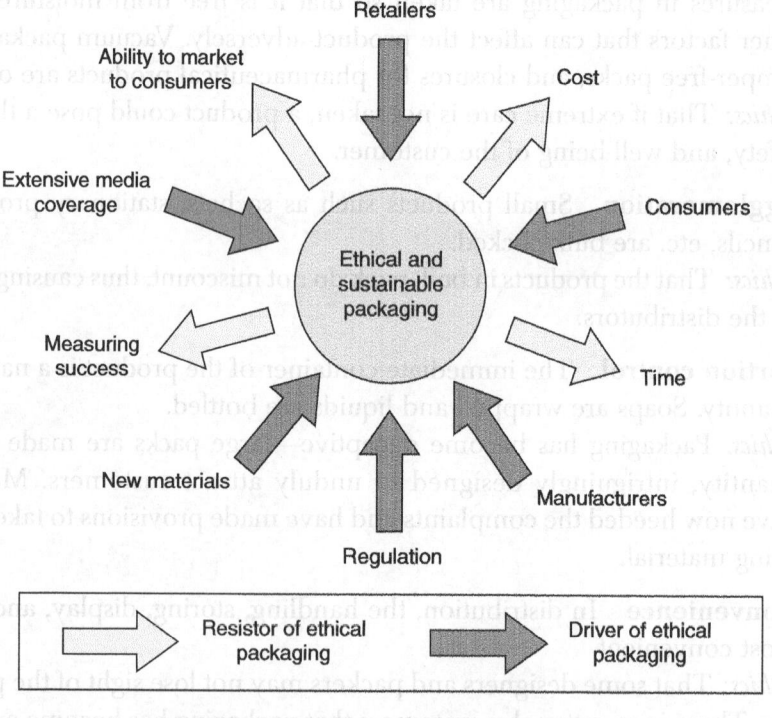

Fig. 6.2   Ethical and sustainable packaging

Source: Business Insights, 'Trends in Ethical and Sustainable Packaging, Innovation by Product Category' at www.globalbusinessinsights.com/consumer.

Labelling

The words of Shakespeare, 'What is in a name? That which we call a rose/by any other name would smell as sweet' are romantic but would fail disastrously as a marketing strategy. Identity by name is what makes the product count. If products are displayed with blank packages, one would not be able to identify the product. The customer is able to choose a product if it has a label with the name and other information about the product, such as the ingredients, the manufacturer, any warrantees or guarantees, product values, nutritional values, date for use, and risks of use. Following are some of the salient features of labelling with the ethical uptake.

Logistical information   There is an immediate communication about what is contained in the package, how to handle it, transport it, place it, and the conditions under which it has to be stored. If the packed products deal with chemicals, foodstuffs, and pharmaceuticals, then extra guidance and symbols are printed.
Ethics: It is important that firms truthfully print the details on the labels so that those who handle or consume them are not harmed. Each country has its own labelling regulations. Labelling plays a greater role in the import-export packages, where misunderstanding of the information is possible due to educational and cultural differences.

Marketing   Labels are a great source of marketing because they directly communicate with the customers. The customer picks up the product and reads it. This is the point of sale. The marketer could not get to the customer nearer than this. The customer makes the decision to buy the product based on the information supplied on the label. The label carries pictures, graphics, ingredients, risks, price, and a host of other information.
Ethics: Customer relationship is at stake here. The marketer has brought the customer from the advertisement in the media to the market and has made the customer notice the product. The transfer from the shelf to the shopping cart is crucial. With what is said on the label and also the appearance of the packaging, the marketer can either trick the customer or help make a well-informed decision. Risks and disclaimers are very often not clear. If the customer is tricked, the marketer will not get to sell to the customer again, but if helped and satisfied with the product, the marketer will have a loyal customer.

Launching

The fast-moving consumer goods (FMCG) market is worth a whopping Rs 85,000 crores. In India, the three major competitors—ITC Ltd, Dabur India, and Marico Ltd—who try to outdo each other as they launch new products. One of the favourite areas where the competition is fierce is the personal care products segment. ITC's strategy is to introduce as many new products as possible. Dabur's strategy is to widen its market net and increase investment in its products, which will give both visibility and availability of its product range to the customers. Marico's new mantra is brand building and new products.[5]

The reality behind these scenes is quite acrimonious: the formation of aggressive strategies to introduce new products and high-voltage advertisements, efforts to drown out competitors through clever product positioning, and carefully choreographed launch strategies. These are the hard realities of running a business successfully. The costs involved in the effort to build awareness and promote the product are very high. Hence, what means would be used to position and introduce the product in the market naturally raises several ethical concerns. Following are some of the strategies and their ethical consequences.

Marketing research   Marketing research is conducted even prior to the creation of a product or service. However, further marketing research is required to determine when and how to launch the product.

Ethics: What rules does the marketing research follow in order to gather intelligence about the launch time and strategies of competitors? The sensitive data acquired about competitors could lead the companies into dispute. The marketing researcher could sell it to a third party.

Communication   It consists of all the available media to publicize about a product to attract customers. It involves all the pitfalls of advertising campaigns, which are very costly. The oldest, time tested, and totally free means of publicity is by word-of-mouth. It can generate a buying storm or it can turn into disastrous rumours and ruin the business. McDonalds introduced a humorous word-of-mouth campaign when they launched chicken for breakfast, 'What came first—the chicken or the egg?' Such a word-of-mouth campaign can bring a change in the customers' behaviour of having chicken instead of eggs for breakfast.

Visibility   Launch is successful only if it is visible. Promotion—from street corners, supermarket entrances, and showroom announcements to exhibitions and fairs—is a fairly high drama. Premiering of movies has all the glamour and the launching of new software programs all the tech-buzz. Problems arise due to the fact that what you see may not be what you get.

Strategy for execution   A launch strategy can make or break a business. After all the publicity blitz, if the product is not launched as promised on time, the customer will not only ridicule the inability to deliver, but would doubt the competency of the product itself. The early bird incentive is an old and tried strategy, but what is the discount rate, and is the incentive true to what it says or a mere gimmick? Or is it that the launch price is intentionally high and after a while, the prices will be reduced? This happens very often at the launches of new car models, and the initial buyers might feel cheated.

---

[5] Lalitha Srinivasan, *The Financial Times*, 'FMCG majors pursue aggressive growth strategy', http://www.financialexpress.com/news/FMCG-majors-pursue-aggressive-growth-strategy/396504/.

Catching the Crook

Blogging as ethical tool

Arlen Pasra, 21, is a student of Columbia College, Chicago, and has set his goal to be a documentary film producer. He loves to blog. His girlfriend told him that he could earn some money on the net by subscribing to work for a company called Belkin,[a] which produces routers, cables, and various iPod accessories. The company had advertised on Amazon's Mechanical Turk. Mike Bayard, Belkin's executive, offered 65 cents per review of the product. Actual use or testing of the product was not necessary to write the review. It was also made clear that negative reviews were not desirable. In fact, he was asked to produce a 5/5 star review for the products.

In Pasra's head there rang warning bells. To his utter disgust, he realized that his family members as well many other friends relied on reviews like these before they made their online purchases. So he decided to find out more about it. First he got on to the search engine and got hold of Bayard's profile. He found that Bayard had advertised on other sites also. Pasra reacted the only way he likes to do—blog.

The Belkin scandal of *astroturfing*, that is, manufacturing fake grassroots, was appealed through fake reviews blogged by Pasra and spread like wildfire on the Internet. Even the traditional media feasted on it. The *New York Times* nominated Arlen Pasra for the Internet Hero of the Week. The Belkin management put up an apology and regretted the deed of its executive as being one of its kind. But the damage was already done. Belkin lost the trust of its customers.

The moral of the above episode shows that to be ethical one does not have to move the mountains; one has got to do just what one does. Pasra loves blogging. He blogged and prevented customers from making a wrong choice.

Questions

(a) Why should one take precautions while launching products and services online?

(b) How powerful could the Internet be to launch a product and sustain it?

(c) Have consumers come of age to appraise and evaluate marketers through blogging?

[a] Renay San Miguel, TechNewsWorld, http://www.technewsworld.com/story/65925.html, accessed on 23 January 2009.

Apart from these, there are several other aspects that need to be examined by the marketer, such as risks, uncertainty of time, matching customers' moods, hurdles by competitors, leak-out of launch plans to the competition or the press, and pre-launch publicity. Doubts both about the viability of the product in the market and credibility of one's own choices in launching will have far-reaching consequences, both ethical as well as commercial.

PRICING AND ITS CONSEQUENCES

The most important among the four marketing Ps (product, promotion, place, and price) is the price. It is the bottom line for the manufacturer, to earn revenues by covering costs and obtaining profits. The economic forces of demand and supply play a great role in the determination of the price. Marketers—manufacturers, advertisers, distributors, retailers—have a stake in the pricing, but the ultimate stakeholder is the customer who withholds the money until he/she buys. To make the customer part with the money, marketers create ingenious plans and strategies. These strategies may be categorized from being fair and customer friendly to downright unfair and fraudulent. Marketers use all possible tools to entice the customer—cognitive tools to convince with reason, emotional tools to appeal to feelings, psychological to exploit human behaviour, fear to warn that prices will go up, promising quality for a higher price, making captive to monopoly, and a myriad other ways. In a command economy, however, there is no room for pricing activity. It is as if the results of the game are pre-determined. The free-market system is interactive and takes on all the hues of human behaviour and social customs and habits. Price plays a big role in the free market ethos and hence the human judgment as to the fairness of this interaction is inevitable.

Objectives of Pricing

The price objectives show the motive, and motive is the basis for ethical judgment.

Competitive pricing In a competitive market, the company cannot pretend that what it has to offer is incomparable to what others offer. So a competitive pricing strategy would be to follow the market leader closely and find other ways and means to attract customers. For instance, offering better quality than that of the competitor for the same quantity and price, engaging in creative marketing, etc.
Ethics: The strategies adopted to re-enforce better quality should be fair and not harmful to the customers.

Prestige pricing The company may have the objective to establish as a higher end, through a limited supply of its product, to enhance its reputation for up-market users. Some car brands such as Lamborghini and Rolls Royce have such pricing objectives.
Ethics: In this game of marketing, the ball is in the customer's court. These exclusive customers, in their turn, will have exclusive problems against the product and may feel that they have not got value for their money. The social responsibility of these companies is always suspect in the eyes of the public at large. There was a time when computers were prestige items. Competition made them common.

Profitability pricing The company has a set stock formula: profits equal revenue minus expenses. This is the most reasonable way to function in the market. The marketer has the work cut out and is supposed to sell more to bring maximum profits. Hence, fair price and high volumes determine good revenues. Such marketers are always very careful as to what is going on in the market and act or react accordingly.
Ethics: The ethical crux is whether the marketer is working under the rules of fair competition, and that the marketer does not undermine competitors or exploit customers.

Volume pricing The marketer adopts the sales maximization principle and hence resorts to volume pricing, that is, depends on the volume of the sale by pricing the units to the lowest possible scale. Such a strategy is possible where production and sale can be done on a mass scale such as building materials, mobile phones, computers, food products, etc.

Ethics: Supermarkets in the retail sector are an example of volume turn-over revenue earners. Problems crop up when individual entrepreneurs and petty businesses come in the firing line of the supermarkets, forcing them to close shop. Social unrest related to this form of marketing is already prevalent in India. The case of retail vegetable sellers in Uttar Pradesh against the Reliance Company's Reliance Fresh is one such case.

Pricing Strategies

Pricing strategies are the actual plans carried out to fix the price and market the product. These actions are the immediate subject matter for an ethical evaluation of the actions of the marketers.

Penetration pricing strategy   A marketer who wants to make a quick impression in the market promotes the product with considerable discount and other freebees. Once the market stabilizes, the freebees are slowly withdrawn and the price is settled to a mean.

Ethics: Such behaviour of the marketer can generate a price war, unfair comparisons in publicity, imperceptible volume reduction in the individual units for the same constant prices, etc.

Price skimming   It consists of gradually lowering the price for the same product or service. The marketer plunges in the marketplace with quite a high price and is able to persuade the customers willing to pay at this rate. When the costs are fairly covered, the price is reduced and more customers who can afford to buy are brought in. This is further repeated with more downward pricing till very large volumes are sold. Thus, methodically, profits are skimmed from all the sections of customers.

Ethics: As a strategy in itself, it could have noble motives. The product is new and the marketer cannot finance the venture without earning some capital from the customers. Gradually, as the sales increase, the marketer passes on the benefit to more number of customers and supplies greater volumes at a lesser price. Ethical problems arise if such a strategy is adopted to eventually wipe out competition and develop monopolistic tendencies.

Competitive pricing   Marketers are watchful of competitors changing their price bar codes. They are conscious that customers are always quite discerning and keep changing their habits. Marketers have to research and analyse the situation and act accordingly.

Ethics: The marketer narrows the gap with the competitor and splits the market. The marketer adopts price shadowing, whereby the marketer closely follows the competitor without raising the price, to wean away customers. Once customers switch loyalty favourably, the option of further lowering the price to take away all the customers from the competitor is available. At times, the marketer can take recourse to price covering, where irrespective of the competitors, the marketer is doing good business and would like to continue with the success by offering even lower prices. These strategies in themselves may not spell unethical behaviour. As long as the competitors feel it is fair and the customers are not exploited, it can remain ethically correct.

However, it is difficult to say when the scales will tip, and in most cases, the result in the end has been price volatility and customer despair.

Price shading   This happens when manufacturers allow distributors a free hand in allowing discounts to customers and also when the demand is high and the manufacturers have the requisite supply.

Ethics: A constant escalation of demand may actually cause a glut in the market. Due to other factors such as seasonal change, catastrophes, or some scandal, markets can take an unpredictable turn and cause losses to distributors who depended on the profits from large volume sales.

Seasonal pricing   FMCGs such as woollen products, air conditioners, summer wears, and fashions fetch higher prices in their season of demand. Marketers offer lesser price and greater discounts at end of season or out of season.

Ethics: Season's clearance is very often an excuse to clear inventory and make place for new products.

Term pricing   Business is booming because of the various credit facilities and schemes of instalment payments available. Marketers give incentives with higher discounts to those who immediately purchase and pay in full. The conditions of payments determine the time allowance for payments. Large industrial buyers profit more from this than individual customers.

Segment pricing   The marketer, after a careful study, targets a particular segment of the market, such as senior citizens or students or children, by giving discounts or freebees as incentive.

Ethics: This turns out to be quite deceptive. On one hand, the company projects itself as socially responsible whereas, on the other hand, makes large profits.

Volume pricing   When the company wants to encourage volume sales then it offers its buyers a scheme, that is, the larger the volume of purchase the greater is the discount on price.

Ethics: Creating demand where it actually does not exist may not have profitable long-term objectives. If the motive of the company is to dump its goods, the consequences could be disastrous.

Consequences of Pricing

The price of a product or service is dynamic in nature. Price responds to the economic forces of demand and supply. The dynamics of these forces comes into play in a free economy. In contrast, in a command economy, where the prices are controlled, the intuitive and dynamic workings of market behaviour come to a standstill.

Free market

Ethical problems arise in a free market system due to the influence, whether right or wrong, exerted by all those who are involved. It happens when marketers try to influence the economic forces through the manipulation of the price mechanism. Marketers lower price to raise demand. If customers feel that the price is too high, they buy less. The price has a completely contrary effect on supply. If the price is high, then the suppliers would like to supply more and earn profits. So, if the price is high, supply rises along with it. However, supply depends on all the economic factors—raw material, labour, and capital. The cost of production may increase or decrease, as the case may be, with a related increase or decrease in prices. How long will this to and fro, a kind of a sea-saw, continue is difficult to say. Ideally, it is possible to achieve a balance between the economic forces of demand and supply, with the prices at equilibrium. It is pure economic utopia, where suppliers and customers are perfectly happy with the prices. It is also an ethical utopia, where there is no more strife between marketers and customers and both parties have reached ideal ethical behaviour.

Monopoly, the death of competition

Just as in our moral actions there is no perfect stage, so also there is no purely ideal economic behaviour between demand and supply and pricing. Market competition could amass such forces that one of the marketers would be able to muster monopoly in supplies and then use this dominant position to enforce a higher price than would be possible in a competitive market.

Monopolies are extremely unethical because they violate the fundamental principle of free market. They violate the right of other competitors to exist. Justice demands that all marketers have a level playing field. Monopolists are guilty of manipulating by illegally controlling supply forces and wantonly pricing their products.

M for Monopoly

The landmark Microsoft antitrust case is well known even to a cursory newspaper reader. Internet entrepreneurs, investors, and millions of Internet users around the world became interested in the case, which is regarded as a global phenomena. Its magnitude lay in the fact that all of them had a stake in it.

The case in the court, dated 18 May 1998, was the United States of America versus Microsoft Corporation. The plaintiffs were the US Department of Justice and twenty states. They accused Microsoft of having abused monopoly power in its handling of operating system sales and web browser sales. Microsoft had bundled its web browser Internet Explorer with its Windows operating system. This allowed the company to monopolize the web browser market, since every Windows user had a copy of Internet Explorer. This gave an undue advantage over other browsers such as Netscape Navigator and Opera. Further, Microsoft had altered or manipulated its application programming interfaces (APIs) to favour Internet Explorer over third-party web browsers. It had also formed restrictive licensing agreements with original equipment manufacturers (OEMs). The plaintiffs tried to establish the intent of Microsoft's conduct to destroy competition and establish itself as a monopoly.

Microsoft defended its actions. It said that due to innovation in product development, the two segments—the browser and the operating system—had become one single product. As a result, Windows customers need purchase only a single product. The defendants countered it by saying that since Microsoft sells Internet Explorer as a separate programme for

Contd

Box Contd

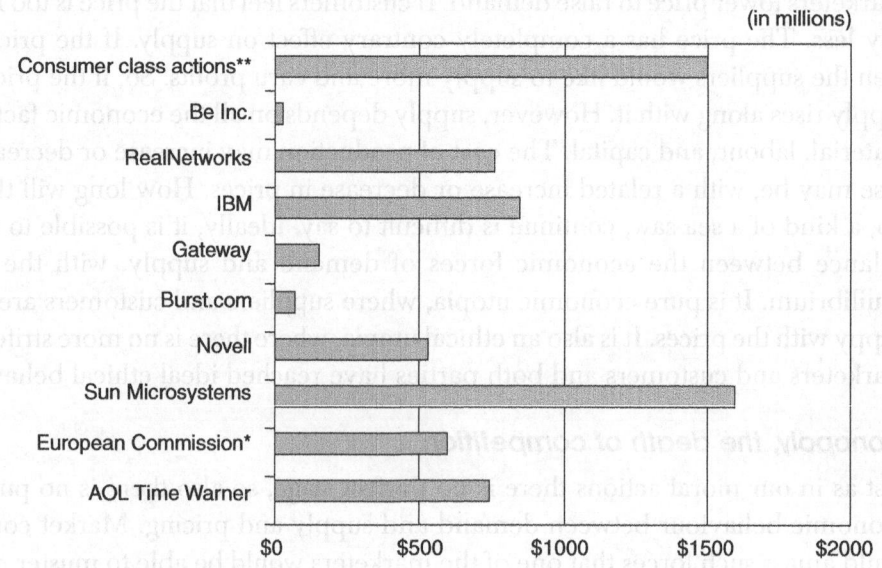

Fig. 6.3 Microsoft's settlement with competitors

Source: http://www.antitrustreview.com/files/2006/07/200607071706.jpg.

Mac OS, there is no question of its being integrated into the Windows operating system and that it was still a distinct product that took away the advantage from its competitors. Further, Internet Explorer's development and marketing raised the price of the Windows operating system, which went to prove Microsoft's claim as false.

In November 2001, the US Department of Justice reached a settlement with Microsoft that the latter would share its APIs with third-party companies and appoint a panel that will have full access to Microsoft's systems, records, and source code for five years. (The settlement has expired in 2007 and has been renewed for the next two years.) Of the twenty states, nine states refused the settlement. In June 2004, the US Appeals Court upheld the settlement. Figure 6.3 is a chart summary

of the settlement dues that Microsoft had to pay to its competitors.

The criticism against Microsoft and the justice it meted out was witnessed across the globe. Critics included the noted Nobel prize winner for economics, Milton Friedman. While Friedman thought it was government interference in technology business, others thought that dismissing it as a packaging problem was unfair.

Questions

(a) Why is monopoly characterized as antitrust?
(b) If the market is truly free, how would monopolies originate, and even if they originate, how long will they last or how effective would they be?
(c) Does the government have a responsibility to prevent monopolies?

Government Control

There are times when the government arrives at the conclusion that marketers (particularly monopolists or those who have formed cartels, or those companies who come together to form a monopoly) are holding people to ransom, or that the nation is suffering from some great economic ill or collapse, and decides to control the prices.

In poor and developing countries, government control becomes necessary lest the market forces ruin those already impoverished. India is a developing country and has made enormous progress, but since the majority of the people still live in poverty, the government has to take measures to ensure that these people get food grains at a lower price. Hence, the public distribution system or rationing of foodstuffs is still prevalent. Further, subsidies to farmers, free health care, lower tariffs on public transport, etc. are the ways in which prices of essential goods and services to the poor masses are kept in check.

Government intervention is also required to protect the economy. Price control helps the producers. The government fixes a base price or floor price. The farmers in India enjoy these fixed prices as support prices, and the government procures the produce at these prices in order to ensure and stabilize the agricultural economy. European countries have adopted the system of subsidies and controlled farming, wherein the government would have to pay compensation for not having farmed the land. Thus, the prices are controlled at the production level.

In order to protect consumers, the government controls prices through price ceiling, the maximum price that can be charged. Thus, for example, to protect tenants from exorbitant and volatile housing rents, the government can put a house rent ceiling. This is done in slabs of rent after classifying the various housing schemes, such as higher income or lower income housing schemes. The government may sometimes freeze prices, if it feels the need to do so. This, however, is too rigid, and it may cause even more problems, since the economic conditions of the people keep changing as do the prices. Frozen prices are unnatural in any economic order.

The ethical problems that surface with government control are related to human freedom. In the name of protecting the poor, India has followed a policy of controlled economy, which has curtailed the entrepreneurial freedom of the people. The people, in turn, have remained indolent and for every need of theirs depend on the government and blame it for not doing enough. This has harmed the self-esteem of the people.

Man is entitled to all forms of freedom, be it political, economic, social, free speech, etc. Economic freedom enables one to aspire for a better and dignified life. The government should be rather vigilant on how businesses function. Whether businesses are fair to the customers, whether cartels are formed to the detriment of the customers, or whether monopolies are destroying the overall economic growth should be observed. Vigilance is a good virtue, and the government must use it for the benefit of the people.

BRAND MANAGEMENT IMPERATIVES

A brand is the identity of a company. What a name is to a person, a brand is to a company. It consists of an insignia, also known as symbol or emblem, and also images, words, signs, sounds (radio, TV), or a combination of all these. The company has a brand when the insignia of the company is registered in accordance with the law

Indian Competition Act

A change of mindset

Independent India remained a command economy till 1990. As the geo-political equations around the world changed and communism collapsed, India was left with no alternative but to reform itself into a market economy. During the days of the command economy, competition was regulated by The Monopolistic and Restrictive Trade Practices (MRTP) Act 1969. It controlled and regulated the growth of enterprises. Any form of commercial dominance was seen as restrictive and bad.

However, in the 1990s, as liberalization took hold, the need for a progressive competition law was felt. The new law enacted was titled The Competition Act 2002. For the purpose of implementation, the Competition Commission of India (CCI) was set up as a quasi-judicial body, with a chairperson and a team of up to ten members, and would have separate prosecuting and investigating wings. Table 6.1 shows some of the contrasting features between the two Acts.

Table 6.1   Indian Competition Act

Monopolistic and Restrictive Trade Practices (MRTP) Act 1969	Competition Act 2002
Basis for determining dominance was size.	Basis for determining dominance is structure.
Compulsory registration of agreements.	Registration of agreements discontinued.
Offences were not well defined or listed but only implied; very complex and verbose; lacked combinations regulation.	Offences well defined and simple to understand; combinations regulated beyond a certain threshold.
Old mindset: Dominance is offensive.	New mindset: Abuse of dominance is wrong.
Competition commission lacked administrative and financial autonomy.	Competition commission enjoys greater autonomy.
No juridical role.	Has both juridical and investigative roles.
Reactive and rigid; had no power to impose penalties.	Proactive; has adequate powers to deal with penalties for offences.

The Competition Act 2002 deals with three areas, which are briefly stated below.

Agreement among enterprises The Act deals only with those agreements between enterprises that have a significant adverse effect on competition. Any anti-competition is to be determined, including those by foreign enterprises, and it should be ensured that cartels are not formed.

Abuse of dominance Dominance is the position of strength in the market. Abuse would include charging or paying unfair prices, initiation of predatory pricing, restriction on quantities, markets, and technical development, and restriction and distortion of competition.

Mergers or combination among enterprises The Act regulates all mergers that may create a position of dominance in the post-merger scenario. It also provides for pre-merger notification and a deemed approval of the merger within ninety days, if there is no response from CCI.

Questions

(a) Why should the government intervene in the market forces?

(b) What is more important for Indian enterprises: government regulation or corporate governance?

(c) How can India be made free from price fixing?

of the state. It becomes the company's unique and singular property. The law protects it from violations of use, counterfeits, close resemblances, or any other infringements. Just as a newborn is registered and recognized by the state, so also a company's brand acquires the right for its individual existence and good name. The goods and services of a company are branded with the company brand and the company is legally responsible to these. Further, a company may have several other companies forming a group of companies with their own insignia. Finally, a company may develop further brands for different goods and services and name them accordingly. Thus, a company becomes a family as it creates more brands for its goods and services.

The basis for the moral responsibility of the brand lies in the fact that the company, by virtue of its registration with the authorities, becomes a moral person and is responsible for its actions. Consumers recognize the brand and they refer to it as such, or to the company itself. In the event of consumer disputes, the brand is referred to and due action is taken against the company from the identity of its brand.

Integration of Ethical Values and Brand Value

A brand has a character. It is shaped by the company internally and recognized by the consumers externally. What the brand stands for is defined by the company, and how that stand is perceived depends on the experience of the customers. It is what we are to ourselves and what others perceive us to be. Thus, the brand character is formed as one's own self and the opinion and experience of others.

The employees of a company proudly display the brand on their sleeves if it has a good name. Brand perception is formed in an ethos; a brand has a cultural background of its own through which it develops its personality. Without the cultural background, the brand stands there empty and characterless. An insignia or a symbol is nothing in itself, except for the meaning that we attach to it. That relevance is bestowed on it by the collective behaviour of the people in the company and the quality of goods and services offered under that particular brand. The total behaviour of the company and the quality of its products are characterized by the brand. Just as we judge a person by his/her actions, so also a brand is known by its performance in the society of consumers. Thus, a good name or good reputation is the essence of brand value.

Brands that connect ethically to society earn reputation. They become members of society. Such brands are grounded in the cultural values and exhibit authenticity.

Brand Citizenship

Brands become citizens when they are accepted in society as distinctly useful partners. If a brand can spell transparency in its dealings, respect its shareholders who are from the society in which they are doing business, and commit to the economic, social, and environmental values, then they are a part of the citizenry.

A brand must grow in human society by association and assimilation. It has to develop a community of loyal customers, it should always innovate, it must employ and manage human capital in an exemplary fashion. A good brand is an inestimable

Living with the Brands

Brand controversies

Union Carbide It has been the worst ever industrial nightmare. On 3 December 1984, ten thousand people in the city of Bhopal went to bed not to rise the next morning. The poisonous gas from the Union Carbide plant killed them all. Since then, thousands of people have succumbed to various illnesses caused due to its after effects and have died. Young mothers today, who were not even born at that time, are carrying with them the aftereffects of the toxins. Their breast milk is unfit for their babies. The brand Union Carbide is a synonym for death in India. For the people of Bhopal, it goes beyond death—the living are still battling for compensation. For these people, Union Carbide is worse than the colonialists who robbed them of everything, their wealth as well as their health.

Exxon Valdez A lady sitting next to Raymond Loewy at dinner struck up a conversation. 'Why', she asked, 'did you put two Xs in Exxon?' 'Why ask?' he asked. 'Because', she said, 'I couldn't help noticing!' 'Well', he responded, 'that's the answer'.[a] In 1989, Exxon Valdez was grounded on Bligh, in Prince William Sound at Alaska. It spilled a phenomenal 11 million gallons of crude oil. It destroyed a coastline of 2500 miles. The damage caused to the flora and fauna was immeasurable. It became another name for sudden and irresponsible, environmental damage. Indeed, one cannot help noticing the disastrous brand.

Nike It gave a motto for the young—'Just do it'. But its own actions spelled exploitation and slow poisoning of its sweatshop workers in Vietnam. In 1996, the media world exploded with the inhuman treatment meted out by Nike to its workers. The media reported tales of mental and physical brutality and appalling working conditions that the workers were subjected to in order to meet the daily quotas. Further investigations brought to light the fact that the workers were exposed to carcinogens that exceeded the legal limits by 177 times. More than 70 per cent of the employees suffered from respiratory problems.

Adidas It is a brand recognized around the globe for sports and sports fashion. When it was revealed that the company used child labour extensively in the third world countries and paid just one-and-a-half dollars for a twelve-hour shift to women, people changed their image of this sports goods giant to that of a slave task master.

De Beers It is the world leader in diamonds and gems. It blemished its name by buying these valuables from African revolutionaries and warlords, who have bloodied the continent. The company thought that business would continue as usual, but it was terribly wrong. The consumers reacted. People gave it a new brand name—Blood Diamonds. They stopped buying from the company. The company had such an overhang of its stocks that its business got strangled. The company buckled and promised to behave. The company changed tracks, and conducted only 'clean' gems business. Business picked up again and the customers enjoyed the benefits of cut-price diamonds passed on to them. People will forgive firms if they show both intention and action to reform.

Protests

It is not that consumers take everything lying down. Green Peace and several other organizations and human rights groups have protested before WTO, UNO, and wherever world summits have taken place. It has brought pressure on these organizations and several brand companies have complied with ethical strictures.

Questions

(a) Does an ethical tag to brands really matter?
(b) Do customers choose a brand because it represents ethical business?
(c) Is buying branded goods more of a status symbol than ethical behaviour?

[a] Alan Fletcher, *The Art of Looking Sideways*, Phaidon Press, 2001.

and intangible asset, which experts think is close to 50 per cent of market capitalization. This is the only way that brands can last for a very long term.

Long-term brand equity, for that is the catch phrase, depends on the firm's ability to implement its mission, which consists of its purpose in the market. Without a comprehensive marketing programme, a brand will become a ghostly shadow, irrelevant to the living. Christopher Betzter says, 'Brand equity is the sum of all the hearts and minds of every single person that comes into contact with your company.'

Citizenship, in reality, lies in the relationships that a company develops with the people. There could be different types of relationships—boss and staff, ruler and subject, parent and child, physician and patient, buyer and seller. For a good business citizenship, however, none of these may help. The only relationship that will help in business in general and brand building in particular is that of partnership. The company must accept shareholders, employees, distributors, retailers, and consumers as partners. It is a partnership in mission, an economic enterprise, where each one is accepted for

---

The Counterfeiters

Brand dilemma

If anyone thinks that there are no smart people outside of the corporations who can beat them at their own game, then they need to rethink. Brand protection has become a big problem for corporations. The challengers are smarter and faster. They counterfeit brands,[a] fill their packs with their own stuff, which are often spurious, and make big money. The fake industry in India is estimated to constitute about 35 per cent of the branded products sold.

The brand problems are compounded when, in the world of designs, it becomes unmanageable to remain unscathed from copycats. Fashion designers, gems and jewellery firms, fashion accessories such as wrist watches, sun glasses, etc. find their designs reproduced and sold as genuinely fake. Consumers who cannot afford high-end branded products do not mind flaunting fakes. Somehow people do love to raise their status symbol, albeit with a fake brand, and gain some social equality with the rich and the famous. The fake designer market appears to be even higher than that of the counterfeited brands.

Consumers in Iraq love Unilever products marked 'Made in France'. To Unilever's chagrin, it does not do any business in France and it closed its last production unit in France a good ten years ago. To its greater disappointment, in India, where it is a market leader in fast-moving consumer goods (FMCGs), it has been established that there are over a hundred imitations of their product Fair & Lovely alone. Some of the other most affected brands are Vicks, Axe, Ariel, Parachute, Johnson & Johnson, Clinic Plus, Dove, Lux, Colgate, and Pears. It has been reported that of the total market share of Rs 1,13,000 crore in FMCGs, the revenue loss due to imitations is Rs 5000 crore. Up to 30 per cent of the packaged toiletries have been reported to be counterfeits.

The economic and social repercussions of counterfeiting the brands are enormous in terms of employment to the people, revenue loss to the companies, and tax loss to the country. The social cost of potential damage to health is enormous.

Questions

(a) How is counterfeiting brands unethical?

(b) If companies price their products reasonably, will brand misuse reduce?

(c) How can you reconcile the fact of 'genuine facts' with genuine business?

[a] *Source:* See Counterfeit Products Dog FMCG Companies Too, http://business-standard.com/india/storypage.php?autono= 346428, 18 January 2009.

his/her role. It is this relationship that makes a brand a household name and wins the confidence of the shareholders, the commitment of the employees, and the trust of the customers.

BUSINESS AS USUAL

Marketing Strategies: Right and Wrong

Marketers very often describe marketing as 'war out there'. Observing today's fierce competition, the analogy may not be an exaggeration at all. Several products fight for the same turf, the same market segment. All is fair in love and war, so goes the saying, but if marketers feel that ethics should take a backseat in so far as marketing is concerned, they should rethink. It is now amply proved through empirical studies that it is only ethical marketing that ultimately wins the battle. Ethical companies become market leaders, and customers respect them by being loyal to them for a very long time.

Some of the strategies mentioned here are like any tool. They can be used or misused.

Deterrence   A war tactic without actually fighting.

Upside: Your product is so imposing qualitatively and quantitatively that it deters competitors.

Downside: You are able to absorb losses; your pricing is so low that it deters competitors from entering the market.

Pre-emptive strike   You simply have the idea before your competitors do. Time is business.

Upside: Use of farsightedness.

Downside: Wrong idea; an idea whose time has not come.

Frontal attack   Aggressive marketing.

Upside: Gather as many customers as possible, leaving a blazing trail that keeps competitors away.

Downside: Customers may dislike too much intrusion and reject the product outright if privacy is disturbed.

Flanking   It is to operate where your competitors have less interest. These are normally safe areas for new entrants. Flanking can become an aggressive strategy. For instance, you cannot sell Coke if you are selling Pepsi. You attack competitors on the flank, the supply and distribution side, and eventually take over the frontal battle line.

Upside: Gives a stable and reasonable start for a new business; good place to mature before the big battle.

Downside: You may go unnoticed and fold up soon and be swamped by competitors' flanks.

Sequential strategies   This one is about the veterans. It is a well-thought-out, long-term marketing process that involves not only main strategies, but also sub-strategies and detailed plans and policies.

Upside: Formalized and well-executed long-term policies have far-reaching consequences for the company.

Downside: One could get bogged down by the bureaucratic processes and slow decision-making processes. As a result, competitors may surge ahead.

Alliances   When marketers feel that undue competition is sapping up their energies, they could come together to form alliances and partnerships so that they do not face cutthroat competition, but are satisfied to have the market share without rocking the boat.

Upside: The competitors turned co-operators could give customers better products and better services.

Downside: The few players in the market can form a cartel and function as a monopoly. The Indian cement industry has been accused of this malpractice.

Defensive   Developing strategies to protect one's market share.

Upside: Facing threats to growth can positively affect rethinking over the prevailing strategies and failures and correct them.

Downside: In the event of protecting one's market share, one might be doing the bidding of the competitor, who will find chinks in the armour and attack weak points.

Counter offence   'Offence is the best form of defence' is a principle that has worked well for many.

Upside: Counter offence takes the competitor by surprise and one might actually win more than hoped for. Keeps a company on its toes.

Downside: Customers and media do not miss market wars and one could end up losing both the market share as well as one's reputation.

Mobile defence   This is a versatile tactic whereby the company keeps its product mix flexible and allows innovation and repositioning of its products.

Upside: Tests the resilience of competitors. Customers benefit if the changes have been for the better.

Downside: A product can lose stability. Competitors see the flanks shift and open, and may take on the challenge head on.

Encirclement   It is a long-term strategy that surrounds the competitor flank by flank, product by product.

Upside: The company has a plan. Through superior products and better services, it is able to edge out mediocre competition.

Downside: May get bogged down with an obsession with the competitor and lose the larger market picture.

Strategic withdrawal   It is a defensive tactic.

Upside: If done with the foresight of an economic downturn, it will save the company from loss, and as the economic situation revives the company may enter the market with a smart product mix.

Downside: Competitors may gain upper hand and it may be difficult to re-enter the market arena.

Leapfrogging It is an innovative strategy coupled with new technology, and thus leaves behind competitors to their old ways of doing business.

Upside: It enables the company to lead with a cutting-edge strategy.

Downside: The tried and tested strategies may prove successful. It is also possible that customers may not take to the new product or gadgetry.

UNUSUAL STRATEGIES: INTEGRAL MARKETING PARADIGM

Creation of Consumer Capacity

Business, as usual, assumes that consumers have money, but they need to be attracted through marketing strategies to spend the money. In social marketing, the assumption is that the consumers have very little money. They cannot afford to buy what the middle class buys. Following strategies target such consumers.

Affordability The marketer, therefore, instead of neglecting this customer who can afford less, sees in him/her a very good customer and packs and sells products and services to suit his/her pocket. Today, sachets from shampoos to dry fruits are available for just Rs 5; the mobile phone top-up card is available for just Rs 10.

Access These customers are like the fly that lives for a day. Their earnings are from their daily wages; their purchases are from day to day. They live in the rural areas and the poor localities of the city. Their shopping begins at sunset. This is a huge market of nearly 70 per cent of the Indian population. Accessibility concerns itself with making all the essential commodities available to them at that time, at their place.

Availability Shortages in India are phenomenal. New methods of supply chain and distribution have to be developed, such as turning some households in the villages into small shops and kiosks. This would create a formidable army of little entrepreneurs.

Innovative products and services Since these customers cannot afford quality products and services, they resign themselves to buying substandard items and, in the long run, stand to lose even more. With innovative ideas and affordable packing, goods and services may be available to this dormant market. Thus, if the up-market customers can enjoy processed foods, so also the people of the lower income group, if these are packed in single, use-and-throw sachets and packages.

Partners in business A mammoth supply and distribution logistic system performs under great tension. The products and services appear without any relationship to the people. But in social marketing, instead of a top-down unmanageable organization, one could create cells of productivity and exchange. Services such as bank loans, marketing of farm produce, manpower management, cottage industry, all these and more can make people partners of the industry and business, not just in commercial exchange but also in production and distribution.

Empowerment and dignity Large companies at times get into philanthropy to assuage their conscience. It only ends by further humiliating the poor. However, in integral marketing, the partnership principle includes the customers as a social part of business. The buyers are part of the economic circle of capital, labour, production, and distribution. By now, the new customers-turned-partners have heightened their capacities as consumers. For these people, once thought to be poor and illiterate, there is hope, dignity, and choice.

Supportive relationship   Business is an exploitative relationship between the marketer and the customer. The marketer somehow takes as much as possible from the customer. Integral marketing is a bonding of the economic and social relationship. Marketers and customers are interdependent by nature on the business in which all of them participate. Such interdependence creates trust naturally. They share an activity that makes them winners. There are no losers in integral marketing.

SUMMARY

- The market consists of people.
- Marketing is an activity in which economic exchanges, transactions of buying and selling, take place.
- Social relationship is the basis for marketing ethics.
- Marketing cannot ignore social realities such as the purchasing power of the people.
- Free-market system functions on its given dynamism of demand and supply.
- The product and its positioning, its promotion and working, fighting, struggling through competition, and creating value addition to the firm and shareholders is the objective of marketing.
- Customer satisfaction is the mission that motivates further growth of the market.
- Marketing practices of product, price, promotion, and place call for ethical evaluation. The

principle of such evaluation is that the means ought to justify the end.
- There is a utilitarian corollary to the afore-mentioned principle: the consequences of the nature of the product, the pricing approach, and its promotional methods, particularly concerning advertising, must be examined for their effects on the consumers.
- Ethics promotes healthy competition, avoids monopolies, and looks for equilibrium between supply and demand.
- Brand business is good for the market.
- Protection of the brands is good for the health of the economy.
- Integral marketing, assimilation of the poor as partners in business, is a challenge to business as usual.

KEY TERMS

Brand   An insignia identifying a firm or a product.

Brand counterfeit   Plagiarized brand.

Brand value   The reputation of a brand, evaluated as an intangible asset, or its potency in market capitalization.

Competition   Contesting to sell goods and services in the free-market system.

Consequential utilitarianism   An action is judged as good or bad by its results, e.g., if milk causes illness, investigations will show that it was adulterated.

Ethical packaging   Packing that consists of correct information causes no harm to the customer and is environmentally sustainable.

Integral marketing   Marketing done to empower the consumers economically; make people with little or no purchasing power, partners in a marketing enterprise; extend the free-market system to include the deprived populace, to enjoy equitable and just distribution of wealth.

Means to end   Ethical principle that it is not the end, but the means that justifies the end.

Monopoly   Complete domination of market by a particular product or service; it is the death of competition. Ethically untenable because it deprives others of their right to do business.

Price   The amount of money for which a good or service is bought or sold.

Social marketing   Marketing with a social objective, e.g., distribution of condoms by the Ministry of Health and Family Welfare.

Societal marketing   Marketing undertaken by corporations as a part of the corporate social responsibility.

Spurious   Bogus product.

CONCEPT REVIEW QUESTIONS

1. What is the role of business ethics in a free-market system?
2. Discuss the ethical implications of product positioning.
3. What kind of packaging is harmful to humans?

4. What are the misuses of MRP?
5. What ethical problems do companies suffer when launching a product?
6. Why are branded goods high-priced?

CRITICAL THINKING QUESTIONS

1. Draw a business model for integral marketing for one essential commodity.
2. What are the other important issues that are not covered in this chapter, for example, product placement? What moral grounds can you provide for its advocacy or disapproval?
3. Discuss the ethical dimension of pricing dynamics.

4. If you had a large amount of money at your disposal, would you buy a car that costs over a crore of rupees? Justify.
5. How would you implement brand management ethics in India?

FURTHER READING

George G. Benkert, *Marketing Ethics*, Wiley Blackwell (2008).

Rama Bijapurkar, *Winning in the Indian Market: Understanding the Transformation of Consumer India*, John Wiley & Sons (2007).

CASE STUDY

Lifebuoy: The Story of a Soap

Unilever's mission is to add vitality to life. We meet everyday needs for nutrition, hygiene, and personal care with brands that help people feel good, look good, and get more out of life.

—Corporate mission statement

Can soap 'buoy' life? The story of this soap demonstrates that it can not only buoy life, but it can save it too. Washing one's hands with soap may seem too simplistic for a life saver. But the hand-washing hygiene campaign in rural India, headed by Hindustan Unilever Limited (HUL), is saving over half a million children annually from death that is caused by diarrhoea. It is not surprising that the *India Post* released a first day cover on the

company's campaign called Swasthya Chetna, the health consciousness programme. The United Nations' World Health Organization (WHO) further strengthened its hand to partner in this massive village hygiene movement.

Market Implications

Soap is a mundane article of use. However, there are few other common commodities other than soap

HUL Timeline

1888 Unloaded crates of soap at the Calcutta harbour, with the emblazoned writing: *Made in England by Lever Brothers.*

1895 More soaps: Pears, Lux, and Vim.

1898 Lipton tea is launched in India by the company for Lipton.

1900 Brooke Bond tea was launched.

1912 Brooke Bond & Co. India Limited was formed.

1918 Vanaspati, the vegetable oil, was launched.

1931 Hindustan Vanaspati Manufacturing Company was formed.

1933 Lever Brothers India Limited came into existence.

1935 United Traders Limited was born.

1937 Dalda, the most famous vegetable oil, also known as the poor man's ghee (clarified butter), was introduced.

1956 Hindustan Vanaspati Manufacturing Company, Lever Brothers India Limited, and United Traders Limited were merged to form Hindustan Unilever Limited (HUL). A public offering of its 10 per cent equity was made. HUL currently holds 52.10 per cent of its equity, while the remainder is with individual and institutional shareholders, numbering to a phenomenal 3,60,675.

1958 Establishment of Hindustan Unilever Research Centre.

1972 Unilever acquires Lipton in 1972.

1977 Lipton Tea (India) Limited is incorporated.

1984 Brooke Bond joined the Unilever fold through an international acquisition.

1986 HUL acquires Ponds (India).

1993 Tata Oil Mills Company (TOMCO) merges with HUL.

1994 Joint venture with Kimberly Clark Corporation of US, which markets Huggies, Diapers, and Kotex Sanitary Pads.

1995 Lakme Limited, a Tata company, forms a fifty-fifty joint venture with HUL.

1996 Brooke Bond India Limited (BBIL) and Lipton India Limited (LIL) merge with HUL.

1998 Lakme sells its brands to HUL and divests of its stake in the joint venture.

2000 The government-owned PSU divests 74 per cent of its equity in HUL and gets into wheat and wheat products.

2002 Acquisition of Modern Foods by HUL.

2003: HUL acquires Amalgam Group, a leader in marine food product exports.

---

that generate so much revenue for the companies who manufacture it and market it. HUL is a company that is over a hundred years old. Its soap crates landed in the Calcutta harbour (now Kolkata), in 1888, and for the next century, it strode the Indian soap market unchallenged, whether under the colonial rule or under the protective market of the independence era. Things changed however, with liberalization in 1992. Although a market leader with a 60 per cent market share, it was under pressure to initiate a change, as multinationals such as Procter & Gamble entered the market.

Redefinition of Vision and Product Positioning Strategy

The Lifebuoy soap cake had almost become synonymous with the product, and yet it felt insecure in an open and competitive market. It redefined its vision for the soap: Making a billion Indians feel safe and secure by meeting all their health and hygiene needs.

In quick succession in 2002, 2004, and 2006, Lifebuoy underwent a metamorphosis. The new mix included a new formulation in appearance,

composition, and quality to suit the times and the customers. With new packaging and labelling, fragrance and varied sizes, the repositioning of the product was intelligent and smart. Lifebuoy Deofresh was targeted at those who looked for freshness, Lifebuoy Nature targeted at nature conscious people, and Lifebuoy Care was targeted for those with sensitive skin. Further, Lifebuoy Handwash and Lifebuoy Clearskin were supplied as liquid soap variants of the hygiene and health promoting products.

Manufacturing

HUL's manufacturing[a] unit is of sheer size. The manufacturing takes place in over 40 factories across India. The operation is carried out by over 2000 suppliers and associates. There is a large network of over 4000 redistribution stockists, 6.3 million retail outlets, and 250 million rural consumers alone.

HUL's range of products is so diversified in FMCGs that these affect two out of every three Indians. This is an enormous manufacturing capability. Home and personal care products, creams, jellies, oils, soaps, detergents, a range of foods and beverages—their mere weight alone amount to four million tons and a whopping Rs 13,718 crore. It is also one of the country's largest exporters, and the Government of India has honoured it as the Golden Super Star Trading House. It has a workforce of 15,000 people, of which 1300 are managers.

Manufacturing has been very successful due to the priority given to research and development. It is known to introduce the latest technology in its production sector. The two centres of Hindustan Unilever Research Centre at Mumbai and Bengaluru employ over two hundred scientists and technologists.

The following products have become household names in India: Lifebuoy, Lux, Surf, Surf Excel, Rin, Wheel, Fair & Lovely, Ponds, Sunsilk, Clinic, Pepsodent, Close-up, Lakme, Brooke Bond, Kissan, Knorr-Annapurna, Kwality Walls, etc.

Genesis of Societal Marketing

With the dawn of the millennium, the world business' focus on economics and lifestyles changed. While on the one hand prosperity became almost scandalous for a few, on the other hand, poverty rose like a hideous mountain in developing countries like India. The United Nations highlighted the plight of the poor and the paucity of service they are rendered. It announced the millennium goals to be achieved, including health and hygiene. Out of the six billion people in the world, four billion live in utter poverty and more than half a billion of them are from India. Even if these were to get a small piece of soap cake every week, the market shares of such a company could soar through the roof. HUL saw a social and business opportunity for their century-old Lifebuoy. If it could tap this market with innovative tact and strategy, it could reach out to these people socially and make more business economically.

A study done by the London School of Hygiene and Tropical Medicine showed that diarrhoea claims a child's life every 10 seconds and one-third of those who die in this manner are children from India. The study revealed that a simple washing of hands with some soap could reduce this death rate by 47 per cent. HUL decided to go rural with a definite and socially targeted programme to help eradicate diarrhoea. It chose the heart of rural India by selecting the states of Uttar Pradesh, Bihar, West Bengal, Orissa, and Maharashtra.

Lifebuoy Swasthya Chetana

A simple but effective programme was drawn, focusing on the health of the children in villages.[b] Over six lakh children alone are the victims of diarrhoea in India. Avoiding it is a simple matter of hygiene that can be effectively achieved by washing hands before eating. If this is demonstrated to the children in their villages and schools, all those

---

[a] See http://www.hul.co.in/knowus/present_stature.asp.

[b] See http://www.hul.co.in/citizen_lever/lifebuoy_chetna.asp.

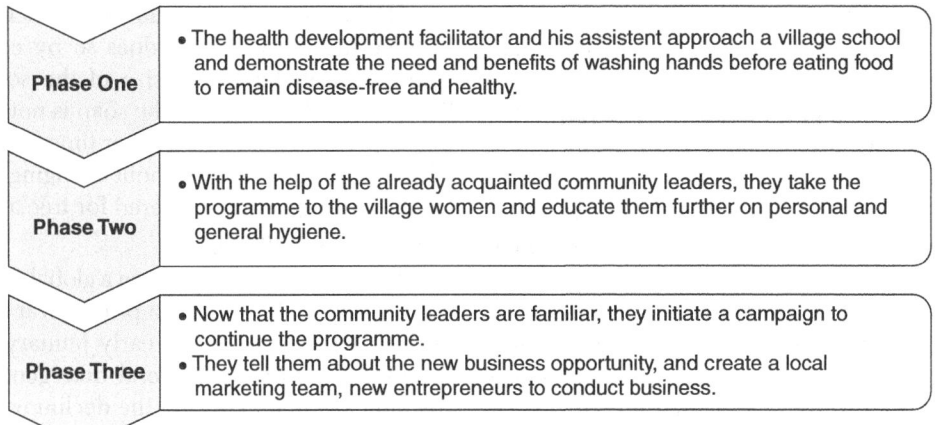

Phase One	• The health development facilitator and his assistent approach a village school and demonstrate the need and benefits of washing hands before eating food to remain disease-free and healthy.
Phase Two	• With the help of the already acquainted community leaders, they take the programme to the village women and educate them further on personal and general hygiene.
Phase Three	• Now that the community leaders are familiar, they initiate a campaign to continue the programme. • They tell them about the new business opportunity, and create a local marketing team, new entrepreneurs to conduct business.

Fig. 6.4 Progressive rural marketing strategy

lives will be saved. This in turn will teach the adults also to do the same.

In all Asian countries, washing one's hands and feet is a cultural practice. People refresh themselves when they return home from work. Water is offered to guests for this very purpose, as a sign of hospitality. Washing and the use of water also has a deep religious significance. Yet, the lack of following this simple ritual seems to have victimized the poor. That the children pay for it with their lives is an unbearable irony of the poverty-stricken people. This lost custom found its saviour in a business opportunity.

The re-education programme was called Swasthya Chetana or health consciousness. A consciousness was ignited through a repeated action, which formed a lasting habit. The organizational behaviourists called this a behaviour change programme for the consumers. HUL introduced a multi-phased education programme in the village schools across the various states of India. See Fig. 6.4. A simple demonstration showed them that what they seemingly saw as clean was actually very dirty and unhygienic. One needed to wash one's hands with soap before touching any food. A further explanation with pictures, posters, and projected images demonstrated what germs were and how they caused various diseases and death. Looking

down at their little palms, the children became ominously aware of the unseen but fatal germs. With this knowledge empowerment, selling a piece of soap cake to get rid of those heinous germs became a cake walk for the sellers.

HUL's next move was to go to the mothers of these children and tell them that the future of their children and health lay with them. They should always insist that their children wash their hands with soap. It is natural that once the children started doing it, the others at home would be compelled to do the same. The household would eventually become health conscious.

Finally, once all the spade work was done, the company made sure that the villagers got a constant supply of soaps and all the other things that were necessary for personal hygiene. They needed small entrepreneurs to run this newly found business. One did not have to go far. Here was an opportunity for the village women to have a go at business.

One of the senior executives summed up the project succinctly: 'Swasthya Chetna is not about philanthropy. It's a marketing programme with social benefits. We recognize that the health of our business is totally interconnected with the health of the communities we serve and if we are to grow sales of our brand, we have to increase the number of people who use soap.'[c]

---

[c] Harpreet Singh Tibb, Senior Product Manager for Lifebuoy, Hindustan Lever Ltd, in 2005.

Micro-enterprise: *Shakti*

When HUL started its rural campaign, the micro paradigm was the most successful business model in the world, including the micro-credit that changed Bangladesh for good. It started its micro-entrepreneurship programme in thousands of villages and attractively called it Shakti. Shakti implies power and is quite resonant in Indian culture. Goddess Durga is the symbol of that shakti. It also gave a new connotation to women's power, since the programme was oriented towards women.

It has a simple modus operandi. The woman interested in selling soap and other HUL products erects a simple outlet, may be on the veranda of her own house. This insignificant retailer is a cog in the giant HUL marketing machine. In 2001, there were approximately 45,000 women covering over 1,35,000 villages and reaching out to 150 million customers. By 2010, the estimates are, there will be over 1,00,000 Shakti entrepreneurs covering 5,00,000 villages and reaching out to 600 million people—more than half the population of India. It is a proud achievement and even the critics of the company agree with the company's self-assessment that states, 'If Hindustan Unilever straddles the Indian corporate world, it is because of being single-minded in identifying itself with Indian aspirations and needs in every walk of life.'

Pricing

That Indians are price conscious customers is a truism in the marketing manual. Indeed, it is true when the customer is able to pay the price. What should be done when the customer is really unable to pay for it because he/she cannot afford it? This is where the principle of social marketing becomes relevant. If the customer cannot afford to pay, then make your product proportionately affordable by offering a less quantity without diminishing its quality. HUL did just that. The soap cake was reduced to 18 grams, with a price tag of just Rs 2. It would be sold, like its sachets, in a strip containing a dozen soaps. In 2003, Lifebuoy registered a 31 per cent growth. This helped HUL penetrate the market by 40 per cent of all HUL's turnover.[d]

HUL has vigorously followed its pricing policy of lowering the prices. It does so by constantly changing the shape and size of the soap cake. Sometimes, the weight of the soap is not changed but its price is lowered. At other times, the weight of the soap is increased without changing its price; so, the extra quantity is offered for free and this is displayed prominently.

The year 2008–09 has been a global slowdown, but not for HUL. There is a pricing war out there in the FMCG market.[e] In early January 2009, it dropped the prices of several detergent brands. Keeping a watchful eye on the declining inflation rate, HUL went for the kill. The relatively cheaper detergent, Wheel Active, has been brought down from Rs 75 to Rs 67 for a 2 kg pack; the weight of the same product of 250 grams has been raised to 275 grams without any change in the price. In fact, the entire family of soaps and detergents have been brought down in prices. A 90-gram soap cake of Lifebuoy, which used to cost Rs 13, is reduced by Re 1; the 150-gram bar now costs Rs 14 instead of Rs 15; the 90-gram multi-pack of three soaps weighing 90 grams is reduced by Rs 2 and now costs Rs 34. Its closest competitor, Proctor and Gamble, are forced into this war of prices.

Conclusion

There are critics who have castigated HUL's societal marketing as merely a marketing gimmick to penetrate the changing rural market of India. With a growth rate closely hovering close to double digits, bigger markets are needed and they are around the corner. Others have criticized the marketing approach of HUL as targeting children's sickness to get into the good books of international non-profit organizations. The UNICEF and WHO have not only endorsed HUL's rural programme for hygiene, but have also recognized it as a fulfilment of their corporate social responsibility. Criticisms have also been levelled against the supporting marketing systems like Shakti micro-enterprises, as a cheap marketing vehicle to push other HUL products.

---

[d] http://www.financialexpress.com/news/HLL-Launches_Lifebuoy-At-Rs-2/92685/.
[e] See http://timesofindia.indiatimes.com/business/india_Business/HUL_starts_a_price_war/articlesshow/4003975.cms, accessed on 20 January 2009.

Lifebuoy, one of the brands of HUL, has almost become a generic name for the common man's soap of India. The jingle '*Lifebuoy hai jahan, tandurusti hai wahan*' (wherever there is Lifebuoy there is good health) seems to have become a part of the Indian culture.

Discussion Questions

1. How complex is a market system?
2. Has HUL missed something important in marketing ethics?
3. Has HUL developed tendencies of monopoly?
4. Discuss the ethical merits and demerits of HUL's rural marketing strategy.
5. Can HUL's method be replicated for alcoholic beverages, tobacco products, lottery tickets, etc.?

6. What ethical principles are at stake in HUL's marketing?
7. Brand Lifebuoy straddles the Indian soap market and no one can dislodge it. Ethically, which model can you come up with to compete with Lifebuoy soap?

Going Further . . .

- Collect outsiders (common folk living close to your company or institute) who are equal in number to those in your group.
- Put into practice the suggestions offered by the local people in the group.
- Build a tradition to continue what you have started.

ETHICAL DEVELOPMENT PROGRAMME

Management Training

Integral Marketing

Identify a small successful business from your own native place. Analyse its strategy. Develop this strategy on the principles of integral marketing. Test it to see whether it can economically empower the customers.

Market Strategy: War Game

Requirements

(a) Objective: To win fairly in a warring marketing situation.
(b) People: At least three groups with the basic following group division (or more, if there are more members)
  (i) Product manager (leader for research, product development, and positioning/competition)
  (ii) Marketing manager (strategist for pricing and packaging)
  (iii) Ad manager (strategist for ads and labelling)
  (iv) Promotion manager (strategist for launching and promotion)
(c) Identify a single product for marketing.
(d) War strategies:

  (i) Defensive marketing
  (ii) Offensive marketing
  (iii) Guerrilla marketing
  (iv) Flanking marketing
  (v) Or any variations of war strategies
(e) How to play? The game is real. The area of operation should be specified to the nearest town or city or part of it. The customer number must be fixed at 100. All the groups will deal with only these 100 identified customers. The time period of the game is five days only.
(f) The participants will file their detailed report to the coordinator.
(g) The coordinator, who had earlier on made an appraisal form and given one to each of the targeted 100 customers, will collect and collate the report and declare the choice made by the customers.

Quiz

Relationship Marketing Development

(a) Relationship marketing is about
  (i) Business-to-business marketing.
  (ii) Direct response marketing campaign.
  (iii) Point of sale transaction.
  (iv) Acquisition of new clients.

(b) Philosophy of relationship marketing ethics is called:

   (i) Ethical transcendentalism

   (ii) Creative ethics

   (iii) Ethics of care

   (iv) Ethical behaviourism

(c) The objective of relationship marketing is

   (i) To build a community of manufacturers, suppliers, service providers, and customers in a mutual and satisfying relationship so as to earn, grow, and retain the concerned businesses.

   (ii) To obtain customer loyalty by offering incentive-oriented schemes.

   (iii) To position products competitively, cultivate select customers, and dedicate to serve them exclusively.

   (iv) To create a monopoly of the products and services, so that the customers are not confused by a surfeit of substandard choices or plagued by the bad decisions taken.

Answers

(a) (ii); (b) (iii); (c) (i)

Marketing Awareness Programme

(a) Carefully draw up an awareness programme that is about ethical/unethical marketing for children's food.

(b) Conduct seminars for local manufacturers and dealers.

(c) Generate ideas for better practices and bigger profits.

Management Mantra

Snow Turns to Gold

'It was the best purchase ever made', said Richard Nixon about Alaska. That it was purchased by the US from the Russian empire is common knowledge. However, what is not so commonly known are the circumstances of this largest land sale deal in the world. A massive 17,17,854 sq. km. real estate was bought for a paltry sum of $7.2 million in 1867. Western Union Company was constructing electric telegraph lines that ran from California up the coast of North America to Alaska and beyond. The company had to go across the Bering Strait that divides the American continent from Russian Asia and establish a connection till Moscow. The work was stopped because the Russians thought the project was not worth its while. The Americans saw this as a great opportunity. Hence, the then Secretary of State, William Seward, was sent to negotiate with the Russians to fund and complete the project on their side. The Russians, to whom Alaska belonged, were smart and thought that the land would be run over by the Americans and Canadians and that it was appropriate to dispose off a land considered as frozen and useless. To make the deal even smarter, they realized that there were now two competitive buyers—Canada and the US. So they tried to play one against the other to raise their stakes. However, the Canadians showed no interest because they thought that this arctic region was useless. The deal was finally sealed between Russia and the US.

To the utter consternation of both the Canadians and the Russians, Alaska has become a treasure trove. Among other innumerable riches, it has the prized gold and oil.

MANTRA   *Know your opportunity.*

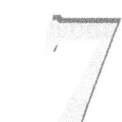

On the Billboard

Advertisements are now so numerous that they are very negligently pursued, and it is therefore become necessary to gain attention by magnificence of promises, and by eloquences sometimes sublime and sometimes pathetic.

—Samuel Johnson

It is insight into human nature that is the key to the communicator's skill. For whereas the writer is concerned with what he puts into his writings, the communicator is concerned with what the reader gets out of it. He therefore becomes a student of how people read or listen.

—William Bernbach

LEARNING OBJECTIVES

After studying this chapter, you will be able to

➤ Discuss about advertising and communication decisions
➤ Understand the exploitative nature of advertising
➤ Differentiate between culture and ad-culture
➤ Understand the lessons from nature

INTRODUCTION

Advertising is the lingua franca of marketing, used for communication between marketers and consumers. An adman's decision on what to say and when and how to depict it forms a complicated moral dimension.

Ads can be hilariously ironical. The pug of the Hutch/Vodafone advertisement is so cute that the market for pugs has skyrocketed. Little children like the pug in the Hutch/Vodafone ad and want a similar one. The pester power of children is so strong that parents are left with no choice but to forego the mobile phone and buy them a pug. The Hutch/Vodafone mobile phone market could have equally grown with some other intelligent advertisement. The product ambassador, although a pug, has became a product himself. But the company is not complaining because it believes that it has endeared itself to the people; neither are the pug breeders complaining, because someone is doing free marketing for them.

However, there is a group of people who are severely complaining about the ad. An animal protection group from Chennai served a notice to the company for causing trauma and distress to the animal: the dog was shown running behind a school bus for a very long time. Ethical questions are no more just about how people behave with each other. Ethics now extends to the treatment of animals too. Ethical sensitiveness has extended not merely to relationships among humans, but also to their relationship with animals and the environment. In such a highly sensitive, ethically developed world, advertisement ethics has serious consequences for the way we do business.

Advertising is akin to the mating season in nature. It is as enthralling as a dancing peacock, as enchanting as a cuckoo's song, as aggressive as a tiger, as absorbing and as entwining as a slithering snake, as cunning as a fox, and as colourful as a chameleon displaying and camouflaging its numerous colours.

Advertising is marketers' way of communicating with customers. An advertisement communicates information and explanation of the goods and services available for the customers. It makes its language attractive and appealing. It shows images that are attractive and alluring. It employs all the five human senses of perception, namely, the sense of smell, taste, touch, hearing, and vision in its communications with its subjects.

It is not uncommon for marketers to employ advertising strategies based on the advice and expertise of ad agencies. These agencies are not really concerned about whether the ad is good or bad for the business. Their interest is to create a product for the business. The ads that they put out need not bring in customers. Ads are nothing but messages to the customers. The right message to the right people will bring a response.

As is the case often, some of the outrageous advertisements could give rise to controversy and generate reams of news and serious debates. This then becomes a social issue in itself. Sexually oriented ads may cause voyeurism, and ads hurting the religious sentiments of the people and abusing their social practices may result in anger or even public outburst. But the moot question for the marketer is whether or not an advertisement has convinced customers to buy the product. It is also seen that good ads—tasteful and artistic in nature and at the same time clearly conveying the product message—are the ones that stay around for a long time. They even become classic customer communication. The Lifebuoy soap ad is one such ad that has been around since the launch of the product, and its jingle has been hummed for generations.

Ethicists often discuss a particular ad and pass their judgment. The adman remains aloof. It would be of importance to know what goes on in the mind of an adman. After all, it is the creator of the ad who must be responsible for its contents. Advertisement ethics must be focused on the ad creator, just as writer ethics on the writer. In this chapter, therefore, we will look into the case of a famous adman, William Bernbach.

ADVERTISING AND COMMUNICATION DECISIONS

An advertisement is communication in the public domain. Just as a media publication has to take care of what it is going to print or broadcast, so also a marketer has to do serious decision making about what it chooses to put up on the billboard. The ethical value of truth is at stake in communication.

Advertising as Information

An advertisement communicates information to potential customers about the goods and services offered by the marketer. An advertisement persuades customers to buy. However, most of the time, what we see is only the persuasion part. For instance, when floating a public issue, companies and financial institutions put out interesting and innovative commercials on television. The commercials invariably end in a super-fast reading of the investment risks involved and the need for customer discretion. This information is statutory. But marketers do not want to waste on ad time and get admen to complete the task in five seconds.

Similarly, the instruction manuals supplied with consumer products, machinery, technical instruments, and banking and investment products are well detailed. Statutory product information goes on the label. This information, for whatever it is worth, is in fine print. It lists the ingredients with percentages, manufacturing date, expiry period, how to dispose the product, some slogan, and a warning about the risks involved in using the product.

The price, of course, is the bottom-line for customers. The ultimate selling point of any product is its price. Advertisers have innumerable tricks up their sleeves to deceive customers. Some of them are as follows.

Types of deceptive pricing

(a) Hidden fees and surcharges such as undisclosed service charges, activation charges, installation charges, taxes, accessories, and several other ingenious ones.

(b) Rebates are given by the manufacturer as a direct benefit to the customer. Factory rate, sale, discount, etc. are recovered through sales tax and other surcharges not disclosed earlier on.

(c) Inflated prices are slashed and reduced prices are shown. This is nothing but blatant lies.

(d) Sale! Sale! Sale! These signs beckon customers. Some establishments are on perpetual sale. Garment shops in India employ other tricks—exhibition cum sale, export quality, export excess, and export rejects—in which one cannot make out defects.

(e) Psychological pricing is done by reducing just a digit, e.g., Rs 99 scores a psychological advantage of not being Rs 100. In car prices, it makes an enormous visual and mental difference. The price of a car shown as Rs 3,99,000 looks much less than Rs 4,00,000.

(f) Freebees offered along with a product attract many customers. A toothpaste, with a toothbrush free, or a soft drink in a 2-litre bottle, with 300 ml extra or gratis, as well as 'buy one get one free' are other alluring terms to attract customers. Sometimes it goes in percentages that are anywhere from 10 per cent to 50 per cent, and may be even more.

(g) Bait and switch is literally to bait or tempt a customer with the promise of a highly reduced price item, and when the customer arrives, he/she is told that the item is already out of stock and is then persuaded to switch to a similar item.

(h) Other forms of price lowering frauds are introductory offers, promotional price, distress sale, MRP not at the rate of X price but offer price, etc.

Advertising as Public Relations

Advertising is to give a clarion call to the consumers in an attractive way. Advertisers decide on the image and logo that will go on the billboard, play on TV, or ride on transport. Very often, advertisers take an image from a world event that has made a great impact. The destruction of the World Trade Towers in New York, known as 9/11 because of the month and date it occurred on, is the most dramatic terrorist act ever committed. Starbucks, the coffee giant, tried to exploit this image by placing two large glasses of iced coffee, towering over the sketches of the city, with the slogan 'Collapse into Cool'. The public took offence to it and the media castigated it. The adman in charge of the campaign had shown utter disregard to the thousands who had died and crass insensitivity towards such a ghastly event. The adman had made an imprudent decision, and Starbucks had showed callousness and lack of appraisal by taking out the ad. The ad succeeded in generating not only aversion, but also distaste and repugnance.

It is, therefore, very important to understand the perspectives of the people from different cultures. One cannot alienate the people and succeed in selling a product. Public relations is the most important factor in communication. Controversial ads may generate media controversy, and an adman may mistake the volume of controversy for popularity. This is a terrible blunder. The fundamental principle of the maintenance of public relationship is courtesy and respect for public norms and sentiments. Starbucks apologized, but the damage was done. The company cut a very sorry figure in public relations. While the financial meltdown of 2008 relatively affected fast food companies like McDonalds, Starbucks had to close down several hundreds of establishments.

Advertisement Dilemma

The greatest dilemma in ads is that what the marketer thinks is a justifiable persuasion, the critics—the media, the moral guardians of society, the law—perceive as misleading, false, and deceptive.

The growth of the advertisement industry in India is encouraging. As the middle class grows, so does consumption. The greater the number of consumers, the greater is the market share for advertisers. It is an approximately Rs 20,000 crore colossus. In 2008, TV ad volumes grew by 23 per cent (in seconds), radio ads grew by 12 per cent (in seconds), and print ad volumes grew by 5 per cent (column centimeters) as compared to the previous year. Despite the global financial meltdown, the industry experienced only a 10 per cent slowdown.[1] The global advertising market is worth hundreds of billions in US dollars. The share of the advertisement industry in the US alone amounts to approximately $200 billion.

The advertisement industry is serious about its business and cannot afford to lose its large market by antagonizing the public. The personnel at the ad creating agencies often miss this big picture. Their personal whims and fancies leak through their creativity, and they are able to convince their clients of the speculated quality and power the ads have to reach out to customers. Problems crop up when the ads backfire, and both the marketer and the ad agency suffer. Both lose their customers and this has an adverse impact on the entire business. Therefore, it is important to make the right decision, both commercially and socially, to be most effective in persuading customers.

Joshi's Secret

Learning from everyday experience

When the Tata Indicom mobile phone ad hit the market, it was a euphoric sale for the company. The protagonists in the ad were the famous film actors from Bollywood, Ajay Devgan and Kajol, who said the most elementary thing about phones, 'Phones are for talking.' It may have been the most naïve thing to say, but the truth couldn't be more simple. Prasoon Joshi, the creator of this ad, is a young and successful adman. He admits that the inspiration for the ad came from his driver, who wanted his advice on which mobile phone to buy. The poor man wanted no fancy stuff; he just wanted a phone to make calls. Joshi hung on to the basic need that was expressed so simply by the driver, and expressed it in his ad. It became the wish of millions of people like that driver.

Joshi observes his immediate surroundings and the people keenly for inspiration. He watches the simple and poor people of India very carefully and listens to what they say. He saw a man drinking water from a mug by holding it high, so that the stream of water poured directly into his mouth. This is the way the people in the villages drink water from pitchers and tumblers. It is a natural process and you have to hold your head backwards in order to drink something that is poured from above. 'Piyo sar uthake' (hold your head high and drink) was the slogan he wrote for one of the most successful ads for Coca-Cola. The slogan gave such a boost to one's emotions of pride and self-esteem that it made the customer feel good.

Questions

(a) What makes Joshi a successful adman?
(b) What ethical values does he employ for his ads?
(c) What is the responsibility of a copywriter?

Source: Shyama Majumdar, http://rediff.com/money/2005/oct/19inter1.htm.

---

[1] See http://economictimes.indiatimes.com/News/News_By_Industry/2008_A_mixed_bag_for_Indian_advertising/articleshow/3938966.cms.

EXPLOITATIVE NATURE OF ADVERTISING

Upon reflection, it would seem that there is an inherent exploitative element in advertising. If we watch nature carefully, we see that animals as well as plants attract and allure their mates or prey with a great deal of deception and camouflage. Human nature is no different. When it is a matter of persuasion, people adopt friendly, aggressive, sociable, exclusive, forceful, insistent, persistent, and violent methods. Some of these approaches are good, while others are not. Some marry through courtship and falling in love, while others marry through some social arrangement, and yet others marry through coercion. Advertising is also a social activity for commercial ends. Ethical problems arise depending on what means the advertiser uses in order to attract and persuade customers. The principle in advertising is that the means used must justify the end. Ads whose means are not fair and justifiable are exploitative in nature. The exploitation extends not only to the ultimate stakeholders, who are the customers, but also to other competitors, shareholders, investors, and society at large. Following are some examples of false and exploitative advertising.

Exploitative Advertising

Disclosure

It is the duty of the marketer to disclose the truth about the product. Nondisclosure of unfavourable information is common in the food and pharmaceutical industries, where the risks involved are not disclosed or partially disclosed, to fulfil statutory obligations. Deciding not to disclose complete product information can endanger the health of the customers.

Insufficient research

In order to stay ahead in competition, companies have very little time for the research results of their products. The cosmetic industry has to take extreme care to ensure the safety of its personal grooming products and, therefore, needs careful research. Talcs and perfumes, creams and oils, soaps and shampoos are used directly on the body. Some people are allergic to certain chemicals. Insufficient or flawed research may result in permanent damage.

Product disparagement

This consists of belittling and vilifying the competitor's product. This is done through a comparison chart that ticks those features that the competitor's product lacks. From cars to detergents, this phenomenon is commonplace. It clearly infringes the rights of the competitor and puts the genuine customer in a quandary about the choice to be made. Some of the comparisons shown are so miniscule that the difference is completely negligible, since it is not going to affect either the quality or the quantity of the product. Such advertisements are outright malicious. These advertisements also start an unsavoury advertisement war and end up harming all the competitors.

Trademark infringement

This consists of aping a brand trademark, sometimes with very insignificant and perceptibly negligible difference. For instance, the brand name Sony is slightly modified, with one of the letters written with a slant or colour variation. The ingenuity of stealing trademarks in China and India are phenomenal. There is a very high rate of litigation in this field and very often, smart lawyers are able to win cases for their clients. Hence, the deception continues.

Parody

It consists of an imitation of any popular phenomena, such as drama, religious icons, characters, or storylines from blockbuster films, public figures, popular programmes and the like. However, these can be caricaturized and trivialized to such an extent that they become obscene and objectionable. Printing religious symbols and names of gods and goddesses on products such as underclothing is a consequence of such parodies. Lampooning of competitors' products with the bad characters from epics is another such distortion. Such advertisements have sometimes offended public sentiments, even resulting in riots and loss of lives.

Remedies for Exploitative Advertising

Remedies for deceptive advertising lie in various approaches such as public protest, recourse to law, and monitoring and control by statutory or voluntary bodies that oversee the activities of marketers and advertising agencies. In India, consumers have all the above choices. Several political parties, social activists, and NGOs also provide a collective voice to consumers. Following are some of the remedial measures.

(a) Complaints to the authorities or agencies that deal with consumer problems brings quicker relief than immediate recourse to law. However, the law is helpful in case of stay orders. This may be needed in areas such as heavy engineering, construction, and heavy machinery, where capital investment is huge.

(b) Each country has its own consumer courts service that deals with general goods and services, and is able to redress quickly. Consumer courts are also competent in dealing with the false claims of advertisers.

(c) Consumer groups and NGOs dealing with consumer woes also deal with unacceptable and offending advertisements.

(d) Public apologies by the concerned firms for unethical ads and the recall and correction of such ads is the duty of the concerned company.

(e) Damages and compensation, if need be, must be paid by the companies as directed by the authorities or the groups responsible such as advertising councils.

CULTURE AND AD-CULTURE

An advertisement is a reflection of the local culture. We notice this when we travel out of our state or country. We encounter the language, the images of the people, their

---

Pricing War Story

Starbucks versus McDonalds

This is a little ad story of two food giants of the world and the price of their prized coffee brew.

McDonalds introduced coffee and charged $1.99, $2 and a cent less than its competitor Starbucks. The message was crass and direct and suggested not to waste money at Starbucks when one could have double the quantity for the same price at McDonalds. Some took it as fun, while others took it as an insult, depending on which fan blog one clicked. One blogger reacted by saying that Starbucks had been unfair to its customers by charging such a high price and blamed the misfortunes and closures of its establishments on fleecing its customers. At the same time, another blogger who supported Starbucks, praised the superior quality of its coffee and its unique experience in taste.

Questions

(a) Is there an ethical problem here?

(b) If you were a shareholder of Starbucks, how would you react to the above story?

(c) If you were a shareholder of McDonalds how would you defend the company?

Source: Laura Petrecca, Theresa Howard, and Bruce Horovitz, 'Ad Track: McDonald's adds expresso as adds taunt Starbucks', *USA Today*, http://usatoday.com/money/advertising/adtrack/2008-12-14-ad-briefs_N.html.

---

customs, their social and cultural vestiges, the new trends among the young, the habits of the old, the role of various actors in society such as women, children, men, and scores of other facets of life portrayed on the billboards, hoardings, and the various media.

When an ad goes up, it is indeed like a company putting forward its credentials for a job. There are several who apply but the people choose only one. The ads tell the people the way these companies would like to serve them. Each company tells them, in the most attractive way possible, why they must choose its products or services over its competition. The choice, at least in the beginning, is influenced by the advertisement. The people will choose, but how long they will employ the company depends upon its usefulness to them. There are some positive steps that may be taken to be both good and successful.

Cultural Consequences of Advertising

An advertisement is a statement meant to highlight the product. But these statements are neither created nor publicized in vacuum. They form the bulk of our mass media, and thanks to advertising, the public enjoys the benefits. One of the economic consequences of advertising is that the businesses layout a large percentage of their earnings as budget for advertising. As a result, the mass media such as newspapers, the radio, television, and the Internet are able to give us programmes that are almost free. Newspapers and TV channels charge the public very little because their real revenue comes from advertising.

However, whatever is played out in the mass media has a profound effect on society. There is constant dilemma. On the one hand, the paymasters of the mass media are the advertisers; on the other hand, the opinion makers in society are the mass media. Who would the mass media listen to? Would they reflect the views of society or promote the commercial values of their clients? The following are some of the effects on the social and cultural lives of the people.

Ads promote consumerism   Ads are made to sell goods and services, but they do it in a manner that goes beyond fulfilling human needs. They become successful in creating a need and demand, making it fashionable to have their products and services. Consumerism is the desire to buy a product not out of need, but to satisfy ego and possess it as a status symbol.

Ads cause price hike   Companies set aside quite a substantial budget for ad campaigns, which has to be realized through the revenues from sales. Hence, the higher the expenditure on ads, the higher the price of the goods or services in question. This upsets the lifestyle of the people and causes hardships, which further deteriorates into social conflicts.

Ads target children   Baby food and milk products bring in large revenues. One of the consequences has been that breast feeding children, which is medically the best, has nearly become extinct. Such is the power of advertising that the child is weaned away at birth from its natural source of nourishment. This has caused enormous health hazards, economic loss, and distress to the people.

Ads have fundamentally changed our society   There are two special pillars of our society—politics that governs the civic life of the people and religion that exercises both secular and spiritual influence on the people. Both these depend heavily on advertising or propaganda. During elections it is all a matter of how one party is able to control and win the media battle. Religious organizations also communicate with the people through the media. Some controversial pamphlets have even generated social hysteria, violence, and mayhem.

Media through advertisement is able to control both our minds and our emotions. It is unthinkable how much our consciousness is shaped by the advertisements and propaganda that are played out round the clock, around the globe, at all times.

LESSONS FROM NATURE

We share our world with animals and plants. We have mentioned that nature persuades animals to either attract preys or attract mates. This is prevalent both in the animal and plant world. What lessons can we learn for advertising from these two coexistent

Amul and the Cultural Revolution

Da Cunha's Little Miss Moppet

Throughout the length and breadth of India, one of the commercial ads that expresses the unity and diversity of the country is undoubtedly the ad for Amul Butter that portrays the cute, delightful, charming, and most endearing moppet called Amul Baby. Just the way Indian films are released every Friday, the Amul Baby ad for Amul Butter appears every Friday, and is based on the leading issue of the week. The visual images are as iconic as R.K. Laxman's *You Said It* cartoons in the daily *Times of India*. The comments are clearly pun intended, but Amul Baby makes it look as smooth as the butter itself, and succeeds in bringing a smile to the viewers/customers lips, across the length and breadth of the country. The ad campaign is being considered for the Guinness Book of World Records as the longest ad campaign.

Sylvester da Cunha, who was running an ad agency called ASP in Bombay (now Mumbai), bagged the offer to create ads for Amul Butter, a product quite staid in

the market since 1945. Da Cunha and his team created the moppet girl with the polka dot dress and a base slogan that read, 'Utterly Butterly Delicious Amul'. The day the ad appeared on the billboards, there were crowds standing under the hoardings, in humorous admiration for the heartwarming, pretty, and sweet moppet. As the ads changed every week, there appeared a theme that highlighted the major events or issues of the country, by giving it a typical 'Amulesque' twist. Some examples are given in Table 7.1.

Table 7.1   Popular Amul Butter ads

Event	Image	Quip
Hare Rama Hare Krishna Movement	Parody of the event.	Hurry Amul, Amul Hurry Hurry.
Dhabol Power Plant Controversy	Two eyes of the Amul Baby in darkness.	Enr on? Or off?
Kargil War between India and Pakistan	Moppet between Defence Minister and Prime Minister on Kargil peak. Amul retain this peak.	Pak up and leave.
The famous Ganesh festival in Bombay	Ganesh festival.	*Ganpati Bappa More Ghya* (pun on the word *morya*, which means praise the deity. Its replaced with *ghya*, which means take more [butter]). Received warning from Shiv Sena, the prominent militant political party.
Film *Cheeni Kum* (less sugar)—the Bollywood megastar Amitabh Bachchan's popular movie	Parody with the actor.	*Cheeni Kum Butter Zyada* (less sugar, more butter).

Contd

Box Contd

The Amul campaign, thus comments on every major event in our country and focuses on all the aspects of the people's lives in a witty and humorous way. It has become an inalienable part and parcel of our popular culture. References to the Amul Baby from households to kindergartens is very common. It is a wonderful conversation topic and also a serious business proposition to the industry.

Source: http://www/amul.com/story.html.

Questions

(a) What importance do you give to cultural assimilation in advertising?

(b) Find out a controversial Amul ad and discuss its ethical implications.

(c) What makes an ad successful?

worlds that we live in? Does nature (plants and animals) teach us some lessons in advertising ethics?

Ethology

Ethics is the study of the moral behaviour (ethos) of humans. Ethology is the study of the behaviour of animals. While humans are rational and intuitive, animals are instinctive. They behave through their inherited tendencies. Their actions do not have moral consequences because they cannot be held responsible for their actions.

Advertisers have found inspiration in animals and use them quite liberally to exploit the emotions that they arouse, such as love and sympathy, aggression and fear, watchfulness and care, and scores of other qualities that we find in animals. The cheetah is used to denote the speed of a car, the eagle to denote the effortless flight of an aircraft, the lion or tiger for macho expressions, cat for femininity, horse for speed and elegance, dove for love, pigeon for communication, elephant for strength, and domestic pets for sympathy and friendship.

Lessons from Animal Kingdom in Advertising

Predation   There are three ways in which animals prey upon their food. First, there are those who attack the prey with great force and aggression. Second, there are those who use skill and deception more than aggression. Third, these are those who use techniques to destabilize their prey.

Very often the media utilizes these predatory practices in the industry. Marketing and advertising is an area where managers seem to take course to the animal strategies of aggression and cunning, and even adopt venomous methods to conquer the turf of the competitors and woo away their customers.

Natural selection versus rational choice   The ad industry, at times, seems to be influenced by natural selection. The animal kingdom develops in a natural fashion and goes through processes to perfect strategies over hundreds of thousands of years. Marketers and advertisers have no such patience, but would like to have the benefits of trapping customers. The deceptive methods of advertising that we have listed all belong here.

Humans have developed natural abilities quite differently than animals. Humans have developed reason as a tool for survival, not only for themselves but for society as well. Society functions on reason, whose products are the values and ethos developed in society and ensured through the rule of law.

The lesson to be learnt from the animal kingdom should be a modified one. It is not natural selection that rules humankind, it is rational choice. Marketers and advertisers have to offer a rational choice to us. Aggression, cunning, and insidious ways will not ensure social rationale of human activities, and business is no exception.

Reproduction versus production strategies   The natural world fulfils its purpose of existence by striving to its natural ends. The animal and plant kingdom has its end in the procreation and propagation of its species. In order to attain its purpose, it has developed some very attractive methods over several millions of years.

Although humans belong to the natural world, they can control their own ends in the society that they have created, through their highly developed reasoning and technological abilities. They too have reproductive tendencies, which they have translated into social customs and certain acceptable and unacceptable sexual behaviour.

Chameleon and the Adman

The united colours of the adman

The chameleon belongs to the lizard family. There are over eighty species in the chameleon family. They change colours according to their environment and respond to temperatures by changing the hues of the colours. The colours are controlled by body chemicals or hormones that affect the pigments in the skin. Chameleons protect themselves through camouflage and use the same to prey upon their prospective food.

Chameleons are used as a symbol or metaphor for the ever-changing behaviour of humans. They have become proverbial because they can camouflage themselves in numerous colours. The proverb 'changing colour like a chameleon' refers to those people who change their opinions to suit the company they are in. They have no fixed views and their behaviour changes according to the situation.

Questions

(a) What are the different ways in which you can use the phrase 'like a chameleon' for managers in general and marketers and advertisers in particular?

(b) As a manager can you afford to be static in your behaviour?

(c) Do moral principles change according to situations?

Note: United Colours of Benetton is an apparel company that steadily puts out controversial ads giving rise to racial and colour controversies; e.g., a black woman breast feeding a white baby.

Peacock

The brand bird of India

Peacock is the national bird of India. Hence, it is not only protected under the law but is also a very intimate part and parcel of our culture, art, and literature. It is a much loved and venerated bird and roams quite freely in the subcontinent, without being harassed. The peacock is the male species of the peafowl; the female is termed a peahen. Because of its beauty, people generally take the peacock to be a female and often refer to it as 'she'.

The peacock is a riot of colours. It has a metallic greenish-blue neck and breast, purplish-blue underbody, and unusually long tail feathers that are aptly called the train, because they resemble the train of a bridal gown. The feathers are in various shades of green and blue and are brilliantly marked with bold spots of dark blue that are in the shape of eyes. These have inspired painters and poets alike. Since the feathers are large, they grow from the back (and not from the tail) to give them added support and strength. During courtship, the feathers are spread in a large, shimmering half-moon of dazzling colours before the peahen, in a tantalizing dance. It is an unforgettable and enduring sight, even to an untrained and unaccustomed pair of eyes. Its beauty is a supreme joy, and the purpose, which is to recreate the world with a dance, divine!

Questions

(a) In what way can you use the image of a peacock to establish brand India?

(b) How can you use a peacock to describe the human behaviour?

(c) What metaphor does a peacock provide for advertising?

Marketers and advertisers use the sexual tendency, its desirableness, and its attraction in a very big way for their purpose. The use of both male and female sexuality in subtle and obvious ways has raised controversies and ethical debates. Sexuality is one of the essential aspects of humanity, which has been elevated to the institution of marriage, and is interwoven with religious and social customs and given legitimacy through law. Hence, there are limitations for marketers and advertisers in the use or exploitation of human sexuality.

SERIOUS PROBLEMS IN CONTEMPORARY ADVERTISING

Reasons for Problems

Consumerism   The Internet and the mobile phone messaging services have also revolutionized marketing practices. They are not only turning customers' needs into wants, but also into must-buys.

Globalization   India's rapid economic development has brought the world to the local markets in India. Marketers are leaving no stones unturned to get noticed.

Exclusion of the poor   As the middle class of India grows by leaps and bounds, marketers are responding fiercely, without paying any heed to the people below the poverty line.

Market segmentation   Marketing research has unduly concentrated on segmenting the market so that marketers may quickly move in to make quick money.

Main Problems

Exploitation of social prejudices   Ads showing fair-skinned people as smart people because they use a particular whitening cream, or children as being intelligent because they drink some food supplement, are typical examples.

Surrogate ads   Alcohol beverages advertised as club sodas, or cigarette packets marketed as CDs, can circumvent the law, but clearly communicate to the consumer.

Subliminal ads   Manipulating the human psyche through pictures and messages cannot be overtly detected, but can influence the choice-making ability of the consumer and thus create demand.

Predatory pricing   How can one come to terms with the unorganized industry producing unbranded goods that are cheap and easily available? Resort to predatory pricing. This will unbalance the livelihood of the small-scale sector, as well as the traditional, local markets. People have been reacting violently to some of the malls and supermarkets, which seem to have invaded the territory of even fresh vegetables.

False and misleading ads   Ads with models posing as doctors and certifying toothpastes and creams, or portraying themselves as building contractors and certifying electrical goods to be installed in buildings, are totally misleading. The comparative charts of the features of cars with tick markings to show qualitative and quantitative differences with the competitors seem even more preposterous but it does leave an impact, however false, on the customers.

Post-purchase dissonance   'On TV it did not look like this' is a constant complaint made by tele-shoppers. The Internet buying or auctioning too has the same complaints. With only pictures as guides and no tangibility, these goods leave the purchasers livid.

Women   Objectification of women, particularly as sexual beings, is constantly castigated and there is no improvement on this front. Marketers have not liberated themselves; they still believe that sex, or rather, sexed-up products sell.

Children   Children are used in ads and the sentiments towards them have been exploited fully. Psychologists, ethicists, social scientists, and religious leaders have been wary of such exploitations.

Alcohol and tobacco   In India, direct ads on these health-injuring products have been banned, but surrogate ads do remain. The deaths caused due to tobacco-induced cancer are phenomenal. However, there is no estimate of the number of lives and families that are destroyed due to the consumption of alcohol.

Privacy There is a blatant swapping of client information by companies across mobile networks. Consequently, in addition to freebies and add-ons, one is literally bombarded with promotional messages. Companies seem to treat the individual information given by the clients as trivial and deserving of no respect.

Copyright and trademark The violations of intellectual property rights are very high in China, followed by in India. It looks as though a 'tit for tat' has been finally served. The consternation and anger among the big brands and the multinationals is understandable. However, one must realize that two wrongs don't make a right.

SUMMARY

- Advertising is a means of persuasion used by the marketer to communicate with the customer.
- The fundamental ethical principle for an advertiser is to seek justifiable means to achieve the ends of selling.
- The marketer and the advertising agency employed have the responsibility to be truthful in their claims.
- Ethical problems arise due to deceptive advertising, which may antagonize customers.

- Deception, dishonesty, and fraud will eventually recoil on the business and destroy it.
- Advertising is a part and parcel of the modern culture and imparts information about the goods and services available to the members of society.
- Those who do not follow ethics may stumble upon breaking the law, which will punish the guilty. Consequently, the business will suffer.
- Nature teaches advertising to be intuitive, artistic, and aesthetically appealing.

KEY TERMS

Advertising Communication in public domain to persuade customers to buy the goods and services offered by the marketer.

Advertising ethics Moral responsibilities in advertising.

Copywriter One who writes quips, quotes, and slogans in advertisements.

Disclosure Accurate information about a product in the ads.

Parody Ads that imitate persons, literature, a successful drama, or cinema imperfectly to highlight some product or service.

Price deception Concealing the real price through false and misleading information.

Product disparagement Vilification of a competitor's product in ads.

Trademark infringement Violation of brands and trademarks to mislead customers into believing that the product is from a superior company.

CONCEPT REVIEW QUESTIONS

1. What is the nature of communication in advertising?
2. How do ethical problems arise in advertising?
3. Why is it necessary to follow the ethics of advertising?
4. Does advertising fulfil the need for accurate information?
5. How does advertising make an impact on culture?
6. Can we learn advertising ethics from nature?

CRITICAL THINKING QUESTIONS

1. How serious is the problem of advertising ethics in India?

2. How can ethics in advertising improve without the interference of law or statutory bodies?

3. Do the social activists and moral vigilante have a positive role in the behaviour of advertisers?

FURTHER READING

Carl Hamilton, *Absolut: The Biography of a Bottle*, Texere (2002).

Tej K. Bhatia, *Advertising in Rural India: Language, Marketing Communication, and Consumerism*, Institute for the Study of Languages and Cultures of Asia and Africa, Tokyo University of Foreign Studies, Tokyo Press, Japan (2000).

CASE STUDY

The Story of an Adman

Bernbach and the Soft-Sell Revolution

The truth isn't the truth until people believe you, and they can't believe you if they don't know what you're saying, and they can't know what you're saying if they don't listen to you, and they won't listen to you if you're not interesting, and you won't be interesting unless you say things imaginatively, originally, freshly.

Truth Advertising

The most powerful element in advertising is the truth.

Ad 1. For Volkswagen Beetle: There in the wide, wide expanse of space rests a small beetle. Caption: *Think small.*

This ad is completely in contradiction to the American dream, where everything big is beautiful. Bernbach presented a product that emphasized the fact that small was not only beautiful and unobtrusive, but also appealed to the common sense to live within one's means. It presented both a smart and intelligent choice. The car sales shot up by 28 per cent!

Ad 2. There is a picture of a small tray at the back of an aircraft's seat, which shows a plateful of sumptuous food that is ensconced with two pairs of cutlery, a coffee cup, a tea cup, a glass of sherry, and two beautiful glasses of red and white wine, a dessert, crusted bakes and even salt dispensers. On top it reads: 'Loosen your seat belt'; beneath the picture

the caption reads: 'American Airlines to New York'.[a] It is a perfect appeal to one's heart through the stomach, as the adage goes. Its literary meaning is the common sign on the aircraft to fasten or unfasten the seat belt. The derived meaning of the ad is to loosen one's belt in order to enjoy all the goodies that the airline is offering. What would be more tempting than to eat such sumptuous offerings till you reach New York from any part of the world?

Ad 3. Face the Goliath of a market leader with a diminutive David attitude: When you're only No. 2, you try harder.

People are actually sick of the barrage of ads that claim to be the best and number one in what they offer. Is there an honest service provider who says that what is offered is not yet the best, but is trying harder to be the best? It is a sincere appeal about one's imperfection. People accept it unconditionally, since everyone agrees that no one is perfect. However, when people see the effort they readily accept and lend their goodwill.

Analysis Ad 1 characterizes a profound thought defined in a simple manner. Ad 2 declares that food is more basic than the mode of transport. This is also food for thought. Ad 3 depicts the nature of man as striving for perfection, and has the appeal of more adventure than the one in which one has already reached the summit.

---

[a] See http://www.ciaadvertising.org/studies/student/98_fall/theory/weirtz/classic.htm.

Think small

Think small.

Our little car is no longer a novelty.

A dozen college kids don't try to squeeze into it any more.

The guy at the gas station does not ask where the gas goes.

Nobody even stares at its hour-glass shape.

In fact, some of the people who drive our little car don't even think of 32 miles to the gallon as 'going great guns'.

Nor do they think of using five pints of oil instead of five quarts.

They don't think of needing an anti-freeze.

Neither do they hesitate racking up 40,000 miles on a set of tyres.

That is because once they get used to some of the economics, they don't even think about such things anymore.

They are happy that they can squeeze into a small parking spot.

Or renew their small insurance.

Or pay a small repair bill.

Or trade their old VW for a new one.

Think it over.[a]

[a] The caption is written for clarity.

The ads are ethically ennobling and are close to the nature of human thought and everyday life. They reflect life in a positive way. One can see Bernbach the philosopher and humorist behind the ads. The ads succeed in giving a perspective. The customer is pleasantly led to think about where to participate and be a part of what is proposed. Even if one were not to buy the products advertised, one would love to describe what is communicated in the advertisement as though one were relating a story. The ad has suddenly become the talk of the people. This, in other words, has become advertisement by word of mouth, the most powerful method of advertisement in the world.

Bernback believed that 'a great ad campaign will make a bad product fail faster. It will get more people to know it's bad.' Hence, truthfulness about the product is the essence of advertising. The rest, that is, the communication can be taken care of through art and creativity.

Communication Is Advertising

Advertising doesn't create a product advantage. It can only convey it.

Bernbach saw his role of a copywriter strictly as a product communicator. He was careful, despite his fame, not to make advertisement as a product in itself. In other words, he explained that people would buy a product or service not because of the advertisement but because of the desirability of the product itself. The advertisement's role is to communicate effectively the desirability of the product. The American Airlines ad was a treat to the eyes. It communicated to the customer that as far as air travel was concerned, he could trust the company and enjoy a wonderful and wholesome meal; the customer could relax and forget all worries, whatever they might be.

As the 1950s dawned, the advertising industry saw a turning point. Till now the advertisers had adopted a cognitive approach. Bernbach realized that communication is possible at a deeper level through emotions. He was not alone. Leo Burnett and David Ogilvy, who are known as equally big visionaries of the art of advertisement, were his contemporaries.

Just as good literature, drama, and music communicate with the people, so too can advertisement create such masterpieces that people will remember them always. He said, 'Advertising isn't a science. It's persuasion. And persuasion is an art.'

Substance in Advertising

Forget words like 'hard sell' and 'soft sell'. That will only confuse you. Just be sure your advertising is saying something with substance, something that will inform and serve the consumer, and be sure you're saying it like it's never been said before.

Perhaps this is easier said than done. The substance is the truth about the product, and art is the way you put it across to the public. The crux of the matter is to give the customer that which will inform and serve. The Volkswagen ad had both information as well as the substance of information to serve the customer: provoked the customer to think small. The metaphor of small, the car, had indeed very big thoughts on savings, from fuel and oil to mileage and small workshop bills. The big cars, on the contrary, were a big resource drain and pointed towards small thinking. Just a gentle command at the end, 'Think it over', made people really stop for a while and re-think. There was so much food for thought in Bernbach's ads that it is not surprising they became classic examples in advertising.

When the substance lacks and the copy is without the truth, gimmick follows. Bernback advocated, 'No matter how skilful you are, you can't invent a product advantage that doesn't exist. And if you do, and it's just a gimmick. It's going to fall apart anyway.'

Advertising Philosophy

Bernbach was a student of philosophy and he leaned completely on the intuitive nature of man. Observation of human nature and the study of human motivation interested him. He deeply delved in the subject of human emotions, wants, needs, and desires. He cared to understand love, hate, greed, jealousy, etc. and centred his work less on rational analysis and more on the emotional aspect of man.

This genuine interest was expressed in his ads, which were simple, intelligent, appealing, and fresh. People at once realized the inner power that expressed itself in the details. He used plain pictures, taking care of every bit of its detailing, particularly the shades and the shadows. The product, not the advertising, was the centre of his work. The Avis Car Rental ad quite simply expresses the truth about the standing of the company in words as well as in the image of a hand showing two fingers, stating that the company is number two in the business of car rentals but is trying to be the best. The ad was a phenomenal success because it stood the probe of the American psyche that always supported the underdog, a fighter who is not first but is fighting wholeheartedly to be number one.

Professional Ethics

Bernbach was a professional to the core. True to Jewish traditions, duty was his first virtue. His duty to his profession was total, and so was his commitment to his family. He would be at work during the stipulated working hours. The rest of the time was meant for his family. He did his work at his office and did not take work home. He insisted that he is a family man and loved his family. At work, he loved his job. He did perfect justice to his work and his legacy stands testimony to it. He retired as per the regulations, at the age of sixty-five. The company was handed over to professional managers.

He had a clear idea of the world he lived in. He said, 'In this very real world, good doesn't drive out evil. Evil doesn't drive out good. But the energetic displaces the passive.' Good and evil are the forces in the world; they exist because we do. Doing our duty with energy and devotion is more important. He advocated that our actions must exude goodness. All his work succeeded in doing just this. The fundamental ethical principle that he set for himself was, 'Let us prove to the world that good taste, good art, and good writing can be good selling.' All of Bernbach's ads are witness to this thought.

Bernbach was highly sensitive to social issues. He used to be a speech writer for various political leaders, and later became an advisor to many businesses and political leaders. He understood the need for social responsibility. He said it very succinctly, 'All of us who professionally use the mass media are the shapers of society. We can vulgarize that society. We can brutalize it. Or we can help lift it onto a higher level.'

Bernbach's ethical philosophy consisted of the following tenets:

(a) Perform your duty with heart and soul.

(b) Let good taste, good art, and good writing be your motto.

(c) Be intuitive.

(d) Be responsible to society.

(e) Look after the family.

Exemplary Life

William Bernbach was born on 13 August 1911 in New York, to a Jewish family. He graduated from the New York University and worked as a clerk in a company called Schenley. In his free time, he created some advertising concepts. The chairman of the company noticed his talent and he was hired by the same company as their adman. He joined Grey Advertising Company in 1945, after he had done his duty in World War II. He moved with his colleagues Ned Doyle and Mac Dane and formed the ad agency Doyle Dane Bernbach (DDB) in 1949 and ran it successfully. The company had a meteoric rise with classic ads, such as Levy's Bread with Indian children, the 'torn ocean', a non-stop flight for the Israeli airliner El Al, the Volkswagen ad, the Avis ad, etc. The company of the three colleagues remained successful until it went public in 1960. In the 1970s, the competition was eating into the clients of DDB and as the 1980s dawned, DDB lost all its good and faithful clients. Bernbach resigned as president and the corporation was taken over by professional management.[b] Bernbach had earned for himself the name of 'Poster Boy of Advertisement'. There were innumerable awards showered on him and he figured in the Copywriters' Hall of Fame. His advice was much sought after by businesses, as well as political establishments. He served on the boards of several public and private organizations.

---

[b] For a present status of the company, visit http://www.ddb.com/.

Bernbach did not live to see further turmoil in his company, as he died in 1982. David Ogilvy, one of the most successful contemporaries of Bernbach gave testimony to his life, 'He was a philosopher. He lived without ostentation, and organized his time with a self-discipline that is rare among heads of agencies. He once told me that he never stayed in the office after five, never took work home, and never worked at weekends. "You see, David, I love my family."'

Discussion Questions

1. What are the qualifications required for an advertising professional?

2. What are the attitudes that a career advertiser must possess?

3. Bernbach was born during the economic depression and started his career in advertising after World War II. He became a successful copywriter and visionary of images for products and services. What role does one's personal life and ideals play in one's professional career?

4. How should an advertiser evaluate the ethical values of the society he lives in?

5. What is the decision-making process involved while creating an ad?

6. What is your opinion on socially, sexually, religiously, and racially provocative ads?

7. Should ads that are explicitly homosexually oriented be permitted?

8. How is the nudity shown in the ads, viewed in different cultures?

9. In this Internet and globally interactive age, do cultural differences in advertising matter?

10. If you are the minister for mass media, how would you regulate advertising in India?

Going Further . . .

A. Choose one of Bernbach's ads:

Have a panel discussion with a group of not more than six persons.

Let each person in the panel represent a different culture and country.

B. Choose an ad of your liking:

Follow the two steps as mentioned above.

C. Create an ad:

Discuss inputs.

Decide what goes in the ad.

Give reasons.

Anticipate cultural and legal problems.

Discuss ethical principles.

D. Make the ad:

Send it for evaluation to an ad agency and get its reaction, e.g., Advertising Agencies Association of India (AAAI).

ETHICAL DEVELOPMENT PROGRAMME

Management Training

As a manager, you will need to make an ad appraisal before you decide to approve an ad for your company. Follow the training steps given below with the help of your instructor:

(a) Apply a suitable ethical principle in each case and write a brief appraisal for them.

(b) Check legal, social, religious, and cultural aspects to assess the acceptability of the ad by the public.

(c) Make a SWAT analysis for the commercial success by suggesting changes and corrections in the ad.

(d) Create an alternative ad and explain its suitability.

Quiz

Advertising Standards Council of India (ASCI)[2]

Go through the cases in Table 7.2 of advertisers, the complaints against them, examine the claims

---

[2] See ASCI at http://www.ascionline.org.

Table 7.2 Certain cases filed against advertisers

Advertiser/agency/ media	Claim/description of ad/TVC	Complaint
1. Axis Bank Ltd (Quick and Easy Personal Loans) Ad printed on their national bill mail service envelope	Ad shows a parakeet picking up a fortune card with the tagline, 'Your wishes are now fulfilled within 48 hours!'	Complainant: Consumer Representational Organization Parakeets are protected under the Wildlife (Protection) Act 1972. The trade and trafficking of these birds is banned, and this includes the caging, displaying, and performance. Any advertisement that uses any kind of animals must have a No Objection Certificate from the prescribed authority, that is, the Animal Welfare Board of India, certifying that the said advertisement has been made in compliance with the Performing Animals (Registration) Rules 2001, framed under the Prevention of Cruelty to Animals Act 1960. Hence, the performance of the bird in the advertisement is in contravention of both the Wildlife Protection Act, as well as the Performing Animals (Registration) Rules 2001.
2. Haier Appliances (India) P. Ltd (Haier ACs) *The Times of India* (27 April 2007)	Claims—'Enjoy 51 per cent power savings', 'Future comfort technology', '… enjoy superior air conditioning', 'Refresh function', 'Intelligent air flow', 'four-stage air filter', 'With the revolutionary digital DC inverter technology', 'Super Ioniser', 'Healthy UV ray generator'.	Claims need to be substantiated with proof, independent data, supporting technical information with details of tests/trials reports from an independent recognised testing institution. Advertiser should prove that other ACs in the market do not have this technology. Advertiser needs to provide proof in support of these claims and also substantiate how these claims can benefit the consumers.
3. Hyundai Motor India Ltd (Hyundai Verna) Ad appeared on company's website	Ad states—Hyundai Verna diesel variant 'CRDI VGT' has a fuel economy of 32.8 Kmpl.	On seeing this advertisement, the complainant purchased the vehicle, under the impression that the vehicle will be economical and will be comparatively cheaper to run. In the one month since the purchase of the vehicle the complainant never measured a fuel economy of over 11 kmpl. The complainant was deceived by this advertisement. Advertiser needs to provide proof in substantiation of this claim.
4. Trent Ltd (Sisley Fall Winter Collection 07) Promotional e-mail	Headline—'You'll melt once inside'. Visual—'a woman in a provocative and seductive pose'.	This advertising should be classified as pornography. Headline, read in conjunction with the visual depiction, appears to be indecent.

Contd

Table 7.2 Contd

Advertiser/agency/ media	Claim/description of ad/TVC	Complaint
5. Kinetic Engineering Ltd (Kinetic SYM Flyte) Publicis Ambience Advertising (*) Auto India (January 2008 issue)	Claims—'it's made by the only two companies that know scooters best—Kinetic and SYM', 'Europe's fastest growing 2-wheeler company', 'Largest 2 Level Storage' 'Our confidence 3 year warranty*, * only for first 10,000 customers'. '4-in-1 magnetic key, for initial customers only'.	Claims need to be substantiated with an independent data. Why is the warranty given only to first ten thousand customers. If the company is confident of its product, it should extend warranty to all customers. Why is the magnetic key given only to initial customers and not to all? The term 'initial customers' appears to be ambiguous.
6. Dabur India Limited (*) (SaniFresh Thick Toilet Cleaner) Ogilvy & Mather (*) *Good Housekeeping* (January 2008 issue)	Headline states—'SaniFresh Thick. The secret of my shiny, silky hair'.	Advertisement that pertains to 'SaniFresh Thick toilet cleaner' projecting itself as a 'hair shampoo'. The advertisement is in bad taste and needs to be withdrawn before any vulnerable teenager actually tries out the product.

and give your judgment. Later, verify it with the actual ruling that the agency gave.

Consequent results

1. January 2008 Chapter III.4. Visual depiction appeared to be performing an act, which was in apparent violation of the Performing Animals (Registration) Rules 2001.

Advertiser assured that the said creative will not be used in any ads.

2. January 2008 Chapter I.1. Claims made in the advertisement and cited in the complaint were not substantiated.

Ad modified.

3. January 2008 Exparte (absence of comments from the advertiser). Chapter I.1. Claim was not substantiated.

Ad discontinued.

4. February 2008 Chapter II. Ad headline, read in conjunction with the visual depiction, is likely to cause grave or widespread offence.

Advertiser assured that ad will be withdrawn, and such ads will not be released again.

5. February 2008 Chapters I.1 and I.4. Claims 'It's made by the only two companies that know scooters best—Kinetic and SYM' and 'Largest 2 Level storage' were not substantiated. Claim of 'for initial customers only' was misleading by ambiguity.

Advertiser assured that ad has been modified.

6. February 2008 Chapter I.4. Visual of 'a lady with lustrous hair', along with the ad headline, is likely to be misconstrued as an advertisement for a 'hair shampoo' and not for a 'toilet cleaner'. Advertisement was misleading.

Ad withdrawn.

Keep in Touch

Join one of the advertising organizations like ASCI. Actively participate in creative foray.

Management Mantra

A Case of Having the Cake and Eating It Too

Richard Branson is a flamboyant businessman from the UK and is known for ostentation. The Tata Group, however, is much staid and demure. The former's Virgin Media tied up with the latter's Tata Teleservices in March 2008. The hybrid that came out was known as Virgin Mobile. The ads in the papers and magazines and on TV and on the billboards screamed, 'Get paid to receive calls.' To the discerning Indian customer, this was an irresistible temptation, and to the Indian youth towards whom the product was targeted, this was a bonanza. For the young and the mobile phone savvy, this offer of endless talk with cronies and less recharge hassles was the wildest dream come true. The offer was that the Virgin Mobile user gets ten paise for every minute of incoming call, irrespective of the originating network. The 'discerning Indian customer' tribe started thinking. One had to get a ten-minute call, in order to collect just one rupee, which is the current rate of a local call in the home network. One had to 'work hard' to pile up ten paise ten times in order to make a single local call. It is no wonder that the market has not shown any customer migration from other networks.

| MANTRA | *Customers enjoy gimmicks but may not take the bait.* |

CHAPTER

Finance and Value

Never ask of money spent
Where the spender thinks it went.
Nobody was ever meant
To remember or invent
What he did with every cent.

—Robert Frost

Any informed borrower is simply less vulnerable to fraud and abuse.[1]

—Alan Greenspan

LEARNING OBJECTIVES

After studying this chapter, you will be able to

> Understand financial accounting and decision making
> Define the financial standards
> State the financial institutional responsibilities
> Describe the capital market and state its regulations

INTRODUCTION

Keeping in mind the Indian business scenario and the developing nature of the economic condition of the country, a manager's social as well as financial responsibility must be handled with sensivity. The fundamental principle of finance is devotion to duty, which translates into the values of truth and trust. All financial dilemmas must be weighed and judged in the light of duty. This principle alone can convey impartiality, dedication, and application, which are required while being responsible to the shareholders and the stakeholders. We will focus our attention on four important themes that are important to an Indian business manager in the discipline of finance management.

---

[1] Alan Greenspan, Ex-chairman of the Board of Governors of the Federal Reserve Systems (1987–2008).

EARLY HISTORY OF FINANCIAL SCAMS

Holland is the land of tulips and to think that tulip bulbs could be the medium of exchange sounds more romantic than real trading. It is a fact of history that in 1634, there was the so-called tulip mania, a pyramid investment scheme in Amsterdam. Tulip bulbs became the craze of speculation and could be bartered for mansion houses. Although the scheme was not as sophisticated as the ones today, with regulators in place and other players who entice people into the scheme, it was a craze hard to describe. The fact that the dreams of the Dutch of using tulip bulbs as a system of barter crashed in just four years and thousands of people lost their money has not taught the following generations any lesson. The tulip business had crashed by 96 per cent. The Dutch nation was shrouded in gloom. The future of tens of thousands of families and their children was doomed.

The public keeps getting lured into the make-belief world of making quick money despite repeated and disastrous failures. The public would like to trust just one more time. The longest pyramid investment scheme, which lasted for seven years, originated in Israel.[2] No one thought that the Israeli banks could ever go bankrupt. The banks offered their own shares to the public. That the price of the shares went up by 2 per cent on a daily basis made the public dream beyond its imagination. The mind-boggling scheme was kept aloft by the banks through the money of more depositors, profits, and even borrowings from abroad. The finance ministry also fell for it and the government supported it wholeheartedly. In October 1983, the house of this mythical Midas touch of a scheme was shattered. The civil unrest that followed could have torn the small country apart. The government of Israel was forced to bail out the banks with a whopping $6 billion.

Investors are often lured into high-yielding schemes that do not materialize because the monies cannot be invested and the yields are harvested very quickly. But the investors are impatient and they need to be paid through the money received from the other investors who are rushing in, or through borrowings. The day of reckoning dawns when the investors cannot be paid for lack of funds. Investors privy to the inside information of the scheme would have withdrawn their investments when the profits were at peak. Others suffer losses.

Financial schemes that turn into financial scams are permeated into the fabric of society and destroy not only wealth, but also the lives of the public. Individuals lose money, families lose livelihoods, and the nation stands in peril. Financial scams are the scourge of society.

However, it is the corporations that have been accused of cooking up the accounts and causing inestimable damage to the businesses and to society at large. The accounts, capital, funds, credit, banking, fiduciary responsibilities, budget, audit, due diligence, salary of the executives, securities, investment, equity, shares, mortgage, bonds, financial instruments, and scores of other themes form the science of managerial finance.

---

[2] See http://www.crowdedsite.com/news-media/article2893.htm.

Finance management is the core of business management. All the decisions that a manager takes finally boil down to financial matters. It is not an exaggeration if it is stated that no other discipline of management is crowded with as many ethical dilemmas as that of finance. Managers, as agents of their principals, have a well-defined fiduciary relationship with their principals. The brief of managers is to make profits for the principal and thus add value to shareholders. Ethicists, on the other hand, think that managers have broader social responsibilities. The shirking of their professional and social responsibilities have caused not only scams like the ones that took place at Enron and WorldCom, but also the total collapse of the developed economies of the West in the so-called global financial meltdown of 2008.

India perhaps grosses the highest number of investment schemes and financial scandals. Chit-funds, small and big lotteries, plantation plans, co-operative banks, derivatives, public work contracts, pay backs in defence deals—even coffins are not spared—and a myriad other schemes and methods of making a quick buck lure people to part with their money and it is eventually lost. Then, there is the entire parallel economy of black money, the unaccounted, untaxed, liberally laundered wealth that is used for corrupt practices by politicians for elections and for funding terrorists and separatist activities.

FINANCIAL ACCOUNTING

Financial Dilemma—Rational Maximizer Paradigm

The principal assumption of the agency theory is that the agent acts professionally in the interest of the principal. The corollary to this assumption is that the agent acts rationally in the mission of seeking to maximize self-interest. Although the principle of self-interest is supreme, the rational maximizer paradigm allows for rationalization in the interest of both the agent and the principal. The dilemma lies in the fact that as a manager, would one be able to sacrifice self-interest for the sake of the principal? If the answer is not in the affirmative, then the paradigm is of no consequence. Thus, it is clear that this concept militates against the basic nature of safeguarding one's own interests. Hence, it is not viable. The need is for a conceptual framework that allows for managerial accountability, primarily in matters of finance.

Accounting—Language of Business Decision Making

Accounting may be defined as a body of principles and conventions, as well as an established general process for capturing financial information related to an entity's resources and their use in meeting the entity's goals. Accounting is a service function that provides information of value to all operating units and to other service functions, such as the headquarters of a large corporation.

Accounting answers two questions: what and how. The 'what' aspect concerns itself with the various branches of accounting such as audit, financial statement analysis, financial accounting, cost accounting, not-for-profit accounting, and financial planning.

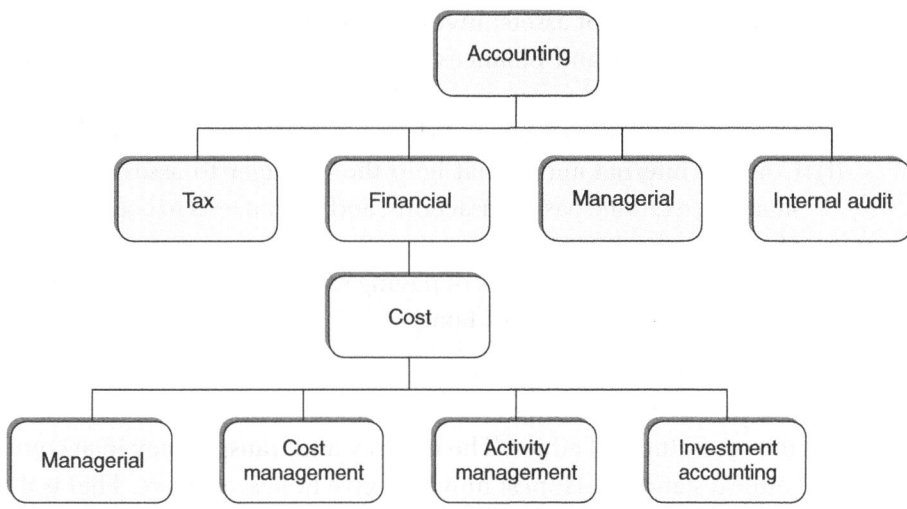

Fig. 8.1   Classification of management accounting

The how aspect deals with the various processes involved in accounting such as book-keeping, measuring, interpreting, communicating financial data, preparing financial statements, and tax planning. See Fig. 8.1.

The subject matter of accounting consists of an accounting unit or entity, which consists of a value exchange transaction or its prediction. The information that is generated is recorded, analysed, and reported. An entire network of information and logical analysis is possible from the financial data generated. This data is used by the manager as the bedrock for financial decision making.

Accountants—Professionals Who Help in Decision Making

Accountants are professionals who deal with accounts and supply managers with the information they need. The ethical aspect of an accountant cannot be underlined enough. An accountant is expected to have a background in economics, statistics, mathematics, law, language, and behavioural sciences. The duties of accountants consist of accumulating the financial facts, estimates, and forecasts, and converting this data to assist the managers in taking financial decisions for the company.

Data collection begins with the traditional book-keeping. Computerization aids in the quick and efficient supply of data. Accountants customize the accounting system to suit the firm's needs in taking financial decisions. Accordingly, a manager is able to take decisions about obtaining resources, organizing operations, and maintaining control. It helps the manager in dealing with employees, investors, creditors, and other stakeholders. It also helps the manager to make both investment and credit decisions.

The accounting system provides the manager with control over the functioning of the firm. It helps to

(a) Implement the policies of the firm and follow the law of the land.
(b) Maintain accounts accurately.

(c) Monitor the use of assets; invest idle money, etc.

(d) Exercise checks and balances to reduce chances of losing assets or incurring liabilities.

(e) Check fraudulent activities, dishonesty of employees, suppliers, etc.

(f) Conduct internal audits that help the manager to assess the current financial situation, examine past transactions, and submit tests to countercheck the veracity of ongoing business.

(g) Conduct the standard tasks of paying salary, provident fund, and other benefits to employees and filing of taxes.

There is no greater and precise standard of morality than the accounting system. Accounting is a perfect mathematical definition of ethics. The correctness of accounts equals the correctness of ethics. The honesty and transparency in accounts reveals the perfect ethical standard. Honest numbers give honest answers. That is the truth. Truth is ethics. The decisions based on truth are always right.

Alan Greenspan

The financial decision-maker

'I have found no greater satisfaction than achieving success through honest dealing and strict adherence to the view that for you to gain, those you deal with should gain as well.'

The above quote from Alan Greenspan (2007) is being true to himself. He is one who believed that the decisions he took for his country's economic policies, which also affected the rest of the world, were taken with an objective towards human happiness. He was a close friend of the famous novelist and thinker Ayn Rand, who advocated that the supreme aim in life is to seek happiness with the most potent human instrument, the power to reason. This philosophy was called objectivism. Greenspan used reason as the core element in his profession as an economist and arrived at decisions through thorough rational processes.

Greenspan's call to public life came in the early 1970s, when he was hired as an economic advisor to Richard Nixon, and later to Gerald Ford. In 1987, Ronald Reagan appointed him as the Chairman of the Board of Governors for the Federal Reserve System. The successive presidents, George W. Bush (Sr), Bill Clinton, and George W. Bush (Jr), confirmed the appointment for their tenures, until he retired in 2006

at the age of 80. The power of his financial decision making was so immaculate that it rose above political loyalties. It was so powerfully convincing that it became indispensable.

Greenspan was a diehard believer of the free-market system. He was wary about inflation. He decried controlling prices but insisted on full employment. He concentrated on inflation, financial market, interest rates, employment, and housing while taking policy decisions.

He came on the scene as the great market crash of 1987 occurred. On the so-called Black Monday in October 1987, the market fell by more than 500 points and over 20 per cent of the wealth of the New York Stock Exchange vanished into thin air. Investors and brokers and institutions lost faith. Insolvency was staring them in the face. There was no money. It was a liquidity crisis. In less than 24 hours, Greenspan was ready with his ominous decision. He said that the Federal Reserve would serve as a source of liquidity to support the economic and financial systems. The market picked up and soared and the Clinton years marked its zenith.

However, the complexities of a free-market economy are very intricate and multifarious, as they depend on

Contd

Box Contd

the decisions made by millions of people. Several million times over, things go seemingly out of control. The dilemma that Greenspan faced was that he was standing against all odds but at the same time had to make policies to control the inflation, the rate of interest, and the budget deficit. The collapse of many federally insured savings and loan institutions was forcing the government to pay out billions of dollars more in the future. Interest rates had to be raised to supplant spending for capital investment in the private sector. On the one hand, future supply productivity was being hampered but demand was also increasing. Economists warned that this trend, popularly known as Reaganomics, since it happened under President Reagan's administration, and the feel-good effect it generated would have disastrous effects in the future. However, Greenspan was confirmed in his post throughout the 1990s, when communism fell and Greenspan's brand of capitalism became the super economic power of the world. There was a widespread feeling around the globe that Greenspan could do no wrong. This was a terrible mistake. He complained that people were making irrational decisions. It was time for him to leave. He left. Markets had reached a point of no return. They started collapsing from all sides. Joseph Stiglitz, a Nobel laureate economist, holds Greenspan responsible for being unwilling to regulate the market. Paul Krugman, another Nobel prize winner for economics, blamed Greenspan for the collapse of housing.

Greenspan penned his biography and named it *The Age of Turbulence: Adventure in a New World*. He advocates unabashed capitalism and believes that it triumphs over all the other systems. People's interests and motivations affect economic decisions. He underlines the importance of education for the success of a free-market. He strongly supports the teaching of mathematics and science for higher standards of living. 'It has been my experience that competency in mathematics, both in numerical manipulations and in understanding its conceptual foundations, enhances a person's ability to handle the more ambiguous and qualitative relationships that dominate our day-to-day financial decision making.'

Greenspan was born in 1926, just on the threshold of the years of depression in America. He became the Chairman of the Federal Reserve just before another economic crisis in 1987, and he retired from his office just before the global financial meltdown in 2006. His philosophy of life may be concluded in his own words: 'I do not deny that many appear to have succeeded in a material way by cutting corners and by manipulating associates, both in their professional and in their personal lives. But material success is possible in this world and far more satisfying when it comes without exploiting others.'

Questions

(a) How important is ethics in financial decision making?

(b) Explain the dynamism of decision making in a free-market economy?

(c) If you were the governor of the Reserve Bank of India, what decision would you take as your first policy decision?

FINANCIAL STANDARDS

Rules pervade all aspects of our lives. Money markets have even more stringent rules. There are standards set both nationally as well as internationally to regulate and standardize financial practices and processes. These rules and regulations are nothing but the norms of applied ethics.

Generally Accepted Accounting Principles

The Generally Accepted Accounting Principles or Processes is generally known by its acronym GAAP. Every country, through the body of chartered accountants, formulates good accounting practices. GAAP includes standards, conventions, and regulations for accountants to follow while preparing financial statements. Following are some salient features of GAAP.

Principle of regularity   There should be conformity to the enforced rules and laws.

Principle of consistency   The same methods should be applied in the prescribed period of time.

Principle of sincerity   The financial statement of the company should reflect its true and real financial status.

Principle of permanence of methods   There should be coherence in financial statements published by the company.

Principle of non-compensation   There should be a complete declaration of the entire financial information without compensating debt with an asset, revenue with an expense, etc.

Principle of prudence   One must show the real picture, without altering the financial facts or camouflaging them.

Principle of continuity   The basic assumption is that business will not be interrupted. Thus, assets do not have to be accounted for at their disposal value but at their historical value.

Principle of periodicity   Each accounting transaction must be assigned a date or period. Even split transactions should be noted as and when transpired. For instance, if a client makes pre-payment as in subscriptions, the given revenue should be split for the subscribed time span and not just for the date of transaction.

Principle of full disclosure and materiality   One should report complete information and values pertaining to the financial position of business.

Thus, to conclude succinctly, accountants are responsible for assembling the financial statements scientifically and reporting them objectively. Third parties should be able to rely on such statements and they have a right to be assured that the data is free from bias and inconsistency.

International Financial Reporting Standards

As the GAAP provisions differ from country to country, and as globalization is taking root, a need for an international institution for financial and accounting processes becomes a natural imperative. A body called International Accounting Standards (IAS) was formed in 1973. In 2001, a committee was formed by the name of International Accounting Standards Committee (IASC) by the International Accounting Standards Board (IASB) and it adopted the International Financial Reporting Standards (IFRS), whose acronym is as well known as that of the GAAP.

With the downfall of Satyam, financial auditing came into limelight for all the wrong reasons of non-compliance and accounting frauds. Many experts opine that there is a huge gap between the Indian GAAP and IFRS and that auditors in India certify audits as true without comparing with the actuals. There are only a few cases that come to the media's notice, but most of the run-off-the-mill stories vanish. In 2001, an International Forum on Accountancy Development (IFAD) was formed[3] to have a general oversight independently and to monitor the accounting processes taking place around the globe. The objectives of the forum are

(a) To promote understanding by national governments of the value of transparency in financial reporting in accordance with good corporate governance
(b) To uphold public interest by defining expectations from the accounting profession, whether for the private or the public sector
(c) To encourage governments to focus on the needs of the developing countries
(d) To advance cooperation between governments, accounts professionals, international financial institutions, regulators, etc.

The positive result of the IFAD efforts has been to seek convergence between national and international standards.

Convergence: IFRS and Indian GAAP

IFRS, as has been already mentioned, are standards and interpretations adopted by the IASB and Indian GAAP and are the standards[4] notified by the Union Government under the Companies Act (Accounting Rules 2006 applicable to all companies as per the requirements of the Companies Act 1956). Table 8.1 shows a few points as a comparison of these two standards. It is merely a sample of some compare and contrast features. There are many differences, from assets to amortization and from taxation to financial instruments. However, it is noteworthy that accounting behaviour is regulated both nationally and internationally. The guidelines provided save accountants and auditors from pitfalls and ethical dilemmas.

RESPONSIBILITY OF FINANCIAL INSTITUTIONS

Mutual funds are runners in India, where small investors put in their hard-earned savings and hope to make some money by trusting in the ability and expertise of the fund managers to give them dividends. Unit Trust of India is a Government of India undertaking, and it was not surprising that people had more faith in its schemes than in those of other private financial institutions. This is because government actions are supported by enacted laws. However, in the post-liberalized economy, Unit Trust bungled and failed. In 1999, the government had to bailout the undertaking with a whopping Rs 4800 crore.

---

[3] See www.ifad.net.
[4] See http://www.iasplus.com, a comprehensive website for accounting standards of the world.

Table 8.1 Comparison of IFRS and Indian GAAP standards

Financial statement	IFRS	Indian GAAP
Primary literature	IAS (2007) Presentation of Financial Statements—effective from 1 January 2007.	AS 1—Disclosure of Accounting Policies/Schedule VI to Companies Act 1956. AS 5 Net Profit Loss for the Period, Prior Period Items and Changes in Accounting Policies.
IAS 1	(a) Financial position (b) Comprehensive income displaying components of profit or loss and another statement displaying profit and loss of other comprehensive income (c) Cash flows (d) Changes in equity (e) Summary of accounting policies and explanatory notes Comparative figures are presented for one year; when a change in accounting policy has been applied retrospectively, or items of financial statements have been restated, a statement of financial position is required as at the beginning of the earliest period presented.	As in Schedule VI to the Companies Act 1956; Schedule III to the Banking Regulation Act 1949 (for banks), the regulations issued by Insurance Regulatory and Development Authority (for insurance companies) and the SEBI guidelines (for mutual Funds) together with Accounting Standards notified under the Companies Rules 2006 Accounting Standards. Components: (a) Balance sheet (b) Profit and loss (c) Cash flow (not for small and medium sized companies) (d) Explanatory notes and summary accounting policies Single entity financial statements are required to be presented by all entities. Public listed companies are required to present consolidated financial statements of the parent in terms of the Listing Agreements with the Stock-Exchanges and the SEBI Guidelines.
IAS I Balance sheet	An entity is required to present current and non-current assets and liabilities as separate statements of the financial position, except when a presentation based on liquidity provides reliable and relevant information.	The Companies Act 1956 or the relevant statues prescribe the form and content of the balance sheet and specify the order in which the items are presented, along with the related disclosures. It is neither classified into current and non-current nor is it in order of liquidity.
IAS 1 Classification of financial liabilities upon violation of covenants	Non-current if the lender has agreed before the end of the reporting period to provide a period of grace of minimum 12 months after the reporting period within which the breach can be rectified and the lender cannot demand immediate repayment.	There is no guidance. Generally undisclosed as the payable within 12 months of the balance sheet date if the lender has agreed after the balance date and before the approval of the financial statements not to demand immediate repayment.

Contd

Table 8.1 Contd

Financial statement	IFRS	Indian GAAP
IAS 2 Inventories scope	IAS 2 does not apply to inventories held by commodity broker-traders, who measure their inventories at the fair value. Fewer costs to sell are recognized in profit or loss in the period of the change.	There is no scope exemption in AS 2 for any inventories held by commodity traders. Work in progress arising in the ordinary course of business of service providers has been scoped out of AS 2.
IAS 8 Accounting policies changes in accounting estimates, changes in accounting policies	Requires retrospective application of changes in accounting policies by adjusting the opening balance of the affected component of equity for the earliest prior period presented, and the other comparative amounts for each period presented, as if the new accounting policy had always been applied.	Changes in accounting policies should be made only if it is required by statute, for compliance with an Accounting Standard, or for a more appropriate presentation of the financial statements on a prospective basis, together with a disclosure of the impact of the same material. Also, if a change in the accounting policy has no material effect on the financial statements for the current period, but is expected to have material effect in the later periods of the same, should be appropriately disclosed.
IFRIC 4 Determining whether an arrangement contains a lease	Arrangements that do not take the legal form of a lease but fulfilment of which depends on the use of specific assets which convey the right to use the assets and are accounted for as lease.	There is no such guidance; payments under such arrangements are recognized in accordance with the nature of the expenses incurred.
SIC 32 Website costs	Costs incurred in application, infrastructure development, and graphic design may be capitalized.	Similar to IFRS.

Anatomy of Financial Crisis

When the times were good and the financial markets were roaring with business, the institutions that supported them, particularly the banks, appeared to have such a glut of money that it was impossible not to dream high. Then, there was a crash and a thud and a crunch and a meltdown and all the money vanished. Let us discuss how this vanishing act takes place.[5]

(a) The central or reserve banks have stopped pegging their currencies to the price of gold. So, money has lost its backing in gold. Money's worth comes only because of the promise to honour the said amount. The currency note is a mere promise without substance, that is, an equivalent of stored wealth to backup

---

[5] Based on Paddy Allen's 'Where did all the money go?' See http://gaurdain.co.uk/business/dan-roberts-on-business-blog/interactive/2009/jan/29/financial-pyramid.

Arthur Anderson & Co

Another name for accounting scandal

Arthur Edward Andersen (1885–1947), the founder of Arthur Anderson & Co., must have turned in his grave in 2001, as the auditor firm founded by him became a synonym for shame in the accounting profession. On 15 August 2001, Sherron Watkins, an employee of Enron, in a single-page letter to its CEO, questioned the company's accounting practices. All hell broke loose. By the time December arrived, Enron, the energy giant that ruled the world, bit dust and along with its accomplice, Arthur Andersen & Co., became the ridicule of the world.

In early January 2002, as the US Justice Department began criminal investigations into Enron's bankruptcy, Arthur Andersen admitted to having destroyed incriminating documents. Before the month end, Clifford Baxter, one of the top Enron executives, had committed suicide. The events of the greatest accounting fraud became news fodder for the daily media. Andersen executives, David Duncan and Nancy Temple, were responsible for shredding the evidence.

In 2002, the firm was convicted by the lower and appellate courts. The conviction was for obstruction of justice. The firm had worked hand in glove with Enron and cooked its account books. It had huge and undeserving remunerations for auditing and consulting. The clients of the auditor firm left in droves. The firm that once had an 85,000 strong workforce, now had closed offices and business interests around the globe. In 2005, as the Supreme Court gave the firm reprieve from the lower court's judgement, there were barely 200 employees left. The firm's name is so tarnished, that there is no other business going on in it, other than attending to over a hundred civil suits. The irony is that it is neither dissolved nor declared bankrupt, and exists merely as a zombie.

Questions

(a) What makes auditors give up on clearly stated professional accounting principles?

(b) If you were a manager in Arthur Andersen & Co., would you have realized the fraud you had committed and admitted it?

(c) Why does the history of accounting fraud repeat itself, such as PricewaterhouseCoopers in the case of the Satyam scandal?

and legitimize the money. So, the money soars on promise, creating a huge balloon of trust; all hope against hope that the trust lasts. In case one runs out of money, and needs more and goes to the bank, the central bank can always print some more!

(b) Of course, due to the complexity of trust or credit, there is more money in the market than mere printed currency. Interest rates come in handy for the increase or decrease in the supply of money. Lower interest rates will bring more money in circulation.

(c) Borrowing and lending on interest is the business of a bank. But all clients do not need money at the same time, which allows banks to lend money several times over their reserves. Banks are required to maintain these fractional reserves with the apex bank, for example, the Reserve Bank of India.

(d) Banks on a business spree offer credits and loans for lower interests and increase the debt.

(e) Special investment banks and hedge funds find innovative ways to borrow more and earn more. In the rush for making more money, they lose sight of the safeguards. It is said that the notional value of the derivatives around the globe went close to a thousand trillion US dollars, which is several times the value of the economic activity of all the people on Earth!

(f) Experts have fixed the total economic value of wealth created by humans just a little above a hundred trillion US dollars. Since, the debt bubble is so large, it cannot sustain itself and gets shattered. The world of credit thus has a crash landing.

(g) The entire world economy, despite the presence of such brilliant people like the economists, policy makers, corporate leaders, political statesmen, could not prevent the crash. This is because these people were financially irresponsible, and now all had to pay the price.

(h) The bailout will not work for the simple reason that no matter how much money is provided as stimulus, it is too little when compared to the castles built in the air.

(i) The lessons learnt will be hard to forget. It also demonstrated in deed that irresponsible and unethical business ruins everyone, including those who have not been directly involved in it. Financial ethics, particularly as practised by financial institutions around the world, have a great global responsibility to sustain people and their livelihoods.

The financial debt build-up bubble, which grows exponentially to the power of a given integer, figuratively explains the meltdown.

There is no more money in the market than the initial money, and its real growth as against the speculated one is shown in the exponential growth of Fig. 8.2. The stimulus money intended to rejuvenate the economy has to come from the existing

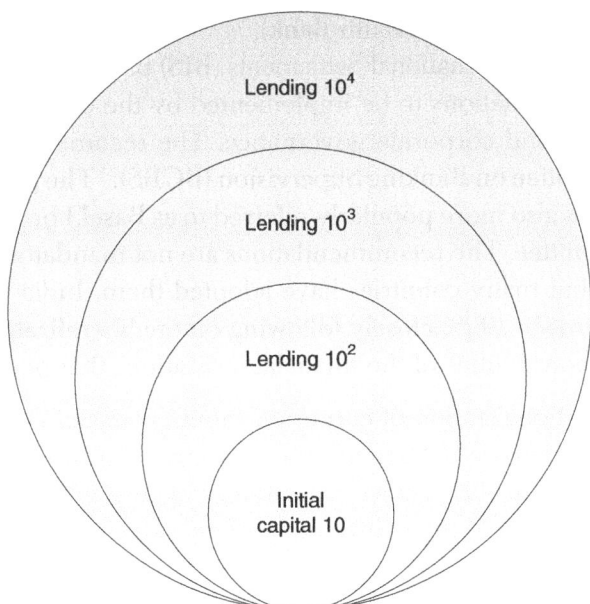

Fig. 8.2   The financial debt build-up bubble

resources, such as the tax payers' money. That is going to be unrealistically insufficient to support a debt giant. Hence, jobs will be lost, industries will be closed, banks will bite insolvencies, stock markets will crash, and the misery will continue. The government and the lending institutions will have to buy stocks of companies to prop them up from bankruptcies, and thus, effectively end the dream of a free-market economy. For now, the government as the owner will regulate the market. It is like going back to command economy and socialism through the backdoor.

The indictment is that it is not the free-market system that has failed; it is the unethical financial behaviour of the concerned people that failed the system. It is greed, at the cost of ruining a system by the people who could be depended upon, that has destroyed a dynamic financial system.

Responsibilities of Financial Institutions

Banks are to an economy what air is to life. They are the financial institutions that manage people's money with the promise of growth and prosperity. There are different types of banks, established with a focused objective, for different purposes. Thus, we have banks that serve the general public by taking in their deposits and lending them their services. There are merchant banks that exclusively devote themselves to all the specialties of trade and industry. They deal with bills of exchange, management of customers' securities, project writing and counselling, portfolio management, under-writing of shares and debentures, and a host of other tasks to help the promoters of the industry. There are also banks set up with a sectoral objective and their names suggest their purpose. In India, we have the Industrial Development Bank of India (IDBI), the National Bank for Agriculture and Rural Development (NABARD), and the Export Import Bank (Exim Bank).

The Bank for International Settlements (BIS) based in Basel, Switzerland, has formulated recommendations to be implemented by the central banks, particularly in risk management and corporate governance. The recommendations are drafted by the Basel Committee on Banking Supervision (BCBS).[6] The process is known as the Basel Accords; it is also more popularly referred to as Basel I or Basel II, as per the conclave of the committee. The recommendations are not mandatory on central banks around the globe, but many countries have adopted them. India became a signatory to the Basel Accords in 1992, closely following on the liberalization process. The following are the responsibilities of the financial institutions that perform banking duties:

(a) Institutionalization of corporate values, codes of conduct, and other standards of appropriate behaviour and a system to ensure compliance.
(b) A well-articulated corporate strategy against which the success of the financial institution and the contribution of employees can be measured.

---

[6] See http://www.nationmaster.com/encyclopedia/Basel-Accord.

Global Trust Bank

Where trust was the victim

There was euphoria in the post-liberalization era. The liberalization of the Indian economy in 1991 opened the banking sector to private enterprise. Well-known financial institutions such as HDFC, ICICI, UTI, etc. began their operations in commercial branches, with their reputation fully backing them. Ramesh Gilli, Sridahar Subasri, and Jayant Madhob were the three big promoters of the newly founded Global Trust Bank (GTB).[a] On its opening day, on 30 October 1994, its collection was a record Rs 100 crore of deposits. GTB's bang catapulted them into the league of big timers.

Ramesh Gilli became a banking genius overnight. A quick network of bank branches with ultra-modern looks, smart front-office executives, quick, efficient, and hassle-free service was a surprisingly refreshing experience for the customers who were the victims of the lethargy of the nationalized banks. ATMs, phone banking, easy money transfers, Internet banking, and dozens of other financial products and services were backed by high tech and modern management systems.

The going was as good as it could get until a certain client by the name Ketan Parikh, the securities wheeler-dealer, came to roost. Gilli, the genius banker, almost pulled another coup when he tried to merge GTB with UTI bank. The Reserve Bank of India (RBI) smelt the rat in the merger and pulled the rug from under the feet, only to expose GTBs misdeeds. Gilli was sacked. The Securities and Exchange Board of India (SEBI), the market regulator, put in place orders that prohibited raising money from the capital market. The stock market dived to the shenanigans of Ketan Parikh. GTB was left with non-performing assets worth Rs 11 billion and a negative net worth.

What went wrong? Gilli, the deposed chairman, maintained that he had delegated the tasks to managers. GTB had indulged in giving 52 per cent of its advances to the stock market, against RBI rules. The erosion of value from this sector sucked the bank. In 2004, the government sanctioned the scheme to amalgamate GTB with the Oriental Bank of Commerce. Accordingly, customers could now continue their normal banking activities with the new bank. Shareholders would be given pro-rata payment if any surplus would remain after paying for all liabilities. The new bank also filed cases against those who were involved in wrongful activities by which the erstwhile GTB was defrauded for hundreds of crore of rupees, such as Unitel Software Ltd, Business India Publications, Petro Energy Products Co. Ltd, Shonk Technologies Ltd, and Pearl Distilleries Ltd.

Greed had claimed GTB. It betrayed the trust of enthusiastic customers and shareholders who had great hopes in a free market and economically growing India. GTB not only struck a blow to those who were immediately related to it, but also to the very idea of economic liberalization.

Questions

(a) What kind of training would you propose to the managers of financial institutions such as banks?

(b) What punishment do you propose for people involved in scams?

(c) Can India trust its financial managers both within the government, who are the regulators, and in the financial institutions from the private sector?

[a] See http://www.banknetindia.com/board/817.html.

(c) Clear assignment of duties and decision-making authorities, incorporating a hierarchy of approvals, from employees to the board of directors.

(d) Establishment of a mechanism for interaction and co-operation among the members of the board of directors, senior management, and auditors.

(e) Institution of strong internal control systems, internal and external audit functions, risk management functions, and other checks and balances.

(f) Special monitoring of risk exposures where conflicts of interest are likely, including business relationships with borrowers affiliated to banks, large shareholders, senior management, and key decision-makers within the financial institution.

(g) Transparent information flow both internally as well as to the public.

Banks are extremely careful in risk taking and run day-to-day business operations efficiently and transparently, and are responsible to all stakeholders, including shareholders, investors, and the community.

CAPITAL MARKET AND ITS REGULATOR

The lesson from each financial scandal, big and small, is that trust is good, but regulation is better. The Indian capital market has a long history. The origins go back to the days of the East India Company, when loan securities trading was initiated. Corporate stocks, bank shares, and cotton presses were the starting point of trading in Bombay (now Mumbai). By 1874, traders used to gather at a street where they formed the Native Share and Stock Brokers' Association. That street is today aptly known as the Dalal Street (*dalal* in Hindi stands for broker), and the association is now known as the Bombay Stock Exchange. Today, India boasts of nearly two dozen stock exchanges, but the Bombay Stock Exchange still towers over all the others, giving it a national identity.

The Securities and Exchange Board of India, known more popularly by its acronym SEBI, is the market regulator set up by the Government of India in 1988. The SEBI Act of 1992 made it into a statutory body and is headquartered in Mumbai. The premises is called the SEBI Bhavan. SEBI has three regional offices situated in Delhi, Kolkata, and Chennai.

Nature of the Indian Capital Market

The Indian capital market, just like its economy, can be distinguished into two sectors: organized and unorganized.

(a) The organized sector consists of the government and corporations, and the supply comes from household savings, institutional investors such as banks, investment trusts, insurance companies, finance corporations, the government, and international financing agencies.

(b) The unorganized sector, mostly characterized by monies spent on consumption, is supplied by the indigenous financiers or moneylenders. This sector is unbridled and efforts to bring it under a regulatory authority have failed.

Professional managers deal with the organized capital market, where they are accountable to their companies and stakeholders. They are also bound by the regulatory authority, SEBI. The responsibilities of the managers have risen since the time the organized capital market has started developing at a quick rate. The reasons for growth are the new economic policies supported by legislation.

There are, however, several difficulties, such as lack of diversity in financial instruments. Financial disclosures are still not controlled fully. The primary market is marred by unofficial trade, prior to issues of shares coming into the market. Growth in the secondary market is still desirable. There is an increased trend in insider trading and manipulation in security prices. Financial institutions have been, more often than not, mute spectators to the malpractices in the capital market.

Structure of the Indian Capital Market

Figure 8.3 is a pictorial depiction of the structure of the Indian capital market.

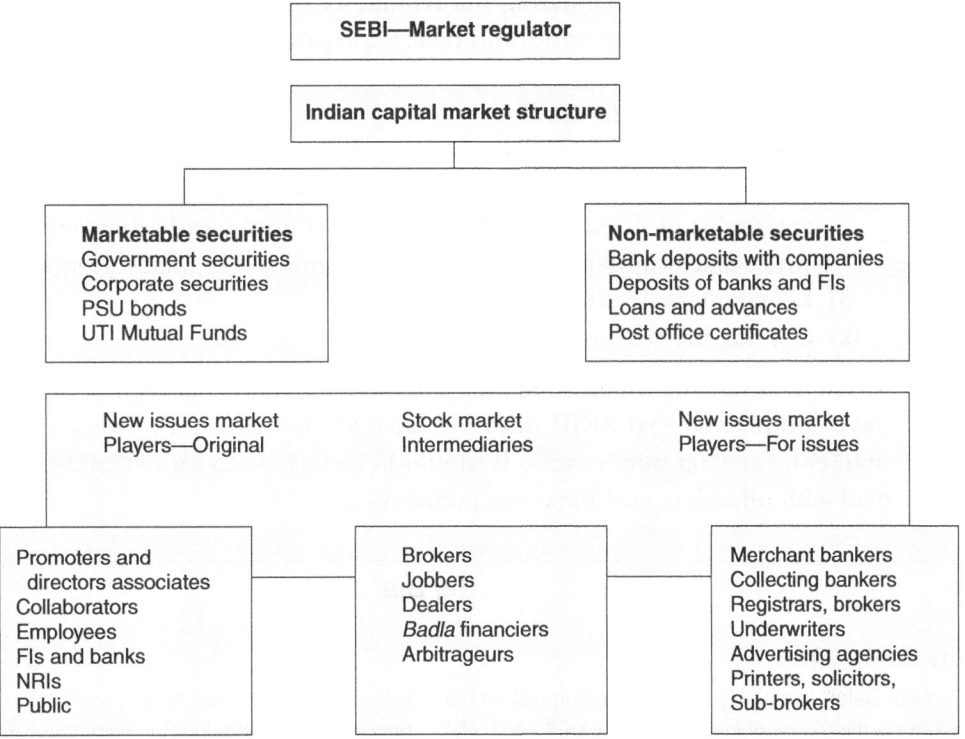

Fig. 8.3 Structure of the Indian capital market

The Capital Market Regulator

As has been already mentioned, SEBI became a statutory body when the SEBI Act 1992 was passed by the Indian Parliament. It was set up with the following objectives:

(a) Protection of investors' interest in securities
(b) Development of the securities market
(c) Regulation of the securities market

SEBI as a regulatory authority is a body instituted to conduct just and fair business in the securities market. For want of a better word, SEBI is an ethical overseer. Some of SEBI's functions are as follows:

(a) Regulating the security exchange business
(b) Registering and regulating the activities of stock brokers, sub-brokers, and share transfer agents, bankers to an issue, trustees of trust deeds, merchant bankers, underwriters, portfolio managers, investment advisors, and other intermediaries who deal with securities
(c) Registering and regulating venture capital funds, collective investment schemes, and mutual funds
(d) Promoting and regulating self-regulatory organizations
(e) Prohibiting unfair and fraudulent trade practices
(f) Promoting investor education
(g) Prohibiting insider trading
(h) Regulating a substantial acquisition of shares and the takeover of companies
(i) Calling for information by undertaking inspection and by conducting inquiries and audits of the stock exchanges, mutual funds, and other persons associated with securities markets, intermediaries, and self-regulatory organizations
(j) Levying fees or other charges
(k) Conducting research

There have been financial scandals in the stock market at regular intervals. Experts have complained that SEBI does not have all the required powers to safeguard the market from economic shocks. It should have powers to immediately and effectively deal with offenders and mete out punishment.

Big Bull

The sinister agent

Sucheta Dalal[a] is a highly respected columnist. In her column in the *Times of India*, dated 23 April 1992, she revealed how Harshad Mehta was actually conducting an illegal banking business to buy shares in the stock market. The modus operandi was almost a comparative model to the old business of pawning. He did ready forwards (RFs). An RF is a secured short-term loan, characteristically of two weeks, from one bank to another. The bank would lend against government securities (just as a pawn broker does against jewellery). The borrowing bank sells the securities to the lending bank and buys them back at the end of the period of the loan, naturally at a slightly higher price.

Harshad took his brokerage commission for the deal between the two banks. But the problem was that there was supposed to be no broker in this kind of financial dealing. Mehta had made his moves so smartly that the buyers and the lenders had no idea of each other. Only the broker made the deal. Mehta made it look perfectly legal by posing himself as conducting business on behalf of some bank or the other. Further, Mehta made things easy for the banks by merely dealing with bank receipts (BRs) without actually moving back and forth the securities. This was not enough for the great mover and shaker of the market. He caught hold of two small and lesser known banks—the Bank of Karad

Contd

Box Contd

(BOK) and the Metropolitan Co-operative Bank (MCB)—who readily issued fake BRs at his behest. What happened next was mere business logic. There were an over-abundance of BRs flying all over and Mehta made merry while others had the pleasure of doing business in government securities. Mehta now had a lot of money and he could really play up to his sobriquet—the Big Bull of the stock market. There was sufficient money made, and everyone got their returns. Even Sucheta Dalal may not have been prepared for the enormity of her exposure. Big Bull's scam caused a loss of Rs 4000 crore. It shocked the nation. Doubts about economic liberalization surfaced.

In the summer of April 1992, it became clear that the banks were drained off, and the stock market hit rock bottom. The select stocks that Mehta had pumped the money into were ACC, Apollo Tyres, Reliance, TISCO, BPL, Sterlite, Videocon, etc. It directly affected nearly a dozen banks and several other foreign banks. The MDs and CMDs of the banks were unceremoniously fired. CBI arrested Harshad Mehta and the investigations continued for another decade. On 31 December 2001,

the Big Bull breathed his last in the prison at Thane, Mumbai.

Harshad Mehta, who began his career in the early 1980s, became a synonym for stock market success by the end of the decade, and the media called him the Big Bull. Every move of his was observed and it affected Sensex, the market index. He lived like a king and acted like a superstar. He had no qualms of conscience in showing off his wealth. Sucheta Dalal admitted that it was his swanky car (he had several imported cars) that pointed towards something not being right. In fact, his Toyota Lexus was the one that she had seen, and that became his nemesis. There are several myths being floated as to where his wealth may have been stashed away.

Questions

(a) Many say that the Harshad Mehta scam taught the stock market some early lessons and helped enact SEBI. Would you justify this comment?
(b) How can stock market ethics become effective?
(c) What role do the media play in stock market ethics?

[a] It is highly recommended to study the journalist's work. See http://www.suchetadalal.com.

SUMMARY

- Financial management is the core of business.
- Ethics in finance is the soul of business.
- Truth is the ethical value at stake in finance.
- Duty is the standard of judgment in accounting.
- Business is built on the financial decisions taken.
- Financial decisions are rationalized to serve the interests of all the stakeholders.
- Accounting is the language of financial decision making.
- Without moral reasoning, financial decisions will cause disastrous consequences, as several financial scandals demonstrate.

- The law has established definite financial standards that reflect fundamental ethical values.
- There are both national as well as international financial standards, and effort is made for harmonious application of both.
- Financial institutions are invested with a special responsibility to safeguard the interests of investors and other stakeholders.
- Modern industrial development depends on the capital market for funds.
- The capital market, like the financial institutions, requires to be regulated.
- SEBI is the lawful authority that regulates the capital market.

KEY TERMS

Accounting decisions   Choices made while recording financial data.

Financial decisions   Choices made for the use of financial products and services.

Financial responsibility   Duties concerning fiscal matters, which may be socially, morally, and legally binding.

Financial scandal (scam)   Gross financial mismanagement causing loss to the stakeholders.

Financial standards   Principles to be followed in conducting financial matters.

Insider trading   Illegal dealing in shares by those who are privy to internal information because of their privileged position, such as an employee in the stock exchange, which is not available to others concerned with it in the public; misuse of exclusive information that materially impacts the value of shares before it is made public.

Objectivism   The philosophy that external reality exists independent of us, and that we can know it through our reason.

Ponzi scheme   Pyramidal financial schemes, which eventually end up causing loss of money.

Regulator   One who is invested with legal or moral authority to exercise power and demand compliance with the rules.

Risk taking   Choices made without the complete knowledge of the circumstances.

CONCEPT REVIEW QUESTIONS

1. Why should finance be within the purview of ethics?

2. If accounting is an objective science, what is the role of ethics in accounting?

3. What is the role of the auditors in maintaining the financial health of corporations?

CRITICAL THINKING QUESTIONS

1. Discuss an insider-trading case. Are there instances of ethical insider trading? In what cases can one divulge insider information?

2. Explain the following comments:

   (a) Accounting is the grammar of finance.

   (b) Ethics is the soul of accounting.

   (c) Regulations are the rules of the game.

3. People like Ketan Parikh have found ways to skirt the regulations of SEBI. Are not more regulations a way of encouraging people involved in scams to find loopholes in the laws?

FURTHER READING

Ashish K. Bhattacharya, *Indian Accounting Standards*, Tata McGraw-Hill (2006).

Alan Greenspan, *The Age of Turbulence: Adventures in a New World*, Penguin Press (2007).

CASE STUDY

Satyameva Jayate—Truth Shall Prevail

The gap in balance sheet arose because of inflated profits over several years... Every attempt to eliminate the gap failed... It was like riding a tiger and not knowing how to get off without being eaten...

—Ramalinga Raju, Satyam Ex-chairman

It is an event of horrifying magnitude. We are in touch with the ministry of company affairs for coordinated action. We need to learn a few lessons from this. This development will have serious implications for the market.

—C.B. Bhave, Chairman SEBI

Introduction

FRAUD! This single-worded headline in the *Financial Times Express* on Thursday, 8 January 2009, summarized the horrible financial disaster in the annals of Indian corporations. That the fraud was committed by a Fortune 500 company, which was decorated with scores of awards around the globe, and was the fourth largest Indian IT company, only added insult to injury. The company's name Satyam, meaning truth in Sanskrit, was the ignominious irony that cast the company to dust for its own lies.

Part I: The Company

The End-Confession

Ramalinga Raju's last task as the chairman of Satyam was to make an honest confession of his dishonest ways of running the reputed corporation. He made this confession in the letter of 7 January 2009 to his board of directors and also sent copies of the same to the chairman of SEBI and other stock exchanges.

(a) The letter had an attachment of the balance sheet dated 30 September 2008 that stated the following facts:

  (i) Inflated (non-existent) cash and bank balance of Rs 5040 crore (as against Rs 5361 crore reflected in the books).

  (ii) An accrued interest of Rs 376 crore, which is non-existent.

  (iii) An understated liability of Rs 1230 crore on account of funds arranged.

  (iv) Over-stated debtor position of Rs 490 crore (as against Rs 2651 crore reflected in the books).

(b) For the September quarter (Q2), we reported a revenue of Rs 2700 crore and an operating margin of Rs 649 crore (24 per cent of revenues) as against the actual revenues of Rs 2112 crore and an actual operating margin of Rs 61 crore (3 per cent of revenue). This has resulted in artificial cash and bank balances going up by Rs 588 crore in Q2 alone.

Every attempt made to eliminate the gap failed, wails the once powerful chairman. As the promoters held a small percentage of the equity, the concern was that the poor performance would result in a takeover, thereby exposing the gap. It was like riding a tiger and not knowing how to get off its back without being eaten. The aborted Maytas (company owned by Raju's son) acquisition deal was the last attempt to fill the fictitious assets with the real ones. Maytas' investors were convinced that this is a good divestment opportunity and a strategic fit. Once Satyam's problem was solved, it was hoped that the Maytas payments could be delayed. But that was not to be. What followed in the last several days is common knowledge.

In the second part of the confession, Raju tried to exonerate his relatives and their spouses who held positions in the company and absolved all the directors, both past and present, of any misdeeds or embezzlements or any personal benefit from the inflated profits.

Raju went on to inform the task force that was formed, to address the situation arising out of the above mentioned Maytas merger. He also suggested the name of the next chairman and interim CEO of the company, Ram Mynampati, to the task force. Merrill Lynch was the law firm suggested to be entrusted to deal with the merger issues.

In a last burst of emotions and nostalgia, Raju glorified the company founded by him that rose to Fortune 500 fame with 53,000 employees operating in 66 countries globally. He hoped that all the Satyamites, along with the banks and other stakeholders and the government would stand by the company. He regretted that under the circumstances he had to resign.

Transformation

The term 'transformation' is a byword at Satyam. The company website prominently highlights its thrust: 'delighting customers', 'assuring investors', 'empowering associates', and 'transforming society'. The company's self-description is as follows: Satyam is a leading global business and information technology company, delivering consulting, systems integration, and outsourcing solutions to clients ... We leverage deep industry and functional expertise, leading technology practices, and an advanced, global delivery model to help clients transform their highest-value business processes and improve their business performance.[a]

The investors, mainly the institutional ones, had great trust in the company. The financial institutions hold over 60 per cent of its equity. The clients, particularly from the developed countries, were happy about both the work ethics, as well as the price tag. Despite the outcry in Europe and the US against outsourcing, the company received very large contracts, mostly from the Fortune 500 companies. The company serves 654 global companies, out of which 186 are from Fortune 500.

It had a meteoric rise before the equally dramatic thud.[b]

1991 Opens on Bombay Stock Exchange with an IPO that is oversubscribed 17 times.

1999 Satyam Infoway (Sify) becomes the first Indian internet company listed on NASDAQ; presence established in 30 countries. Satyam sold it six years later.

2001 Listed on the New York Stock Exchange with trading name SAY.

2006 Revenue exceeds $1 billion; sets up the first 'Global Innovation Hub' in Singapore and operations in Guangzhou, China.

2007 Becomes the official IT services provider for the FIFA World Cups, 2010 (South Africa) and 2014 (Brazil); Ramalinga Raju named the 'Ernst and Young Entrepreneur of the Year'.

2008 Revenue crosses the $2 billion mark.

16 December 2008 Announces plan to buy two Maytas firms to 'close the gap' of the inflated balance sheet; calls off the deal within hours, in the face of shareholders' opposition; share prices tumble.

18 December 2008 Announces board meeting on 29 December 2008 to consider share buyback as markets hammer the shares.

23 December 2008 World Bank confirms blacklisting Satyam for eight years on grounds of data theft and bribing bank officials.

26 December 2008 The crisis takes its first toll—Mangalam Srinivasan, an independent director, quits.

28 December 2008 Puts off board meet to 10 January 2009.

29 December 2008 Three more directors quit.

2 January 2009 Founder-promoters stake falls from 8.64 per cent to 5.13 per cent, as the financial institutions with whom the entire stake was pledged dump the shares.

6 January 2009 Promoters' stake falls further, as lenders offload more pledged shares.

7 January 2009 Ramalinga Raju resigns after confessing to the fraud. The shares fall by 78 per cent.

8 January 2009 The business world is in awe and shock. The corporate bosses speak against their colleague and his company and bemoan the lack of business ethics. Institutional investors, who hold the major equity, want to take over the company. SEBI takes action. Satyam is promptly delisted. Government orders probe. The employees feel cheated. There is no money to pay their salaries. Except for the chairman, who confessed, all the other employees, from the directors to the last office bearers of the company, deny knowledge of the fraud. The internal auditors, who won an award for their work, become deaf and dumb. The external auditors, an internationally famed company called PricewaterhouseCoopers, hides behind 'client confidentiality'. Even M. Srinivas, the Chief Financial Officer had no clue about the fraud. The interim chairman, who was a part of the establishment, puts up a brave face before the TV cameras and asks the clients for their support, and shows great concern for the employees. The reaction from the politicians is muted towards the loss of a benefactor. The public at large is neither surprised, nor aghast, nor awed or shocked. Their reaction may be summarized in a single statement: 'There are many more Satyams in the Indian corporate world.'

Part II: The Scandal

The Crime

Capital market makes the corporate ride high, and cooking the books is a bait to rake in as much liquidity as possible. It makes the financial institutions go into a frenzy by weaving dreams for the

---

[a] See http://satyam.com/about/index.asp.
[b] See http://sify.com/finance/fullstory.php?id=14832496&?vsv=TopHP3.

Satyam Company Brief Profile

Established on 24 June 1987

Global headquarters Hyderabad, India

Registered office

Satyam Computer Services Ltd
1st Floor, Mayfair Centre, SP Road
Secunderabad—500003
Andhra Pradesh, India
Phone +91-40-30654343
Fax +91-40-27840058
E-mail MediaRelations@satyam.com

Management

Executive directors
Ramalinga Raju, founder and chairman
Rama Raju, co-founder and CEO
Ram Mynampati, member of the board and president

Non-executive directors
T.R. Prasad
Prof. V.S. Raju

Services offered
Application services, BI & PM, business process
outsourcing, business value enhancement, consulting
and enterprise solutions, infrastructure management
services, integrated engineering solutions, MES and
LIMS, Oracle solutions, product and application testing,
product lifecycle management (PLM), SAP solutions,
Six Sigma consulting, supplier relationship
management, and supply chain management

Development centres
Bangalore, Basingstoke, Beijing, Bhubaneswar,
Budapest, California, Chennai, Chicago, Dalian,
Georgia, Guangzhou, Gorgon, Hartford, Hyderabad,
Kuala Lumpur, Melbourne, Mumbai, Munich,
Mississauga, New Jersey, Ontario, Pune, Sao Paulo,
Shanghai, Singapore, Sydney, Tokyo, Wiesbaden

Subsidiaries
Satyam BPO
Citisoft
CA Satyam
STI China
Bridge Consultancy

Joint ventures
Satyam Venture Engineering Services Pvt. Ltd

Financial summary
Consolidated Indian GAAP Highlights for FY 2008:
Revenue: Rs 8473.49 crore; a growth of 30.7 per cent
over fiscal 2007
Net profit after tax: Rs 1687.89 crore; a growth of
20.2 per cent over fiscal 2007

Employee strength
52,865[a] (including employees in subsidiaries and joint
ventures)

Source: http://www.satyam.com/about/quick_facts.asp.
[a] Figures as of 30 September 2008.

---

individual investors, who in turn cannot wait but entrust all their money to be managed by the highly skilled MBAs who man these companies and institutions. The Americans have been a leader in dreaming these money dreams. As the new millennium dawned, Enron, the American energy giant, became synonymous with enormous accounting fraud. With the dawn of the 2009, Satyam bit the dust by cooking its books.

(a) Cooking books: Ramalinga Raju admitted in his confession to a fraud of over Rs 7000 crore. The account figures had been inflated to show increased profits and revenue figures. In September 2008, the books showed over Rs 5000 crore of fictitious cash in the current account of the banks. The liabilities amounting to Rs 1230 crore were no where in sight.

(b) Nepotism: The chairman, in a last effort to 'close the gap', wanted to merge the two firms of his two sons, under the name of Maytas (Satyam spelled backwards). The investors had had enough and halted the buyout and demanded accountability.

(c) Omission of duty: There are hundreds of managers in Satyam who manage the business, run contracts, and see to the cash flow. It does not take rocket science to realize what is amiss. Shirking such responsibility is tantamount to criminal negligence. The wrongdoings of the company were kept efficiently undercover.

(d) Irresponsible directors: All the directors including the chief accounts officer denied any knowledge of the wrongdoings. They abdicated their duty to the whims and fancies of the promoter's family. They were awed by his business acumen and political clout.

(e) Nelson's eye by regulatory authority: SEBI was dour when the scandal broke out and showed no prior knowledge of the motives of the market moves by the company.

(f) Promoters selling shares before the fall: The promoter's family had 26.1 per cent of shares in 2001, which came down to 3.6 per cent by 6 January 2009. Experts believe that the promoter's family made room for certain eventualities such as broadening of the investor base and pledging their shares to creditors, yet the estimates are that the promoters profited over Rs 1000 crore.[c]

(g) Institutional investors: Just like market regulators, institutional investors are highly qualified and are duty bound to keep their checks and balances. If an individual citizen cannot get away with the bank rules and regulations, should not these institutions be more careful about their corporate clients?

(h) Political establishment: It is common knowledge that corporations are closely connected with politicians and their parties and develop a bipartisan relationship for mutual benefit. This became clear when the scam was exposed and the political establishments pressed the mute mode.

The culprits

(a) Ramalinga Raju and his family, as promoters and perpetrators of the fraud, for at least ten of the twenty years of the company's existence.

(b) The accountants: Internal auditors an external auditors who actually falsified and certified the accounts.

(c) Executive and independent directors for shirking their responsibilities as the decision-making body of the company.

(d) Senior managers and executives, particularly those connected with the financial responsibilities for helping to cover up illegally.

(e) Regulatory authorities: Even the simple citizen who reads the newspaper is able to analyse the role of the capital market regulator, SEBI. This regulatory authority failed to detect the market trend of the company or just shirked from doing so, for extraneous reasons.

(f) Political establishment: The politician-corporate nexus is highlighted by the media. The politicians quickly deflect from the issue, by expressing their concern for the thousands of employees.

The accomplice

The audit firm, PricewaterhouseCoopers, is considered an accomplice, for not doing their professional duty. Only investigations will reveal the role of the auditing firm. Forty-eight hours after the scandal broke out, the firm was smarting from the accusing fingers pointed towards it. The editorials have already dubbed it as Arthur Andersen & Co., which was the accomplice in the Enron debacle. It was the largest audit firm of the world and bit the dust along with the company for which it certified the account books. However, by the last of week of January 2009, two senior auditors were taken into custody.

Part III: The Fallout

Shock and awe

Ramlinga Raju's confession caused a huge short circuit in the stock market. Satyam stocks plummeted by 91 per cent. Sensex shed over 749 points. Satyam disappeared from the New York Stock Exchange. The external auditor, who certified the inflated revenue figures and made the liabilities disappear, ran for cover. The directors feigned having no knowledge of the figure fudging. The investors' money was wiped out. The media revelled in breaking the story. The employees of Satyam fished for the 'Satyam spirit', more out of

---

[c] See 'Promoters did sell part of stake earlier', *Times of India* (Goa edn), 9 January 2009, p. 11.

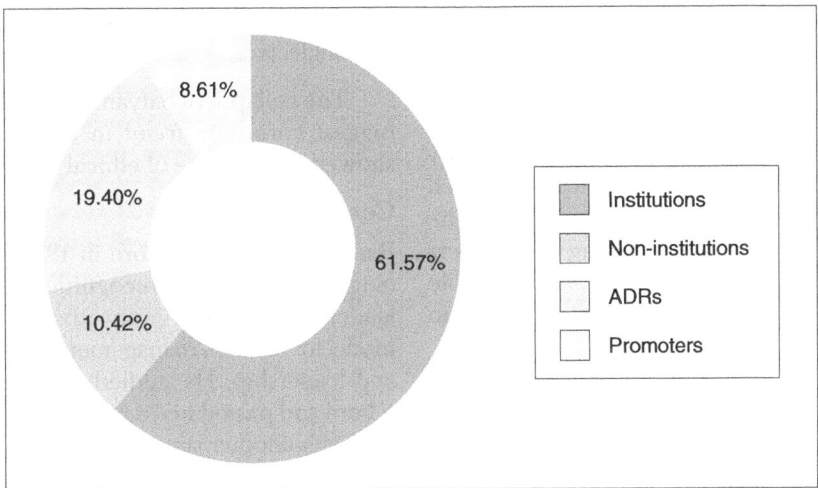

Fig. 8.4   Shares of the investors

economic compulsion than ethical responsibility. Industry magnates spouted business ethics. The dean of the Indian School of Business (ISB), who was one of the independent directors, resigned from the prestigious business school. Even he was helpless and did not understand how the fraud occurred. The image of India as an IT superpower was dented. Only politicians glibly pouted the oft repeated statement that the scam was not going to affect the economy adversely.

Institutional investor activism

'Investor's want to take over' ran the headline in the business section of the *Times of India*. In his confession, Raju had said that none of the directors were responsible for what went wrong. The financial institutions having stakes in the company (see Fig. 8.4) retorted that if this was the case, the directors were incompetent. The management could not be trusted and hence, the institutional investors who had the majority stake should take over the company.

The financial institutions held the largest number of shares, which amounted to 61.57 per cent of the shares. These are the well-known financial institutions who suffered losses (see Table 8.2).

Individual investors have been asking disturbing questions, such as what has been the relationship between these institutions and the company? Are they taking up cudgels because they are becoming wiser after the event?

Table 8.2   Financial institutions who suffered loss at Satyam

Name	Shares (in crores)
Aberdeen Asset Managers Ltd	3.44
Fidelity	2.30
ICICI Prudential Life Insurance	1.66
Lazard Asset Management	1.45
Life Insurance Corporation of India	1
Others	Less than 1 crore

Legal tangle

Section 23 of the Securities Contract Regulation Act 1956 empowers the SEBI to convict the offender to ten years of imprisonment and charge a fine of Rs 25 crore. All involved are liable to punishment, whether it is the chairman, the directors or the officials of the company, for violating the listing agreement by making false and inaccurate disclosures in the company's quarterly and annual reports.

Section 24 of the SEBI Act 1992 further imposes an imprisonment of one year for fraudulent and unfair practices.

Section 477–A of the Indian Penal Code may convict the offenders to seven years of imprisonment. This may be imposed by the police on their own, with the recommendation of the Serious Fraud Investigation Office and punish those who have been found to possess falsified accounts.

The Satyam chairman's confession has helped the law enforcing agencies to peg the guilt not only on the chairman, but also on the executive, as well as non-executive directors and other officials. The law does not recognize the shielding of offenders by the declaration of the chairman. All are liable for penalty of fine and imprisonment for failing in due diligence.

Part III: Ethical Analysis

Dilemma   One could not have put it better than Ramalinga Raju, the disgraced chairman of Satyam, who in his lengthy confession said, 'The gap in balance sheet arose because of inflated profits over several years... Every attempt to eliminate the gap failed... It was like riding a tiger and not knowing how to get off without being eaten.'

There is no excuse when the figures in the accountant's book speak for themselves. If the written facts do not conform to reality, the discrepancy is glaring. Fudged accounts are a futile effort to prove the existence of non-existing funds and cover up the liabilities. All the intelligence and skills of a learned manager come to a naught, when facts do not represent reality. Ethics is about being in conformity with reality. It is about running a business truthfully. At Satyam,

(a) Instead of the benefit of the stakeholders, only greed guided the management.

(b) Instead of dedication to duty, the investors were taken for a ride, and more were allured into the net by showing inflated profits.

(c) Instead of the means justifying the ends of the company, only personal ends mattered and accounts were fudged.

(d) Instead of being just and fair to the customers and employees who trusted the competence of the management, the company betrayed them.

(e) Instead of showing corporate social responsibility, the conscience was hardened to siphon off money.

(f) Instead of using the learning and experience and thus exercising prudence, outsmarting and one-upmanship was exercised, political and corporate power was exercised.

(g) Corporate governance or prudence was neglected.

The collapse of Satyam, which resulted in the biggest corporate fraud in Indian history, also showed the collapse of ethical values.

Conclusion

Ramalinga Raju was born in 1954 and was at the height of his global recognition as a corporate leader of enormous innovative skills and a role model for efficient management, entrepreneurship, and leadership. He studied in a renowned Jesuit school and passed his MBA from Ohio University US, with another stint at the famed Harvard Business School. He was also known as an IT Czar who won awards and also academic honours for the kind of progressive leadership he showed, and millions of young Indians looked up to him as their role model. Success, however, in the ultimate analysis is measured by one's intentions and motives and not the temporary fame.

Silver lining in employees

The company and over 53,000 of its employees lived up to their ideals. Several awards are a testimony to their highly professional commitment. The chairman and the directors left the ship to sink. Over two thousand executives, all with MBAs, gave up immediately. The rest of the employees stuck to their tasks and invented the so-called 'Satyam spirit'. The employees did not give up. Amid gloom, they showed grit. However, given the Indian situation, the courage shown was perhaps inevitable, due to the compulsion of choosing between having a job or losing it. The news that thousands would be laid off only made their resolve stronger.

Discussion Questions

1. This case was written when the Satyam incident came to light. Hence, list all the developments that took place since the latter part of January 2009.

2. What was the fundamental principle that was breached?

3. Would the Satyam case have seen the light of day if its own chairman did not make the public confession?

4. Why did no one blow the whistle? Were the employees and all the internal auditors not aware of the malpractices?

5. What are the negatives of the Satyam case?

6. What similarities and contrasts can you find between Enron and Satyam?

7. Do not all corporations indulge in an inflation of profits in their accounts?

8. Is it systemically possible that no one in the capital market, be it SEBI or the brokers or the financial institutions, know what was going on in Satyam?

9. Do not the people who are concerned with Satyam Corporation have a responsibility to reveal the wrongdoings of the company?

10. How was the Satyam board of directors governed?

11. What role did nepotism play in the Satyam debacle?

12. If you were a part of the SEBI board, how would you proceed with the case? Would you be restricted by the law to do anything against the company? How would you be accountable to the investors?

13. What systemic solutions would you suggest so that another Satyam debacle does not take place?

14. What positive changes do you expect will happen within the law in general and the capital market regulator, SEBI, in particular?

15. Make a code of conduct for Satyam to implement.

Going Further . . .

- Have extensive discussions to inform you thoroughly about the ethical issues of the case.
- Make two separate governing boards:
  (i) The old Satyam board of directors
  (ii) The new Satyam board of directors
- Make committees to formulate a code of corporate conduct.

ETHICAL DEVELOPMENT PROGRAMME

Management Training

Do It Yourself

Guidance: The following is an exercise in professional training. The questions below are instructive, and are merely to conduct your own self-training and guide others. Here are some suggestions:

(a) Make these questions your research markers.

(b) Make questionnaires, conduct surveys, and compile findings.

(c) Draw up a finance code for your company.

(d) Make a personal finance management code for yourself.

(e) Instruct and guide an organization in your community, such as a Traders' Union or an NGO or a school or a temple committee or a cultural organization, etc., about ethical financial management.

(a) Finance is the central point of business management and accounting is its soul. In an MBA classroom, referring to the notorious financial scandals such as Enron and WorldCom is considered fashionable and common. However, in the more sober situations of management, business managers have problems managing the finance. What rule of thumb should a manager follow in everyday financial management without fail?

(b) It is believed that Indian companies cook their accounts. The accountants work furiously, producing several drafts of balance-sheets every quarter. The promoters then publish the one that it is favourable to them. The credit rating agency, CRISIL, has come out with a research about the unethical practices of our companies. The manager is caught between the accounting firm and the promoter. What measures should the manager take to be redeemed from this difficult situation?

(c) We read and hear so much about the financial disclosures of the companies. What does this involve? What are the responsibilities of a manager in handling such matters?

(d) The nature of our tax regime is voluntary. It is commonly perceived that Indian companies avoid paying corporate tax. It means that these presumably rich companies, including the manager of the company, who is an employee and a salaried tax payer, take a free-ride on the backs of the ordinary tax payers. What remedies do you suggest?

(e) Is there a code of conduct for the company's finance controller? In the event of a financial mismanagement, can criminal proceedings be undertaken against the financial controller rather than against the promoters of the company?

(f) In 2003, the managing director of finance of a highly reputed company was charged with insider trading, and was eventually banned by the SEBI for five years from securities trading. Insider trading is a crime against the general investors. It profits only a few who use the information in securities trading. Some suggest that those who are employed in the securities exchange cannot help leaking some information wittingly or unwittingly. Hence, some kind of limited insider trading should be allowed. To a normal investor, this sounds catastrophic. Is such a thing possible?

(g) In 2002, when UTI failed to deliver and investors across India lost their hard-earned money, the fund managers seemed to have lost their voice. In what way are the fund managers responsible to the investors?

(h) India is home to a large number of non-profit organizations where professional managers, accountants, and auditors are employed. How does a manager, who is working in such an organization, prepare for an audit?

(i) Scandals of the misuse of public funds or their instruments are not new, and have shaken India several times in such scandals as the Bofors-Gun kickbacks, the infamous coffin scam after the Kargil war, etc. Recently (2008), the Union Minister for Information Technology allotted the 2G Spectrum for the mobile services, and that too, more than the stipulated 6.2 megahertz, rather than going for a global auction. It is reported that the Central Vigilance Commission questioned the motives of the allocation. The estimated loss for the country was Rs 60,000 crore, which an auction could have

otherwise brought in as revenues. What steps can be taken to eradicate such corporate corruption within the people's government?

(j) Is it possible to train management students in the management of financial uprightness? As a finance manager what code of conduct would you draw for your employees?

Game I

Bulls and bears

(a) This game consists of a simulation of the current capital market, in real time.

(b) Objective is to monitor the ethical behaviour of all the stakeholders.

(c) Choose one of the markets—BSE, NSE, NYSE, CAC, Hang Sang FTSE, DAX, etc.

(d) Depending on the numbers, divide the group, as is convenient, into market players: promoters, financial institutions, bankers, investors, brokers, etc., all with a stipulated initial working capital.

(e) Appoint a regulatory authority. These will be responsible for monitoring the game and dealing with 'cases' and award penalties.

(f) The duration of the game is six weeks, real time.

Rating

- **Excellent** Completion of six weeks with quality performance and an 'A' grade from the 'Regulator'.

- **Very good** Completion of six weeks with some breakdowns, disputes—major or minor—but solved and a 'B' grade from the 'Regulator'.

- **Good** Completion of five weeks, with serious disputes, some of which are unsolved and a 'C' grade from the 'Regulator'.

- **Unsatisfactory** Not able to complete three weeks, serious accusations, quarrels, breakdowns and disruption with a 'ban' by the 'Regulator'.

Game II

Ponzi

(a) Develop a Ponzi scheme for the people in your establishment.

(b) Play it for six weeks.

(c) The game should be kept absolutely confidential during the time it is being played to make it real.

(d) All the money must be kept very safely and under supervision with a third party, preferably the authorities or administrators of your establishment, so that when the game period is over, the people who played can get their full money back.

(e) The game should be played with the express and written permission of the authorities of your establishment, with the serious undertaking that the money will be returned to their rightful owners.

(f) Keep all the records impeccably, with the authorities.

(g) The objective of the game is to impart a lesson to all the players that they should be careful with their money and learn to invest it intelligently. This is known as practical ethics.

Management Mantra

When Life Equals Money

The global financial meltdown claimed the lives of several enterprising businessmen.

Adolf Merckle, a noted billionaire of Germany, invested heavily in Volkswagen AG, the leading German automaker. He was also one of the foremost investors in Rationpharm, the pharmaceutical giant. The firms suffered heavy financial losses. Moreover, their ethical reputation became controversial. Both the companies suffered financial meltdowns. Merckle lost in billions. He threw himself before a running train and died. He is survived by his wife and four children.

At 47, Kirk Stephenson of London was a highly successful COO of Olivant, the private equity house. At West London Railway Station, he jumped before a speeding train. He is survived by his wife and a young son.

Venkata Reddy, 55, from Bangalore ran a garment export business, which became a victim of the financial meltdown. On 31 December 2008, he returned home with a heavy heart after losing the business completely. He convinced his wife and his two grown-up daughters—the older girl was a student of medicine, and the younger one was a student of commerce—that it was the end of their lives. They fulfilled a suicide pact by eating poisoned *jalebis* after their dinner.

These and several others around the world have equated their lives with only money. Wives and children, relatives and friends, home and love, and many more good and beautiful things in life did not matter to them.

MANTRA   *When life equals money, you lose both life and money.*

Part Three

Managers and Workplaces

Managing People in the Organization

Managing People in the Organization

The Way of Defining a Manager in an Organization

To leave footprints on the sands of time, wear work shoes.

—Anonymous

To idealise the real which more often than not is full of inequities is a very selfish thing to do. It is only when a person finds a personal advantage in things, as they are, that he tries to idealise the real. To proceed to make such an ideal real is nothing short of criminal. It means perpetuating inequity on the ground that whatever is settled is settled for all times. Such a view is opposed to all morality. No society with ideal conscience has ever accepted it. On the contrary whatever progress in improving the terms of associated life between individuals and classes has been made in the course of history is due entirely to the recognition of the ethical doctrine that whatever is wrongly settled is never settled and must be resettled.[1]

—B.R. Ambedkar

'Workplace' is a term that IBM popularized for a set of strategies and system software technologies for developing future products. But the term became generic to mean where people work, and ever since, it just means what it announces. The term has become so common that it has even dislodged the term 'office'.

MANAGER'S OLD PARADIGM

A manager is in charge of a workplace. There are employees working under the instructions of the manager. The manager wields professional power over the employees. The manager has authority over the employees because the latter work under the former's instructions. The authority of the manager needs to be responded to with obedience by performing the task. The process has problems. Employees may not want to perform a task in the way the manager wants it to be done. The wants, desires/wishes, and wills of the two clash. The exercise of authority and obedience are the two important moral issues at a workplace, which have often clashed and created a conflict.

The authority–obedience paradigm is power or authority centred. Commands are given and must be obeyed. Contemporary managerial systems are power centred and are entrenched in hierarchical decision making. Decisions trickle down after an obedience feedback of the employees is sent up. Employees wait with great anticipation of what will befall them next. Managers devise strategies to control the employees, sometimes with a carrot and sometimes with a stick. The stick is used most of the time. The employees learn their ropes and devise their own strategies by coming together to attack. The managerial dictatorship is ready for a fight, with superior powers of authority and influence. There is a fight. There is a war. There is destruction. There is death.

Figure P3.1 shows the top-down leadership at a workplace. It is an efficient model to extract work and increase productivity. This is a very complex, systemic network in which strategies

---

[1] See quotations of Dr B.R. Ambedkar at http://www.ambedkar.org/.

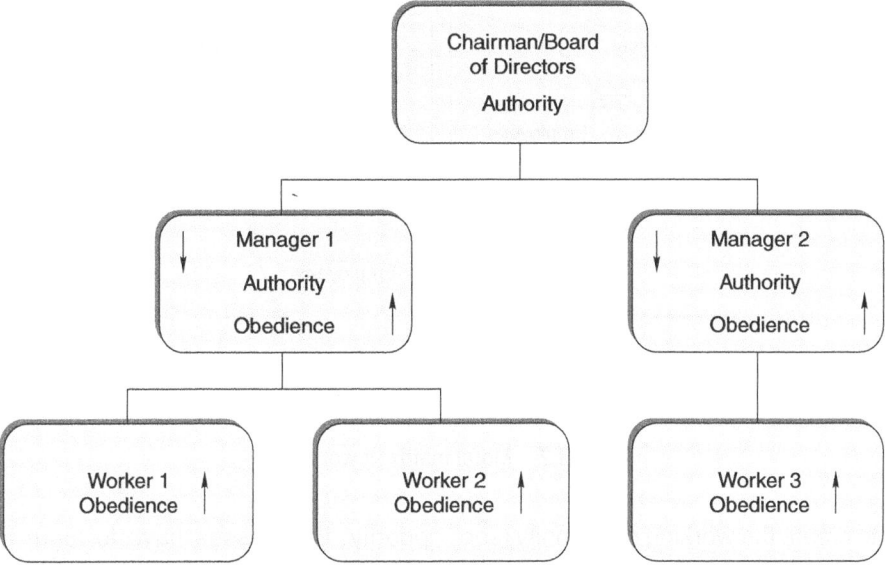

Fig. P3.1   Authority–obedience workplace

for efficiency are conceived. The managers try and fix employees to suit the workplace. They set targets and put the employees to work to achieve the targets. When the targets are met, managers are acclaimed as leaders.

This model has served for a long time and has been used right from the period when enlightenment and moral consciousness were not given prominence. As a result, we experience very difficult odds at work on a daily basis. It appears as if the entire organizational structure is impinging on the employees to do more work. Psychological powers are also used to motivate the employees to give greater outputs. Yet, there are more problems at the workplace than any manager can solve.

MANAGER'S NEW PARADIGM

Initially both the manager and the employee are bound by their respective duties. Duties can create differences of opinion. This can generate a debate and even create a conflict. There should be justice. Justice needs justification, but each one has her/his view. The goals are questioned, the means are probed, the purposes are examined, and yet there is a deadlock.

Further, an appeal is made to reason, commonsense, and the conscience. Wisdom dawns only when the manager dons the mantle of stewardship and shares it with, not his/her 'employees', but his/her 'colleagues'. A change in the moral attitude at the workplace defines the success of the manager.

In the new paradigm, the manager's role is that of a steward who seeks the cooperation of his/her colleagues. This new realization gives a new direction to the goals and purposes that have to be accomplished. Individuals are replaced by the community, consciences are clear, and reasoning and commonsense are utilized to the utmost. There is a new consciousness in the organization. It functions like a living organ, a living system. The workplace becomes a living place of the people.

The workplace, as the living place of the people, has morality at its core. Both the managers and the employees are part and parcel of the same reality, the workplace. Their roles are different, but their spirit is one. They are not machines but people made of flesh and blood, who bring diverse backgrounds into this new place to enrich it. All the aspects of human life, whether physical, psychological, social, or legal, come to bear on

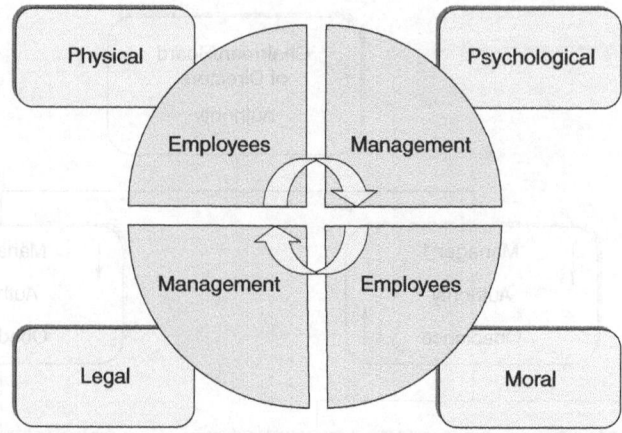

Fig. P3.2 Moral matrix at workplace

each other to create the working community (see Fig. P3.2).

The new work-cycle is powered by morale, not motivation. Motivation works on incentives, sometimes even disincentives. The morale is fired by an ideal. Employees with high morale are confident and their self-esteem is high. Their self-esteem is high because the company that they work for has a noble ideal. Business as usual pumps up motivation but it collapses in the face of adversity. Employees who have morale are not afraid of adversities and problems. Employees with morale challenge these difficulties. The greater the difficulty, the greater is their spirit to face up. The greater the challenge, the greater is their morale.

A manager is a leader who boosts the morale of the employees. Inspiration needs to be more important than bookish intelligence. A good leader is created by life's experiences, where she/he makes challenging moral decisions.

WORKPLACE IS A REPUBLIC

Our contemporary world is a republic. It is a people's world. The business world is no exception. We no longer have tribal leaders and aristocrats, or kings and queens, who exercise the arbitrary powers bestowed upon them. Even in those countries where the worst forms of dictatorship exist, people are given the top-most

priority. Businesses have to learn to be good citizens, and managers have to represent what people and employees expect from them.

It is the shareholders who elect a board of governors to manage their affairs. The managers in their various capacities deal with people—at the workplace, with employees; in the market-place, with customers; at the supplies, with suppliers; and when dealing with money, with accountants and regulators.

In addition to this, the workplace is a republic because the employees are its immediate stakeholders. Without their interest, there is no workplace. The new paradigm demands democratic principles to be followed. Dictatorships will not last long.

OBJECTIVES OF PART III

Bees buzz. People talk. Bees make honey. People make money. Bees live in a colony. People live in a society. Bees live to work. People work to live. We could go on extolling the virtues of the bees and draw lessons for ourselves. If it is work that defines a bee, a manager would like to be as busy as the bee. Experts have studied the behaviour of the bees intensely and have tried to implement their work model, better known as work ethic (that is, the attitude of the employees to work). Further, this attitude or work ethic is based on a definite, desirable conduct that society has developed. Employees want fair treatment, just wages, and respect. Promoters or managers expect employees to do their duty and help the organization get due returns so that the employees can be paid and the organization can make profits from the invested capital. Thus,

(a) work, employees, and the workplace is the first concern when focusing on the rights, duties, personnel policies, just wages, and the morality of employees' unions.

(b) work and home, the moral concerns about informed consent, health matters, and privacy are the pressing problems of employees.

(c) the contemporary manager has advanced in the modern world and so have the problems concerning conflict of interest, whistleblowing, abuse of one's position, and kickbacks.

(d) the Indian manager has myriad problems to face at the workplace, such as discrimination, sexual harassment, job reservation, etc.

The responsibility of the Indian manager is quite different from that of the other managers around the world. The poor constitute the bulk of the Indian population. At the workplace too, it is the people from this bulk of the nation who try to eke out an existence. The Indian history is a wounded history of horrendous exploitations, not only by India's conquerors and colonialists, but tragically by her own people as well. Poverty and social discrimination are the greatest evils that the country faces. Without a social conscience and a high degree of moral integrity, the Indian manager will not be effective.

Grooming to Work

I am sure that nothing has such a decisive influence upon a man's course as his personal appearance, and not so much his appearance as his belief in its attractiveness or unattractiveness.[a]

—Leo Tolstoy

Well-groomed executives are a *sine-qua-non* at the workplace. That working women are self-conscious about appearance is but natural. These days, even male executives are taking a leaf out of their female counterparts' book. It is wonderful to know that at least in the area of grooming, men are on an equal footing with women. In the *Times of India*, there was a report with the following title: *Are you groomed enough for the workplace?*[b] The report describes how young executives spend as much as Rs 4000 to Rs 5000 every month for services such as facials, manicures, pedicures, hair styling, massages, etc. This encourages

business in the area of personal care. The phenomenal rise in the personal care industry in India is a clear sign that the so far one-sided demand by the fairer sex has now extended to the men folk. It is all good for business. It is also good for the workplace.

Today, HR consultants are specialized in good manners and grooming strategies for the employees of large corporations. The philosophy is that good manners and good looks make a good executive. However, fake Western accents and use of slang language should be avoided.

Manners, of course, is a matter of customs and culture. Certain customs do come along with the fashion package. You cannot wear a three-piece suit along with a Gandhi cap. Nowadays, it is not just work that matters; good grooming and good manners are also equally essential.

[a] See Leo Tolstoy quote at http://motivationempire.com/inspirational_quote_for_the_workplace.php.

[b] Debojyoti Ghosh and Swati Anand (1998).

CHAPTER 9

Workers and Morals

The only safeguard of order and discipline in the modern world is a standardized worker with interchangeable parts. That would solve the entire problem of management.

—Jean Giraudoux

A nation is building in India today before the eyes of the world... This is the faith in which the Karmayogin puts his hand to the work and will persist in it, refusing to be discouraged by difficulties however immense and apparently insuperable.

—Sri Aurobindo

LEARNING OBJECTIVES

After studying this chapter, you will be able to

> Discuss the rights and duties of employees
> State personnel policies and procedures
> Define just wages
> Describe union morality

INTRODUCTION

We shall study four themes in this chapter, which will help you analyse your place in an organization, know your rights and duties, understand well-laid-out policies, terms and conditions, wages, and the relevance of unions in an ever-stronger free-market economy.

Workplace Insecurity

Rupa works at an auto insurance call centre in Hyderabad. She left her family behind in Madurai, Tamil Nadu, and lives in Hyderabad as a paying guest with a family of five. Despite the company pick-up and drop-off facility she finds it difficult to adjust to the shift system, particularly the nightshift. This is because when she gets back home, she does not get the much required sleep, as the household is bustling with activity. At work, she dreads when a caller is going to yell at her in frustration. Meenakshi shudders at the thought of the name calling and crude sexual remarks she has to face. She is afraid to complain to the supervisor because her colleague who did so had to bear the brunt of his wrath and was forced to leave. Her colleagues tell her that these things happen and she should not take them personally. She also came to know that one of the young men who was not able to take the barrage of abuse committed suicide. She wants to work, or rather, she has to stay back and work, because if she returns home, her parents will get her married against her wishes, which she feels would be a 'lifelong suicide'.

The contemporary workplace differs a great deal from the traditional one in a manufacturing unit. Though a workplace with tools and machinery may be routine and monotonous and one may feel less important than the machines one is working with, one could pass snide remarks at the foreman while at work, and yet forget about workplace worries once home. Today for many people, work-from-home is an option. There are other kinds of employment as well, but the tribe of executives has multiplied, and many think that they lead very high-end lives. But they live in constant insecurity because the competition for their posts is also very high. Their subordinates dislike them, while their superiors keep them away from better opportunities. Even senior managers are worried as to who is going to push them over the edge for the topmost place. Thus, insecurity haunts everyone at the workplace, from the lowest to the highest.

TeamLease, a company that provides staff, conducted a research to discover some traits of workplace behaviour. Table 9.1 shows the results. Another interesting finding was that approximately 50 per cent of the managers thought that the ideas of the subordinates did not require acknowledgement, but all agreed without exception that 'leaders must walk the talk'.

Table 9.1 Traits of workplace behaviour

	Workplace action	Ethical judgment
(a)	Coming late to work	45 per cent say latecoming is not wrong.
(b)	Making personal calls from the office phone	46.8 per cent say it is not wrong.
(c)	Details of office expenses	55.7 per cent say fudging details is not wrong.
(d)	Leave application	60 per cent say telling lies is not wrong.
(e)	Promise to the customer	60 per cent say making false promises is not wrong.
(f)	Means of getting competitor information	62 per cent say that the means adopted to get the required information are not wrong.
(g)	Use of office stationery for personal use	61 per cent say it is not wrong.
(h)	Doing personal work during office hours	63 per cent say there is nothing wrong in it.

Source: http://www.pluggd.in/indian-it-industry/workplace-ethics-indian-companies-teamlease-survey-2373/, accessed on 3 November 2008.

RIGHTS AND DUTIES OF EMPLOYEES

Managers manage employees not arbitrarily but under the terms and conditions of employment. Human resource management is the human face of business. For a business to succeed, there has to be harmony among the management, the workers, and society. Authority plays a role, but today it is expected that authority be more of a facilitator than a task master. Society has got rid of the command economy. There is a choice of industry and employment for people, as well as a choice of goods and services for consumers. In this situation, organizations have developed themselves to empower their employees. Democracy and good citizenship is expected from corporations, and employees too have their share in team work and decision making.

Employees and Duties

It is obvious that people take up employment with the knowledge that they are obliged to work. Their duty is to work. They have no other right other than the right to work. They have their right to pay because they work. If they did not work, they would not get paid. Their obligation is to the firm. They are hired because it is the firm's need and can be fired when the firm does not need them. As long as they are under the contract of the firm, they cannot indulge in any other employment, nor do anything that will conflict with their loyalty to the firm.

Consider the case of Shridhar Kelapure (see box titled Occupational Hazard), a railway employee who claimed compensation for contracting an allergy at the workplace. After examining the evidence, the court declared that the allergy was unique to him and that it was not an occupational hazard, hence no compensation would be given. The court's judgement shows that employees have the duty to render the services for which they are paid. If it is made clear that for an employee it is duty that is essential, several disputes could be nipped in the bud and companies could benefit from lesser litigation and focus more on their productive work. However, an employer does not have rights over the employee for things that are not relevant to the workplace.

Indian Labour Laws

- The Child Labour (Prohibition and Regulation) Act 1986[a]
- The E.P.F. and Miscellaneous Provisions Act 1952
- Industrial Disputes Act 1947
- The Maternity Benefit Act 1961
- Minimum Wages Act 1948
- Payment of Bonus Act 1965
- Payment of Gratuity Act 1972

- Payment of Wages Act 1936
- Payment of Wages (Amendment) Act 2005
- Public Provident Fund Act 1968
- Workmen's Compensation Act 1923
- Factories Act 1948
- ESI Act 1948 (Employees State Insurance Act 1948)

[a] See http://www.laws4india.com/acts/labourlaws/, accessed on 3 November 2008.

Employees and Rights

Rights have their basis in freedom, the fundamental and inalienable right of an individual. In fact, ethics is all about freedom, the freedom of the will, the faculty of decision making. The employees' first right is either to accept or reject employment. If they accept employment, they sign a contract and it is valid until termination in accordance with the contract. Secondly, employees have the right to reasonable working conditions and safety. Thirdly, they have the right to just wages, without discrimination of caste, creed, or race. The principle of equal work for equal pay must be upheld. Fourthly, with experience and productive work, job promotion is a right that cannot be denied.

The cited case of allergy contracted from the worksite and demanding a compensation for the same is one such case that even the courts find difficult to handle because they apply a clause of the law without regard to the context of application. The law is applied here to the letter; the spirit of the lawgiver is absent. Laws are based on the utilitarian principle and this is one reason why the application fails. The law, apropos utilitarianism, states that if 500 co-workers do not find diesel hazardous,

---

Occupational Hazard

Allergic to worker's right

Shridhar Kelapure from Nagpur is now aged 65 and an ex-employee of the South Eastern Railways. He joined the Indian Railways in 1962 as a *khalasi* or cleaner. He was appointed as a diesel cleaner in the shed. He appeared to have developed some allergy due to the diesel fumes and it grew worse as he got older. Doctors advised him against his working conditions, but he continued to work as he had no other alternative offered by the Railways. His kidney and liver got affected badly and disfiguration set in his face (Thomas, 2008).

Kelapure approached the Labour Court for compensation from the Railways, pleading under the Workmen's Compensation Act. The Railways defended their decision for not compensating him by advocating that what he suffered was an allergy, not a work hazard at the workplace. The Labour Court upheld the employer, that is, the Railways, and Kelapure lost his case.

Kelapure then approached the High Court with all the relevant medical records to support his case for compensation. The court clarified by referring to the Act under which he had appealed: 'If any person contracts any disease as occupational disease it should be treated as an injury and the claimant or employee would be entitled to compensation.' But there was a caveat to the provision: the disease must be peculiar to that occupation. In other words, all persons working in similar conditions should contract a similar disease to be eligible for compensation. The court also examined 500 other reports of people working in similar situations and handling similar substances, but none had contracted the ailment suffered by Kelapure. The judge ruled that only Kelapure suffered from the allergy and no one else in a similar situation had contracted it. Hence, it was not an occupational disease.

Questions

(a) On what moral grounds is the health of employees the responsibility of the employer?
(b) Do generalizations like the one that the judge made in the above case help to solve individual problems?
(c) How many people would have to get sick so that Kelapure gets compensation?

there is no reason why one should find it so. Is it the real will of the lawgiver to deny a person his/her right just because the other 500 do not have a reason to claim theirs? Therefore, in conclusion to the argument, we could say that a case must be considered on its individual merits if the law has to uphold the rights of those who come under it.

Factoring Rights and Duties

From the above pro and contra arguments on rights and duties and the corroborative case that further sharpens the conflict of rights and duties, it becomes clear that merely factoring one without the other leads to complication of roles of the employee vis-à-vis the employer. The rights that one may claim have meaning only if one is willing to give or do one's duty in return. Duty is a moral obligation that employees bind themselves to; employee rights, on the other hand, are the obligations of the employer. Thus, we see that one kind of duty demands another kind of duty, depending on the relation of the persons. In our case, the relation is between the employee and the employer. The fundamental relation is built on the give and take of work and wages. Further, relations of rights and obligations involve social, legal, economic, and other factors that influence the basic employee–employer relationship. It will become clear as we study the list of the rights and duties of an employee, given in Table 9.2.

Table 9.2   Important rights and duties

Rights	Duties
1. Work contract—letter of appointment.	Acceptance of terms and conditions of work—ratification of the contract.
2. Wages—equal pay.	Work—equal work.
3. Working hours—as per the legal provisions. Eight hours work has been the general standard.	Expected work delivery.
4. Benefits—medical, provident fund, gratuity, allowances for housing, travel, etc.	Diligence at duty to justify the benefits.
5. Holidays, casual leaves, and sick leaves.	Attendance at work and punctuality.
6. Membership to employee union.	Transparency about the membership to the management.
7. Freedom of thought is a constitutional right that cannot be gagged by the firm if the employee becomes a whistleblower.	Not to misuse one's rights to the detriment of the firm. For example, publicize information about the superiors merely to embarrass them.
8. Privacy and personal information.	Not to raise undue attention to private matters without relevance. If surveillance and monitoring systems intrude on privacy, it is one's duty to bring it to the notice of the management before taking legal recourse.

Contd

Table 9.2 Contd

Rights	Duties
9. Compensation due to damage suffered at workplace or retrenchment.	Care in following all the instructions of the firm on safety and the use of the given equipments for the purpose, e.g., wearing work suits, helmets, or protective gear.
10. Non-discrimination based on caste, creed, race, gender, etc.	Not to discriminate fellow workers on the basis of caste, creed, colour, or gender.
11. Dispute redress system, e.g., ombudsman.	Not to misuse the system or hinder others from using it.

Warning about Workplaces

Wages of workplace $237 billion and rising

The World Health Organization has bad news for an economically resurgent India. By the year 2015, Indian workplaces[a] will cost the people a whopping $237 billion and above. China would stand to lose double that amount. Non-communicable and lifestyle diseases such as diabetes and heart ailments are on the rise. Promotion of a healthy workplace becomes an imperative for corporations. Unless plans are mooted to make the workplace healthier through innovative work culture, physical exercise, and healthy diet, the losses would be enormous to calculate. In 2005 alone, 35 million people died due to non-communicable diseases, making workplaces so much poorer in talent and experience. Addressing the health problems of workplaces will not only save money and lives but will also enhance the productivity and reputation of the corporation.

What is the moral question here? Indeed there are very serious ones.

Questions

(a) What right do corporations have to endanger the health of so many millions?
(b) Would corporations bear the responsibility for those families who have lost their breadwinners?
(c) How can ethics help?

[a] WHO, Geneva, 19 May 2008; see newspaper reports of 20 May 2008.

PERSONNEL POLICIES AND PROCEDURES

The rights of workers brings to the fore a firm's human resource policies, the procedures and implementation. We shall consider this mainly under three themes, namely, placement, promotion, and discipline and discharge. Just wages and unions also are a part and parcel of the policies and procedures, but we shall treat them separately due to the special considerations they demand.

Placement

The term 'placement' has evolved from the old-fashioned 'hiring' and 'recruitment'. Those who were hired were hirelings, those recruited were recruits, while those placed are trainees. The terms suggest an attribute of the new employees in relation to their skills. Hirelings were barely skilled, the recruits were capable of being skilled, but the trainees already have definite competencies that need to be directed for a particular purpose and they should be trained on the job. In the entire process, the personnel manager cannot take his/her eyes away from the cost to the company against each chosen candidate.

Personnel managers have to be highly competitive and skilled in their jobs. It is a highly responsible job because an underproductive trainee is going to cost the company dearly. Further, if new employees do not deliver as has been desired by the company, the head of the personnel manager will be on the block, because there is a great competition for his/her position.

Placement may involve several moral problems for the company. The integrity of the personnel manager is crucial. Newspapers and other sources of public knowledge of events in this country give us a depraved picture. Jobs are actually on for sale. People pay huge bribes to get jobs in public services, and this, like cancer, has spread to private enterprises too. Promotions and transfers too involve corruption at all levels.

There are also brokers involved in placements. Today placement companies are a big business. Shady agents are involved in what is known as human trafficking. The media has brought out various such scandals involving celebrities, artists, and even members of parliament. The United Nations has taken up this issue and has a task force to contain the malaise. One of the ugliest global problems faced today is that these agents offer glamorous job specifications to young ladies, including minor girls, and force them into call girl and *nautch* girl rackets, and forced prostitution. The casting couch, seeking sexual favours for jobs, is as old as the world of cinema, but not merely restricted to it.

Remedies: Policies

A clear policy on placement is imperative for any firm. Job specifications, especially the eligibility of the candidates, must be clearly spelt out. Candidates must have the opportunity to get full information about the nature and requirements of the job. Companies outsourcing the placement service must make clear their policy on placement to the placement agency.

Job Specifications

This consists of giving all the essential information to the prospective candidates, such as educational qualification, training, and experience. Factors such as age limits and physical requirements such as height, fitness, etc. are essential for the jobs in the police and defence forces. Gender-specified jobs and jobs for the disabled must be clearly mentioned with the purpose to avoid contravention of the law. The purpose of job specifications is both beneficial to the personnel manager, whose list of applicants can now be made selective, and to candidates, who will not have to waste their time or lose better prospects elsewhere.

Tests

The requisite qualifications need verification against fraud. Some of the factors for verification include the date of birth. Age is an important factor in hiring because it involves determination of benefits. Educational qualifications that make a person eligible for a given job need to be verified due to the frequent instances of fraudulent certificates being furnished. In the Gulf countries, employers are apprehensive of the degrees issued in India and the other countries in the region. In India, on the other hand, there is a penchant for over-qualification. (See case box.) The attitude in India is that an over-qualified person is better than an adequately qualified one, though common sense tells us that a sufficiently qualified person will be able to deliver efficiently. Consequently, candidates in India produce long bio-datas that run into several pages. It would make the employer wonder why such a person would need this meagre job? The bio-datas of management students are guided by the management institute's placement policy guidelines and read like that of a senior manager.

Aptitude test

Companies want to avoid recruitments based on trial and error and would like their personnel managers or placement agents to get them candidates based on scientific screening. Aptitude tests have been commonly used to evaluate a candidate's verbal and psychomotor abilities, quantitative and logical skills, etc. This is done to measure the required proficiency for the said job. Validity and reliability of these tests is very important. If the tests are merely an exercise to fulfil some policy obligation, the companies are going to harm themselves and their shareholders as well. Once people sense that such a procedure is irrelevant, the companies will come into bad repute.

Penchant for Over-qualification

A pilot to drive a taxi

Meenakshi had done her M.A. in history and, for a while, found nothing worthwhile to do. So she began to give tuitions at home to small children. The children were from a close-by kindergarten, quite simply known in local parlance as nursery. Since the competition to get into good schools is very high, despite the Supreme Court discouraging the mushrooming of nurseries and a ban on interviews for school admissions, the trend goes on unabated. Anxious parents want their children to learn, read, and write even before they get to Class I.

Meenakshi was comfortable with the children and the parents saw that she was good. One of the parents suggested that Meenakshi teach at the nearby kindergarten. Meenakshi inquired at the school and, to her utter shock, found that they take only those with a B.Ed! The nursery that advertises as a playway school for three-year-olds boasts of having highly qualified teachers with MA and B.Ed degrees. Meenakshi put forward a metaphorical argument that it would be equivalent to a pilot driving a taxi. She was promptly asked to leave the office.

Questions

(a) Why do employers seek over-qualified people?
(b) How does one explain to the above employer that the stand taken by the school is untenable?
(c) How can companies be made responsible for specifying qualifications?

Nowadays, however, screening has become a very thorny issue. AIDS is spreading fast and organizations that have employees who are HIV positive are facing colossal human problems of coping with the disease. Laws around the globe are made not to discriminate HIV positive people from legitimately seeking employment. But in the workplace, there is a psychological barrier among the employees. Knowingly recruiting a person who is HIV positive is to inherit a workplace problem; but refusing to employ would be in contravention of the law. The dilemma is difficult to solve. Homosexuality is another issue that is difficult for organizations to handle, and the law favours equal opportunity employment, irrespective of a candidate's sexual choices.

Interview

An interview is a critical situation where the employer or the employer's representative, the personnel manager, and the prospective employee come face to face and the personnel manager evaluates the prospect's personal and professional data. The human need to work for a living has brought the candidate before the interviewer. What the interviewer must not forget is the fact that candidates must be treated with dignity. The interviewer would do a good job if he/she keeps away from cultural, racial, or religious biases. It would be extremely imprudent to make comments on the looks and other physical traits of the interviewee. Organizations should have clearly defined profile portfolio for personnel recruitment, and adhering to it will create both professionalism and goodwill among the future employees.

Promotions

Promotion consists of moving from an existing position to a higher position within an organization; the opposite is called demotion. The image of promotion is that of a person climbing a ladder, starting at some stage on the rung of the ladder and working his/her way to the top. Organizations have definite criteria for promotional activity. In some organizations, promotion is based on seniority in the service of the organization, whereas in others the basis is productivity or meritocracy. The fundamental issue concerning promotions in an organization is based on the principle of justice. Deciding who should be promoted or who is eligible for promotion and why causes a lot of stress and consumes tremendous energy of the authorities, which could be better used for running the business efficiently. Seniority, inbreeding, and nepotism could damage the concept of promotions.

Seniority

Mrs Indira Gandhi, the former Prime Minister of India, created a furore in the 1970s when she promoted three judges over their immediate seniors, on the bench of the Supreme Court of India. Irrespective of the kind of organization, whether public or private, superseding the seniors is considered both unfair, as well as emotionally iniquitous. Government organizations generally follow the principle of seniority in the service as the criteria for promotion, which is an easy way out of industrial conflict. But if justice or fairness be the principle of promotion, then merit or performance should take precedence over seniority. Such promotions, however, involve emotional issues and an organization has to be extremely dexterous and transparently fair in order to avoid situations that can cause severe conflicts. Today, companies are increasingly aware of this problem, since disputes of this nature may cost them good employees. The criteria for promotion must be spelt out not only in the general policy regarding human resource management, but also in the appointment letter and during the initiation of the employee in the company.

Following are some of the factors that can be considered along with seniority.

Skill   The skill of a person may help promote him/her rather than the colleague who joined the organization at the same time but has not exhibited the same skill.

Merit   A person who has put in more work, for example a train driver who has clocked more hours of running the train than his colleague.

Loyalty   A loyal employee may not only be given promotion but be also allowed to supersede colleagues if during a crisis, while others just followed the crowd, this employee stood by the management and cooperated to resolve the crisis. Naturally, such a promotion could lead to discontent among colleagues, who may charge the employee with being a favour seeker and not a team player. The employee could also incur the wrath of the union.

If the policy of the company is to merely promote an employee on the basis of the time spent in the organization, then it does not follow any business logic for the progress of the firm. One shudders to think of the national loss incurred when hundreds of thousands of government officers and workers in this country are promoted merely on this narrow principle of seniority. On the other hand, if only qualifications and nothing else becomes the policy to promote, then other human qualities of loyalty and goodwill seem to lose all value. Indian companies value the loyalty of their workers as much as they value their seniority, which is defined as experience by the company. Traditional companies such as the Tatas, the Birlas, and the Godrejs have flourished on these values and they have expressly shown this through the special care of the workers' families.

Human resource managers have their tasks well cut-out to balance the various variables for promotion. It is they who are supposed to balance the principles of seniority along with the loyalty of the workers and usher in reforms with a human face, which will benefit the companies in the long run.

Inbreeding

In-house development, cultivation of talent, and competence is required to furnish a loyal and familial workforce. In reality, however, inbreeding is resented because it dwells on exclusivity and is unable to attract good and competent people from outside. Moral problems arise if inbreeding is the fundamental and guiding principle of recruitment and promotion. The exclusion of others would mean infringing the principle of equal opportunity employment.

The moral dilemma of the human resource manager is unenviable. What are his/her options, given the choice of external competence and internal loyalty? Should the manager employ someone who is qualified and has proven competencies, but comes from outside the firm, or someone whose loyalty to the firm is never in doubt, but is an in-house person? Human resource managers who constantly look outside the firm may be blamed for not valuing the fidelity and reliability of the persons at hand. Again, particularly among the well-established and traditional companies, too many outsiders may in fact destroy the very culture for which the company is known. Hence, depending on the nature of the firm, its longevity in society, and several other policy and social factors, managers would have to balance their act of promotion of employees.

Nepotism

Nepotism is a negative concept, wherein one is discriminated against because he/she is not related to the employer in any way. It is a preferential treatment given to a person not because of his/her professional competence, but because he/she is somehow related to the employer. The only claim for promotion is kinship, and the person is recommended or granted a special favour without actually deserving it and without going through the procedures laid down.

Although nepotism is easy to detect, the nepotist may or may not always be morally clear. His/her moral character is not clear if, for instance, in the public services, favours are granted through the ministers in the government or the officials of the bureaucracy. But in family-owned companies, it is expected that certain posts in the company are manned by the members of the family and preference is given to relatives. However, as Indian companies are now being professionally managed, family members are taking a backseat.

Discipline and Discharge

Discipline, the right behaviour, is the core of morality. Workplace discipline concerns quite strictly with the behaviour that is becoming of a workplace. The employee's manual, consisting of clear clauses and descriptions of acceptable and non-acceptable behaviour, is handed over to the workers at induction. Even senior managers are given the company's code of conduct, wherein their service rules, regulations on perks, and policies on receiving gifts, etc. are clearly documented. When discipline is breached, discharge is an extreme action. However, two or three infringements are duly noted, memos are sent, and warnings are given before any drastic action is taken. Firms have very clear directions for the dismissal of employees on the grounds of indiscipline.

Dress Code

For hospital staff, wearing the prescribed uniform is not only essential to maintain a professional image, but also to facilitate their work and guard them against certain infections. Hence, wearing gloves and caps and mouth flaps are prescribed by code. Similarly, industrial helmets at the construction site and factory overalls in the automobile factory ensure safety. People who deal with hazardous wastes need special equipment to protect them. Thus, workplace discipline is primarily related to its practical consequences.

Discipline of Human Interaction

Where two or more people gather, a social group is formed, and if this group is gathered professionally and works together at the workplace, the relationship, howsoever professional, is a human relationship with all its positive and negative aspects. Views and counterviews as well as agreements and disagreements that lead to verbal and even physical conflicts are natural. In addition, the workplace also faces gender-related problems. Today, the workplace is not just a place for males and females. People belonging to the same sex are into relationships and this is accepted as normal. Problems arise due to sexual harassment and misbehaviour. There are other social problems too that get transferred from the life outside the workplace. Discrimination based on race, religion, caste, and gender crop up from time to time. Problems such as HIV/AIDS and physical and mental disabilities can affect the atmosphere of the workplace negatively. If conflicts become severe and unproductive for the firm, the management will have to resort to the discharge of the employee, responsible for the same after the due procedure of disciplining him/her has failed.

Punctuality and Order

For an organization, time is money and it cannot afford to lose man hours. Firms maintain strict working hours and check-in and check-out regimes. It is also expected that employees maintain a predetermined order of work, so that precision and efficiency are ensured. In the service sector, since firms are directly in contact with customers, care is taken to maintain punctuality and the order of service. A constant breach of this discipline may definitely and rightly call for a discharge.

Privacy

A personnel manager's position enables him/her to be privy to employee information, whether social or professional. He/she has to treat it with utmost confidentiality. Information on illnesses, sexual bias, and personal status of the employee are extremely sensitive. The code on privacy is very strict, and in case of a conflict, the employee may drag the firm to court, where the employee may claim hefty sums as compensation.

Civic Liberties

We see very often that a gag order is placed by professional sports organizations on their hired players to check certain stories from being blown out of proportion in the media and thus causing loss of reputation and money. However, these gag orders are only for a limited period. No organization has the authority to curb the basic freedom of a citizen of a free country. Though the citizen may be an employee of a firm and contracted to offer his/her services, it does not imply forgoing fundamental rights. The empowerment of the employees to whistleblow comes from the civil liberties enshrined in the country's constitution.

Discharge

Keeping in mind the above essential points, the discharge of an employee is not as easy as the old hire-and-fire policy. Social awareness towards the employees is very high. In other words, the moral obligation of firms towards their employees is very serious. The firms, apart from their regular code of conduct, often appoint disciplinary or ethical committees to deal with problems of discipline and discharge. Clear and unambiguous regulations are drawn up and also given to the unions to which the employees belong. A record of the lapses, memos, warnings, and notices is maintained and the employee is well informed about these procedures. Discharge is always a very painful human experience. Firms have realized this aspect and have introduced counselling for such persons. This helps avoid any legal tangles in the event that an ex-employee approaches the court.

A discharge from work may occur for different reasons.

Dismissal   This may be due to very serious reasons of gross insubordination, causing great loss to man and material or bringing the firm to disrepute.

Termination   As per the clauses in the code of conduct, if employees show incompetence through poor performance, a discharge is given.

Layoff   Some employees are hired on a contract basis. Their discharge occurs when the assigned work is over or the contract has expired. Layoff does call for a re-call.

Retrenchment   A firm wants to cut down its workforce due to the various economic reasons forced on it. In Western Europe, as the economic growth rate is hardly a digit strong, firms have to eliminate several work positions, or some factories have to be closed down completely.

Any of the above procedures is not easy to implement. In April 2008, the Arcelor Mittal steel plant workers in France went berserk and destroyed property due to the retrenchment drive. Care and preparation are the watchwords for human resource management. Care must be taken that discharges do not occur without the stipulated notice period. The human resource department must be careful that the employee is notified in normal circumstances and not, for instance, on the day of the spouse's tragic death or the serious illness of a child. Firms must be socially conscious and prepare the employees for the eventuality of closure. The employer will do well to submit the process to professionals, who will not only prepare the employees for the loss of jobs, but also show them several opportunities for new jobs and entrepreneurship. Social leadership must be exercised so that out of a serious challenge, there emerge

---

Top Ten Great Places to Work

Best workplaces 2008 awards

In May 2008, at a function held in Mumbai by the Confederation of the Indian Industry (CII), awards were given to ten companies adjudged as the best workplaces for their employees. These companies have adopted and institutionalized some fundamental values that made them what they are today. Some of the outstanding attributes of the companies have been inspiration to success, approachable management, and pride in corporate image, ethical practices, employee development, and transparency, caring environment, sharing power, and empowering employees.

Following are the top ten companies:

1. RMSI Pvt. Ltd
2. Marriot Hotel, India
3. Google India Pvt. Ltd
4. Agilent Technologies
5. Classic Stripes Pvt. Ltd
6. American Express Bank, India
7. Cadbury India Ltd
8. NTPC Ltd
9. Godrej Consumer Products Ltd
10. HILTI India Ltd

---

opportunities that are so far unseen. If done in this sensitive manner, one does not really know what turnarounds may take place, for the employees may have some brilliant ideas that could save the firm. The example of Telco that belongs to the Tata group has been often cited. When Telco was nose-diving and the management put its hands up in surrender, the employees came up with new suggestions that have now made the company globally successful.

JUST WAGES

The very phrase 'just wages' is morally loaded. 'Nothing is to be had for nothing,' said the Greek philosopher Epictetus, and the same sentiment is repeated today with the phrase 'there is no such thing as a free lunch.' Somewhere, someone has to pay for the work or service done. The question is whether what we pay is fair and just or not. Today, we see an immense disparity in the payment of wages. In the developing world, people work the entire day to earn just a dollar, whereas in the business world, executives amass so much wealth that it can shame the budgets of some small nations!

Constitution of Just Wage

What constitutes the just wage? The answer remains elusive because the problem has never been solved. For most of the working people in the world, the wages are never enough; for a few, they are extravagant. Both cases present serious moral problems. Let us consider a few problems regarding wages. A wage is the price that an employer pays to the employee for the work done. The payment is based on both time and the work done, depending on the contract between the employer and the employee. We generally observe that time-based wages are common. Thus, the workers may be paid hourly, daily, weekly, or monthly.

Wages as income   Wages are the income of the workers. Wages may be distinguished as money wages and real wages. Money wages are the actual amount that a worker receives from the employer. Real wages, on the other hand, consist of the amount of goods and services that the wage money can buy. In other words, it refers to the purchasing power of the money. Money wages may increase but may not be proportionate to the purchasing power. In fact, at inflationary phases, the purchasing power of money goes down, although the real wages may substantially rise, and yet not be proportionate to the earlier value. This may cause severe labour disputes and personnel managers would have insoluble problems at hand. Just wages would be those that validate the money wages to that of real wages.

Fringe benefits   Pension benefits, house rentals, medical insurance, paid holidays, travel expenses, dearness allowances, perquisites such as company car or transport, etc. are seen by the employer as part of the wages, rather than additional benefits.

Indexation   A system of indexation has been developed to overcome the problems of wages whereby wages, prices, taxes, and the rate of inflation have been tied up to demonstrate the actual value of the wages. An escalator clause helps one to look into all the factors to adjust the wages fairly. A consumer price index is commonly used to measure the scale of inflation. Accordingly, governments are able to fix taxation and employers are able to decide the wages of employees. But there is another factor that has become very important, and it is the cost of living. Cost of living consists of the people's basic needs, their family needs, and their social needs. As the standards of living rise, so do the costs of living. The just wage has to cover the cost of living. It is this that ensures the economic progress of the workers.

Rules of Thumb

The law   Follow the law of the land without compromising on the minimum wages fixed by the government, and revise the same, following the revisions by the government. The scales determined by the nation's pay commission are the most practical directives to follow.

Best practices   Follow the best practices on wages in the industry.

The nature of the job   Keeping in mind the nature of the job while determining the wages is very important. The job in a chemical unit could be hazardous, while a scientist's work may be slow and trying; a pilot's job is technically high on skills, while that of a construction worker at a high-rise building is physically tiring and highly dangerous. Keeping the nature of the job in mind, the wages must be determined according to the conventions followed in those areas, as well as in the international standards prescribed by the United Nations International Labour Organization (ILO).

Firm's ability to pay   This is a crucial moral issue. Companies in developing countries often contract undersalaried work force. The exploitation of local conditions, as well as the use of illegal and child labour to reduce production costs, makes the companies morally corrupt. The so-called sweat shops and mass manufacturing units with negligible wage costs have become a festering social issue in India and China. Cheap labour has catapulted the income of these companies without improving the lot of the workers in the same proportion.

Negotiated wages These days, the personnel manager resorts to negotiated wages. Instead of offering standard wages for a definite work, the personnel manager resorts to negotiations with the prospective employee. Thus, it is possible to find people on the same work floor doing the same work for different wages. Depending on the need, a prospective employee agrees to a much lower wage.

Cost of living Cost of living differs from place to place and city to city. In India, every state has its own living standards and locally determined wages. This is an important factor, and people may not be willing to go to a certain city even though the wages offered there are higher because the cost of living is proportionately even higher. The irony of wages in a city like Mumbai would be that one could readily get a highly paid job, and yet all that good money may not help to rent a decent apartment.

Every worker deserves just wages, and to be honest, there should be really very little difficulty in fixing the wages. The problem, more often than not, is how to curtail those wages through a jugglery of financial wizardry and moral inaptitude.

Minimum Wages

The inevitable question that arises is how does one determine the quantum of wages? The simple answer would be to comply with the legally established wage system. The government enacts labour laws according to which a minimum wage is fixed. The system is usually developed by the ministry of labour and involves scientifically factored inputs that give a definite logic to the wage schemes. Indexation and the factors involved therein have been mentioned above. Apart from this, governments form pay commissions from time to time, which assess all economic factors in order to determine salaries and wages. What we should not forget is that governments attempt to arrive at a reasonable sum to be paid to workers for a definite work. The law demands the least minimum. Morality must go beyond the mere fulfilment of the tenets of the law.

Family Wages

The concept of family wages was originally developed through the teachings of the Catholic Church over a century ago, and is now being considered by corporations as their responsibility. Under the ethics of care, corporations are increasingly realizing that if the family is taken into consideration while determining wages, it would be an investment whose returns would be in the form of employees' commitment, efficiency, and productivity. At the same time, it would prepare the next generation of employees, who would take pride inheriting the job from their parents. The example of such best practices is to be found in the Tata group of companies. J.R.D. Tata had made compassion the guiding principle of the enterprise, and the young generation is ever eager to join the company. Although family wages makes a great case for moral justification, companies could have problems while determining the family wage without any discrimination.

TRADE UNIONS

Trade unions are also known as labour unions. These are associations of workers who make a collective bid for just wages. Historically, their origin is attributed to the industrial revolution, and their development is credited to the subsequent social philosophies, namely socialism and communism. The core purpose of trade unionism is to collectively negotiate the salaries and benefits of workers with their employers.

Top of the World

Ten highest paid Indian executives

There is a perennial debate in society about the unjustifiable remuneration of executives. In a country where the majority of the population is poor, how can one justify such high salaries and perks? This question is constantly debated in the public domain. While more than half the population of this country subsists on less than Rs 50 a day, how could one morally justify the following list of remunerations of these top executives?[a]

Name	Group	Designation	Rupees in lakh
1. Mukesh D. Ambani	Reliance Industries	CMD	3046
2. P.R.R. Rajha	Madras Cements	CMD	2478.52
3. Kalanithi Maran	Sun TV	CMD	2326
4. Kaveri Kalanithi	Sun TV	Jt. MD	2326
5. Sunil Bharati Mittal	Bharati Airtel	CMD	1495.62
6. K. Anji Reddy	Dr Reddy's	Chairman	1439.62
7. Brijmohan L. Munjal	Hero Honda	Chairman	1399.52
8. Pawan Munjal	Hero Honda	MD & CEO	1388.82
9. Toshiaki Nakagawa	Hero Honda	Jt. MD	1344.08
10. Takao Eguchi	Hero Honda	WTD	1332.27

Questions

(a) On what moral principle do executives get paid?

(b) Are we conscious about the basic needs of the labourers in India?

(c) Can Indian workers hope for justice?

[a] For an exhaustive list of 1500 executives from the listed companies who are earning Rs 50 lakh and above, see Rajan Bhatia's article in *Business India*, dated 2 December 2007. In the 2000–01 list, there were only 100 executives earning Rs 50 lakh and above. (Jt stands for *Joint*; WTD stands for *Whole Time Director*.)

The purpose is a simple one: to demand just wages for its members. The consequences, however, are very complex and involve economic, political, legal, and social dimensions in their extreme sharpness. Hence, the moral gravity of all the issues involved in labour relations is of utmost importance to businesses. There is a conflict of not only ideologies such as socialism and capitalism, but also livelihoods and all the social and cultural relations. The social ideologies developed by Marx and Engels were for a definitive social revolution. Their objectives were the destruction of capitalism and the establishment of labour as the ideal of a classless society, where work is done as per skills and rewards distributed as per needs.

Evolution of Trade Unions and the Related Morality

Trade unions originated out of the sheer need to improve wages and the working conditions of the workers. A study of the evolution and development of trade unions may help banish some of our prejudices against the working class.

Guilds in Medieval Europe

Medieval Europe had guilds formed by craftsmen. Although a group of craftsmen such as weavers would be a guild, there were also guilds of collective craftsmen. Guild halls, where the meetings of the members of these guilds were held, were built with architectural grandeur. These still remain the signature buildings of the old European cities. These centres had little to do with bargaining with the employers; rather, they were the places of learning for young apprentices and journeymen till they became masters in their trade.

Then trade developed in Europe and the guilds became less influential. Traders, who dressed dandily in liveries, succeeded the masters and the entrepreneurs and their numbers increased. By the end of seventeenth century and the beginning of the eighteenth century, as the industrial revolution took over, an enormous change took place. The industrial revolution brought the issue of the worker to the centre stage and it has remained there ever since.

Industrial Revolution and Marx

The Industrial Revolution created a new world. Production from homes and guilds disappeared and large factories were set up, where mass production of goods began. Factories were fitted with large machines and these machines were operated by workers. Labour became increasingly skill-oriented. People migrated from rural areas to industrial centres. The simple agrarian society suddenly turned into an industrial one, with the growing number of entrepreneurs, financial institutions, investors, bankers, manufacturers, and businessmen. In the new industrial world, the worker was the key to production and thus an indispensable catalyst to the new economy.

Middle class   There grew a new class called the middle class, who owned factories and ran businesses, operated banks and other institutions of trade and commerce, and became very prosperous. A large multitude of workers streamed in from the villages to seek work in factories and in other institutions as labourers. Their economic conditions as against the middle class saw a growing and yawning gap. This disparity clearly showed the injustice of the industrial revolution. The middle class was now firmly entrenched in the philosophy of capitalism and the right to private ownership, and it vigorously advocated and succeeded greatly in the economic logic of supply and demand. The supply of cheap labour made the rich richer and the poor labourers poorer. Further, the injustices that were heaped on the labourers were unregulated working hours, unhealthy working conditions, lack of safety measures, lack of housing, and unbearable living conditions. This finally made the workers hit back.

Injustice to workers   It is at this juncture of extreme moral depravity of justice to workers that the ideas of Karl Marx became meaningful. Marx's ideas included the labour force, the common ownership, the class struggle, the destruction of bourgeois, the end of capitalism, the abolition of private property, the establishment of the dictatorship of the proletariat, and the supremacy of the state. In short, social justice was the sole aim of socialism.

Trade union legislation   As early as the 1840s, legislation in Great Britain, Germany, and several other countries was passed to legalize trade unions. Labour laws were enacted for regulating the number of working hours, the safety and security of workers, and the provisions of housing and health. However, to supply to the great demand at home, European countries resorted to colonial occupation of countries in other continents, and pursued imperialism as a legitimate policy. The Americas, the whole of Asia, and Africa fell to the colonialists, and scores of countries around the globe suffered. These countries were not only robbed of their nationality and dignity, but also of their enormous wealth. It left them impoverished, while Europe flourished at their cost.

Thus, in the nineteenth century, socialism had issues that were fundamentally humanistic and based on social justice. It stood against imperialism and capitalism. The Russian communist revolution helped to establish a worker-state, while China and several other countries fought against the Japanese colonialists to establish an imperialist-free country. India too with its socialist agenda, although not of a communist kind, won its freedom from the colonial rulers to form a free, democratic, and socialist country. The countries of South America too fought wars of independence and the US helped several of them by issuing warnings against the European colonial powers.

Change of employer–employee relationship   The social relations, the basis of any morality, changed from a master–servant relationship to an employer–employee relationship. In the entire development mentioned above, one single issue of morality has been at stake, that is, the principle of distributive justice, to give one his/her due. While capitalism robbed workers of their fair wages, imperialism robbed nations of their wealth and reduced the populace to poverty. Thus, history stands witness to the fact that justice was grossly violated both individually and collectively.

Collective Bargaining

Grounds for Demands

Workers have demands. The morality of those demands question whether such demands are right or not. If the demands are exorbitant and beyond the reasonable means of the employer, they would be termed unfair. Now, let us assume that workers put forward their just demands through their unions. The question is, what is the morality of the collective demand or of bargaining to fulfil the demands? There are several moral problems that arise from collective bargaining:

(a) Is it not a strong-arm tactic against the employer?
(b) If the employees do not like the employment terms or working conditions, are they not free to seek employment elsewhere?
(c) If the demands are going to drain the employer's resources, how is the employer going to invest and improve his/her enterprise?

Morality of Collective Bargaining

The reason for collective bargaining is quite compelling. An individual employee is no match to the employer. To overcome this imbalance in bargaining, individual workers form a union and they elect a representative to present their case before the management or the employer.

However, the problems are many and the bargaining is not merely bilateral, that is, between the employee or the trade union and the employer. There are at least three elements—the trade union representing the employees, the employer or the board of governors of a company, and the legal apparatus represented by the government. In the case of the Bombay Textile mill workers (see box), the law stood in the way of the negotiations and 3,00,000 mill workers lost their jobs and livelihoods. The moral responsibility of such negotiations is enormous and when the representatives of the workers fail to deliver, the suffering of the affected workers is appalling.

How would managers handle such situations? Would a manager have the courage to stand up to a union leader and demand to know whether his interests represent that of the workers? Is it not that the union leader wants to position himself politically? Is the union leader justified in using the power of the working force to his personal ends? The history of union representatives is replete with failed negotiations. This leads us to ask, what then is the morality of industrial action?

Morality of Industrial Action

Firstly, the morality of industrial action or striking from work is based on the term 'just cause'. What is a just cause? This calls for a sharp debate. We need to justify it through a thorough process of both economic and moral reasoning. Indeed, wages as well as working conditions must be raised according to the levels of inflation and the cost of living. Such a condition could be a just cause. The second term of reference is 'proper authorization'. Primarily, it consists of workers authorizing their representatives

Doctor of Trade Union

The mill workers of Bombay

Mumbai, which was till a few years ago known as Bombay, the colonial legacy, was also known as the Manchester of the East, because Manchester is the city of textile mills of Great Britain. Today's Gen-X, who mill around in these large mega malls, which once upon a time were the textile mills that made India as famous as today's IT, may not truly realize the significance of these workplaces of the tens of thousands of mill-workers, who lost their livelihoods and became perfect examples of the lost power of collective bargain.

To say that Dr Datta Samant was a famous union leader of the textile mill workers of Bombay in the 1970s and 1980s would be an enormous understatement. Samant donned several hats, including the powerful ones. He was a Maratha. He came from a middle-class family in Deobag, Konkan, and was brought up in Ghatkopar, Mumbai. He was a medical doctor by profession. He subscribed to communist ideology but was politically affiliated to the Congress Party under the leadership of Mrs Indira Gandhi. He headed the Rashtriya Mill Mazdoor Sangh, an affiliate of the Indian National Trade Union Congress (INTUC), which is the trade union wing of the Congress Party. He became a legislator of the Maharastra Assembly, as a member of the Congress Party. Later on, in the 1980s, he became a Member of the Parliament. But above all else, he had found a place in the hearts and minds of the mill workers. He was god for them and they referred to him as Doctorsaheb.

At the fag end of 1981, Samant led twin negotiations with the Bombay Mill Owners Association and the government. The demands from the former were for higher wages and better working conditions for the workers, and from the latter, to scrap the Bombay Industrial Act of 1947. The phase of negotiations catapulted Samant to the front pages of the national dailies. He and his associates grew in enormous power as the battle of wills kept the nation in suspense. The negotiations failed. Samant organized a year-long strike of over 3,00,000 mill workers and hogged most of the space in the national dailies. Mrs Gandhi's directives were clear and unbending and Samant was adamant in his demands.

The end result of this great battle of industrial negotiations was a great disaster for the tens of thousands of workers who had put their absolute faith in the abilities of their Doctorsaheb, who could do no wrong. The mill workers lost their jobs and livelihoods; some perished in misery, some returned to their rural roots, and some found little solace in alternate jobs. The textile industry closed down in Mumbai and it relocated itself in different parts of the country. Most of the mills modernized and established themselves in Gujarat.

The mill owners' association earned a blessing in disguise by getting rid of the old workforce and garnering the soaring real estate value of their landed assets. The totally abandoned mills today fetch the owners thousands of crore of rupees. Mega malls have been set up on these very grounds where the mill workers sweated and earned their money to take care of their families. If one such mill worker were to return today and see the towering stacks now donning some hoarding of an MNC product, it would be an unbearable insult to his injury.

Questions

(a) If you were a mill worker how would you justify the mill workers' strike?

(b) Does poverty rob even the moral right of an Indian worker?

(c) Have the trade union leaders of India done more harm than good to the workers?

to take action. For those who know what a strike is, this might sound self-contradictory. However, now that strikes are recognized as a legitimate weapon for collective bargaining, both legal as well as moral support can been garnered for the action. The third term of reference for the morality of strike is that it is adopted only as a last resort. Unions are obliged by the law to give adequate notice of the strike to the management. Unions must also show a record of the failed negotiations to arrive at a decisive solution, to prove that they had threatened to strike from work as no other choice was available.

In the face of the confrontation between the union and the employers, there could never be a consensus on these three terms of reference for the justification of strikes, because these are the very contentious issues upon which the impending industrial action is sought. It is quite logical therefore that one proposes and the other disposes. The only exception to this case is the state of West Bengal, where the Communist Party of India (Marxist) rules and sponsors strikes or city *bandhs* through its union affiliates!

The present-day unions have lost most of their credibility. Many employees think that their right to join a particular union is infringed because of the closed-shop principle, wherein an employer is able to employ workers only from a definite union. In some cases, the unions divide the territories and give the employees time to join once they take up employment. Some unions give the employees the freedom not to join the union, provided they pay the fees!

With the end of communism in Europe, trade unions have lost their clout and the market economy has much satisfactory answers to their employees. In the developing countries, unions still have much power but have lost the trust of their members due to the lack of commitment by the union leadership to the cause of the workers.

Morality of Lockouts

A strike is work stoppage by employees to forward their demands. A lockout is the employer's refusal to allow the employees to work and thereby depriving them of the wages. The lockout is a powerful weapon in the hands of the employer, quite simply because the employer has the resources to hold out longer, whereas a worker may be able to survive for only a short period of time. The unions, having lost much of their clout and resources, would not be able to support their members for long either. Thus, the employer can force the workers to agree to his/her conditions if they wish to be taken again on board. The morality of lockouts is a very difficult issue to justify, and yet if there are just causes, moral support to the employer is not misplaced. If employees go on strike repeatedly, and the enterprise is economically doomed and is becoming insolvent, then the employer has no choice, as the establishment comes to an automatic halt. Transparency by the management and correct information could win over the employees. The best practices in corporate governance in Germany invariably include union representatives on the board of directors. As a result, labour relations are smooth and the partnership between the employees and employers becomes commendable.

Managers and Trade Unions

From what we have seen above, it makes enormous management sense to develop and nourish better labour relations. We have seen in the stages of moral development

The preacher and the slave

'The Preacher and the Slave' is a song dedicated to the workers of the world by Joe Hill, whose real name was Joel Hagglund. He was born in Sweden in 1879. At the beginning of the twentieth century, he migrated to the US and spent his time doing several odd jobs. He was a passionate songwriter. He joined the Industrial Workers of the World (IWW), which was an American labour organization. Its philosophy was to replace the contemporary American system of government with a government by the workers of America. Joe Hill was instrumental in popularizing the ideology of the organization through songs. 'Casey Jones—The Union Scab' was one of his popular songs. In 1914, he was convicted with capital punishment for the murder of two people. President Woodrow Wilson's influence, the endeavours of the Swedish government, and the pressure of the people around the world could not save him from the firing squad on 19 November 1915. He is revered as a great hero of the workers even today, in America and in the communist world.

Questions

(a) Do songs and music have a role in trade unions?
(b) Why do workers feel motivated by songs?
(c) Do songs bear a moral message?

the kind of relationship that exists among the agents of moral action. Today, we must rule out the pre-conventional theory of top-down management, or command management strategy. The conventional management that functions to the letter of the law—pay, benefits, perks, etc.—may bring in some efficiency of the kind that was introduced by Frederick Taylor. This may even satisfy the unions very well, since all tenets of the labour law are followed assiduously. But one would certainly feel that a touch of humanity is missing. It is said that Ford Motors, which followed Taylorism to the core, concentrated on the number of cars on the production line. It worked for a while, and then, the slump began. The company changed the motto from the number of cars produced to 'Quality is Job 1'. The focus shifted from machine to man, and the turnaround took place.

Moral Principles for HR Manager

There are three fundamental moral principles that have significance for the human resource manager—human dignity, dignity of labour, and dialogue. Before the manager deals with the trade union, it would be logical that he/she deal with the members, who are the employees working under the manager. If the manager takes care of the workers, the unions will be automatically taken care of.

People work for money out of economic need, but they do not pawn their dignity to their employer just because the employer is the pay master. Both the employer and the employee partake in the same humanness, and it has to be respected for its own sake. The roles of a manager or a worker or an entrepreneur are rather incidental in the world of economics, for today's labourer could be an entrepreneur tomorrow. Alos, the dignity of labour must be treated as supreme. Work in all its forms is work and it creates wealth with a social purpose, and should therefore be respected. When

---

UNSNA

Inclusions and exclusion in statistical concepts

'Cost to the company' is a commonly used term. But 'compensation of employees', known by the acronym CE, is a statistical concept in use with the national accounts, which refers to the total pre-tax wages paid by the employer in a financial year or accounting period, such as half-yearly accounting. The United Nations System of National Accounts (UNSNA) was formed to understand the value that is contributed by labour, along with the other factors of production. Following is a list of the items included and excluded in CE.

Inclusions in the statistical concept	Exclusions from the statistical concept
Gross wages and salaries	Unpaid voluntary work
Cash allowances, overtime pay, bonuses, commissions, tips, and gratuities	Income from self-employment, unemployed, unpaid family workers
Remuneration in kind valued at purchaser price: meals, drinks, accommodation, uniform used outside the workplace, vehicles and other durables, travel, child care or crèches, subsidies, etc.	Property income, income of outworkers
Income tax and social contributions by the employer on behalf of the employee	Social benefits paid directly by government
Income of students from paid work	Job seek expenses, relocation
Income received by shareholder employees	Benefits paid by employer with respect to dependents
Income by contract workers	Payment made for absentee work
The interest foregone by the employer for house loans and other consumables	Severance payments to workers or survivors for sickness, accident, or death

a manager acknowledges a fellow worker as being as worthy as himself and respects his contribution at work, there ensues a mature human relationship. The manager and the worker will be able to relate to each other on the same level. This relation or communication between the manager and the worker is called a dialogue. This dialogue may consist of very little verbal exchange. The exchange is at a deeper human level of attitude, which creates a mutual understanding. This relationship continues to strengthen their trust in each other, which is the cause of the empowerment of the worker and the transformation of the business. The manager becomes a morally responsive being and is able to impart servant-leadership, that is, leading by example. With such leadership, the company can only progress in both wealth and moral values.

Employees of such companies need no unions to bargain for their wages and benefits. Even if such trade unions do exist, their mission will change, for they too will participate in the governance and be responsible not just to the workers, but also to society. Thus, managers can deal with trade unions in a mature moral environment, which will create co-operation, progress, and prosperity.

SUMMARY

- The employer and employee come into a working relationship under a contract.

- The employee, while having the right to wages and benefits, is duty bound to offer a sincere service and justify the wages and benefits received.

- The employee enjoys the human rights conferred on him/her by society, as well as all the lawful rights as a worker, according to the law of the land.

- The personnel manager has duties and responsibilities towards the worker—from hiring to discharge, interviewing to negotiation of wages.

- The personnel manager strives not only to marshal the human resources at hand for

profitable returns for the company, but also provides moral leadership.

- The trade union upholds the demands of the workers in a collective bargain.

- The morality of the collective bargain and any planned industrial action depends on the just cause, proper authorization, and the decision to go on a strike only as a last resort.

- Good labour relations are very important for all the stakeholders in a company.

- Partnership of the trade unions or the workers with the management of the company is an ideal worth striving for.

- A lockout is a serious moral issue, since it involves the livelihood of those who cannot economically hold out or bargain successfully.

KEY TERMS

Closed shop   A company where all employees must belong to a definite trade union and the employer is bound to employ people from a definite trade union only.

Collective bargain   Negotiation between an employer and trade union.

Competency   Abilities required for a professional, consisting of educational qualifications and skills.

Contract   An agreement with terms and conditions.

Cost of living   Expenses one has to bear to live a normal family life in a given locality.

Dialogue   A potent solution to solve human problems of differences of opinion, strife, and conflict; open and transparent communication among people on differing issues, to find the most acceptable means to move ahead.

Dignity of labour   Work, irrespective of its nature, is directly related to individuals and hence to their dignity or honour.

Discharge   Dismissal of an employee from service; severing of the work contract.

Discipline   Regulation in the workplace.

Dismissal   Discharge from duties.

Duty   Assumed obligation under a contract.

Escalator clause   The clause in a contract permitting adjustments of the wages because various factors diminish the value of the wage money.

Family wages   The wages of an individual, sufficient to look after his/her family.

Fringe benefits   Benefits received other than the salary and the usual benefits.

Hire   To contract for the agreed remuneration; both goods and services may be hired for which payment is assumed.

Human dignity   Universal and inviolable self-esteem and respect.

Human resource   One of the factors of production, also known as human capital; in moral applications, one has to be careful not to treat humans as commodities or objects.

Human trafficking   The corrupt practice of supply of manpower, often involving the trade of minors, particularly girls, or migrant workers from poor countries to developed countries, to work unaccountably as cheap labourers.

Inbreeding   Cultivation and development of employees from within the organization.

Industrial action   Any adverse action such as strike, pickets, sympathetic strike, etc. initiated by trade unions against employers when the bargaining of their demands fail.

Just wages   The pay for work that satisfies the criterion of at least the legal minimum wages.

Labour law   Enacted laws of the land concerning workers, wages, and their social and economic well being.

Layoff   Suspension of contracted labour.

Lockout   Halting of work by employers to make workers bow down to their demands.

Loyalty   The emotional bond that exists between an employee and the employer's enterprise; it also creates a sense of belongingness and readiness to face hardships for the sake of the organization.

Merit   The requisite value needed for employment or admission.

Minimum wages   Wages declared as lawful by the state authorities.

Money wages   Actual wages accounted for in terms of currency.

Nepotism   Misuse of one's power to grant undue favours and promotions to relatives and friends.

Obligation   Duty to honour contract.

Open shop   Freedom for workers to join any trade union or for employers to hire from any trade union.

Over-qualification   Educational and skill qualifications over and above the requisite factors for gainful employment.

Real wages   Wages according to the purchasing power parity.

Recruit   To enlist the services of an employee

Retrenchment   Economizing on or cutting down of the workforce due to economic reasons such as recession.

Right   What is good, right (as opposed to wrong), and lawful; what ought to be and belonging justly to a person.

Seniority   Pre-eminence of position by way of experience in an organization.

Strike   To keep away from work of the employer.

Taylorism   A detailed system of organizing factory work to make it more efficient by measuring time and motion involved at work.

Termination   Scrapping of employment contract.

Trade union   Also known as labour union; it is an association of workers to safeguard and promote their interests.

Workplace   Where work is done; today one can work from home during office working hours; thus workplace is both space and time related.

CONCEPT REVIEW QUESTIONS

1. What do you understand by the term 'working conditions' in a call centre?
2. Justify some of the factors in just wages.
3. What personal questions are objectionable at an interview and why?
4. Is employing over-qualified persons morally right? Give reasons.

CRITICAL THINKING QUESTIONS

1. Is Taylorism successful?
2. Analyse the family wages of a bank clerk in the State Bank of India and compare to see whether the present wages justify as family wages.
3. As a personnel manager of a city mall retailer, would you like to know from your applicant whether she is a single mother? Give reasons for or against this query.
4. You are the personnel manager of a paints and chemicals marketing company in which the promoter's son also works as a marketing executive. The senior executive of marketing has shifted to another company and the post is vacant. There are two executives in the company who are senior to the above mentioned son of the promoter. The son has strongly positioned himself to take up the post. If you

promote one of the seniors, you fear the wrath of the father and son. But you have also learnt from your sources that if you promote the son, the promoter is going to discharge you for deviating from the company policy. You need your job desperately due to family reasons and cannot afford to look for a new job. Provide a successful solution for this dilemma.

FURTHER READING

Karl Marx, *Das Kapital*, available at the Gutenberg Project site.

CASE STUDY

Cool Dudes Bunking Work

HR Practice at BPO

The BPO

The company offers its customers technical product support. The activity consists of customer call service, data monitoring, and quality audits. It is a very busy workstation with three shifts.

HR Head

He is a seasoned manager, who has had his share of dealing with the young employees. He follows a personal philosophy of employing good people, that is, those whose attitude match the company's work culture; he then trains them as required. He found a similar trait in the HR manager when he signed him on. The new HR manager was from a tea estate HR management background, but he was willing to learn the industrial HR management skills. The HR head has given him two months to prove himself.

Problem

Six disgruntled shift workers have a grievance. They are underpaid as compared to those who have joined the company after them. So they walk up to the HR manager and tell him exactly how they feel about the issue of their pay and give him a day's ultimatum to sort it out. Two days go by but the HR manager does not attend to the problem. The workers walk out and do not report to work.[a] The Operations Manager intervenes and patches up. He even succeeds in getting the entire unit of the firm to agree to work for longer hours and at weekends also, when the business increases

manifold. Things continue as before and the workers realize that there is going to be no end to it. The increase in their remuneration is not materializing, nor do they have any idea about the volume of the work involved and how long the provisional period of extra work will go on. So now, they want to quit. But the company cannot afford to lose them. What should the HR head, the HR manager, the Operations Manager and the supervisor do?

Knowledge Workers

These unhappy workers are young, modern, Gen X, just-out-of-college group of individuals with new age thinking, live fast lives, and have a fling at BPOs to make quick money. They couldn't care less for the corporate hierarchy and neither are they in awe of the managers. They are straightforward, upfront, and if they do not like something, they walk out without arguing. They know exactly what is going on and are also aware of their importance to the company. Their first priority is, in fact, not the raise in their remuneration, but that the HR manager speaks to them or rather listens to them. Neglect by the HR manager is an insult to them. They sulk. Instead of working, they sit at the coffee shop and perhaps call the HR manager names.

HR Manager

He is a fine man and understands his duty well. He expects everyone else to understand his or her duty as well, and turn up for work. He easily forgets the ultimatum given by the shift team because

---

[a] Meera Seth, 'To Grow a Giant Oak' in *Business World*, 29 April 2008, pp. 53–56. Adapted with a suitable format and summarized to focus on the problem. The names have been omitted, only designations are mentioned.

he thinks that normally employees do not carry out such threats and that these problems can be sorted out in time. It is a blessing that the Operations Manager usually understands the youngsters. However, he is perplexed why these six workers threaten to quit at the drop of a hat. He fails to understand why these cannot let things take their own course. Sometimes there is more work and at other times, there will be a lean season just as it is in the tea estate.

Operations Manager

He has a definite experience in dealing with the young people and he does not mind condescending to speak to them or go after them. He finds them in the coffee shop just as he had expected. So he sits down with them and asks them what's wrong. The youngsters tell him and he just listens to their grievance without saying a word. The youngsters then return to their workstations. The Operations Manager shows his human understanding, and the skill and attitude that a manager must exercise when there is a huge volume of business spurt. A new product launch caught the imagination of the people and its demand was an all-time high. The Operations Manager decides to give it as a gift to this entire unit of shift workers during the festival season. The manager skilfully manoeuvres the entire troupe of six into working overtime, without taking the weekends' and holidays' off. But perhaps he too becomes a victim of his own strategies. He does not disclose to the employees about the burgeoning load of work. He reasons that he need not disclose this because after all, they have to only attend to a single call at a time. The employees have agreed to work longer, so what difference does it make? The Operations Manager, who always understood his employees, cannot understand the problem of the six youngsters who would now like to quit.

Supervisor

The Supervisor knows the problem of the youth at the BPO; he is aware that they have spoken to the HR manager. He is a sensitive man who observes everything that is going on but reserves his judgment. He is the key to what is going on. On a sophisticated apparatus, he monitors the workload that comes in and the calls are directed to the teller's desk. They do not get to see the data; only he knows

about the volume of business transactions happening on the floor.

Epilogue

There is no epilogue! The story ends here but the suspense must continue. It is expected that the students, managers, or readers make up their minds about this situation which is taking place practically everyday at the BPOs. Many management practitioners and thinkers are apprehensive about this industry and are concerned about the young employees working here. These youngsters, who are in the prime of their youth, are exposed to enormous verbal abuse, ghostly working hours, and are forced into a life-style that is unreal, and has very little longevity. Stability in life and the security of life are the trade offs. If young people get frustrated despite the so-called 'good money' that they earn, it only shows that their foundations are shaky.

The HR managers too are caught up in a web. How do they deal with the young employees? One comes up with the banal exercise of 'listening' to the youngsters, but does not care to do anything about it.

Practitioners and thinkers are often very critical about the BPO industry and liken it to the sophisticated sweatshops. The 'silicon valley' nomenclature has been changed to the 'coolie valley'. To think that this is the industry that has catapulted India to new global heights is sad. Is this what our young employees should look forward to? What kind of a country are these citizens going to build? The future looks gloomy.

Discussion Questions

1. What is the outstanding issue of the case?

2. Why is the issue ethical?

3. What is the attitude of young people towards authority at their first stint at work?

4. Is there an age culture that affects human relationships at workplace?

5. Is it necessary that the employees should know everything? Is it not fair that they do their duty?

6. Is it fair to threaten to quit, or just walk out without prior notice? What is the responsibility of an employee?

7. Should the BPOs not have a union? Apart from an instance in West Bengal where

BPOs have a union, there is no such phenomenon reported so far. This should be because a union functions under the law. Even industrial action has to follow a procedure of giving prior warnings to the employer and sufficient time to consider the demands. At the same time, unions make it obligatory that employees perform their duties. They also monitor employees' work memos, attendance register, warnings, etc., given by the employer.

8. What stage of moral maturity is shown by the different characters in this case?

Going Further . . .
- Simulate a BPO setting and role play the discussions with the HR manager.
- Call a small group of young BPO employees, as well as a couple of executives, to recount their experiences.

ETHICAL DEVELOPMENT PROGRAMME

Management Training

Make a synopsis of The Minimum Wages Act 1948 and examine the moral reasoning of the provisions.

Develop Moral Leadership

Conceive an adventurous and challenging project to become a part of the workers union:

Attend meetings. Speak to the member workers. Record their life and grievances as employees, survey their families and home conditions, etc. Take up any cause of the people of your society. See where it is going to lead you. (While doing her PhD research, Medha Patkar, an alumnus of the Tata Institute of Social Sciences, took up a similar challenging adventure that changed her life into a leader of the Narmada Bachao Andolan and made her the voice of the displaced people.)

This is not meant for every one. This is not a call to profession. It is a vocation, a special call from one's conscience. It is where a leader is formed to inspire and suffer. This is a challenge of moral leadership. Only very rare persons, who can conceptualise and crystallize the will of the people, will embrace it. This is not a career. It is to lead people by example, strength, and fearlessness. The only qualification required, which is contrary to the fundamental principle of business, is selflessness.

Management Mantra

Arbeit, Arbeiter, and Arbeitskraft

By labour-power or capacity for labour is to be understood the aggregate of those mental and physical capabilities existing in a human being, which he exercises whenever he produces a use-value of any description.

Karl Marx (1818–1883), the German philosopher and revolutionary, may be called the discoverer of the workers' power. How did Marx get the idea of the worker being the central point in civil society? One does not have to go very far. Work is the attribute by which a German may be defined. Germans honour work to the extent that it becomes their identity. *Arbeit* implies work, *Arbeiter* is the worker, and *Arbeitskraft* is literally work-power, now translated as labour force and is attributed to the lexicon of Marxism as the most important factor in production economics and as the most potent socio-political factor. In the background of the industrial revolution, Marx saw the rise of capitalism and, at the same time, the exploitation of workers. Marx himself did very little to support himself and his family that comprised his wife and six children. It was his friend and co-author, Friedrich Engels, who looked after them when they settled in England.

MANTRA   *Workers of the world unite!*

The Workplace and the Individual

The test of the artist does not lie in the will with which he goes to work, but in the excellence of the work he produces.[1]

—Thomas Aquinas

So much of what we call management consists in making it difficult for people to work.[2]

—Peter Drucker

LEARNING OBJECTIVES

After studying this chapter, you will be able to

➤ Distinguish between professional and personal ethics
➤ Understand the morality of informed consent
➤ Differentiate between workplace surveillance and privacy
➤ Discuss health and safety hazards

INTRODUCTION

A manager's ethical standard of judging self is stewardship at the workplace and prudence at home. Generally, professional fulfilment is more than mere duty. Yet, duty is the minimum to begin with, to be fair to the employer, fellow employees, and other stakeholders. If a worker enjoys the work, then the tediousness of merely performing it is replaced by self-satisfaction. Satisfying work always motivates an individual. However, there are serious workplace problems that include both professional as well as social issues. When prospective employees seek jobs, their focus is only on getting the job and they pay less attention to the terms and conditions

---

[1] Thomas Aquinas (1225–1274), the medieval scholastic thinker, is considered as one of the most systematic thinkers the world has ever produced.

[2] Peter Drucker (1909–2005), the management thinker of the twentieth century, proposed ethics as the cornerstone of business management.

of employment. When they study these terms and conditions later on, they become disenchanted because some of the terms and conditions are personally and socially detrimental to them. Employees have a right to informed consent. If managers have failed to convey this to them, then it is a serious breach of human rights. Privacy and surveillance are becoming increasingly difficult in a technologically advanced workplace. Problems of workplace safety have plagued the industrial society always. We will study these problems under the themes mentioned above.

NEED FOR WORKPLACE ETHICS

Thomas Aquinas' and Peter Drucker's thoughts aptly describe the scope of this chapter, the workplace ethics. A product gets judged by its quality. The quality of a product depends on the workmanship that has produced it. The workmanship comes from the worker. The worker works in a workplace. The manager manages workers at the workplace by evolving a system for the workers to function. The system could facilitate or make it difficult for the workers to perform. The interaction between the manager and the worker creates a work culture, which we may call work ethic or the system to perform. Ethics consists of the rules on which this system is built.

We are wholly and integrally involved in whatever action we perform. We cannot artificially develop a schizophrenic personality and be one person at home and another person in the office. Our home life influences our workplace performance, and vice-versa. What influence does your organization have on you? It could be total.

Let us imagine that you are a plant manager of a very sensitive and controversial weaponry system at an ordinance factory. These factories come under the Ministry of Defence, Government of India. You are bound to secrecy and there are certain matters that you cannot mention to even your family members or closest friends. You have been transferred regularly. You are also under surveillance, as a result of which your communications such as phone calls, emails, etc. are monitored. In the beginning, you seemed to like all these personal intrusions, since it gave you a sense of pride and prestige for playing an important part in the national life of your country. However, after making a few unintentional mistakes, you received memos. So now, you have become extremely wary of your surroundings and feel uncomfortable at the workplace. You tend to look over your shoulders all the time and are always stressed. Your religion has also come under scrutiny. You know definitely that you are being followed. When you complain to your senior officer, he assures you that it is natural to feel that way after receiving those memos and spending several years in the organization. He further assures you that the memos and warnings were mere formality. You still feel intuitively that something is not right somewhere. Then late one night, there is a knock on your door. You are led to the military headquarters for interrogation. You see a file lying on the table before your interrogator. You recognize it at once. You remember bringing it home over the weekend to work on it, so that it could be ready for the coming week. But you got ill overnight. So you called your friend and colleague, who is also of the rank of a major like you. You handed over the file to him in confidence, because he would need to work on it in the coming week. When you now see that very file with your interrogator, you realize its ominous implications. You shudder to think that you are a cog in the enemy spy net. One look at your interrogator tells you that it is the end of the world for you. The faces of your wife and children swim before your eyes. You think you will collapse. The military discipline in you roots you to the ground. It has been a long time since then. Now sitting behind the bars, you still wonder whether your family too has condemned you.[3]

Whatever high or low credential a manager may possess, he/she has to face another individual, whatever be his/her status at the workplace.

PROFESSIONAL VERSUS PERSONAL

Is professional ethics different from personal ethics? This simple question presents several dilemmas for a professional. One of the most natural things that happens at the workplace is the sharing of personal information. We slip into a quandary of exactly how much information to divulge. In what light will colleagues see us if we were to say that we are divorced or have AIDS? Further, professionals have to face a host of dilemmas on the home front. They wonder about whether to share their workplace problems with their family. If they do, they will make the family equally sad or unhappy. But if they do not say anything, the family might become suspicious. These professionals feel guilty for taking out their frustrations on their family members, particularly their wives and children, who are vulnerable. Thus, the problems and dilemmas that professionals face both at the workplace and at the home front are serious and have moral implications.

At the Workplace

The philosophy of work-life balance is patronized and propagated by human resource management (HRM). HRM professionals train employees in the art of balancing their personal and professional lives, using time management techniques such as prioritizing and meditation. Ethics is also dealt with in the personal as well as professional front. HRM professionals train employees on how to identify the issues, balance them, and then cope with them.

Personal ethics is a private matter. An individual's view about right and wrong is a personal affair. A man may believe that women should not have the same social and religious rights as men. However, at work, if a woman is his senior manager, he does not let his personal beliefs interfere with his professional duties. He performs his duty as per his contract of employment. His manager, in turn, may not be concerned with the man's personal matters, such as his being divorced, not returning borrowed money,

---

[3] The story is a figment of my imagination and intends to highlight the dilemmas in professional and personal life.

and having no respect for his elders. However, the man's poor reputation may negatively influence the boss's thinking about him: his being divorced may be because of his association with a certain female colleague; since he does not return borrowed money, he may also be fudging the accounts; and his disrespect for his elders is reflected in his disrespect for his co-workers. HR professionals work at resolving such problems.

Ethics is fundamentally the deliberate choices that we make in life, whether in personal and professional matters. For instance, you are a finance controller and your immediate task is to see that there is sufficient cash flow. On one occasion, 'on technical grounds', you had to ask your accountants to inflate some transactions. You personally consider this a financial fraud that only serves to pander the ego of the promoters and give a bright picture of the company to the shareholders. You remember that diversion of certain funds in the previous quarter had not been right and were not accounted for. You know that if these matters had been attended to promptly, the need for inflating transactions would not have arisen. If you were to follow your personal ethics, you would not inflate the accounts. It is that simple. Your company may face a cash crunch, but will never face a financial scam. Knowing what the company's present predicament is and deciding not to inflate the accounts could indeed be a very difficult choice to make. But as a smart finance controller, if you chose to follow your professional compulsion of utilizing a technical ground, it would be a rather easy choice you made. However, there is a distant risk that if discovered some day, it would be the first step towards a scam in your company.

Peter Drucker, one of the greatest management teachers, was never tired of advocating that there is only one ethics, business or otherwise. The laws of nature are same for everybody, irrespective of the subject. The law of gravity works on all things and brings down whatever is thrown up. The solar system also functions according to the law of gravity. In the same way, ethics has a fundamental universality when it comes to the principles of honesty, truth, and justice. Personal, professional, or otherwise, these principles apply to all equally.

However, certain matters may not seem as watertight as they are imagined to be. Is universal ethics hypothetical? Has it no relevance to professional ethics?

Workplace versus Home Front

In India, which is rapidly growing economically, women are increasingly coming out of their traditional household roles and assuming competitive careers. However, the reality in most of the cases is that their burdens seem to have simply doubled. No one has substituted for their housework. They have to put in extra time to complete their household chores and then rush to work. At times, the burdens and pressures from the family are so much that they are in the dilemma of prioritizing their homes over their careers.

The present working world is literally a war front. The term 'war front' was prevalent in history ever since man went to war. It was only during World Wars I and II that the term 'home front' was coined. While men were at war at one front or the other, life was equally difficult for women at home. In Europe and America, women, apart from looking after their households, also started working in war-related industries. Thus, women fought not only on the war fronts but also on the home fronts.

Today's battle fronts, both at home and at work, are economic in nature. In order to meet the needs of modern living, the traditional breadwinner's earnings for the family are inadequate. The role of men and women is mixed; they are there at both the fronts. It implies that life's choices are determined by the economic choices. Working men and women have to plan not only their budgets, but also how many children to have and how to time their arrival. They have to plan for their homes, manage their

---

A Decision That Went Sour

Airline employee layoff grounds management

In mid-October 2008, in the middle of the festival season in India, the employees of Jet Airways were in for a rude surprise. The employees, 1900 in all, including 800 permanent employees with more than a decade's service in the organization, were given notices of their retrenchment. Some were informed through SMS only.

The $6 billion aviation industry in India suffered a total loss of $2 billion till March 2009. Jet Airways and Kingfisher Airlines struck a strategic alliance to counter the slowdown in the aviation industry, which caused them a loss of Rs 10 crore daily. Putting plans of expansion on hold and agreeing to a code-sharing alliance with Kingfisher, Jet Airways expected to break even in 2010. The layoff decision was a part of this business plan.

Mumbai became the epicentre of the employee action: Hundreds of employees of Jet Airways, including pilots, the cabin crew, and ground staff came out openly and agitated.[a] They enlisted the sympathy and support of the Maharashtra Navnirman Sena (MNS), a rightist political party, and pleaded with its leader, Raj Thackeray, to support their cause. They wept bitterly before the TV cameras and several of them claimed that they were the only breadwinners in their family and that they would be forced into starvation.

When the media approached one of Jet Airway's executive directors, he apparently gave the management's decision quite dispassionately. He said that the layoff was not unusual, but agreed that it was a bit sudden. The company had to take the decision to save itself.

MNS decided to ground Jet Airways in Maharashtra. Naresh Goyal, the chairman of Jet Airways, reacted immediately. He said that his management had taken a bad decision, but now he was going to take a decision that was beyond the management. Every one of the 1900 employees would be reinstated and they could celebrate their festival season without further worries. He went on to say that he was the father of his company and could not bear to see tears in the eyes of his large family.

Questions

(a) Are business decisions devoid of moral sensitivity?

(b) On what grounds can a chairman unilaterally overrule a decision that is arrived at after serious business deliberation?

(c) What choice does the management have when it faces political pressure?

[a] See the *Times of India* and the *Indian Express* from 15–18 October 2009; also visit http://www.businessworld.in/index.php/Aviation/Jet-Reinstates-Sacked-Employees.html, http://www.indianairlinesblog.com/2008/10/1900-employees-to-lose-jobs-jet-airways/.

transfers, deal with the troubles of moving house, their children's schooling, and their own professional update and development. Managing career and a home at the same time need both skill and moral strength.

In ethics, philosophers advocate, virtue lies in the middle. In other words, a prudent and balanced manner of decision making is called for. Companies do bear the responsibility of helping the cause of their employees. It has now become a normal practice for companies to open day-care centres for the babies and young children of working mothers. In contrast to former times, when only women got maternity leave, companies have now adopted policies to give leave to men also to take care of their newborns. This is a part of the 'ethics of care' programme run by companies.

MORALITY OF INFORMED CONSENT

Suchita is a nurse and has specialized in midwifery. When she took up an assignment in a local polyclinic, she was in for a shock. She had to assist in medical termination of pregnancies (MTPs), commonly known as abortion. She knew very well that an abortion up to twenty weeks was legal and clinics such as the one she was working for normally had a legal MTP registration. However, she had been told while taking up the assignment that her specific duty would be midwifery. The same was stated in her appointment letter. But most of the time, she ended up at the MTPs. When she enquired from her employer, she was told that midwifery technically included abortions. She contended that she took up the job as a midwife to give prenatal care, assist at childbirth, and provide postpartum care to the infants, and protested that midwifery technically did not include abortion.

Consent: The Essence of Morality

Consent is a philosophical concept, an act of the will (see Chapter 4), known as moral act or human act, which we commonly understand as decision. Figuratively speaking, a decision is a long document and a consent is its approval/disapproval seal. A consent may be expressed or implied. It may be expressly given in words, produced in documents such as a bequeathing will, through pledges, oaths, vows, such as when assuming public office, in social ceremonies and religious rituals such as marriages, and in partnerships. Consent has implications in all aspects of our life.

Moral consent   A decision that binds one morally through codes, customs, ethics, manners, personal integrity, and the responsibility to the consequent action, through words and deeds, is called a moral consent. A moral act is synonymous with the human act, that is, a rational act, which presupposes full knowledge and deliberation of the act in question. The process of a moral act is also known as moral reasoning. All the other forms of consent given below are mere descriptions of consent in a particular context. The essence of morality is consent, and ethics is a philosophical system that studies the nature of consent in given cases or human actions.

Legal consent   The law of the land determines the age of consent. Accordingly, those who have reached the age of consent are held responsible for their actions. Making a will, registering a property, proceedings in a court of law to ensure the nature of consent between the litigants, etc., are a few examples.

Social consent   The activities that follow the customs and conventions of society such as public ceremonies of marriage, resolutions of various institutions and public bodies, etc. have a social consent.

Political consent   In a democracy, voting is an elaborate consent given by the people, a mandate to rule for a given period of time.

Medical consent   This is the agreement or approval of a patient to undergo treatment.

Employer/employee consent   The offer and acceptance of the terms and conditions of employment at the workplace.

A consent may involve one or several of the above aspects at the same time. Thus, marriage between two people—male and female—can have religious, social, and legal aspects. An employment contract may have legal and social aspects. But all have one aspect in common—the moral consent. For without it, one may not be able to impute responsibility for the action.

Impediments to Consent

Consent is given under certain circumstances. The circumstances of the situation may lighten or aggravate the seriousness of the act that follows from a particular consent. For instance, if a young woman is forced to marry the man chosen by her parents against her wishes, then such a marriage is null and void. A consent free and devoid of force constitutes a true marriage. If two adults have sexual intercourse willingly, it is known as consensual sex, but if one of the partners is forced into it, then the law will rule it as rape. Thus, following are some of the examples that will invalidate the consent and the actions that follow from it.

(a) Consent is expressed out of fear or social pressures or under threat of violence, but is withheld within one's own mind.

(b) A person may state that he/she understands what he/she has been consented to, but in fact is completely ignorant about it. For example, persons who are imbalanced or mentally retarded or totally ignorant of the event in question.

(c) Legal impediment of age, mental health, etc. form impediments to consent.

(d) Among family members or friends, in matters regarding money, gifts, etc., consent is not expressly brought out but is implied. As long as there is no protest by the other, it is assumed that consent is given. Only expressing rejection would imply that consent is not given.

When there is a dispute about the validity of an action, the principle is to work back to find out the motive of the action, which in turn determines whether the subject in question consented or not. If consent was given, then under what circumstances was it elicited and whether the subject was in full knowledge of the matter before taking a deliberate decision to consent are found out.

Informed Consent Concept

The concept of informed consent originated in the medical field. As people became more knowledgeable about medicine and health care, they increasingly questioned the decisions made for them by their doctors about their illness and treatment. Therefore, a system has been developed to inform patients about their illnesses and the measures, particularly the surgical ones, that are required to be undertaken, and a document of informed consent is duly signed. However, in cases where the patient's judgment is impaired due to retardation, or Alzheimer's disease, or because he/she is a minor and hence not reached the legal age of consent, a legal guardian or a close relative recognized by the law is required to give consent on behalf of the person in question.

Informed Consent at the Workplace

It would seem that in Suchita's case mentioned earlier, she had failed to read her contract carefully and had she done it, she would not have got into the unhappy situation she found herself in at the workplace. However, informed consent at the workplace is a very complex and, ethically, a very poignant issue. There are two aspects to workplace information: employer information and employee information.

(a) On taking up a job, a document specifying the duties and responsibilities and also the terms and conditions of employment is given to the employee, so that the employee knows what exactly is expected of him/her. This information must be adequate for the employee to give informed consent. The employee in turn would have already supplied adequate information when she/he had applied for the job, along with a signed declaration for the correctness of information. However, some of the information given may be false, such as date of birth, educational qualifications, work experiences, projects undertaken, recommendations, etc. Even the certifying documents could be forged or falsified.

(b) Employee privacy is a major workplace concern. Apart from the information that the employee has given, the employer may devise ways and means to get more employee information, which may be illegal and morally detrimental to the employee. Following are some methods used to garner information against employees.

Polygraph test   Commonly known as the lie detector test, it is a medical procedure for determining whether a person is telling the truth or a lie in response to a question by monitoring the pulse rate, blood pressure, respiration, perspiration, etc. A company may say that it has made this policy to screen prospective employees. It may cite the advantages of recruiting good and honest people: once selected, these new employees would need less supervision and monitoring, saving the company money. The prospects may feel that their freedom is curtailed. They may feel criminalized and if selected, they may never feel at ease at the workplace. However, their greater apprehensions are about what the company would do with such intimate information about them. Would it be used against them sometime in the future at the workplace, or in a court of law? Would the information be misused when they leave the job? Would it be shared with other employers?

In India, lie detector tests like polygraph or narco analysis of the brain do not stand in the court of law as evidence. The government has pleaded before the Supreme Court to be allowed to use it as evidence in cases of serious crime and terrorism. In some such cases, courts may allow the investigating agencies to conduct such tests, but not admit the tests as prima facie evidence.

Personality test   Companies very often would like, as it were, to get information through the back door. Personality tests, aptitude tests, etc. are quite handy. Subtle questions can give insight into one's personality. For instance, 'Do you feel a sense of power when you drive your car?' or 'When did you stop playing with dolls?' or 'Given an open opportunity what adventure would you like to undertake?'

There are several other subtle and not-so-subtle means of getting non-voluntary information from the employees or prospective employees. Some companies have devised tests for detecting narcotic addiction, homosexuality, AIDS, etc. Such indirect ways of testing and getting information without the express knowledge and consent of employees or prospective employees is morally reprehensible. Further, using such information against the present and future interests of these people is devoid of both moral and legal sanction.

WORKPLACE SURVEILLANCE VERSUS PRIVACY

When the employees of a well-known company received mobile phones for free with subsidized recharge schemes, they were more than happy. Very soon, they realized that this enabled their employer not only to contact them and assign them duties, or change their schedules as the case may be, but also to monitor their location and find out, subtly of course, what they were doing. The new technological wonder made them suddenly less than happy.

Employee Privacy in the Indian Context

An article in *Business Today* of August 2007 highlighted the Indian situation about privacy at the workplace. Four situations were starkly put before the readers for their judgment.

(a) The CEO of a profitable and reputed company keeps a micro recorder in his pocket and records the conversations of employees without their knowledge.

Tables Turned

Narcotest for managers

Malegaon, a town in the Nashik district of Maharashtra, has a sizeable Muslim population. It was a Friday and also a holy day called Shab-e-Bara'at. Just after 1 o'clock in the afternoon, there was a blast, or rather two, in the cemetery adjoining a mosque. There was great panic, followed by stampede. The death count rose to thirty-seven, and over a hundred people were injured.

The bomb blasts in Malegaon, on 8 September 2006, shook the country even though terrorist attacks have become common. The attacks generally come from Islamist terrorist organizations. To begin with, it was no different: one or the other Muslim group, both within and outside the country, were under suspicion. However, the Anti-Terrorist Squad (ATS) eventually found out that the alleged Malegaon blasts came from a right-wing Hindu organization.[a] A *sadhvi* (Hindu nun) and two other men were arrested by the ATS on 24 October 2008 as suspects of the Malegaon blasts.

In the case of the Malegaon terrorist attacks, the issue became highly politicized, since the criminals happened to be right-wing Hindu activists. The mainstream Bharatiya Janata Party (BJP) took a sympathetic stand towards the accused. It was of the view that the persons in question were incapable of such acts and it is a political conspiracy to blemish the party. The spokesperson of the party questioned the probe into the Malegaon blasts and demanded that the officers of the ATS undergo narco tests to detect whose orders they were functioning under.[b] Thus, the integrity of the probe was questioned and it was alleged that the probe was directed by the party in power for their vested interests. In addition to this, the ATS did not have a free hand in the investigations.[c]

The ATS is a special branch of the Maharashtra Police and was instituted in 2004. The officers of the ATS are highly qualified professionals in crime busting. These are selected officers with training and record, to tackle terrorist attacks and conduct investigations in the aftermath of these attacks. These form a highly motivated team, who know how to manage terror attacks on civilian targets. The extent of their competence and ability to deal with terror attacks was tested on 26 November 2008 in Mumbai. It was a turning point for Indian polity. Several of these officers laid down their lives, including their leader, Hemant Karkare.

Questions

(a) What ethical principle does the narco test infringe?

(b) Is narco test meant only for the suspects, or also for those who cast suspicion? If so, could the president, prime minister, high-level bureaucrats, CEOs, managers of companies, the army generals, and the judges also be subjected to narco tests?

(c) Is narco testing a back door to the breach of one's right to silence?

[a] See http://www.indianexpress.com/news/malegaon-blasts-murder-charges-on-sadhvi-2-others/377519/ accessed on 24 October 2008.

[b] See http://www.expressindia.com/latest-news/BJP-wants-narcotest-of-ATS-officials/389965/2/ accessed on 24 November 2008.

[c] See http://indiancurrentaffairs.blogspot.com/2007_04_28_archive.html.

(b) A BPO company with several branches in the country has embedded chips in the ID tags to track the whereabouts of its employees.

(c) The system administrators of a company go through all the email accounts of its employees every weekend, with an excuse of routine maintenance.

(d) In a high-tech company, employees are asked to go through medical examination in which they are tested for HIV/AIDS without their knowledge.

These and other similar practices with technical intrusions are going on in Indian companies quite unchecked. There is no clear law for employee workplace privacy. Companies have utilized this loophole, or rather the absence of the law, to monitor their employees through whatever means possible. When employee raise questions, the answers are ready and flow effortlessly. They are told that the practices will benefit all, or that there are security reasons, or that prevention of terrorism is important.

Measures against intrusion of privacy at the workplace

In places where there is absence of protection by law, employees must use their discretion and take measures to safeguard their privacy. They should be aware of the surveillance systems already in place. Following are some guidelines for safeguarding privacy:

(a) Use the Internet only for professional work and not personal work.

(b) Keep your personal communication private.

(c) Agree to any health test or treatment only after you are satisfied that it is proper and needed and that there is adequacy of health record privacy.

(d) Be careful about who handles your personal records, and when taken for a valid purpose, follow up and ensure that the records are returned to authorized storage.

(e) Educate and train yourself in matters of personal privacy, under technically competitive instructors or institutions.

Safeguarding Employees' Privacy

As employers, companies legally possess enormous amounts of information about their employees: personal, educational, past employers, health and fitness, and other data. These records are the intimate and private rights of their employees. The employees have let the companies have the information only to help determine their position, duties, and remuneration. Thus, companies are morally obliged to protect the privacy of the employees. Following are some moral obligations of employers:

(a) The employer must state the reasons for collecting certain information and specify the uses. The forms provided by the employer must be clear, clause by clause, without giving ambiguity to words and meanings.

(b) Special care must be taken to ensure the safety and security of the records. They should be handed back to the employees when they leave the organization.

(c) If record systems are created, these must be done after consulting the experts on the matter, especially the legal branch. The computer system networking, etc., must be handled with technical expertise.

(d) Authorization must be obtained if records are to be disclosed.

(e) Even those with legitimate authorization should exercise great prudence and never reveal any information either directly or indirectly to a third party.

(f) Only such information may be given which is required, irrespective of the authorization for information.

(g) The physical and administrative systems should be put in order so that the records can be filed and are easy to access.

Companies would do well to act on the above points and others that they deem necessary. The organization in its memorandum, or the bylaws of the company, must devote clauses to annunciate the privacy policy.

The Privacy Dilemma

Irony of economic development

The London-based Privacy International[a] is an organization dedicated to protect and promote the privacy of people, whether in organizations or in societies. The organization, like any human rights organization, has a tradition of ranking countries for the surveillance of the respective societies. Countries that have the worst ranking denote poor privacy performance and those that have the lowest ranking have a high level of surveillance. India belongs to the former; most of the European countries and the US belong to the latter. About fifty countries are under Privacy International's scanner.

In the surveillance map of the world, shown in Fig. 10.1, developed countries seem to be the worst violators of privacy. Both European and North American countries are very heavily involved in the surveillance of their societies. There is hardly a public place or workplace, where people are not constantly watched. The workplaces, shopping centres, supermarkets, transport nodes such as bus stops, railway stations, airports, and roads are fitted with surveillance technology in the name of providing security.

The assessment for India was as follows:

(a) No explicit right to privacy, though Supreme Court sees it as implicit under article 21 on the right to liberty.

(b) General right to privacy law, requiring warrants for searches.

(c) No comprehensive privacy law, though sectoral laws do provide some protections. Though there is great pressure to implement a privacy law, little is being done.

(d) Fraud and identity theft in the outsourcing industry continues.

(e) History of the abuse of wiretapping, and NGOs complain of their communications being intercepted.

(f) Law requires disclosure of encryption keys, and there are stiff penalties for failing to provide the requested information to authorities.

The dilemma seems to be manifold. Firstly, if surveillance is practised, then safety and security is assured; if surveillance is not practised, danger is imminent. Secondly, as economic development rises, organizations increase both production as well as the surveillance of their employees to protect the interests of the company. Lack of surveillance results in a loss to companies. Finally, as the necessities of modern life, such as the Internet, telephones, travel, global business, increase, surveillance also increases, but privacy decreases.

Some of the findings of Privacy International's 2007 report given below are causes for concern.

The trend in surveillance is worsening, that is, privacy protection safeguards are violated.

Immigration for better prospects in developed countries has increased the detailed use of the data base of the people, such as their identities, finger prints, etc., where it is ascertained that the person is stripped of every bit of private data.

The authorities' archive have all the geographic, financial, and personal data.

Countries have started keeping an increasing amount of data of the people entering the country.

Contd

Box Contd

Map of Surveillance Societies around the World

Consistently upholds human rights standards
Significant protections and safeguards
Adequate safeguards against abuse
Some safeguards but weakened protections
Systemic failure to uphold safeguards
Extensive surveillance societies
Endemic surveillance societies

Source: Map developed from http://english.freemap.jp.

Fig. 10.1   Surveillance map of the world[b]

Technology has made it possible for instant collection of data, pictures, and finger prints.

The trend across the globe is that as countries develop economically, surveillance practices too increase.

The surveillance industry, which is a very lucrative industry, is progressing at the cost of people's privacy.

Questions

(a) Is the issue of privacy an ethical issue?
(b) What alternatives could you offer to surveillance at a workplace?
(c) Can you give an example where excessive surveillance caused great harm?

[a] See http://www.privacyinternational.org/phr.
[b] See www.privacyinternational.org/article.shtml.

HEALTH AND SAFETY HAZARDS

When we think about health and safety at the workplace, we cannot help thinking about the Bhopal gas tragedy. The concerned company, Union Carbide, became synonymous with the industrial tragedy of the greatest proportion. The silent death of over 10,000 people, as well as the suffering spanning over a full generation of hundreds of thousands of people, is a reminder of the negligence of the safety norms at the workplace. That may well be the case, and yet, it appears as though lessons have not been learnt. The public perception is that in India, people do not care for safety and security issues at the workplace. This is exhibited by the industrial tragedies that take place on a daily basis across the country.

Occupational Safety and Health

'Occupational health should aim at the promotion and maintenance of the highest degree of physical, mental, and social well-being of workers in all occupations; the prevention amongst workers of departures from health caused by their working conditions; the protection of workers in their employment from risks resulting from factors adverse to health; the placing and maintenance of the worker in an occupational environment adapted to his physiological and psychological capabilities; and, to summarize, the adaptation of work to man and of each man to his job'.[4] The International Labour Organization (ILO) and the World Health Organization (WHO) have adopted the above definition for workplace safety and health, and their mission is to promote the same.

In India, apart from the usual workplace problems of safety, health, sanitation, environmental and noise pollution, there are also severe caste and creed problems. Severe social pressures make the workplace hell for the employees. The heartrending stories of children being hired in factories, foundries, and tanneries, for carpet weaving, as roadside mechanics, and in food outlets seem to have become a part of our inevitable and unchangeable culture.

Take the case of a woman called Sumitra Bai, a widow who belongs to the Valmiki community of Madhya Pradesh and works as a manual scavenger. She collects human excreta from dry toilets and transports it in a vessel to a waste deposit.[5] She is above fifty years old and has been doing this menial task for over three decades to support her children. Initially, however, upon the insistence of her children, she had given up scavenging and taken a loan of Rs 20,000 from a local cooperative bank to set up a small cloth shop. Some social workers supported her through counselling; they thought this was the best form of women's empowerment. But the society that she lived in was not ready for it. The elders of the village sent out a diktat and not even one person turned up at her shop. She was in for an even greater surprise, when no one from her

---

[4] For definition of occupational safety and health adopted by ILO and WHO, see www.ilo.org and http://www.who.int/en/ .respectively.

[5] See http://newsblaze.com/story/20090203122329zzzz.nb/topstory.html, accessed on 3 February 2009.

own Valmiki community showed up. She had to close the shop, return the bank loan, and go back to her menial task.

Indeed society, the depository of ethical values, can be very cruel where prejudice and not moral reasoning rules.

Legal Provisions

A slew of Indian legislation will give us an idea of both the seriousness and the need to regulate workplace safety and health.[6]

- (a) Factories Act 1948.
- (b) The Dock Workers (Regulation of Employment) Act 1948.
- (c) The Plantation Labour Act 1951.
- (d) The Mines Act 1952.
- (e) The Working Journalists and Other Newspaper Employees' (Conditions of Service and Miscellaneous Provisions) Act 1955.
- (f) The Working Journalists and Other Newspaper Employees' (Conditions of Service and Miscellaneous Provisions) Rules 1957.
- (g) The Merchant Shipping Act 1958.
- (h) The Motor Transport Workers Act 1961.
- (i) The Inter-State Migrant Workmen (Regulation of Employment and Conditions of Service) Act 1979.
- (j) The Shops and Establishments Act.
- (k) The Cinema Workers and Cinema Theatre Workers (Regulation of Employment) Act 1981.
- (l) The Cinema Workers and Cinema Theatre Workers (Regulation of Employment) Rules 1984.
- (m) The Cine Workers' Welfare Fund Act 1981.
- (n) The Dock Workers (Safety, Health & Welfare) Act 1986.
- (o) The Building & Other Construction Workers (Regulation of Employment & Conditions of Service) Act 1996.
- (p) The Dock Workers (Regulation of Employment) (inapplicability to Major Ports) Act 1997.
- (q) The Mica Mines Labour Welfare Fund Act 1946.
- (r) The Limestone & Dolomite Mines Labour Welfare Fund Act 1972.
- (s) The Beedi Workers Welfare Fund Act 1976.
- (t) The Iron Ore Mines, Manganese Ore Mines & Chrome Ore Mines Labour Welfare Fund Act 1976.
- (u) The Cine Workers Welfare Fund Act 1981.
- (v) The Employment of Manual Scavengers and Construction of Dry Latrines Prohibition Act 1993.

---

[6] For Acts and their full text, see http://labour.nic.in/welcome.html.

These and other individual state legislations indicate to us the seriousness of the safety and health problems in India's workplaces. That even in the twenty-first century we have been burdened with the problems of manual scavenging is an indicator to us of the work that lies ahead of us, to make our workplaces both safe and healthy.

Workplace Measures for Safety and Health

As long as man was a nomad, and then a pastoral being, dependent on agriculture for his livelihood, safety at work and health concerns hardly existed and neither did anyone care. Even slavery and bonded labour did not raise any ethical questions. However, as industrialization became part of our civilization, both education and human welfare grew hand in hand. Since the workplace is where we spend most of our time, the employer's moral obligation towards our safety and health is all the more important.

Thus, from the moral point of view, an employee does not have to risk injury or health hazard at work. From the point of economics, it does not make sense to risk the employee's health; healthy employees are better for the economy. From the law's point of view, the workplace needs to be regulated, so that fairness and justice is enjoyed by all at the workplace, in the same measure (see Table 10.1).

Table 10.1   Hazards at the workplace

Physical	Mechanical	Biological/ chemical	Social/ psychological
Collisions, confined space, slips, trips, falling from heights, struck by objects, transport accidents at work, electric shocks, etc.	Noise, vibrations, lighting, pressures (barotraumas), compressed air, crushing, cutting, entanglement, etc.	Bacteria, virus, acids, radiation, lead, solvents, body disorders, malfunction of the body systems— respiratory, circulation, muscular, sight, hearing, reproductive, etc.	Violence, bullying, mobbing, verbal assault, sexual harassment, stress, compulsion to overwork

Measures for Safety and Health at the Workplace

National governments, as well as ILO and WHO, have been putting in efforts to improve the lot of employees. In the US, the Occupational Safety and Health Administration (OSHA) is the most progressive organization of its kind, which has developed measures for the safety and health of employees. International Standards Organization (ISO) has also developed a series of measures that are important for workplaces to implement to get its sanction. The subjects that get elaborate treatment are occupational hygiene, occupational illness, and occupational rehabilitation.[7]

---

[7] Some important links: Workers Health and Safety Centre—a leading Canadian workplace health and safety training organization, ILO International Occupational Safety and Health Information Centre, Society for Occupational Health Psychology, etc.

Recently, in February 2009, Oscar Fernandes, the Minister of State for Labour and Employment, assured the Parliament that the Factories Act 1948 would be amended comprehensively to meet the current needs of employees at the workplace.[8] The ILO conventions related to the use of asbestos, occupational health services, the use of chemicals, and safety and health issues will be incorporated. Four labour institutes

---

Curse for the Children

Cracker factory

Sabera Begum, who lives in Huturia village in West Bengal, was a poor but happy woman. Her husband was a labourer. They had four children. However, Begum's world fell apart when her husband died. She started begging in the village to feed her four children. But what she earned couldn't sustain her and her children any more unless they too did some work. Mujibur and Bapi, her two sons, and Jyotsna and Sharmila, her daughters, began to work in a factory that produced fireworks.[a] The name of the factory was Nawab Cracker Factory, and it was situated at Bagnan, in the Howrah District. Begum's children were all minors, that is, those who had not attained the age of fourteen, and were legally not suitable for work according to the Factory Act 1948. They earned between Rs 50 and Rs 60 a week.

On a fateful day, 11 September 1995, the Nawab Cracker Factory was gutted in a fire, and along with it, twenty-three child labourers became the victims of the flaming factory. These children belonged to thirteen families. Of the twenty-three children who died, four belonged to Begum, all charred beyond recognition. She was left alone to suffer the unbearable loss of her entire family.

As if this suffering was not enough, Begum and the other dozen families now had to wait to see what the concerned parties would do, which included the Government of West Bengal. Sadly, nothing happened. No one did anything, until a well-meaning advocate called Mrinmay Shau came along and filed a public interest litigation. In 1998, the High Court directed the Additional District Magistrate of Howrah to distribute a compensation comprising of Rs 11 lakh to the family members of the victims. Again, nothing happened and the victims' families received no compensation. The government paid only Rs 20,000 for each of the victims of the families. The case continued.

On 5 December 2008, the court took cognizance of the violation of its earlier order and directed the government to hand over a cheque of Rs 18.40 lakh as compensation, with an addition of interest at the rate of 9 per cent for the lost time. Begum, who had received Rs 80,000 for losing four children in 2000, would now receive Rs 3.20 lakh. The only good that came from the tragedy is that from now onwards, she may not have to beg.

Questions

(a) What measures would you take to educate cracker factory owners in the country of the moral responsibility they should bear?

(b) How effectively can the government implement the Factory Act 1948 and its amendment in 1987?

(c) It is believed that all the cracker factories throughout the length and breadth of the country utilize child labour. What are the justifications put forward by the owners of these factories? How can you counter them by suggesting a morally good and economically sound business plan?

[a] See http://www.expressindia.com/latest-news/finally-families-of-95-factory-fire-victims-get-compensation/397989/, accessed on 13 December 2008.

---

[8] See http://www.zeenews.com/nation/2009-02-11/506411news.html.

in India will be asked to provide research, training, and consultation services to the industries.

Moral strength: The source of leadership

Recession time tests families both morally and professionally. Making the right decisions at testing times gives us moral strength, and moral strength at testing times helps us make the right decisions. This may be a cycle, but they are one and the same.

SUMMARY

- Modern man works for economic reasons and aims to produce excellent work.
- Managing work at the workplace is the task of a manager, whose ingenuity can make it efficient and profitable.
- Man is made up of many parts, which are his individual self, his working self, and his professional self.
- Fundamentally, ethics is one; the basic principles of duty, justice, conscience, etc. remain the same.
- The modern workplace is a very complex and morally complicated place.
- Employees have the right to know about the nature of their employment.

- Making people work without their express consent is not only morally wrong, but also legally untenable.
- The law has developed to protect the rights of the worker, among which the right to privacy is essential.
- The moral law also gets expression in the enacted laws of safety and health of the employees.
- Morality comprises both the dignity of labour and the labourer.
- Free, prior, and informed consent, whether of an individual or of a community, is a precondition to undertake any work or enterprise.

KEY TERMS

Consent Willingness or unwillingness to a moral action; freedom of the will.

Impediment to consent Something that obstructs or hinders a free and informed consent.

Individual A person capable of human action; one who can decide for himself.

Informed consent Consent given after adequate knowledge of the subject.

Intrusion of privacy Meddling in private matters.

Moral consent Involves free will, complete knowledge of action, and the action being of good or bad impact.

Personal ethics One's own beliefs of right and wrong.

Privacy Matters that belong to individual domain; personal affairs that a person does not want to disclose.

Professional ethics Defined code of conduct for a workplace or a profession.

Work An occupation, employed or self-employed, taken upon as an economic activity; its ethical value lies in its rightness or wrongness, with relation to oneself or to others.

Workplace ethics Employer–employee relations, workplace safety and security, freedom of the individual, and duties.

Workplace surveillance Supervision or close watch without the employee's express knowledge, or immediate consciousness; the employee may be aware of it, but may not be immediately and always conscious of it.

CONCEPT REVIEW QUESTIONS

1. What moral reasoning can you propose in favour of keeping professional ethics distinct from personal ethics?

2. What ethical principles would be required to explain informed consent?

3. How does one determine the guidelines for surveillance at a workplace?

4 How important are regulations for health and safety at the workplace?

CRITICAL THINKING QUESTIONS

1. Are dignity of labour and dignity of man distinct?

2. Why is free, prior, and informed consent important in moral action?

3. Does doing away with surveillance help one to maintain one's privacy?

4. Hazards at the workplace are natural; they are a part and parcel of the job. Why should there be moral and legal obligations about these issues?

FURTHER READING

James Roughton, *Developing an Effective Safety Culture: A Leadership Approach*, Butterworth-Heinemann (2002).

CASE STUDY

Consensual SEZ

Special Economic Zones and the Will of the People

Zamin amcha hakka chi, Nahin konacha bappa chi (in Marathi: The land is ours by right, it is not anyone's paternal property).[a]

—SEZ protest slogan of March 2007

Introduction

Consensual SEZ, the title of this case, is an allusion to consensual sex. It portrays the sensitivity of acquisition of someone's land without consent, the land upon which someone depends for livelihood and life itself. Anything that is taken away from someone without consent is both immoral and illegal; it is robbery, injustice, and exploitation. We have said repeatedly that ethics is about human relationships, and these are not tenable without consent. A human action gets its approval through one's consent and disapproval through nonconsent. Thus, without consent there is no marriage, no buying and selling, no legal transaction, not even the enacting of a law. Anything in violation of consent is in contravention of one's will; what is against one's will is devoid of moral sanction.

Part A

The SEZ problem

The farmers in India are used to their lands getting devastated by floods, droughts, and pests, but no one has tried to take away their land so far. In independent India, farmers have enjoyed a favoured position. The government has always made sure that farmers enjoy irrigation facilities, subsidies for electric power, fertilizers, seed procurement, and several other benefits. The

---

[a] SEZ protestors' slogan in Maharashtra, March 2007.

Fig. 10.2 Protest against POSCO in Orissa[b]

Source: Courtesy http://cache.daylife.com/imageserve/ 0dM7c6V98V4jY/340x.jpg.

government has also ensured land reforms, through which the tiller received the occupancy rights and the Zamindari system got abolished. The farmer's land cannot be alienated. The Special Economic Zones Act 2005[c] hit the farmers of India with a force that was greater than any natural calamity that they had encountered so far. It must be most ironic that in independent India, where the successive governments went overboard to assure the farmers their lands and their produce, the current government decided to take away their land and turn them into industries. (Figure 10.2 shows a farmer protest.) From the acquired land of the farmers, which is their self-owned workplace of food production, the government wants to create Special Economic Zones (SEZs). These are modern industrial production centres, which are deemed foreign territories that are legally set aside for the purposes of non-taxation and several other exemptions.

SEZ Proposals by the Ministry of Commerce

SEZs come under the Ministry of Commerce.

Objects of SEZs include

(a) Generation of additional economic activity

(b) Promotion of exports of goods and services

(c) Promotion of investment from domestic and foreign sources

(d) Creation of employment opportunities

(e) Development of infrastructure facilities

The above will accelerate economic activity, foreign trade, employment, and inflow of foreign capital.

The land will be acquired and provided by the government as per Land Acquisition 1894. The ministry states that the total land requirement for the formal approvals that have been granted till date is approximately 67,680 hectares, out of which about 109 approvals are for state industrial development corporations (SIDCs)/state government ventures, which account for over 20,853 hectares. In these cases, the land already available with the state governments or SIDCs or with private companies has been utilized for setting up SEZ. The land for the 270 notified SEZs, where operations have since commenced, is approximately over 31,405 hectares only. Out of the total land area of 29,73,190 sq km in India, total agricultural land is of the order of 16,20,388 sq km (54.5 per cent). It is interesting to note that out of this total land area, the land in possession of the 270 notified SEZs amounts to approximately over 314 sq km only. The formal approvals that have been granted also work out to only around 676 sq km. Out of the 531 formal approvals given till date, 174 approvals are for sector specific and multi-product SEZs for the manufacture of textiles and apparels, leather footwear, and automobile components.[d]

The consent of the people and land use

The farmers' land is not limited to the cultivated land. Apart from the farm holdings in several states, there is common land that provides people with

[b] For a full understanding of SEZ, see SEZ ACT 2005; link: Ministry of Commerce, Government of India: http://sezindia.nic.in/ HTMLS/SEZ%20Act,%202005.pdf.

[c] For details, see http://sezindia.nic.in/HTMLS/about.htm.

[d] See http://timesofindia.indiatimes.com/articleshow/2151679.cms.

grazing land for domestic animals, fodder, and firewood, and they depend on it for several other day-to-day needs. The government has categorized this land quite simply as waste land. This is the excuse upon which it is trying to acquire land for the industry.[e] The reasoning is that it is not depriving the farmer of his tilling land and productive land. This so-called waste land comprises of approximately 20 per cent of the total geographical area, on which 12 per cent of the population depends for a living. Since the government's definition of land use is inconsistent and unpredictable, it has a much easier way to acquire it. Thus, in most cases, tilling farms, forests, and, in the coastal areas like the Western Ghats, the rainforest areas too get included. This is not only going to take away the land from the farmers, but is also going to cause environmental disaster. Further, quite a sizeable area of land that is under actual cultivation is not shown in the land records, nor is it transferred to the farmers. In Raigarh, where Reliance Industries has acquired 12,000 hectares of land for its SEZ, it is actually known as *dali* land, which has been under cultivation by the local tribes since independence. The same is the case in Orissa; since the land is not regularized, problems have arisen because the industries are ready to acquire land. For instance, the SEZ of Pohang Steel Company would have to evict 300 families from their farm holdings. Since these farmers do not have legal documents due to the government's apathy to regularize the holdings, now hundreds of families in the declared SEZ areas will lose their land and livelihoods, and are legally not entitled to any compensation.

The land use management by the government failed. Now, with its decision on SEZ, farmers are going to be made the victims for no fault of theirs. Timely interventions with legal instruments are necessary, even to manage the lives of the traditional farmers. People elect their government to govern and manage their affairs. The government, in a democracy, needs the consent of the people to bring a fundamental change. SEZ has never been a poll issue upon which a government has been elected or thrown out of power. Hence, people have got united and have agitated against the acquisition of land against their will. The political parties know it. Therefore, as the general elections of 2009 came close, they have shelved these burning issues.

The will of the people versus contravention of the law

From the government's view, it would seem that people are breaking the law with impunity, by opposing the SEZ law. The government thinks it is acquiring land as per law. It has a larger aim—the development of the country, where it thinks hundreds of thousands of people would find a suitable workplace to improve their standard of life, rather than work as farmers, trying to eke out their existence. Hence, the government in its wisdom set out to acquire approximately 1,20,000 hectares of land for about 200 SEZs across the country. It went about its business as per its records of the land use. Thus, the tillers of the land who did not hold legal documents such as ownership papers, *pattas*, etc. were seen as unlawful occupiers of the land. The land on their records was a wasteland and hence, the government felt that there was nothing morally wrong in acquiring the same and turning it into an SEZ.

People argued that the government couldn't care less to examine the ground realities. They felt cheated by the government agencies for neglecting the fulfilment of their legal needs. Through protests, the media's help, and the sympathy of various organizations, the farmers tried to blame the governments, both at the centre as well as at the concerned states, for their plight. They claimed to be the victims of unjust and unfair laws and their implementation.

Figure 10.3 shows the people in Maharashtra—fisher folk, farmers, etc.,—announcing to the government that the land is theirs, not the SEZs' or their promoters'.[f]

---

[e] *Source:* http://images.google.co.in/imgres?imgurl=http://www.east-indians.com/News_clippings/AntiGoraiSEZ1_web.jpg.

[f] For a sample of the opinions of ordinary farmers and their advocates, see http://www.hindustan.org/forum/showthread.php?p=6596.

Fig. 10.3   Protecters of SEZ in Maharashtra

The people versus the government

'We don't want SEZ at all. Our land is very fertile. What it lacks is proper arrangement of irrigation, which the successive governments of Haryana have

failed to ensure in the last 60 years. Give us water not SEZ. The government should listen clearly that we are ready to go to any extent to save our land.' These are the words of a farmer from Haryana.[g] All the protests of the people may be summarized in a single proposition: stealing farmers to gift capitalists.

Table 10.2 presents a few instances where people confronted the government directly.[h]

Figure 10.4 gives us a picture of the land for SEZ acquisition.

Table 10.3 contains a list of eight states where major SEZs have been allotted land and protests and agitations are going on.[i]

By August 2007, the SEZ approvals exceeded more than 350, of which half of them were already notified. All of these have confronted rejection by the people, but in most cases to no avail. Violence has left several dead and hundreds of thousands homeless.

Table 10.2   Anti-SEZ agitation

State	Anti-SEZ agitation	Consequences
West Bengal	Agitations led to the deaths of at least 14 villagers on 14 March, and a severe government crackdown in November 2007.	Proposed SEZ in Nandigram to be relocated.
Goa	Goa Bachao Andolan (GBA), Goa's Movement Against SEZs (GMAS), SEZ Virodhi Manch, and the Catholic Church conducted a unified movement.	All 15 SEZs were scrapped in the state on 31 December 2007; de-notification of three approved SEZs is awaited.
Karnataka	Under the umbrella organization Nandagudi Raitha Hitarakshana Samithi, 21,000 farmers from 36 villages were resisting land acquisition for an over 12,000 acre SEZ.	In October 2007, protestors managed to send back an SEZ survey team.
Maharashtra (Raigad)	Protesting farmers from at least 24 villages being supported by multiple partisan and non-partisan umbrella organizations.	1000 protestors burnt land acquisition notices in June 2007 and 5000 farmers blocked a highway.
Orissa (Jagatsinghpur)	Farmers resisting an SEZ project by Pohang Steel Company, popularly known by its acronym POSCO (considered India's largest FDI project).	2000 villagers potentially affected by land acquisition, the agitations are going on.

[g] See Jonathan Jones' India's *Democracy Has a Heartbeat* in http://www.india-seminar.com/2008/582/582_jonathan_jones.htm.
[h] See http://in.diarealestate.com/2008/07/india-sez-statewise-statistics.html.
[i] Steven Herz, Johanthan Sohn, and Antonio La Vina, Development without Conflict, The Business Case for Community Consent, WRI, 2007.

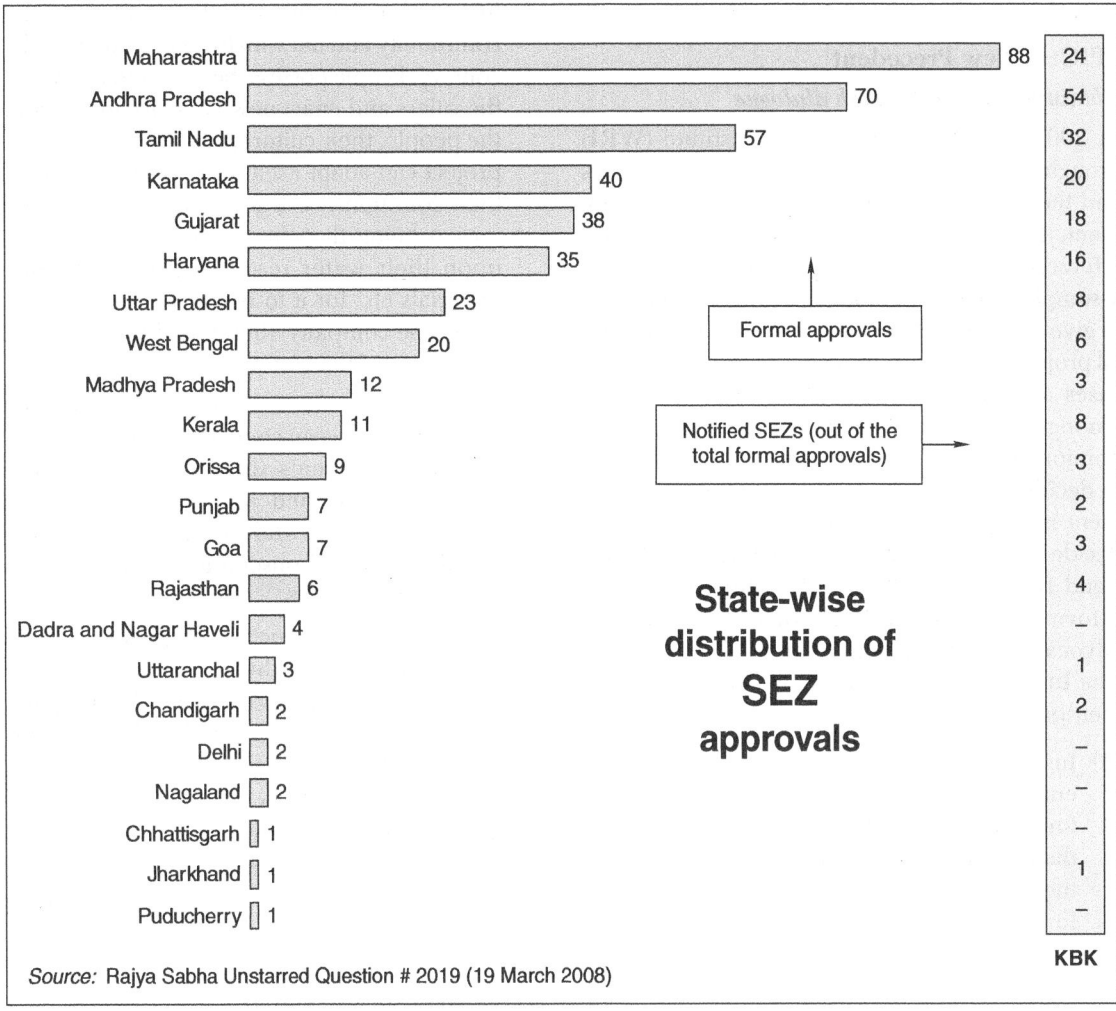

Source: Rajya Sabha Unstarred Question # 2019 (19 March 2008)

KBK

Fig. 10.4 Land for SEZ acquisition

The SEZ promoters promise the sky before they acquire the land—a job for every member of the family, land to build a house, education for the children, etc., but none of these materialize. The people of India are questioning those who manage their affairs. The managers do not seem to hear them.

Table 10.3 Land allocation to SEZs

	State	No. of SEZs	Size of land in hectare
1.	Maharashtra	126	42,714
2.	Haryana	55	29,100
3.	Gujarat	48	22,376
4.	Rajasthan	17	16,029
5.	Tamil Nadu	71	12,419
6.	Andhra Pradesh	78	12,071
7.	Karnataka	51	9,057
8.	West Bengal	35	8,905

Part B

FPIC: A New Precedent

Obtaining consent through dialogue

In 2007, The World Resources Institute (WRI) brought out a path-breaking report on the progress and the assent of the people for such a development. The title of the work was self-explanatory (Herz et al. 2007). The report is based on the assumption that people have a fundamental right to give or withhold their consent for developmental projects. The assumption has been proved from cases around the world. The Indian SEZs are among them, the people increasingly voice their opinions and fight for their rights. They would like to decide for themselves, what kind of a development is good for them. They would also like to decide what they want and when they want it. This trend is termed by the WRI as free, prior, and informed consent (FPIC). In other words, it advocates obtaining of consent through dialogue. The Indian SEZs need this new strategy to solve their problems.

(a) Justice: It is the will of the people that has enacted the law. The will of the people is fundamental; the laws obtain legitimacy with the sanction of the people, not vice-versa. If there are laws that come in the way of people's fundamental rights, the laws need to be changed. It is rather ironic that the people concerned require the consent of the banks, insurance companies, sponsors, etc. after due information, in order to run a project, but do not think its necessary to take the consent of those people who are affected by the project.

(b) It makes good business sense to get the consent of the people for a project that is planned for them. Avoiding conflict with the community is the first premise. Getting their cooperation is half the battle won. Once the people who are the main stakeholders in any business are involved as a community, the business finds its right bearings and can depend on the people for its success. An imposed project, despite its merits, is against the will of the people and is doomed.

(c) FPIC quite simply implies that anyone who wants to start a project in the community must first have a dialogue with the members of the community and not with the elites who rule the country. People possess the power to throw out the rulers and enact new laws. To understand the people, their culture, and analyse how the project can adapt itself to becoming a part of their community is a good starting point. The reason being that the project has to depend upon their water resources, minerals, raw materials etc. for it to be carried out on their land. The company, therefore, has to become a member of that community.

(d) The company must clearly understand the distinction between consultation and consent. The WRI presents three cases where the companies curried for favours with the governments, but rode roughshod with the people and failed miserably, and bore losses in billions of dollars.

The Esquel Project in Argentina, a gold mining venture of the US-based Meridian Gold, had to be abandoned after the company failed to answer the safety and health questions of open mining.

The Samut Prakarn, a wastewater management plant in Thailand, had to be abandoned almost towards the end of its completion because the people were not taken into confidence.

Then, there was another case in Peru, the Yanacocha gold mine project, which was opposed by the people. The confrontation became so serious that the company had to make public apologies and shut down the project.

(e) One company that succeeded was Shell (Royal/Dutch Shell). It took up a project called Malampaya Deep Water Gas-to-Power in the Philippines. They put up the proposal before the community and faced some initial problems. The company learnt quickly enough that it would be judicious to understand what the people were telling them. They rectified the proposed plans to include the suggestions of the community, where the project was based. The community then gave their full support. The project was completed ahead of schedule, and the company has ever since applied this model of FPIC in all its following projects very successfully.

Struggle of the old workplaces with the new workplaces

The Indian economy has been expanding even by the global meltdown standards India is indeed booming with over 6 per cent of annual growth and is aiming at 9 per cent. There is a burgeoning need for infra-structure, power, roads, manufacturing every kind of product, and services from IT to steel, from pharmaceuticals to gems and jewellery. The need for industrial expansion is real. These are new and challenging times for businesses, which need to be discussed with new and innovative solutions. Merely taking a recourse to the antiquated laws of land acquisition and making tall promises, like the leaders in political parties do, is old hat for the people who have been continuously under one kind of oppression or the other. Today, people have decided that 'enough is enough; we will decide what we want.'

Following are some of the points for a free, prior, and informed consent:

(a) Establish communication with the community in which the project has to be established.

(b) Create free and fair exchange of ideas.

(c) Make a draft of the plan and put it up for further discussion and amendments.

(d) Having educated—that is, informed—the people and having taken their prior consent, which is free and not induced or won by allurements, obtain a formal consent of the people. Earning people's confidence and approval before starting a project is the cornerstone of people's assent.

(e) Go through the government procedures to obtain a legal status. Without the corrupt practices that are otherwise involved in such ventures, you will earn quick approval and backing of the people.

(f) Let the community be the ultimate stake-holder.

Part C

Conclusion

There is news for the government and the corporations

We, Polepalli SEZ Vyathireka Aikya Sanghatana, are contesting these elections, as we find all political groups have cheated the poor farmers and are responsible for their deaths. All political parties are silent on this major crime that's taking the lives of people in the name of the SEZ.[j] A Dalit group of thirteen members, who came from the village of Polepalli in Andhra Pradesh, declared the above statement. Three of them were women. They told the press that their village land was acquired on the pretext of turning it into a green park and that they would be employed in it. Several lies and rumours about its development and their employment circulated, and over a thousand acres of land was acquired from the surrounding villages. They declared that now, they have come together to contest elections against the regular politicians. Then, all of a sudden, there was an announcement that the SEZ would be scrapped. The politicians bought time. They reneged on the promise. People suffered intensely and received a measly compensation. Corruption ruled the roost.

But the story is not over. The simple and illiterate people of India seem to be on the march. Individual disappointments have not dampened their spirits. The SEZ operation has been going on since its institution in 2005, and both—the governments at the centre, as well as in the states, and the corporations—have lost their battle.[k]

The message for the government and the corporations is to obtain free, prior, and informed consent.

Discussion Questions

1. Children, for instance, are not asked for their consent before any medicine is administered to them, or they are sent to school. Why is it necessary to obtain consent for good public works?

---

[j] See http://www.tehelka.com/story_main40.asp?filename=cr090808landfrom_landless.asp.

[k] See http://www.indiatogether.org/2009/jan/eco-sezbust.htm.

2. In a democratic and law-abiding country, why should corporations go for another mandate with the people?

3. SEZs are not different workplaces, they only work differently. Comment.

4. What ethical principle is utilized by the government and the corporations to convince that what they are doing is for the people's development?

5. Do you think the consequences of SEZ, such as displacement, migration, sinking into deeper poverty, and deprivation of traditional livelihood are ethically justifiable?

6. Why are the legal means used by the government to acquire land ethically untenable?

7. What ethical principles can be used to support those who are against SEZs?

8. Do the people opposing SEZs have a moral right to do so?

9. What is the moral worth of FPIC?

10 What recommendation would you give to governments and corporations?

Going Further . . .

- Central point of discussion: free, prior, informed consent. Other points: safety and health, privacy, workplaces (agricultural versus industrial).

- Panel discussion with a group of NGOs involved in anti-SEZ movement, local officials—panchayat, ministry/directorate of industries, etc.

ETHICAL DEVELOPMENT PROGRAMME

Management Training

Programme A

(a) Study the SEZ Act 2005 and the subsequent rules.

(b) Identify specific cases such as Nandigram, POSCO, Raigad, etc.

(c) Make alternative proposals and send them to the concerned corporations and the Ministry of Commerce.

Programme B

(a) Propose an alternative for industrial development in your locality for your company.

(b) Draw a programme for FPIC.

(c) Pay attention to the health and safety of the people working on the project.

Programme C

Game

Boss Is Faking[9]

Objective

Find out whether the leadership of a manager is real or fake.

Method

Time frame: About six weeks.

Make a group of at least a dozen people.

The group may be a commercial company or a non-profitable organization.

Activity: Assign a small project or ask to simulate a project.

Monitors/Judges

Appoint two monitors/judges for each group.

Create checklists under three headings: concepts, skills, and values.

Concepts will judge knowledge.

Skills will judge professional competencies.

Values will judge ethical/moral standing.

Award

At the end of the game declare the result.

Optional: You may institute an award or a certificate.

---

[9] Jeffrey Kluger, 'Competence: Is Your Boss Faking It?' in http://www.time.com/time/health/article/0,8599,1878358,00.html.

Management Mantra

Rehana: Challenging Moral Mindsets

Rehana is a 42-year-old Muslim woman, who hails from Tarana village, in the Ujjain district of Madhya Pradesh.[10] Her workplace is a living hell. Although Islam is against any caste, in India the caste system still prevails, irrespective of religion. Rehana belongs to the Haila cast whose job is to scavenge human excreta and clean toilettes. She was just 14 years old when she was married off to Arshad. She was still a small girl and she had not done any such work before her marriage, but marriage changed her world. To her utter disgust and despair, she was forced into the traditional trade of her caste. The custom is that the new bride must take over this work from her mother-in-law.

Her work began early in the morning. She went with a broom, a piece of tin plate, and a vessel on her head to the assigned houses where there were dry latrines, small holes in toilet cubicles. She would bend down to scavenge with the tin plate and the broom and collect the excreta in the vessel. After attending to several houses, when the vessel was full, she would carry it either on her hip or on her head, and walk to the assigned sanitary dump.

According to the law, neither Rehana's marriage, nor her work has any legal validity. Those who married her off and those who forced her to do this work ought to be behind bars. Both, the marriage of minors as well as the scavenging of dry latrines, has been banned by respective laws, and are to be punished with fines and imprisonment. However, people in rural India do not seem to have much respect for the law. In Madhya Pradesh, 90 per cent of those involved in scavenging are women like Rehana. They earn about Rs 5 per house and one *chapati*. Their husbands too are normally employed at the local municipality for sanitary work.

Rehana's young daughter felt terrible about what her mother was doing and urged her to leave her traditional job of scavenging. Her husband and family members opposed tooth and nail by saying that respecting the customs of the community was important for the safety of their lives. She listened to the voice of reason from her little daughter and gave up the hideous toil. Her husband and family did not accept her decision. She left her house with her daughter. She learnt sewing and stitching from an NGO. She was despised by her community, but she remained steadfast. Rehana and her daughter faced a hostile world, but they continued their fight and met all the challenges bravely. In their new trade, they flourished and even built a house. This development brought a change in Rehana's husband's attitude, and he too joined her in her venture. They married off their daughter proudly. A large number of people attended the marriage. It was a sign that not only had the community accepted her, but they even honoured her. Rehana knew that no one would have come for the marriage if she was still a scavenger. She was also happy to know that her daughter did not have to take over the dreadful task from her mother-in-law. Rehana has given a *mantra* for success.

> MANTRA   *The honour of a person is most important.*

---

[10] Shuriah Niazi, 'Dirt Poor but Defiant: These Women Dump Tradition', in http://newsblaze.com/story/20090210141421tsop.nb/topstory.html. The mantra is in Rehana's own words.

CHAPTER

11

The Contemporary Worker

*No servant can be the slave of two masters: he will either hate the first and love the
second, or be attached to the first and despise the second. You cannot be the slave
both of God and of money.*

—Luke 16:13, The New Jerusalem Bible

*There is no denying the fact that corruption is rampant in our country. Be it Government,
public sector or private sector—everywhere, it has crept into the system. It is so deep
rooted and channelized that when a whistle blower tries to raise his voice against
corrupt practices from within the system, his voice is scuttled and he is made to suffer
because of his audacity for his outburst.[1]*

—The Whistleblowers Bill 2006

LEARNING OBJECTIVES

After studying this chapter, you will be able to

> State the meaning of conflict of interest
> Define whistleblowing
> Discuss about the abuse of official position
> Define a bribe

INTRODUCTION

In this chapter, we will concentrate on the four main issues that confront the contemporary manager. We should be able to get an insight into the problems a manager
faces and also the necessary qualities a manager should possess to grapple with such
problems. The examples of courageous whistleblowers should inspire everyone.

In this chapter, we will also introduce a new idea—contemporary worker
consciousness—and understand the contemporary worker in that light. The old concept

---

[1] These are the opening words of The Whistleblowers (Protection in Public Interest Disclosures) Bill, which was introduced in
the Rajya Sabha on 3 March 2006, and is still pending in Parliament.

of the worker is being replaced by a new one. The old worker had nothing to think about, except do the assigned duty. Whatever right or wrong that was happening at the workplace was the responsibility of the owner or the promoter of the company, and the worker took no moral responsibility. There is a difference now. The worker has become an employee and has a different consciousness. An employee is one of the very important stakeholders in the company. Employees are conscious of this and are responsible for their actions. The modern manager is not there to tout some policies of the company, but has the powers to make decisions in the assigned area, and is conscious of what is going on. Today, managers are able to set their standards high, higher than the mission of their companies. They will not even worry about losing their jobs if they are doing the right thing. The difference lies in the self-understanding, or the new consciousness. Normally, a manager makes choices to earn a large amount of money for the company. There are some rare instances when managers make choices that go beyond the issue of making money. These choices are made in the larger interest of the company, the employees, and society.

India's image on integrity is very low. The world has seen India fall from a high position of conscience to a corruption-ridden country. It is a big downfall. Corruption seems to have become the sub-culture of the country. As the country is growing into an economic power, it is marred by rampant instances of corruption, both political and corporate. Corporations look forward to employing upright managers and employees, but these are rare commodities. Corporations have been requesting management schools to train managers of high integrity, who would exercise moral leadership for their companies. There have been some exemplary managers who have become well-known as whistleblowers. However, these are a few exceptions.

There is another term that we use for the renewed consciousness of an awakened manager. It is called conscience. It is the sense of right and wrong that each of us develops. Today, managers are empowered to listen to their conscience due to several factors, such as economic stability, opportunities of alternative careers, etc., which help them take strong steps and abide by personal decisions of right and wrong.

CONFLICT OF INTEREST

In 2005, the Indian Parliament rocked with an interesting case of conflict of interest. The issue was that the finance minister's wife had represented the Income Tax Department, which was under her husband's charge. The implication was that the finance minister's wife was unduly misusing her husband's position of political and governmental power. When a person's personal concerns stand to benefit from the professional ones, a case is made for conflict of interest. For instance, a law firm is hired by both the plaintiff and the defendant; or a judge has to give a ruling in a case in which one of the litigants is his own relative; a personnel manager interviews to hire his own family member. These are cases of nepotism, favouritism, corruption, and unduly profiting from one's public position. Responsible fiduciary duty demands that not only justice should be done in such cases, but the manifestations of justice should be visible to all. The consequences of conflict of interest are serious. They may not only create legal problems, but may also irreparably damage a company's or a professional's reputation and career as well. Let us study the measures to avoid conflict of interest, and in the event of an occurrence, the measures to rectify the mistake.

Kinds of Conflict of Interest

Here are a few examples of the various kinds of conflict of interest[2]:

(a) Public–private conflict: When interests of public office or business influence private concerns.
(b) Outside employment: Where interests of one job are unduly connected with the other.
(c) Receiving gifts from vendors to the company.
(d) Pump and dump: Artificial inflation and deflation of stocks.
(e) Self-policing: When an organization is asked to investigate its own affairs, it will make exceptions to suit itself.
(f) Claims adjustment: The insurance company's adjuster manages to convince the client for less than the entitled settlement, working for the company's undue profit. It is impossible to establish partiality.
(g) The purchasing manager buys only from those suppliers who are friends or relatives.
(h) Revolving door: It is where officials quitting public offices get into corporations and pass insider information.

These and several other methods constitute conflict of interest. All of them have characteristics of deception, self-profiting, non-disclosure, and self-justification, which a manager needs to be impartial to in the discharge of duties.

Measures to Avoid Conflict of Interest

Even if no impropriety is intended and the manager conducts the fiduciary duties admirably, in certain situations, breach of trust may be suspected. For instance, even when a bank manager sanctions a loan to a close relative, with all the paper work and other formalities done impartially and without any prejudice or favour, to the bank personnel, as well as some of the customers acquainted with both the parties, it may not appear above board. They may always have some room for suspicion. Following are some guidelines for avoiding suspicion.

Prevention Before taking a fiduciary position, carefully examine whether there are any impediments that may cause conflict of interest. For instance, before assuming a

---

[2] See http://en.wikipedia.org/wiki/Conflict_of_interest.

political office, sell all corporate stocks and thus avoid any future impropriety. One could also form a trust to conduct such business, where the person concerned does not have a say.

Disclosure   In India, the rule to disclose assets for a person seeking political office is already in force. It is also suggested that the members of the judiciary do the same. It makes great ethical sense if promoters as well board of directors declare their assets.

Recusal   It is a withdrawal of one's position to facilitate free and fair transaction. For instance, if one of the directors on the board is connected with a company that the board has on its list of suppliers, then the director can recuse from voting on supplier-related decisions.

Third-party evaluation   Third-party evaluators are called when a transaction involves people from within the company, e.g., when there is a need to fix a fair price or to charter a fair course of action.

Code of ethics   Well-established codes of ethics are a great help in conducting affairs impartially. If the code of conduct is followed both in letter and in spirit to the satisfaction of all, conflict of interest could be a avoided.

In fact, the code of ethics in an organization should take care of all the rest of the points in ensuring morally right choices for the company and its employees. The code of conduct has, in its wisdom, to separate the private and the public affairs.

Measures to Solve Conflict of Interest

People are not robots to function exactly and precisely as predetermined by a programme. Human actions are subtle; they express the will in a unique way. Hence, each action is singularly different from the rest. Thus, in an organization, the employees' actions and interactions inevitably produce enough complexity and wrongdoings, such as favouritism, bending the rules, double standards, etc. Moral sanctions and legal hassles may be solved with the following measures (Hartman & Chatterjee 2007).

Admit possible conflict of interest   If you are an upright person and you know that you have done nothing wrong, and yet are being accused of conflict of interest, be open to investigation. It is natural to resist in order to defend your image, but in the case of conflict of interest, appearances do matter. Mere investigation does not prove guilt. Re-examination of the issue will reveal the exact nature of the transaction and also clarify if there was any conflict of interest involved. Thus, a conflict-of-interest investigation is a good management strategy, making the case public and bringing accountability to and application of a single standard of judgment.

Determine conflict of interest   You cannot admit to a possible conflict of interest and sit pretty. You must begin the process of identifying the nature of the conflict. Most of the conflicts may be determined easily and rectified by disclosures and recusals.

However, there are some irreconcilable conflicts of interests; for instance, a single party such as an investor or a legal firm representing merger and acquisition process. In such cases, corrective action should be taken.

Take immediate action　Action needs to be taken immediately once conflict of interest is identified. If a politician holding a minister's post is charged with conflict of interest, it is morally advisable to resign from the public post until cleared of the charges.

Create a code of conduct　The event of a conflict of interest should teach you to create a code of personal conduct. Make efforts to re-study and rework the code of conduct for your firm and put it into practice.

Apply　After a bad experience of conflict of interest, the organization must set out to implement its new code of conduct like a good learning organization.

With a little bit of the good old virtue of humility, which is a handy business tool, you can avoid most of the conflict-of-interest situations by admittance and prompt action.

WHISTLEBLOWING

In early December 2008, *The New York Times*[3] published a story that transported one to the Stalinist era in the former Soviet Union. Since the story happened in China, you could safely say that it went back to the cultural purges of the early Maoean era of the communist revolution in China. In the Shandong province, local officials reportedly sent whistleblowers to mental hospitals. A farmer in his fifties was caught and sent to the mental hospital, where he was given the medicines and sedatives meant for a patient with mental illness. He complained to the doctor, saying that he had lost his land to a coal mining company. He had protested and exposed the corruption of the local officials. He told the doctor that he was not sick. The doctor expressed his helplessness and put him on medication. An investigation by the federal authorities showed eighteen such patients.

In the field of sports, the referee blows the whistle whenever an infringement occurs. This image has been borrowed into the business world to apply to an employee who brings to light the prevalent wrongdoings. Such an employee is called the whistleblower. Whistleblowers are seen by the establishment as troublemakers and the establishment will go to any extent to eradicate the menace.

Whistleblowing may be done by the present or past employees of a company, and even outsiders to a firm. In India, these external sources of whistleblowing may be those who file public interest litigation (PIL) in a court of law.

---

[3] Andrew Jacobs, 'Whistle-Blowers in Chinese City Sent to Mental Hospital' at http://www.nytimes.com/2008/12/09/world/asia/09china.html?ref=todayspaper.

Palaniappan Chidambaram's Conflict of Interest

Palaniappan Chidambaram, popularly known as just PC, has been the Finance Minister of India under different regimes and has an enviable reputation of a clean politician, able administrator, and, above all, an architect of the Indian economic liberalization. Before he became the finance minister, he was the commerce minister, and in the aftermath of the Mumbai terrorist attacks of 29 November 2008, he has been made the home minister, which is a further admission of his unique abilities of managing such a vast country.

In 1992,[a] it came to the notice of the media that he and his wife, Nalini Chidambaram, had invested shares in Fairgrowth Financial Services Ltd. The company was involved in a share market scandal, which involved a corrupt banker and the notorious share broker Harshad Mehta, better known as the Big Bull. Chidambaram, the then commerce minister of state in Narasihma Rao's government, set an example by tendering his resignation. To his disappointment, the prime minister accepted the resignation. This action motivated the Janata Party president, Subramanian Swamy, to file a case against Chidambaram, arguing that the latter had used his influence to invest shares at face value, although the real value was much higher. An investigation was launched by the Central Board of Investigation. The minister was represented by a lawyer, Arun Jaitley, who has now become the leader of the opposition in the Rajya Sabha. Chidambaram won the case and was reinstated to his position.

In 2004, Chidambaram was not holding any government position. He went back to practice law. Chidambaram was Enron Corporation's legal representative. Enron's Dabhol project in India had generated immense political heat and financial seasaws. Chidambaram withdrew, or rather, recused himself from the negotiations between the company and the government, citing potential conflict of interest.

Later in 2004, Chidambaram became the Finance Minister of India under the premiership of Manmohan Singh. An income tax case of the Income Tax Department that he had taken up had to be discontinued, since he had become a minister in the government. His wife Nalini, also a lawyer, took up the case. Thus, she represented the case as a lawyer of the Income Tax Department, which was under the Ministry of Finance, where her husband was the minister-in-charge. This clearly and indubitably formed a conflict of interest case.

For the third time in his life, Chidambaram found himself in the same situation again. He had taken the right decisions earlier: in the first instance he had resigned and in the second, he had recused himself. But on this third occasion, Chidambaram chose not to recognize any conflict of interest. He did not offer to resign. In the following session of the Parliament, there was furore. He defended himself by saying that his wife had dealt with matters that were purely within the law. He gave several precedents of rulings by the Supreme Court. Finally, he denied any knowledge of his wife representing the Income Tax Department. This statement amused the members of the Parliament, who said that the husband and wife were not in talking terms. The media criticized him by saying that if the finance minister did not know what was going on in his own household, how was he expected to know what was going on in the country.[b]

Questions

(a) How do you determine a conflict of interest?
(b) What is the moral damage caused by conflict of interest to a firm and the manager?
(c) Is it realistic to avoid conflict of interest situations?

[a] Paranjoy Guha Thakurta, 'Chidambaram, a magnet to controversy', http://www.rediff.com/money/2005/sep/08pc1.htm (8.9.05).

[b] See *Conflict of Interest* at http://greatbong.net/2005/08/29/conflict-of-interest/.

Necessary Conditions for Whistleblowing

Whistleblowing is an act by an employee to expose the wrongdoings within an organization in the hope of stopping it. In normal circumstances, the whistleblower goes through the routine channels of the organization as prescribed in the code of ethics. However, if not heeded to, the whistleblower then takes the serious step of making it public, that is, exposing it through the available media. Hence, one of the preconditions for whistle-blowing is that it is done in the interest of justice and for the benefit of the organization and its employees, and its motive is not some kind of personal revenge.

The conditions may be divided into three groups (Johnson 2007). See Table 11.1. The imperative of whistleblowing lies in an overriding motive. When the grounds of misdemeanours and wrongdoings are so evident that there is a true public interest involved, a responsible employee takes up the initiative to make the wrongdoings public. A whistleblower is an extraordinary leader whose interests go beyond satisfying personal economic needs. His/her interests lie in justice for all. He/she is an intense listener of own conscience. His/her conviction inspires colleagues to think and do their duty with a higher and nobler end. A whistleblower's sincerity and the justness of the cause are sufficient reasons to constitute the case for whistleblowing.

Whistleblowing Dilemma

The inevitable charge by the organization and colleagues will be one of betrayal. How can one go against the very organization that has given employment? The dilemma is whether to blow the whistle or remain loyal. If you blow the whistle, you are disloyal. If you are loyal, then you are going to allow the wrongdoings to continue. 'Couldn't someone else do it' is what your family members will say and put you on the defensive. But your conscience will say, 'You cannot let it happen; you cannot let so many people suffer; you cannot let so much money go waste.'

Table 11.1   Conditions and characteristics for whistleblowing

Conditions	Characteristics
Dissent	Seriousness of the accusation. Accurate facts. Impending danger or threat. Role of the accused. The public good it would achieve.
Loyalty	Exhaustion of routine channels. Lack of time for routine channels. Internal channels are part of the corruption. As a last resort.
Accusation	Fair accusations. Who has the right to know? When should the public know?

Existential dilemma   A whistleblower is an employee of the organization, has joined the organization with the economic motive of earning a living for self and family, and depends on the organization. How could this person now turn against an agency that provides for his/her well-being? Further, after all that has happened, no other organization will give the whistleblower a job.

Cultural dilemma   Whistleblowing is not done overnight. The family knows directly or indirectly through the whistleblower's disturbed and changed behaviour that he/she is going to take a drastic step. Colleagues give a hundred reasons to be careful and not to lose the job. The plight of the whistleblower can be tragic—loss of job and friends and ever divorce.

Loyalty dilemma   The first victim of whistleblowing is the whistleblower. The organization, colleagues, and even the family are apprehensive about the whistleblower's intentions. They do not trust him/her anymore. Can a whistleblower risk the very value 'trust' that is the cornerstone of all healthy relationships?

Conscience dilemma   In the mission of whistleblowing, when abandoned by all, the whistleblower's conscience has been the constant companion and solace. But now doubts seem to creep in: Is what I did right? Why is the media now probing into the motives? Why are they raking up the past?

These and several other moral conflicts explode in the mind of a whistleblower. Doubts come to torment. Only those who take leadership of the highest kind seriously will be able to come out of such battles unscathed and stronger. The history of great leaders, such as Mahatma Gandhi, Nelson Mandela, and even the much lesser known Satyendra Kumar Dubey, the manager of a prestigious highway project of the Government of India, shows us that they valued and cared for moral principles more than any economic gain.

ABUSE OF OFFICIAL POSITION

Philip Zimbardo, a professor of psychology at the Stanford University, conducted a game called prison experiment in 1971.[4] It was just a role play, a game involving cops and criminals. A mock prison was designated at the psychology department's basement, where twenty-four undergraduates agreed to play the game, which was slated to last for fourteen days. The group was divided and assigned roles of guard and prisoner. Soon enough, the players assumed their roles seriously. The guards exercised so much abuse that the prisoners were traumatised both physically and psychologically. The situation became unbearable and the experiment had to be stopped on the sixth day. The resultant controversy snowballed and went out of the precincts of the university. There was public outcry and the players were acrimonious to each other publicly.

---

[4] See http://en.wikipedia.org/wiki/Stanford_prison_experiment.

Student versus Teacher

A matter of conscience

Walter DeNino[a] is a medical student at the University of Vermont, Canada. His area of specialization is prevention and treatment of obesity. DeNino nourished a vision for his career. He saw that obesity is a global problem affecting millions of people. He envisioned his role as medicine man in an innovative way. He wanted to confront the problem of obesity through his medical knowledge and a sports activity like triathlon, to be precise.

His professor, Eric Poehlman,[b] had built his reputation as a researcher in the field of obesity and aging. To his utter shock, DeNino, who was a student then and was assisting the professor as a lab technician, found that his professor's research was bogus. What was even more surprising was that he was regularly falsifying the data and applying for research funds, which he got.

DeNino's conscience was disquiet. He felt that he could not remain silent to the double injustice being done, first towards obese patients, and second, with the public grant of money. He approached the university authorities and exposed Poehlman's double treachery. In the court proceedings that followed, the professor was accused of scientific misconduct and misuse of funds. Poehlman pleaded guilty to scientific dishonesty and seventeen grant applications. He was sentenced to a year in prison and was ordered to return $180,000; he had to also reimburse the legal fees of his student to the tune of $16,000. The prosecutors had charged that Poehlman's fraud amounted to $2.9 million.

DeNino later admitted that he experienced an enormous sense of responsibility, and after the court verdict, felt that his cause was vindicated. He found it difficult to believe that he had accomplished so much for the scientific community.

Questions

(a) What is special about whistleblowers?
(b) Does our conscience have the power to change the world around us?
(c) Would you do what DeNino did?

[a] See http://en.wikipedia.org/wiki/Walter_DeNino.
[b] See http://en.wikipedia.org/wiki/Eric_Poehlman.

If a mere game could take such an ugly turn, what would be the reality where officials, executives, managers, generals, etc. have real authority and the right to exercise power over others? This incident appeared to be a fore-shadow of the prison atrocities at Abu Ghraib in Iraq since 2003. The far-too-common news of custodial deaths in India, abuse of power by bureaucrats, even professionals such as medical doctors and petty local officials, these and other such abusive deeds, mark our society. Our workplaces, offices, and other establishments are full of stories of the abuse of official power, which creates trauma, stress, depression, and even loss of job when the victim cannot put up with it anymore.

Kinds of Abuse by the Dominant Position

The crux of the abuse of position lies essentially in the dominant position that the perpetrator enjoys. A glaring example of this kind of abuse is that of the casting couch. In 2004, an actress called Preeti Jain filed a police complaint against the well-known

Hindi film director Madhur Bhandarkar. She alleged that the director had asked for sexual favours prior to casting her in a movie role. Hollywood too has a long history of casting couch cases, law suits, and even movies depicting real stories.

The dominant position of a manager or a person of authority encourages the following crimes:

Economic
(a) Bribe: To get a job, to get promotion, to consider favourably for transfer, to grant leave, etc.

(c) Fraud: Accountants/auditors cook books; managers embezzle money; brokers involve in insider trading, etc.

Workplace
(a) Body language: Aggressive, hostile, cold, ignoring, disregard, condescending attitude.

(b) Verbal: Intimidation, slurs, sarcasm, mocking, disdain, bad mouthing, threatening, humiliating.

(c) Bullying: Use authorized power to change work duties, timings, shifts, tactically separate friends working at one workstation and replace one of them with a person who is not liked by the other. Use the above methods to settle scores, to show the power of authority. Use power to exceed one's own power, by raising the bar of bullying methods.

(d) Strategic misuse: Use the system cleverly to the disadvantage of the employees. Give damaging memos for every instance, send bad reports to the higher management, refuse to recommend the deserving, systematically force the person to resign.

(e) Undue patronizing: Even goodness can be manipulated. The employee thinks the boss is good and well-meaning. However, the boss's intentions are not as noble as the employee thinks. The boss uses an ethical ploy to obtain an unethical end, e.g., to gain total and unquestioning personal loyalty, to endorse all the boss's plans in the meetings without discussion, to get close to a family member of the employee, etc.

(f) Violence: There are times at the workplace when a heated argument may end up with fisticuffs. Violence at the workplace is becoming common, particularly in instances when the manager has to face a union, and may degenerate into conspiring violence against certain key employees. Violence may also be through sabotage of machinery or even destruction, which the manager would be in a position to blame upon an employee or employee group.

Social
Due to the position that certain employees enjoy in a reputed organization, they also enjoy social prestige and approbation. They are considered as rendering service to society. This goodwill may be misused by the employees for their own undue gains.

Chairman-cum-Managing Director

Coal Is cool

To be a chairman and a managing director (CMD) at the same time and that too of a public sector unit (PSU) in India is next to being the Indian royalty in its heyday. Mr N.K. Sharma was exactly that. He was the most enviable twin title-holder of Coal India Ltd (CIL). In mid-June 2003, *The Hindu* brought out a news story with the title 'CIL Chief Abused Official Position'.[a] The report said that the chairman-cum-managing director was suspended from his post on alleged corruption charges and the abuse of official position.

The then Union Coal Minister, Karia Munda, after briefing Prime Minister A.B. Vajpayee, took the decision to suspend the CMD because the norms and guidelines stipulated for the sale and purchase of coal had been violated. Sharma had favoured a party while opening a tender for a job. The CMD did not even bother to open any other tender. One such tender that was not opened happened to be from another PSU, Heavy Engineering Corporation (HEC) Ltd. During the investigations, it was revealed that H.E.C. Ltd was the lowest bidder. Further, the CMD had sold coal at the rate of Rs 60 per ton, as against Rs 20 per ton, and had pocketed the difference. The case was handed over to the Central Bureau of Investigation.

Questions

(a) How would ethics help to eschew the misuse of official position?

(b) If a manager uses his influence to get a bit of extra money on the side, which he would use for the welfare of the employees, would that be morally a good action?

(c) If managers do not follow the laid down rules and regulations strictly because they are outdated, and following them would hinder quick decisions, such as the bid of tenders, taking a few short cuts could cut bureaucratic hassles and increase efficiency and bring in profits. Comment.

[a] See http://www.hinduonnet.com/2003/06/06/stories/2003060602281600.htm.

(a) Misuse of influence to recommend undeserving people for jobs and other public favours.

(b) Misuse of influence to induce political gains; gather votes for political banks, the ensured vote segment due to caste, creed, and community.

(c) Misuse of influence for personal gains, to promote close relatives, etc.

There is, however, a big problem when we want to determine the guilt of such crimes. Crimes of direct violence are easy enough to pin down as compared to the subtle methods of body language, sexual advances, systemic uses of memos and warnings, and other forms of harassment.

BRIBE

R.K. Laxman, India's best-known cartoonist, has had a great time poking fun at the bribe culture of India. In one cartoon, he has this setting in a minister's office. The workers have placed an oversized table. The personal aide to the minister quips that such a table is needed because all the work of the minister is done 'under the table', a synonym for rampant bribery in India. Indeed, bribery is not just limited to the political class; it pervades the entire Indian society. Transparency International's Corruption Perceptions Index of 2008, ranks India way down at 85.

The sheer versatility of terms used for bribe gives us an indication of its widespread prevalence that permeates all strata of society. Some of the terms are as follows—inducement, backhander, enticement, kickback, carrot, sweetener, grease the palm, under the table, commission, something-for-your-efforts, for the service, extra incentive, softener, reward, cut, hush money, and several more that differ from area to area, language to language, country to country. In India, the commonly used terms are *baksheesh, maska,* commission, etc.

Bribe involves a transaction. There is a giver and a receiver. Both bear the responsibility of moral culpability. In most countries, taking a bribe is a legal offence, although giving it may not be considered with such seriousness. These days, there are several countries that consider both giving and receiving bribes as constituting a legal offence.

Definition of Bribe

Bribe is one of the most corrupt practices, both morally and legally. Corruption may be understood as a moral disability of integrity, a moral depravity, or decay and is prone to inducements, impropriety, unlawful deeds, and a deviation from the normal course of action. Bribe is something of value given voluntarily but stealthily, such as money, favour, or influence to a person in a position of trust, in expectation of a special favour outside the normal course of business.

The act of bribing is bribery. The *Encyclopaedia of Britannica* describes it as giving a benefit, that is, money. There is a corrupt purpose involved in bribery. Further, the *Encyclopaedia of Everyday Law* describes it as offering, giving, receiving, or soliciting something of value for the purpose of influencing the action of an official in the discharge of duties. There are also instances when such an official may proactively peddle influence, rather than wait passively for people to make an offer. Such an act is called peddling influence.

The constitution of a bribe may consist of immediate payment of money, in cash or kind, or even a promise of later payment. No written agreement is necessary to prove bribery, yet the onus is on the prosecutor to prove the intent of corruption. The very intention to pay the bribe is morally wrong. The actual action, which comes under the legal provisions and could be judged as both immoral and illegal, comes later. The people involved may either be officials, corporate leaders, managers, or simple individuals. The severity of bribery may reach felony, a serious crime for which the criminal courts have very stringent punishments.

What is notable in bribery is that when such an act takes place, there instantly results another crime, the conflict of interest. The person receiving the bribe has clearly put the interest of another legitimate person or persons in jeopardy by giving a favourable treatment to someone else.

Bribery and Indian Corporate World

KPMG India, an international audit firm of repute, has some grim predictions for the Indian corporate world.[5] The agency has done a corporate research across the wide spectrum of the Indian industry. It states that over 70 per cent of the respondents believe that fraud in India will increase over the next two years. Supplier kickback would be the most prevalent form of fraud. The reasons given are that there are no adequate anti-fraud measures and that unethical behaviour of employees is high. These two elements, namely, anti-fraud measures and unethical behaviour, will lead to an environment where both inclination and opportunity will co-exist. Without quick and effective measures, Indian corporations will become breeding grounds for bribes by their employees and will stand to lose enormously. While 80 per cent of the respondents agreed that fraud is the biggest problem, 70 per cent said that it will increase, not decrease. As compared to the earlier findings in the research report of 2006, the report of 2008 shows an increase of 54 per cent kickbacks among employees.

The report further emphasizes the need to rein in measures of employee ethics and regulations. The respondents believed that the threat to the industry is from within. It also depicted that greater threats would emanate from senior managers. This is because they enjoy trusted positions, have access to confidential information of the company, and possess the power to override decisions.

Bribery and Code of Corporate Conduct

Companies are increasingly feeling the need to include strict guidelines against bribery and receiving of gifts in their code of conduct. In the example that follows, Proctor & Gamble has clear directives to its directors and managers.[6]

(a) The core of the company's ethics is 'doing the right thing'.
(b) Standard of right, 'Would I feel happy if others know what I have done?'
(c) Treat colleagues with respect, without any form of discrimination.
(d) No bribery—neither give nor receive.
(e) No money laundering, making unlawful financial transactions appear lawful.
(f) Neither individual nor company bribery is tolerated.

If companies take a little care to safeguard themselves from hush money, influence peddling, and seeking favours from government officials, it would only help them build a good and strong reputation. They will have strong character, the self-esteem of the employees will rise, and the companies will save a considerable amount of money, which can be rolled back to give more benefits to customers.

Companies may tune up their ethics by conducting periodical interactions among employees and also by training them in new trends in ethics and behavioural science.

---

[5] See http://www.indiaprwire.com/pdf/pressrelease/200803188150.pdf.
[6] For the full code of conduct of P&G, visit http://www.pghhcl.in/download/codeofconduct.pdf.

This becomes imperative since business is changing quickly around the globe, and so is the way that people behave and interact with each other.

Bribery and Law

Despite periodic anticorruption laws and also the most supportive Right to Information Law, India is perceived as going down the corruption index.[7] The thrust of the legal instruments has been the public services. However, as the Indian economic situation is changing for the better, the economic offences appear to be worsening.

One of the bribery scandals, the one that followed the Bofors, was the Jain Hawala scam of the 1990s.[8] Ironically, the politicians who agitated against Bofors found themselves implicated in this case, the prominent among them being Lal Krishna Advani, the leader of the opposition party. The Central Bureau of Investigation again failed to nail the culprits, much to the chagrin of the Indian public, and all those who were chargesheeted left their posts by 1998.

In terms of money, the scam was of Rs 65 crore, a crore more than the Bofors scam. There were a record thirty-five charge sheets. The case began with the arrest of two Kashmiri militants in 1991. They informed the investigating agency that they were funded through hawala transactions. Two brothers, N.K. Jain and S.K. Jain, were the kingpins of these transactions. Upon their arrest, they spilled the beans by saying that they had bribed a number of politicians, including the prime minister and the leader of the opposition. Their dairy of payments was provided as proof. This failed in the court to make any good evidence. Although a lot of upheavals took place, the case finally ended as a damp squib.

The anti-bribery laws, and even the one that is regarded as the most effective, the Right to Information Act, have failed to stem the tide of corruption. This clearly shows that something more basic has to be done. All professionals, including politicians, public servants, and business executives, have to be trained in fundamental moral values. The value training that begins at home is good enough for the household; what is learnt at school is good enough for society; and what is learnt in higher education will prepare professionals for careers. The moral value system has to be so developed that during each stage of life, a person is able to deal with the difficult moral choices to be made.

Law and fear of punishment is a poor deterrent. We have seen that both in the Bofors case and in the Jain Hawala case, law could not give results, that is, justice. Crime and punishment are important ingredients of a civil society, but these are for those who live on the fringes of crime.

---

[7] For an eye opener on Indian bribery, see http://www.transparencyindia.org/BPI_2008_Indian_Press_Release.pdf.
[8] See http://www.indianexpress.com/ie/daily/19980916/25951004.html.

Guns and Notes

Bofors kickbacks

India is perceived as a corrupt country; it is a *baksheesh* country. But never did one single case of bribery epitomize the Indian bribery culture the way the Bofors kickback[a] scandal that began in the 1980s did. It still continues to fester, and will remain a metaphor for the hideous underbelly of India.

The Indian Army needed a field gun. Several arms manufacturers from around the globe offered sample pieces. Finally, the French Sofma, the Austrian Voest Alpine, and the Swedish Bofors were shortlisted. In 1986, the Swedish Prime Minister Olof Palme visited India and with his counterpart, the Prime Minister of India Rajiv Gandhi, agreed to have no middlemen. The same year, the Government of India and the Swedish Bofors AB signed a deal for Rs 1437 crore, for the supply of 400 of its 155 mm Howitzer guns.

In Sweden, an engineer of Bofors, Ingvar Bratt, blew the whistle. He told a Swedish radio that his company had paid a bribe to get the contract. In India, this was picked up by two reputed journalists of *The Hindu*, Chitra Subramaniam and N. Ram. The investigation unearthed a Rs 64-crore kickback alleging industrialists like the Hinduja brothers, the agent Win Chadda, the officials in the defence ministry, the Army brass, which included the Army chief, the Italian industrialist and arms dealer, Ottavio Quattrocchi, who was supposed to have acted on behalf of the Congress Party, and, finally, the Prime Minister of India himself, the President of the Congress Party.

The whole of India suddenly became aware that something terrible had hit them at the core. The moral fabric of the country was in tatters. Day after day, week after week, month after month, and year after year the story was broadcast. The irony of covering a moral demeanour is that the more you cover it up the more it exposes itself. The lies to cover up more lies end up creating bigger lies that become more obvious than before. A Joint Parliamentary Committee (JPC) was formed to investigate the charges. Except for the Congress, the rest of the parties refused to take part in the committee.

The 1989, general elections became indirectly a referendum as to how the people of India perceived the scandal. V.P. Singh, one of Gandhi's closest confidants, had taken the higher ground and had quit the party and now spearheaded the election against Gandhi. The Congress and, along with it, Gandhi lost power at the centre. The people's verdict convicted those involved in the Bofors scandal. However, the vagaries of politics unseated Singh, and even the next prime minister, Chandra Shekhar, did not last very long, for he had made a mess of the economy. Elections were declared in 1991. The Bofors issue was still the number one issue. However, during the elections, Gandhi met his fate at the hands of the LTTE terrorists and died.

The following election was won by the Congress, and Narasihma Rao succeeded to premiership. Under his leadership, his foreign minister, Madhavsinh Solanki, was accused of asking his Swedish counterpart to stop the investigations into the Bofors case. He had to resign. Rao lost the elections in 1996. He was succeeded by H.D. Deve Gowda, with the support of the Congress. He picked Joginder Singh as the head of the Central Bureau of Investigations, who managed to get the much publicized Bofors documents to India. But the rug was pulled from under his feet by the Congress, and Gowda had to resign.

In 1999, there ensued the Kargil war with Pakistan. Bofors guns boomed, and in a sweet irony, the guns stole the victory show.

Under the premiership of Atal Behari Vajpayee, a charge sheet was filed against the accused, which included S.K. Bhatnagar, W.N. Chadha alias Win Chadha, Ottavio Quattrocchi, Martin Ardbo, Messrs AB Bofors, and Rajiv Gandhi for entering into criminal conspiracy and abuse of official position. The Hinduja brothers were chargesheeted a year later.

Rajiv Gandhi was already dead. Some more deaths followed, such as that of Bhatnagar and Win Chaddha. Quatrocchi could not be extradited. In February 2005, the Delhi High Court acquitted Gandhi for lack of

Contd

Box Contd

convincing evidence of his complicity. The court also quashed the case against the Hinduja brothers. Upon the elapse of three months, and the Central Bureau of Investigation's unwillingness to appeal, the case was buried.

However, for the people of India the Bofors ghost still lives on.

Questions

(a) During the Bofors scam's peak days, the Indians abroad felt ashamed of their nationality. Explain why such a moral degradation is felt, despite non-involvement.

(b) Bofors AB of Sweden and the Hindujas of India were considered highly respectable in the business world. Their reputation, which was built over generations, was shattered. What systemic and training measures would you suggest for the corporations to safeguard their moral stature?

(c) What moral principles are important to avoid another scam like the Bofors?

[a] See N. Ram's 'Know Your Bofors' in *Frontline* 16(24), 13–26 November 1999, and visit http://www.indianexpress.com/oldstory.php?storyid=86371.

SUMMARY

- Good business decisions are possible where moral values are more important than money.

- Managers are expected to be conscientious leaders.

- The employees of today have a heightened sense of consciousness about their roles in the organization.

- Positions of responsibility confront difficult choices where the interests conflict.

- Good managers are able to overcome conflicts of interests through transparency in their choice of actions.

- Conflicts of interests may be avoided through a strict professional code.

- Managers who are in difficult situations have to assume a higher moral ground and if need be blow the whistle on the organization.

- Whistleblowing is the last resort to make the organization morally responsible for its actions.

- A whistleblower has the purpose of bringing unethical practices to light so that the perpetrators of the crime face the law of the land the larger interest of all the stakeholders is safeguarded.

- Whistleblowers are exceptional leaders who are not afraid of personal losses, such as loss of job or reputation.

- It is a great temptation to utilize one's position for personal gains.

- India is notorious for its culture of bribery.

- The termination of bribery would lift India, both economically and morally.

- Corruption in higher places, both in the political as well as the corporate world, is the bane of India.

- India needs managers with a good conscience.

KEY TERMS

Abuse Improper use of any idea, action, substance, person, position, etc; misuse of anything that brings moral approbation.

Bribe Offering or soliciting of favour in cash or kind; undue and illegal payments in exchange for favours or influence.

Conscience A faculty within human beings that enables personal judgment about right and wrong; awareness of moral responsibility.

Consciousness Judgment that follows from all the faculties that man possesses—sensory and cognitive—to become aware and be responsive to human experience.

Employee   A person with a definite contract from the employer, with well-determined rights and duties; exercises moral responsibility.

Interest   Something or someone of benefit.

Official position   A public or responsible office, with power designated to such an office, such as a

government official, a manager in the corporation, etc.

Whistleblowing   Reporting of misconduct in the workplace by an employee, or a former employee.

Worker   A person with an occupation, who performs tasks as deputed, with no moral curiosity.

CONCEPT REVIEW QUESTIONS

1. How different is today's employee from the employee of a generation ago?

2. Why should conflict of interest be considered as a case in ethics?

3. What are the moral grounds for whistle-blowing?

4. How does the abuse of official power occur?

5. Why is bribing wrong?

6. Does poverty lead employees to solicit bribes?

CRITICAL THINKING QUESTIONS

1. Why is moral leadership important in today's corporate world?

2. Is whistleblowing justified in a company where the employer is facing insurmountable financial problems and the action could lead to a closure, thereby rendering all the employees unemployed?

3. Can you think of instances of ethical dilemmas in which an official takes care of all the rules and regulations?

4. Is there a way to make bribe legal?

FURTHER READING

C.P. Srivastava, *Corruption, India's Enemy Within*, McMillan Publications (2000).

Reena Raj, *Whistleblowing*, ICFAI University Press (2008).

CASE STUDY

Dubey's Dream

Golden Quadrilateral

[The Golden Quadrilateral] *a dream project of unparalleled importance to the nation but in reality a great loot of public money because of very poor implementation at every stage.*[a]

—Satyendra Kumar Dubey

It was an early November morning in 2003. The train from Varanasi reached Gaya at the ungodly hour of 3 a.m. Satyendra Kumar Dubey alighted

from the train. The railway platform was cold with the wintry wind. I will be happy to get into my car, he thought, and be cosy. But there was no car in

---

[a] A quote from S.K. Dubey's letter to the prime minister; visit http://en.wikipedia.org/wiki/Satyendra_Dubey. For complete coverage, see http://www.ivarta.com.

sight. He called to find out. His driver said that the battery was out of order. Nothing unusual, he thought, and decided to take a cycle rickshaw to his suburban apartment. There was nothing unusual in hiring a rickshaw to go home. Dubey was shot dead somewhere along the way. This again was not unusual in the crime infested state of Bihar.

Dubey's a not-so-ordinary decision resulted in his murder, and became the most sensational news of the year. It rocked the country, and had some far-reaching consequences: it resulted in a new legislation passed by the Parliament.

Shared Dream

The then Prime Minister, Atal Bihari Vajpayee, has been a much-loved leader of the country, irrespective of party affiliations, cultural divides, and generation gaps. He was very shocked by Dubey's assassination. Dubey was one of the project directors of the National Highway Authority of India (NHAI) at Koderma, Bihar. He was managing the Golden Quadrilateral (GQ), a mega highway project, conceived by the prime minister himself, and the country supported him in this dream project. The GQ would connect all the major cities of the country from North to South, and from East to West, superimposing the whole country with a network designed like a quadrilateral. With the death of Dubey, a link in the GQ was snapped. The dream dimmed. Dubey was eliminated for exposing the loot in the project.

Stupor

The governments at the state level and at the centre were stunned for different reasons. The media exposed the pretended stupor of the state government, and the fact that it did not want to take any action. The murder suspects, who had been arrested and put behind bars, escaped. While the media reported in disbelief and people around the country expressed their deep displeasure (see Fig. 11.1), the state government still snoozed. The surface transport ministry at the centre was also in stupor, since Dubey had earlier on sent a letter to the prime minister, and its copy to the concerned

Fig. 11.1   People's outrage and demand for whistleblowers law

Courtesy: http://www.hinduonnet.com/fline/fl2104/images/20040227004603001.jpg.

ministry, revealing the horrendous corruption in his area of management. The Central Bureau of Investigation was asked to solve the case. The agency did it quite quickly. Its findings were that Dubey was a victim of a wayside mugging. He was killed with a *katta*, a country-made pistol. Figure 11.2 shows the CBI report. Even the murderer and his accomplice were caught, but they managed to escape. They were found, but one of them escaped again in 2006. This is nothing unusual in Bihar, it is said.

Golden Quadrilateral

NHAI

The NHAI[b] was constituted by an Act of Parliament, the National Highways Authority of India Act 1988. It is responsible for the development, maintenance, and management of the national highways entrusted to it and for matters connected or incidental thereto. The NHAI came into operation in 1995.

The GQ is one of the mega projects of India. Just as Jawaharlal Nehru, the first Prime Minister of India, had dreamt of mega projects in irrigation and built several famous dams, so also A.B. Vajpayee had the dream of surface transport,

[b] See www.nhai.org/.

Satyendra Dubey Murder Case
RC 12(S)/2003/SCR.III/ND

Central Bureau of Investigation, Special Crime Region-III. New Delhi had investigated Satyendra Dubey Murder Case and Charge-sheeted three accused persons including Mantu Kumar s/o Sh. Lachhu Singh, R/o Village Katari RS: Chandoti, Distt. Gaya Bihar who had shot dead Sh. Satyendra Dubey on 27.11.2003.

Presently, the case is pending trial in the court of Addl. Distt. & Session Judge, Patna at the state of prosecution evidence and the last date of hearing was 13.09.2005. On 13.09.2005 all the three accused were brought to Patna court from Beur jail by the escort of Bihar Police. While the accused were being taken to the court from the court lock up, accused Mantu Kumar escaped from the Police custody.

The Director General of Police, Bihar Patna as well as other concerned Distt. SSP of Bihar have been requested to make all out efforts to apprehend the aforesaid accused. The Director CBI has also announced a cash reward of Rs. 1 Lakh for the apprehension of the said accused.

Fig. 11.2 The CBI report of Dubey's murder

Source: http://www.cbi.gov.in/seekinfo/s_dubey_case.php.

roads to connect all the major cities and towns of India into a network. Young engineers like Dubey shared this dream.

GQ consists of building 5846 km of four- and six-lane express highways connecting Delhi, Mumbai, Kolkata, and Chennai (forming a quadrilateral of sorts) (see Fig. 11.3) at a cost of Rs 60,000 crore. The benefits of the highways are far reaching, as they would connect cities and towns and major ports on the coasts, and, like the railways, would be the arteries of industrial development. They would provide very high job opportunities and increase the demand for building materials.

Corruption

With hundreds of thousands of crore rupees involved in the project, it attracted undesirable elements and corruption became rampant. The main contractors would subcontract to the local mafia and pocket huge amounts of money. Unskilled labour and substandard use of materials, further helped in inflating the accounts and profiting the money on the side. In 2006, for instance, the highway sank into the ground in some places, leaving gaping holes in large stretches of the road.

The Letter

Dubey, by the sheer dint of his efforts, had become a project manager in the NHAI and was assigned

the work at Koderma in Jharkhand. He understood the people and the place very well, since he was born and brought up in a village in Bihar called Shapur. (Until recently, Koderma and Jharkhand were a part of the state of Bihar.) In 2003, Dubey was transferred to another section of the highway. This time it was in Gaya, in his home state Bihar. He saw the abyss of corruption in both Koderma and Gaya.

Although Dubey was from Bihar and knew that corruption was nothing unusual in the notorious state, he could not bear to see the money being drained out from the project in which he was the project manager. His conscience was disturbed. He had been offered bribes several times, but he had refused with characteristic disgust, which his friends and classmates at IIT Kanpur were quite familiar with. He was nicknamed 'police' in the best sense of the term because he would not tolerate corruption.

He wrote a letter directly to Prime Minister Vajpayee (see Fig. 11.4). He wrote about the dream project of which he was also a part. He mentioned how NHAI officials transferred funds with undue haste: the minute the contract was signed, the money was transferred. He further stated how the primary contractors and well-known multinationals were subcontracting the work to unskilled and unprofessional people. He exposed the irony of

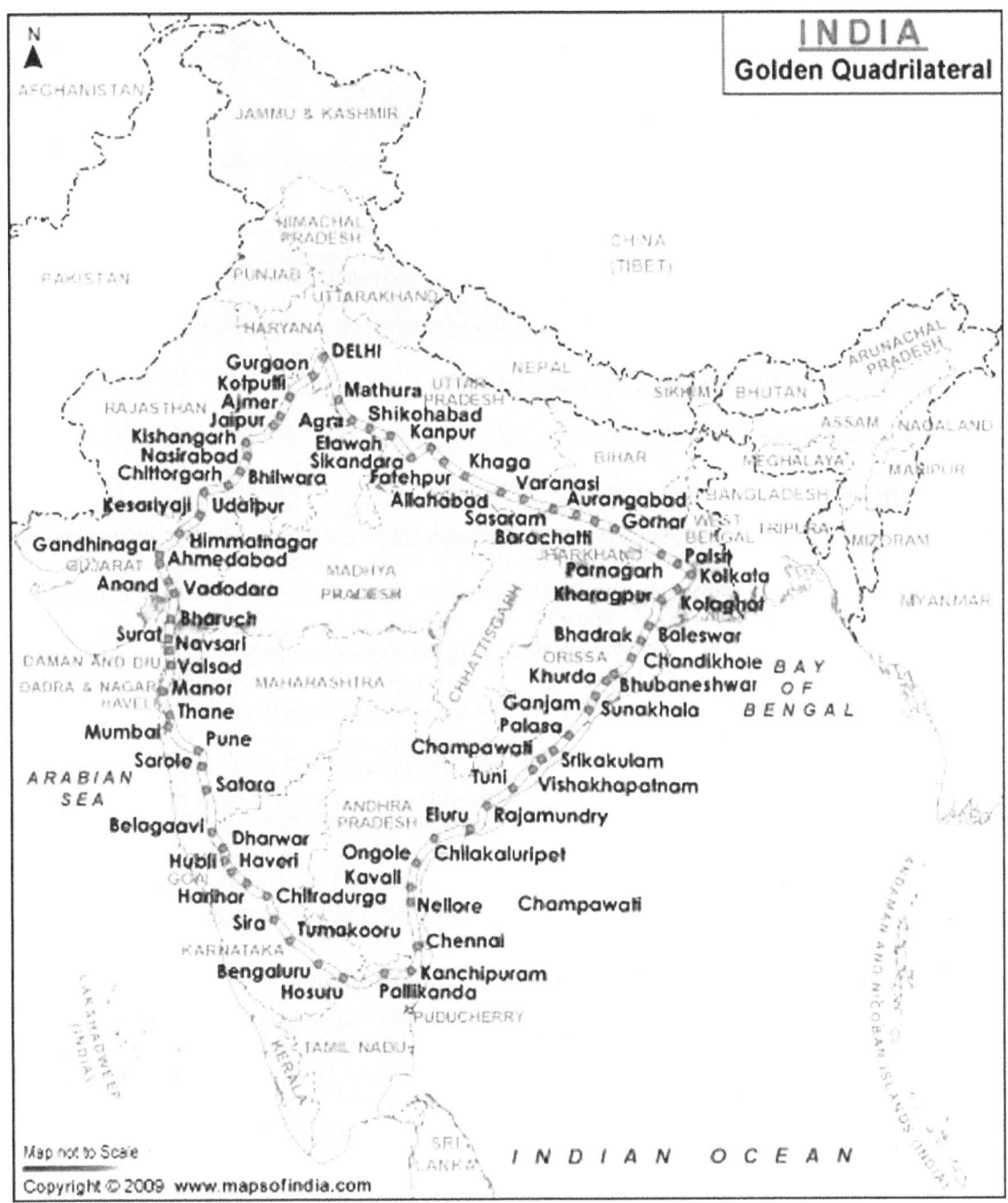

Fig. 11.3   The Golden Quadrilateral

Source: www.mapsofindia.com/roads/golden-quadrilateral.gi.

To

The Prime Minister
Republic of India
Prime Minister's office
New Delhi - 110001

Subject   : National Highways Development Project (Golden
                                  Quadrilateral and North-South, East-West Corridors) –
                                  A dream project of unparalleled importance to the
                                  Nation but in reality a great loot of public money
                                  because of very poor implementation at every stage.

Fig. 11.4   Dubey's letter addressed to the PM

Source: Sunday Express, 30 November 2003.

how the NHAI had actually gone for the best and competitive bidding, to procure the most competent civil contractors, and yet, the execution of it all was done by unprofessional people. He stated that all the officials of the NHAI knew the reality of the subcontracts and were benefiting from it. He lamented that a dream project that was unparalleled was going down due to the loot and poor implementation of the work. He concluded his letter with the promise that he would not stop pursuing the issue and would do everything in his limited capacity, in his assigned place, till the matter was resolved.

The Emperor Is Naked

Dubey had sent his letter to the prime minister's office, and a copy of the same to the NHAI. Dubey was immediately, officially cautioned that it was improper to write to the prime minister directly, and that he had not followed the right procedures of going through the proper channels. Knowing the corrupt officials, it does not take great imagination to guess that the letter came to the knowledge of the subcontracting mafia of Gaya. True to his name, Satyendra (the god of truth) had shouted loud and clear that the emperor was naked. The mafia had no option. They had to silence him if they had to save their garment. Dubey knew what

was happening to him. He repeatedly told his superiors of the death threats that he was getting. But, as we have seen, there was nothing unusual about it. But Dubey's death changed that.

Bihar's Director General of Police was quoted in *Indian Express* as saying, 'The criminalization of contractors is an unfortunate but true fact ... Most of the contracts go to the mafia. I am shocked to hear how an honest man died. I will take personal interest and ensure that we book the culprits'.[c] It was, of course, nothing unusual that all the culprits were not booked. Some of those booked were released later, only to be found dead, which the police declared as suicide. Others who were booked had escaped from high security jail, not once but twice.

Whistleblowers Act

The country had had enough. The media, particularly, the *Indian Express,* spearheaded the movement for Dubey. Thousands of IITians from around the globe signed lengthy memorandums. The institutes of higher education in the country became aware of the magnitude of the Dubey issue. It became increasingly clear that whistleblowers need the protection of the law. People argued that if had Dubey received the protection of the law, then, as a whistleblower, his identity would have been kept

---

[c] *Sunday Express,* 30 November 2003.

A BILL *to provide for protection from criminal or avail liability, department inquiry, demotion, harassment and discrimination of whistle blowers, i.e., The persons who bring to light specific instances of illegality, criminality, corruption, miscarriage of justice, any danger to public health and safety in any Government, public or private enterprise to an authority designated for the purposes and matters connected therewith and incidental thereto*

BE it enacted by Parliament in the Fifty-seventh Year of the Republic of India as follows:

1. (*1*) This Act may be called the Whistle blowers (Protection in Public Interest Disclosures) Act 2006.

Fig. 11.5 Specimen of the beginning of the bill

Source: Rajya Sabha Bill, Bill No. XI of 200.

secret. Dubey was very intelligent. However, even though he had taken the precaution of not signing the letter, he had made the mistake of attaching his bio-data. Upon receipt, the concerned officials should have detached the bio-data and then taken the necessary action, without revealing the identity of the whistleblower.

These officers, who were trained professionals, should have used their prudence to understand the seriousness of the matter and treated it as Dubey had so clearly mentioned. The characteristic lackadaisical attitude of the Indian bureaucracy gave away Dubey's secret to the entire NHAI. The NHAI in turn cautioned Dubey officially about his impropriety. It was shocking even to the common man that such a sensitive matter was treated in such an insensitive way.

It was only in March 2006 that the whistleblower bill (see Fig. 11.5) was introduced in the Rajya Sabha, the Upper House of the Parliament of India.

Dubey's Journey (1973–2003)

Dubey was born in 1973 in a village named Shapur, Bihar, and went to a local school. The Dubey family, consisting of father, mother, and seven children, lived a humble life with a small landholding. The father worked in the local sugar mill as a clerk. Dubey was both brilliant and studious. Although the family could not afford it, he was sent to Allahabad to complete graduation. On completion, he got admission to IIT Kanpur. He was the first person from Shapur to get admission to IIT. He passed out with flying colours in 1994. There were plenty of job opportunities for him, but he

wanted to do something better. He applied for the Indian Engineering Service, which is in charge of public building projects. After working for a while in Delhi, he joined the NHAI and eventually, in quick time, due to his dedication, got designated as project manager and was headquartered in Koderma, Jharkhand. Later on, as part of his supervisory duties, he went to Gaya in Bihar. He has been awarded posthumously by several organizations, including his alma mater, IIT Kanpur, and Transparency International, London. The daily *Indian Express* has instituted a scholarship in his name.

Discussion Questions

1. Is whistleblowing an emotional or ethical issue?
2. Were Dubey's intentions honest?
3. Did Dubey bring it on himself?
4. Do whistleblowers have a role in the Indian industry and business?
5. Is whistleblowing a matter of conscience?
6. Do whistleblowers blow away trust from an organization?
7. What is the difference between a whistleblower and a spy or mole in the organization?
8. How can we be sure that our conscience is always right?
9. Would two people's consciences function in the same way and give a similar judgment?
10. If corruption is so widespread, why should it not be accepted as a way of life?
11. If bureaucrats are employed on a commission basis, which is fixed transparently and as per

market forces, the government could save money and society will be rid of corruption. Comment.

12. Why is the Indian criminal justice system corrupt?

13. What can the whistleblower law do in a country that is perceived as being corrupt?

14. Would the enacting of a law guarantee the privacy and secrecy of employees who expose the wrongdoings of employers?

Going Further . . .

Stage one   As the instructor, make a deal with the group that you will only observe and not interfere with the discussion. Next, each member identifies all the issues in GQ, both ethical and non-ethical, and writes them in the order of importance.

Stage two (i) The group tries to reach a consensus by making a common list of the issues, based on priorities. (ii) Carefully observe the prioritizing process by keeping your presence very low-key, and the ensuing discussion will produce an honest report. Do not disturb the discussion by veering off to personal experiences, work experiences, criticisms of the current establishment. Allow free and frank, disturbing and acrimonious discussions to continue. If the members come to you to solve the problem being discussed and help them to bring in some order, remind them of the deal you made with them.

Stage three   If you are in a position to discuss Dubey's case, then proceed.

ETHICAL DEVELOPMENT PROGRAMME

Management Training

Research Experiment

- Objective: People-oriented approach to management.

- There are six people mentioned below for conducting the research.

- Collect all the necessary information about them.

- Step into the shoes of the subject of your research, that is, you become the protagonist of the story and write the story.

- Assessment: Depending upon your confidence, you could assess it with (a) peer, (b) boss, (c) junior, (d) rival, (e) the Internet community, (f) blog it, etc.

  (a) M.N. Vijayakumar (help link: http://fightcorruption.wikidot.com).

  (b) Dr Rita Pal (help link: http://www.ward87.blogspot.com).

  (c) S. Manjunath (help link: http://www.indianexpress.com/res/web/pIe/full_coverage.php?cov).

  (d) Mordechai Vanunu (help link: http://www.vanunu.org).

  (e) Shiv Chopra (help link: http://shivchopra.com).

  (f) Jeffrey Wigand (help link: http://www.jeffreywigand.com).

Quiz

Organizational Loyalty

You and Your Peers

Put yourself in the following situations.

Grade yourself and your peers (Cullinan et al. 2008) on a scale of 1–10, as shown in Table 11.2.

Table 11.2 Organizational loyalty

Situations	Grading scale 1–10
1. You are the purchasing manager. You have to purchase a large information system. You have examined two of them. System A is cheap, but has higher operating costs. The purchase cost will be borne by your department, and the operation cost by the department of technology.	Your chances of buying: _____ Peers' chances of buying: _____
2. Owing to some technical error, your department erroneously overstated the projected sales. Your dilemma is that if you report the error, the financial community will think your firm is unreliable and this will affect your firm in raising capital.	Your chances of announcing the error: _____ Peers' chances of announcing the error: _____
3. You are on a business trip. You invite your friends there for dinner. You wonder whether you should include the bill for reimbursement as a part of the trip expense report.	Your chances of including the bill in the reimbursement report: _____ Your peers' chances of including the bill in the reimbursement report: _____
4. As finance manager, you will apply for an extension of credit soon after the financial statements are prepared. Unrest in the city prevented your supply for a couple of days. If you could keep open the books for a couple of days, that is, a day after the year end, then you could make up for the lack of sales due to disturbances in the city.	Your chances of holding the books open: _____ Peers' chances of holding the books open: _____
5. Your brief is restructuring of the firm. One of the plants needs to be closed. Your estimate of doing it is 10 per cent of income, which includes both identifiable costs and reasonable allowances for contingencies. A strategic move of increasing the charges by 14 per cent would reduce the current earnings, but could position the firm better to achieve better in the future.	Your chances of increasing the restructuring charges: _____ Peers' chances of increasing the restructuring charges: _____
6. You are a senior manager and you travel often. If you take the frequent flyers' scheme, you would stand to benefit personally, with offers such as a small vacation, gifts, etc. But the airlines does not always charge cheap and your firm pays for it.	Your chances of taking the lowest fare flight: _____ Peers' chances of taking the lowest fare flight: _____

Management Mantra

Here is a contemporary twist on Hans Christian Anderson's celebrated story *The Emperor's New Clothes*.

Original narrative	Contemporary narrative
There lived a great emperor who spent his wealth on clothes and wore new fashionable robes each hour of the day.	We, the customers, we love vanity.
There lived two clever entrepreneurs.	There exist chief executives, managers, politicians, business tycoons—in short, EC, the executive class.
They developed a business plan and approached the king with a novel design.	The EC always has a trick or two up its sleeves.
They got funds sanctioned that far exceeded their wildest dreams.	The EC never feels the liquidity crunch.
The entrepreneurs set up spinning yarns.	The EC loves to spin yarns.
They informed the emperor, his courtiers, and the people in an ad blitz that only those who were not stupid and worthy of their station would be able to see the new clothes from their yarn.	We, the customers, are not stupid; we are always right.
The emperor saw himself clothed. His courtiers and the people saw the emperor's newly yarned clothes and expressed great happiness amidst great pomp.	We, the customers, like fashion; we are smart.
But a boy in the crowd shouted, 'The emperor has nothing on!'	Ah, the Whistleblower!
After a while, even the people started whispering that the emperor was naked.	We, the customers, are the herd.
The emperor then realized that he was naked, but strode on nonchalantly.	We, the customers, we have a way!

MANTRA   *All is a metaphor.*

12

On-the-Job Problems

The right to move the Supreme Court by appropriate proceedings for the enforcement of the rights conferred by this Part is guaranteed.[1]

—The Constitution of India

Manners are not idle, but the fruit
Of loyal nature and of noble mind.

—Alfred Lord Tennyson

LEARNING OBJECTIVES

After studying this chapter, you will be able to

> Identify the various forms of discrimination and their morality
> Describe affirmative action or job reservation as a form of social justice
> Discuss about sexual harassment at the workplace
> Understand the importance of manners for managers

INTRODUCTION

The purpose of this chapter is to inculcate a deep sense of justice and an understanding that all people are equal. If a manager is able to deal justly with on-the-job problems, then half the battle is won. Further, the good manners or etiquette of the manager will make day-to-day work a matter of joy and satisfaction.

The report Equality at Work—Tackling the Challenges[2] by the International Labour Organization (ILO) pointed out the caste discrimination suffered by Dalits, the lower castes of India. The report indicted that Dalits are excluded from work opportunities in the areas of production, processing, or sale of food items, and services in the private and public sectors of India. Untouchability is prohibited by the law, yet it is

---

[1] Constitution of India, Article, 32/1, Fundamental Rights; see http://india.gov.in/govt/documents/english/coi_part_full.pdf.
[2] See ILO Report 2007 at http://ilo.org.

practised in India and Nepal, concludes the report.[3] However, some people would counter and say that such communities have been given job reservations. In addition to this, government schemes for education, mid-day meals, and reservations in institutes of higher education go to form a system of social justice and equality. The National Rural Employment Guarantee Act 2005 only shows the resolve of the public policy against the injustices meted out to the economically backward classes of India.

We will also address another serious issue, that is, of sexual harassment at the workplace. Indian women, both in the rural as well as urban areas, are increasingly becoming career oriented. Although there are several problems that need to be addressed here, sexual harassment and gender bias are the major issues that women face at work. Social discrimination may be remedied by affirmative action, by giving the discriminated groups preferential options for their development, and by granting them work and equality. However, people need a change in their attitude with regard to sexual discrimination and criminal acts of harassment towards women.

Gender issues are very difficult to deal with. In the workplace, a manager comes across several ethical dilemmas, and has to decide for the people, according to their gender. Suppose, you are the manager and a female employee comes and tells you that she has been due for promotion for a long time but many of her male colleagues have already been promoted and moved ahead in their careers. There is a slot open for promotion, which your seniors want you to give to the man they have recommended. If you follow their wishes, you will have to consider dropping the female employee in question. But if you do not listen to your seniors, they can make your work life difficult. You attempt to wriggle out of the situation by trying to convince the female employee that if she is promoted, the increased workload will not allow her to get home early. Furthermore, she will be the only woman in the senior ranks, and some of those men up there are mean. At the same time, to overcome the policy problems of the company, you try to convince her to write and declare to the company that she is not interested in the vacant position for her own personal reasons and that the company could go ahead and appoint someone else. By trying to solve the problem in this manner, you can land yourself in a sticky patch. The female employee could complicate matters by recanting her letter and accusing you of misleading her. She could even bring legal proceedings against you. The issue starts to weigh heavily on your conscience. You may lose the moral ground to defend yourself. You may be seen as a failure because you could not implement justice, nor could you follow the company directives. Thus, your moral and professional fecklessness may be exposed.

How to manage the workplace peacefully, without clashes and without human strife, depends on a manager's management skills. It is the task of a manager, by definition, to handle not only the economic resources, but also the human resources. You may be a brilliant professional and an able organizer. However, if you are unable

---

[3] Sandip Das, 'Caste discrimination at workplace...' in *Down to Earth*, 15 June 2007, at http://www.downtoearth.org.in/.

to control your anger, banish prejudices against socially different people, respect them, and conduct yourself honourably before men and women, all your abilities will be in vain. We would have to reinvent the dictum 'good manners maketh a man' in this chapter. After all that is said, what remains is that something has to be done. Management is all about action, working efficiently, and working with others in a workplace.

DISCRIMINATION

Discrimination is the opposite of equality. Discrimination may be understood in other synonymous terms such as bias, favouritism, prejudice, unfairness, inequity, bigotry, intolerance, chauvinism, narrow-mindedness, sexism, injustice, inequality, disparity, disproportion, and imbalance. Discrimination is an unfair way of treating others. Equality, on the other hand, may be seen in terms of equal opportunity, parity, impartiality, egalitarianism, justice, fairness, and other similar ethical behaviour towards others.

Discrimination at the social level comprises unequal treatment of people on the basis of their race, sex, colour, nationality, disability, religion, or sexual orientation. The law prohibits any such discrimination in areas such as employment, housing, voting rights, education, and access to public facilities. Equality, liberty, and fraternity in all the areas mentioned above have been enshrined in our constitution as fundamental rights.

Direct and Indirect Discrimination

All countries with constitutional laws have ensured equality as a fundamental right of the people. The businesses in such countries have to abide by the law of the land and they cannot override it. Discrimination can be direct or indirect. The former consists of a direct reference to age, race, colour, gender, sexual orientation, physical disability, caste, etc., with openly exhibited prejudice and slur. At the workplace, this comes out starkly in the following instances:

(a) Selection of a person for promotion
(b) Selection of a person to represent the firm for a business meet, travel, etc.
(c) Exceptions to the rules made when an offence is committed
(d) Outbursts at conflicts
(e) Following of normal procedures

However, many workplaces do exercise some form of discrimination in a subtle way. Remarks that are understated and made unconsciously may be couched in people's speech and behaviour so as to humiliate someone else's region, race, colour, gender, creed, or community. People could say things like, 'Oh! I did not recognize your voice, I thought it was Y', to a lady employee who has a rough, manly voice. It could be twisted around to belittle a man also.

Cultural Discrimination

India is a pluralistic society with different religions, regions, languages, races, colours, customs, and historical backgrounds.

Religions   India is a place where several religions and cultural minorities exist. The very names of the people distinguish and categorize them. Thus, the Hindus, Muslims, Sikhs, Christians, and Zoroastrians have typical names that immediately categorize them into stereotypes. Further, the names and family names of the Hindus betray their castes within the Hindu fold. At the workplace, accounts betray caste and creed, and this subtle insight into culture draws lines of superiority and inferiority.

Languages   Indian languages are very subtle, and in matters of discrimination they take even finer hues. For instance, people use the plural forms of pronouns and verbs while addressing someone respectfully. In a family, the elders are often addressed by the plural forms of pronouns and verbs, whereas the singular forms are used while addressing friends. In the caste-ridden culture of India, the higher castes use the singular forms for the lower castes. At the workplace, language unconsciously continues to place a subtle partition. A person belonging to a higher caste will address someone of the lower caste with the singular forms, and the lower caste respond in the plural forms. However, people avoid it now-a-days, and cleverly camouflage the discrimination with English. English is a leveller in so far as such addressing is concerned. But even here, Indians have been able to introduce the subtle partitions by invariably addressing the higher ones with 'Sir' and *ji*, the more respectable suffix from Hindi, several times over, which shows subservience.

Food   Food in India is a labeller of cultures. Who eats what determines the culture of that religion or community. This is exhibited very clearly in a canteen at the workplace. Very often, only members of the same community share the same table. Those belonging to the lower class will sit at some distance, at another table. If the boss belongs to a lower class, the higher caste employees will fill up the vacant places at the table before the boss comes in for tea or lunch.

Age Discrimination

Age discrimination occurs at the workplace when decisions about employment, promotion, and retirement are made. A competent person may be left behind because of the age factor, due to the principle of seniority to be followed for promotion. The Government of India has adopted this policy for its employees. Are we justified to question such a discriminatory policy? Our educational institutions and age old corporations follow seniority for the three stages of a student's or an employee's life at the workplace, respectively.

Adultism   It is discrimination against young people, and is generally practised at recruitments. The employer does not hire a person because that person is too young, although he/she has reached the age of majority, the legal age to work. Young employees are very often at the receiving end at the workplace, as they are often derided for having no experience. Sometimes, the employer exploits them by making them work more, with the justification that this will give them on-the-job training and an opportunity to learn. Management trainees literally get ragged in such situations and become the butt of jokes for other employees.

Gerontophobia It is the fear of growing old, or hatred or fear of the elderly. As employees get old and near the retirement age, the employer becomes apprehensive of a possible decrease in their productivity and waits for an opportunity to dispense with them. The employer often worries about whether the aging employees will ask for an extension. Such employees also become the target of layoffs. Many older employees, who are in their forties fifties, get stressed and worried about being transferred or retrenched. If they lose their job, they may not get another because of their age.

Gender Discrimination

Gender discrimination in India is so common that it passes off as normal. There are horrendous social and religious discriminations directed against women. Women seem to be targeted even before birth, while still in their mothers' wombs. Detection and termination of the female foetus is commonplace. A large percentage of the labour force of the country is formed by women, who are almost always paid less than their male counterparts.

Masculinity and femininity are forms of gender expression, and it could be argued that they influence the attitudes that people have towards one another. However, gender discrimination must be distinguished from sexual harassment. Gender discrimination in the workplace occurs when the male and female employees are not treated equally. Thus, paying unequal salaries for equal work done is gender discrimination. Women are discriminated against. The ethical aim in resolving gender issues is to arrive at gender parity. It is to treat men and women as equals at the workplace and give them equal benefits to enjoy. The law allows this equality. Hence, women are found in the defence forces, corporations, and politics. They are selected on merit.

Following are some areas of gender bias at the workplace.

Recruitment During recruitment, women are subjected to reprehensible questioning about their ability to attend work due to marriage and pregnancy.

Remuneration In the lower rungs of semi-skilled and unskilled work, women are invariably paid less. In the higher and skilled employment areas, men are not ready to accept women's ability and competence in senior management positions. According to an ILO report, even in these areas, 30 per cent of the women suffer unequal pay.

Corporations include in their mission statement, among others, equality of genders. Corporations are bound by the law to offer equal opportunity employment, opportunities for education and up-gradation, equal pay for equal work, strict policy implementation without gender bias for promotions, and other benefits.

Sexual Orientation

Although in many developed parts of the world, sexual orientation of employees is being openly debated to find equitable solutions, in India and other parts of Asia, the issue is a social taboo. However, there is growing recognition of the rights of homosexuals. Companies need to address the issue of homosexuality in their policies so that they are transparent about their stand. Homosexuals are present in every walk of life, be it economic, political, social, cultural, or religious, and no company can avoid them.

Companies have to look at their human resource objectively, and look for competencies, skills, and values. An employee's sexual orientation, just like all other aspects of private life, should be no concern of the company.

If companies have to keep the welfare of their employees in mind, then they would do well to formulate employee policies that remove discrimination, from recruitment to retirement. Here are some measures that need to be followed:

(a) No seeking information about sexual orientation at recruitment
(b) No allusions to be made at the interview
(c) Even if voluntarily disclosed by the employee at some stage, there would not be any professional difference made; privacy and confidentiality to be maintained

Caste Discrimination in India

Caste, in its original objective, was created as a system of determining occupation in society. It was a sort of division of labour, by birth. The occupational structure became a social structure. It was abused, since one could not cross the boundaries of caste. According to UNICEF, over a quarter of a billion people in the world are directly affected by it. Most of these caste systems are to be found in the Asian countries. They are particularly strong in the sub-continent and have spread till Japan. The caste system is strong in Africa too. However, seen from an economic perspective, the people of the entire old world were somehow classified according to economic segmentation, whereby the lower classes carried a stigma. Thus, in reality, the caste system appears to have been universal. Today, all law-abiding countries have constitutionally declared that any form of discriminatory human classification is illegal and against the fundamental rights of the people.

Sadly, India is still plagued by the residue of the caste system, despite sixty years of independence.[4] Workplaces in India are not free from caste prejudices. We get to read about workplace discrimination and harassment even in well-established institutions such as the higher centres of learning, industry, and services.

---

[4] Bahujan Students Network, 'Premier Institute or the Hub of Caste Discrimination', at http://www.ambedkar.org/News/IISc_Suicide.pdf. This is an account painstakingly put together by a group of Dalit students, Bahujan Students Network (BSN), in September 2007. It is about a young Dalit from Andhra Pradesh who entertained dreams of becoming like Dr B.R. Ambedkar, an untouchable who became the most erudite man of India and the architect of her constitution.

We shall deal with discrimination in greater detail, when we deal with human rights. Here, we will suggest a few measures that can help a manager to remain above caste discrimination in dealing with employees.

(a) Remove the idea of discrimination from your psyche. In India, irrespective of one's station in life, inferiority and superiority complexes are created due to deeply embedded cultural prejudices. Dark-coloured people are considered to be of a lower caste. The skin crèmes advertised in India, for instance, suggest that you apply the cream, become light skinned, and your employer will think that you belong to a higher caste and give you the job. If an advertisement could be so blatant, how blatant would the workplace be to denigrate human dignity?

(b) Make human dignity the cornerstone of your workplace. It is very simple to practice if the manager is conscientious that others are also human beings just like her/him and deserve equal respect.

(c) Respect your employees. Respect is an ethical value. It consists of a relationship between self-esteem and the recognition of the same in the other. Respect at the workplace tests relationships. Mutual respect builds work teams beyond the barriers of any dissimilarity.

Dilemma for the employer

So far we have discussed how a company must frame policies for its HIV/AIDS employees. However, when a company employs people, it has a right to employ

---

Ajay Sree Chandra

Something foul at the seat of learning

Ajay Sree Chandra was an exceptionally intelligent student. He always scored over 80 per cent. He would have got into any institute of higher education on merit. But since he belonged to a scheduled caste, he was given a seat under this quota, although he was among the top twelve selected for the PhD programme in biological sciences at the Indian Institute of Sciences (IISc), Bangalore.

Fellow students certified anonymously that he was harassed by two faculty members who belonged to higher castes. It became unbearable for him. He was abused and humiliated in the lab. Chandra used to shiver at the very sight of them. When some pages of his dairy were later released, the following words were found written in it, 'Those eyes scare me... Those eyes scare me lot. My legs pain...'

Chandra wrote a lengthy suicide note, which was found in the room he had hanged himself in. His diary and the note were confiscated by the police, who registered the case as suicide. It is said that the diary and the suicide note were destroyed. After several pleas, a couple of pages of his dairy were given to Chandra's father, where the words mentioned earlier were found written.[a]

Questions

(a) What is the morality of suicide?
(b) What moral responsibility does a person bear who leads another to commit suicide?
(c) How will you convince others that you did not realize your normal remonstrations would lead your employee to suicide?

[a] See http://www.tehelka.com/story_main34.asp?filename=Ne201007INFAMY_ENROLS.asp.

healthy people. The interests of the company cannot be served by potential HIV/ AIDs employees. On the contrary, if and when health breakdown occurs, the company will suffer heavy losses as the above policies can be counter productive. This is a dilemma that companies have to face. The only solution they have is to keep their promise and suffer the loss.

In 2005, the International Labour Organization (ILO) had conducted a study at the Singareni Collieries Company Limited (SCCL) in Andhra Pradesh. SCCL has

---

HIV/AIDS

ITC, founded in 1910, is one of the largest Indian conglomerates. From being Imperial Tobacco Company Limited, today its acronym ITC suffices as its brand name and has diversified into several branches of the industry. It has over 21,000 employees and works from about sixty hubs across the country.[a] It has been the target of public ridicule for promoting tobacco products and at the same time taking up projects in the health care industry. Hence, it is very conscious about the health of its employees. Since its interests also lie in the hospitality and fast moving consumer goods (FMCG) industry, it has an elaborate policy on employee health. Let us look at its policy on HIV/AIDS for its employees.[b]

Health
(a) Safe and healthy environment for all employees.
(b) People with HIV/AIDS do not pose a risk of transmitting the virus to co-workers by casual, non-sexual contact in the normal work setting.
(c) Compliance with all relevant central and state legislation. The company will implement all policies and directions of the government regarding HIV/ AIDS whenever issued.
(d) Prevention through awareness. The company will provide its employees sensitive, accurate, and latest information about risk reduction strategies in their personal lives, with the objectives of reducing the stigma of HIV/AIDS, encouraging safe behaviour, and improving their understanding of the treatment.
(e) Access to health services to prevent and manage HIV/AIDS.

Non-discrimination
(a) No discrimination against any employee infected by HIV/AIDS with regard to promotions, training, and other privileges and benefits applicable to all employees.
(b) HIV positive employees will be allowed to continue to work unless medically advised. If the case demands, reasonable alternative conditions will be provided.
(c) When medically advised not to perform duties, the employee will be given help for rehabilitation.
(d) The company will not make pre-employment HIV/ AIDS screening mandatory as a part of its fitness-to-work assessment. Screening of this kind refers to direct methods (HIV testing), indirect methods (assessment of risk behaviour), and questions about HIV tests already taken.
(e) HIV/AIDS test will not be a part of the annual health check-ups, unless specifically requested for by an employee.

Confidentiality
(a) Voluntary testing for HIV/AIDS when requested for by the employee will be carried out by private or community health services and not at the workplace.
(b) There will no obligation on the part of the employees to inform the company about their clinical status in relation to HIV/AIDS.
(c) Information on the clinical diagnosis, his/her HIV/ AIDS status, if advised to the company, will be kept strictly confidential.

[a] See http://www.itcportal.com/.

[b] For a comprehensive HR policy of the company, visit http://www.itcportal.com/our_values/hr_policy.html.

over 300 employees with HIV/AIDS. It spent Rs 65 lakh on disbursement of terminal benefits to twenty-nine employees declared unfit due to HIV/AIDS related illnesses during the last five years. In addition to this, the company had to bear the rising costs due to absenteeism and loss of manpower due to HIV/AIDS. When all the affected employees will finally claim benefits, it will cost Rs 9.33 crore in the coming years. The company can only hope that better medicines for the anti-retroviral treatment would cost less.[5]

Other forms of workplace discriminations

The discriminations present in society creep into the workplace. Let us discuss in brief the other forms of discrimination at the workplace, which have not been explained above.

Migrant workers   Workers, mainly the unskilled ones, migrate from their home states, especially Bihar and Orissa, to escape poverty and hunger or from political and social unrest, especially from regions in Kashmir or Assam. People living in state border areas also seek employment in their neighbouring states. Migrants are discriminated against when it comes to hours of work, pay, and housing facilities.

Region   Not only migrant workers, but also those who have moved out of their states for professional reasons face discrimination and social ostracism—from derogatory remarks to various acts of violence. In Maharashtra, a hate campaign was launched in 2008 against thousands of workers who came mainly from the northern states of the country.

Language   India is divided into states on the basis of linguistics. Whether migrant workers or professionals, when people work in states other than their native one, communication becomes a problem. Despite learning the local language, migrants are the butt of jokes because of their different accent, food habits, or dress style.

Racism   There is a debate whether discrimination on the basis of one's caste should be treated as racism. In India, racism is found even in well-known workplaces. The racial mistreatment meted out to the people from the northeastern states of the country has constantly been in news. Foreign students, particularly those from African countries, have been subjected to racial discrimination and humiliation.

Colour   That Indians are colour conscious is a sad truism. The matrimonial columns of our dailies alone are ample proof of it. Only those girls who have 'very fair, fair, or wheatish complexions' are proposed to or accepted as brides. It has been generally perceived that the people of South India, the tribals, and the *adivasis* around the country are dark skinned. Colour has been a serious element of discrimination even in employing someone.

---

[5] See http://www.indiatogether.org/cgi-bin/tools/pfriend.cgi.

Disability It will not be wrong to say that India as a civic community has failed terribly towards its most vulnerable citizens, the mentally and physically disabled. Some progress has been made towards the non-discrimination of the physically disabled: referred to in the past as physically challenged, but now as differently abled. However, these people have shown that they are much more resilient than those who are able-bodied. So, this proof should suffice to offer them employment with equal opportunities.

Professional discrimination Professional discrimination occurs when a person is discriminated at the workplace due to the previous professional assignment. There was a time when some companies preferred to employ government bureaucrats. However, present companies are reluctant because they believe that these employees will bring into the work culture lethargic bureaucratic work ethic and, worse still, proneness to bribery.

Ideology Political, religious, and economic ideologies strongly divide people. These orientations could hinder a person from getting a job for which she/he is qualified. It may happen that people of certain communities are accepted for interviews, to fulfil the legal obligations of equal opportunity, but get sidetracked surreptitiously. For the ones who manage to get employed, the behaviour of the colleagues is often unsettling.

The ways of discrimination are as complex and as complicated as human ingenuity can drive. It would heal society and the workplace to first accept that such moral deformities do exist and then try to remedy them with goodwill and understanding.

AFFIRMATIVE ACTION OR JOB RESERVATION

The term 'discrimination' is often used negatively. It describes unfair and unethical behaviour, the unequal treatment meted out due to all the discriminatory factors we enumerated. However, society has become conscious about the injustice meted out to its less fortunate members. This new consciousness for fairness and equal treatment stems from the moral ground that all human beings are equal. The problem is that since in the past society failed in its fundamental duty of eliminating unlawful discrimination, it must undertake something drastic to overcome and reverse the discrimination. This reversal is a positive effort to give opportunity to those people who had been neglected and left behind in the social, political, and economic growth. This positive effort is known as reverse discrimination and, for want of a better term, it is well-known across the world as affirmative action. In India, since independence, affirmative action is called reservation, by the action taken. At times, it is also called the quota system, which describes the jobs reserved for the select classes of people who have so far been discriminated against.

When positive discrimination gets legal sanction, it is called affirmative action. A common example of positive discrimination is the practice of 'women and children

Off-track Sex Test

In January 2007, the Olympic Council of Asia (OCA) took an ominous decision. It declared that Santhi Soundarajan, the winner of the silver medal for 800m at the Asian Games at Doha, Qatar, was disqualified for failing the sex test. Santhi was shattered. She wanted to commit suicide.

Indian Olympic Association (IOA), the Indian counter part of OCA, merely confirmed what the latter said. Santhi, the 25-year-old athlete hailing from Tamil Nadu, was disqualified for violating the rules of the Olympic Games—she had failed the gender test. In plain words, Santhi had deceived the sports authority about her gender. She had competed as a woman, when actually, she was a man.

Everyone who knew Santhi, including her parents, coaches, sports officials, and even the Government of Tamil Nadu, vouched that she was a woman. There was utter shock, disbelief, and humiliation. The IOA tamely said that she had failed the gender test.

The wisdom of science was sought. An expert gynaecologist said that it is difficult to determine whether a person is male or female merely by the external appearance of the genitalia. Some people are born with ambiguous sex organs. Women and men are distinguished through their chromosomes. A female has two X chromosomes (XX) in her cell and a male has an X and a Y chromosome (XY). There are some exceptional cases, where a Y cell owner has all the physical characteristics of a female, including the external sexual organs, yet fails to have any female internal sexual organs. This is due to a genetic defect, which does not produce testosterone. Such a person has the medical condition known as androgen insensitivity syndrome (AIS). Even though such a person has XY chromosomes, due to the inactivity of the testosterone, which is the hormone that makes one a male, the individual cannot be considered a male.

Since the person's body does not produce testosterone, the body does not respond to it. Hence, AIS does not give the female athlete any benefit of a male's advantages, such as muscles and strength.

In the 1996 Olympics at Atlanta, seven women had Y chromosomes; they had the AIS and they competed legally. The IOA has given up the gender test to avoid confusion; but why its Asian branch is still practising it and why Indians are supporting it is not known. In Santhi's case, she had successfully competed in athletics.

Santhi comes from a very poor family, from a small village called Kathakkurichi, which is in the Pudukottai district of Tamil Nadu. Her parents work in a brick-kiln as labourers. She became a sportswoman by overcoming the problems of poverty and malnutrition. She trained with great passion and dedication. She has set a national record for 3000m in the steeplechase, clocking 10:45:65. At the National Games in Bangalore in 2005, she won the 800m, the 1500m, and the 3000m athletics events. In the same year at the Asian Championships in Incheon, South Korea, she won a silver medal for 800m.[a] It was at the 2006 Asian Games at Doha, after she won the silver medal for 800m, that the officials made her undergo a sex test and declared that she was faking. Despite her ordeal and humiliation, the Government of Tamil Nadu took a proactive stance and recognized her as an athlete who had made a contribution to sports and to the state. She was awarded Rs 15 lakh in appreciation.

Questions

(a) Does scientific testing aggravate gender discrimination?

(b) Can gender testing be considered morally wrong? What principles are violated in the process?

(c) Can a male, after a sex change operation, compete or work in a role designated for females?

[a] See http://en.wikipedia.org/wiki/Santhi_Soundarajan.

first'. It is in this moral sense that affirmative action is justified. In our moral journey, we have travelled quite a distance from the principle of 'survival of the fittest'. If our workplaces must become more human, then the principle of equality must rule.

Reservation or Job Quota

Reservation in the Indian Constitutional Law consists of a certain percentage of seats being reserved in the public sector, union and state civil services, government departments, public and private educational institutions (except religious and linguistic minorities), for the scheduled tribes, scheduled castes, the backward classes, other backward classes, and some notified forward classes. Recently, there has been a very strong proposal for an extension of such reserved jobs and educational privileges in the private sector too.

See Table 12.1 for some arguments for and against reservation.

The history of reservation dates back to the Hunter Commission of 1882 during the British rule. Ever since, it has been a highly divisive issue in India. In independent India, the reservation policy has overshadowed every other issue. There have been debates, hundreds of cases in courts, agitations, strikes, violence, and loss of lives and property. It is one of the unsolvable problems of India. The reason for this state of affairs is a moral one, which has snowballed into a legal one. It is morally untenable that one human being be considered higher or lower to another. Legally, different standards for different people are also equally untenable. Whoever occupies the decision-making position, such as in the parliament and the courts, has the greatest

Table 12.1   Arguments on reservation

Pro-reservation	Anti-reservation
1. Practised in both developed and developing countries with very good results in education, employment, and standard of life.	We do not have to emulate bad examples that will lead to greater inequality.
2. India is already a good example of how it has helped to include the people who have been neglected for centuries.	India's reservation system has become ridiculous, as in many cases it has overshot the 50 per cent quota.
3. It is a potent instrument of social justice. It has helped to remove prejudices such as untouchability and lack of education for women.	Equality cannot be achieved through unequal means. Natural justice is a better principle than artificially induced equality.
4. States such as Tamil Nadu have been able to do justice to reverse affirmative action, as these underprivileged classes have even gone ahead of the forward classes.	Reversal of roles merely equals to revenge; nothing else is achieved positively. It has merely helped in establishing political vote banks.
5. Caste is the biggest problem that reservation resolves to solve in all the areas of human activity.	Poverty is the biggest problem. It makes no distinction between caste, creed, and other categories.
6. It is a programme for the equality of man. It will help earn meritocracy. In India, occupations are caste oriented. Only a Brahmin can become a temple priest. Reservation will change the way people work and establish their careers.	A programme for equality must be for all; selectiveness creates bias and bias creates strife, which leads to division and violence.

Contd

Table 12.1 Contd

Pro-reservation	Anti-reservation
7. The argument of the anti-reservationist that reservation should be based on economic backwardness and not on social segmentations of caste is incorrect. Indian reality shows that an overwhelming number of people belonging to the reservation category are poor in every way, namely socially, economically, politically, educationally, and work-wise.	The reality is poverty. The poor are deprived of everything; even dignity is not spared. Where there is dignity, caste has no power. The power comes from education and employment. This is the right of all individuals, not just those in the reserved category.
8. Anti-reservationist allegations that the reserved people have brought in incompetency and lethargy within the government and the public sector is unfair. It is not due to their incompetence, it is due to the poorly implemented management systems.	The accusation that the reserved category has brought in incompetence and lethargy is a factual statement. All the people of our country suffer from incompetence and lethargy of the people in the public service.

moral dilemma of how to reconcile the principle of equality to social justice. If you promote social justice, then you have to make a preferential option for the marginalized people. However, if you do so, then the principle of equality is violated, for you have given a preferential option. The very same dilemma has hit companies, which are under pressure to introduce reservation.

Mandal Commission and Social Justice Dilemma

In 1979, the Janata Party appointed the well-known Parliamentarian Bindheshwari Prasad Mandal (1918–1982) as the chairman of a commission that bore his name, for the purpose of reservation for various classes and to make recommendations for the same. It is the most comprehensive and far-reaching report ever made, where the recommended reservations jumped from 27 per cent to 49 per cent.[6]

The commission adopted eleven criteria to identify a class or group of people eligible for reservation. These were classified under social, that is caste; educational, again castes under various age groups for educational purposes; economic, yet again based on caste, determining the different strata of the poverty line. It was found with great trepidation that at least 52 per cent of the total population of India came under these categories. It squashed the argument of merit by saying that it is elitist and that the categorized classes were disadvantaged. It also noted with disdain how the British rule had destroyed the Indian society and had introduced the Western concepts of justice. In addition, the phenomenon of *Sanskritization* (another word for Brahmanical system) had created divisions in society, thus becoming a cause for division and violence. It spelled out an elaborate system of reservations, almost turning the logic of reservation on its head, as it closed in on the 50 per cent mark. The report also

---

[6] See http://www.pucl.org/from-archives/Dalit-tribal/mandal-2.htm. Other useful links are http://en.wikipedia.org/wiki/Mandal_Commission and http://sify.com/itihaas/fullstory.php?id=13383406.

recommended total structural changes in order to implement the reservations. Hence, the entire government machinery would be set up to implement the mammoth social reform and restructuring.

The Janata Party, as well as B.P. Mandal, left the scene. The party had an inglorious exit and the chairman of the commission died a natural death. No one remembered the Mandal Commission until V.P. Singh, the eighth Prime Minister of India, resurrected it in 1989, exactly a decade after its formation. Its implementation set India literally in flames. A student of Delhi University immolated himself; several more self-immolations took place in protest against the commission. Figure 12.1 shows the population estimation and reservation percentage of various communities.

This shows that even in the best of schemes for social engineering, people see some deformity of moral nature, which outrages them. In India's job reservation or job quota case, those who were for and against it had equally sound moral grounds to justify their case. The disadvantaged wanted justice; others refused to give in. The former cited their historical disadvantage; the latter argued that their future would be in jeopardy and that India's educational institutions, industry, and enterprise would not be the same. In the labour history of India, the Mandal Commission will remain a watershed for better or for worse.

SEXUAL HARASSMENT

Human beings are sexual by nature; when they come together, their sexual element becomes a part of that togetherness. Workplaces are a meeting point for men and women and sexual attraction is natural. Society has created institutions within which

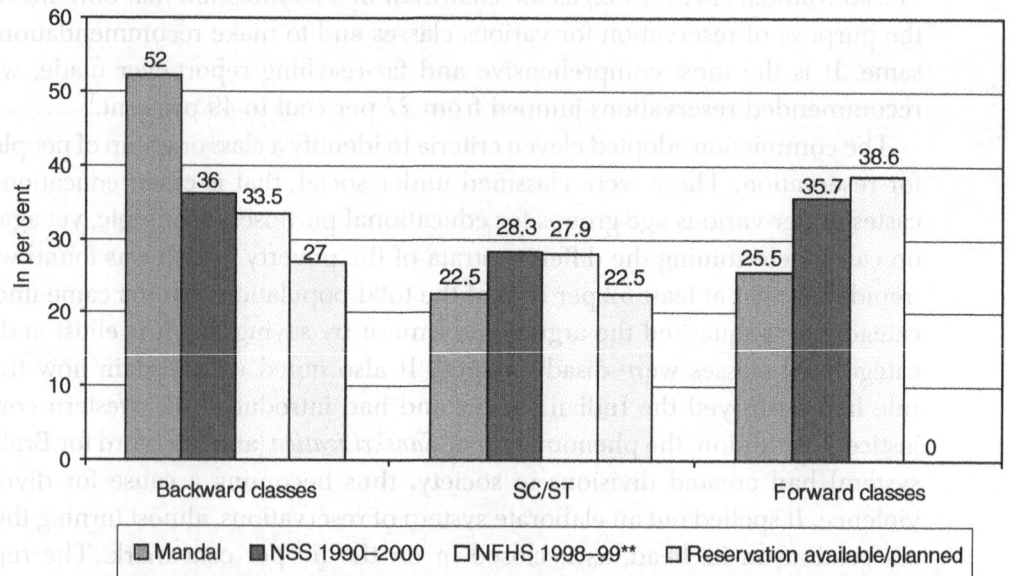

Fig. 12.1 Population estimation and reservation percentage of various communities

Source: http://en.wikipedia.org/wiki/Mandal_Commission.

Dr B.R. Ambedkar: The Prophet of Affirmative Action

If Mahatma Gandhi inspired India to attain political freedom, it is Dr Ambedkar who stirred the conscience of the poor, the powerless, and the outcasts that such freedom has no relevance without social and economic freedom for all the people. He said, 'Constitutional morality is not a natural sentiment. It has to be cultivated. We must realize that our people have yet to learn it. Democracy in India is only a top dressing on an Indian soil which is essentially undemocratic.' He clearly pointed out that the majority of Indians belonging to the lower castes—the tribes and untouchables, that is, the Dalits—were not yet free.

As early as 1930, Ambedkar saw no solution of equality in the political freedom. On 5 August 1930, in the conference of the so-called 'depressed classes', he announced, "We must shape our course ourselves and by ourselves... Political power cannot be a panacea for the ills of the depressed classes. Their salvation lies in their social elevation. They must cleanse their evil habits. They must improve their bad ways of living.... They must be educated.... There is a great necessity to disturb their pathetic contentment and to instil into them that divine discontent which is the spring of all elevation'.[a]

Religion is very important for Indians, realized Ambedkar. Hinduism had systematically discriminated the Dalits, he felt. He wanted to bring all the Dalits under a respectable religious banner. From 1950 onwards, there began mass conversions of Dalits to Buddhism. He rejected the name Harijan (God's people), given by

Gandhiji to the untouchables, as another humiliating epithet.

Above all, Ambedkar, as the architect of the Indian Constitution, made sure of the constitutional rights of all the people and the abolition of untouchability. He enshrined in the constitution extensive economic and social rights for women. He introduced the system of reservation, which was taken forward in every schedule of the Parliament that followed. He completed the work of the Constitution of India on 26 November 1949 and it was adopted by the Constituent Assembly.

Bhimrao Ramji Ambedkar was born on 14 April 1891. His family belonged to the Mahar community of untouchables. With a little luck and by the sheer dint of his efforts, he rose in life. Since his father served in the British Army, he got an opportunity to go to school. Later, he studied in the London School of Economics and Columbia University. He returned home with incredible academic laurels from these universities, with a series of PhDs in political science, economics, and law. He became instantly famous in India. He took part in the political movement of India, and was a Parliamentarian when he died of illness on 6 December 1956.[b]

Questions

(a) What ideas of morality should one who is born as an untouchable form?
(b) What is the moral justification for affirmative action?
(c) Can an affirmative action be morally wrong?

[a] See http://en.wikipedia.org/wiki/Ambedkar.
[b] See http://www.ambedkar.org/.

such natural attraction finds its full expression. Marriage and family ennobles sexuality. This then is the morality of human sexuality, to seek fulfilment in life through faithfulness towards one's partner.

The foundation of sexual morality lies in the consent of the partners. Sexual attraction and courtship are within moral limits when both the partners consent. If one does not consent to another's efforts for sexual response, it can be construed as sexual harassment because it is unwanted. What is against the wishes and will of another constitutes grounds for violence. This violence may be called harassment when gestures and insinuations, physical closeness and touch, verbal suggestions of a sexual relationship, behavioural contexts, and colouration occur. The violence can be completely physical, leading to a non-consensual sexual attempt or molestation, or the actual sexual act termed as rape. Further, the law supports the moral law and lists sexual atrocities from harassment to rape as serious crimes, and metes out just punishment.

Sexual Harassment at the Workplace

Sexual harassment at the workplace is increasingly becoming a problem. A victim may perceive sexual harassment even where no physical closeness, touch, or even verbal exchange is found. The body language, various workplace situations, and atmospheres are enough for a perverted mind to seek satisfaction of carnal desire. Table 12.2 lists the kinds of sexual harassment a person may suffer at the workplace.

A manager needs to take extreme care that the workplace remains free from sexual harassment. The manager has to know, both morally and legally, what constitutes sexual harassment. There is no other action at the workplace that is as damaging as the one that is sexually demeaning in nature. Further, a person, who is perceived as sexually harassing others, stands to lose the job and also the respect of his family and community.

Humiliation of the Victim

The rape cases that we come across are of a horrendous nature. After going through the trauma of sexual harassment, the victims also undergo tremendous humiliation. The victims are further victimized during the medical examination, filing of the first information report at the police station, and then at the court hearings. The defence lawyer would like to prove that the woman was of loose character. The victim goes through the traumatic experience innumerable times. Some of these victims commit suicide.

The most infamous is the Mathura rape[7] case in the 1970s that brought to light the complete violence that a victim suffers. Mathura, a tribal from Maharashtra, had eloped with her boyfriend. At the filing of a complaint by her family, the policeman raped her in the police station. The lower court dismissed the case by saying that Mathura was used to sexual intercourse and that she was of a loose character. The furore that followed made the rape law amendment[8] possible. Accordingly, the character of the woman was ruled as not relevant for the violence that was perpetrated on her person.

Disciplinary Counselling

Corporations have realized the seriousness of the offences at the workplace and have established codes of conduct concerning discrimination and sexual harassment.

---

[7] See http://infochangeindia.org/200811117484/Women/Backgrounder/Violence-Against-Women.html.
[8] See http://ncw.nic.in/Amendments%20to%20laws%20relating%20to%20women.pdf.

Table 12.2   Kinds of sexual harassment

Type	Nature
1. Misuse of position of power	Deal—job, promotion, grades, credentials, orders—only if sexual favour is granted.
2. Protective role players (parents, seniors, mentors, etc.)	Deceptive ploy to get close to the subject at the workplace, an educational institution, etc.
3. One-of-the-gang	In a mixed sex group where one wants to impress, one is open, loud, and lewd; it can happen openly at celebrations, gatherings, or festivities.
4. Third party	Where the harasser uses employees or peers, who are not themselves the target; occurs in situations such as quid pro quo and misuse of position of power.
5. Serial	A harasser who plans well and strikes, and no proof can be given.
6. Groper	Sly harasser who tries to fondle and press, irrespective of the place, public or private.
7. Opportunist	Taking advantage of a situation or creating a situation such as one-to-one meeting, travel, and workplace closeness.
8. Bully	To punish an employee or peer or junior with sexual aggression, when the victim resists or complains to the superiors.
9. Confidant	Akin to a protective role, where a superior gains confidence through sharing personal stories, etc., it creates an atmosphere of trust and takes advantage of the situation.
10. Situational	Such a harasser is under some stress or trauma, such as psychological or marriage problems, and vents frustration through sexual gratification.
11. Pest	One who never gives up harassing the victim.
12. Great gallant	One who gets his way through flattering the victim's gender, appearance, or stares leeringly, and makes obvious sexual signs.
13. Intellectual	In offices and educational institutions, one who pretends to be highly intellectual and uses the excuses of study, research, etc., to create a suitable sexual context.
14. Inept	They are quiet but want the attention of their targets; if the attention does not come forth, they can become bullies.
15. Stalking	Following the victim everywhere; the victim feels extremely threatened.
16. Unintentional	The perception of harassment is actually in the mind of the harasser; the so-called harasser's words, gestures, or actions are misconstrued to be sexually offending.

Grievance procedures, counselling, and therapy have become a part of the workplace. The human resource department has another very human and delicate task to perform.

It is responsible for the employees' psychological, emotional, and spiritual health. The persons who need counselling could either be offenders or victims.

It is not our task to tell the counsellors how they should go about their work. There are some aspects for the moral grounds of the grievance cell or the labour relations cell or the counselling cell, by whatever name it is called, to be sound. The following moral grounds are similar to the moral decision-making process:

(a) Understand the grievance or the offence, as the case may be.
(b) Clearly distinguish the issues involved, into various aspects relating to the workplace.
(c) Discuss the relationships involved and the actual facts as they happened during the incident in question.
(d) Determine what moral and legal problems are involved.
(e) Take steps to address them.
(f) Decide the course of action.
(g) Implement the course of action—reconciliation, disciplinary action, legal action, etc.—in the way it is planned.

If the conflict situations are such that they can be solved through dialogue and reconciliation, the company is going to safeguard its interests by keeping matters within the workplace. However, if a legal action is necessary, then it must be taken.

MANNERS AND MANAGERS

Sometime ago, there was some media hype about the management students of the Indian Institute of Management, Ahmadabad, learning good manners. Actually, what was shown on TV and written in the papers was about table etiquette. However, good manners should go beyond knowing how to hold a knife, fork, and spoon and use a napkin. Another term for good manners is 'civilized behaviour'. This term has several synonyms, which give us a glimpse into the meaning of good manners, that is, cultured, refined, enlightened, educated, polite, elegant, sophisticated, and urbane.

Today, good manners are considered as social rules that make relationships agreeable. The term 'etiquette' is also used when a definite kind of action is involved, such as at social functions, lunch or dinner, etc. From these etiquettes, the governing class developed a protocol. Today, state protocols are very stringent. They represent the correct manner that officials and heads of state, military, and other state organs must follow while in the public eye. Each and every function of the state is as per protocol, whether it is the running of the parliament or an official visit of the local officer.

What has business ethics got to do with good manners? The simplest definition of good manners is that it is ethics in action. Manners refers to the way we behave with others. With some commonsense and a conscious effort about what is going on around us, we can overcome any cultural barrier, although we may be initially ignorant of the local business culture. A manager with an appreciable sense of observation and an attitude of consideration towards others can win not only hearts but also very good business deals. A successful manager is always a person of personal integrity, whether with one's own duties, colleagues, subjects, or superiors. This shows that the person's morals are impeccable.

Workplace Manners

Good impressions are important for good business. Hence, good manners are not only necessary for the employees in sales and marketing, but is also of paramount importance to others in the organization, from the chairman down to the last employee. From airlines to banking, from restaurants to malls to cinema halls, good manners ensure good business. Managers can make their businesses successful by following these basic guidelines.

Respect for culture   Seek to understand the culture of your employees and fit in.

Fair play   See that you are fair both in word and deed.

Orientation of newcomers   Make newcomers feel welcome and familiarize them with their work and colleagues.

Gender interactions   Be knowledgeable about the rules for gender interaction in the workplace.

Conflict management   In a conflict situation, handle the situation maturely, impartially, and with respect to all the parties. Conduct dialogue, not monologue, when the situation has subsided.

Dealing with difficult people   While good manners are like a balm when dealing with good people, firmness of principles and kindness in words can set difficult minds to think differently.

Criticism   Have a good sense of humour to put up with negative feedback and destructive criticism. Have a positive mind to think of criticism as an instrument to refine whatever you are doing.

Conducting business   Prepare your brief, keep to the protocol, document proceedings, and be polite in negotiations.

Foreign culture   Be prepared to receive your foreign guest by knowing some basic customs of the visitor's country. Make sure that you clearly explain the customs and traditions you are following. Learning from each other is the best for good manners and is a lot of fun.

Sixth sense   Employ commonsense. The situation immediately tells you if something is the matter. Show your openness to know and learn. Remember, good manners are not rigid.

As the rules of good manners keep changing, it is important to keep abreast. Reading about different cultures, religions, ways of life, food habits, festivals, bereavements, etc. will do a world of good to your career as a manager. The one principle that can save a manager even in most difficult situations is never to betray trust.

Some Fundamental Shibboleths for Managers

The Constitution of India

Preamble

We, the People of India, have solemnly resolved to constitute India into a **Soverign Socialist Secular Democratic Republic** and to secure to all its citizens:

Justice, social, economic and political;
Liberty of thought, expression, belief, faith and worship;
Equality of status and opportunity;

and to promote among them all.

Fraternity assuring the dignity of the individual and unity and integrity of the Nation;

In Our Constituent Assembly this twenty-sixth day of November 1949, do **Hereby Adopt, Enact and Give to Ourselves this constitution**.

Fundamental Rights
(a) Right to equality—Articles 14, 15, 16, 17, and 18
(b) Right to freedom—Articles 19 to 22
(c) Right against exploitation—Articles 23 and 24
(d) Right to freedom of religion—Articles 25 to 28
(e) Cultural and educational rights—Articles 29 and 30
(f) Right to constitutional remedies—Articles 32 to 35

1. Right to equality
(a) Article 14 provides the Right of **Equality before Law**.
(b) Article 15 provides Rights for **Prohibition of Discrimination on Grounds of Religion, Race, Caste, Sex or Place of Birth**.
(c) Article 16 gives the Right to **Equality of Opportunity in Matters of Public Employment**.
(d) Article 17 deals with Rights associated with the **Abolition of Untouchability**.
(e) Article 18 deals with Rights associated with the **Abolition of Titles**.

2. Right to freedom

(A) Article 19 on **Protection of Certain Rights Regarding Freedom of Speech** that:

(1) All citizens shall have the right
  (a) to freedom of speech and expression
  (b) to assemble peaceably and without arms
  (c) to form association or unions
  (d) to move freely throughout the territory of India
  (e) to reside and settle in any part of the territory of India
  (f) to practice any profession, or to carry on any occupation, trade, or business

At the same-time, vide part (2) of the same Article 19, the Constitution allows the Operation of any existing law, permits the States to make any law to impose restrictions on the above rights that can be considered as reasonable.

(B) Article 20 gives the Rights of **Protection in Respect of Conviction for Offences**, in some unfair or unjust manner.

(C) Article 21 gives the Rights of **Protection of Life and Personal Liberty**.

(D) Article 22 gives the Rights for **Protection Against Arrest and Detention in Certain Cases**, in some unfair and unjust manner.

3. Right against exploitation
(a) Article 23 deals with **Prohibition of Traffic in Human Beings and Forced Labour**.
(b) Article 24 deals with **Prohibition of Employment of Children in Factories**, etc.

Right to Seek Justice from the Supreme Court

Article 32, in fact, is the most important provision of the Constitution, forming part of Part III on fundamental rights. It provides every citizen and every individual the right to move the Supreme Court by appropriate proceedings for the enforcement of the rights.

SUMMARY

- The Indian workplace is as complex as the country itself, and problems of discrimination, sexual harassment, and affirmative action afflict the polity.
- Discrimination at the workplace is based on several factors like age, sex, sexual orientation, disability, caste, diseases such as AIDS, language, regionalism, racism, etc.
- Affirmative action or job reservation is a reverse remedy taken to address the problems of long-standing discrimination problems.
- The legal system, with all its powers, has not been able to solve the dilemma of discrimination and affirmative action. Both are seen as discrimination, one way or the other.

- The fundamental principle at the workplace should be equality. The ethical standard of judgment is justice.
- Disciplinary action at the workplace is necessary.
- One of the effective ways to overcome harassment and make the workplace comfortable to working is good manners, which will help professional behaviour and relationships.
- It is recommended that employees know the laws of the workplace for their own benefit. The knowledge of the law gives the citizen the power to act.

KEY TERMS

Affirmative action   Positive discrimination, an action taken for the underprivileged to come up to the standard of others.

Discrimination   Unjust preference of one over the other.

Equality   A moral principle that all are born equal, irrespective of their birth, race, colour, etc.

Fundamental rights   Our rights enshrined in the constitution.

Good manners   Agreeable form of behaviour.

Harassment   Unwelcome behaviour.

Justice   Giving one the rightful due.

Social justice   The concept of bringing equality to the entire society.

CONCEPT REVIEW QUESTIONS

1. What is the morality of discrimination at the workplace?
2. Is there a universal agreement on the reservation of jobs?
3. Why is sexual harassment morally wrong and a criminal offence?

4. How can workplace sexual harassment be controlled?
5. Should an employee who causes sexual harassment be dismissed from the job?
6. How important are good manners for a manager?

CRITICAL THINKING QUESTIONS

1. How serious is the caste system in contemporary India?
2. Is it not an exaggeration to say that Indian workplaces are ridden with caste discrimination?
3. Can one type of discrimination—caste, backwardness, etc.—be cured by another type of

discrimination, that is, reservation of seats in educational institutions and in jobs?
4. Sexual harassment is not a moral issue; it is a legal issue. Comment.
5. Do good manners promote snobbish values?

FURTHER READING

International Labour Organization, *Equality at Work: Tackling the Challenges*, Report of the Director-General, Geneva (2007); http://www.ilo.org/wcmsp5/groups/public/—dgreports/—dcomm/—webdev/documents/publication/wcms_082607.pdf.

CASE STUDY

Vishaka

Benchmarking Behaviour

While a murderer destroys the physical frame of the victim, a rapist degrades and defiles the soul of a helpless female.

—Justice Pasayat

Part I

Transgression

Child marriages and multiple marriages are rampant in the state of Rajasthan. The Government of Rajasthan has a social programme for the welfare of children. Under the programme, the government has focused its objective to prevent child marriages. Child marriages and multiple marriages are against the law, and the government is determined to enforce this programme. It has appointed social workers to run it. The social worker, who is invariably a woman, is known as *sathin*. Bhanwari Devi was one such sathin.

Ramkaran Gujjar's daughter was not even one year old when they got her married. Bhanwari Devi[a] tried to stop it, but the marriage was carried out despite her best efforts. The Gujjar community was very unhappy with her. They started harassing her and ostracized her. In September 1992, Ramkaran Gujjar, along with four other men, gang raped her in front of her husband.

Insult to Injury

Bhanwari needed medical examination as evidence to prove the crime. She went to the Primary Health Centre, where the only doctor on duty, who happened to be a male, refused to examine her. Then she went to Jaipur, where the doctor did nothing else but merely confirmed her age. There was no mention of any rape in the medical report. At the police station, she was taunted by the police constables. Finally, the case was heard. The trial court acquitted the five accused.

Strength of the Spirit

This was the beginning and not the end of Bhanwari Devi's suffering. Unlike other women who have been snubbed in the dust never to be heard of again, Bhanwari Devi is made up of a different mettle. She waged her battle by taking the help of the law of the land.

Her colleagues, the other sathins, were amazed by the strength of her spirit. She told them that she would fight for justice. She told them that she had done nothing to be ashamed of. It is those men who raped her, who had done wrong and who should be ashamed. This resolution in Bhanwari Devi ignited a spark not only in the women of the state but across the country. Like-minded non-governmental agencies and social workers came together to form Vishaka.

Vishaka

Vishaka launched a systematic campaign and the case reached the high court. In December 1993, the court gave its verdict, 'It was a gang rape committed out of revenge.' Emboldened by the judgment, Vishaka broadened its scope. It approached the Supreme Court of India to give directions regarding sexual harassment that women face at the workplace.

The Supreme Court accepted that sexual harassment in the workplace violated women's

---

[a] See http://www.elaw.org/resources/text.asp?id=1831.

equality rights and that employers were obligated to provide a mechanism for the prevention of sexual harassment. The court set out guidelines on the law of the land, under the Constitution of India, Article 141, until further action were taken by the legislature.

On 13 August 1997, the Supreme Court of India gave well-defined directions.

Part II

Benchmark

The following is a brief summary of the directives given by the Supreme Court of India.

Title Vishaka and others versus State of Rajasthan and others (1997) 6 SCC 241, AIR 1997 SC 3011, (1998) BHRC 261, (1997) 3 LRC 361, (1997) 2 CHRLD 202.[b]

Bench J.S. Verma, the Chief Justice of India, Justices Mrs Sujata V. Manohar and B.N. Kirpal.

Jurisdiction Supreme Court of India.

Date of decision 13 August 1997.

Litigation The litigation resulted from a brutal gang rape of a publicly employed social worker, in a village in Rajasthan, during the course of her employment. The petitioners bringing the action were various social activists and non-governmental organizations. The primary basis of bringing such an action to the Supreme Court of India was to find suitable methods for the realization of the true concept of 'gender equality' in the workplace for women. In turn, the prevention of sexual harassment of women would be addressed by applying the judicial process. Under Article 32 of the Indian Constitution, an action was filed in order to establish the enforcement of the fundamental rights relating to the women in the workplace. It sought in particular, to establish the enforcement of Articles 14, 15, 19(1)(g), and 21 of the Constitution of India and Articles 11 and 24 of the Convention on the Elimination of All Forms of Discrimination against Women.

Law

Constitution of India

- Article 14 (the right to equality)
- Article 15 (the right to non-discrimination)
- Article 19(1)(g) (the right to practise one's profession)
- Article 21 (the right to life)

Convention on the Elimination of All Forms of Discrimination against Women (CEDAW)

- Article 11 ([State] takes all appropriate measures to eliminate discrimination against women in the field of employment)
- Article 24 ([State shall] undertake to adopt all necessary measures at the national level aimed at achieving the full realization)

Decision

In disposing of the writ petition with directions, it was held that 'the fundamental right to carry on any occupation, trade, or profession depends on the availability of a "safe" working environment. The right to life means life with dignity. The primary responsibility for ensuring such safety and dignity through suitable legislation, and the creation of a mechanism for its enforcement, belongs to the legislature and the executive. When, however, instances of sexual harassment resulting in violations of Articles 14, 19 and 21 are brought under Article 32, effective redress requires that some guidelines for the protection of these rights should be laid down to fill the legislative vacuum.'

In light of these deliberations, the court outlined guidelines that were to be observed in order to enforce the rights of gender equality and to prevent discrimination of women at the workplace. These guidelines included the responsibility upon the employer to prevent or deter the commission of acts of sexual harassment and to apply the appropriate settlement and resolutions and a definition of sexual harassment, which includes unwelcome sexually determined behaviour (whether directly or by implication) such as

---

[b] See http://ncw.nic.in/pdfreports/Sexual%20Harassment%20at%20Workplace%20 (English).pdf.

(a) Physical contact and advances

(b) A demand or request for sexual favours

(c) Sexually coloured remarks

(d) Showing pornography

(e) Any other unwelcome physical, verbal, or non-verbal conduct of a sexual nature

Furthermore, the guidelines set out that persons in charge of a workplace, in the public or private sector, would be responsible for taking the appropriate steps to prevent sexual harassment that included

(a) The prohibition of sexual harassment should be published in the appropriate ways and provided with the appropriate penalties against the offender.

(b) For private employees, the guidelines should be included in the relevant employment guidelines.

(c) To provide appropriate working conditions and environments for women, which are not hostile, in order to avoid grounds for discrimination.

(d) The employer should ensure the protection of potential petitioners against victimisation or discrimination during potential proceedings.

(e) An appropriate complaints mechanism should be established in the workplace with the appropriate redress mechanism.

(f) Where sexual harassment occurs as a result of an act or omission by any third party or outsider, the employer and person-in-charge will take all steps that are necessary and reasonable to assist the affected person in terms of support and preventive action.

Finally, the court stated that the guidelines are to be treated as a declaration of law in accordance with Article 141 of the Constitution until the enactment of appropriate legislation and that the guidelines do not prejudice any rights available under the Protection of Human Rights Act 1993.

Part III

Words of Wisdom

The Supreme Court of India puts on record that harassment at the workplace is not a mere violation of any law. It is the violation of a fundamental right and states that 'where public functionaries are involved and the matter relates to the violation of fundamental rights or the enforcement of public duties, the remedy would be avoidable under public law. It was more so when it was not a mere violation of any ordinary right, but the violation of fundamental rights was involved—as the petitioner was a victim of rape, which is a violation of fundamental right of every person guaranteed under Article 21 of the Constitution.'

Justice Saghir Ahmad expressed his view, considering the plight of the women and the dilemma of the law: 'Unfortunately a woman in our country belongs to a class or group of society who are in a disadvantaged position on account of several social barriers and impediments and have, therefore, been victims of tyranny at the hands of men with whom they, unfortunately, under the Constitution enjoy equal status.'

Kiran Bedi, the former Commissioner of Police and presently an activist for social causes, feels that the law cannot be understood and applied piecemeal. It must be understood and applied in a comprehensive manner. 'The law of rape is not just a few sentences. It is a whole book, which has clearly demarcated chapters and cannot be read selectively. We cannot read the preamble and suddenly reach the last chapter and claim to have understood and applied it.'[c]

Conclusion

Now that equality and liberty are claimed by both men and women, there appears to be a war between the two. It is amazing that in a world where half the population comprises of women, they are subjected to unspeakable atrocities. It is a shame on the twenty-first century civilization that with all the progress made, there still persists such discrimi-

---

[c] See http://www.combatlaw.org/information.php?article_id=277&issue_id=11.

nation. Women lived in an overprotected world for a long time; rather they were made to live there. A workplace is where men and women meet, perform their duties, create wealth, run businesses, and make life possible. The workplace is the grand meeting place.

Discussion Questions

1. What is the relationship between ethics and law?

2. In what way does the Constitution of India bear moral responsibility?

3. Is not sexual harassment, in someway, natural?

4. Is our society overtly concerned about sexual issues?

5. How serious is the sexual abuse in the workplaces of India? Give instances and cases.

6. It takes a very long time to get justice. In what way can ethical training help to overcome the menace of sexual harassment at the workplace?

7. How serious is sexual violation in terms of body language, groping and touching, verbal insinuations, third-party participation (not directly involved but as a mere observer), bullying, sadistic behaviour, showing pornog-raphy, sending obscene SMSs, emails, and letters?

8. How serious is the offence of rape in moral terms?

9. Does the moral seriousness of the offense of rape change from culture to culture and religion to religion?

10. Should a rapist be awarded the death penalty?

11. Is there a reverse sexual harassment—females against males?

12. Is the law biased against males?

13. Can ethics be biased against males?

14. What sexual conduct would you adopt for your workplace?

Going Further . . .

Panel discussion

Compere: One or two assistants.

Panel: An NGO with four students, two judges, two lawyers (pro and contra).

Rules: Formulate the rules of discussion.

Time: Strict time management (Recommended: 90 minutes).

ETHICAL DEVELOPMENT PROGRAMME

Management Training

Attendance at Court Proceedings

1. **Object** As a manager you would be required, if necessary, to manage court matters, which include the selection of lawyers, preparation of cases, and actual attendance at the court. Familiarity with court proceedings will go a long way to help you represent your company.

2. **Select cases** Attend the proceedings of those cases that pertain to your workplace. If your area of management is finance, then attend those trials pertaining to audit, money laundering, taxation, etc. If you are managing the human resources of your company, attend those cases that are related to other departments.

3. **Diary** Maintain a separate diary for the purpose.

4. **Research** Collect judgments, orders, gazettes, notifications, and journalistic reports of the case.

5. **Use** Analyse the learning points and make guidelines for your workplace.

This exercise needs unlimited time. Court proceedings are stretched. If you are a student, you may continue the research. However, your instructor may grade you for the work that you have done up to the date you attended the proceedings in the court. If you are a professional, your research may not only help you, but will also be useful to educate your area of functioning on matters concerning the workplace laws.

Management Mantra

This write-up is based on a joke.

Company policy This is our company. You work for our company. We appreciate your loyalty.

Motto Follow the rules.

Rules

(a) Leave: There is no company policy on leave.

(b) Sick leave: A doctor's certificate is not required. If you can get to the doctor, you can get to work as well.

(c) Vacation: For one calendar year, 104 days. The days are known as Saturday and Sunday. You are welcome to work for at least half a day on Saturdays, since good employees will feel guilty not working for two full days in a week.

(d) Surgery: It is banned. Remember, the company employed you wholly and integrally. It is against the employment contract to have any addition to or deletion of body organs.

(e) Public holidays: The holiday is for the public, not for you.

(f) Bereavement leave: There is nothing you can do for the dead. Loyal employees have no excuse for staying away.

(g) Internet: Never forget that this is our company.

We are glad that you like our company. If you have any problems, frustrations, complaints, grievances, etc., send them somewhere else, away from our company.

MANTRA	*The sense of humour is the best sense at the workplace.*

Part Four

Managers and Corporations

Corporate Citizens: Organizations in the World

Corporate Citizens: Organizations in the World

The Way of the New Person in Society

In nature there is fundamental unity running through all the diversity we see about us.

—Mahatma Gandhi

The leaders who work most effectively, it seems to me, never say 'I'. And that's not because they have trained themselves not to say 'I'. They don't think 'I'. They think 'we'; they think 'team'. They understand their job to be to make the team function. They accept responsibility and don't sidestep it, but 'we' gets the credit.... This is what creates trust, what enables you to get the task done.

—Peter F. Drucker

REPUBLIC RULES

Our idea of business as a republic is steadily widening. Earlier on, we had applied the metaphor of the republic to the market, wherein we had stated that just as the citizen is the ultimate stakeholder of democratic governance in a country, the customer is the ultimate stakeholder in a free market. The metaphor will get internalized when employees become citizens of their organizations. In this part we shall see how corporate governance can be systematized or formalized. It is similar to the governance of a country, where the citizens of the country give themselves a constitution and elect the members of parliament, which provides for the legislative, executive, and judicial branches of the people's republic.

REPUBLIC AS AN IMAGE OF NATURE

An organic model of governance seems best suited to conduct human affairs, whether political, cultural, or economic, because it is just natural to do so. When it comes to governance, the best way to understand the logic of authority and its implementation is our own body. The various systems of our body—nervous, respiratory, skeletal, muscular, digestive, cardio-vascular or circulatory,

endocrinal, reproductive, urinary, integumentary or the skin organ—function harmoniously. All these systems and their functions are controlled by our nervous system. The nervous system has the brain as its centre of intelligence, from which information is sent to and received from every cell of the body. The natural law of the living, that is, breathing, feeling, muscular movements, skeletal formations, digestive processes, reproduction, and cleansing and disposal, make the body function naturally.

Corporate governance hopes to achieve harmony among all the areas of a corporation's functioning, such as production, marketing, advertising, distribution, sales, and above all, human resource management. The board of directors, the brain of the business, combines and harmonizes these independent systems to function as one body with a definite goal (see Fig. P4.1). The fundamental explanation for its smooth functioning is the inbuilt system, the moral law.

HUMAN BODY AS THE IMAGE OF CORPORATION

It is not by accident that a corporation is called so. It exactly implies what it says in Latin, *corpus*

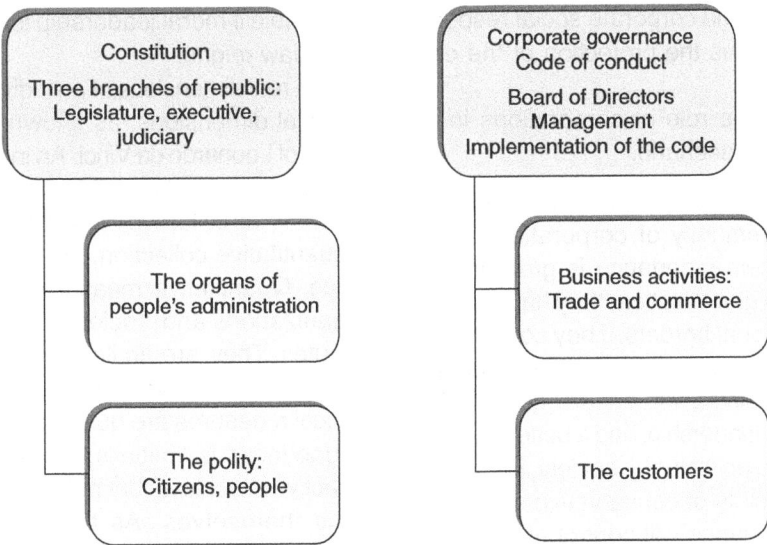

Fig. P4.1 People are the masters of their own fate. Customers decide what they want

meaning body. A given number of people come to form a body, with a definite purpose of achieving an end. In our case a number of people, entrepreneurs, and shareholders come together to form a business body with the legal sanction of the government of the land.

In this section, the model for governance is our own body. The board of directors is the head of the organization that decides the policies and processes. Its responsibility is that all the systems and subsystems in the body co-ordinate and function as perfectly as possible.

Sickness of the Body or Moral Failure of the Corporation

The application of the organic metaphor becomes even more acute when the natural law obstructs the body and it falls ill. So too is the failure of the moral law in a corporation, which leads to its sickness, disrepute, and bankruptcy. Table P4.1 illustrates the body and corporate governance metaphor. That the world's largest credit institutions and multinational businesses bit the dust in the great financial meltdown of 2008, and appear to continue in the year or years to come, is a clear example of the ethical epidemic that hit corporations. The result of such an epidemic is the death

of corporations, as well as the livelihoods of the people on a mass scale.

Mens sana in corpore sano, meaning 'a healthy mind in a healthy body', is a famous Latin proverb. A good diet and regular exercise keeps the body fit, which helps the mind to think well. Adoption of good principles and their regular exercise make corporations healthy and wealthy.

OBJECTIVES OF PART IV

The fundamental objective of Part IV is to discuss how and why a corporation should be based on moral law. The need for corporate governance was felt because too many corporations were declared sick. Here we will pursue the following objectives:

(a) To realize that corporations are moral entities and are responsible to the entire humanity and that they are the stewards who will preserve and increase the wealth of nations and the well-being of the citizens.

(b) To understand the role of corporations in implementing the code of conduct and developing best practices to advance the enterprise for all the stakeholders.

(c) To understand corporate social responsibility, such as the protection of the environment.

(d) To study the role of corporations in the geopolitical scenario.

What corporations should not forget is that they belong to a community of corporations. Their numbers and their importance is growing phenomenally. With globalization, they have already crossed the national borders. They could help in achieving a world without national boundaries. The above objectives will ensure good governance, collective leadership, and a better future for all and will create an inclusive society, rather than an exclusive society of conservative capitalism. Corporate governance will control an unbridled market and unfair distribution of wealth. This dream is possible if moral leadership is realized and the moral law reigns.

The real dimensions of an individual are not the physical dimensions, as shown in the *Vitruvian* model of Leonardo da Vinci. An individual is judged by his/her virtue. The measure of human organizations is the collective virtue, that is, ethics. It is not a quantitative collection, but a qualitative excellence. Quantitative measurements that govern organizations and societies are the laws and statutes. They are limited and restricted. Their objective is to restrain people from doing bad. Ethical measures are qualitative and their scope to goodness is limitless. They do not have an objective to achieve, but rather they are the objectives themselves. As the great philosopher Socrates observed, 'Virtue is its own reward.'

Table P4.1   Body and corporate governance metaphor

System	Body	Corporation
Nervous	The central control of all functions; it receives information from the senses, processes it, analyses it, decides and informs how to act. Brain thinks, decides, is conscious of, or knows everything subconsciously. Peripheral too aids the central system function as sense receptors, impulses, etc. Autonomic is a special part of the peripheral system and regulates the automatic functions of the body such as heart beats.	The board of directors, the decision makers,—adopt processes, customs, draw policies, appoint managers, communicate, monitor, and control all the cells or departments of the company.
Respiratory	Supplies oxygen to each and every cell of the body and gets rid of the carbon dioxide present in the body.	Supplies finance that breaths life into the company; safeguards the interests of the shareholders and investors; draws finances from the capital market.
Skeletal	Body architect that holds together all parts and muscles of the body, facilitates movement, shields bone marrow that produces blood cells, and keeps the blood healthy.	The infrastructure of the company to which all the processes of running the company are attached.
Muscular	Causes movement (17 muscles needed to smile, 43 to frown, 202 to take a step)	The employees of the company; the best utilization of the human resource.

Contd

Table P4.1 Contd

System	Body	Corporation
Digestive	Teeth break the food down and grind them to small pieces, salivary glands pour saliva to aid the grinding through moisture to the stomach; after the most complex processes in the stomach, the food passes through the small intestine, where even more complex processes of absorption occur; the liver is the greatest manager in this chain of events; the large intestine takes care of absorbing most of the water and minerals, and supplies them to the blood stream; the waste is sent down to the rectum as faeces.	The operations of the company, whether in production or service sector; production processes, assemblies, supplies, absorptions, and even effluents and disposal management.
Circulatory	Supply blood, that is, food and oxygen to the whole body and carries back carbon dioxide and other wastes; heart is a hollow muscle, has two pumps side by side; left side is more powerful and receives oxygen-rich blood from the lungs and sends it to the cells throughout the body; the used blood with waste returns to the right side of the heart, and with its weaker power, pumps the blood to the lungs to get oxygenated, and so the process goes on till the death of the person.	The workplace, the work ethic ensure punctuality and order; the work force functions as a team, to network all the functions of the company; the moral behaviour of every cell, department, and every employee ensures the success of the company.
Endocrine	Glands produce hormones, which have several critical functions in the body.	Training and upgradation, diversification, emoluments and wages, motivation and spirituality of the workplace.
Reproductive	Creation of new life through the fertilization of the female egg by the male sperm, development of the child in the womb.	Corporate social responsibility, adoption of sustainable development policies, care of environment, and and diversification of the company.
Urinary	Blood filtering and waste management.	Constant monitoring and control of quality, cleaner technologies, better working conditions, etc.
Integumentary (the skin, largest organ of the body)	Body pack, protection from vagaries of environment, of body temperature and sweat management, constant replacement of epithelial cells to provide new pack of skin every 7–14 days.	Brand, good governance, enhancement of the reputation of the company.

The Perfect Man

The Vitruvian man

The *Vitruvian Man* is the famous painting by the renaissance artist and genius Leonardo da Vinci. It depicts a male figure in two superimposed positions, with arms and legs apart, and is at the same time within a circle and a square. The artist wanted to achieve the ideal human proportions, to produce a specimen of the perfect man, or a prototype, which would be known as the Canon of Proportions. He has used all the possible measurements known during his time, which are altogether fourteen in number. In short, it was to be the ultimate measure or standard for man.

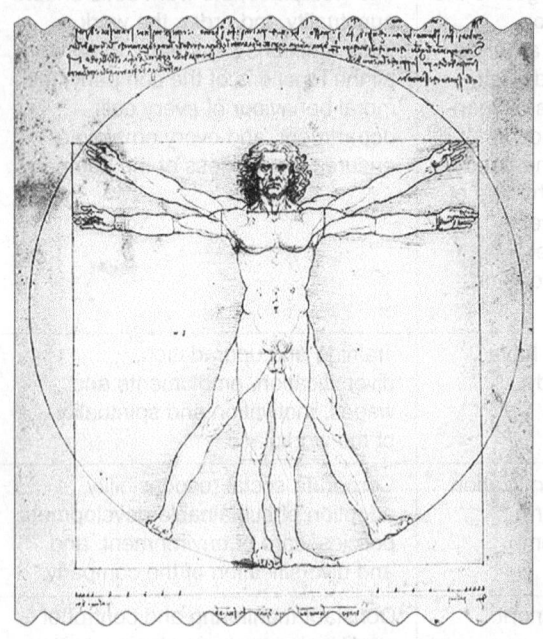

Da Vinci, who was also a highly recognized mathematician, scientist, and an astronomer, considered the human body as the perfect microcosm of the functioning of the universe. Today, the picture is used wherever one wants to depict perfection and proportion. Technologies have adopted it as a paradigm expression of the technical precision. In India, it has also been adopted as the symbol of good health. The picture is also the motive of the Italian euro coins. Da Vinci's inspiration to draw the perfect man came from the famous Roman architect, Vitruvius—hence, the drawing bears his name and is preserved in the Gallerie dell'Accademia in Venice.

The trillion-dollar question: When is the business world going to adopt the symbol of the Vitruvian Man?

Leonardo Da Vinci's *The Vitruvian Man* and the text

From the roots of his hair to the bottom of his chin is 1/10 of a man's height; from the bottom of the chin to the top of the head is 1/8 of his height; from the top of the breast to the roots of the hair will be the seventh part of the whole man. From the nipples to the top of the head will be the fourth part of man. The greatest width of the shoulders contains in itself the fourth part of man. From the elbow to the tip of the hand will be the fifth part of man; and from the elbow to the angle of the armpit will be the eighth part of man. The whole hand will be the tenth part of man. The distance from the bottom of the chin to the nose and from the roots of the hair to the eyebrows is, in each case the same, and like the ear, a third of the face.

13

Corporate Governance

The most effective way to restrict democracy is to transfer decision making from the public arena to unaccountable institutions: kings and princes, priestly castes, military juntas, party dictatorships, or modern corporations.

—Noam Chomsky

The most important mission for a Japanese manager is to develop a healthy relationship with his employees, to create a family—like feeling within the corporation, a feeling that employees and managers share the same fate.

—Akio Morita

LEARNING OBJECTIVES

After studying this chapter, you will be able to

> Understand that a corporation is a moral person
> Describe corporate governance
> State the corporate governance theories
> Determine the salient features of good corporate governance

INTRODUCTION

A corporation comes into existence as a collective of entrepreneurs, stockholders, and investors. Hence, the principle of stewardship or trusteeship is at the core of its functioning. Natural justice demands that a corporation is responsible to those who have contributed their monies for the enterprise. At the same time, just as an individual is responsible for his/her acts that affect others, so too are corporations responsible to the human society. The moot ethical question behind every issue and every case is: are corporations benefiting at the expense of others?

In ancient Rome, there was a custom to carry fasces as a standard before the emperor or his officials. This standard called fasces was made up of an axe blade tied to a few wooden rods with a red ribbon. To whomsoever this honour was granted, he was a fascist, that is, a person with official powers. Benito Mussolini who ruled Italy from 1922 to 1943 and Adolf Hitler who ruled Germany from 1933 to 1945 were called fascists. These rulers changed the meaning of the word fascist from a mere person of political influence to a person with a diabolical design bent upon destroying humanity. All that they did was wage wars and cause destruction. The fascist economic policy, unlike that of the communists, not only permitted but also encouraged large-scale private enterprises. It supported large corporations and ensured productivity at all costs. Consequently unions, strikes, and all other activities that hindered productivity were outlawed. The government created corporations that consisted of both the workers as well as the management. The entire exercise was focused and efficiently executed to promote the government and its programme—Pogrom (repression of Jews and minorities) and war. Many famed German corporations of today, despite vehement denials, were nursed by these fascist dictators. As a matter of fact, the fascist state was called a corporative state.

One may be tempted to say that times have changed and that we have come a long way in making corporations responsible, making them companies with good governance. However, facts prove otherwise. Corporations still look for large favours from the government, such as land for factories, which leads to eviction and large-scale migration of poor farmers, tax reliefs, lax labour laws, trade protectionist laws, tolerance towards cartels, relaxation of environmental strictures, and, in the event of bankruptcy, a bail out!

In this chapter, we will examine the character of corporations and their impact on society. We will investigate some aspects of corporate governance.

It must be remembered that corporations are not faceless. They have an identity; that is, they are persons who take decisions and are responsible for those decisions just as individuals are. The only difference with corporations is that they are a collective of persons. In short, they too are the subjects of moral behaviour.

CORPORATION AS A MORAL PERSON

Understanding Corporation

Indian corporations come under the Companies Act 1956. Business corporations, generally known as companies, are legal entities. People come together with an objective to establish an enterprise. The law of the land makes provision for such groups or associations of people. These are corporations or bodies (*corpus* in Latin means body) that are formed by a given number of individual persons. To distinguish them from real persons, they are also called as artificial persons. In the eyes of the law, however, artificial persons will be held responsible for their actions, just as the natural persons will be. (A natural person is a human being, as opposed to an artificial or legal person.)

Corporation

A corporation is like a moral person who is responsible for his/her actions, and exercises power to perform actions that have definite functions. These actions are based on the regulation of society. This is termed as governance. However, the corporation does not live in isolation from society. Its position is well observed and its role is rated by not only the clients of the corporation, but also by the people at large. The corporation not only has a legal obligation to the law of the land, but also has a responsibility to act as a good global citizen. Just as an individual faces moral choices, so also a corporation encounters difficult situations and faces a collective responsibility for the decisions to be taken and implemented. All the seven standards of judgment (see Chapter 4) come into play in the life of the corporation. However, the principles of stewardship and justice are paramount.

Definition of Corporation

Once we have determined the essential character of the corporation as an artificial person with moral responsibility, there follows a logical definition. *Business Encyclopaedia* defines it as: A business corporation is a legal entity permitted by law in every state to exist for the purpose of engaging in lawful activities of a business nature. It is an artificial person created by law, with many of the same rights and responsibilities possessed by humans. Corporations are widely prevalent in the US; today, virtually every large enterprise is a corporation.[1]

We could further describe it as one that exists only in the eyes of the law, and could find its end when the law terminates it. It may own property, incur debts, sue and be sued, just like a natural person. Although it does not have a soul like the natural person, it has a seal as its identity and a perpetual succession.

Some Salient Features Determining Nature of Corporation

Incorporated association   A corporation is a registered body under the appropriate act of the land. According to the Companies Act 1956, a minimum of seven persons may form a public company and a minimum of two persons may form a private company.

Distinct from its members   An incorporated company is distinct from its members who constitute it. All the assets and liabilities of the company are owned by the company, and not by the individuals who form it. Thus, the company has to be distinguished even from its shareholders. It is not the individual directors or shareholders but the company as a whole that would be responsible for all the decisions taken in its name. The company has fundamental rights also; for instance, the right to own property.

Limited liability   A company is distinct from its members. Hence, the latter are not liable for the former's debts. The liability of the members is limited to the value of the shares held by them.

Unlimited liability   A member of a limited company may have unlimited liability in a case of insolvency if the law decides that it is the responsibility of those members who may have brought about this situation to defraud the creditors.

---

[1] See *Business Encyclopaedia* at http://www.answers.com/library, accessed on 21 October 2008.

Separate property A company is a distinct person and the property it holds is distinct from the shareholders. Even in the instance where a shareholder may hold a majority of the shares or all of them, he/she will not have an insurable interest in the property of the company.

Transferability of shares Since the company is distinct from its members, the members may transfer their shares. They have ownership of their shares only, not of the company.

Perpetual existence Unlike a person who can be incapacitated by illness or finds death as an end, a company continues to exist beyond the departures or deaths of its members, as long as its existence is in conformity with the law.

Common seal A person has an identity and it is expressed through the acts of the citizen, such as certificates and a signature. A company shows its presence through the functioning of its members, particularly those who govern its activities, such as a board of directors. To certify their acts, the company must have a seal of approval. Conventionally, a seal is designed with a logo and the name of the company, which becomes the signature of the company. No document will be valid and the signature of the company executive will have no appeal if the document does not bear the imprint of the seal.

Citizen Corporation

A corporation is like a moral person and is responsible for all its actions. Since it has a domicile, that is, a name and an address, rightfully owns property, can exercise freedom of speech, and do several other things that a natural person does, it can be called a citizen. The constitution of India makes it quite clear that the citizenship in its strict sense is conferred only on a natural person. Moreover, once the company is formed, its business is to achieve the objective that it is formed for, and not for the business of exercising citizenship. Citizens, the natural persons, exercise their franchise to choose their government; but companies do not enjoy such a privilege.

Lifting the Corporate Veil

We have established that a corporation is distinct from the members who form it and has a consummate and complete identity of its own. This distinct and independent identity of the corporation is the cornerstone of its being. The law does not try to find out who are behind it and what kind of benefit they derive from it. There is a distinct separation, a veil as it were, between the corporation and its members.

However, in very rare circumstances when affairs are pushed to unnatural limits, the law steps in and if necessary, exposes the members behind the corporation's veil. This may be done either under statutory provisions or judicial pronouncements. Such circumstances arise when the stated membership expires and is not renewed within six months, or there is misrepresentation in the prospectus of the company, a failure to return the application money, misuse of financial instruments by the officers of the company, investigation of ownership of companies and fraudulent trading, contempt of court, bounced cheques, or where the company is a mere sham or cloak.

Moral of the Corporation

We see that the lawgiver has given the people an opportunity to conduct businesses and institutionalize them. These bodies or corporations or companies pursue their object to conduct business like natural persons, but on a larger scale. The lawgiver takes into account the needs of society and allows for such distinct legal entities.

Having become a corporation, that is, a person in society, it is now subject to the law of society. Its identity is recognized and people expect it to behave ethically. They appreciate its good work and if it does not conform to the norms of society, they adjudicate it with approbation. Therefore, it is important that a corporation is not merely a person, but a moral person. In general terms, it has to be a good citizen.

The unique feature of a corporation is that although it is created by mortal human beings, it outlives those who created it. It is like a man sowing a seed, and the seed growing into a very large tree with numerous branches bearing fruit. The fruits are enjoyed by not just the sower, but also by several others who have helped the tree grow and by those who take shelter under its shade. This is the ingenuity of the human collective: a living entity that is created by the living people, which continues due to the people living in it and through it. It is an institution with all the human characteristics of good and evil and comes to the service of human purposes and endeavours.

CORPORATE GOVERNANCE

We elucidated above the concept of corporation. We will now develop the concept of governance. The concept is at once quite simple as we generally speak about it everyday in the affairs of managing a household or a business or a government, but becomes difficult when we have to draw household rules or business strategies or government policies. Thus, governance is quite a complex concept of management.

Understanding Governance

We may understand governance in two preliminary ways:

1. Governance is to exercise legitimate power or authority over the affairs of others. Thus, governance implies a legitimate course of action directed towards the benefit of an individual or the entire society. Our elected governments do this by exercising the powers enshrined in our constitution.
2. Governance is to rule. For instance, the arbitrary power exercised by dictators and despots may lack the processes of enacting laws, formulating policies, and implementing them.

Hiding behind the Veil

Salomon versus Salomon & Co.

Salomon versus Salomon & Co. is a case over a century old (1897), and company secretaries, chartered accountants, business managers, journalists, and lawyers have the facts on their fingertips. The case comes under the purview of the British Companies Act 1862, to which India too was a subject, and is still cited as a precedent par excellence.

Aaron Salomon was a merchant, who formed a limited company called Salomon & Co. Ltd, in 1892, along with his sons. Out of a total of 20,007 shares, Salomon owned 20,001 shares. His wife and five children were each given a share from the remaining six shares. So, Salomon was not only the company's chief shareholder, but creditor as well. The company went bankrupt. The liquidator put forth the argument that since the intention of the principal shareholder was based on fraud, the debentures used by Salomon as a security for the debt should be declared as invalid. The judge concurred, adding that Salomon had created the company to transfer his business to it. He had misused the company as his agency, and as the principal shareholder was liable for the debts to the unsecured creditors. There was appeal. The court of appeal also upheld the earlier judgement and added that Salomon had clearly abused the privileges of a corporation of limited liability to commit a fraud.

But the House of Lords, the final appellate authority, overturned the verdict. They rejected the arguments of agency and fraud. They asserted that under the Companies Act 1862, one could create a limited liability company as legal persons, separate and distinct from its members. The House of Lords resolution read, 'Either the limited company was a legal entity or it was not. If it were, the business belonged to it and not to Mr Salomon. If it was not, there was no person and no thing to be an agent [of] at all; and it is impossible to say at the same time that there is a company and there is not.'

Even to this day, courts all over the world cite this case for distinct existence of the company. However, the moral debate goes on.

Questions

(a) Does not simple commonsense tell us that Salomon intended to misuse the company as an agency to perpetuate a fraud?

(b) When society sees that a fraud has been deliberately committed, should not the lawmakers make provisions to amend the law?

(c) What is the purpose of an unamended law if it is going to uphold something that is wrong?

(d) What should prevail, moral existence or legal argument?

(e) When can the law expose the members behind the façade of a company?

The above explanation leads us to understand governance as an orderly process of maintaining good order in all the things that we do. Such an order or governance is a necessity in all the human institutions such as marriage and family, schools and colleges, cultural organizations, and governments; business management is no exception. The one who is entrusted with the task of maintaining such good order is known as the head of the family, principal, king, governor, manager, or chief executive officer, as may be the case, and exercises appropriate authority.

Governance is not a new concept. It is as old as when man said, 'I will do this,' or 'I will not do that,' 'It should be like this,' or 'It should not be like that,' and 'You ought to do this,' or 'You ought not to do that.' These three simple sets of expressions show us the core of governance.

(a) There is a state of affairs that man has created for himself—facts.
(b) He sets rules to manage the state of affairs—operations.
(c) He determines the nature of the rules—conduct of operations.

All the three aspects form governance in the simple form. Moral problems arise because of the authority it exercises in relation to the people over whom it is imposed or implemented. Problems arise regarding the fairness of the rules, the methods of governance, and the way the subjects respond.

Understanding Good Corporate Governance

There is no definite definition for corporate governance because the definition could vary depending on the kind of theory we accept. There are several theories on corporate governance, depending upon the kind of principles corporations are based on. However, let us have a working definition of corporate governance as follows.

Just as a natural person adheres to the ethical principles of society to be a good citizen, so also a corporation, an artificial person with legal existence, imbibes the same ethical principles to be a good citizen in society. In this context, corporate governance consists of making moral decisions and implementing them with responsibility.

The following are a few aspects of understanding the concept of corporate governance:

(a) Corporate governance is to work for the goals of the shareholders, which is to create wealth within the bounds of law.
(b) Corporate governance is to maintain good relationships with all the participants of the corporate body and thus give right direction for its activities.
(c) Corporate governance consists of an ethical or a moral framework to guide the decision-making process for the benefit of all the stakeholders—primary shareholders, board of directors, and the management and secondary stakeholders, such as employees, creditors, suppliers, customers, and the community.

Definition of Good Corporate Governance

The following attributes of good corporate governance shed light on the essence of governance. The essence of governance consists of the following four principles.

Transparency   The governing board or the board of directors has to lay down unambiguous policies for the management.

Accountability   The system must work for all equally, with periodic reporting and communication to keep all the stakeholders well informed and to help them make independent judgments about the company and comply with the regulatory authorities.

Justice   Just and fair dealings with all the stakeholders.

Social responsibility   It has citizenship in the community and so it must be sensitive to the special issues of poverty, ecology, and other social concerns.

All the above four characteristics express the ethical standards that we have discussed. Keeping in mind the above characteristics for good corporate governance, let us define it in the following terms.

The Committee on Corporate Governance constituted by the Securities and Exchange Board of India (SEBI), under the chairmanship of the well-known entrepreneur N.R. Narayana Murthy, declared: Corporate governance is the acceptance by the management of the inalienable rights of shareholders as the true owners of the corporation and of their own role as trustees on behalf of the shareholders. It is about commitment to values, about ethical business conduct and about making a distinction between personal and corporate funds in the management of a company.

The Institute of Company Secretaries of India emphasizes on the ethical values by stating that corporate governance is the application of best management practices, compliance of law in true letter and spirit and adherence to ethical standards for effective management and distribution of wealth and discharge of social responsibility for sustainable development of all stakeholders.

The definition by the Confederation of Indian Industry emphasizes the terms 'informed decision making' and 'good' in corporate governance.

Corporate governance deals with laws, procedures, practices, and implicit rules that determine a company's ability to take informed managerial decisions with regard its claimants—its shareholders, creditors, customers, the state, and its employees. There is a global consensus about the objective of 'good' corporate governance—maximizing long-term shareholder value.[2]

The Organization for Economic Co-operation and Development, Standard & Poor's, and Cadbury have codes of conduct that stress the need for good corporate governance through values and controls. It goes to prove that the very core of governing the companies is founded on the values of ethics. It is only through ethical means that long-term shareholder values and all societal expectations are attained.

CORPORATE GOVERNANCE THEORIES

Just as natural persons have different philosophies of life, corporations also adopt different doctrines. We may classify these under the following four theories.

Agency Theory

The very term 'agency' suggests a relationship between two elements or entities. In this case, it is between the principals or promoters of a company and their agents or managers who implement the former's brief. In actual practice, however, managers do not exactly function in the way principals plan. This results in costs that would not have been incurred if the principals themselves were at the helm of affairs. Such costs

---

[2] Desirable Corporate Governance—A Code by CII, in *Business Week*, issue no. 84, 25 November 1996.

Investors' Favourite

Indian corporations

In February 2009, equitymaster.com, an investor-oriented portal took a survey of 1000 investors.[a] The portals pie chart in Fig. 13.1 clearly shows the most-investor friendly companies.

The parameters were

- Integrity
- Transparency and good corporate governance

- Ethical and professional management
- Rewarding all stakeholders
- World-class business practices

The picture clearly shows that just two companies—the TATAs and Infosys—make it to double-digit percentage.

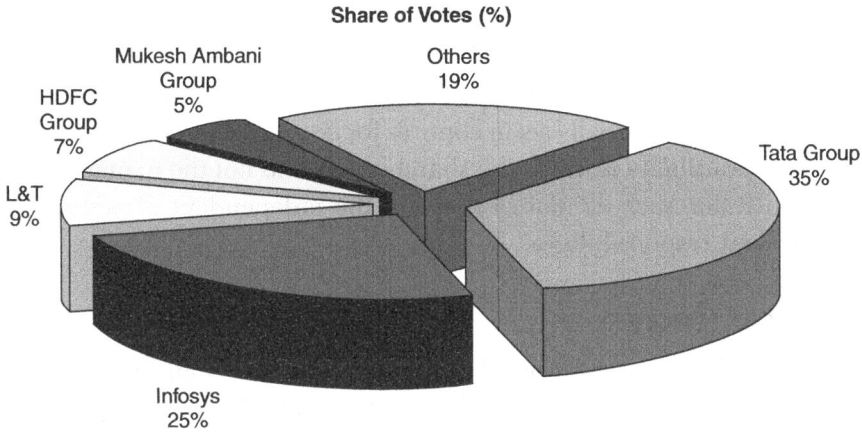

Share of Votes (%)

Mukesh Ambani Group 5%
HDFC Group 7%
L&T 9%
Infosys 25%
Others 19%
Tata Group 35%

Fig. 13.1   Investors' favourite companies

Courtesy: http://www.equitymaster.com.

Questions

(a) Is too much made about corporate governance by the Indian companies in their visions and mission statements, while the investors do not think they measure up?

(b) Is the idea of corporate governance a waste? Is it a waste to maintain the market regulator SEBI?

(c) How can corporate governance enhance the moral behaviour of the companies?

[a] For details and graphics, see http://www.equitymaster.com/detail.asp?date=2/18/2009&story=3.

---

are known as agency costs. The agency theory consists of working out a way to control the agency costs. This then becomes the crux of governance.

Paul Milgrom and John Roberts (1992) put forward the following four principles of agency theory. Howsoever one may try, one will not have optimum information about the principals and the managers. In such a case, the principals gauge the performance by the effort levels and duly compensate the same. This leads to the second principle, that is, incentive intensity principle. This in itself, apart from being unprofitable for the principals, may not yield any result if the first principle is not well adhered to. In other words, the principals must know the returns of incremental incentives and the risk proficiency of the managers. Complementary to the second principle is the monitoring principle, where intense incentives correspond to the optimal level of monitoring. Finally, the principals follow the equal compensation principle, wherein the activities that are equally valued by the principals must also be equally rewarded whether as compensation, perks, or due respect.

There are two major measures through which the principal–agency problems are solved.

Financial disclosures   Financial disclosures are an effective measure to control costs. The services of accountants and auditors are engaged. Further problems arise, of course, about the fairness of the disclosures and their accuracy. Many companies have faced bankruptcy in the 2008 meltdown as a result of the failure of this measure.

Independent board of directors   The principals appoint an independent board of directors who will impartially set in controls for good governance. The board has direct fiduciary responsibility towards the shareholders and not the managers. In the recent scandals in India, such as that of Satyam, the independent directors had allegedly abdicated their responsibilities.

Stewardship Theory

The stewardship theory assumes that managers are good and trustworthy. They are appointed mainly due to their good reputation. The board of directors is generally composed of all insiders to the company, who trust their managers to deliver and hence, do not put vigorous disclosure measures. This is done with the intention to cut bureaucracy and increase motivation, which will help the managers take quick decisions.

The stewardship theory is an ideal theory. If it functions ethically, it will cut agency costs considerably. The biggest problem here, in the face of a lesser regulatory system, is that the board of directors must assume greater responsibility towards their shareholders. The risks are greater for the principals and the shareholders.

Religious organizations and family enterprises adopt this trust-based system. Mahatma Gandhi had advocated that the government and the industries must function on the stewardship principle. In the Asian culture, which spans from the Gulf countries to the Southeast Asian countries, employers are held in high honour because they provide the people their livelihoods. People regard the employers as divine stewards.

Table 13.1 compares and contrasts the managers in these two systems to find out which one of them scores a higher moral ground.

Shareholder Theory

This theory stems from the conservative capitalist theory. The most important assumptions are that an individual has a complete and inalienable right to a private property and that individual liberty ensures it. Holding stocks or shares in a company

Table 13.1 Comparison of agency theory and stewardship theory

Manager as agent	Manager as steward
Agent of the principals	Steward of the enterprise
Motivation lies in self-interest	Motivation lies in common interest
Function under the system of monitoring and controls	Function to facilitate and empower others
Averse to risks; if risks are taken, they are done under a controlled system	Not averse to risks; risks are taken under justifiable reasons
Authority is institutionalized	Power is an instrument to serve and preserve
Formalized relations	Informal relations that are based on mutual respect

are a form of private property ownership, and the shareholder alone is its rightful owner. It goes without saying that all value addition is solely the shareholder's privilege. Is this a very selfish and uncaring socialism? The proponents of the theory disagree that it is unfair. They advocate that private property is the incentive to create more wealth, and freedom is the tool for it. This is a universal right. Hence, people have no right to blame others for being rich. Those who work hard become rich. They castigate the stakeholder theory for creating parasites and dependents that drag society into poverty. The advocates of the shareholder theory are criticized for increasing the divide between the haves and the have-nots. They are also accused of causing economic disparities and conflicts within society.

Stakeholder Theory

The stakeholder theory stems from the assumption that individuals are not above the community. The social principle of justice is at stake here. The individual is a part of society and has a responsibility towards it. Such individual privilege would not have been possible if the individual were not a part of the community. Hence, corporations have a wider responsibility than merely adding value to the shareholders. Corporations have a responsibility towards society. The stakeholder theory holds a holistic view of society and lays down normative principles for governance.

John Rawls' *A Theory of Justice* emphasized this fact by going back to the foundations of the formation of society as a contract. Corporations cannot abdicate their responsibility to this contract. The members of society have the right to their livelihood from the enterprise in society. It is imperative on the part of corporations to act fairly. It is also sometimes called the ethics of care.

The stakeholder theory has been criticized for being overtly idealistic and delivering very little in real terms. Money is diverted from corporations towards wasteful programmes. There is also scope for large-scale corruption, since funds can be easily diverted to imaginary causes and schemes. This sort of waste and corruption is a greater moral evil than the conservative principle of shareholder value, wherein there is accountability. Further, it is unjust to take away the rightfully earned profits of the shareholders and invest in proposed philanthropies and social development schemes.

GOOD CORPORATE GOVERNANCE

A corporation in the modern world is not an island. It is influenced by the external environment—social, economic, political, and cultural. It is one among numerous organizations, such as cultural and religious associations, political parties, and special interest groups, governmental and non-governmental institutions. To maximize shareholder value, a business must commit itself to good corporate governance. Features of good corporate governance include strategy setting and planning; risk management; consultation; roles and responsibilities; skills, independence, and resources; conduct and ethics; performance; succession planning; financial and operational reporting; and audit committees.

Role of Board of Governors

As per the directions of the Companies Act 1956, a duly constituted board becomes an artificial person or a legal entity, and to function, it must have a decision-making body. This decision-making body that comes into being according to the wishes of the principals or the shareholders constitutes a body to govern the affairs of the company.

In corporate governance, the board of governors is the highest decision-making body and it exercises threefold powers:

(a) Legislative powers: To formulate bylaws for the company; draw new policies for business and employees

(b) Executive powers: To appoint executives and empower them to the planned tasks

(c) Judicial powers: To attend to the grievances not solved at the managerial level and take appropriate action, as per company policies, against the offending managers and employees

The following are the objectives of corporate governance:

(a) A properly structured board to take independent and responsible decisions: Clearly defined powers, board meetings, and board independence.

(b) The board is to be represented by an adequate number of executive and non-executive directors, who will represent the interests of all the stakeholders: Appointment of qualified and skilled persons to the board.

(c) It takes transparent decisions and adopts such procedures that are unambiguous.

(d) It has effective machinery and policy instruments to safeguard the interests of the stakeholders: Code of conduct.

Unity in Diversity

Indian corporate governance

How many types of corporate governances are there? The broad answer is, as many as the corporations in existence. The narrow answer is, as per their objectives:

(a) Anglo-American: Shareholder value
(b) German: Long-term corporate value
(c) Japanese: Long-term community value
(d) Indian: Mixed value—shareholder and community value

The character of Indian corporations is Indian by nature, although more often than not, they try to ape the West. When it comes to some important parameters such as people management, social responsibility, employee benefits, they are typically Indian. 'Typically Indian' can be best expressed in the Bollywood song—*Thodi si beimani, phir bhi dil hai Hindustani* (It is perhaps a little dishonest, but the Indian heart is still at its best)—which is an appeal to the Indian conscience or compassion.

Some important characteristics:

(a) Corporate objective: Shareholder value
(b) Shareholding: Directors and family members, other corporations, foreign investors, lending institutions, and the government
(c) Governance focus: Maximize surplus
(d) Measure of success: Returns on financial capital
(e) Decision making: Exclusively the directors, outside stakeholders excluded
(f) Control: Linked with owners
(g) Capital market, primary and secondary: More dependence on institutional funding
(h) Dividend: Low and uncertain
(i) Strength: Recent measures of corporate governance
(j) Weakness: Secret and corrupt practices
(k) Opportunity: Incorporate corporate social responsibility
(l) Challenge: Board independence over management

We must realize that the Indian corporations are in their nascent stage of corporate governance. It is only after the economic reforms that the corporations are realizing their responsibility to govern in the interest of the larger community.

Questions

(a) Trace the moral stages of development of Indian corporations.
(b) What kind of corporate leadership is desirable from corporations?
(c) Illustrate what is meant by typically Indian in the moral sense.

(e) It informs the shareholders of all the relevant developments: Strategies, risk management, financial reporting, and audit.
(f) It is always vigilant and monitors the functioning of the management: Operational reporting.
(g) It remains in effective control of the company at all times: Board independence.

In this manner, the board of governors, which is an exemplar of the people's republic, emulates a constitution, a body of governance, and judicial justice. While it focuses on its objective to create wealth, it also pays utmost attention to the means to attain it.

Factors Influencing Quality of Corporate Governance

We have to look at the larger picture of corporate governance—the environment in which it operates. The quality of corporate governance depends on the following factors.

Ability of the board It has been observed that Indian corporate governance lacks the ability of the board to give directions to the company. It has been alleged that the board members are appointed because of vested interests; at times, merely to fulfil formality. Incompetent board members play into the hands of the promoters. This has been sighted very often as the reason for failures and scams.

Commitment of individual members It has been alleged that most of the Indian corporate board members are merely for decorative intentions. The CVs of well-known CEOs and entrepreneurs list an incredible number of companies that they represent as board of directors. So it is obviously impossible to offer dedicated and undivided attention to the affairs of the company.

Participation of stakeholders India has adopted an Anglo-American system of corporate governance, wherein it is the business of the shareholders to appoint a board of directors who are directly responsible to them. There are no other stakeholders in the decision-making body, whereas in Germany, employees and trade unions are also represented in the highest decision-making body.

Adequacy of processes Monitoring the process of the system, operational and financial reporting, internal and external audit, and disclosures and legal compliances make up for a system of adequate control and systematic administration.

Integrity of the management It depends on the philosophy of the company—whether it subscribes to a shareholder theory or a stakeholder theory. The former will appoint managers as agents, who will look after the interests of the shareholders and seek their value addition. It would also make provisions for the cost effectiveness of the agents. The latter will appoint managers as stewards of the company, entrust them with the management of its affairs, and expect steady and long-term returns from them, for the shareholders, as well as endeavour to be good corporate citizens. An ethical framework will help to uphold the integrity of the management, no matter what philosophy the company adopts.

Quality of corporate reporting Corporate reporting has suffered the most in India. There is a culture of veil rather than transparency in the corporate function. Many blame it on the colonial yoke and the adoption of a socialist economy, which made corporations wary of revealing a true picture of the state of affairs. The quarterly reports and the chairman's annual report are seen as being ceremonious rather than substantive. The shareholders and investors do not have the means to know the real picture of the company. If this were not the case, then frauds such as the one at Satyam would not have taken place.

Corporate Governance through Listing Agreement

SEBI had appointed commissions at different intervals to seek guidance for listed companies. The Kumara Mangalam Birla Committee Report of 1999 is considered the most comprehensive in terms of reference—amendments to listing agreement, a code of corporate governance, and safeguards against insider trading. SEBI gave the following directions to companies,[3] revising its existing Clause 49 of the Listing Agreement for the new entrants and the existing ones.

(a) Under Listing Agreement: They must obtain a certificate from either practicing company secretaries or auditors regarding compliance with Clause 49 of the Listing Agreement. The certificate will be sent to the shareholders along with the director's report.

(b) The certificate will also be sent to stock exchanges.

(c) Companies are supposed to file a quarterly report to the stock exchange within fifteen days of the closure of the quarter.

Compliance under Companies Act 1956

The Companies Act 1956 amended in 2000 provides for the following: companies having a paid-up share capital of Rs 10 lakh or more and not requiring to employ a whole-time secretary are required to file with the registrar of companies a compliance certificate from a secretary in whole-time practice.

Ethical Nature of Corporate Governance

An ordinary consumer in the market recognizes the various common brands, for instance, Lipton (tea), Bata (shoes), McDonald's (food), Tata Motors (cars), Nokia (mobile phones). Thousands of companies that supply to the varied needs of the consumer jostle for a place in the consumer's heart and mind. These companies would like to build a good reputation and present themselves as most ethical. In this manner, they build a good corporate culture. Good governance is the only instrument for the purpose.

We have already advocated the view that a corporation is not only a distinct person from its members, but also a moral person. Therefore, before the law, it is responsible for all its actions. The decisions that the members take and implement in the name of the corporation are collective decisions and not the decisions of individual members. It is natural that the ethical background of members influences the corporation through decisions and implementation, and through its existence in society, whereby its behaviour becomes transparent and affects others in such a manner that it is steadily able to develop a personality of its own.

There are two ways in which the moral responsibility is fixed on corporations. First, being a subject of the law, the company will be held accountable for all actions that are not in conformity with the law. Second, customers observe through their personal experience of the company, and through the free press and media, who are the opinion makers in society, and give an appropriate verdict, which results in the acceptance or rejection of what the company has to offer.

---

[3] See SEBI Circular SEBI/CFD/DIL/CG 1, dated 12 October 2004.

Changing Course Mid-stream

World Bank versus Wipro

Wipro Technologies Ltd is a highly reputed Indian company that has helped to establish Indian credibility across the globe. It is also one of the most admired companies and is known for good governance practices. It was a shock to the Indian industry in January 2009 when the World Bank declared that under its revised rules of disclosure of 2007, Wipro had violated its code and hence will be debarred from doing business with it till 2011. Infosys, the other famous IT company of India, too was debarred. The industry and the media asked questions about the motives of the World Bank.

As a part of its best practices, Wipro involves employees and customers with the public offering to expand the recognition and brand. In 2000, in connection with its initial public offering (IPO) of American Depository Shares (ADS) in the US, Wipro offered a commonly utilized, and Securities and Exchange Commission approved, directed share programme (DSP) that allowed employees and clients to purchase ADSs at the IPO market price. Through its chief information officer and a senior staff, Wipro offered the World Bank to participate in the programme and directed this offer to the members of their family and friends as well. The aggregate number of shares purchased by them was 1750, for approximately $72,000 at the IPO price. All participants in the programme signed a conflict of interest statement that their purchase did not violate any ethics or conflict of interest policies of their company.

Wipro's credentials have been excellent, and it has a history of sharing the company shares with its employees and other investors. It is this value of the community creating wealth together and also sharing it that has made the company one of the most admired ones.

Questions

(a) Is the World Bank guilty of selective application of ethical standards?

(b) What is the importance of time gap in the application of a rule in the above case?

(c) How can Wipro counter the World Bank charges with moral arguments?

Source: http://www.cxotoday.com/India/News/Wipro_Cant_Contest_Direct_WB_Contracts_Till_2011/551-97638-911.html.

SUMMARY

- A corporation is an association of entrepreneurs, shareholders, and investors and functions under the trusteeship of its governors.

- The guiding ethical principle is stewardship of the company.

- A corporation is a legal entity and has the responsibility of a moral person.

- Unlike a natural person, a corporation has permanency.

- A corporation is required to be a responsible person and hence works within the rules and regulations and provides good governance to the organization.

- It is essential for the growth of a company that it takes its investors into confidence and is transparent in all its dealings.

- Although the dominance of the agency theory cannot be denied, corporate governance demands stakeholder responsibility and hence the stewardship theory is ideal to govern the company well.

- The most important feature of corporate governance is the separation between ownership and governance.

- Corporate social responsibility is the most salutary feature of corporate governance.

KEY TERMS

Agency costs   The cost that the company bears to run the management.

Agents   The managers of the company.

Corporate social responsibility   Corporation's responsibility beyond the shareholders, towards the other stakeholders, and society at large.

Corporation   Formation of an association of the people for a definite purpose.

Good governance   Ethical exercise of authority or power with well-formed regulations and social practices.

Governance   Exercise of authority or power in an organization.

Legal person   An artificially created body of people or an association of people, which has legal sanctions to exist in society and perform its functions and is responsible for its actions before the law of the land.

Market regulator   The government-appointed securities controller.

Moral person   A person, moral or legal, for whose actions moral responsibility—the right and wrong of such actions—may be fixed; a corporation is a moral person, as opposed to a natural person.

Person   A human being, a corporation, or any legal entity recognized by law as having rights and duties.

Transparency   Voluntary disclosures by a company.

Veil   The enduring distinction between the human person and the legal person.

CONCEPT REVIEW QUESTIONS

1. How do corporations come into existence and what is their purpose?

2. Why is an individual different from a corporation, which is but a group of several individuals?

3. Which theory of corporate governance do you personally advocate? Give valid reasons.

4. What is the 'good' in corporate governance?

CRITICAL THINKING QUESTIONS

1. Why do human beings form associations and give them rights and demand duties of them?

2. What is the difference between personal discipline and corporate governance?

3. Are not corporations outdated? What is the alternative to corporations?

4. Can common good be enhanced by corporations? Give a critical comment.

FURTHER READING

S.K. Chakraborty, *Value and Ethics for Organizations, Theory and Practice*, Oxford University Press, New Delhi (1998).

CASE STUDY

Trial of Warren Hastings

The CEO of a Corporation That Ruled the World

Our liberty is as much in danger as our honour and our national character. We, who here appear representing the Commons of England, are not wild enough not to tremble both for ourselves and for our constituents at the effect of riches. Opum metuenda potestas! We dread the operation of money. Do we not know that there are many men who wait, and who indeed hardly wait, the event of this prosecution, to let loose all the corrupt wealth of India, acquired by the oppression of that country, for the corruption of all the liberties of this, and to fill Parliament with men who are now the object of its indignation? Today, the Commons of Great Britain prosecute the delinquents of India: tomorrow the delinquents of India may be the Commons of Great Britain. We know, I say, and feel the force of money; and we now call upon your Lordships for justice in this cause of money. We call upon you for the preservation of our manners, of our virtues. We call upon you for our national character. We call upon you for our liberties; and hope that the freedom of the Commons will be preserved by the justice of the Lords.[a]

—Edmund Burke

Part I

Objective of the Case

The British East India Company is a monumental historical case. It commands all the superlatives— first multinational, largest company, richest corporation, long lived, varied, global, greatest monopoly, most powerful, most influential, most political, culturally most diverse, the only company to found an empire and rule it like a dynasty, most corrupt, least principled, most insensitive to human misery, misgovernance, most blood on hand, and the list goes on.

To sharpen the ethical focus, rather than delve at length into history, I have chosen the trial of Warren Hastings, the first Governor General of India, whose impeachment trial was held at the Westminster, the British Parliament. The proceedings against the defendant were conducted under the leadership of Edmund Burke, the well-known philosopher and parliamentarian, who laid bare the moral degradation of the company and its leader.

The trial is about the most important lesson— accountability—that should be learnt by every corporation and its leadership. For Indian companies and organizations, there are two most important issues to be encountered—corruption and misgovernance. Over three centuries after this trial, we are still struggling with the same problems within corporations: endangerment of innocent lives, corruption, favouritism, inhumanity, bankruptcy, unethical management practices, monopoly, enrichment at others' expense, maltreatment of the employees, a fat bonus to the top officials, and downright injustice to the workers. The much touted corporate governance came to a naught in 2008, with the worst ever global stock market meltdown. Just the way 1857 has gone down in history as the year the British Government intervened and put an end to the East India Company, 2008 will also go down in history as the year when the

governments of the countries following the capitalist system of economy intervened to control the free reign of the corporations, and thus demolished its central principle of free-market economy.

For managers and students of management, there are rich treasures of knowledge in their chosen profession. A deeper study of the East India Company in general, and its social and moral implications, should raise their consciousness to the business of doing business rightly. It would be easy to sit in judgment of this company. It will be a lesson to reflect upon what it teaches, but will be very difficult to put into practice the principles that could have made this company unique, humane, and changed the world for the better.

Finally, whether we like it or not, all Indians share their history with the East India Company. Whether it is for better or for worse, we are the company's children. Our education, our careers, our lives, and the lives of our future generations are inextricably bound to this company.

Part II

Some Historical Landmarks Preceding Hastings

Founding (1600 AD)

On 31 December 1600, Queen Elizabeth I of Great Britain granted the Royal Charter, conferring on Honourable East India Company, the privileges of trade in India. It was known elaborately as The Company of Merchants of London Trading into the East Indies. The company would be known quite simply as the East India Company, and later as British East India Company. In India, it earned nicknames, such as 'Company Bahadur' and John Company. It was not just the British who had an East India Company, but the Portuguese and the Dutch also obtained charters from their respective governments to conduct trade in the Indies. The Portuguese were the first in India, followed by the Dutch. The British, in comparison to their

---

[a] For an extract from the prosecution speech of Edmund Burke, 7 May 1789, see http://www.ourcivilisation.com/smartboard/shop/burkee/extracts/chap14.htm, accessed on 25 October 2008.

European cousins, were much weaker. They satis-fied themselves with trade that was based in Surat and Bombay (now Mumbai) on the west coast, and Madras (now Chennai) and Calcutta (Kolkata) on the east coast.

First Voyage (1601 AD)

The ships set out to trade woollen cloth and silver for spices. They met Arab, Turkish, Gujarati, Bengali, Malay, and Chinese merchants on the voyage. The commerce consisted of spices, drugs, silk, porcelain, precious stones, carpets, foodstuffs, and perfumes.

Surat (1612 AD)

The first ship landed at Surat. The company obtained rights to establish a factory from the Mughal ruler Jahangir.

Madras (1640 AD)

The company obtained permission from the Vijayanagar ruler to start a new factory and trading post at Madras, and traded Indian cottons to other countries in the East Indies. There, the fabrics were traded for spices.

Bombay (1668 AD–1687 AD)

The company leased the island of Bombay and established trade and commerce. The island was given in dowry to the British Crown by the Portuguese when Charles II married the Portuguese princess Catherine de Braganza. In 1687, the company moved its headquarters from Surat to Bombay.

Calcutta (1690 AD)

The company obtained permission for settlement in Calcutta from the Mughal emperor, and system-atically expanded its influence. The demand in England and the rest of Europe for handwoven textiles and silks shot up; the company hired hoards of craftsmen and labourers, who toiled to meet the demand but with very poor pay. The people suffered under famine and extreme poverty. The company, however, had no concept of welfare of the workers. While the natives were enslaved by their masters for hard work, the company pros-pered and the shareholders got rich dividends.

English Traders' Protest (1697 AD)

There were protests in Britain by weavers, dyers, and other professionals, as a repercussion of the company's monopoly over textiles and other goods. Initially, the company diverted its trade to other European countries. But as the market forces demanded, the protests drowned amidst the popu-larity of the Indian goods.

Expansion to China (1700 AD)

A century of most successful trade and profits made the company invincible. It now looked further to expand its trade still further to the east, that is, China. It dealt with tea, porcelain, and silk. Tea alone amounted to more than 60 per cent of the trade with China. The company paid in silver, but disliked lots of the metal going out of the home-land. Hence, it found the wonder material called opium, which not only spread the drug problem, but destroyed families and lives as well.

Founding the Empire (1757 AD)

This was the year of the company's turning point, from a trader to a ruler. Robert Clive made history by winning the battle of Plassey or Palashi. He was a well-experienced general and had served the company since 1743. He had won remarkable victories against the Dutch and the French forces in India. The Mughal Empire was weak and wars broke out everywhere in the famed empire. Siraj-ud-Daula was the Nawab of Bengal and he did not like the English. A year earlier in 1756, he had captured some English; Warren Hastings was one among them. The battle of Plassey vanquished the Nawab and for the first time, the British East India Company put its foundation of the empire in Bengal, which was then the richest province of India. It took exactly 157 years for the company to achieve this remarkable and singular feat, the trans-formation of a business corporation into a political ruler. And what a rule! Immediately, unbearable tax burdens were put on the people to multiply the profits for the shareholders. In the famine that followed, it is said that one-third of Bengal's popu-lation succumbed to death. Millions of survivors were dispossessed of their landholdings. The company and Clive both thrived!

Battle of Buxar (1764 AD)

Shah Alam II of Bihar was defeated at the battle of Buxar.

Governor General (1773 AD)

The company was a villain for the people of Britain, because it not only amassed wealth, but also stripped the natives of all their dignity and sustenance, and subjected them to abject poverty, with no regard for any humanity. Thus, the British government was compelled to take action, curb the power of the company, and appointed its own custodian for the British territories in India, who would be called the governor general.

Warren Hastings (1773 AD–1785 AD)

The first Governor General of India had an express mandate from its government that the newly established colony must be governed by the rule of law. Four events took place under his tenure: the Bengal famine and the three wars of Rohilla, Maratha, and Mysore. There were efforts at reforms but the mismanagement and ill treatment of the natives continued unabated. Added to this was the infamous opium trade.

Pitts India Act (1784 AD)

The public opinion was against the profligacy of the company. Britain was shocked by the mismanagement and atrocities committed in India. The government was forced to take greater control over the affairs of the company through the Pitts India Act.

Resignation of Hastings (1785 AD)

Hastings found out that his powers had been curbed by the Pitts India Act, and resigned from the company and returned to England.

Trial of Hastings (1788 AD–1795 AD)

Impeachment proceedings were conducted before the British Parliament under the charges of corruption, mismanagement of company affairs, plunder and exploitation, and misuse of power against the natives. Hastings was acquitted.

Part III

Trial of Warren Hastings and Prosecution by Edmund Burke

The trial began on 13 February 1788. There were twenty charges levied by the prosecution, headed by Edmund Burke, in the House of Commons in the British Parliament. Historians agree on one point that it was the single-most spectacular event of the eighteenth century. It was an epic, seven-year-long trial. The parliament hall was crammed with politicians, nobles, aristocrats of every hue, journalists, painters, historians, celebrities, actors and actresses, and all the who is who of the then British realm. It became a status symbol to attend the trial.

The trial was The House of Commons and the People of India versus East India Company, under the Governorship of Lord Warren Hastings. The prosecution consisted of the most brilliant speakers from the House of Commons: Edmund Burke, Charles James Fox, Richard Brinsley Sheridan, and Charles Grey. They were called the managers of the prosecution.

Charge of Genocide
(Reminiscent of Union Carbide, Bhopal Gas Tragedy)

Hastings had renegotiated a treaty with Shuja-ud-Daula, the Wazir of Avadh, that was earlier concluded by Robert Clive. This was to ward off the threat posed by the Maratha federation against Avadh and Bengal. The treaty was that the Wazir subsidizes maintenance of the British troops and that if needed, he would march against the Rohillas who had invaded North India from Afghanistan. In 1774, the British army and Wazir's army fought against the Rohillas. There was not only plunder and pillage, but wanton killing also in the aftermath of the war. The complicity of Hastings was implicit.

Charge of Mismanagement
(Reminiscent of Meltdown 2008)

The company was now involved in a vortex of Indian rulers and their very complex change of loyalties and sudden and unexpected geopolitical modifications and reincarnations. The company's sole interest was to accumulate as much revenue as possible by devising ways to play on the loyalties and disloyalties of the rulers. Thus, for instance, in 1775 when Shuja-ud-Daula the Avadh ruler died, his widow and mother, the Begums of Avadh, were given guarantees to pass on the wealth of the diseased. But Hastings needed money for the wars on several fronts. He reneged on the promise to the Begums, charged them for inciting Chait Singh,

| Warren Hastings' Timeline ||
Year	Event
1732	Hastings born to a noble, but impoverished family
1750	Sent to Bengal as a clerk for the East India Company
1751	Siege of Arcot—Britain defeats the French and their Indian allies
1756	While working at Cossimbar, factory was taken. Hastings was captured and released
1757	Battle of Plassey: Britain gains control of Bengal
1758	Appointed resident at Murshidabad for three years
1761	Promoted to council of president Vansittart
1764	Resigned post and sailed for England
1770	Worst famine on record in Bengal
1772	Returned to Bengal as second-in-command
1773	Appointed governor-general for five years
1775	Brahman Nandkumar is hanged
1776	Became involved in First Maratha War
1780	Injures Philip Francis in a duel. Francis returns to Britain
1780	Became involved in Second Mysore War
1785	Sails from India after resigning governorship
1788	Hastings put on trial for corruption. Prosecuted by Burke
1795	Hastings acquitted of wrong-doing
1818	Death of Warren Hastings

the Maharaja of Benares, and thus robbed them of their sustenance. The problem was that a watchful England was aware that on the one hand, the company was depleted of funds and that the government would have to bail it out, and on the other hand, the company officials were returning back home laden with wealth, so much so that they were nicknamed as nawabs!

Hanging of the Dewan

(Reminiscent of scapegoat syndrome and blame game in the economic and political spheres)

The company had invented a dual system for revenue collection. After it won a battle with the local king, the company not only appointed him as a puppet king, but also appointed a *dewan*, a collector of revenues for the company, in the court of the local king. Nandkumar, an appointee of the company, was the Dewan of Bengal. He grew powerful and played political games in the same way as the company did. Nandkumar threatened to bring forgery charges against Hastings, of which he possessed evidence. Hastings had become famous in India for not imposing the British law on the locals, but had studied the Hindu and Islamic laws and implemented the same for the locals. In 1775 as the threat of Nandkumar loomed large, Hastings changed track and charged Nandkumar with corruption. In the trial that ensued, Nandkumar was found guilty as charged and was hanged according to the British law.

Arbitrary Administration of the Law

(Reminiscent of some lower court judgments that discriminate people on basis of caste and gender)

Hastings' duty was to enforce the law as was enshrined in the constitution, and not create his own law at random and feign to administer justice. There was no semblance of administered justice, as rulers were bought and sold. The posts of collectors and other officials too went for a price. There was complete disregard for the local community.

The conquest did not endow one with the gift of arbitrary law. For both the governor and the governed, the law was one and the same.

Corruption and Revenue Collectors
(Reminiscent of bureaucratic corruption)

The brief for Hastings was to raise money for the company, with the twin purposes of expanding and consolidating its rule in India. Bengal was known for its agriculture and craftsmanship. The company devised ways and means to implement and extort money tax revenues. With this money, the company not only raised and maintained a large army of Indian soldiers who were commanded by the British officers, but the company officers hugely enriched themselves from the corruption in revenue collection, and also from their independent businesses, which were allowed by the law. But they carried it out to the extent that it was beyond the discretion of the law. They depleted the resources of the Indians and subjected them to abject poverty. Hastings did nothing to control his officers from looting the Indians.

Opium Trade
(Reminiscent of Prohibition in Gujarat, spurious liquor tragedies, and drug peddling in other parts of India)

The company had used silver as the medium of exchange for its trade. It was very strange and devoid of any moral qualms when it adopted opium as a medium of exchange to conduct its trade with China. It served two purposes. It saved its silver currency and brought in revenues to support the expansionist plans in India. During Hastings' tenure, it wrought catastrophe in China, when a great number of its population got addicted to opium and hundreds of thousands of people died and thousands of families were destroyed.

Private Business
(Reminiscent of the parliamentarians, bureaucrats, and public servants running parallel trade or office of profit)

When Hastings arrived in England, he was welcomed with great pomp and recognition, only because he had made a name for himself as a very successful executive and was immensely rich. For the twenty-five years that he spent in India, he had developed vast business interests. The officers of the company were allowed to supplement their small emoluments with private commercial activity, but it became a huge embarrassment for the government, when the company officers enriched themselves at the cost of the poor Indians.

Humanity Violated
(Reminiscent of bonded labour, child labour, sub-human conditions in which people live in Indian city slums, construction sites and villages)

There was ample evidence in public knowledge, created through the newspapers, which reported the violation of basic humanity. Hastings' regime was ruthless in the extortion of revenues. Hastings was completely complicit in the atrocities perpetrated on the natives. Women were brought out into the public, paraded naked, and their limbs were mutilated. Fear and terror was instilled in the natives mercilessly, with total disregard for humanity.

The next two-and-half centuries would make this company not merely a global monopoly par excellence, but also a military superpower. No other company in the world has been as vast, as rich, and as powerful as the East India Company, and perhaps will never be. However, the giant that was considered omnipotent and immortal suffered a mortal blow as a band of simple Indian patriots challenged the company's military might and rose in rebellion. History records it as the Mutiny of 1857. Following this historical event, the company became defunct and an act of the British Parliament, the East India Stock Dividend Act of 1874, dissolved the company.

Part IV

Epilogue

Every aspect of this case has been analysed—as a story, history, politics, armies, wars, science, technology, cities, railways, economics, management, language, culture, money, and people. There is no dearth of lessons to be drawn for modern corporate governance, the idea of globalization, and the value addition to the shareholders. There is no shortage of ethical problems that have not been highlighted and investigated and promptly castigated. What then is the objective of delving into such an enormous case of an early corporation,

The Indictment

Burke's speech

(Edmund Burke's oratory was par excellence. Here is a sample of that genius, from Para 7–20.)

My lords, I do not mean now to go farther than just to remind your lordships of this—that Mr Hastings' government was one whole system of oppression, of robbery of individuals, of spoliation of the public, and of supersession of the whole system of the English government, in order to vest in the worst of the natives all the power that could possibly exist in any government; in order to defeat the ends which all governments ought, in common, to have in view. In the name of the Commons of England, I charge all this villainy upon Warren Hastings, in this last moment of my application to you.

My lords, what is it that we want here, to a great act of national justice? Do we want a cause, my lords? You have the cause of oppressed princes, of undone women of the first rank, of desolated provinces, and of wasted kingdoms.

Do you want a criminal, my lords? When was there so much iniquity ever laid to the charge of any one? No, my lords, you must not look to punish any other such delinquent from India. Warren Hastings has not left substance enough in India to nourish such another delinquent.

My lords, is it a prosecutor you want? You have before you the Commons of Great Britain as prosecutors; and I believe, my lords, that the sun, in his beneficent progress round the world, does not behold a more glorious sight than that of men, separated from a remote people by the material bounds and barriers of nature, united by the bond of a social and moral community—all the Commons of England resenting, as their own, the indignities and cruelties that are offered to all the people of India.

Do we want a tribunal? My lords, no example of antiquity, nothing in the modern world, nothing in the range of human imagination, can supply us with a tribunal like this. We commit safely the interests of India and humanity into your hands. Therefore, it is with confidence that, ordered by the Commons.

I impeach Warren Hastings, Esquire, of high crimes and misdemeanours.

I impeach him in the name of the Commons of Great Britain in Parliament assembled, whose parliamentary trust he has betrayed.

I impeach him in the name of all the Commons of Great Britain, whose national character he has dishonoured.

I impeach him in the name of the people of India, whose laws, rights and liberties he has subverted; whose properties he has destroyed; whose country he has laid waste and desolate.

I impeach him in the name and by virtue of those eternal laws of justice which he has violated. (Para 16)

I impeach him in the name of human nature itself, which he has cruelly outraged, injured and oppressed, in both sexes, in every age, rank, situation, and condition of life.

My lords, at this awful close, in the name of the Commons and surrounded by them, I attest the retiring, I attest the advancing generations, between which, as a link in the great chain of eternal order, we stand. We call this nation, we call the world to witness, that the Commons have shrunk from no labour; that we have been guilty of no prevarication; that we have made no compromise with crime; that we have not feared any odium whatsoever, in the long warfare which we have carried on with the crimes, with the vices, with the exorbitant wealth, with the enormous and overpowering influence of Eastern corruption.

My lords, it has pleased Providence to place us in such a state that we appear every moment to be upon the verge of some great mutations. There is one thing, and one thing only, which defies all mutation: that which existed before the world, and will survive the fabric of the world itself—I mean justice; that justice which, emanating from the Divinity, has a place in the breast of every one of us, given us for our guide with regard to ourselves and with regard to others, and which will stand, after this globe is burned to ashes, our advocate or our accuser, before the great Judge, when He comes to call upon us for the tenor of a well-spent life.

My lords, the Commons will share in every fate with your lordships; there is nothing sinister which can

Contd

Box Contd

happen to you, in which we shall not all be involved; and, if it should so happen that we shall be subjected to some of those frightful changes which we have seen—if it should happen that your lordships, stripped of all the decorous distinctions of human society, should, by hands at once base and cruel, be led to those scaffolds and machines of murder upon which great kings and glorious queens have shed their blood, amidst the prelates, amidst the nobles, amidst the magistrates, who supported their throne—may you in those moments feel that consolation which I am persuaded they felt in the critical moments of their dreadful agony!

My lords, if you must fall, may you so fall! but, if you stand—and stand I trust you will—together with the fortune of this ancient monarchy, together with the ancient laws and liberties of this great and illustrious kingdom, may you stand as unimpeached in honour as in power; may you stand, not as a substitute for virtue, but as an ornament of virtue, as a security for virtue; may you stand long, and long stand the terror of tyrants; may you stand the refuge of afflicted nations; may you stand a sacred temple, for the perpetual residence of an inviolable justice!

Source: The World's Famous Orations, Ireland (1775–1902) (1906) III, At the Trial of Warren Hastings, Edmund Burke (1729–1788), http://www.bartleby.com/268/6/3.html, accessed on 7 September 2008.

---

when the science of management was not even seminally conceived?

We want to live. We want to be immortal. The truth is, we may live but we cannot be immortal. Man devised ways to become immortal—create progeny, build cities, discover the hidden, invent machines, create wealth, build institutions, found organizations, establish religions, constitute nations, and enjoy civilization. People die, tribes are lost, wealth is lost, institutions fade, organizations collapse, and civilizations come to an end. So there is nothing unnatural if the British East India Company came to an end just as the great British Empire did, on which the sun set much against the dreams of many.

There is however one point, a singular characteristic, which the historians, the politicians, the social scientists, litterateurs, prophets, and journalists have lost. This is the point on which the organization depends. It is the singularity from which the organization proceeds and expands. It is called trust. This trust was entrusted to the company at the highest level, by the government of the people with the approval and seal of the head of state.

Discussion Questions

Historical

1. How do events that become historically important take place?

2. Was the East India Company conscious of its role in history?

3. What were the decisions made by the company that changed the course of history?

4. What would have been India's history without the East India Company?

5. The US of America was also a British colony. Draw some historical similarities and dissimilarities to analyse and understand the past, present, and future of these two countries.

6. What is the role of morality in history?

Trial

1. What was the most outstanding issue at the trial of Hastings?

2. Show the moral dimensions of the trial.

3. What ethical lessons can we draw from the trial?

4. What laws did Hastings break?

5. How do business governance and politics get mixed?

6. Which one of the following was Hastings' interest—the company's interest, the interest of his country, the interests of the natives of the colonized country?

7. What aspects of the trial bring out the moral responsibility of a leader in the events that take place?

8. Is a leader called so because he/she bears a moral responsibility towards her/his office?

9. How is a leader responsible for those actions which do not turn out as they were planned out to be, such as famine and opium trade?

Governance

1. In what way was Hastings responsible for mismanagement?

2. In the absence of the guidelines that were set for management, how can Hastings be held responsible for the crimes against humanity?

3. Are corporate leaders of today brought to rigorous justice as during Hastings' time?

4. Are today's corporate leaders subjected to a detailed scrutiny?

5. What are the instruments of governance for such kind of scrutiny?

6. Name a few companies that have lasted for more than a century. Find out what social, political, economic, and ethical reasons helped their longevity. If they are defunct, what caused their end?

7. In what way did the East India Company influence the political process, interfere with the government policies, and meddle in the functioning of the government? Give an example of such a contemporary Indian corporation and illustrate it.

8. Do corporations enrich themselves at the expense of their employees? Illustrate this with a recent case.

9. Make a list of the merits and demerits of the East India Company. Draw an ethical governance model.

10 In what way does the company show the best and the worst in human nature? Name some companies of today that influence people for better or the worse.

Personal

1. Your education is in English, your political system is based on the British law, your economy still follows the East India Company model, which is the free-market economy, your bureaucracy is a continuation of the company's system, and your businesses follow in the footsteps of the company... Are you not, as an Indian or any other person from the subcontinent or wherever the company had its influence, that is, as a person living in the Commonwealth country, a child of the East India Company?

2. What moral qualities do you possess to be a good corporate leader?

3. As a manager of a company, whose interests would you represent, your company's or that of the country's?

4. In a terrorist attack on your company's headquarters, would you kill the attacker if you got an opportunity?

5. What would you do if your company brought false charges against you and dragged you to the court, where before the court and the media of the country, you were declared a felon?

Going Further . . .

- Pre-requisite: Read a standard Indian history book from the period 1600 AD to 1858 AD.

- Enact the trial to understand the historical and contemporary seriousness of the case.

- Any discussion of the case in any manner must have relevance to the present manner of doing and managing business.

- A serious reflection or meditation must be conducted to realize the shocking, stunning, troubling, failing, struggling, helping, healing aspects of this case, which have affected our ancestors, and is affecting us and our future generations.

ETHICAL DEVELOPMENT PROGRAMME

Management Training

(A) Set up a company

Come together as a group of not less than seven, and form a company under the Companies Act 1956 by formulating the memorandum of the company to be registered.

(a) Objective: Learn by doing.

(b) If the group members are earnest, they may found a real company by forming a group as stockholders.

   (i) If you are a group of MBA students, your course time of six weeks should be sufficient to conceive, plan, and draw a memorandum for registration in consultation with a company secretary.

   (ii) If you are an executive, plan your timeframe and carry on with the business.

(B) Game

Play coordination game:

(a) Go to link http://viswiki.com/en/Coordination_game.

(b) Pick a game for each group.

(c) Determine the payoffs.

(d) Decide the objective such as behaviour, strategy, risk measurement, etc.

Management Mantra

The Corporation: The Real Person

The Corporation is a simple Canadian documentary with relevant topics, cases, and interviews that highlight the modern corporation as a real person who can turn dangerous. It evaluates corporations and their actions and analyzes their behaviour. A specimen of the following dialogue illustrates what we already know, but what it makes us do is to rethink.

Narrator: *150 years ago, the business corporation was a relatively insignificant institution. Today, it is all-pervasive. Like the Church, the Monarchy, and the Communist Party in other times and places, the corporation is today's dominant institution. This documentary examines the nature, evolution, impacts, and possible futures of the modern business corporation. Initially given a narrow legal mandate, what has allowed today's corporation to achieve such extraordinary power and influence over our lives? We begin our inquiry as scandals threaten to trigger a wide debate about the lack of public control over big corporations.*

Narrator: *Through the voices of CEOs, whistleblowers, brokers, gurus and spies, insiders and outsiders, we present the corporation as a paradox, an institution that creates great wealth, but causes enormous, and often hidden harms.*

Ira Jackson: *The eagle, soaring, clear-eyed, competitive, prepared to strike, but not a vulture. Noble, visionary, majestic, that people can believe in and be inspired by, that creates such a lift that it soars. I can see that being a good logo for the principled company.*

Robert Keyes: *The word corporate gets attached in almost, you know, in a pejorative sense to and gets married with the word a-gen-da. And one hears a lot about the corporate a-gen-da as though it is evil, as though it is an agenda, which is trying to take over the world. Personally, I don't use the word corporation. I use the word business. I will use the word... use the word company. I will use the words business community because I think that is a much fairer representation than zeroing in on just this word corporation.*

Interesting topics like a business plot, Dwight D. Eisenhower, Bovine Growth Hormone, Fox News Channel, Fanta, IBM, Nazis, privatization, water supply, Bechtel Corporation, Corporation turned psychopath, and more become parts of the cases and opinions.

The documentary was produced and directed by Mark Achbar. Bart Simpson was the co-producer and Jennifer Abbott was the co-director. The documentary is highly recommended for intense discussion.

> MANTRA   *Warning! Corporation control!*

Institutionalization of Ethical Governance for Corporations

The speciality of corporate governance is that it pre-empts the need for government or other regulatory interferences in matters of business. It is, in fact, the business of business.[1]

—K.V. Krishnamurthy

To be a leader and partner in initiatives for corporate reforms, good governance and enlightened regulation with a view to promote and facilitate effective corporate functioning and investor protection.

—Vision of Ministry of Corporate Affairs

LEARNING OBJECTIVES

After studying this chapter, you will be able to

> Understand the emergence of the corporate governance code
> Describe the development of Indian corporate governance
> Discern the assumption of best practices
> Analyse the failure of corporate governance

INTRODUCTION

The objective of this chapter is to understand the ethical principle of stewardship in corporate governance beyond its present application. In order to analyse the deeper ethical nuances, we would have to examine the origins of corporate governance and its development as relevant to us in India, and study its espoused best practices. We will also analyse the factors that led to the failure of corporate governance.

Organized commerce has been around since ancient times, when there were famous trade routes, exotic caravan trades, dealings in precious metals, highly prized silk, and spices, and sea routes of flotillas with treasures from distant islands and pirates. There would also have been governance related to business houses. Having read the

---

[1] K.V. Krishnamurthy (former chairman and managing director of Bank of India), as quoted in *Corporate Governance*, ICSI, p. 66.

case about the trial of Warren Hastings in the previous chapter, one would like to make a safe guess that colonial British India inspired it and that it was enacted at the Westminster Palace. Europeans would think that it was one of the inventions of resurging renaissance and the age of enlightenment. Americans would wager that it was done during the civil war, to control the free flow of arms between the two armies, by corrupt gun producers and suppliers. All the guesses are mere guesses and none of them actually took place. The trial was triggered by a series of corporate failures in the previous three decades. Following are some more examples of corporate failures from the past:

(a) The Watergate scandal that unseated the US President Richard Nixon revealed the underbelly of the corporations that funded the political causes and bribed bureaucrats, which resulted in the enactment of the Foreign and Corrupt Practices Act 1977.

(b) In the UK, the biggest financial scandal took place in the reputed Bank of Credit and Commerce International. It was immediately followed by the bankruptcy of Barings Bank, which led to four subsequent reports being written to control the practices of corporations.

(c) In India, in the aftermath of the bull run at the Bombay Stock Exchange and the fall of Harshad Mehta, and the end of command economy at the fall of communism, followed by the economic reforms, the Government of India formed several committees to regulate corporations.

In the new millennium, corporate governance was seen as a dire need in the face of blatant frauds by managers, which shattered the economies of corporations, sheared shareholders of their investments, and forced other stakeholders to bear the consequences of these failures for which they were not responsible. The very managers who had chided that ethics in business is an oxymoron and that they believed in value addition to shareholders betrayed their clients and ended up behind prison bars. The world had had enough of Enrons, WorldComs, Big Bulls, Leesons, etc. A new direction was needed. There emerged a slew of reports from committees that were set up for better corporate governance. The purpose of these measures was to win back the trust of investors and put them back into business.

These corporate failures had made it very clear that mere legislation was not adequate to anticipate every wrong and regulate unwanted behaviour. The need for self-control, self-restrain, self-censorship, and self-regulation was considered as a reasonable option to being goaded by innumerable laws. In short, it was back to the basics—ethics. As we shall see in the latter part of this chapter why corporate governance failed, it suffices to say here that corporate governance mistook regulation for ethics. As a result, several governmental statutory bodies occupied the gap and flooded it with mandatory and non-mandatory stipulations, and considered them nothing short of law. The chapter-end case study on corporate disputes of ownership will further highlight the failure of corporate governance.

EMERGENCE OF CORPORATE GOVERNANCE CODE

It is dreadful if your house is burgled, but the good thing about it is that you would get wiser and ensure that it is fortified against future attacks. A similar situation took place in the business world. This is not to say that businesses in the past were impeccable. There were horrible instances of frauds and loot. But in the recent decades there has been a cascade of business scandals, and corporations have realized that they must put their houses in order, because the burglars in their case were not from outside, but from among those within.

Here we shall see some well-known measures taken by various committees. The report of each committee bears the name of the chairman who had been called to formulate a regulatory system specific to the context or the country.

Cadbury Committee

Ian Robert Maxwell (1923–1991)[2] was a businessman, who not only ruled over a media empire after his name, but was also a Member of the Parliament of Great Britain and was a decorated citizen, awarded with the military cross. After his death a trail of frauds and deceits was discovered, which included looting the pension funds of his own employees. If this was not enough for the Britons, their famous bank, the Bank of Credit and Commerce International, defrauded its depositors, shareholders, and employees of billions of pounds. There were other frauds as well that were perpetrated on the stakeholders and the public was getting restive. The government of Great Britain appointed one of its most upright citizens and a businessman of repute, Sir George Hayhurst Cadbury of the famous chocolate business conglomerate, to serve guidelines to companies on good governance.[3] The report was published in 1992 and was immediately recognized as a brilliant piece of administrative regulation. It was adopted by the European Union, the US, and the World Bank. Following are some of its most important recommendations.

Board of directors or governors

(a) The board of governors must retain control over the management and monitor its executives by meeting regularly with a formal schedule.

(b) There should be a clear division of responsibilities at the highest decision-making level and it must be collective, and no single person should exercise monopoly. If the chairman is also the executive head, then there should be independent directors on the board who are senior and are reputed for their maturity.

(c) There should be non-executive directors of sufficient calibre and number.

(d) The directors must be well informed to make decisions. Hence, they should be able to take external expert advice at the company's expense.

---

[2] See http://en.wikipedia.org/wiki/Robert_Maxwell.

[3] See http://www.cbr.cam.ac.uk/pdf/wp277.pdf.

(e) There should be an agreed procedure for all the directors of the board and they should have access to the company secretary, who will make sure that all the formalities of the board are fulfilled. Removal of a company secretary depends on the entire board of governors.

Executive directors

(a) Their contract should not exceed three years without shareholders' approval.
(b) Their complete financial position must be disclosed, which include emoluments, pension contributions, and stock options. Salary and performance-oriented earnings must be shown separately.
(c) Their pay must be subject to the recommendations of a committee that is wholly constituted of non-executive directors.

Non-executive directors

(a) They must bring independent judgment concerning issues of strategy, performance, resources, including key appointments, and standards of conduct.
(b) The majority of them should be independent, that is, they should not be related with the business of the company, which would conflict with their independent judgment; their fee should reflect the time that they commit to the work of the company.
(c) Their appointment must be for a stipulated period, with no automatic reappointment.
(d) They should be selected through a formal system introduced by the board.

Reporting practices

(a) It is the board's duty to give a balanced and comprehensible assessment of the company's position.
(b) The board should maintain an objective and professional relationship with the auditors.
(c) The audit committee of the board must have at least three non-executive directors.
(d) The directors should explain their responsibility for preparing the accounts, next to a statement by the auditors about their reporting responsibilities.
(e) The directors should also report on the effectiveness of the system of controls.
(f) The directors must report the ongoing business concern, with supporting assumptions or qualifications, as is deemed necessary.

For the first time in the history of corporations, a clear and comprehensive code was established. The selection of the non-executive directors was a mechanism to keep a watch over the governing system, impartially and objectively. The setting up of auditors and audit reporting practices was to ensure accountability. The most controversial measure was that of the directors' obligation to report on the effectiveness of the company's system of internal control, which went beyond financial matters. The report won approbation because of its twin principles—self-governance and accountability.

Organization for Economic Co-operation and Development

In 1948, some time after World War II, in the face of the expansion of communist ideology, the democratic countries of Europe came together to form the Organization for European Economic Co-operation (OEEC), with the twin objective of strengthening democracy and free market. In 1961, the organization changed its name to Organization for Economic Co-operation and Development (OECD)[4] and also admitted members from outside Europe, such as Canada, the US, Australia, and other developed countries, which are thirty in number today. The headquarters are situated in Paris.

The OECD Principles of Corporate Governance were formulated in 1999 and later revised and promulgated in April 2004.[5] They are as follows:

(a) Rights of shareholders: Shareholders have the right to secure their ownership of shares, the right to disclosure of information, voting rights, the right to participation in the sale or modification of the assets of the corporation, mergers, and new share issues.

(b) Equitable treatment of shareholders: There should be concern for the protection of minority shareholders and prohibition of insider trading. Directors must disclose any material interests regarding transactions.

(c) Stakeholders in corporate governance: Besides shareholders, the other stakeholders are banks, bondholders, and employees, whose interests must be protected as much as that of the shareholders.

(d) Disclosure and transparency: There should be transparency in the reporting procedures regarding the decisions of the board, financial reporting, and directors and their remuneration.

The above principles may be too general and their application to specific countries would need well-defined policy directions. The right to private property needs emphasis so that shareholders may claim their rights. Also, countries must be able to maintain a shareholder database so that the minority and individual investors are not discriminated. Finally, the independence of the external auditors cannot be underlined more.

Sarbanes–Oxley Act 2002

As expected from the number one economy in the world, the US has a surfeit of financial scandals, and also the highest number of legislations. One could safely form a general law—the greater the number of scams, the greater the number of laws.

---

[4] See http://www.oecd.org.
[5] See http://www.oecd.org/document/49/0,3343,en_2649_34813_31530865_1_1_1_1,00.html.

Senator Paul Sarbanes, a member of the Democratic Party, and Michael G. Oxley, a Republican Congressman, formulated a bill called Public Company Accounting Reform and Investor Protection Act 2002, which came to be referred to as the Sarbanes–Oxley Act 2002[6] or SOX. Following are some of the important reform areas:

(a) Audit committee: It consists of independent directors of the board who appoint auditors and establish and review the procedures for the receipt retention, and treatment of complaints. The audit committee also handles the treatment of the accounts, the internal control, and the audit complaints received by the company from the affected parties.

(b) Accounting firms should not perform audit service for a publicly traded company if any top officer of the firm was employed by the company a year preceding the date of initiation of the audit.

(c) Audit partner rotation: It is mandatory to rotate the lead audit, or co-ordinate the partner and the partner reviewing audit, every 5 years.

(d) Improper influence on conduct of audits: The director or executives of the company are legally barred from influencing the auditors in any manner.

(e) Auditors: Auditors are prohibited from rendering any non-audit services such as book-keeping, and any similar services of the recording of accounts, financial information system, its design and implementation, appraisal or valuation services, actual services, internal audit outsourcing services, management functions or human resources, broker, dealer, investment or banking services, legal services, or expert advice. However, non-audit services such as taxation could be allowed only if it has been previously permitted by the audit committee.

(f) CEO and CFO must affirm financials: Financials must be reported to the Securities Exchange Board in case of impropriety or fraud. If the financials have to be restated, then the concerned officials will lose their bonuses. False and improper certification attracts $1 million to $5 million in fine, or ten years of imprisonment, or both.

(g) Loans to directors: The directors are prohibited with securities traded within the country, although the existing loans are allowed to exist or continue.

(h) Attorneys: They are required to report any material violation of the securities law or the breach of fiduciary duty to the CEO or CFO, and if action is not taken, they must report to the audit committee and the board.

(i) Securities analysts: No broker or trader should withhold any information from a researcher.

(j) Penalties: Heavy penalties of fines and imprisonment for any breach range from $1 million to $5 million and imprisonments up to 20 years for the offenders.

SOX indeed provided a stiff legislation to discourage fraud on shareholders and other investors. It has been regarded as a landmark law and would have far-reaching

---

[6] See http://www.soxlaw.com/.

Baring the Bank

Barings Bank buried

People at the London end of Barings were all so know-all that nobody dared ask a stupid question in case they looked silly in front of everyone else.

—Nick Leeson (1996)

Could you ever, in your wildest dreams, dream about buying a famous bank for just a pound? Someone did. The Dutch bank ING only had to pay a single pound to buy one of the prestigious banks in the world, Barings Bank, with an elegant coat of arms of a star surrounded by two wings.

Nick Leeson was operating arbitrage from Singapore between Osaka Securities Exchange in Japan with that of the Singapore International Monetary Exchange. It consisted of taking advantage of the price differences in publicly traded futures contract. Since the margins on such trading are low, only very large transactions would ensure returns, although the risks are low and hedged. But Leeson was a genius; BCCI was in awe of his abilities and would not dare to ask anything lest they be proved dim-witted about derivatives. The bold bull Leeson, instead of hedging his positions, gambled on the future direction of the Japanese markets. Unpredictable things were happening in the market and Leeson lost sight of his losses, which were a phenomenal US$1.4 billion, by the end of January 1995. This was twice as much as the bank's trading capital. So it was no wonder then that it was disposed off for a nominal price of £1 to ING, which accepted it with all its liabilities.

Leeson failed on two counts. He was holding two positions in the company: that of the floor manager in Singapore and the head of settlement operations, for which accurate accounting was needed. Leeson later blamed the bank for not doing its duty of questioning him, and pointed out that had they done it, the bank would not have collapsed. The bank was declared insolvent on 25 February 1995. The British Parliament blamed the bank for not knowing even the basics of its business and stated that the executives lacked the simple commonsense of a layman.

The Barings Bank was established by a German family in 1752 in London, and is the oldest merchant bank. It played some controversial role during the Napoleonic wars, but survived and prospered well. The Barings family was very close to the royal family and enjoyed its patronage through the conferring of several peerages. The bank also went through the two world wars successfully, and in the latter half of the twentieth century, it was regarded as one of the finest financial institutions. Its culture was proverbially English and it earned the trust of the common man.

Questions

(a) How important is prudence or commonsense to run a complex business such as derivatives?

(b) Would a common man take the kind of risk that Leeson took with other people's money?

(c) If a bank with over 250 years of experience could not use governing mechanisms, what could be expected of lesser organizations?

---

consequences on the functioning of the markets. How far this effort has borne fruit will be seen as we explore the world of corporate governance.

DEVELOPMENT OF INDIAN CORPORATE GOVERNANCE

It goes to the credit of India that it has not only kept abreast with corporate governance developments in other countries, but has also contributed to the global think tank on various aspects of corporate governance. As it set to reform the economy in 1991, India took advantage of including corporate governance as its fundamental principle of democratic governance. Today, India can be happy about its structural framework in corporate governance. The following institutions are the stewards of corporate governance:

(a) Ministry of Corporate Affairs
(b) Securities and Exchange Board of India
(c) National Federation for Corporate Governance
(d) The Institute of Chartered Accountants of India
(e) The Institute of Company Secretaries of India
(f) Association of Chambers of Commerce and Industry
(g) The Confederation of Indian Industry
(h) Federation of Indian Chambers of Commerce and Industry

Misgovernance and Corruption

Although Indians are considered as shrewd businessmen around the world, they are not viewed as honest. In the post-independence era, business became a synonym for cheating and corruption. The well-known *licence raj* further institutionalized corruption. While private firms paid scant respect to the age-old values of honesty and integrity and fleeced shareholders, investors, employees, and other stakeholders, public sector undertakings, which enjoyed protected and monopolistic positions, carried on with atrocious misgovernance and passed on the costs to customers. Following are some of those unethical practices:

(a) Cornering of industrial licences: *Licence raj* thrived in a commercially insulated and ideologically socialist economy. The industrialists of the private sector soon realized that they could also establish monopolistic positions by cornering licences and thus deprive competitors entry into their areas.

(b) Import licences: The prized licences were import licences that enabled the holders to make quick money.

(c) Money abroad: Money illegally held abroad for investments and business expenses.

(d) Corruption culture: The whole protected economy, coupled with the feudal mindset, contributed to corruption. Donations to politicians, political parties, and government officials became well entrenched as part and parcel of business. This culture still persists two generations down the line after independence.

(e) Tax evasion: Misgovernance led to phenomenal costs, which the government had to recover by levying higher taxes. But corporations found devious ways to evade the same. Thus, compensation packages for the senior and middle managers sky rocketed. Residences, holidays abroad, and even clothing and furniture were shown as being used for work.

(f) Scandals: The securities scam headed by Harshad Mehta, the thousands of crore of rupees lost in the vanishing companies, the plantation scam, the mutual funds scam, and others looted the shareholders and investors to the most intolerable limits.

The reasons for the above unethical practices and the loss of money of the investors were that they happened in an atmosphere that encouraged corruption. Transparency and accountability were shrouded for some obscure reasons of state security and obscurantist philosophy of socialism.

Emergence of Corporate Governance

Unlike in the Western countries, where a strong shareholder activism prompted corporate governance, in India it was a handful of reputed listed companies that took the lead in corporate governance. In 1996–98, the Confederation of Indian Industry (CII) framed a code of governance to be followed voluntarily. In the following couple of years, about thirty Indian listed companies that accounted for 25 per cent of the market capitalization adopted the code. In 1999, the Securities and Exchange Board of India (SEBI) appointed a committee under the chairmanship of Kumara Mangalam Birla to recommend a corporate governance code. By mid-2003, all the listed companies came under SEBI and the code.

The root cause for such a paradigm change in the Indian industry was clearly due to the changed atmosphere of the economic reforms. Companies had to regulate themselves because the shareholder base widened appreciably every quarter. Now investors had voice and it was carried directly and clearly to the corporations. Businesses were growing exponentially and the promoters were losing out on their percentage of shares proportionally. At the same time, investors, both individual as well as powerful institutions, demanded accountability.

The evolution of corporate governance has a very short history, but it has been quite impressive. However, the problem is that SEBI still does not have enough statutory powers to act more decisively and effectively. Table 14.1 shows a list of the evolution of corporate governance codes.

Some Salient Features

The processes of corporate governance ensure adequate disclosures and effective decision making to achieve the objectives of good governance. This consists of a responsible board, which complies with the regulator, protects the interests of shareholders, commits itself to ethical values, and proves that the corporation is a good citizen in society. Thus, in short, a corporation has political (legal), social, and economic responsibilities. We may summarize the following features as a sum of good governance practices desired by the regulator.

Role and powers of the board   The board takes responsibility for the policies and decisions of the company. It clearly identifies roles, responsibilities, and accountability of the directors, executives, and managers.

Table 14.1 Corporate governance codes

Year	Name and description
1998	CII Code on Corporate Governance: The first of its kind in the history of India and a precedent for subsequent reports
1999	Kumara Mangalam Birla Committee on Corporate Governance: Sustainable amendments to listing agreement and safeguards against insider trading
2002	Recommendations of the Naresh Chandra Committee Report on Corporate Audit and Governance: Auditors, independent directors, etc.
2003	Narayana Murthy Committee Report (SEBI)
2004	First National Conference on Corporate Governance Trends in India (Delhi): Under the auspices of the Ministry of Corporate Affairs, CII, ICSI, and ICAI, the National Federation for Corporate Governance (NFCG) was set up
2004	Concept Paper on Companies Bill 2004 (CII): The Companies Act 1956 amended 20 times, hence needed to clear complications
2004	Clause 49 (SEBI): Listed companies with a paid-up capital of Rs 3 crore or more to comply with Corporate Governance Code
2004	Dr J.J. Irani Report on New Companies Act: Structural review of the views of the stakeholders in the development of company law
2004	Review of Companies: Issue of Indian Depository Receipts Rules
2007	Proposed changes in Clause 49 of Listing Agreement
2008	The Companies Bill 2008
2008	The Limited Liability Partnership Bill

Legislation The board must function under the legislative and regulatory framework to render effective governance.

Code of conduct The code of conduct of the organization is issued to all, from the directors to the executives, down to employees and investors. It must be clearly understood by all the stakeholders and there should be a periodic review and evaluation of it.

Board independence Independent and professional governance is the cornerstone for good administration. The board is also capable of objectively assessing the management and the commercial activity of the company. This will help avoid all perceived and real conflicts.

Board skills The board members must possess diverse qualifications and qualities. This makes them an effective and talented team to guide their company. Theoretical, technical, and operational expertise, financial and legal skills, as well as the knowledge of the functioning of the government are assets the board members must possess.

Management environment Where there is a spirit of openness, freedom, and adventure, there is also an environment of high motivation and clear objectives. When a definite direction is given, the company can muster all its resources and even take risks confidently. Following simple but effective ethical standards ensures trusting relationships.

Board positions   Only those people who are highly competent and relevant to the company must form the board of governors. The processes of selection and appointments or reappointments must be strictly adhered to.

Board induction and training   The board members must not only appear to be competent but must be really competent. The directors must be knowledgeable about all the governance issues.

Board meetings   These are forums to discuss and discern and make mature decisions. Both intellectual honesty and personal integrity are important so that the inputs of information help make good decisions. The meetings must be planned, the agenda discussed beforehand, and the minutes maintained professionally.

Strategy setting   The company's short- and long-term strategies must be clearly documented. These must be achievable and must have measureable performance targets and milestones.

Business and community obligations   Corporations are public persons and they cannot function outside of society. In fact, their existence has meaning because of society. The responsibility of the company to society at large can never be adequately underlined. Society must be aware of the company's plans and how it intends to carry them out.

Financial and operational reporting   The regulatory authority SEBI has laid down mandatory and non-mandatory guidelines, which the company must comply with. In order to comply, the board requires comprehensive, regular, reliable, timely, correct, and relevant information, which is qualitatively the finest, so that it may discharge its duty of monitoring and performance appraising.

Audit committee   The audit committee occupies a pivotal position in governance. It is responsible for the examination of the financial health of the company, and monitors the internal auditors. It discharges duties impartially without conflict of interest, and presents an objective picture of the financial status of the company.

Risk management   Business management ultimately boils down to risk management. The procedures must be clearly laid down to identify, analyse, and measure risks. The board is ultimately responsible for all the risks it takes and is answerable to the shareholders.

Thus, good corporate governance aims at not only adding value to the shareholders, but also to other stakeholders. Ultimately, corporate governance is in the best interests of corporations themselves.

ASSUMPTION OF BEST PRACTICES

Corporate governance is a way of business. It is not just business for business' sake, but a profit-driven machine; it is not even a legally driven institution. Trying to make profits and staying overboard with legal situations is business as usual. What makes corporations pursue unusual businesses are the adoption of distinct practices and the development of relationships, wherever and with whosoever business is carried out. The corporation draws policies, which distinguish it over and above the legal compliances required. These practices make it an ethically sound and good corporate citizen in the community, where all its stakeholders feel happy about its existence and continuance. The objective of the following practices is that it should go beyond the obligations of Clause 49 of the market regulator SEBI.

Code of Ethical Conduct

The board of directors is more responsible for the company than all its stakeholders. The board owes its existence to the shareholders and can win their confidence through the disclosures and transparency in operations. For its operation, the board must consist of both directors and independent directors. Its direct responsibility is also towards the management, the audit committee, the employees, the customers, and society at large. For all these constituents to work harmoniously, an ethical culture is important. The board of directors needs to draw up a detailed code of conduct or company

---

Corporate Chimera

Vanishing act

In the pre-corporate governance regime, there was a statutory body called the Controller of Capital Issues. This was abolished in 1992, since SEBI was now the watchdog of the new and reformed capital market. Between April 1992 and March 1996, over 4000 companies registered and raised a phenomenal Rs 54,000 crore from the investors, through public and highbred issues. Another 1500 companies raised an incredible Rs 34,000 crore at a very high premium through rights issues. These companies had a field day. SEBI merely listed them, and the Department of Company Affairs and, later on, the Ministry of Corporate Affairs (MCA) remained the proverbial bystanders. When the investors enquired about their money, the companies had disappeared. Thousands of companies just evaporated into thin air, with loads of real money. The capital market regulator could only list them lamely as vanishing companies.[a] Although the MCA claims that they have identified a few of these companies and prosecutions have begun, it is rather too late and not enough. Knowing the efficiency of the Indian courts, the Indian investor can only blame his/her own fate.

Questions

(a) Why do regulations fail?

(b) Can the law plug all the possible loopholes in the laws it enacts?

(c) How can ethics help?

[a] S. Sivakumar, 'Menace of Vanishing Cos.,' in *The Hindu Business Line*. For full details, see http://www.blonnet.com/iw/2002/07/07/stories/2002070700620700.htm.

ethics. This helps in professionally defining the relationships. Some important points that may help form this code are

   (a) Core organizational values in relationship with all stakeholders
   (b) A history of the equity of the company
   (c) A dividend history of the company
   (d) Human resource accounting
   (e) Brand valuation
   (f) Financial disclosures
   (g) Loans
   (h) Employee welfare
   (i) Women's development
   (j) Environment protection measures

Board of Directors

Corporate governance is fundamentally about the separation of ownership from governance, so that a company may be governed independently of the promoters and professionally in keeping with the best practices. The board of directors that is appointed and confirmed by the shareholders is the highest decision-making body of the company, who is invested with the powers of governance. (See Fig. 14.1.) To facilitate complete impartiality, it is composed of executive and non-executive directors.

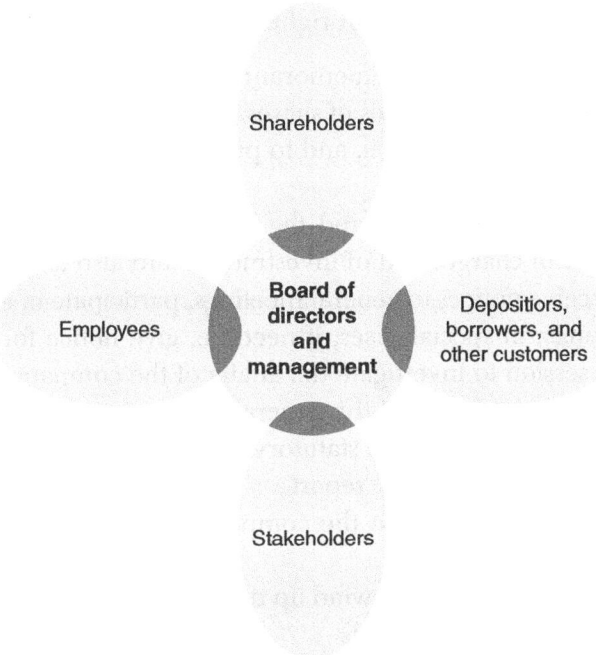

Fig. 14.1   Constituents of a corporation

However, the stakes for the directors are very high and could be easily amenable to malpractices. Certain practices like the ones mentioned below will ensure honesty and transparency:

(a) A manageable size of the board with clear vision and objectives
(b) Competence, diversity of skills, and well-informed board members
(c) Clear and just policies
(d) Transparency in self-remuneration and prohibition of tax-free payments

Management

A corporation is known by its actions. The management keeps an eye on the actions. Apart from professional competencies and duties, there are certain practices that would contribute essentially to the governance of the company:

(a) Responsibility to the board
(b) Protection of company's assets
(c) Scientific management
(d) Employee relationship
(e) Rewards

Protection of Rights and Privileges of Shareholders

The shareholders are the rightful owners of the company in a twofold way—as legislated by the Companies Act and also as signatories to the memorandum or articles of association. The most important rights are as follows:

(a) To obtain copies of the memorandum or articles of association of the company
(b) To obtain the certificates of shares, to transfer them or appeal to the company if aggrieved of their rights, and to preferential right to purchase shares on a pro-rata basis
(c) To inspect the register and the index of the members, their annual returns, register of charges and of investments, and also take extracts from them
(d) To receive notices to general meetings, participate in elections and vote at such meetings; in special cases, if need be, give notice for a general or extra-ordi-nary session to investigate the affairs of the company
(e) To demand minutes of the general meetings
(f) To receive a copy of the statutory report, annual report of the directors, annual accounts, and auditors' report
(g) To make application to the company for relief in the case of oppression and mismanagement
(h) To petition the court to wind up the company's operations and to participate in the company's final assets

Auditing Practices

The objective of the auditing committee is to give accurate, timely, and proper disclosures and transparency of the integrity and quality of financial reporting. Following are some of the important points for good auditing practices:

(a) Composition of the auditing committee
(b) Responsibilities of the committee
(c) Relationship with independent and internal auditors
(d) Disclosure requirements
(e) Meetings and reports
(f) Delegation of authority

Investor Protection

Investor protection is the most important practice for a company to raise money from the capital market. Investors are both institutions as well as individuals. Individual investors are important because they number in hundreds of thousands of ordinary people. When they invest money in companies, they do know that there are risks. Yet, they depend on the competence and reputation of the company when they invest their hard-earned savings and expect the companies to do well and await their rewards in dividends. The trust that the investor has shown must be protected. Strict vigilance, particularly against insider dealings, must be maintained. Transparent and timely information about the behaviour of the investments and the payments of the dividends must be ascertained by

(a) Affirming legal protection to the investor
(b) Ensuring transparency in all dealings
(c) Ascertaining timely payment of dividends
(d) Ensuring through the regulator the veracity of the companies who raise money
(e) Addressing investor grievance at all levels—company, stock-broker, SEBI, Ministry of Corporate Affairs, Reserve Bank of India, and Consumer Courts

Institutional Investors and Bankers

Financial institutions and banks are in reality a collective of the individual investors, where the latter entrust their money to the former. These are financial companies and they must practice corporate governance themselves and safeguard the interest of their customers. The fund managers of these establishments have a special fiduciary duty to represent and uphold the investors' interests. 1n 1998, the Bank of International Settlement, known as the Basil Committee, came out with reforms for banks in the interest of the investors:

(a) Generate economic returns for the owners.
(b) Run day-to-day operations for the investors.
(c) Align corporate activities in alliance with the applicable laws.

Creditors

From a corporation's point of view, investors are the creditors on whom the corporation depends for funds. A system of creditor monitoring control must be set up. The following practices will help create a strong creditor–debtor relationship that is based on the proposed controls:

(a) Information: Lenders, since they are parting with their funds, must have clear information about the debtors, such as their creditworthiness, by knowing the true value of their companies' firm value.

(b) Creditor incentives: The natural incentive is a higher margin of profit. But what makes creditors happy is the high growth of the company and its consolidation in times of intense competition, which ensures long-term relationships between creditors and debtors.

(c) Debt collection: Appropriate legal framework and effective procedures of debt collection are the mechanisms required to monitor and control credit. If debt collection discipline is not inculcated, then creditors will lose faith in the company.

Employees

Corporations are no more profit mills, but rather organizations of the people. Investors are people who make business happen, just like the employees. Maintaining labour relations is the obvious and immediate task. Today, apart from the recognition of trade unions, profit and equity sharing, and team production, the following are also being considered:

(a) Equal opportunities of employment
(b) Model human resource policy
(c) Scientific management planning
(d) Technical and managerial training
(e) Just compensation
(f) Responsive and sensitive systems tailored to the needs of the employees
(g) Employee health, safety, and privacy
(h) Participation in management
(i) Whistleblowing
(j) Ombudsman

To provide the highest standards of openness, probity, and accountability; corporations may appoint ombudsman, who ensure that all employees have the right to express and redress their grievances without fear or compromise of human dignity.

Government

The government is of the people. It is the regulator for the companies that function within the community. It is the government who has established rules and regulations of corporate governance. It is to its regulator SEBI, that the companies have to file their reports. The best practice is that the company attaches a good governance or best practices report along with a mandatory report. In this manner, it gives a voluntary account of itself to the government of the people.

The government expects the following from corporations:

(a) Compliance to the mandatory regulations of the market regulator
(b) Best governing practices report
(c) Due diligence to government monitoring and control
(d) In the event of bankruptcy, takeover of the company by the government, in the interest of the investors and the people

Community

Corporations are a part of the community. Today, well-known corporations have gained their reputation to be so because of their involvement in community building. These acts go beyond philanthropy. The aim of community exercise is not charity, but the empowerment of the people. The corporations work on the following principles:

(a) Respect and dignity for all
(b) Financial responsibility for the community programmes
(c) Concern for the environment
(d) Better social and economic standard of life

Clash of Colonial Cousins

ITC versus BAT

British American Tobacco Company (BAT) is just over a century old. It was founded in 1905. Five years later, it set up a full-fledged Imperial Tobacco Company (ITC) in India that focused on the tobacco business. Its headquarters are in Kolkata. Today, it is one of the most diversified companies, with a turnover of nearly $5 billion.

BAT[a] has a 32 per cent stake in ITC and is the non-institutional shareholder. In March 1995, BAT dropped a bombshell. It demanded the resignation of ITC's CEO, K.L. Chugh. Chugh made the mistake of reporting that BAT was trying to increase its stake in the company in a takeover bid. But BAT clarified and said that the CEO was asked to resign because there were financial irregularities in the company, and that he should resign in the interest of the shareholders and the employees.

Chugh chided BAT for throwing tantrums and said that its real intention was to prevent ITC from diversifying into the energy sector, since it was planning for a takeover. The CEO declared independence in a style worthy of India's freedom movement—ITC does not need BAT.

It is said that the entire crisis ended in a damp squib, as Chugh was pacified with attractive settlements.

Questions

(a) Does the quarrel between these two corporations show immaturity?
(b) What went morally wrong in the relationship?
(c) How should corporations maintain public behaviour?

[a] See 'Ringside View of the Battle' at http://economictimes.indiatimes.com/articleshow/msid-2183724,prtpage-1.cms.

In this manner the best practices should be the best, that is, they must go beyond the prescriptions of the regulatory authority who ask for the good corporate governance report along with other compliances. Although the Indian industry has its ethical problems, it must be acknowledged that it is the efforts and leadership with a public conscience that have initiated these practices in the country. As more and more investors and institutional investors from the public participate in the development of our industries, corporations are increasingly becoming public property. Our idea that corporations are a republic is being actualized on an everyday basis. The greater the participation of the people, the greater will be the responsibility of the corporations towards them.

FAILURE OF CORPORATE GOVERNANCE

From 2008 onwards, we have seen a clear example of not only the failure of corporate governance, but its total collapse due to the financial crisis. Coorporate governance suffered because corporations mistook the shibboleths of responsibility and a list of best practices that were attached to the reports sent to the regulator as corporate governance. It failed because at a time when people needed support and confidence from corporations, the corporations just shirked every responsibility, lay off employees, and let the nation drown in debt. The freedom of free market was abused and credit was allowed to inflate, to make people live beyond their dreams, by creating false dreams and shattering lives for generations to come.

The main reason for the financial crisis has been a lack of transparency and accountability, which are the two pillars of corporate governance. The risk management funding schemes were envisaged without any regulatory mechanism.

Financial Crisis and Banking Blunder

The World Bank[7] says that the financial crisis of 2008 will shrink the world's economy for the first time since World War II. The worst sufferers of the crisis are the developing countries, who are just the bystanders. The developed countries that professed high standards of corporate governance actually conducted very bad business and lost the value of their assets. Their banking failed, the financial bubble burst, their stock markets crashed, recession set in—all because the simple economic principle of living within one's means was abandoned as un-businesslike. It was also because the moral principles of economic life, the principles of creation of wealth, the fiduciary duties towards investors, and, above all, the stewardship of organizations was not taken seriously. Here is what happened:

(a) Banks that supply and manage credit are not only catalysts of industrial development but also corporations in their own right. Hence, they have a solemn duty as mediators between the investors and the business corporations. They

---

[7] CNN, World News, 9 March 2009.

hold the stakes for the customers as well as the entrepreneurs. However, in the 2008 financial crisis, the banks responsible for the crisis just failed to anticipate the bank run, that is, a large number of investors demanded their money back because they thought the bank will fail.

(b) The banks failed to learn from their experiences. The banking failures are phenomenal and yet, with all the modern wherewithal of technology and managerial skills, the banks neglected their fiduciary duty towards the investors. They did not do their basic homework of maintaining reserves. The credit crunch that they themselves created crushed them. Some of these banks are Lehman Brothers, Bear Stearns, Northern Rock, IndyMac, AIG, etc.

Failure of Regulators

The entire financial crisis saw corporations abandoning their investors. Regulatory authorities can only keep a watch over the trends. A regulator cannot regulate the crisis. Regulators from developed countries are quick to point out who failed, but are not taking any proactive action to do something about the market behaviour. The very concept of regulatory authority has suffered an identity crisis due to the following reasons:

(a) A market regulator has three powers—legislative, executive, and judicial. Yet, regulators have failed to take action on short selling and dumping of shares. Even if some people get caught, how have they been treated? Dozens of scamsters, such as Bernard Madoff, who have siphoned away billions of dollars, are some kind of vintage heroes who have outsmarted the system.

(b) Regulators have abdicated their duty to ensure that financial institutions have sufficient assets to meet their contractual obligations through reserve require-ments, capital requirements, and other limits of leverage.

(c) The failure of regulators to take steps against undue risk-taking has been con-sidered as a serious cause for financial crises. The International Monetary Fund feels that there are no adequate safeguards and regulations against risk-taking. This mindset of wanting more regulations for the regulator defeats the very essence of corporate governance, which is supposed to be decrease legislation and increase responsibility, transparency, and compliance.

Failure of Indian Regulator

In the mid-1980s, the Indian capital market picked up appreciably and by 1990, the market was growing even better. As the economic reforms fell into place, a brand new capital market regulator was established. The SEBI was established on 12 April 1992, through an Act of the parliament. Its objective was, 'To protect the interests of investors in securities and to promote the development of, and to regulate the securities market and for matters connected therewith or incidental thereto.'[8]

---

[8] See http://www.sebi.gov.in/Index.jsp?contentDisp=AboutSEBI.

SEBI initiated the following reforms in the capital market:

(a) It abolished capital issues control and retained the sole authority for new capital issues.

(b) It armed itself with adequate powers: legislative—appointing commissions and committees, drafting regulations; executive—conducting investigation and enforcing action; judicial—passing rulings and orders.

(c) It took over the regulation of stock exchanges.

(d) It brought primary and secondary markets under its control.

(e) It enforced that companies disclose all material facts and risk factors while going in for a public issue.

However, every year since its inception, there has been a major financial scam, which has had a ripple effect on the business in the country. For instance in 1999–2000, companies with IT firm-like names came up. They had prefixes or suffixes like soft, info, sys, and tech. People believed that these were highly valued blue-chip companies. Thousands of crore of rupees of gullible investors just vanished with these vanishing companies.

SEBI and some financial market experts think that the regulator does not have enough powers to regulate corporations and demand compliance to corporate governance. With the recommendations of every committee, it manages to get more powers, and yet the scams keep rolling. So, they insist on more regulation and also legislation. Following are some of the weak points of the regulator:

(a) Poor tackling of price manipulation and insider trading

(b) Poor conviction rate against errant market players

(c) Inadequate manpower skills

(d) Excessive regulations—so many that they overlap each other and implementation becomes almost impossible

(e) Low quality of disclosure

(f) Poor grip on IPOs and mutual funds

The problem with SEBI has been its desire to acquire more and more bureaucratic power. Greater legislation and more regulation is proving unhelpful and even contradictory to the purpose of corporate governance. The practice of corporate governance is supposed to initiate and sustain the culture of business ethics. Good corporate governance is a synonym for good business ethics.

Ethics and Corporate Governance

One may safely assert that there are three branches of business ethics—professional ethics, corporate governance, and corporate social responsibility.

(a) Professional ethics: Part I, Part II, and Part III of this book have been devoted to professional business ethics.

(b) Corporate governance: Part IV is devoted to corporate governance.

Human, Only Too Human

The regulator

Sucheta Dalal, an investigative journalist and an expert on Indian capital market, feels that SEBI, the Indian capital market regulator, is selective in its duty.

The story is that on 5 November 2001, Reliance hiked its stake of 4.38 per cent in Larsen & Toubro (L&T) to 10.5 per cent over the next 10 days, till 16 November 2001. The scrip rose sharply from Rs 167 to Rs 209. By some coincidence, Grasim approached Reliance for a possible block sale of shares from the latter. The former's board recorded the deal as being an offer from Reliance. It arranged for a 10 per cent premium for the L&T shares. This pointed out to a transaction due to some prior knowledge. On the appointed day, that is, 16 November 2001, Grasim made an offer of 47 per cent premium, Rs 309 per share to the prevailing market price for a block of 10.05 per cent of the holding of Reliance. On 18 November, the deal was finalized. The investment banker is close to both the parties. Reliance insisted that it had no prior knowledge that the deal would materialize. Dalal, however, thinks that SEBI did not apply the same standard of rule to Reliance and was selective and soft.

Questions

(a) Do bigger corporations have a bigger say in the application of the rules of market regulation?

(b) Is SEBI responsible for the safeguard against insider information?

(c) What is the morality of a prior, mutual understanding that is reached to transact in the capital market?

(c) Corporate social responsibility: The final chapters of Part IV and Part V are devoted to corporate social responsibility and the larger issues of global business ethics.

Ethics is concerned with the cultivation of a morally sound ethos or culture. We need to learn this form of business behaviour not from the West, which has repeatedly failed in ethical responsibility, but from a very successful country in the East: Japan. The Japanese business culture does not depend on overtly legislative and legalistic bodies. It depends on societal values; the way of life and the way of doing business are inclusive. Nothing is businesslike, as it were. Business is not a separate part of life; it is just a part of life. Thus, it would seem that we would have to change our national culture.

SUMMARY

- Corporate governance is about the self-regulation of a corporation.
- Problems in corporations have resulted in setting up self-regulatory systems within the corporation's administration.
- A systematic code of governance emerged in a short period of time during the economic reforms.

- The capital market regulator has legislative, executive, and judicial powers to deal with the problems of the market.
- The recent financial crisis has revealed the shortcomings of corporate governance, and it has revealed the need for a greater accountability.

- Accountability, disclosures, governance, and corporate social responsibility are the pillars for future corporations to build their business.

- The most important factor is to train corporations in adopting and implementing codes of

good conduct and honour ethical values, for no amount of regulation is going to be fruitful unless it is undertaken with the right attitude.

KEY TERMS

Code Clear and unambiguous guidelines for management.

Corruption Dishonest practices, deviation from normal application of rules and receiving of undeserved rewards.

Ethical governance Corporate governance driven with ethical values.

Institutionalization System of adoption and implementation of code of governance.

Reporting practices Mandatory and non-mandatory disclosure rules.

CONCEPT REVIEW QUESTIONS

1. How can you distinguish governance from ethical governance?

2. What lessons do we learn from the emergence of corporate governance code?

3. Are best practices contradictory to ethical practices? Give your reasons.

4. Why do ethical codes fail?

CRITICAL THINKING QUESTIONS

1. What standard of moral judgment is required in good corporate governance?

2. Can a CEO who has no faith in ethical values make a morally right judgment?

3. If there is an adequate code, would ethics be required?

4. If you are CEO of Pepsi Co, what best practices would you adopt?

FURTHER READING

S. Rao Ballabhaneni, *Corporate Management, Governance, and Ethics Best Practices,* John Wiley & Sons (2008).

Hamish McDonald, *The Polyester Prince, The Rise of Dhirubhiai Ambani,* Unwin, Australia (1999).

CASE STUDY

Riddle of Reliance

Acrimony over Corporate Inheritance

This new star, which rose on the horizon of the Indian industry three decades ago, remained on the top till the end by virtue of his ability to dream big and translate it into reality through the strength of his tenacity and perseverance.[a]

—P.C. Alexander, Governor of Maharashtra

---

[a] *Financial Express,* 8 July 2002.

I am confident that both Mukesh and Anil, will resolutely uphold the values of their father and work towards protecting and enhancing value for over three million shareholders of the Reliance Group, which has been the foundational principle on which my husband built India's largest private sector enterprise.[b]

—Kokilaben

Reliance genesis and growth

In 1962, Dhirubhai Ambani started an import business of polyester yarn and called his company Reliance Commercial Corporation, with a capital of a meagre Rs 15,000. In exactly 40 years between its establishment and his death, he had created a corporation that was worth Rs 99,000 crore. Such a wealth creation has never happened in the history of India.

Ambani was always on the move and was constantly in touch with all sorts of people. He had a way of dealing with one and all, from a simple employee to a political big wig. His secret of success was his openness and humility. To put it smartly, he was a business diplomat. His critics accused him of using unfair means to get his work done through bureaucrats and politicians. His supporters felt that he was working in their interest.

Ambani's second secret of success was the timing of risk-taking. He exported spices at a loss, and used replenishment licences to import rayon. When India produced rayon, he exported rayon at a loss and imported nylon. With the imported items heavily in demand, his profit margins soared to 300 per cent under the command economy regime. He was not only a step ahead of his critics, but several miles ahead of his competitors.

In 1977, Ambani ventured into the textile business and the brand Vimal made its own history, an independent story of business success in India. The World Bank certified it as 'excellent even by developed country standards'. In the same year, Reliance's IPO was subscribed by more than 58,000 investors. It was a phenomenon in India's corporate history that the Reliance annual general meetings had to be held in stadiums, and generated greater euphoria than cricket in India. In 1986, Ambani addressed the investor throng at the open grounds, the famed Cross Maidan of Bombay, with an investor crowd of over 35,000 people. Reliance grew at a fast pace and became the numero uno private sector company of India.

The corporate empire of Ambani in 2003, as per *Business Today*, consisted of

- 17 per cent of the total profits of the private sector
- 7 per cent of the entire corporate sector
- 6 per cent of the total market capitalization
- 13 per cent weightage on BSE Sensex
- 10 per cent weightage on Nifty Index

Ambani led a corporate movement. This is the kind of development that India needed in the business world. On 24 June 2002, he died of a heart failure. The funeral was fit for a head of state. Not just the tens of thousands of investors, but the country as a whole paid homage to the Indian corporate patriarch. He truly left behind an empire in every sense of wealth and a shared wealth among thousands of employees and investors. He was survived by his widow Kokilaben, two daughters, and two sons, Mukesh and Anil. The sons carried on his legacy, or rather, they divided it.

Reliance family dispute and demerger

Reliance continued its upward graph in the corporate world, and the investors, buoyed by the booming market as well as the idealism of Ambani, surged ahead. There were some rumours about a tussle between the two brothers. It appears that the tension within the family would burst at any time. It did so when Mukesh, the older sibling, at an unguarded moment, made a passing remark about the ownership issues.

Sparks of accusations flew between the brothers, with the mother caught in the crossfire. There followed a flood of allegations and the one that hit the hardest was that there was no real corporate governance in the company. What was even more unsettling was the revelation that

---

[b] For details, see *Kokila forces Reliance peace*, dated 18 June 2005 in http://www.expressindia.com/news/fullstory.php?newsid=49050.

Ambani had left no will. The investors were flabbergasted. How could such a big entrepreneur leave out such an important detail? Investment experts opinionated that had Ambani made a will, it would have revealed the maze of investments made by him. Hence, Ambani decided to give the will a go-by.

Table 14.2 shows the time-line of the dispute, which gives us a glimpse into the war games of a business empire, concentrated within a single family.[c]

Reliance corporate governance and investor plight

On 15 December 2004, Anil Ambani, the younger brother of Mukesh Ambani, sent a 500-page document to the Reliance Industries Limited (RIL) board of directors, pointing out in detail the corporate governance lapses. This was the oddest thing to happen. Mukesh was the chairman and Anil was the vice-chairman. Anil had blamed his own company, where he was the vice-chairman, of every possible corporate misgovernance—non-disclosures, non-transparency of transactions, cover ups, silence, etc. This was whistleblowing par excellence.

For the Indian public, which is used to serials that are also known as TV soaps, the warring brothers' business battles were a reality stranger than fiction. But it is the investors who waited with bated breaths. Their dilemma and anxiety was indescribable. They felt the brothers did not care about the investors. They realized that Dhirubhai, who had built the business empire, had worked hard for their money. Here were his sons fighting over the ownership of their father's wealth, which in truth belonged to the investors. They questioned about the missing stewardship.

But as has been the case, in reality it was stranger than fiction that the vice-chairman of the board of directors had blown the whistle with such precise and clear infringements against the corporate governance. What the non-existent will could not reveal, the 500-page charge sheet of Anil revealed with every sordid detail about the money and the people behind it. On hindsight, the

investors reviewed the Excellence in Corporate Governance Award conferred on the company by the Institute of Company Secretaries of India (ICSI) in 2003.

All along the troubled path, the RIL governing board worked and performed and passed resolutions as if nothing had happened. One of Anil's supporters observed that there was very little that one person (Anil) could do against the eleven on the board. Anil had questioned the business deals, such as

(a) Non-disclosure of marketing agreement between RIL and Reliance Infocomm

(b) Mukesh's conflict of interest as CMD of RIL, Reliance Communications, and Reliance Infocomm

(c) If one goes on the RIL website, it is clear to the whole world that the independent directors having holdings in the company could never be real

(d) According to Clause 49 Listing Agreement of SEBI, 50 per cent directors have to be independent, which was not the case with Reliance

These and several other issues flouted the practices of corporate governance as per the Listing Agreement.

Reliance settlement and split of shares to the shareholders

With mother Kokilaben and K.V. Kamath, the well-known CEO of ICICI Bank, and a family friend acting as mediators, the brothers came together to accept a settlement. The settlement was arrived at after days of marathon negotiations between the teams representing the brothers. The mother intoned, 'Mukesh will have responsibility for Reliance Industries and IPCL, while Anil will have responsibility for Reliance Infocomm, Reliance Energy, and Reliance Capital. I am confident that both Mukesh and Anil will resolutely uphold the values of their father and work towards protecting and enhancing value for over three million share holders of the Reliance group.'[d]

---

[c] See http://www.rediff.com/money/2005/jun/18ril10.htm.

[d] See http://www.expressindia.com/news/fullstory.php?newsid=49050, accessed on 19 June 2005.

Table 14.2 Ambani versus Ambani

Date	Particulars
18 November 2005	Mukesh Ambani admits to 'ownership issues' in the Reliance group and his differences with Anil
19 November 2005	News surfaces that Dhirubhai did not leave a will
22 November 2005	Mukesh clarifies, says Dhirubhai had settled ownership issues during his lifetime
23 November 2005	Mukesh writes letter to 80,000 employees saying the CMD is the final authority
25 November 2005	Six directors quit Reliance Energy
25 November 2005	Emails show Anil unhappy over clause re-defining Mukesh's powers in 27 July 2005 RIL board meet
5 December 2005	Talk of settlement in the air
6 December 2005	Anil spurns Mukesh's settlement offer
8 December 2005	Anil camp questions ownership claims of Mukesh
10 December 2005	Row over news that Mukesh got 12 per cent stake in Infocomm as sweat equity
15 December 2005	Anil seeks RIL board meet to discuss developments
23 December 2005	Mukesh Ambani gives up sweat equity deal
27 December 2005	RIL says Anil is against the buyback for personal reasons. RIL board backs Mukesh
3 January 2006	Anil quits IPCL board. Blames director Anand Jain for conspiracy to divide the two brothers
5 January 2006	Mukesh accuses Anil of running a malicious campaign against him
7 January 2006	Finance Minister, P Chidambaram advises Ambani brothers to settle the dispute
9 March 2006	Family friend K.V. Kamath, CEO of ICICI Bank completes RIL valuation. Kokilaben holds talks with sons
8 April 2006	Anil complains to the government that his phones are being tapped
27 April 2006	Anil Ambani says its RIL XI versus me; abstains from signing RIL accounts claiming that relevant details and information are missing
28 April 2006	Anil says RIL shares are undervalued and accuses RIL board of rejecting his requests for clarifications at the board meeting. RIL board denies allegation
15 June 2006	Sources say settlement likely on 24 June 2006, on Dhirubhai's death anniversary
16 June 2006	Reliance settlement is most likely to be structured around a demerger. Reliance Industries' stake in Reliance Energy, Reliance Capital and Reliance Infocomm will get de-merged into a separate company
18 June 2006	Under K.V. Kamath's plan and the guidance of the mother of the warring siblings, the ownership issue is settled

Anil Ambani resigned from RIL, and Anand Jain, who was intensely disliked by Anil for being a confidant of Mukesh, was axed from IPCL as a part of the deal. The big Ambani corporate cake was divided among the shareholders:

(a) The firm value stood at Rs 1,00,000 crore.

(b) The flagship RIL's three holdings—Reliance Capital, Reliance Energy, and Reliance Telecom ventures—went to Anil.

(c) The transfer will come about through special purpose vehicles (SPVs).

(d) The RIL shareholders will be allotted shares through SPVs in the same proportion as their holdings in RIL. For every hundred shares held, the RIL shareholder will get five shares of Reliance Capital, seven of Reliance Energy, and a hundred shares of Reliance Communications Ventures Limited, which is a new holding company for its telecom ventures.

(e) The RIL shareholder will also get a hundred shares of Global Fuel Management Services, Anil's proposed project in Uttar Pradesh.

Some felt that Muskesh's side got a better share, while others felt that the new economy's telecommunication had better prospects for Anil.

After eight months of a bitter and open feud between the Ambanis, the investors around the country, who were over 3,00,000 in number, heaved a sigh of relief. The uncertainty was over and the market welcomed it with increased stock value.

Dhirubhai—the beginning

Dhirajlal Hirachand Ambani[e] saw the light of the day on 28 December 1932. His father was a teacher. Early in life, he supplemented the modest family income by selling snacks to pilgrims. At the age of sixteen, he left his country to work in Aden, Yemen. He worked at a gas filling station and became its manager. In 1962, he returned to India and along with his cousin Champaklal Damani sowed the seeds of business.

He had little formal education but his open mind gathered experiences of the world at large, where he learnt all the lessons of life. He married and brought up a family, upholding traditional values. More than his wealth, he gathered wisdom. Some of those gems are here below:

Growth has no limit at Reliance. I keep revising my vision. Only when you dream it you can do it.

Think big, think fast, think ahead. Ideas are no one's monopoly.

Our dreams have to be bigger. Our ambitions higher. Our commitment deeper. And our efforts greater. This is my dream for Reliance and for India.

You do not require an invitation to make profits.

If you work with determination and with perfection, success will follow.

Pursue your goals even in the face of difficulties, and convert adversities into opportunities.

Give the youth a proper environment. Motivate them. Extend them the support they need. Each one of them has infinite source of energy. They will deliver.

Between my past, the present, and the future, there is one common factor: relationship and trust. This is the foundation of our growth.

We bet on people.

Meeting the deadlines is not good enough, beating the deadlines is my expectation.

Don't give up. Courage is my conviction.

Dhurubai's secret to his learning, training, and wisdom was his fundamental principle of open-mindedness. He learnt from every person he met and every situation he experienced. It was from these encounters and experiences that he formed his business theory and put it into practice and created the world of Reliance.

Reliance Reconciliation

The Reliance story lives on. The media sniffed a family reconciliation on the cards. Kokilaben was going to be seventy-five years, an occasion for the family to come together. At a time when corporate mergers made sense, the shareholders couldn't hope for anything less. On 25 February 2009, the family came under one roof with all the who's who of the business, as well as the political establishment, to an invitation that was sent jointly by the Ambani brothers.

Discussion Questions

Investors

1. In the Ambani saga, what are the basic investor-related issues?

2. How are they related to ethics?

---

[e] See http://www.indiaprofile.com/people/dhirubhaiambani.htm.

3. What is the singular ethical issue the investor can fight for?

4. What means can one undertake to rescue investment?

5. Why did the investors not organize themselves to protect their investment?

6. Is it the government's duty to protect the investor?

Indian Family Business

1. On what values is the Indian family business based?

2. What is the ethics of family feuds holding the investors to ransom?

3. What ethical principles are at stake in a family-owned business?

4. What is better, corporate governance of SEBI or a family business based on Indian values of trust?

5. What dangers of Indian family business does the Reliance story expose?

Governance

1. Why is corporate governance required in family-owned businesses?

2. How do best practices of corporate governance promote ethical values in corporations?

3. What is the moral role of the market regulator?

4. Why did SEBI not interfere in the Ambani dispute to protect the investors?

5. What ethical principle should the market regulator follow?

Regulation versus Ethics

1. What is the difference between the rules of the regulator and ethical imperatives?

2. How can the market regulator provide rules for all transactions and monitor every action of corporations?

3. Besides regulation, what else can SEBI do to improve disclosure and compliance?

4. Is regulation self-defeating?

5. What is your advice to the Reliance board of governors, the investors, and the public?

Going Further . . .

Enact a board of governors meeting with complete details:

- Prior to the meeting: Preparation of an agreed agenda
- The board must be consistent in expressing the opinions of executive directors, non-executive directors, independent directors
- Office bearers
- Audit committee
- External observers (optional)

ETHICAL DEVELOPMENT PROGRAMME

Management Training

Quiz

A. Tick right or wrong   (1 × 5)

It is almost a truism that the adequacy and the quality of corporate governance shape the growth and the future of any capital market and economy.

Corporations pool capital from a large investor base, both in the domestic and in the international capital markets. In this context, investment is ultimately not an act of faith in the ability of a corporation's management.

Investors have suffered on account of unscrupulous management of companies, which have raised capital from the market at high valuations and have performed much worse than the past reported figures, or the future projections at the time of raising the money.

Corporate governance is the acceptance by the management of the inalienable rights of shareholders as the true owners of the corporation, and of their own role as trustees on behalf of the shareholders. It is about commitment to values, about ethical business conduct, and about making a distinction between personal and corporate funds in the management of a company.

Corporate governance extends beyond corporate law. Its fundamental objective is not to merely fulfil the requirements of the law, but to ensure the commitment of the board in managing the company in a transparent manner, for maximizing long-term shareholder value.

B. Fill in the blanks with the best option   (1 × 5)

(a) _____ governance is the key element in improving the economic efficiency of a firm.

(i) environmental (ii) fiscal (iii) strategic (iv) corporate

(b) Good corporate governance also helps ensure that corporations take into account the interests of _____ as well as of the communities within which they operate.

(i) a wide range of constituencies (ii) shareholders (iii) stockholders (iv) independent directors

(c) Further, it ensures that corporate boards are accountable to the _____.

(i) shareholders (ii) foreign investors (iii) institutional investors (iv) World Bank

(d) This in turn helps assure that corporations operate for the benefit of the _____.

(i) government as a whole (ii) society as a whole (iii) industry as a whole (iv) business as a whole

(e) While large profits can be made by taking advantage of the asymmetry between stakeholders in the short run, balancing the _____ of all stakeholders alone will ensure survival and growth in the long run. This includes, for instance, taking into account societal concerns about labour and the environment.

(i) interests (ii) payments (iii) dividends (iv) debts

C. Match the following

(1 × 5)

Kumar Managalam Birla Report	Securities and Exchange Board of India
N.R. Narayana Murthy Report	Instituted in 1999, completed in 2000
SEBI	Institute of Chartered Accountants of India
ICAI	Instituted in 2002, completed in 2003

D. Answer in single sentences   (1 + 1 + 3)

The committee noted that accounting policies and principles are selected by a company's management. Consequently, the onus should be on the management to explain why they believe their selection is more representative of the underlying business transactions. The auditor's responsibility is to express a qualification, in case he disagrees with the explanation given by the company's management. The responsibility should not be cast on the auditor to justify such departures from the accounting standard. The members were of the view that the auditor may either concur or disagree with the management's viewpoint. The auditor may draw reference to this footnote without necessarily making it the subject matter of an audit qualification, unless he disagrees with the departure from the accounting standard; in this case, he would be required to issue a qualification.

(a) What is the role of the managers?

(b) What is the role of the auditors?

(c) Do managers and auditors conflict?

E. Classify the functions of the board of directors

The board directs the company by formulating and reviewing the company's policies, strategies, major plans of action, risk policy, annual budgets, and business plans, setting performance objectives, monitoring implementation and corporate performance, and overseeing major capital expenditures, acquisitions and divestitures, change in financial control and compliance with applicable laws, taking into account the interests of the stakeholders. It controls the company and its management by laying down the code of conduct, overseeing the process of disclosure and communications, ensuring that appropriate systems for financial control and reporting and monitoring risk are in place, evaluating the performance of the management, the chief executive, and the executive directors, and providing checks and balances to reduce potential conflict between the specific interests of the management and the wider interests of the company and shareholders, including the misuse of corporate assets and the abuse in related party transactions. It is accountable to the shareholders for creating, protecting, and enhancing wealth and resources for the company, and reporting to them on the performance in a timely and transparent manner. However, it is not involved in the day-to-day management of the company, which is the responsibility of the management.

F. Choose the correct option (1 × 5)

The committee therefore recommends that

(a) The audit committee should have a minimum of three members, all being _____, with the majority being independent, and with at least one director having financial and accounting knowledge.

(a) executive directors (b) non-executive directors

(b) The chairman of the committee should be _____.

(a) independent director (b) not necessarily an independent director

(c) The chairman _____ at the annual general meeting to answer the shareholder queries.

(a) should be present (b) should not be present

(d) The audit committee should invite those executives as it considers appropriate (and particularly the head of the finance function) to be present at the meetings of the committee; but on occasions it may also meet _____ the presence of any executives of the company. The finance director and the head of internal audit, and when required, a representative of the external auditor, should be present as invitees for the meetings of the audit committee.

(a) with (b) without

(e) The company secretary _____ as the secretary to the committee.

(a) should act (b) should not act

Management Mantra

Humpty Dumpty Had a Great Fall: Meltdown of Values

Humpty Dumpty sat on a wall,
Humpty Dumpty had a great fall;
All the King's horses and all the King's men,
Could'nt put Humpty together again.

It is said that nursery rhymes are not as innocent as they sound. They were an indirect criticism of the social issues of the time, because direct criticism of the powers that be would have brought certain death. Fables, parables, and rhymes were the literary forms used to criticize those in authority, such as religious and political figures. However, the above rhyme was supposed to be a critique of society itself. It is said that Humpty Dumpty was, in fact, an egg. It sat on a wall and fell. Nothing could make the egg whole again. And that's where the rhyme ends.

Our values, if ensconced in our hearts, can create a new life. But if we are careless like Humpty Dumpty and make a morally bad decision, we will fall and shatter.

> Mantra *If money is lost, nothing is lost; if health is lost, something is lost; if character is lost, everything is lost.*

(c) The Chairman _____ at the annual general meeting to answer the shareholder queries.
(d) should be present (b) should not be
(d) The auditor or his authorised representative, if any, shall be entitled to attend the general meeting.

CHAPTER
15

Corporate Social Responsibility

The real power of money is the power to give it away.[1]

—Narayana Murthy

Power said to the world, 'You are mine.'
The world kept it prisoner on the throne.
Love said to the world, 'I am thine.'
The world gave it the freedom of her house.[2]

—Rabindranath Tagore

LEARNING OBJECTIVES

After studying this chapter, you will be able to

> Understand corporate social responsibility
> Analyse the moral arguments for corporate social responsibility
> Identify the issues in corporate social responsibility
> Study the development of corporate conscience as the moral principle of corporate social responsibility

INTRODUCTION

Our objectives in this chapter are pointed towards the sharpening of the universal principle of conscience. Conscience is a personal standard of judgment that one develops in the environment of one's own world, with the entire cultural, religious, economic, and political milieu. Corporations too are persons, albeit artificial, but consist of real people and relate to real people. It is within this context that we shall delineate our subject under the four lead concepts mentioned above.

The horrors and excesses of the East India Company, which we earlier glimpsed through the trial of Warren Hastings, should provide all Indians with sufficient

---

[1] See quotes of Narayana Murthy at http://en.wikipedia.org/wiki/Narayana_murthy.
[2] Rabindranath Tagore, *Stray Birds* (1916); http://www.gutenberg.org/etext/6524.

ideological and moral reasons to believe and advocate the philosophy and practice of corporate social responsibility (CSR). For those who have doubts, the following chapter is an endeavour to persuade, not to prove, the validity of CSR.

Below are the parameters and results of a recent Forbes online polling on CSR.[3] The voting issue was: Can public companies save the world?

(a) Yes, through corporate social responsibility programmes. (39%)
(b) Yes, through environmental initiatives. (11%)
(c) Yes, by maximizing profits. (3%)
(d) No, companies are inherently evil. (4%)
(e) No, companies do not have social obligations. (3%)
(f) No, the world's problems are intractable. (2%)
(g) Maybe they can do a limited amount of good. (13%)
(h) They shouldn't try to save the world. (1%)
(i) They already are, by employing people and by innovating. (20%)
(j) I don't know. (5%)

We live in a free and open world where the lenses of TV cameras are omnipresent. Media news teams, constantly competing to be the first to break a story, dig up on everything: from common people's stories to corporate indiscretions. Corporate executives and their lifestyles, employees and their plight, and products and services are under constant media glare. Though corporations will want to only benefit from the media and hide misdeeds, nothing can escape media attention.

A daily dose of corporate news is a part of modern life, as corporations have a tremendous impact on our lives. We depend on corporations, and corporations in turn depend on us. Corporations, however, are manned by people, and we expect these people to behave with conscience, just as we expect our neighbours, friends, or co-workers to do so. The answer to the question, what is a corporation, is then settled. A corporation is a part of our community; it ought to be good citizen. Thus, companies are by the people, for the people, and of the people. Our model of the republic, adapted early in the book, is apt. The republic confers not only rights but also duties, and duties are responsibilities.

CSR is not philanthropy. Philanthropy is almsgiving on a large scale. CSR is taking the responsibility to empower people both socially and economically. Though empowering the people is the responsibility of the government, we must remember that the government is already a republic; it is a corporation at the national level. The government is under the charter of the people, governing the country with the ascent of the people, and business corporations are a part of the larger whole that includes the government. Just as a citizen has duties, so also the group of citizens who form a

---

business corporation has duties. Corporations do not exist in a vacuum. They exist within society and are under the law of the land.

Corporations who advocate that the business of corporations is to seek profits and increase shareholder value do not understand that they have to act like corporations. They have to act like full-fledged members of society, with duties and responsibilities.

The new world needs a new world order. Narrow-minded corporations seeking their own profit cannot survive today's competitive market conditions. Corporations need to be broad-minded and reach out to the communities they function in.

UNDERSTANDING CSR

Corporate social responsibility, though a heavy terminology, is self-explanatory when broken down into individual terms. *Corporate* refers to the corporation, a legal entity created with the objective of profit. *Social* refers to the community of people among whom and for whom the corporation runs its business and depends on for its monetary returns. *Responsibility* is the trait of being answerable.

Definition of CSR

In the above definition of CSR, we could use the terms 'company', 'firm', or 'group' instead of 'corporation'. A business organization with two or more owners can be registered as a company. The organization could start more companies to diversify into other areas of business, and thus form a group. Sometimes the word family is used for a group of companies. Thus, we have the TATA family, the Reliance family, the Infosys family, and the Sahara family. The companies that came into existence later within the group are known as the sister companies. The first company of the group is called the mother company. This demonstrates that corporations unconsciously perceive themselves as a family of people, and function in society accordingly. We may thus define CSR as one's duty towards others.

Let us make the term company more clear. The word is formed from the two Latin terms *cum* and *panis*, and literally means breaking bread. Breaking bread is a figurative phrase for sharing a meal. CSR is precisely that, that is, to share one's wealth with others. For modern corporations, wealth and welfare go hand in hand.

Having understood the contextual meaning of CSR, let us define it as follows:

(a) CSR is the firm's concerning itself with the interests of society.

(b) CSR is the dual duty of a firm towards its shareholders and stakeholders.

(c) CSR assesses the impact of the actions of the company on not only its shareholders, but also its employees, customers, communities, and the environment.

(d) CSR is the moral arm of corporate governance.

Conflicting Outlooks on CSR

Corporate governance serves the shareholders as well as the stakeholders. The role of the shareholders is quite obvious, whereas the stakeholders are often questioned as to why they should be treated at par with the shareholders. However, without the stakeholders, the logic of business is futile. For, the stakeholders are the employees, the suppliers, the marketers, and the customers; and all of them, including the shareholders, form the community. If the community at large is served, the company has the benefit of serving its shareholders, immediate stakeholders, and distant stakeholders.

Shareholder outlook   Conservative thinkers such as Milton Freedman strictly follow the theory proposed in *The Wealth of Nations* by Adam Smith, and propose that the business of business is business. The only business of a corporation is to perform its fundamental duty, which is to conduct business efficiently and justify it with profits, which is the return on investments of the shareholders. The best form of CSR for a company is to provide the best of products and services to its customers. It is wise to leave social duties to those who are entrusted with it, such as the government and other institutions within the community. Business institutions should not meddle in the business of others. Adam Smith's view was that a business entrepreneur puts to work his capital, with his own interests in mind. He actually does not know how beneficial he has been to the people at large, but what he does know is how secure his interests are. He works on the givens of the market and the price, and becomes a part of a phenomenon in society, of which he has no idea. It is possible that good things may happen because of his activity, but that was not his direct intention.

Stakeholder outlook   In contrast to the above view, what we must realize is that we have come a long way in history since Adam Smith's world and the guidance of the 'invisible hand'. The law of reason tells us that if things happen, they do happen for a reason. All human activity has a moral dimension because they proceed from one's intentions or free will. Business decisions are highly moral decisions, as they affect the lives of people.

We must also realize that we have travelled a long way from the pure agency theory. Presently, what is essential for corporations is accountability. Profitability is a very narrow view of business, and that businesses must be measured by their profits sounds crude unless those profits are utilized in the larger interest of society. Business corporations must realize that not-for-profit organizations are increasing in numbers all around the globe and are generating more wealth than corporations. Not-for-profits are profitable to their management, employees, suppliers, and the receivers of their products and services. Not-for-profits are also in the same business as for-profits, such as manufacturing, co-operative banking, healthcare, and education. Hence, when corporations are pointed out their duties in society, they cannot afford to say that their business is to only run a business. In the new world order, everyone is in some business, whether profit-oriented or not. Stakeholdership is the new principle of business operation.

Use and Abuse of Water

Coca-Cola

In India, the brand Coca-Cola has suffered for years because it is mired in controversy with the farmers of Kerala. The company has been accused of not only the abuse of water, but of large-scale environmental damage and water shortage.

Now the company is running programmes such as Jal Yatra, Jal Bima Abhiyan, and Jal Sanchay Ahbiyan, which translate to 'movement for water,' 'water insurance,' and 'water conservation movement,' respectively. Ever since R.K. Pachauri's Intercontinental Panel on Climate Change won the Nobel Prize, there is an increased consciousness in the Indian companies, to conserve water. The Confederation of Indian Industry has encouraged programmes on water management. The Coca-Cola initiative is one of them.

The situation is really alarming. India's per capita water availability has slid from 5000 cubic metres per annum in 1950 to less than 2000 cubic metres at present. The industrial use of water has been quite pathetic when it comes to effluents. The industries on the banks of the river Yamuna are an example of how these effluents are causing damage to the celebrated Taj Mahal.

The problem now is that water itself is scarce. Atul Singh, the President and CEO of Coca-Cola, India, says, 'We at Coca-Cola are committed to refresh the lives of communities on an everyday, all day basis. As part of the same strategy, sustainable water management remains our top priority. We will continue to find innovative solutions in all areas of water management through our integrated 4R strategy—reduce, recycle, reuse, and recharge.'[a] The time, as well as the water, is running out.

Questions

(a) Why is the abuse of water wrong?

(b) How is ethics relevant to conserving water resources?

(c) What more can the companies do to restore this most important resource?

---

[a] See http://www.business-standard.com/bs_csr/news.php?autono=303353.

MORAL ARGUMENTS FOR CSR

We cannot see the woods for trees when we are bombarded with the imperatives of CSR. The entire media appears to come down on those companies who are not known much for CSR. Corporations, it appears, are sometimes forced into CSR because insiders and strategy consultants tell them that it is in vogue, and it is a very good strategy. If Bill and Melinda Gates have gone in for founding the largest non-profit foundation for healthcare, then others cannot be left behind. The CSR activities of the company make those CEOs who pout the mantra of 'giving back to society' highly visible. Then, there are impressive and famous foundations such as Ford and Carnegie, and, in India, the Birla trusts, the TATA charitable institutions, etc. However, for-profit institutions are a *sine qua non* for the economic well-being of a society. All these catapult the corporations as 'good corporate citizens'. Can there be a reasonable and convincing argument in favour of CSR in such a confused scenario? Let us now discuss why CSR is relevant, and therefore desirable.

CSR is natural   There is a relationship of dependence between corporations and communities. Corporations are, in fact, creatures of the community. Corporations are formed and given a legal existence through real persons, who have also made sure that the corporations will have permanency of existence beyond the biological lives of its members. Therefore, it behoves that corporations work naturally for the community. Thus, CSR is a natural response to the community.

Profit is no sin   In general, the perception that is steeped with socialistic ideology or some religious ideology that profits are inherently bad is an untenable argument. If wages can be just and moral for the worker, and rent to the property owner, then profits are just rewards for the investor's capital. After all, the capital is earned by its owner. Further, it takes all the skills of the entrepreneur and an enormous risk to venture into business. In this way, profits are just and fair rewards.

The egalitarian ideal   If business has to grow, it needs investment. Future investments come from profit, loans, and borrowings. It is fair to reward shareholders. However, with growth in business, it is possible for corporations to participate in community building, and this egalitarianism creates a social market economy.

CSR as Duty

Corporations cannot say that their business is only to attend to their own business and earn profits for shareholders. It is the community that supplies the infrastructure, employees, and security (by the police), legal protection, and several other services, both tangible and intangible, and corporations cannot ignore this fact. On the contrary, corporations are guilty of misusing natural and human resources, polluting the environment, and causing various crises in society. It is the duty of corporations to mitigate the damages that they have done, stop perpetrating further damage to the environment, give equal pay for equal work without gender discrimination, maintain safety and security at the workplace, and maintain confidentiality. These are the first and essential duties of CSR. Further, though philanthropy and social work are welcome, it is a good CSR programme that will help corporations reap rich rewards by building a better brand, perhaps at costs lesser than what is spent on advertising and marketing. Thus, CSR is not a favour done to society. It is a bounden duty to be performed.

CSR with Conscience

People live by their conscience. Corporations, which are associations of the people, have a collective conscience, whereby all their decisions express this moral quality. Thus, for instance, letting out untreated effluents, paying unjust wages, rigging the price, giving false information, deceiving the market regulator, etc. are sins against conscience. In a similar fashion, the behaviour in the community exhibits the conscience of corporation. CSR is a visible image of the conscience of the corporation.

Conclusion: One Ethics for All

Corporations are no exceptions to morality. They cannot have a separate set of moral rules. The only difference between individual human beings and corporations is that the latter bear an even greater and collective responsibility for their actions.

Corporations with CSR show that they are conscious about the community they live in. Since they have both collective manpower, as well as economic strength, they could take up leadership roles in society and become motivators for the people in the common mission of a better life for all.

Thus, CSR makes companies realize the common good. It is this sense of common good that makes us human beings and gives us a broader vision to understand and solve human problems.

ISSUES IN CSR

Peter Drucker had predicted that the twenty-first century would belong to the social sector organization. The financial crisis of 2008 has taught the world a hard lesson for not taking sufficient interest in the social economy. It is due to the work of the social service organizations, non-governmental agencies, and not-for-profit organizations that there is some sense of sanity in the world, and people are able to cope with crises. Now there are some more positive signs. Corporate governance is taking hold, and a more active CSR will help in all the issues that humanity faces—from environmental problems to healthcare, from employment to standards of living.

Tsunami

TVS and CSR

TV Sundaram Iyangar & Sons[a] is more popular by its acronym TVS. This very old company founded in 1929 has a special place in the hearts of the people of Tamil Nadu because of the company's social engagement even before the more fashionable CSR came on the scene. The Srinivasan Service Trust (SST) is the social arm of the company. Tsunami relief is just one example of its social work.

On 26 December 2004, a disastrous tsunami hit the East Coast of South India, causing inestimable damage to life and property. SST swung into action immediately.

The company took in its fold about 15,000 people for relief, food, and medicines. Medical aid was rushed to the four affected districts and volunteers and professionals worked to give succour to the hungry and the sick. The company also provided for sanitary facilities.

The company has further mooted a plan for the long term development of villages. It has adopted a number of villages for the purpose.

Questions

(a) What is wrong if companies take up CSR to build their brands?

(b) What makes an action moral, the intention or the end result?

(c) A company is not a real individual who can feel good or bad. Who then enjoys the moral dividends or desserts of CSR?

[a] See http://www.tvssst.*org*.

Trusteeship

A corporation is created under a trusteeship. Individual shareholders are not the owners of a corporation as in the sense of owning a private property. The law has it that shareholders are merely residual claimants. Moreover, managers are not agents of shareholders, but rather stewards who exercise fiduciary duty. Thus, the idea of trusteeship adopts a realistic philosophy of the corporation as a social institution.

A corporation is a public person. When a corporation fails, it is the public that takes it up as its own and saves it. We have seen in numerous instances of financial crises around the world how governments have rallied and tried to save corporations with tax payers' money. If the respective communities had also adopted a hardened attitude that the business of business is to do profitable business only, these corporations would have folded up immediately. The shutdowns would have been disastrous, leaving employees with no shelter or livelihood. Hence, corporations are social institutions and ultimately belong to the people, who rescue them with their hard-earned money. Hence, CSR is not charity done by corporations to the community. It is fair to say that it is the community that shows charity towards corporations.

Corporate Governance

The issue of trusteeship logically leads to good corporate governance. Corporate financial scandals can seriously hurt the stakeholders. People expect corporations to be mature, responsible, transparent, and accountable. Just as ordinary citizens serve the country in myriad ways—electing a government, and demanding accountability from it, paying taxes and taking care of the entire country and its needs, from economics to defence, from health and education to cultural activities—so too corporations should serve the community. Corporations do no one a favour by being good corporate citizens. It is their duty to do so, and corporate governance is a worthy instrument to do it with.

CSR and State Partnership

Non-governmental agencies are citizens' initiatives to help the government with the ever-growing range of social issues. Similarly, there are working partnerships between the government and the corporations who form CSR foundations and help the social causes of the people.

The Infosys CSR case at the end of the chapter shows us a good example of state–corporation partnership. Government hospitals get annexes and modern equipment donated by corporations. Likewise, school libraries get refurbished, mid-day meal programmes supported, rehabilitation of people in times of disaster coordinated, and several other social causes supported. Such cooperation between corporations and the government will double up the efforts and bring speedy solutions.

CSR and Citizen Partnership

Similar to the partnership between the state and the corporations, partnerships have been formed between NGOs or non-profit organizations and corporations for effective solutions in healthcare, education, and women's empowerment. Poverty and the illiteracy of the masses in India have presented corporations with a challenge. They see an opportunity for the future in this challenge: it is from these masses that more corporations will arise, more human resources will be created, and a better world will be formed.

There is now a positive trend in India, where we see that all corporations, whether big or small, have some item of CSR on their agenda. The idea that shareholders will grudge a portion of the profits that will go towards these activities is outdated. Investors are happy that their firms are taking a leadership role in society on their behalf.

CSR Trends in India

'Wealth is not to be earned for the purpose of self-indulgence or for satisfaction of greed. Wealth should be treated as the citizen's instrument of helpfulness. The word is not just helpfulness but helpfulness combined with a sense of duty' said Thiruvallvar, India's ancient sage, in his work *Kural*, which is considered as one of the best guides to the art of living. In 2001, the Tata Energy and Research Institute (TERI) undertook a survey of CSR in India. It found that Indian corporations were quite spirited about community services, although their models were different. Some had adopted the Gandhian method of voluntary commitment to welfare, particularly rural welfare. Others were more statist, like Nehru, for a centralized model. Some corporations were quite conservative and insisted that good business is CSR. An overwhelming majority were for the stakeholder model. The following were the main concerns expressed by all the corporations:

(a) Environmental pollution
(b) Good quality products and services at affordable prices
(c) Faith in the NGOs to carry out the work of welfare

Triple Bottom-Line Approach to CSR

One of the most recommended approaches to CSR is the triple bottom line (TBL). This was proposed by John Ellington in 1997, and is known by its acronym TBL. Previously, there was only one bottom line for corporations, to reap profits for shareholders. But CSR has three of them—shareholders, environment, and social. Thus, there came the system of environmental management, which has taken the central role in industry and social auditing. Now there are parameters on which companies can measure themselves for CSR and its reporting practices. In this manner, corporations are encouraged to be members of the community and responsible citizens.

Good Citizens

Companies known for CSR

It is not possible to recount the CSR performances of every company. However, a short list of the following companies with their special thrust encourages us to know that CSR is not just a gimmick. It has come to stay as a part of the companies' culture.

Company	CSR
Asian Paints	Local resource management for farming communities
BHEL	Rural health and family welfare
Brooke Bond	Veterinary services
Colgate Palmolive	Sports
Escorts Ltd	Agricultural development
SAIL	Dairy, poultry, and fisheries development
Tata Steel	Rural industrialization

Questions

(a) What is the difference between social work and CSR?

(b) If so many companies are doing so much good, why do we not see any difference in the lives of the people?

(c) How ethical is the diversion of funds for CSR?

DEVELOPMENT OF CORPORATE CONSCIENCE AS MORAL PRINCIPLE OF CSR

It is puerile to define conscience as an intermittent inner voice that declares us guilty on hindsight, when we have done something wrong. It is equally puerile to state that conscience is an inbuilt moral cop waiting to catch us if we falter. It is also negative to say that conscience is an unbending normative faculty that society cleverly uses to subjugate its people.[4]

Conscience is a faculty that represents the nature of a person in his/her voluntary actions. It is a moral compass that each person develops in a given social environment, where he/she learns to live and become conscious about the deliberate choices to be made while journeying through life, building and understanding human relationships,[5] realizing the fundamental values of truth, trust, compassion, justice, and the like, and being sensitive to issues concerning general human conditions. It concerns all our voluntary actions, actions for which we are responsible, and such responsibility is fulfilled through a steady development of moral actions, which form in us good habits. Habits are those repeated acts, which when repeated as often as possible, become

---

[4] 'Morality is the best of all devices for leading mankind by the nose,' Friedrich Nietzsche, nineteenth-century German philosopher.
[5] 'The first step in the evolution of ethics is a sense of solidarity with other human beings,' Albert Schweitzer, early twentieth-century German Nobel Peace Prize-winning mission doctor and theologian.

second nature. This second nature can be safely called the formation of a good conscience. The formation of a good conscience goes through an empirical process of learning, development, and progress, depending on the demands made on it. With a well-formed conscience, a person does not need to go through the arduous tasks of deliberation in each case, amid difficult moral choices. Thus, it becomes clear that good education in moral values is a precondition for a well-formed conscience. It epitomizes fundamental values existing in our society and demands the practice of those values that represent individual character on a daily basis. Individuals reflect upon what kind of persons they ought to be, what goals merit pursuit, and how they should relate to other people. In a specialized world, people obtain competence in their chosen fields and become professionals, whether in academics, science, business, or any other vocation of life. These professionals bear even greater responsibility to understand the ethical and legal requirements of their chosen profession, and become prudent in making their choices, and perceptive in recognizing and resolving ethical conflicts.

We have advocated conscience as one of the standards of moral judgment. For professionals, conscience is a constant and personal guide. Conscience is the moral system that we build within us as we grow up in a multilayered environment. Its judgment is indeed very subjective. Though peculiar to a person, it reflects what is objectively acceptable or not acceptable in society. Hence, it is an objective judgment because society has first influenced it. It is subjective because an individual makes it. It is again objective because the person is a part of the society from where the knowledge of such judgments has come. Corporations are also guided by the people whose decisions represent the minds of the corporations. Thus, corporations are capable of making conscientious judgments. Let us delineate the corporate conscience.

Corporate Conscience

Do corporations have a conscience that can be mapped through their words? *The Financial Times* of 20 April 2002 had the following title for its editorial: 'corporate social responsibility—CII and FICCI must speak out on Gujarat'. The alleged silence of the Confederation of Indian Industry and the Federation of Indian Chambers of Commerce and Industry corroborated the general belief that corporations care more about profits than people. The editorial noted that although on a personal score, the tycoons of the industry were perturbed, they did not want to make their feelings public.[6] Obviously, they did not want to displease their political bosses, with whom

---

[6] Industry bore the brunt of the columnists like their political godfathers with thick hides, 'Narendra Modi has made himself an accomplice in the carnage that followed Godhra through his unsympathetic statements in the press... By defending him in Parliament, L.K. Advani has also made the Centre an accomplice in the Gujarat killings...Not the Centre, not the state, not a single political party, not a single industry association has even thought of setting up a relief fund to which concerned citizens can contribute to facilitate their rehabilitation. With such callousness at home, we will soon not need Pakistan or Kashmir to breed our terrorists for us.' Prem Shankar Jha, columnist, in *The Hindustan Times* (15 March 2002).

they dined and wined and did business. The paper was concerned. 'After all, business has been hurt badly in Gujarat. Not only has it been directly hurt by the targeted destruction of shops, factories, and work premises, but also by the reckless looting of shops and the prolonged imposition of curfew thereafter, in many parts. Political parties have protested; the media has spoken its mind out; non-governmental organizations have been pro-active. Surely it is time for the corporate sector to do its bit too.' When fingers were pointed at the industry, and thousands of crores of rupees of business was lost, they took some notice and issued protest resolutions; otherwise, it was business as usual.[7] The Gujarat carnage, sparked by the Godhra railway arson, and the dereliction of the CSR by the industry, amply exhibited that Indian corporations lacked conscience.

Negligence of Conscience Leads to Moral Degradation

In the history of corporate negligence and the loss of conscience, there has been an instance of unparalleled proportions: the 1984 Union Carbide gas leak that caused the Bhopal tragedy. The industrial disaster, also termed as the 'chemical Hiroshima', killed over 10,000 people overnight. It is still festering, and even after nearly two decades, tens of thousands of people are suffering, to the extent that even the mothers' breast milk contains toxins. The Bhopal gas tragedy is a monument of discredit to a corporate with a decrepit and deplorable conscience.

Each and every corporate house in India wastes reams of paper and thousands of web pages on mission statements and adherence to high values, gender equality, empowerment, dignity of labour, and high standards of quality, but cannot listen to its own inner voice to protest against the injustice done to people, the very same people who are the stakeholders—the employees, investors, and customers at large. It is a great social concern that the executives being churned out from reputed business schools lose the voice of their conscience as money starts to jingle in their pockets. They are in competition to climb the corporate ladder in quick time.

Corporate Governance with Conscience

One of the concrete evidence of governing with a conscience is to possess CSR. In a recession-ridden economy, and in the midst of globalization, competition, challenging corporate governance reforms, pressures of performance, etc., CSR is the last thing on the board of directors' agenda. But Rajat Gupta, the managing director of McKinsey & Company, and Paul Coombes, the Director of Corporate Governance Practice at the same agency, think otherwise. In their combined research work *Accentuating the Positive*,[8] they call for a change in corporate priorities: 'Corporate social

---

[7] The captains of industry also had elaborate dinner diplomacy in the capital—*India Inc. takes Modi out to dinner* 15 April 2003, Times News Network.
[8] Rajat Gupta, *Accentuating the Positive.* For more details, visit http://www.mckinsey.com/knowledge/articles/pdf/Coombesv2.pdf.

responsibility should not be simply a reactive affair. Companies should become more proactive in engaging NGOs and other organizations in full debate, and promote the positive aspects of their agendas.' In their research, they account for five major developments in favour of CSR:

(a) Globalization, whose consequences in view of the estimated power and reach of the MNCs is immense.
(b) Failures of governments to respond to the challenges of their models, to supervise the growing corporate power, and to check environmental issues.
(c) End of the non-market economies and generation of 'failed states'.
(d) The growth of the power of NGOs and pressure groups.
(e) The power of communication and provision of instant information through the Internet.

What these researchers try to establish here is that the classical corporate responsibility fulfilled through philanthropy along the lines of Cadburys, Rowntrees, Fords, Rockefellers, Tatas, Wipros, and Infosys is not enough. Dolling out largesse is no more impressive. The priorities at the global level have changed to human rights, labour practices, and the environment. MNCs that thrived on brandishing their brands have to think twice, since global activists have started anti-branding campaigns and have made global corporations extremely vulnerable. In fact, philanthropy performed with the best of intentions can be misunderstood as brand campaigning.

In January 2009 when McKinsey & Company's great leader Marvin Bower died at the ripe age of ninety-nine, the *New York Times* called him 'a pioneering consultant steeped in ethics'.[9] His company, which he preferred to call a 'firm', conducted business as a 'practice' and job as an 'engagement' and bears witness to the fact that the character of a company makes it what it is. It is no wonder that they called him 'the father of the consulting profession', for he excelled in selling corporate advice as a fine art of human endeavour in education and was a living lesson on conscientious corporate governance.

The need of the hour for the corporations is not to jump on the bandwagon of philanthropy and have the 'give back to society' banner emblazoned across the offices in the country. Charity begins at home, and so do education and the other values that go with it. The first priority of corporations is, therefore, to establish sustained value education and its implementation within their corporate environment.[10]

---

[9] Douglas Martin, *The New York Times*, 24 January 2003.

[10] The new entrants on the philanthropy banner are Infosys and Wipro. Both are dedicating about 1 per cent of their income to rural education, which is laudable. However, the point here is that there must be in-house training of one's own employees. See *Business Standard Billionaire Club* at http://www.businessstandard.com/special/billion/year2001/billion15.htm.

Thirukural

A Guide to Corporate Conscience Formation

Sri Thiruvallvar is an ancient Tamil poet (2nd century BC) who is revered by Indians in general and Tamils in particular as a prophet and guide for practical life. His immortal work *Thirukural*, meaning the sacred writing, consists of 133 chapters known as *athikarma*, divided into three main themes: conscience (*Aram*), facts of life (*Porul*), and man-woman relationship (*Inbam*). Today, there stands a statue of Sri Valluvar in Kanyakumari, 133 feet tall with three outstretched fingers, symbolizing his work. Following are some select verses from Thirukural:[a]

Virtue yields heaven's honour and earth's wealth. What is there then that is more fruitful for a man? (*Verse 32*)

He who understands his duty to society truly lives. All others shall be counted among the dead. (*Verse 215*)

Among the wealthy, compassionate men claim the richest wealth, For material wealth is possessed by even contemptible men. (*Verse 242*)

The supreme principle is this: Never knowingly Harm anyone at any time in any way. (*Verse 318*)

All knowledge acquired through the five senses is worthless To those without knowledge of truth. (*Verse 355*)

Learn perfectly all that you learn, and Thereafter keep your conduct worthy of that learning. (*Verse 392*)

The wise never undertake an enterprise Which rashly risks existing capital to reach for potential profits. (*Verse 464*)

Employ those men who discern the good and the bad effects In every undertaking and choose the good. (*Verse 512*)

Those who possess persevering industry Will never say in despair, 'We have lost our wealth.' (*Verse 594*)

When a decision is reached, deliberation ends. To delay that decision's execution is detrimental. (*Verse 672*)

Wealth that is acquired by proper means in a manner That harms none will yield both virtue and happiness. (*Verse 755*)

The world goes on because civilized men exist. Without them it would collapse into mere dust. (*Verse 997*)

Strangers will one day seize his wealth, who, To pile it high, preferred self-denial, forsaking love and dharma. (*Verse 1010*)

Questions

(a) Are the above principles practical for corporations?
(b) How to form a good conscience?
(c) Why conscience is important for civic life?

[a] P.S. Sundaram (tr), *Thiruvalluvar. The Kural*, London: Penguin, 1990; also available at http://www.a1tamilnatu.com/images/kural.pdf.

SUMMARY

- Social responsibility is a community duty.
- Corporations, being persons or citizens of the community, take upon themselves to be responsible towards the community.
- CSR is not philanthropy. It is a commitment to the community for the empowerment of its people.
- CSR is participating in the common good and contributing towards it through active participation.

- Acceptance of CSR has dislodged the old view that businesses are only concerned about earning profits for the shareholders.
- The broad view of CSR is that companies have a duty to perform in the society they function in.
- The moral values of conscience, duty, equality, and freedom that are present in society are sufficient reasons for CSR.
- The fundamental issue in CSR is trusteeship of the community.

- Corporations must develop a good conscience, which is the true source of motivation for CSR.

- The development of corporate conscience must be deliberate so that companies are constantly aware of their duty to society.

KEY TERMS

Common good   The good of a community.

Conscience   Individual sense of right and wrong.

Development of conscience   Nurturing and upbringing of a person in good values.

Egalitarian   Concerning equality among human beings, non-discriminatory.

Good   Ethical excellence of human action.

Mapping the conscience   Ethical analysis of one's words and actions.

Philanthropy   Money given away in charity.

Social responsibility   Duty towards society.

CONCEPT REVIEW QUESTIONS

1. Why must companies adopt CSR?
2. What are the main issues in CSR and how can these be tackled?
3. How can companies become sensitive towards the community?
4. What duties does a company have when the community faces problems of strife?

CRITICAL THINKING QUESTIONS

1. How can you convince a CEO about CSR with moral arguments?
2. Of what benefit is CSR to a company that does not honestly believe in its inherent goodness?
3. Do moral arguments have an effect on the people you want to convince about CSR?
4. Is corporate conscience a relevant subject? Examine it critically.
5. Is conscience a reliable guide?

FURTHER READING

Philip Kotler and Nancy Lee, *Doing the Most Good for Your Company and Your Cause,* John Wiley & Sons, (2004).

Thiruvallvar, *Kural,* translated by C. Rajagopalachari, Bharatiya Vidya Bhavan. *Kural* is also available at: http://acharya.iitm.ac.in/mirrors/vv/literature/tirukkural/kuralint.html.

CASE STUDY

Wealth for the People
Infosys, the Most Admired Company

In life's journey, we all meet strange people and undergo many experiences that touch us and sometimes even change us. If you have a sensitive mind, you will see your life too in the vast storehouse of stories. For me, it is something closest to my heart. Initially, I was a mother to it but somewhere along the line, it has become the mother and I the child.[a]

—Sudha Narayana Murthy

---

[a] Sudha Narayana Murthy, founder Infosys Foundation, in an interview with CNBC on 12 June 2007. The interview is available at http://www.rediff.com/money/2007/jun/12sudha.htm.

Part I

Wealth with Values

Seed

Narayana Murthy, an electrical engineer, was working at Patni Computer Systems when he met Sudha, also an electrical engineer, who was working at the Tata Engineering and Locomotive Co. Ltd in Pune. It was sometime in the mid 1970s. They got married on 10 February 1978. Murthy expressed his desire to found an IT company. Sudha's money, Rs 10,000, was the only money with which Infosys saw the light of day. The rest, of course, is history. Even earlier on in Pune, when they used to meet and go out together, Murthy never seemed to have money to pay for the restaurant bills. Sudha recalls that he had asked her to keep an account. The total amounted to Rs 4000. She says that she tore up the account sheet after their marriage.[b]

Growth

Seven men, namely, N.R. Narayana Murthy, Nandan Nilekani, N.S. Raghavan, Kris Gopalakrishnan, S.D. Shibulal, K. Dinesh, and Ashok Arora incorporated their company as Infosys Consultants Pvt. Ltd, with Sudha's loan. The registered office was at Raghavan's house in Matunga, Bombay.

The tree grew well, branched out, and bore fruit millions of times over, with Sudha's loan.[c] Table 15.1 lists the key milestones in the company's growth.

Secret of success

In an interview,[d] Murthy spelt out the secret of Infosys' success. He enumerated five points:

1. Openness to learn: Openness to subordinate your ego, to take ideas from others.
2. Meritocracy: The best ideas are adopted and implemented using data, to arrive at the best decision.
3. Speed: Assuring to do things faster, compared to yesterday and the last quarter.
4. Imagination: To continually bring better ideas and better innovation to the table.
5. Excellence in execution: Implementation of these great ideas with a higher level of excellence today, than was done yesterday.

Wealth creation for shareholders

Murthy said, 'Our assets walk out of the door each evening. We have to make sure that they come back the next morning.' Right from its founding days, Sudha Murthy's invisible mark was visible to all. The spirit got translated into the vision of the company, which was to be the best commercially and also ethically.

Founded on ethics

(a) Customers: Delight of the customer, surpassing one's expectations
(b) Leadership: Precedent rather than prescription
(c) Ethics: Integrity and transparency
(d) Fairness: Business based on trust and earned respect
(e) Excellence: Relentless pursuit of quality

Sudha once reported that, while watching a movie, her husband was restless and kept telling her about how the quality of production could be improved.

Governance

It is a well-known fact that Murthy was tasked by SEBI to chair the committee on corporate governance. The market regulator wanted to formally introduce the ethical principles that Murthy had practised at Infosys into Clause 49 of the Listing Agreement. The corporate governance at Infosys has been exemplary:

(a) Clear and transparent information to shareholders and stakeholders. The Infosys report has been benchmarked by the Securities Exchange Commission of the US.
(b) Timely declaration of dividends has made the shareholders happy beyond their expectations.

---

[b] 'The Amazing Story of Infosys' is available at http://specials.rediff.com/money/2006/jul/11sld3.htm.
[c] For timeline, see http://en.wikipedia.org/wiki/Infosys_Foundation.
[d] See Narayana Murthy's five tips to success at http://in.rediff.com/money/2006/jun/21murthy.htm.

Table 15.1 Infosys's growth

Dates	Details
1981	Founded: Pune/Bombay (now Mumbai)
1983	Moved the headquarters to Bangalore
1987	First foreign client: Data Basics Corporation, US
1992	First overseas office: Boston, US
1993	Listed. Initial public offering of Rs 13 crore
1996	First office in Europe: Milton Keynes, UK
1997	Office: Toronto, Canada
1999	First Indian company to be listed on NASDAQ
2000	Offices in France and Hong Kong Padma Shri, the civilian award of India, to N.R. Narayrana Murthy
2001	Offices in United Arab Emirates and Argentina
2002	■ Offices in Holland, Singapore, and Switzerland ■ Named as 'India's Most Respected Company' by *Business World* ■ Progeon, a business process outsourcing subsidiary is founded
2003	100 per cent acquisition of Expert Information Services Pvt. Ltd, Australia, and changed into Infosys Australia Pvt. Ltd
2004	Founded Infosys Consulting Inc., US in California
2006	■ Murthy steps down as the executive chairman and is called the mentor ■ Acquisition of 23 per cent in Infosys BPO Ltd ■ Progeon becomes the wholly owned subsidiary with the new name Infosys BPO Ltd ■ First company to make it to NASDAQ 100 ■ NASDAQ honours it with stock market opening bell ■ Padma Shri, the civilian award of India, to Sudha Murthy
2007	■ Kris Gopalakrishnan takes over from Nilekani as CEO ■ Nilekani becomes the chairman ■ Royal Philips Electronics offers multi-million dollar contract for finance and accounting services ■ Founded wholly owned subsidiary Infosys Technologies S. de R. L. de C. V in Monterrey, Mexico
2008	■ Bid to buy the UK Axon Group Plc fails over the bid of HCL Technologies, but gains Rs 180 million in the deal ■ Padma Vibhushan, the second highest civilian award, to Murthy ■ Légion d'honneur, the highest French civilian award to Murthy

(c) The company's performance is measured through various techniques, such as brand value, economic value addition, intangible asset scoreboard, current-cost-adjusted financial statements, human resource accounting, and its endeavour to improve on these parameters.

Murthy set an example for all the corporate leaders to follow when he stepped down as the chairman and devoted his full time to Sudha's mission of CSR. He remains the philosopher of the company, a mentor for it's employees, from the topmost to the bottommost in the corporate ladder. He has set a perfect example of servant leadership, a leader who leads through example and lives by ideals.

Part II

Wealth and Welfare

Welfare of stakeholders

The Infosys philosophy stems from the middle-class values of moderate India. The company is a part of the community and has a sacred duty to perform, which is working towards the welfare of those who are underprivileged. Wealth without welfare seems fruitless. Infosys turned the value into a strategy to create wealth, and turned the wealth to give value addition to both the shareholders, as well as the stakeholders. The welfare of its stakeholders is the CSR of Infosys. This philosophy gave birth to the Infosys Foundation in 1996.

Infosys foundation

'Through creating opportunities and working towards a more equitable society, the Infosys Foundation has made small, but effective strides in the areas of healthcare, education, social rehabilitation, and the arts. Promoted by Infosys Technologies Limited, the Foundation offers the promise of a better tomorrow through its projects across India.'[e] This simple and straightforward statement on the Infosys Foundation website tells us two things—the means and its ends.

According to Sudha Murthy, the company's ultimate goal is the objective of the Foundation, the promise for a better tomorrow for all Indians. All the iconic campuses of Infosys and more than a 100,000 employees who are working towards this goal will make sense only if this can be seen on the faces of the underprivileged children in the remote villages of Karnataka and the rest of India. Her achievements, perhaps, surpass that of her husband's. Equally educated in the science of electrical engineering, it is her initial investment that has brought the company to this stage. However, she went ahead, raised children, worked as an engineer in well-known companies, taught as a teacher, and wrote thirteen books. Her son sent a birthday card to her with these words: Every mother works for her children, my mom works for somebody else's child ... Happy Birthday.[f]

Finance

The Foundation is funded with the profits of Infosys; 1 per cent of the profits are allotted for developmental work. The projects are in healthcare, social rehabilitation, education, arts and culture, and disaster relief.

Healthcare project

The Foundation[g] has built state-of-the-art hospitals and healthcare centres for both the urban and the rural people, who cannot receive quality healthcare:

(a) Super-specialty hospital: The Infosys Super-specialty Hospital, on the Sassoon Hospital premises in Pune.

(b) Donations: Medicines are provided to the aged and poor patients suffering from cancer, leprosy, and defects of the heart/kidney, mental illnesses, and other major disorders. It meets the substantial medical expenses of this section of society, and assures them of a steady source of income for their treatment.

(c) Software systems: Office management software has been installed at the KEM Hospital in Mumbai. This enables the hospital to manage store requirements, keep accounts, as well as publish hospital papers and other information on the Web.

(d) Hospital extension: Additional blocks have been built at the Swami Sivananda Centenary Charitable Hospital at Tirunelveli, Tamil Nadu.

(e) Accommodation for hospital visitors: A *dharmashala* was constructed at the Kidwai Cancer Institute, Bangalore.

(f) Paediatric hospital: Capitol Hospital in Bhubaneswar caters to poor child patients.

(g) Cancer hospital: There is an annex to a cancer hospital in Kancheepuram.

[e] See http://www.infosys.com/infosys_foundation/index.htm.
[f] See http://www.rediff.com/money/2007/jun/12sudha.htm.
[g] For the complete activities of the foundations, see http://www.infosys.com/infosys_foundation.

(h) Hospital: H.D. Kote is a hospital that has been built specially for the tribals at Mysore.

These are only a few of the projects. The foundation conducts health camps and donates equipment to hospitals.

Rural upliftment and rehabilitation

The rural upliftment programme is targeted towards empowering the poor and the destitute. Programmes such as tailoring training and distribution of sewing machines, orphanages, relief camps, disaster relief, etc. are undertaken. The Foundation has worked in the tsunami-affected areas of Tamil Nadu and the Andaman Islands, the earthquake-affected areas of Kutch, the cyclone-devastated areas of Orissa, the tribal areas of Kalahandi in Orissa, and the drought-hit areas of Andhra Pradesh.

Some of the programmes affect the very existence of the poor. Mid-day meal schemes are funded and carried out along with other partners and schools. The Foundation has rehabilitated the *devdasis* in North Karnataka. It has aided and worked with thousands of physically challenged and mentally retarded people by partnering with the Red-Cross Society.

The Foundation has built and maintains orphanages in Karnataka and Tamil Nadu, relief camps in Orissa, schools for the physically challenged, and destitute centres, along with its partnering institutions such as the Ramakrishna Mission, government agencies, and NGOs, to directly facilitate the above programmes.

Learning and education

Being a teacher, Sudha has made this programme the central activity of the Foundation. The Murthys stress upon learning and education as the key to India's progress. The Foundation has educational programmes for the underprivileged, in the states of Karnataka, Andhra Pradesh, Orissa, Tamil Nadu, and Kerala. It generally works through the existing educational institutions and NGOs, and helps them build their libraries and labs by providing them with computers and training. Several schools are reconstructed and refurbished. Thrust is given to the learning of sciences, vocational training, and self-employment courses.

Arts

The Murthys come from a state that has a rich cultural heritage. The cultural programmes organized by the Foundation communicate very powerful messages. These motivate people to seek better professions or to revive the old ones like weaving, send children to school, put ideas to practical use, and earn a better living. The Foundation encourages artisans, painters, writers, and musicians. Famous puppet shows, folk dances, and songs are back. These not only enrich culture, but provide gainful employment to the performing artists and others who organize and manage these events, and work with them.

Critics and conclusions

Reams of paper and TV hours have been consumed on Infosys and the Murthys. The high profile case of Phaneesh Murthy, who brought disrepute to the firm in the sexual harassment case, and politicians taking umbrage at Narayana Murthy's comments on the lack of infrastructure in the country, were no doubt controversial. But, there are no two opinions about Sudha Murthy heading the Infosys Foundation. Even the worst critics of Infosys Corporation have the highest praise for the CSR of the company.

Discussion Questions

After reading the above case, draw up questions on at least twelve issues that begin with the interrogative why and how.

Going Further . . .

Have a panel/group discussion by arranging groups behind the ideologies of the following:

Amartya Sen	Human development
Milton Freedman	Value addition to shareholders
Mahatma Gandhi	Rural Indian economy
J.R.D. Tata	Social work
Deng Xiao Ping	Modernization
Akio Morita	Quality of life
G.D. Birla	Patriotism

ETHICAL DEVELOPMENT PROGRAMME

Management Training

Personal Social Responsibility

All human beings in society have to bear a personal responsibility towards others. We do this naturally at home and with our loved ones. However, social concern goes beyond the boundaries of the acquaintances.

(a) Getting enrolled in a non-governmental, charitable institution, or any other non-profit organization helps to understand the importance of personal social responsibility.

(b) These community experiences will give a social direction to your career at your institute or as an executive at your company.

Careers in CSR

Careers in CSR are increasing, and more and more trained, skilled, and professionally sound managers are required to run this area of business corporations.

The CSR activities are also productive and self-sufficient. Most of them function as non-profit organizations, and are managed in just the same efficient manner as profitable businesses.

People working in CSR-related organizations are highly respected in society.

There is an increasing demand from employees, customers, and government bodies that businesses to be more open about their activities and reach and maintain acceptable standards in business practices. For employers, CSR is now seen as an important way to increase competitive advantage, protect and raise brand awareness, and build their trust with customers and employees.

Focus

- Working in partnership with local communities
- Socially responsible investment (SRI)
- Developing relationships with employees and customers
- Environmental protection and sustainability

Private sector Larger companies may have CSR departments, or have CSR functions located within particular areas of their organization, including marketing, communications, environmental management, public affairs, investor relations, finance, operations, and human resources. Opportunities are also opening up in large accounting and consulting firms, many of which are trying to compete with the niche that CSR consulting firms have carved by offering their own CSR client services.

Public sector CSR career options can be found in both national government agencies and international organizations.

The United Nations has launched the Global Compact—an initiative by the United Nations Secretary General to convince international companies to commit themselves to universal principles in relation to protection of human rights, labour rights, and the environment.

Nonprofits and research There is a wide variety of non-governmental organizations (NGOs), industry associations, think tanks, and academic institutions engaging in learning and/or advocacy within the CSR arena. Such groups promote and examine the use of CSR concepts within the private and public spheres.

Skills

Business skills Building insight, communication skills, decision-making, commercial awareness, IT, innovation, strategic awareness, leadership, handling complexity, and problem-solving skills

People skills Adaptability and empathy, developing others, influencing without power, open mindedness, integrity, political awareness, self-development and learning, building partnerships, team working, and questioning 'business as usual'

Technical skills Technical expertise, understanding impacts, stakeholder dialogue, internal consultancy, selling the business case, understanding human rights, and understanding sustainability

Competencies

Six core competencies for managers involved with CSR in organizations have been developed:

- Understanding society

- Building capacity
- Questioning business as usual
- Stakeholder relations
- Strategic view
- Harnessing diversity

Training

There are three main types of training providers:

Business schools Typically, there is little formal structure to CSR training, although issues such as business ethics, SRI, governance, sustainability, and corporate citizenship are being incorporated into existing modules.

Universities There are a growing number of specialist postgraduate degrees in CSR and sustainable business, and universities have also started including CSR as modules in other programmes and degrees.

Independent training providers These tend to provide executive, specialist, and short courses in CSR.

Areas of training

- Development work
- Health and safety
- Public relations
- Marketing
- Investment management
- Human resources
- Administration
- Environmental protection
- Environmental management
- Scientific research and development
- Social research

The opportunities for careers in CSR will increase due to the interest being taken by corporations.

Management Mantra

Slumdog Millionaire: Love's Mystery

The much acclaimed movie *Slumdog Millionaire* (2008) is built around a plot of winning Rs 2,00,00,000 on a quiz show. Despite so much motivation for making money, the movie is not about money at all. It is about love. The protagonist's motive to contest in the show is to appear on national TV, so that his long lost childhood friend could see him and eventually find him. It is a story about two young people, separated in childhood by the vicissitudes of life, longing for each other.

MANTRA   *Love. Money will follow.*

Corporations in the Geopolitical World

Do not wait for leaders; do it alone, person to person.

—Mother Teresa

If we aren't willing to pay a price for our values, if we aren't willing to make some sacrifices in order to realize them, then we should ask ourselves whether we truly believe in them at all.

—Barack Obama

LEARNING OBJECTIVES

After studying this chapter, you will be able to

➤ Understand global trends
➤ State what is economic justice
➤ Determine the cause for the failure to reach out economic services to the poor
➤ Explain why corporations should be service organizations in a globalized world

INTRODUCTION

The objectives of this chapter are of global proportions. Achieving the common good is the greatest goal of a contemporary corporation, which begins with providing services to the neediest and empowering them economically. The geopolitical situation in the world and the current economic crisis call for instilling a lead idea of global responsibility by business corporations, political establishments, and social institutions.

Some years ago, a young man called Laxmi Mittal was sent abroad by his father for better opportunities. He became an entrepreneur who produces steel, and is today called the Steel King of the world for setting up companies that produce steel in several dozen countries. There was another young man who left the shores of India at the tender age of sixteen to support his modest family, and worked in a Gulf country. When he came back, he started a company with just Rs 15,000, and before he died, he had established a multinational that was worth Rs 1,00,000 crore. Dhirubhai Ambani's company had succeeded in beating even the oldest Indian conglomerate, the TATAs, to become the largest private sector company of India. So, with all the expert philosophies of shareholders and stakeholders, we cannot say that these companies are any different from the multinationals of the Western hemisphere. Our companies are no more local in character; they have become global. They are now known as multinational companies.

Since it is difficult for us to understand the nature of multinational, we get terrorized by these big companies who set foot in our neighbourhoods and gobble up our little businesses. The reason for this fear is not far to seek. The first ever multinational that came into India usurped the entire country. Even after centuries, the Indian psyche is battered by the misdeeds the East India Company.

Today, the world has shrunk to a few hours journey around the globe. Businesses that we once only heard of have found their way into our neighbourhoods. So now, we can just walk into a mall and see a wide range of products from around the world, trying to woo us into buying. Although this is fine and desirable, the real global picture in which people live is grim. Out of every six people in the world, four go hungry to bed. The world's largest number of physically challenged, poorly clad, poorly fed, poor in health, and hunger-stricken people are found in India. Our country seems to be a very scary place to live in.

The political situation around the globe is scary too. From nuclear armaments to the whims of terrorists, from the misery of third-world countries to the uncertainty of the second world and the economic chaos in the first world, humanity has more than its share of problems. We need to manage our political, economic, and social life in a better way. The wisdom that we are endowed with allows us to do it. The good values that have been passed down through the ages can aid us. Change can happen only when we change. We have the power to adopt change for the better.

We need global social responsibility. The objectives of this responsibility would be to build a world-wide egalitarian society that will also include the poor people of the world. Attitudes will have to change, and so also the geopolitical thinking and the economic policies. Humanity must strive together for the common good.

There is a positive element in multinational companies. Despite all odds, multinationals have been able to transcend national and ideological boundaries. However, the recent financial crisis has dented the image of responsible corporations who could have been a beacon of hope for the people. The hope was that they could create more wealth to include those who were outside the fold of good life and would share the common good. In Barak Obama's words that are filled with hope, it is these hard times which should make us have the 'audacity of hope'.

Hope, however, is meaningless and will turn to despair if there are no leaders who can lead and make things happen. In this task, we need something more than efficient management. We need inspiration. Inspiration is not a miracle; it does not happen out of nothing. It only happens with effort. Inspiration is in the action. It comes from just one person, by doing just one thing. 'One person may not be able to feed a hundred people,' said Mother Teresa of Calcutta, 'but one person could at least feed one more person.' Hunger is a matter of numbers, which we can reduce if we are willing to act as individuals for the individuals.

THE GLOBAL PICTURE

Even after several thousands of years of civilization, the questions that disturb us are, 'What does it mean to be a human being?' 'Can human beings live as social beings?' 'Can we co-operate to build one world and be one people?' and 'Can business provide a service leadership and serve humanity?' We will try to find answers to these questions in this section.

Global Political Economy

Our end is happiness, which does not merely consist of the satisfaction of all wants, as the old science of political economy[1] advocates, but includes venturing into new venues of human development and progress, transformation from the old world order into a new one, and the hope that keeps us on the mission of quest and perfection, which we have learnt from historical experiences, examples of the leaders, and self-reflection. The fundamental relevance of the existence of political economy stems from the providential endowment of a social nature of human being upon which the social categorical imperative is based, thus laying the foundation for a just society. Any discrimination or disparity in such determination would then be tantamount to injustice.

Enterprise and Duty to Serve

Service to society is not a favour but a duty performed. It finds its expression through righteousness—recognition of the dignity of man, promotion of the common good, participation and achievement in the community, working towards the just cause of the poor, renouncing conflict and violence, and above all, bearing responsibility individually and as a community in relationship with other individuals and communities. The obligation of a citizen is to make it possible to have a self-determined existence that is free and meaningful, be an agent of change to create conditions to respect human rights, irrespective of creed, colour, region, or religion, and work for peace, democracy, and solidarity.

The obligation translated into contemporaneous application entails a preferential option for the poor, where the world community cannot afford to neglect the less fortunate, for they have the same right to livelihood, property, and respect as the more fortunate ones. It recognizes the claim of the deprived for equality, liberty, and justice. In concrete terms, the duty of society and its members is to be at the service of

---

[1] *Oikonomia politike* (Gk), management of household, implies the doctrine that the state has the responsibility to work for the welfare of its people.

others who are less fortunate and lack opportunities. People do not expect doled out food and healthcare, as was the case in the past, but need education and training to find gainful employment that would build good and healthy families, and raise the living standards of people, worthy of human dignity.

Economic enterprise, the mainstay of human existence is embroiled in the adoption of a correct theory that has divided the world into blocks of free-market economy and command economy, capitalist and socialist paradigms, conservative and liberal labels, economists' and bankers' cartels, first-world and third-world economies, sectarian economic interpretations by religions, activists of various causes, and interest groups with different ideologies that cloud the objective of human fulfilment.

Phenomenon of Globalization

Globalization is the new phenomenon of the new-world order that originates from a quicker and efficient interaction of the people worldwide in social, economic, cultural, and political activities. These activities have been unilaterally and equivocally comprehended as corporate globalization, for very powerful reasons of economic well-being. Figure 16.1 shows a pictorial representation of the issues involved in globalization.

North-South global divide

The genesis of the North-South global divide lies in the divisive policies of the G-8 countries, their sympathizers, and their institutions, which comprise the WTO, IMF,

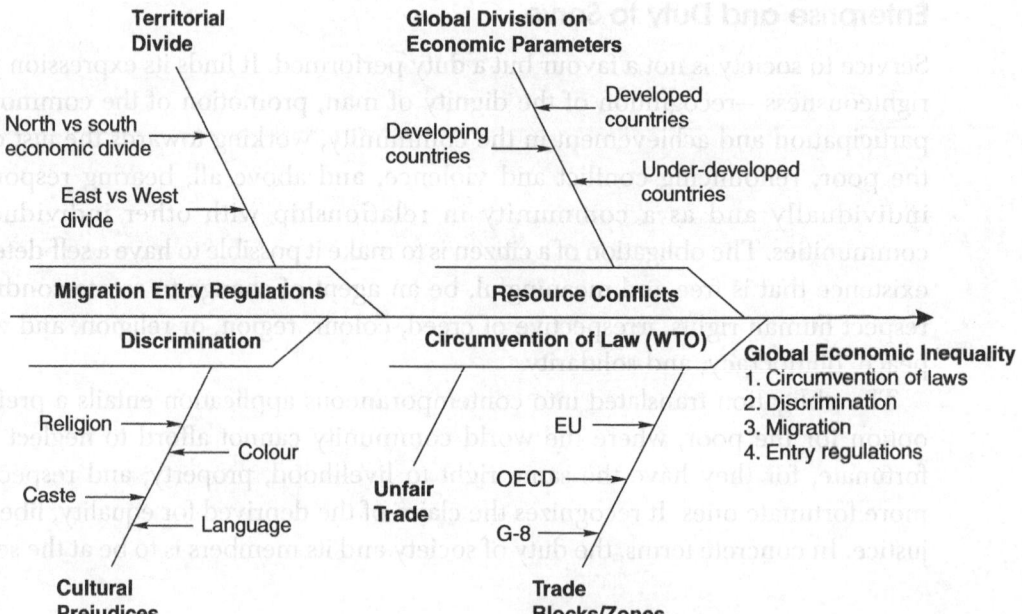

Fig.16.1   Fish-fin diagram of globalization

and WB. These policies strengthened the institutional and legal instruments such that profits override the needs of the poor. Tariff regimes that established unfair trade practices, and exploitation of the natural resources to the detriment of the Earth's environment, contributed to the challenges of a humane global family. However, the strategy of the G-8 seems to be recoiling upon itself: for instance, in the field of agriculture, which is the constituency of the bulk voters[2] on either side of the great divide, which no politician dare challenge. Consequently, they are at loggerheads over bananas, cotton, subsidies, and tariffs, which caused not just headaches on either side of the Atlantic, but had all the makings of turning the great NATO into a midget. Moral: boomerang justice.

Textiles, which the developing countries excel in, suddenly found no market in the developed countries that had earlier enticed them with the pie of free and fair trade in the WTO heaven. Further, more immigration restrictions were imposed. There were threats to stop outsourcing, denigration of credit rating, and fear of sanctions. Moral: don't trust the fox to protect the chickens. Globalization of the past was an imperfect historical process by the people who pushed their barriers by war, colonial expansion, religious zeal, political and economic hegemony, cultural onslaught, and ideological imperialism. The last century globalized the military conflicts twice on a large scale and learned a lesson through the horrendous evil that humanity suffered. It changed the political landscape, the social and cultural exchanges, and the establishment of world institutions.

Global image of man

The first steps into the twenty-first century have carried forward the economic agenda of the last decade of the previous century, accompanied by an enormous scientific and technological network with the consciousness that contrary to the past mindset of exploited riches and profit-at-all-costs, to a win-win situation for both corporations and consumers *sans* political, social, and cultural barriers. The contemporary image of man is that of a conscious person who experiences the world in the living room through a TV box and communicates with the outside world in real time on the Internet. Millions of people around the globe experience a momentous event or entertainment live, and communicate verbally and visually beyond the physical, cultural, political, racial, and other barriers. Contemporary man is a global being.

The limits of our communication were previously confined to the extent of our reach within the world but that has now physically gone beyond the orbit of the earth. This has been made possible by our constant effort in our curiosity to know and manage resources and put them to good use. Now, in a similar fashion, we have to overcome the psychological barriers that separate one neighbour from the other,

---

[2] The farmers of France, for instance, are the most politically active segment that force the government to maintain subsidies.

the barriers of strife and hate between the nation-states, and the barriers of haves and have-nots between the rich and the poor.

ECONOMIC JUSTICE

Nothing happens without a reason. The priori principle of cause and effect explains the *raison d'être* for the existence of poverty in the world: poverty stems from the consequence of economic injustice senselessly perpetrated for the narrow personal ends of the political leaders of the rich nations, the narrow nationalistic interests and the ostensible defence of ideologies that have robbed the basic human freedoms of food, shelter, and security.

Inspirational Leader

Mother Teresa

I try to give to the poor people for love what the rich could get for money. No, I wouldn't touch a leper for a thousand pounds; yet I willingly cure him for the love of God.

—Mother Teresa

It is not unusual to see a picture of Mother Teresa in corporate offices, and if one of the entrepreneurs had had an opportunity to be a part of that picture, then it would surely be displayed. The corporate leadership sees in her an inspirational leader. She is a picture of clear distinction between a manager and an inspirational leader.

Mother Teresa was a symbol of selfless service. She founded an order called the Missionaries of Charity. Today it has spread to 150 countries, with the help of approximately 5000 of her followers. The followers are not paid. They live in communities called convents, which house the poor, the sick, and the destitute. The service is free. The order only depends on donations from the public.

Mother Teresa was popularly known as Mother because she cared for the poorest of the poor; the connotation in mother also implies a goddess. She was known as the Angel of Mercy and the Saint of the

Gutters—all referring to the care and love she inspired, to give to those who were despised and neglected by society. She had no time for the intellectual debates regarding her work. She thought that if each individual cared for just one more person, no one would be in such a subhuman condition. She refused to acknowledge that she encouraged poverty, but insisted that through the little that she did, at least that bit of poverty would be eradicated. She said, 'If you can't feed a hundred people, then feed just one.'

Mother Teresa was born in Skopje, formerly in Albania and presently in Macedonia, on 26 August 1910. She died on 5 September 1997 in Kolkata, the headquarters of her order. There was no award that was not conferred on her. From the Bharat Ratna to the Nobel Prize, practically the highest awards from scores of countries around the world were bestowed on her.

Questions

(a) Is poverty a moral virtue or evil?
(b) Why is service leadership essential?
(c) How can corporations adopt and implement Mother Teresa's principles of service to the poor?

Economic Disparities

The economic disparities[3] are appallingly glaring where half the population of the world lives without sanitation, electricity, and earn fewer than \$2 a day.[4] Five hundred billionaires share half of the world's total wealth, one in six people around the globe is illiterate, 20 per cent of the people in the developed countries consume 86 per cent of the world's goods, and the GDP of the fifty poorest countries approximately equals to the three richest people.[5]

Every year, two million children die[6] because no one cares about the holocausts that take place because of the negligence of the nations who fail to keep their words, the pharmaceuticals do not budge on tariffs, and the conflicts that do not allow the aid to go through. Such problems show the stubbornness of the will of those who rule. They can change the world through policy change, but do not want to do so. This is the greatest stumbling block in the alleviation of misery in the world.

The debt trap is the stranglehold that makes the poor nations poorer.[7] The burden of debt replacement increases to twelve times more than the initial amount. Thus, for every dollar of debt, the burden of repayment is \$12. This vividly exhibits that the governments and their leaders did bad business by borrowing and lending, mainly for arms purchases, and then failed to own up to their mistakes and cancel the same as bad debts. This has resulted in an unbearable burden for the unsuspecting citizens.

Ideally, the elimination of poverty is not difficult if the very same tool of globalization is used rightly[8] by eliminating the three monopolies—land, technology, and finance capital—and applying the principle of equal pay for equal work to equalize the purchasing power, both within the states and internationally. Consequently, wealth

---

[3] 'Never before have had so many people had so much in common, but never before have the things that divide them been so obvious', *Sir Shridath Ramphal* (WDR, 2004).

[4] 'Almost half the world's population lives on less than two dollars a day, yet even this statistic fails to capture the humiliation, powerlessness and brutal hardship that is the daily lot of the world's poor', Message of the United Nations Secretary-General Kofi Annan on the International Day for the Eradication of Poverty, 17 October 2000.

[5] The growing gap between the richest and the poorest countries was 3:1 in 1820, 11:1 in 1913, 35:1 in 1950, 44:1 in 1973, and 72:1 in 1992.

See World Fact Book at http://www.cia.gov/cia/publications/factbook/ accessed on 7 June 2004.

[6] 'This is nothing short of a global scandal. The needless deaths of millions of children should haunt all those governments that pledged to deal with this blight on humanity and have failed to live up to their promises. The world has the resources to save those children's lives. It is feasible and attainable. What is missing is the political leadership to make conference commitments a reality. In the last five years there has been a shameful litany of aid budgets being cut, debt rising, trade barriers costing poor countries billions in lost earnings, and health and education budgets slashed,' Kevin Watkins, Oxfam's Senior Policy Adviser. For more details, see http://www.oxfam.org.uk/press/releases/target.htm accessed on 8 June 2004.

[7] 'Debt reduction has been delayed for many years because governments have been unwilling to admit they have made bad loans, and it is only pressure by Jubilee 2000 and other groups that has made the difference,' admits a former IMF and British Treasury insider, in a candid article in the prestigious journal *Development Policy Review* of September 1999. More details are available at http://www.jubilee2000uk.org/jubilee2000/news/imf2010.html accessed on 24 June 2004.

[8] 'Globalization can be a strong force in the fight against poverty. But globalization must mean more than creating bigger markets, and experience confirms that growth alone cannot reduce poverty and income inequality. Economic policy must be combined with effective social policies aimed at education for all, health for all and gender equality. This is essential if globalization is to work for all the world's peoples, and if we are to meet the goal of halving, by the year 2015, the proportion of people living in extreme poverty', Kofi Annan, United Nations Secretary-General, on the International Day for the Eradication of Poverty, 17 October 2000.

distribution and economic efficiency will rise, and wealth will increase in a co-operative paradigm, which is at once co-operative and democratic (Smith 2003).

Economics for People

The contemporary world order is people centric. Whether they are political ideologies, economic theories, religious proclamations, or cultural repertoire, the well-being of all the people is the aim that has set the world to a complex stage of human relationships in all the aspects of life, particularly the intricate relationship of political, economic, and social equations in the globalized atmosphere. All this has raised concerns about life's fulfilment. The question of economic justice arises when the benefits of the globalized economy are not equitably shared among the nations and their people. The struggle for equal justice for all is taking shape globally among the social-conscious people, who believe in the common destiny of humanity for freedom, fulfilment, and the absence of war.

Oil, the largest energy resource of the world, for instance, has been the source of strife between nations, the stronger powers maintaining the hardest stands at the cost of the fledgling global economies, the exploited third-world countries, the appeasement or subjugation of rebel countries, and total disregard to the environmental problems, arising out of the consumption of the fossil fuels. The unrealistic triumphalism of capitalist economies over the socialistic economies has sent the governing economic factors for a toss due to the confusion in drawing micro and macro policies that militate. While individual freedoms are seen as a necessity to create a consumerist and free-market society, the nation-states are withholding their rights against globalization for a free and fair trade.

Globalization as a Process towards Supra-State

Today, globalization is generally seen as a supra-state corporatization, where the multi-national companies carve out niche markets for their products, but where the states are not willing to allow other states equal opportunity status. At the same time, people are expected to comply with the global citizenship of a consumer society. There are glaring disparities in a shrunk world. The global village of a hundred people—fifty-seven Asians, twenty-one Europeans, fourteen Americans and eight Africans—have the following ratios: non-white and white, 70:30, Non-Christian and Christian, 70:30 (non-Catholics and Catholics 6:1), illiterate 65, malnutrition 50, substandard living 80. Out of these, only one has college education and just six possess 50 per cent of the total wealth.[9] The challenges of inequalities are great, and aid alone will not be able to bridge the gap created by large-scale poverty, growing economic insecurity, poor governance, unsubstantial policies, unstable political atmosphere, and ideological warps. But it becomes an imperative to introduce global mechanisms that will be nationally and locally responsive to spur reforms, both in the agricultural and industrial

---

[9] See http://www.freemaninstitute.com/diversityvil.htm accessed on 16 June 2004.

sectors. Although conceptually, one could very well construe the link between economic inequality and the lack of economic growth, experts at the World Bank have conducted extensive studies to show that there exists a link between inequality, poverty, and growth prospects, wherever inequalities show a clear empirical impact that works negatively for economic growth.[10] Figure 16.2 shows a graphical representation on income inequality.[11]

The two vicious circles of inequality cause poverty that leads to discrimination. This in turn causes loss of human dignity and can only be overcome by optimum equality through education that affects employment. Employment works for the common good, which is prosperity and a better standard of living. This gives rise to equality that affects peace. If education is one wing of economic development of humanity, health is the other one. With these two well placed and strong and working in tandem, poverty can be eradicated from the world in merely ten years, only if the existing bodies at the service of the people implement their programmes, prioritize their commitments, and make a definite choice for the education and health sectors in the world.

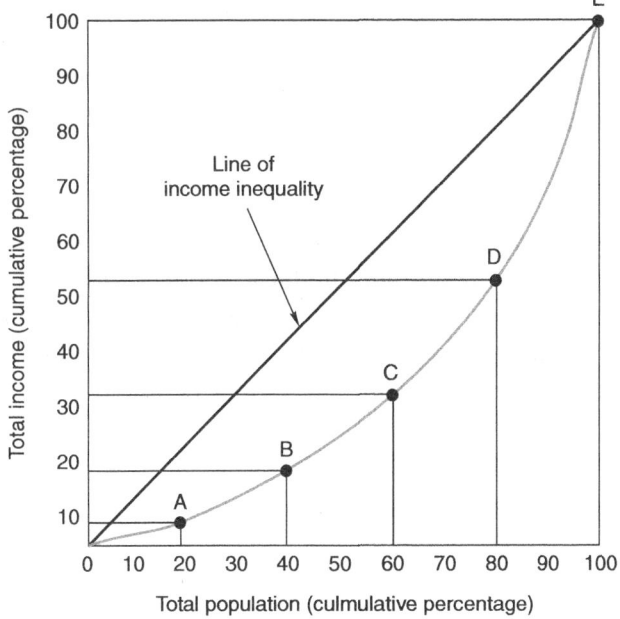

Fig. 16.2   Lorenz curve of income

Source: http://www.worldbank.org/poverty/wdrpoverty/report/index.htm.

---

[10] The World Development Report 2001/2; it is available at http://www.worldbank.org/poverty/wdrpoverty/report/index.htm.
[11] Max O Lorenz's (1880–1962). This graph depicts a Lorenz curve, which plots the cumulative share of income against the cumulative population share. The diagonal represents perfect income equality. The further away the curve is from the diagonal, the more unequal the society. Powerful theorems associated with Lorenz dominance have made this curve something of a symbol of inequality measurement and analysis. Thus, for instance, in the above curve the poorest 20 per cent of the population receives 7 per cent of the economy's total income, and the poorest 100 per cent of the population (the entire population) must receive 100 per cent of the economy's total income.

Bahujan Samaj Party

Socio-political revolution

The party name Bahujan Samaj Party literally means majority community party. It implies that the majority of the population of India belong to the people of the lowest caste, the *sudras*. These are the people who have been under the yoke of the upper castes and have been oppressed for all the known centuries of human civilization. What the oppressors did not realize until recently was that now they have been outnumbered and if democracy has its way, the oppressed are going to take political power.

Ambedkar, who gave the outcasts of India a voice by grouping them under the nomenclature of *dalits*, first accorded them respect by leading them into the fold of Buddhism. He castigated Hinduism for making them and keeping them as untouchables in religious, social, and political arenas. In 1984, Kanshi Ram from Uttar Pradesh, who had followed Ambedkar, founded a party called the Bahujan Samaj Party and fielded candidates for elections. He started a revolution, which was a quiet one at the beginning, and did not take off immediately.

But fifteen years down the line, under his and his disciple Mayawati's leadership, the party won fourteen Lok Sabha seats to the Parliament. Ever since, Indian politics has not been the same. Every party, big or small, promises a piece of heaven to the Dalits.

Power has come to the poor and the oppressed, and it has been consolidated after the elections in May 2009. It has shown the world that without the support of the poor and the oppressed, geopolitical existence is impossible. The Indian order and, eventually, the world order will change because of the *bahujan*, the oppressed and poor of this world, because they are in majority. A revolution is on the way.

Questions

(a) Is democracy a moral principle? Can rightness or wrongness be decided by the majority?
(b) Is caste system morally wrong?
(c) Are the poor manipulated politically and economically by the upper castes and the rich?

The fundamental problem is not the non-existence of intelligent schemes, which in fact are in surfeit to provide the basic services to the poor like food, clothing and shelter,[12] road, water, and power,[13] but is the absence of simple managerial skills of implementation, prevalence of rabid corruption, and the never-ending bureaucratic muddle[14] that succeed in keeping the poor people poor.

FAILURE TO PROVIDE ECONOMIC SERVICES TO POOR

Poor Lack Economic Services

That services fail to reach the poor is evidenced without doubt. It has become a truism, an axiom that seems to have gained validity due to the failure of social and

---

[12] The slogan *roti* (food), *kapra* (clothing) *aur makan* (shelter) brought India's Indira Gandhi to power, and she became one of the highly respected world leaders. However, the political power did not translate the mandate of the people, and India's poor are still struggling.

[13] The promise of roads, drinking and irrigation water, electricity, and even free electricity has been made repeatedly by Indian politicians. They have won and lost elections on this issue. Yet, the problems remain as severe as before. India's is a classic example of mismanagement of the public funds that are meant for poverty irradiation.

[14] 'The counterproductive nature of some of the governmental restrictions, controls, and regulations has been clear for a long time. They have not only interfered with the efficiency of economic operations (especially for modern industries), but also have often failed lamentably to pronounce any kind of real equity in distributional matters.'—Amartya Sen, 'Radical Needs and Moderate Reforms', in Jean Dreze & Amartya Sen (eds), *Indian Development, Selected Regional Perspectives*, Oxford University Press, New Delhi, 1997, pp. 8, 9.

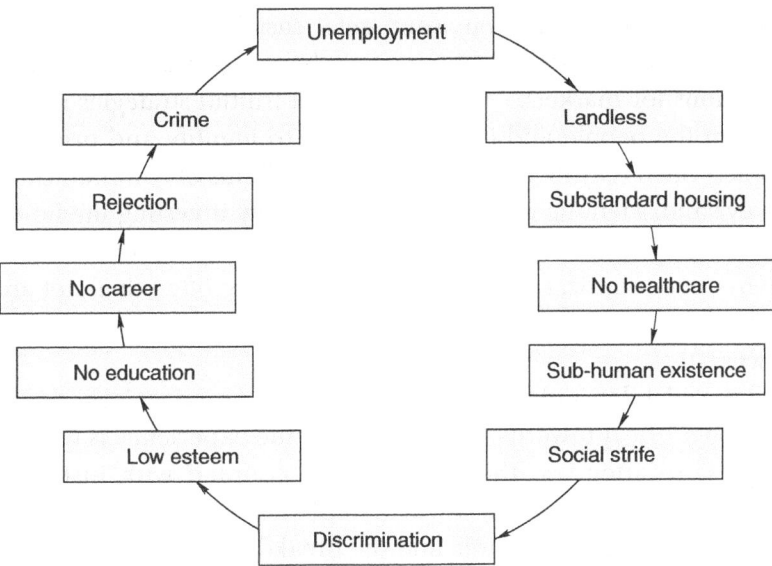

Fig. 16.3 The vicious circle of poverty

political institutions. It is an irrational, inexplicable phenomenon that poverty should exist in the present century, when there is a slew of scientific and technological measures to ensure progress, prosperity, and a better standard of living, the global wealth abounds, and the sophisticated international institutions, both governmental and financial, work around the clock, and yet half the humanity goes hungry to bed. Figure 16.3 the vicious circle of poverty.

In the present global state-of-affairs, a two-fold approach to solve the global problems of economic inequality may be adopted, where on one hand the government fulfils its public social responsibility (PSR) and on the other hand, the industry comes forward as a capable and competent member of society to fulfil its corporate social responsibility (CSR). Governments are the standard bearers of political economy. Hence, such policies have to be formed that make the services reach the people. Neither growth-oriented schemes nor technical introduction with public spending may affect the desired results. Only a constant vigil of those services through citizen action groups and a vigilant press can make the services available to the people.[15]

Political economy necessitates that policy makers in the government lay out plans to make the best of the market forces—and not vice-versa as the present global phenomena exhibit—and draw a strategic time-bound plan for eradication of poverty and hunger, attain universal primary education, promote empowerment of women, reduce infant mortality and increase maternal care, combat HIV/AIDS, malaria, and

---

[15] As the city of Bangalore saw increasingly the economic growth in the 1990s, yet the services fell short and corruption shot up, until a report card system was developed by an action group and was publicized by the press. See WDR, 2004, p. 42.

other epidemics, ensure environmental sustainability[16] and encourage sustainable development, transform institutions, enhance growth and quality of life, and build institutions for markets.[17] One of the most fruitful strategies is to develop a dialogue between the people and the government to identify and prioritize the needs of the people, which may be done through the mediums of communication, and conducting surveys and scientific research, and judiciously investing the funds.[18] This will result in an orderly growth as per the needs of the people and not as one imposed by the experts, economists, and monetarists, who more often than not are blind to the basic needs of the people, and are only interested in the measurement of wealth and market indices.[19]

The availability and the non-availability of the services is proportionate to the attitude the agents[20] bear towards the clients,[21] for the experience is that the former could not care less to attend to their work. This, coupled with institutional failure, weak commitment, lack of political will in implementation, and general apathy by the latter has resulted in a blame game and the breakdown in social relationships.

The positive attitude of the agents, as well as the clients and their growing relationship, makes for the success of services.[22] The affirmative mind-set is the result of not merely one's upbringing, but speaks of the entire social and religious culture, and political and economic conditions. Hence, the relationship between the clients and the agents of services too would operate in the given milieu affecting success or failure.

Establishing Economic Relationship with the Poor

Establishing relationships is as complex as what we take fancy to and what we reject, where indefinable and non-measurable criteria apply. However, a stable government that is ready to go beyond the public sector and involve corporations and a strong sense of mission and implementation of strategy helps in building an atmosphere that is conducive for both the clients and the agents, where mechanisms may be created

---

[16] This is the World Bank's time-bound programme known as The Eight Millennium Development Goals, starting from 1990 to 2015, by introducing system-wide reforms, health, and focused strategies.

[17] World Development Report 2002 had the theme: Building institutions for markets. It provided a blue print for firms, governments, and societies in institution building and finding fair markets for products.

[18] For instance, loan facilities to farmers, artisans, and those involved in the cottage industry. The Bangladesh model of bank credit facilities has done wonders for production of fabric articles.

[19] In Porto Alegre, Brazil, an experiment was done on the budget exercise, in consultation with the public. The results speak for themselves—100 per cent access to water, sewage facilities, doubling of school enrolment, and, most surprisingly, an increase in the city revenue by 50 per cent!

[20] Agents are the employees, workers, of the service sector.

[21] Clients are people at the receiving end of the services.

[22] A spotlight on the education service in Kerala (southern state of India) and Uttar Pradesh (northern state of India) has clearly exhibited this attitude as the primary reason for success and failure of educational programmes. Both the states benefit from the same schemes and yet, Kerala because of its attitude of commitment to primary education, gender equality, and the will to perform is a fully literate and well-informed state. Uttar Pradesh, on the other hand, is exactly the opposite. This proves that the human agent is the centre of action, while the agencies merely play a supporting role. See Jean Dreze and Amartya Sen, *India Development and Participation.*

for competitive markets. These in turn create accountability, which in turn fetches consumer satisfaction.[23]

System or bureaucracy

A framework for public service involves bureaucracy, which in turn for the purposes of checks and balances creates officialdom and loses sight of the real work and purpose of its activity. Such problems may be overcome by the introduction of efficient managerial mechanisms, decentralization of services system, service contracting, health insurance system, introduction of intelligent technology, etc. in all the service areas.[24] The world of the service provider and the client is becoming increasingly involved, where the service providers are private parties and the clients are those who have been once the victims of bureaucratic wrangles.[25] With increasing economic reforms and an increased purchasing power, people are becoming more conscious and have clear and intelligent demands, which the service providers cannot ignore.

System of monitoring

The strategy to utilize funds through contracting is a better route to monitoring than giving to communities, where accountability will be difficult, as experience has shown so far.[26] In addition to this, the realities of heterogeneous communities with various needs would only further strengthen the strategy and help enhance client power.

Developing democracies have clearly shown that services are very powerful political tools and politicians have veered around and developed their clientele or have built powerful constituencies as vote-banks and harmed the interests of the people at large. But after a while, these have been punished by the consumer when realization dawned. One can only progress to the extent the other countries progress.[27]

In this era of global awareness,[28] even among the poorest of the poor, there is a powerful aspiration to change one's life for the better. Aspiration is the primary and necessary condition for change, which once embedded in the soul, starts to change

---

[23] Vouchers for education and public distribution have been successfully experimented in several countries, which bring in private sector in distribution and automatic accountability, since wastage is plugged and the private players do legitimate business.

[24] China has made strides, particularly by privatizing the insurance sector, which in turn makes its services available to all the service sectors. This has had beneficial results, particularly in health. See Dreze & Sen, *India Development and Participation.*

[25] The Indian sub-continent has seen economic reforms, however partially, and has tasted the quality and promptness of the private service providers. Commendable in this sector are the new telecom services, airlines, and choices in consumer goods. People have shown preference to private enterprise and this has given boost to economic reforms. Those who adhere to Marxist ideologies have put hurdles. While private health services have been beneficial and timely and cost effective in the long run, the public health in India is a public money guzzler and apathy towards the clients involves corruption to buy healthcare.

[26] See WDR 200, p. 75.

[27] The General Election 2004 threw out the government that was run by the right-wing party, which made communalism its vote plank, justified discrimination, and decimation of minorities. Moral: politically conscious people will not tolerate development at the cost of others' lives.

[28] If one visits Mother Teresa's home for the destitute in Kolkata, or for that matter anywhere in the world, the inmates here, the poorest of the poor, know what it means to have a better and dignified life. They even know what it means to have a glamorous life through what they see on TV. They are also aware of the present situation in the world, through watching the news.

Popular Plot for the Poor

NREGA

The Economist described it as the world's biggest public-works project that just got bigger.[a] In state after state in India, the semi-skilled and the unskilled have suddenly found some flickering hope—work. India is not very well known for managing public works, but this one is a success by Indian standards. In some states it is accepted well and doing good work. Other states are lagging behind, but are slowly and surely catching up. In these tough times, when farmers are led to commit suicide due to economic problems, the National Rural Employment Guarantee Scheme (NREGS) does exactly what its name says.

On 25 August 2005, the lower house of the Parliament enacted a bill called The National Rural Employment Guarantee Act.[b] The bill was Sonia Gandhi's idea, who is the president of the ruling Congress Party. It was drawn by Prime Minister Manmohan Singh, who is also a noted economist, and Jean Drèze, the well-known scholar at the Delhi School of Economics. The work under this Act is called the NREGS.

The central government will work in tandem with the state governments by meeting three-fourths of the costs and the administrative costs. According to the scheme, the adult member of the family registers himself at the local *panchayat*. The programme officer takes care of the requisite formalities. Employment will be provided within a radius of 5 kilometres. The scheme for the unemployed lasts for hundred days of the financial year.

Questions

(a) The largest welfare scheme also uses the largest funds. How is it justifiable to pour money into projects whose implementation is doubtful and where corruption is rampant?

(b) The guarantee of employment may demotivate rural folks from seeking employment.

(c) What responsibility should the government exercise in implementing large-scale schemes? Suggest some good alternatives.

[a] See 'Shovelling for their supper' in http://www.economist.com/world/asia/displaystory.cfm?story_id=11090559.

[b] For complete details, see http://nrega.nic.in/.

the world despite all seemingly insurmountable difficulties, and if restrained, would charge down in a fury of avalanche, a social revolution that changes the face of the earth. Beware, the wrath of the poor is rising, their voices rising from all the corners of the Earth. Those who listened to the voice of the poor[29] have endeavoured to better their lot by setting achievable objectives and delivering the services, providing management, that is, creating effective frontline organizations through teaching and training, and look at them as clients.[30]

Failure, the cause for social disaster

The wrath of the poor who are in a burgeoning majority in the world cannot be shackled long to economic slavery because they have become conscious of their power,

---

[29] Going beyond *vox populi vox dei*, i.e, beyond the expression of the will of the citizens, by actually taking stock of the activity of the politicians and policy makers.

[30] WDR pp. 113–16.

the people's power. Therefore, misleading them into the war-mongering game,[31] dividing people on the basis of race and religion, or discriminating them for their gender will result in the overthrow of the governments and vacating of the corporations who have been thus far fleecing people and enjoying the creamy layer of the good earth.

CORPORATIONS AS SERVICE ORGANIZATIONS IN A GLOBALIZED WORLD ORDER

The idealism to use the service-tool can motivate to establish a network of education and training institutions. This is because there is no greater tool for economic consciousness, employment, and development than the knowledge through education, which is the ideal tool to eradicate poverty and usher in a renaissance of sustainable development and desirable transformation in the lives of people.

Education

Education is the most powerful route to break free from poverty, and this has been realized as the singular mission by global organizations such as the United Nations. Along with various global organs, the UNO has been striving towards a world literacy programme. The West-dominated world reigned with ideologies of democracy, socialism, and market economy, but without ethical consequences introduced the industrial revolution. However, without respect to ecological balance, they pioneered technology without any concern for the human spirit and treated the limited science as a god, at the cost of commonsense and wisdom.[32]

The end of the modern era challenges us to look forward into a post-modern era of a new ideology called globalism that consists of short physical distances, quick communication, all-pervasive information, global interdependence in politics, macro–micro interplay of economics, social and cultural blending. It also challenges us to look at antagonisms: nationalism versus globalism, safety and security versus terrorism, ethics versus consumerism, militarism, technocracy, and science.

Genesis of New Global Ethos

Globalism is the new paradigm that must be affirmed for all its positive values of universality of humanity, material and spiritual freedom, values of equality, and human rights. It must be negated for what may hamper these values, such as narrow nationalism, religious intolerance, racial discrimination, restriction of territorial movement, sectarian wars, and must transcend into a pluralistic and holistic synthesis

---

[31] The US has been misusing its leadership for war mongering (as in Kuwait and Iraq), while an increasing number of its population is struggling under poverty. The dictators in Africa too are misleading the people by putting one person against another. In Asia, corrupt politicians have been made to pay a heavy price.

[32] In Hans Küng's *Projekt Weltethos*, the author develops a theory for global ethos based on faith in religion. The majority of the people in the world do believe in the transcendental and at the same time, have faith in themselves to follow a moral that is beyond ideologies and organized religions, which unites the world through definite norms and values.

of universal ethos.[33] A new world order is not possible without such a global ethos, which is much more fundamental than enacting laws. Knowledge, information, behavioural sciences, and technology, have their own place in our lives, but their relevance to living meaningful lives must be developed by community-living, in the global village.

Rights The rights of man, proclaimed and enshrined in the highest body in the world, the UNO, need a foundation in universal morality. Making a law before its sense has been developed in a global society, and the behaviour in response to a variety of causes, would merely end up misleading humanity, losing the relevance of the reason for the laws, the meaning of life, and the ultimate end of man, who is the origin of a global social culture.

Business behaviour The example of a world market economy would bring to light better, and in a truly existential way, the effects of share market indexes around the globe, the pricing of goods, which is a commentary of what is happening in the world, and the job market that gives livelihood to people. All this and more function in a global ethos of business behaviour, where even the slightest dishonesty is quantitatively measurable in terms of gain or loss of money, goodwill, and future prospects, the origins of a global market culture.

Business corporation of the world The twenty-first century corporations are going to diminish the nation-states, just as nation-states once banished the aristocratic world order. From among the top hundred economies of the world, fifty-one are multi-national corporations. As sovereign states lose power and submit to the larger economic zones, and these in turn again lose power to form global conglomeration, there is fear that desperate terrorist groups too will join hands and target the new establishments. Hence, a renaissance in the economic life of the people will make the transition less painful, because it would be served by good education and empowerment of the poor.

Rise of customer value The economic power of the corporations will transcend the power of the democracies, for the voter value will decline and the customer value will rise. The representative governments will give in to the more practical exigencies of business, so much so that it will have to follow the dictates of the prevailing trade, industry, and fiscal environment rather than the will of the people, which is hard to define and discern. But, the financial matters are measurable and predictable and can be laid down into logical policy making.

Governance strategies Even the ideologically socialist governments would have to give up the state-managed economy, and employ managers and market strategists for governance, and as a consequence, the sympathetic workers' unions that dominated the last century would have to be dismantled after hefty strife with their political

---

[33] Hans Küng, *Projekt Weltethos*, p. 45.

mentors[34] and find a rightful place in the corporate organization as per personal competence, without the support of the powerful members of a trade union.

Wider corporate responsibilities   Corporations too are mutating and evolving at high-speed for the public ownership of the companies is sky-rocketing and the corporate bosses and the corporate business management are taking their responsibility seriously towards their investors in particular and society in general. As more and more people become part of corporations, a greater democracy will evolve in the economic affairs, whose engines of management are corporations, just as democracy in political affairs, whose engine of administration of public affairs is the government.

The government's motto to serve the people failed. Corporations will adopt a new win-win business paradigm and will see their new members as fellow partners for sustainable growth and development. Typical of the post-modern businessman, customer satisfaction will be the *leitmotif.* The economic cycle determines the social and cultural areas of man. Consumerism and not political ideologies will measure the will of the people, that is, what people want in order to maintain a better standard of life.

Global Environment Culture

Likewise, ecological system responses are quite sensitive. The stressed environment is felt beyond the fences and borders of nation-states, the rising of the water levels, and the depletion of the ozone layer, desertification, deforestation, and pollution. All of these affect the people globally, and a global ethos of environmental ethics is being formed, which expresses itself through various action groups that are raising consciousness, finding scientific and technological solutions, changing their lifestyles, forming habits conducive to the stewardship of nature—the origins of a global environment culture.

Egalitarianism as Business Philosophy

Egalitarianism is a businessman's dream in which he is able to welcome people of all creeds and faiths, the young and the old, the sick and the infirm, black, white, yellow, or brown, clans and tribes, and nations and continents, which make use of his services and enable him to earn his entitlements. But such a dream has remained a nightmare due to base greed, resulting in a divided world of cutting-edge ultra-modern living and over-the-edge minimum existence. For a businessman, egalitarianism[35] is shorn of all ideologies, faiths, territories, and many of the prejudices that human beings may inflict upon one another. It quite simply implies the equitability in the purchasing

---

[34] Trade unions are becoming increasingly irrelevant in Great Britain and Germany, despite the labour-friendly social governments being in power.

[35] French égalité for equality has the entire revolution to explain the meaning of social, political, and social equality. The human spirit cannot be suppressed forever. If corrective measures in removing inequalities are not taken, revolutions will take place in the world in one form or the other. The current trend of terrorism ultimately has a reason in political inequality, whether it is in the Middle East, India, Ireland, Spain, Rwanda, Zimbabwe, etc.

power of the client,[36] which empowers people to spend, save, and invest. Economic empowerment results in a decline in poverty, rise in education, decline in unemployment, rise in the standard of living, decline in diseases, and rise in health services.

Purchasing power parity After the adjustment of the purchasing power parity (PPP), 25 per cent of the world's population receives 75 per cent of the world's income. This means that the poorest 75 per cent of the population ekes out its existence with a mere 25 per cent of the world's income. Recent studies indicate an even worse scenario, where within the richer countries of Europe and North America also, the PPP gap is widening. Such state-of-affairs spells the end of the egalitarian dream.

Choice The egalitarian society is a desirable precondition for global economics that is value[37] oriented, which is resolved through price determination. Price determination is the result of a reasoning in the general theory of choice whose scope it is to study the fundamental concepts of decision and action, where a plurality of agents may be consistently accommodated to one another within the existing social system—globalism.

Choice and laws of economics This theory of choice and accommodation functions as per the laws of economics that govern production, consumption, distribution, and exchange of goods and services, and their related fields, which may be drawn both deductively and inductively, elucidating the causal relationship. However, no certitude may be attained, since such a relationship depends on the unpredictability of complex human actions and reactions and their probable inferences.[38]

Freedom of choice The modern economic science is one of the youngest social sciences. The ecclesial social thinking on the other hand is as old as her foundations, which found theological expression in the scholastic social analysis that had its influence in purely secular definitions as laid down by the Austrian School of Economics.[39] It based its theory on the fundamental assumption of individual freedom, decision-making, right to private property, the nature of economic value, and the inherent catalectic or exchange and free-market mechanism.

---

[36] Amartya Sen's two works *On Economic Inequality* (1973) and *Inequality Re-examined* (1992) deal extensively on egalitarianism under the criteria of diversity, efficiency, and Rawls' distributive justice but does not investige into seeking equality in the purchasing power of the people, where despite disparate incomes, people may enjoy equitable purchasing power resulting in equitable standard of living.

[37] Economics was initially known as the science of value (J.S. Mill, Henry Sidgwick, and Adam Smith). Indeed, the study of value in exchange; the positivists try to shear it off ethical value—*Wertfrei* that is, value free but failed, since the human behaviour here is closely related to decision making, choices that are good and bad, and other such fundamental ethical values.

[38] 'Economic laws, or statements of economic tendencies, are those social laws that relate to the branches of conduct in which the strength of the motives chiefly concerned can be measured by a money price,' Marshall, Alfred, *Principles of Economics*, Library of Economics and Liberty, http://www.econlib.org/library/Marshall/marP3.html accessed on 7 June 2004.

[39] Carl Menger, the founder of the Austrian School of Economics, has a scholastic approach to the investigation of economic phenomena. In the true spirit of his friend Franz Brentano, the Catholic priest from Würzburg, Germany, who later joined the University of Vienna, is the forerunner of phenomenology. In true Aristotelian-Thomistic tradition, he made the mental act—intentionality—as the presupposition for his philosophy. See Barry Smith, *Austrian Philosophy*, Open Court Publishing, Chicago, (1994).

Economic phenomena The economic phenomena present themselves as individual decisions taken by the members of a given society. Today in the globalized world, millions upon millions of people exercise their economic right in decision-making by valuation of goods and services, and form a large pattern of operation that is clearly explainable in cause-effect parlance, without having to explain it as 'the work of an unseen hand.'[40]

Economic theory Value is not an inherent part of the goods, but rather a product of the mind that reveals the attitude of the subject in the process of continuous decision-making. This, when extended from individuals to the entire gamut of society, which is made up of individual decision makers, develops a pattern of common behaviour called the essence of human cognition and action, also known as praxeology.[41] It is the economic philosophy that holds the individual responsible for the economic decisions taken, the actions which form a deliberate design or logic, whose laws are fundamental to acts of thinking and inferring, so fundamental that they may be called a priori, that is, they are true in a self-evident manner.

Economic practice Economic *praxis* is possible only when the decision-making process is free to the individual who has been ensured by private property, where without it, there would be no market for the means of production; and without the market for a means of production, there will be no monetary prices for the same. Without these monetary prices, it will be impossible to calculate the alternative use of capital goods, for decisions have to be arrived at as to how to use scarce capital resources among the competing uses.[42]

Service to people The significance of economic *praxis* lies in its service to man, and not vice-versa as political ideologies and economic theories want it to be. Consequently, in respect to his freedom, man has not alienated himself from the rights of private property, productive work, fair wages, and just demands through unions and organizations. No individual or group or country arbitrates for itself the right over others to amass wealth that denies others the means of a respectable and decent living.

Justice Justice—commutative, distributive, and social—is the minimum fulfilment of the commandment of love and must be the motive for an economic relationship, which should avoid disparities and inequalities and generate the spirit of re-creation of economic opportunities for people around the globe, so as to create and share wealth and transform humanity into a caring society.

---

[40] It is Adam Smith's famous dictum. It explains the mechanism of the functioning of the economic phenomena.

[41] 'The science of human action that strives for universally valid knowledge is the theoretical system whose hitherto best elaborated branch is economics. In all of its branches, this science is a priori, not empirical. Like logic and mathematics, it is not derived from experience; it is prior to experience. It is, as it were, the logic of action and deed.' See Ludwig von Moses, *The Epistemological Problems of Economics* (1976 translated edition).

[42] Peter J. Boettke's 'Economic Calculation: The Austrian Contribution to Political Economy' can be accessed at http://www.econ.nyu.edu/user/boettke/calculat.htm, accessed on 7 July 2004.

A for Apple

Most admired company

In early March 2009, the *Fortune* magazine announced the most admired companies in the world.[a] Apple is the world's most admired company according to the magazine. Of the 363 companies mentioned in *Fortune*'s list, 273 are from the US, 19 are from Japan, and 17 are from Germany. Unfortunately, not a single Indian company is on the list. The parameters for judging the companies were as follows:

- Innovation
- People management
- Use of assets
- Social responsibility
- Management quality
- Financial soundness
- Long-term investment
- Product quality
- Global competitiveness

The company posted revenues worth $10.17 billion with a net profit of $1.61 billion for the quarter that ended on 27 December 2008. During this period, Apple sold 25,24,000 Macintosh, which was a 9 per cent growth over the previous year's quarter. In 2008, Apple sold 10 million iPhones and more than 54 million iPods—a record 2,27,27,000 iPods were sold in the December quarter itself. Founded by Steve Jobs and Steven Wozniak in California on 1 April 1976 and incorporated in 1977, the company was called Apple Computer Inc for thirty long years.

It is the second year in a row that Apple is at the top of the list of most admired companies. Apple products under Jobs' leadership continue to win mass appeal. Today, Apple has 35,000 employees worldwide. Jobs had an unusual background, from being an adopted child, to embracing Buddhism.

Jobs' business model, in his own woods: My model for business is The Beatles: They were four guys that kept each other's negative tendencies in check; they balanced each other. And the total was greater than the sum of the parts. Great things in business are not done by one person; they are done by a team of people.

Steve was born in 1955 and had a difficult childhood and an equally difficult adolescence, where drugs and unruly behaviour was common. He even worked as a strongman for an insurance company, to collect car loans. But hard work, study, and varied experiences such as learning calligraphy helped him to be innovative when he built Apple personal computer.

Questions

(a) Can an individual overcome personal defects in moral values within a team?
(b) How can collective morality help in a corporation?
(c) What lessons can Indian companies learn from Apple?

[a] See http://money.cnn.com/magazines/fortune/mostadmired/2009/snapshots/670.html.

Summary

- The world has become one global human community.
- Political leadership matters in running the world.
- Corporations have a big influence on the people and politics.
- A majority of the people of the world suffer economic and political injustice.
- Both politics and economics have failed in their objectives to reach out to the poor of the world.
- Corporations that have crossed the national boundaries have a responsibility to reach out to the poor.
- Corporations must make their products and services affordable to the poor.
- The poor do not need charity. They need empowerment to help themselves.

- Businesses can build a partnership with the disadvantaged for the advantage of both the people and themselves.

- Individual leadership matters in overcoming poverty and injustice.

KEY TERMS

Economic justice Equitable distribution of economic resources.

Geopolitical Concerning political interaction across the nation-states.

Global Concerning the whole humanity.

Human end Individual and collective goal of humanity.

Human existence Minimum economic condition.

Leader One who takes the initiative to do something good for others.

Poverty Privation of resources.

Service To help a helpless one.

Supra-state Above the national state power.

CONCEPT REVIEW QUESTIONS

1. Describe the social nature of the modern man.
2. What is more important in the world, economics or politics?
3. What do you understand by economic justice?
4. How can corporations fulfil their responsibility towards the poor?
5. What does empowerment entail?
6. Do international institutions such as the United Nations, World Bank, and International Monitory Fund have a role to play in human development?

CRITICAL THINKING QUESTIONS

1. Is internationalism a failure?
2. What features should a world without nations have?
3. How is human development possible?
4. What is the role of the corporations in human development?

FURTHER READING

Benn Steil and Manuel Hinds, *Money, Markets and Sovereignty*, Yale University Press (2009).

CASE STUDY

The Shrinking Feeling

Financial Crisis

We've got to fix the system. We've got fundamental problems in the system. Main Street is paying a penalty for the excesses and greed in Washington, D.C., and in Wall Street there is no doubt that we have a long way to go.

—John McCain

My attitude is we've got to grow the economy from the bottom up.[a]

—Barak Obama

---

[a] The quotes have been taken from the presidential election debate, Oxford Mississippi.

Part I

Once upon a time in America

It happened in the US, not once but several times. But Americans, just like people in other places, do not learn from history, not even from their history of economic disasters, depressions, and recessions. It happened in 2007 rather slowly. Americans enjoyed the boom in the real estate. They loved it. There were many firms that offered credit. People lapped it up. They bought homes. They invested in hedge funds and ponzi schemes. There seemed to be no end to money. So they went on shopping sprees. They still had plenty of money left. So they chased more dream cars and went on tour splurges.

Just as the fun was getting even better, Wall Street, the American purse (burses) said, 'We have sold America.' The people questioned, 'How could you do that?' They replied, 'See how you spent all that money!' The government was in a fix and produced a solution, 'We will bail out.' People were angry at the people on Wall Street and said, 'Send them to jail.' This is the kind of comedy Americans love, but this time the joke was on them.

Night without dawn in sight

The financial crisis consisted of a severe credit crunch, banking failure, currency problems, and a downturn in trade on a global scale. It began in 2007 with the housing loans debacle known as subprime mortgage, which was followed by the collapses and bankruptcies in the bank, and resulted in a liquidity scarcity. This in turn was followed by an industrial slowdown and the closure of commercial enterprises.[b]

September 2008: Great Fall

This was the month in which the crisis was recognized for real. The banks—investment banks, mortgage banks, and subprime mortgage agencies—in the US and across Europe became unstable due to bad debts and debt insurance. The credit crises led to a slowdown in their economic activities. The impact was sudden and immediate. The stock indexes around the globe reacted and plummeted unabated. This led to large reductions in the market value of equities and commodities. Another

immediate effect was the beginning of a decrease in the international trade.

The world leaders, whether G-8 or G-20, held, confabulations, but the slump continued. The famous bank Lehman Brothers filed for bankruptcy. Alan Greenspan, the former treasury secretary prophesied a greater gloom. Another US bank, Merrill Lynch, was also on the way out, while the US Federal Reserve tried to take over AIG, the biggest insurance company. Washington Mutual also went down and Lloyds TSB took over HBOS, the mortgage lender in the UK. Fortis, another European giant in insurance, was nationalized, followed by Bradford & Bingley. Even in the prosperous and cool Iceland, Glitnir was taken over by the government. Banks after banks fell like a pack of cards and the governments tried to prop them up. In Ireland, the government assured the investors of their investments.

October 2008: The Fight-back

The US House of Representatives passed $700 billion to rescue the financial sector. Measures were announced in Germany and UK for billions of dollars for saving the falling financial paper tigers. France announced its own plans to unfreeze the credit. It was a nationalization spree in Europe, without using the word. The new terms were 'stimulus' and 'bailout'. But the indexes fell. Dow Jones had a hit of 8 per cent on a single day's trading.

November 2008: Crisis Spreads

The situation was hopeless and the crisis spread. There was recession but no one admitted to it. The US was disillusioned. The G-20 world leaders gathered in Washington and pledged to take long-term measures. There was no relief, as even the most powerful Citigroup was in the dumps. Interest rate cuts did not boast of investments. A reduction in the taxes in the UK attracted no one. Recovery plans were mooted by governments but there was no end in sight to the crisis. However, there was a new president elected in the US from whom the people hoped that the Wall Street will be illuminated again. But one had to wait till late January for new policies, which naturally would consist of bigger bailouts.

---

[b] See http://news.bbc.co.uk/2/hi/business/7521250.stm.

December 2008: Recession

The promise of bailouts did not convince anyone. There was no trust. Finally, the truth that governments reluctantly admitted to recession, not only hit them in the face but knocked them down as well. The governments felt that the only way out of this crisis was to bail out these financial institutions with more of the taxpayers' money, who themselves were without money. The job losses were in millions. The car industry had come to a screeching halt. There was nothing to celebrate as the year ended.

January 2009: Gloom

There were no fireworks, not even a whimper in the New Year. There was gloom everywhere. People had lost jobs not only in the developed countries, but also in the developing countries. In India, despite the denials by the government, the exports had fallen, people had lost jobs, the thriving IT was circumspect as the demand for their services fell, the economic growth slowed down, and the industry fell behind. China marked the biggest decline in a decade. The world economic growth fell. IMF was worried.

February 2009: Hope against Hope

Barak Obama, the new president of the US, came in off the block with a phenomenal $787 billion as not just a stimulus, but with also a plan. People were hoping against hope that he would succeed. The whole world wanted him to succeed (except the opposition, the Republican Party, under whose rule the catastrophe occurred).[c]

Part II

Eye on India

The leaders of the Indian corporations are often honoured and addressed as the 'Captains of Industry'. However, with the mere onset of the signs of a storm, they get prepared to abandon the ship. All of them cry out in unison, 'The Govern-ment must help.' When these captains appear on TV, they present themselves as leaders and wear their ethical values on their sleeves. The media lionizes them for its own reasons of winning their patronage. The government also buckles under the corporate pressure and concedes concessions, such as assuring credit availability and providing concessions in excise and customs duties. The government also likes this kind of tinkering at the top to keep the captains happy.[d]

Falling Demand in Traditional Exports

There are 35 million people employed in textiles, which is the largest industry in the country and 50 per cent of the produce is exported.[e] By the end of 2008, 7,00,000 workers had already lost their jobs, and the Confederation of the Textile Industries estimated that another 5,00,000 would be retrenched before the first quarter in 2009. Three months after the financial crisis, exports showed a 10 per cent climb down.

Gems, jewellery and handicrafts

Gems, jewellery, and handicrafts are India's traditional exports. In October 2008, the trade took a blow of 16 per cent, resulting in 5,00,000 job losses. The exports were falling quickly because during recession these commodities were not on the priority list of the customers.

Agriculture

India's agricultural exports have increased over the years and till recently, these have been at 12 per cent of the country's total exports. Rice, sugar, cotton, spices, tea, and coffee have fallen in demand. India is the third largest producer of cotton in the world and China is the major importer of its fabric industry that dominates the world supplies. The Chinese garment trade has been hit hard by the recession in Europe and America, which are the main markets for China. Hence, it is now importing less cotton from India and this has hurt the Indian agriculture.

---

[c] These are the last lines that could be written on the subject before this book was published. However, whatever happens next in the financial world will be an Obama history.

[d] See http://www.indiatogether.org/economy/.

[e] Kannan Kasturi's, 'Financial Crisis in India' is available at http://www.indiatogether.org/2008/dec/agrarhit.htm.

Part III

Failure of corporate governance in banks

In the final analysis, the banks of the developed countries, with the best brains in the business, merely ended up as runners of ponzi schemes. Despite all the laws and the induced best practices of corporate governance, nothing was practiced in reality. Transparency was the first casualty.

Ever since the Reagan administration, the banks enjoyed some freedom in adolescent delinquency. Reaganomics, as it was called, was based on a small government, reduced taxes, minimum legislation, and reduced control. The same laissez-faire philosophy of Milton Freedman was introduced. It became an ideology of the Republican Party in the US and that of the Conservative Party in Britain, under the leadership of Margaret Thatcher. In addition to this, a total disregard for the environmental norms of the industry, with no control over the credit and spending laid the foundation stone for the financial disaster, two decades later.

World financial institutions

The International Monetary Fund (IMF) and the World Trade Organizations (WTO) are international organizations with 185 member countries.[f] The former works on monetary systems around the world, and the latter on trade and commerce. These institutions have very large agendas to help the developing nations. While IMF struggles with currency problems, loans for developments, etc., the latter deals with trade tariffs and the opening of the world markets. These, however, are victims of geopolitical movements and in matters of the financial crisis of the present nature have very little voice. These institutions have a great deal of goodwill within themselves, but others do not trust them. Wherever they meet, the third-world countries hold demonstrations to demand relief from their debts. Most of the time, these agencies are seen as instruments in the hands of the developed countries, whose funding they depend upon. Hence, geopolitical considerations play a great role. More is demanded from the aided countries, without giving them relief from their age-old, centuries-old debts. Hence, if the third-world countries consider them another tool of oppression, that would not be very far from the truth. Now that the financial crisis has hit the big donors, the situation in the third-world countries will be unthinkable to figure out.

Reserve Bank of India

Although India was always in the denial mode during the financial crisis, the Reserve Bank of India intervened at the right time. It injected Rs 2.8 lakh crore, which was a wise decision. But unfortunately, the think-tanks of both the nationalized as well as the private banks were empty. The Reserve Bank of India parked this enormous monetary incentive in the safety of government securities. Yet the bankers were apprehensive, circumspect, and were reluctant to lend. Among all the G-20 countries, perhaps this initiative was the only silver lining. But Indian banks know how to fritter away an opportunity amid challenges.

Executive immorality

It does not need complicated economic quantitative methods to find out what the corporations did with the money. There was a systemic failure in the financial management. In plain language, the corporations had messed up with the public money.[g]

Some examples are as follows—Citigroup collected $45 billion. Its executives spent 50 million from it for their corporate jet. The CEO of Merrill Lynch spent $1.22 million for redecorating his office. AIG received $85 billion bailout. Its executives went on the costliest holidays to the gambling resorts of Las Vegas. The executives on Wall Street paid themselves $18 billion in 2008. These were the very people who mismanaged the funds and caused the meltdown.

Part IV

Financial crisis and geopolitical turmoil

The slowdown started showing in the developing countries. These countries started facing a currency

[f] See http://www.imf.org/external/np/exr/facts/imfwto.htm.

[g] P. Sainath, 'Whose Crisis it, anyway?' For more details, log onto http://www.indiatogether.org/2008/dec/agr.

crisis, with investors transferring vast capital resources into stronger currencies such as the yen, the dollar, and the Swiss franc. They were forced to seek aid from the International Monetary Fund. However, more than their financial dues, it is the bottom of the political establishment in these countries that is being knocked out. Most of the poor countries in the world are in debt. The debt trap has them in a vice, where even the rudimentary reforms are not possible. In addition to this, these countries, particularly Africa, are in political turmoil due to the civil wars and destabilizing political upheavals. These countries, which depend mainly on the aid of the developed countries, have now become almost destitute. The economically reformed countries, that is, the BRIC—Brazil, Russia, India, and China—which depend on the developed countries for their exports, suddenly find their growth cut down by critical percentage points, despite having strong domestic economies.

The continued financial crisis has hit the oil-rich Middle Eastern countries. Just before the crisis broke out, they had revelled in soaring oil prices, but they came down with a thud as the demand receded, the recession set in, and the prices plummeted. Their economies are now suffering a slow down, and the biggest indicator of the Gulf, which is the real estate, is slowly coming to a standstill. This has increased political tensions in the area. Iran wants to go nuclear. Israel tried to subdue the Palestinian territory through a merciless war.

The crisis has further worsened the issue of terrorism in the world. The allies at war against terrorists in Iraq and Afghanistan are in recession. The crisis has made them rethink about the costly war in the above two countries. However, the greatest dilemma is that they cannot abandon this cause without embracing greater perils of terrorist attacks at home. The financial crisis seems to have come as a relief for the terrorist organizations such as *Al Qaida*. The stranglehold has become lose and now they have another country in their grip, Pakistan. This portends enormous signs of anxiety for not just India, but for the entire sub-continent.

Impending geopolitical earthquake

José Miguel Alonso Trabanco, a Mexican expert on geopolitical and military affairs, warns the world of a geopolitical disaster.[h] It goes without saying that the happenings at this scale of the financial crisis will have not just a financial outfall, but a disastrous political one too. One cannot separate economics from politics, and vice-versa. The business of the people will always be called political economy.

One of the first things that will get affected is the balance of power. The US will no longer command like a lone superpower. As the year 2008 came to an end, the US had already lost considerable geopolitical power. China pranced like a tiger and danced the dragon dance, and hosted the great Olympic Games to herald that it had taken a prominent place in the power structure of the world. It clearly signalled the end of the uni-polar world order of the US, which the US enjoyed ever since the collapse of communism in 1991.

Russia too flexed its muscles. It threatened to aim its missiles at western Europe. It turned off the gas supply to Ukraine in the coldest winter months, and since the pipeline was connected to western Europe, its supply also effectively came to an end. With the baggage of communism and the tragic experience of Afghanistan behind it, Russia is once again asserting itself. The world is becoming multi-polar. The financial crisis is redrawing the political balance of power in the NATO countries of Europe, the US, Russia, and China, and also in the other strong regional powers such as India, Israel, Brazil, and South Africa.

It implies that now there will be tectonic shifts in international policies. Financial policies will have to be subservient to political interests.

The once powerful US has played into the hands of the countries of the world. It is presently the largest debtor in the world, almost closing in on its total GDP. When will it be able to offload this mountain of debt? What if all the creditors demand their money back? What happens if the US refuses to pay?

---

[h] José Miguel Alonso Trabanco, 'An Impending Geopolitical Earthquake?' See http://www.warandpeace.ru/en/commentaries/vprint/32890/, accessed on 22 February 2009.

With such a financial crisis, the countries in crisis will have to trim their budgets and, with it, the defence allocations as well. The military power of the NATO could be well challenged by the Asian giants such as China and India, and, for a good measure, by Russia also. The economic downturn has already played havoc on all the Western European countries, and political instability is quite imminent.

We do not know what the future holds for the people of the world. However, we know that it is the financial mismanagement that has wrought so much havoc. All are a part of this crisis. There are no bystanders.

Conclusion

Warren Buffet, the ever-optimistic American entrepreneur, says, 'Never invest in a business you cannot understand.' This advice is not new. What is new is that it befits the new realities of our times of financial crisis to indulge in retrospection at how little we knew when we gave away our hard-earned money to the banks or invested in shares. However, history has taught us that in matters concerning money, we never learn enough. Risks will be taken and money will be lost. The history of money will repeat itself.

Discussion Questions

1. What are the main issues of the financial crisis?
2. Are financial issues ethical issues?
3. What conflicts do financial issues cause?
4. Why is bankruptcy an ethical issue?
5. What is the ethics of executives ameliorating themselves in times of a financial crisis?
6. What is the morality of spending the taxpayers' money to bailout the corporations?
7. What is inherently wrong with corporate governance?
8. What moral responsibility does India bear towards the economic well-being of its citizens?
9. What moral role does India have in the geopolitical situation in the world?
10. How can India demand justice for the people who have lost their jobs and livelihoods due to the financial crisis?

Going Further . . .

- Conduct a symposium, followed by an intensive workshop.

ETHICAL DEVELOPMENT PROGRAMME

Management Training

Moral assessment of geopolitical history

Here, you are supplied with some turning points in the history of political economy. At each stage, the judgments taken by the leaders and supported by the people have changed the course of history. Here is an opportunity to review those historical events and learn how to cope with a similar eventuality with lesser anxiety in the future.

(a) Objective: To train you to observe a historical event and take a moral stand from the ensuing issues, in order to seek direction in your undertakings.

(b) Moral arguments are your assessment from an ethical point of view.

(c) You may use the seven standards of moral judgment that we have been following in this book.

(d) For each historical event give two arguments, one that approves the event/decision and the other that disapproves it. For instance: In 1991 Manmohan Singh, the then finance minister of India, introduced economic reforms.

Words in italics suggest the ethical concepts/ standards of judgment.

(i) The economic reforms were good. One of the biggest evils of the earlier economic model of India, which was centralized in its planning, failed to bring prosperity to the people. Due to a licensing system, it bred corruption within the enterprise. The social aim of economic equality and greatest benefit to the greatest number failed miserably. The economic reforms to deregulate and grant freedom to the people to pursue the enterprise of their choice, were prudent. The reforms would encourage fair means rather than corrupt ones to attain prosperity.

(ii) The economic reforms are a boon and not a curse. These merely help the rich to become richer. This increased gap between the rich and the poor causes social conflict and social injustice. The corporations do not have the interest of the poor at heart; only profits are on their minds. The consequences of reforms have resulted in the acquisition of the farmers' lands and deprived them of their fundamental rights to own property; the failure to pay compensation is outright injustice. Farmers have been evicted in large numbers from their lands for the benefit of a few industrialists. In the process, the government has abdicated its duty to the people to protect their lives and properties.

Political Economy Facts

1776: Wealth of nations

At a time when a war was raging in North America and the British colonies over there were fighting for independence, a British economist named Adam Smith published a seminal text that defended the modern liberal economic theory, *An Inquiry into the Nature and Causes of the Wealth of Nations*. The book, which is often referred to simply as *The Wealth of Nations*, advocates free-market economy and promotes the idea that individuals pursuing their own economic self-interest can create unintended positive side effects for the overall economy.[43]

1820: Industrial revolution

The development of the Watt steam engine in the late eighteenth century spurred a wave of industrial development in Europe and the US. It came to be known as the Industrial Revolution. Major changes altered the face of agriculture, manufacturing, and transportation, and rewrote the economic status quo that had dominated Europe for centuries.

1846: Corn laws repealed

Britain repealed its Corn laws, which were a system of tariffs aimed at bolstering British competition against foreign imports. The move signalled a shift away from the British mercantilism—a theory of trade that held the global volume of trade as unchangeable and thus focused on building a positive balance of trade with other nations. It marked a significant step towards increasing free trade internationally.

1848: Communist capitalist divide

With unrest erupting across Europe, the German philosophers Karl Marx and Friedrich Engels published *The Communist Manifesto*, the founding work of communist economic and social theory. The same year, the British philosopher John Stuart Mill published *The Principles of Political Economy*, which became the dominant textbook on economics through most of the remainder of the nineteenth century. These two works coincided with the rise of laissez-faire economics, which espoused limited government intervention in the economy and took hold, particularly in Britain, during the middle part of the 1800s. The growing popularity of *The Economist*, a British news publication founded in 1843 that advocated the liberal economic theory, accompanied this tide.

1884: Fabien socialism

An elite British intellectual group was founded in 1884 and called itself the Fabien Society after the Roman general, Fabius. It promoted a strand of utopian socialism by drawing from the ideas of Karl Marx, but eschewed the violent revolutionary tactics of some of his followers. The group was known for its essays and literary works. Its ranks included prominent intellectuals Sidney and Beatrice Webb, George Bernard Shaw, H.G. Wells, and Virginia Woolf. The society promoted ideas such as the nationalization of property and the implementation of a minimum wage. Its followers figured prominently in the founding of the British Labour Party in 1900.

---

[43] Visit Centre for Foreign Relations at http://www.cfr.org/publication/18709/.

1913: Federal reserve system created

Following a financial panic in 1907, calls for banking and currency reforms led to the creation of the Federal Reserve System, in which a central government bank lent to regional banks. The primary purpose of the system was to increase financial liquidity and give the US government better control over its currency.

1917: Russian Revolution

With World War I raging across Europe, the Bolsheviks seized power in a coup in Russia and gave power to Communist groups called the soviets (councils). This eventually led to the establishment of the Soviet Union in 1922. For the better part of the twentieth century, the Communist Soviet Union was capitalism's main rival and a competing power base of economic ideology. Two years after the Russian Revolution in 1919, the publication of the Fascist manifesto set the stage for pockets of fascism to emerge in Europe. Fascism and communism fought for supremacy in Germany's Weimar Republic, until National Socialism, or Nazism, came to dominate with the rise of Adolf Hitler.

1922: State corporatism

The idea of corporatism, in which a ruling party mediated between civic groups that represented various economic or social interests, rose to prominence in the early 1920s, with Benito Mussolini's ascendance as Italy's prime minister. In the corporate economic model, alliances representing different industries and worker groups were a part of the ruling mechanism of the state. Corporatist models were implemented in Italy, Spain, Germany, Japan, and other countries in the run-up to World War II, and were often accompanied by a brand of authoritarian nationalism known as fascism. The model largely disappeared following the World War II, but authoritarian economies like China and Russia adopted elements of state corporatism in their post-Cold War models.

1935: Keynes economic rethink

A reassessment of markets took root, following the stock market crash of 1929, more than half a decade of economic depression, and a series of massive government interventions in the economy, including new regulatory strictures implemented by President Franklin Roosevelt. The British economist John Maynard Keynes came to represent the new thinking and suggested several changes to the status quo of economic thought. Among other points, Keynes argued that capitalism would not 'self-correct' and would require ongoing government supervision.

1944: Bretton Woods

Following two years of negotiations and half a decade of war, world leaders met in Bretton Woods, New Hampshire, and drafted the first framework intended to govern monetary relations among the world's largest economies. The conference resulted in a system of fixed exchange rates, the creation of the World Bank and the International Monetary Fund, and planned for a third organization, aimed at governing world trade that was eventually founded in 1947 as the General Agreement on Tariffs and Trade.

1949: Chinese Revolution

Towards the end of the Chinese civil war that began in 1946, the Communist Party of China led by Mao Zedong, seized power in 1949. It implemented a communist government that alongside the Soviet Union would oppose US capitalist ideology throughout much of the twentieth century. Within a decade, Mao broke up with Moscow over doctrinal disputes relating to industrialization and collectivization of agriculture.

1956: Peak Oil

A geophysicist named M. King Hubbert theorized that the rate of oil production in any given geographical area tended to follow a bell-shaped curve. Hubbert correctly predicted that oil production in the US would be at its peak between 1965 and 1970, lending credence to theorists who used a similar model to predict the date at which oil production would peak on a global scale—a theory that became known as 'peak oil.' In 1960, new fears over global oil production coincided with the formation of the Organization of the Petroleum Exporting Countries, or OPEC, as a cartel bringing together many of the world's leading oil producers.

1960: Milton Friedman's influence

Healthy economic times in the US during the 1960s coincided with the rise of Milton Friedman, an economist who argued strongly in support of laissez-faire, the libertarian economic principles that stood in contrast to the theories of John Maynard Keynes. Friedman also spread the theory of monetarism, a school of economic thought in which the supply of money in an economy was used as the primary tool to affect the country's rate of inflation.

1978: Socialism with Chinese characteristics

Beginning in 1978, pragmatists within China's Communist party, led by Deng Xiaoping, spearheaded a series of economic reforms aimed at generating economic surplus and modernizing the Chinese economy. These reforms were generally credited with lifting millions of Chinese out of poverty during the final decades of the twentieth century. Analysts in the West commonly characterized these reforms as a part of a gradual Chinese shift towards a capitalist system, but Beijing rebuffed such claims by saying that the Chinese economic liberalization did not undermine the Marxist principles, followed by the country's government, or the Chinese Communist Party itself.

1979: Stagflation and de-industrialization

Paul Volcker took the helm at the US Federal Reserve during a period of stagflation—a combination of economic stagnation and inflation. Volcker implemented the monetarism espoused by economist Milton Friedman as a counter-inflation strategy. This provoked a deep recession that accelerated the shift of the US economy from manufacturing to services and laid the foundation for a steady growth during the 1980s.

1981: Reaganomics and Laffer Curve

Ronald Reagan assumed the US presidency in 1981, preaching the four pillars of economic policy that came to be known as Reaganomics. It involved reducing government spending, reducing marginal taxes on labour and income, reducing government regulation of the economy, and using monetary policy to keep inflation rates low. This theory of economics was bolstered by the 'Laffer curve,' a concept popularized by the economist Arthur Laffer, which argued that increases in taxation rates do not necessarily increase overall tax revenue.

1991: Post-cold war globalization

The collapse of the Soviet Union and the end of the Cold War functioned as enabling mechanisms by spurring a period of globalization and economic liberalization across many countries. This shift was exemplified in 1995 by the establishment of the World Trade Organization, an organization tasked with supervising and standardizing oversight of international trade and liberalizing the global trade agenda. The shift towards globalization came with discontents, however. The vulnerabilities engendered by a more liberalized international financial network became clear during the second half of the 1990s, as financial crises broke out in several emerging economies, including Mexico, several East Asian countries, Russia, and Brazil. The International Monetary Fund (IMF) made emergency loans to many of these countries, but imposed political restrictions as a condition for the loans. The shock of these crises and irritation over the IMF's loan conditions changed the way the affected countries thought about reserve capital.

1992: Economic blocks coalesce

The establishment of the European Union signalled a period in which several groups of countries sought to integrate their economies with those of their neighbours through regional economic blocs. The European Union expanded throughout the 1990s and 2000s. In 1993, the US, Canada, and Mexico signed the North American Free Trade Agreement, or NAFTA, thus binding their economies much more comprehensively. Other blocs, including Mercosur in Latin America and ASEAN in Southeast Asia, sought to expand their influence over the course of the decade. The culmination of this trend was the establishment of the euro, a common currency adopted by a group of EU member states in 2002.

2000–2006: Climax of deregulation

By the latter part of the 1990s, with the US economy booming, a dissenting opinion about the free market's ability to 'self-correct' had faded. The US President, George W. Bush, pressed an agenda, initiated by the administration of President Bill Clinton, that encouraged home ownership as a major economic priority. Alongside major tax cuts, the Bush administration followed this policy course throughout the first half of the 2000s. Meanwhile, in 2004, the US Securities and Exchange Commission lifted a regulation limiting the extent to which major investment banks could leverage their investments. Increased borrowing, taken alongside US spending on the wars in Iraq and Afghanistan, worked to balloon the US budget deficit. Eventually, a bubble in the US housing market burst, and brought major problems for the US subprime-lending outfits, such as sparking the financial crisis of the late 2000s, leading to a broader rethink of when and how markets should be regulated.

Management Mantra

Audacity of Hope: Barack Obama

In 2006, Barack Obama's second book, *The Audacity of Hope*, was published and was received with great hope by not only the people of the US, but also by the rest of the world. The great hope was that this young senator would one day become the president of his country. He did not belie people's expectations, and declared his candidacy for the post of the president of the US soon after he had autographed the copies of the book.

Obama published his memoirs *Dreams from My Father* in 1995, in which he revealed his struggle to find an identity. As the son of a Kenyan immigrant father and an American mother, Obama grew up in a black and white racial divide. When Obama was still a toddler, his father decided to return to Kenya, but his mother took Obama to Indonesia. The identity got even more complicated. As a youngster, he lived in Hawaii with his white grandparents and completed his schooling. He graduated from Columbia University and took his law degree from Harvard Law School, where he was the first African-American student to become its president. He worked as a community organizer and also taught constitutional law.

In 1997, he came into politics as a Democratic Party legislator in Illinois, and in 2005 he became the Senator, and in 2008 he became President of the US. In his campaign he promised, 'Change we can believe in—a change of values in governance.' He considered Abraham Lincoln as his role model, and identified with the civil rights leader Martin Luther King Jr. Through his words of maturity and wisdom, Obama inspired not just his fellow Americans, but it appeared as though he was running for the presidency of the world.

When he won the presidency on 4 November 2008, he declared in his victory acceptance speech, 'Change has come to America....Yes, we can.' In his personal journey of his own discovery of identity, he learnt more about himself in a complex and complicated world of money and race, power and politics, service and honesty. He learnt to distinguish them and use them for the common good. He found his identity in the dreams that he could achieve through his family and through his career. His journey, which was a journey of hope, was realized because he stepped out of his own little world and worked for his community and country. He is expected to have the greatest ever geopolitical influence in the coming decade.

MANTRA　*Yes, we can.*

Part Five

Managers and the International Community

Challenges of the New Age World

Challenges of the New Age World
The Way of Encountering the Future

What I cannot do now is the sign of what I shall do hereafter. The sense of impossibility is the beginning of all possibilities.[1]

—Sri Aurobindo

In the name of democracy, let us use that power! Let us all unite! Let us fight for a new world, a decent world that will give men a chance to work, that will give youth a future and old age security. By the promise of these things, brutes have risen to power, but they lie! They do not fulfil their promise; they never will. Dictators free themselves, but they enslave the people! Now, let us fight to fulfil that promise! Let us fight to free the world, to do away with national barriers, to do away with greed, with hate and intolerance. Let us fight for a world of reason, a world where science and progress will lead to all men's happiness.[2]

—Charles Spencer Chaplin

OUR CHOICES MAKE OUR WORLD

What does it mean to be human? Questioning our very own existence makes us ask, 'What am I doing here?' We reflect on what we are and what we are not, and what we can be. We reflect on what we are doing and what we are not, and what we can do. By striving to be what we are not but what we can become, and by doing what we have not been doing, we become who we are, and yet we see who we are not. We are evolving endlessly. It demonstrates that when we arrive at a stage, we have to go yet further. This in short has been the story of civilization. How this story will be further written depends upon us, and the future generation will either thank us for it or detest us for what we have left for them. We take upon ourselves the duty to leave behind a world of social harmony, economic well-being, and political unity. We would like to be citizens of the world, not of a country in the world. We would like to

believe in our convictions, and work and travel to any part of the world. We would not like to be discriminated on the basis of race, creed, religion, or language. We are now what we are and we are trying to become what we are not. Our choices will make our world.

George Herbert Mead (1863–1931) was a pragmatic philosopher, who described human existence as evolving towards an open future in his work *Mind, Self and Future Society*. The ideal of human action is to achieve a universal community, which will be the harbinger of human progress. In this universal community, every member will recognize the interests of the other. The golden rule of conduct is to make the interests of others one's own. It is an ideal that is implicit in the history of mankind. Spirituality, economic processes, and communication are the historical forces leading us towards our ideal. However, we have a long way to go. The next four chapters will reflect how we would have to come together and be

---

[1] Sri Aurobindo, *Thoughts and Glimpses.* See http://sabda.sriaurobindoashram.org/.

[2] Charles Spencer Chaplin (Charlie Chaplin) in the last part of the movie *The Great Dictator*, made in 1940. Chaplin plays the dual roles of Adenoid Hynkel, the dictator of Tomania, and a Jewish barber. This quote is the closing speech of the Jewish barber, after being mistaken for Hynkel.

a part of these processes, to form a universal community.

ONE WORLD AND UNIVERSAL VALUES

On 10 December 1948, the General Assembly of the United Nations (UN) adopted and proclaimed the Universal Declaration of Human Rights. This was one single and universal affirmation by the people of all races and creeds, cultures and religions, the strong and the weak, the rich and the poor that all human beings are equal and have the right to enjoy liberty, justice, and peace.[3]

The Declaration, a document most sacred in its content and intent, has been the highest achievement in human consciousness of the universal ethical values. It is a perfect testimony of what human beings can produce in their good will. That it came to be drawn after two dreadful world wars, which were a result of the evil will to destroy and kill, shows that human beings are basically endowed with a good will, for they can rise above the consequences of their own evil deeds and give themselves the commandments of the highest moral value.

Over the sixty years of the Declaration's existence, we have traversed quite far. Globalization

Mad Hatter's bungalow in *Alice in Wonderland*, a symbol of our world of endless possibilities

seems to be the most used term today in business, politics, and the cultural life of people. In a previous paragraph, we read about Mead's prediction about the universal community coming together spiritually and economically because of communication. Technology has achieved communication, and globalization has made it possible for a greater integration of the world through trade and commerce, political influences, and people to people communication.

The world has crossed the national boundaries in several spheres.

Economic processes   These include trade, commerce, market capitalization around the world round the clock, real-time communication, mobility and travel, global labour migration, and job market.

Cultural processes   People-to-people contact, intercultural knowledge, reduction in prejudices, and a breakdown in racial and religious barriers are the cultural processes that have helped to integrate the world.

Political processes   The UN has become a community of the nations of the world and its people. There have been more and more interventions of the UN in the military, which was earlier considered exclusive. The UN has worked towards achieving the sovereign rights of the states. The UN also brokers peace between warring nation-states and gives them a chance to debate and dialogue at its assembly. Its health, labour, economic development, and other organizations form a part of its political processes.

Environmental processes   The little, blue planet of the solar system that is called the Earth has become endangered from within. This globe cannot be partitioned with boundaries of its peripheries except the ones determined by its larger universe. Its protection is important for the survival of all its inhabitants. The fundamental need for survival brings all together.

---

[3] See http://www.un.org/Overview/rights.html.

The global community is increasingly an inter-dependent community. We have not achieved all that is possible, but we have achieved some of what was once considered impossible. The world map has changed since the fall of communism in 1990, and political and economic processes that were previously unthinkable are now taking place.

GLOBAL COMMUNITY AND ITS PROBLEMS

In the global community, with such vast diversity, the problems of relationship are also highly complex and difficult.

States at war and the arms race   We still have nation-states that are at war with each other. There is such a huge arms race that most of the resources are spent or rather wasted on them, which could have helped eradicate poverty from the face of the Earth.

Economic problems   Ideologies, trade barriers, and poverty have made an unequal distribution of the Earth's resources.

Consequences of bad economic and political processes   Refugees, labour migration, child labour, abuse of human rights, gender bias, and cruelty to animals are the outcome of bad economic and political processes.

Natural disasters   Natural disasters such as earthquakes, storms, floods, and droughts are beyond human control, but technology helps to overcome the consequences, though most of it is still not available to the needy.

Terrorism   Terror attacks by self-interested groups on the life and property of defenceless people is the new global phenomenon. It is the enemy of humanity and exhibits extreme irra-tionality and immorality.

Although the above points affect us negatively, since they are common to us all, they also give us a reason to unite ourselves against the com-mon enemy. This enemy can be overcome, first and foremost, by the attitude we employ to encounter it. These attitudes are well-articulated in the articles of the Declaration on Human Rights

of the United Nations. We may happily admit that it is a charter of ethics for the world.

The individual   Human dignity defines the individual, irrespective of gender, race, creed, culture, religion, or any other distinguishing and discriminatory categorization.

Communities   The associations of the indivi-duals are unique, but they may not infringe the basic human dignity.

World community   It is the peaceful existence of individuals, communities, and nations within the universal values of social and economic justice.

Earth   It is the responsibility of the individuals to form a communion of the world community, to protect the natural environment.

OBJECTIVES OF PART V

With the above perspective on universal commu-nity in the following four chapters of the final part of this book, we will focus on the contemporary challenges.

Environment   The protection of the environ-ment is a global issue that needs to be discussed beyond the national borders. We would have to find solutions for the sustainability of the re-sources. This is a management task with an attitude. We need to deeply analyse the issues in environmental management.

Communication   We saw above what brings the global community together. Communication has broken down all barriers and today, we do business with people and organizations we have never got acquainted with personally. We have turned the earth into a virtual world. But our attitudes, both good and bad, have also travelled over in cyberspace. This has increased our ethical problems and we need to find ethical solutions for them.

Conflicts   We have mentioned above that despite our best efforts, there are political, economic, and cultural clashes and conflicts. Whether these are military wars or economic ones, terror on innocents or cultural battles, all of these reflect human imperfections, and at the same time, the ability to rise above these problems and form a code that we may not fall back on in the same morass. The possibilities to do something good are immense.

Special challenges   There are some states of affairs among human beings that, despite all the good, will still slip into undesirable regions. Intellectual honesty, non-discriminatory action based on sex, and the way we treat animals are concerns whose solutions seem distant. We must, however, exercise *dharma* to achieve this goal.

Sri Aurobindo taught us that in our imperfection, we must always remember that man is a product of evolution. However, man has succeeded in using his free will and his limited intelligence to come so far in the journey of evolution, and is one day going to mutate from the present status to a superman species.

Community of Ants

The ant world

They make their way inside your sugar bowl. You find them on your oil-smeared pillow. They ruin the cake you just bought for your child's first birthday. You see them everywhere. They are found everywhere, except at the two poles of the Earth; at least, we have not found them there as yet.

Is man a social animal? Wait a minute! Ants have been upon the Earth before man evolved. It is not a big deal that they are social. They have built farms, developed architecture, organized seamless colonies, and created integrated information and communication systems. They conceived all this and more in their powerful little brains, and implemented the projects mentioned above more than 150 million years ago.

Do you want to know about diversity? There are more than 14,000 kinds of ant species! They are small. Some of them are very small, and measure only 0.1 cm in length; the largest ones are 2.5 cm long. They have really small eyes, but their eyes have to be the most beautiful and powerful in the world, because they possess close to a 1000 lenses! They can lift objects that are nearly fifty times that of their body weight! They may be small, but they build the largest super-organisms. It is said that the total weight of all the ants is equal to the weight of the entire human population of the world![a]

To give a typical 'ant' example, let us take the leaf cutters found in the rain forests of South America.[b] They are a photographer's delight when they cheerfully carry leaves towering over their backs, which they have cut with astonishing precision, to their colonies. They can defoliate an entire citrus tree in a single day. They harvest approximately one-fifth of the annual growth, which is more vegetation than that harvested by any other animal. In a single lifetime, which may vary from one to five years, a single leafcutter colony turns over and aerates forty tons of soil!

This shows how valuable the ants are to planet Earth. These ants process the top soil of the planet. Without them, life would be impossible. The ants aerate the soil. Without them, dead leaves, small animals, and insects will litter and cover the surface of the Earth. Pests would flourish, the Earth will be stripped of her vegetation, and the green cover will vanish. In other words, nothing will survive. Life will become extinct upon the Earth.

All this may be very humbling for us human beings. It is from this virtue that we need to learn a lesson that we are all interdependent and our survival lies in forming a super-organism of people. There may be a great truth behind the workings of the ant world—it is governed, or perhaps prompted by a Queen Mother!

[a] For more details, see 'Ant' in the World Book CD.

[b] See http://www.guardian.co.uk/environment/2009/mar/09/ants-nature-research.

CHAPTER

17

Challenges of Environment

*As we watch the sun go down, evening after evening, through the smog across the
poisoned waters of our native earth, we must ask ourselves seriously whether we
really wish some future universal historian on another planet to say about us: 'With all
their genius and with all their skill, they ran out of foresight and air and food and water
and ideas,' or, 'They went on playing politics until their world collapsed around them.'*

—U. Thant, U.N. Secretary General

*A technological society has two choices. First it can wait until catastrophic failures
expose systemic deficiencies, distortion and self-deceptions... Secondly, a culture
can provide social checks and balances to correct for systemic distortion prior to
catastrophic failures.*

—M.K. Gandhi

LEARNING OBJECTIVES

After studying this chapter, you will be able to

> State the principles of environmental ethics
> Illustrate environmental challenges as business opportunities
> Describe the role of government
> Define multi-stakeholdership

INTRODUCTION

Environmental ethics is our main objective, and the guiding ethical standard is
stewardship. With stewardship, we draw on the principles of conservation,
sustainability, and moral responsibility. Corporations have started to develop
responsibility towards society. They will have to bear the responsibilities of
environmental conservation and sustainability of resources for the common good of
humanity and its future.

Let us look at a positive story on wildlife conservation. Junona is a small hamlet
tucked away in a forest cove situated about 15 km from Chandrapur in Maharashtra.
A new family came into the village to settle down. It comprised a tigress with two

cubs and a male tiger, which was identified as the father of the cubs by the villagers. This family was lucky to escape danger and destitution. Sometime ago, the villagers had found three orphaned cubs. The mother had probably become a victim of poaching.

These days children are taught early in school to take care of their environment. The primary schoolgoers may not have seen a live tiger, but they study about the importance of preserving the tiger as a means to environmental conservation. The tiger is a link in the ecological chain. If the tiger has to be saved, then the forests have to be saved. If the forests have to be saved, then the trees have to be saved, and if the trees have to be saved, then one must not only stop clearing the forests, but plant more trees. When we plant more trees, the entire ecological system will start to work. The forests will support wildlife—from the tiniest to the biggest and fiercest creatures— the water tables will get reset, pollution will disappear, and the good earth will flourish. If the project for tiger preservation has been allocated Rs 600 crores as funds, and the Prime Minister of India is the chairman of the Indian Board for Wildlife, it shows the seriousness and importance of the project.

The problem in Chandrapur and the surrounding areas is that this area, which is a declared Tiger Reserve, is now in danger of being taken over by the mining industry. If the central government awards the licence to the mining industry, then twenty-one coal mines will be setting shop in this area—and Chandrapur will become a coal city. The forest will disappear and so will the wildlife. It will adversely affect human life. What choice will the people of Chandrapur be allowed? If they opt for industrial development, then they opt out of a clean environment, which will result in paying heavily for healthcare and will perhaps cost them their lives.

We make the desert bloom with our ingenuity, and turn the forest into a desert in such utter mockery of our intelligence. Somehow, we have failed to intelligently sustain and manage the resources of nature, the primary source of the supply chain. If the air that we breathe is polluted, the water that we drink is contaminated, and the earth that grows food has toxins, then something must be terribly wrong with the way we work, produce food, and live. There is a grave problem here for humanity and it needs to be tackled strategically, with great skill and dexterity. Such a task is performed through management.

In an industrialized world, man's life revolves around what the firms produce and supply in the market. What these firms do has a great impact on the environment. The production of goods for the consumption and leisure activities of man involves processing of raw materials that generates waste in solid, liquid, and gaseous forms, and is let off in the atmosphere to the detriment of the environment. The entire network of the infrastructure involved, such as maintenance of machinery, packaging, and transport, puts great pressure on the environment. The products that the consumers use or consume find their way back into the environment yet again in a different way, which is harmful to the environment. For instance, the consumption of fossil fuels adds to the air pollution and real estate development adds to noise pollution. Even the service sector adds to the environmental problems, since it uses various products of the industry that have negative consequences, more intensively than normal consumers do.

We have traversed from our primitive existence into a highly modernized, complex, and, more often than not, complicated urban lifestyle. To do this, we have exploited far too many resources and mindlessly wasted most of them. Today, the very cities that were our pride have become traps. We cannot sustain them. The resources are failing. There is not enough energy to run the industries and manage the cities. The cities have become intolerable and unsustainable. Water is depleting and garbage is mounting. Pollution is taking its toll on the health of people, and they have to spend a substantial amount of their incomes on healthcare. It is difficult to fathom, unless something is done drastically to enable the future generations to cope with the tragedy that today's generation is perpetrating.

Hence, environmental management is neither a myth, nor a shibboleth of the pass-time activists' mode, but a necessary measure in crisis. It consists of a proper and efficient organization of those activities of a firm, which have or may have impact on the environment.

PRINCIPLES OF ENVIRONMENTAL ETHICS

Environmental ethics consists of the human relationship with the natural environment and all that there is in it. Its scope moves beyond the relationship of humans with the natural environment and animals. Although our relationship with nature has been a topic in ethics, it developed as a separate discipline in the 1960s. The pictures of our planet taken from space was the tipping point to consider the vulnerability of the planet Earth, for the way we exploited the resources, and in the rush of industrialization neglected the fact that our behaviour towards our environment was destructive. Our responsibility therefore was pointed towards saving ourselves. Later, however, ethicists and environmental thinkers and activists advocated that the environment and the other animal inhabitants in it had value in themselves, that animals too had their own rights, and that both nature and animals needed to be recognized and treated ethically.

Extending Our Moral Stand

The general notion about environmental ethics is that if we are not responsible towards our environment, we will destroy it and, in turn, we will destroy ourselves too. In other words, the objective of environmental ethics is to safeguard ourselves. This is known as anthropocentric environmental ethics, which means, human centred. Thus, the question is whether we can relate environmental ethics only to ourselves or whether we can also extend it to others who share the environment and nature.

Human beings   It is natural to be anthropocentric in understanding and applying environmental ethics because without the primary relation to human beings, environmental ethics is not relevant. Thus, for instance, pollution diminishes our health, resource depletion threatens our standards of living, climatic changes put our homes at risk, the reduction in biodiversity results in the loss of potential medicines, and the eradication of wilderness means we lose a source of awe and beauty. Thus, we need to respect and protect the environment for the sake of mankind. It is a worthy moral ideal. That we think of saving the future generations by doing our duty to protect the environment is also morally worthy.

Animals   Because of the raised consciousness of animal rights issues, we now understand that animals too have senses of perception and feel pleasure and pain. They also have emotions of happiness and suffering. These lead us to extend moral values to animals. Upon reflection, we understand that these animals possess consciousness. Hence, our behaviour towards them must be judged as right or wrong. Further, we can understand that because of the very fact that they have life, it becomes our obligation to protect them. Thus, when animals are used for consumption or for experimentation in labs, it is ethically wrong. The utilitarian principle that they are for the use of human beings is null and void. The debate on animal ethics has sharpened in this manner.

Living organisms   Ethicists have gone another step further and said that ethical values be extended to all forms of life. The Hindu scriptures, saints, and traditions have always upheld the sanctity of all living organisms. The principle is that compassion must be shown to all living forms because they have life. If this is so, human beings should not be even allowed to breathe for fear of destroying the organisms that are a part of the atmosphere. Logic requires taking a balanced and reasonable stand on this issue.

Holistic entities   Aldo Leopold, one of the pioneers in environmental ethics, advocated the extension of ethical standards to holistic entities, which he called land ethic. He proposed that we should stop exploiting the land as a mere source of resource. In the Indian tradition, land is given the status of a mother and is called Mother Earth because it brings forth everything into the world. The scriptures and the saints teach us to respect the earth the way we respect our mothers.

At times, the moral arguments presented by ethicists cross the limits of prudence. The Indian tradition lays great worth on the intuitive understanding of ethical actions. The Indian virtue of avoiding extremes and striking a balance by using our prudence is important. In Buddhism, it is known as the middle path of right living.

Radical Ecology

The ethics of radical ecology consists of moving away from extending ethical positions, especially from the point of view of human beings. In other words, the anthropocentric position is an old one and we must find a new ethical paradigm. It implies that we make ethics ecology centred. Since humans are only a part of the ecological system, extending ethics to ecology is to make a part larger than the whole. Humans would have to act within the ecological system in accordance with ecological ethics, and not a human one. This will cause fundamental changes in our society and its institutions.

Deep ecology   The proponents of this theory reject anthropocentric environmental ethics, calling it shallow because of its limited interest in the environment—it is interested only in so far as it is helpful to human beings. Deep ecology rejects such utilitarian view and advocates a radical view:

(i)   Both human and non-human lives have intrinsic value. The anthropocentric position recognizes only a relative value.

(ii)   Except to satisfy their vital needs, humans have no right over environment.

(iii)   Exponential population growth is an infringement of ecological ethics, since the ecosystems are not meant to support more than their capacity.

(iv)   The present human interference with nature and its resources is excessive.

(v)   One must distinguish between the quality of life and the standard of living. The former is eco-friendly, the latter exploitative.

This kind of thinking has been called as ecosophy (ecological philosophy), in contrast to the usual philosophy that concentrates only on human values. Ecosophy aims at raising the human consciousness to ecological values.

Social ecology   The advocates of this theory believe that environmental problems are directly related to social problems, and can be traced to the fact of dominance. Social systems, economics included, create a dominant system, which works according to a superior and subject-related hierarchy. It is the same hierarchical relationship of master-servant that is extended to the environment. In fact, the economic free-market system has reduced both human beings as well as nature to commodities, and exercises control over them. Hence, the environment must be liberated from such dominance of the economic system. The advocates of social ecology propose that there is no dominance of species within the ecosystems. The relationship is mutual between the various systems of ecology. Society must change in accordance with the law of ecology, abandon hierarchy, and promote mutual interdependence.

Eco-feminism   Within the fold of deep ecology, the advocates of eco-feminism take the idea of social dominance to its logical conclusion of sexual domination. One such idea relates to our nature of moral arguments. Traditionally, it is held that only reason is capable of presenting correct moral argument. Emotions such as sentiments of affections, anger, and other human feelings are excluded. The dominance of masculine rational logic is the cause for subjugating the feminine emotional dimension. Domination always divides reason and emotion, mind and body, man and woman, superior and inferior. Eco-feminism challenges such dualism. Thus, in application to the environment, the distinction between man and nature must be obliterated so that humans do not find any reason to exploit the environment. To create a fair society, there must be an end to the divisions of domination and subordination. Feminism is the answer to reconcile these divisions and create harmony.

Conclusion

Environmental ethics is still in its nascent stage. In other words, we have not fully become conscious about the notions proposed by experts. Until such consciousness percolates to all members of society, the larger masses will remain insensitive to environmental concerns. Economics in general and businesses in particular must now address these concerns. For, these are real concerns and to neglect them would be grossly irresponsible.

Damning the Dam

Narmada Bachao Andolan—Long struggle
(Narmada Bachao Andolan song)[a]

Whose are the forests and the land?
Ours, they are ours.
Whose are the wood, the fuel?
Ours, they are ours.
Whose, the flowers and the grass?
Ours, they are ours.
Whose are the cow, the cattle?
Ours, they are ours.
Whose are the bamboo groves?
Ours, they are ours.

Narmada bachao manave bachao (Save Narmada save humanity) is the motto of the Narmada Bachao Andolan (NBA). It is a non-governmental organization (NGO), whose leadership is in the hands of its founder, Medha Patkar, who has become a symbol of contradiction on the issues of environmental ethics. The aim of NBA is a just and equitable society in India. The case at hand, although complex, complicated, and long drawn, consists in the Gujarat government's activity of building 30 large, 135 medium, and 3000 small dams across the Narmada River and its tributaries. The government and its supporters claim that this mega project, Narmada Valley Development Plan, will ensure the required water resources to millions of people across the states of Madhya Pradesh, Maharashtra, and Gujarat. It will also generate hydro-electricity and hosts of other advantages that will result from the provision of water resources. The opponents of the project, NBA, argue that the plan is flawed, not equitable, and unjust; and that the cost-benefit analysis is inflated because the plans are drawn on unfounded assumptions of hydrology and seismological presumptions. The project displaces a big portion of the population of the surrounding areas. The displacement has caused untold misery on the impoverished communities and rampant violation of human rights. The NBA makes alternative proposals of using technology and socially just and environmentally sustainable planning.[b]

The conception of the use of the vast resources of the Narmada River took place during the late 1940s, and Jawaharlal Nehru laid the foundation stone of the project in 1961.[c] The river originates in the Vindhya mountain ranges and traverses through the states of Madhya Pradesh, Maharashtra, and Gujarat. It covers a distance of 1312 km and flows into the Arabian Sea at Bharuch, Gujarat. It is also considered as one of the sacred rivers of India, and innumerable temples and pilgrim centres are situated along its banks. It bears great geological importance, for its valleys are blocks of layers of the earth's crust. Emerging through the valleys and the marble rocks, it meanders through the plains forming the fertile Narmada basin, of approx 98,796 sq km. From the point of view of ecology, it

Contd

Box Contd

possesses incredible biodiversity and nurtures very rich wildlife. The forests and sanctuaries along the river cover a total area of 169,598 sq km and are home to 76 species of animals and 276 species of birds. These are the jungles that Rudyard Kipling describes in his famous book *The Jungle Book.* There are several anthropological sites dating back to the epic periods, rare rock paintings, and enormous caves along the way.

The project took off only in 1979, with a loan of $450 million from the World Bank. The first road block was the interstate dispute for the allocation of water share. Finally, when it was settled by the tribunal, the project hit another road block, the Ministry of Environment and Forests. Finally, when the tribunal solved even this problem, the biggest problem arose with the public interest litigation filed by the NBA in 1985. The court battle as well as the protest movement took several twists and turns, fasts, strikes, blockages, media exposure, arrests, beatings, more protests for unjust settlements, etc. In 1991, the World Bank conducted a review of the project. After a long deliberation, it withdrew from the project in 1995.

The Supreme Court of India[d] took cognizance of the benefits of the project, which would irrigate an estimated two million hectares of land, generate over 3500 MW hydro-power, and provide drinking water to 135 towns and 8000 villages, and benefit close to twenty million people. The bench comprising three judges approved the project, with two of them assenting that the above benefits far outweighed the disadvantages in the ratio of 100:1. The judge who dissented was concerned with the dislocation of the *adivasi* people, the danger to biodiversity due to inundation, the enormous material and social costs, and above all, obfuscated details about the project itself.

Questions

(a) Is the judgement of the Supreme Court ethically right?

(b) Does NBA care for the national interest, which is of a greater utilitarian value?

(c) Give ecologically sound moral arguments regarding the consequences of the Narmada Valley Development project.

[a] See http://www.narmada.org/resources/books/silenced_rivers.html.

[b] See http://www.narmada.org/introduction.html.

[c] See http://en.wikipedia.org/wiki/Narmada_River.

[d] See http://judis.nic.in/supremecourt/qrydisp.asp?tfnm=17165.

ENVIRONMENTAL CHALLENGES AS BUSINESS OPPORTUNITIES

In early February 2009, there was a Summit on Sustainable Development organized by The Energy and Resources Institute (TERI) under the leadership of R.K. Pachauri, the head of the Nobel Prize winning UN Intergovernmental Panel on Climate Change. One of the speakers was Thomas Friedman, the highly acclaimed *New York Times* columnist, whose syndicated writings appear in India's English language papers. In his submission, Friedman brought out the basic assumption of his recent work *Hot, Flat and Crowded: Why the World Needs a Green Revolution—and How We Can Renew Our Global Future.* By the middle of this century, another three billion people will be added to the nearly six and half billion people existing today. Then there are other problems such as climate changes due to global warming, excess carbon, energy poverty, and so on. How can these problems be solved? He suggests a revolution—a green revolution. Not a red revolution as the historical bloody revolution, or the red that suggests the American way of life that exploits nature mindlessly, or the red in the American flag.

The failure is on two fronts. The industrial world, for most of its part, has failed to fulfil its responsibility towards changing its strategies about the use of both natural resources and the technology that is used to exploit such resources. On the other hand, governments have not been able to form policies for an equitable distribution of wealth. Thus, two things are important for an ethical society—environmentally sustainable strategies for business and economic equity for the people. We will propose below the advantages that businesses have in the adoption of sustainable practices; economic empowerment will follow as a consequence.

Sustainable Development as Corporate Strategy

Sustainability as a business strategy is no more a strange subject for corporations. In the new millennium, corporations are realizing that in less than a decade's time, that is, before 2020, they would have to manage resources sustainably with advanced technology and according to what customers want. Customers want a pollution-free environment, so industries have to change the way they manufacture. In order to do this, they need to use clean technologies. Clean technologies demand clean energy, and clean energy lies not in the traditional sources of coal and oil, but in the sun, the wind, and hydrogen.

Resource management through recycling Steve Morris[1] is an owner of toner and inkjet cartridges. It struck him that sooner or later, printer manufacturers would one day have to switch to sustainable management. If he could find a way to do so, he could have a profitable business. The solution lay in using cheaper and environmentally friendly cartridges. So, he approached the users of printers—individuals, institutions, and businesses—and collected their used cartridges and other imaging consumables without any charge, and they were happy to get rid of them, too. He then conducted his business in such a way that not a single can of toner or cartridge became a part of the landfill. He produced recycling and manufactured toners and inkjets, which were completely environmentally friendly. Today, Morris' Australian company, which goes by the name *Close the Loop*, is cited as an example of a zero-waste company because it is able to recycle all of the used up products. It supplies its products world wide. Today it is encouraging to note that every manufacturing industry—housing, transport, FMCGs—in the world is trying to find ways and means to recycle. The greatest advantage of recycling is that it cuts costs on raw materials.

Competitive advantage strategy Corporations thus far have been following David Ricardo's theory of cheaper input costs, such as raw material, labour, and capital. The bottom-line is that cost effectiveness results in greater profits. Where such downsizing on one side and higher returns on the other do not work, sustainability gives a greater advantage. In the recent past, corporations have downsized everything, beginning

---

[1] See *Natural Advantage of Nations*, pp. 75–77.

with retrenchment of labour, and then outsourced to cut costs. Corporations will benefit more if they follow the following four strategies:

(i) Take advantage of the new technologies to design new products.
(ii) Focus on customer needs.
(iii) Innovate to gain increased market share.
(iv) Commit to best practices and improvement.

Business ethics or corporate governance Sustainability is an ethical principle that underlines the ethical and intelligent use of resources. Companies imbibing the values of good governance practices scale higher in the estimation of customers. Companies have come to realize that by putting stress on environmental and societal interests and through corporate governance they can increase their customer base and customer loyalty.

Shifting Nature of Competition in Emerging Economies

So far, the world economy was uni-polar. In other words, there was no competition for industries of the developed world, which also gobbled up all the available resources. However, with the new trends in sustainability, emerging economies are posing a huge competition to their more powerful competitors. The advantage emerging economies have is that it is much easier for them to leap-frog technology. The examples in Table 17.1 are a mere drop in the ocean of the increased best practices around the globe. These companies are increasing by leaps and bounds in emerging economies despite the challenges posed to them by their more powerful competitors. Table 17.2 lists the drivers for sustainable development in emerging economies. It shows how

Table 17.1 Advantages of emerging economies

Country	Industry	Natural advantage
India	Wireless Internet access	Midas Communications Technologies Pvt. Ltd and Analog Devices Inc. of the US, developed Wireless in Local Loop in Chennai, which has leapfrogged telephone and Internet connectivity in India, thereby eliminating costly wiring and accessories such as the modem. This technology is now adopted around the world.
Thailand	Pharmaceutical	Development of the new drug dihydroartemisinen (DHA) to fight the most resistant malaria. It has been acclaimed by the WHO.
Brazil	Personal hygiene	Natura, the cosmetics company of Brazil, in collaboration with UN Global Compact to create natural personal hygiene products. The company supports environmental restoration programmes in Brazil.
Bangladesh, India	Micro-credit	The idea originated in Bangladesh. Very small credit is given to poor but willing entrepreneurs (mostly women) as self-help. Microcredits have the best repayment reputation (which the big businesses are yet to learn) and have now helped millions of poor people around the world and empowered them economically.

Table 17.2   Drivers for sustainable development in emerging economies

Drivers	Development
Economic and business opportunities	▪ Increased productivity and product differentiation ▪ Lean thinking and total quality management ▪ Ethically, environmentally responsible investment ▪ Risk reduction
Population	▪ Population decrease in developed economies and increase in emerging economies ▪ Urbanization and migration
Technology	▪ Clean technology and renewable energy
Environmental crisis	▪ Restoration natural capital, management environmental disasters
Inequality	▪ Refugees, services to the poor, trade barriers
Ethics/staying ahead of regulation	▪ Corporate best practices, ethical investing, marketing

civil society has not only influenced business, but also how it is steadily taking over the responsibility for development. Civil societies across the globe are taking matters into their hands through their demand and participation in the development of a sustainable world. The world is becoming people centred. This offers new opportunities for businesses to differentiate their products to suit customers.

New Opportunities of Product Differentiation

In business, product differentiation plays a significant role to win an edge over competition. If a product is based on the sustainability principle, and also excels over the products of the usual competitors, then it is not just a product of a higher quality, but also an environmentally and ethically sound product. Today, the market is moving away from fuel efficient, energy efficient, and reduced emission level products, such as cars and electric bulbs, towards those that use alternative energy sources such as solar, wind, and hydrogen. According to Hargroves (2005), product differentiation is based on:

(a) Reduced emission levels of toxic material
(b) Measurement of prosperity by less activity and less use of what is environmentally damaging
(c) Going beyond the compliance levels of regulation and setting new benchmarks
(d) Smaller amounts wasted
(e) No wastes, but 100 per cent recycling

The concept of sustainability can be explained through natural ecosystems. For instance, let us examine the food chain. Vegetation grows and prospers in the abundance of sunlight, water, and nutrients, and is consumed by insects, birds, and animals, both big and small. Their nourishment creates waste, which in turn becomes nourishment for the vegetation, and the cycle repeats itself. In the same way, if human beings have to be eco-efficient, they have to use, produce, consume, and transform waste into raw material for production, by recycling it.

Increasing Profitability and Minimizing Risk

Every business is oriented towards profit and minimizing risks.

There are five forces that affect the competition in an industry[2]:

    (a) Rivalry among existing competitors
    (b) Threat of new entrants
    (c) Threat of substitute products
    (d) Bargaining power of suppliers
    (e) Bargaining power of customers

It is the sustainability principle that will allow not merely survival in the competition, but also excellence. This is, however, good when sustainability is a novelty. What happens when all the competitors become sustainable? How can one increase the profits and minimize the risks?

Such a scenario is already happening. The competition for sustainable products is increasing. By adopting the principle of sustainability, businesses break their old vicious circle of exploitation of resources, production, and waste into a virtuous circle of production, consumption, reconversion or recycling, and back to production. The sustainability principles have the inner dynamism to allow the regeneration of resources and the saving of ecology.

The pattern of old competition stated above also breaks down. The new principle changes the attitudes or approaches to business. One of the first things that the competitors realize is that they have to change their old negative or aggressive competition into a sustainable social behaviour. Businesses would succeed only if they become social institutions. They would have to move beyond regulated corporate governance to voluntary ethical behaviour. Only good companies will be able to do good business.

ROLE OF THE GOVERNMENT

Without better policies and institutions, social and environmental strains may derail development progress, leading to higher poverty levels and a decline in the quality of life for everybody. Misguided policies and weak governance in past decades have contributed to environmental disasters, income inequality, and social upheavals in some countries, often resulting in deep deprivation, riots, or refugees fleeing famine or civil wars.[3]

---

[2] See *Natural Advantage of Nations*, pp. 104–08.
[3] World Bank Development Report 2003 is available at http://econ.worldbank.org/wdr/.

Answer Is in the Wind

Suzlon

Tulsi Tanti is closing in on a decade of wonderful business experiences, which he merely stumbled upon out of sheer need. In the mid-1990s, he faced difficulties to get adequate power supply to his upcoming textile factory in Gujarat. The state supply, apart from being costly, was erratic. Constantly looking for energy alternatives, he finally decided to erect two windmills to supply a dependable source of energy for his factory.

With the help of his friends from Rajkot, he set up the factory, with its headquarters in Pune. The rest is a short but very impressive history. There is a phenomenal growth in world wind power. Suzlon is one of the top five competitors. For a company that is growing at the rate of 24 per cent a year, competition is not a threat. The company's aggregate booked orders amount to $4304 that is 3454 MW. The domestic orders alone stand at $208 million. Some of the major firms such as ONGC, TATA, Reliance Energy, DLF, HPCL, and several others are its customers. It has the following impressive ventures and achievements:

(a) Asia's largest wind-park in Dhule, Maharashtra, with over 1000 MW when completed
(b) Operations in 20 countries—Western European, North and South American, and Eastern European countries
(c) Ranked fifth as the largest supplier of wind turbines in the world, with 10.5 per cent of global market share
(d) Over 14 000 employees of several nationalities
(e) Manufacturing capability to provide turbines to various wind and geographical conditions.

Tulsi Tanti, the indefatigable chairman of Suzlon hails from the state of Gujarat. He graduated in commerce and earned a diploma in mechanical engineering. He is passionately involved in advancing the wind turbine business around the globe. Today, he is one of the top ten richest persons in India. However, the difference is that this alternative sustainable business has catapulted him to that position in less than fifteen years, where others took scores of years, and some, even a century. Sustainable dreams are indeed sustainable business propositions.

Questions

(a) Why is sustainability an ethical principle?
(b) How can an ethical principle encourage competition?
(c) Does sustainability increase profits and reduce risks?

The above words from the World Bank Report 2003 express the magnitude of the responsibility governments bear in public policy-making and policy implementation. In India, in the year 1977, Article 48A was introduced through the 42nd Amendment. It stated that 'the state shall endeavour to protect and improve the environment and to safeguard the forests and wildlife of the country.'

Serious environmental concerns were being expressed since 1970. In 1972 the UN organized a conference in Stockholm, which began on a dire note declaring that there may be barely a decade more left to improve human environment. Indeed, it makes sense only if efforts are made by all the stakeholders, which calls for the participation of all nations and people. Only if they work together will they be able to save the planet.

Indian Legal Framework for Environmental Protection

We have mentioned above that the Parliament amended the Constitution of India with the historical 42nd Amendment. Article 48A was added to the Directive Principles of State Policy. Through Article 51(g), a new chapter entitled Fundamental Duties was added, in which the constitution imposed duties on citizens to be responsible for the human environment and to protect the natural resources. Table 17.3 is a compilation of Acts passed for environmental protection.

Table 17.3   Acts passed for environmental protection

Acts	Functions
42nd Amendment	State responsibilities, rights and duties of the citizens.
Indian Forest Act 1927	Although prior to independence and the 42nd Amendment, it was to be read in the new light of the Amendment and the directions of the courts.
Factories Act 1948	Amendments were made in 1987 to counter hazardous industrial waste. The local authorities were empowered to take action. The manager of the factory would be held responsible.
Atomic Energy Act 1962	To control radiation protection. Rules in this regard were formed in 1971. The central government is empowered to take action.
Insecticide Act 1968	It was enacted after the severe cases of food poisoning in Kerala and Tamil Nadu. The Central Insecticides Board was established. It is supposed to monitor pesticide residue. It has become very important, as more and more cases of pesticides are to be found in soft drinks, foodstuffs, and even in bottled water.
Wildlife Protection Act 1972	Wildlife advisory boards established in the states, establishment of parks and sanctuaries, hunting regulations, protection of endangered species. The Act was amended in 1982, permitting capture and transportation of wild animals for the scientific management of their population.
The Water Prevention and Control of Pollution Act 1974	Came into existence after a decade of deliberations. The central and state water boards work in tandem and enforce effluent standards. Amendment in 1988 further empowered the boards to impose stringent penalties.
Water Prevention and Control of Pollution Cess Act 1977	Establishments and industries to pay cess to meet the expenses of the central and state boards. Also incentives given for pollution control.
Forest Conservation Act 1980	To stop rapid deforestation. Amended in 1988 to make it necessary for the states to get central permission for the purposes of non-forest use.
Air Prevention and Control of Pollution Act 1981	To implement the decisions of the international bodies such as UNO, so that an integrated global approach may be facilitated.
Environment Protection Act 1986	After the Bhopal gas leak tragedy, the Act provided for a comprehensive environment protection instrument. It defined and explained all the aspects of the environment like air, water, earth, forests, animals, organisms, micro-organism. It defined environmental pollution and hazardous substances. In 1989, it again concentrated on the hazardous substances, chemicals, waste, and their regulation. A detailed list of penalties was also specified.

Environmental Policy

The National Environmental Policy (NEP) 2004 was released by the Ministry of Environment and Forests (MoEF) as a draft. The public discussion and debate has been going on. The objectives are

(a) Conservation of critical environmental resources
(b) Intra-generational equity, livelihood security for the poor
(c) Integration of environmental concerns in economic and social development
(d) Efficiency in environmental resource use
(e) Environmental governance

Resources like finance, technology, management skills, traditional knowledge, and social capital have been enhanced for environmental conservation. There are some fundamental principles and assumptions to attain the goal. The foremost principle is the eradication of poverty and empowerment of the poor, for all have a right to development. Sustainable and right developments are the two watchwords. Governance with justice and making the polluter pay are the keys to operation.

MULTI-STAKEHOLDERSHIP

The stakeholder concept is already familiar to those of us who have an interest in any organization, not in the sense of curiosity, but rather in the sense of a significant motive that affects us in some way. For instance, when a tannery comes up in a locality, the neighbours will have a stake in it even if they are neither shareholders, nor employees, nor suppliers, and not even customers. Their stake or interest or motive of being close to the tannery is primarily for health concerns, since a tannery generates foul smell and pollutants. Its environmental concerns, such as effluents, too affect the neighbours. Thus, all the people who are connected with it directly as promoters, employees, or customers and indirectly connected as neighbours, children, visitors, or tourists are also stakeholders. The idea of multi-stakeholdership expresses the ancient wisdom that no one is an island. We live interdependently and we impact others, either positively or negatively. For corporations, multi-stakeholdership is now a reality.

Multi-stakeholdership and Its Relevance

The Agenda 21 of the United Nations defines the role of the different stakeholders. It defines that the points of the agenda are possible to implement only with the cooperation of all the related stakeholders.

Earth Summit Rio de Janeiro, Brazil, 1992

This summit of the United Nations, named as the Earth Summit, was historical not only for it being an unprecedented event in the history of mankind, but for the kind of programme it proposed to the world on human development that was mutually connected to sustainable development. The governments of the world recognized the

Ki Khabo?

West Bengal Food Riots 2007

Kemon aachhen? Ki khabo? In Bengali, this phrase literally stands for 'How are you? What will you have?' But there is more to this little phrase than just eating or casual greeting. The phrase embodies the body and spirit, down-to-earth wisdom, and cultivated cultural heritage, all neatly and pleasantly bundled into this common, but lovely phrase.

The days of October 2007 were the heady days when the communists, led by the Communist Party of India, (Marxist) CPI(M), even while supporting the central government, were vehemently leading protests against India's nuclear agreement with the US. The CPI(M) cadres would descend upon the villages in West Bengal to instruct their constituents about the nuclear deal and why the party was against it, and why they must now unite and take to the streets in protests. However, the party workers were surprised when the people countered their campaign and targeted them with angry abuses and physical assaults. It began in merely one or two districts, and spread like wildfire across the entire state. Over three hundred people were injured. Several ration distributors committed suicide.

There was no food for the people. But the governing CPI(M) and its allies went into denial mode. They blamed the central government for a corrupt distribution system. In a knee-jerk reaction, the state issued notices to ration shops, and action was taken against several dozens of food inspectors.

What happened in Bengal happened all over in the developing world. This was, however, not unexpected. There were skirmishes for food, and riots[a] took place in the empty grocery shops from Mexico to Nepal, and from Africa to Jamaica. Food prices rose to 18 per cent in China and 13 per cent in Pakistan and Indonesia. In Latin America, Russia, and India, wheat and maize prices doubled. The Food and Agricultural Organization (FAO) of the UN feared that global food reserves were at the lowest in a quarter of a century. All through 2008 and early 2009, through the financial crisis in the developed world, the rest of the world had to fight for their share of two square meals a day.

While hundreds of billions of dollars have been poured into failed financial companies that have whiled away people's money, the people have had to worry about their next meal. Even the rich had to think twice before they threw a party. The lack of food dampened the spirit of the world. That human beings with such imagination and capability were unable to feed themselves adequately speaks of a universe that is light years away from sustainability.

Questions

(a) Why is food an ethical subject?
(b) Do governments really care for the people or are the people just duty bound?
(c) In what way does the UNO play a moral role for the people of the world?

[a] See http://www.hindu.com/2007/10/24/stories/2007102454341500.htm; http://www.expressindia.com/latest-news/CPIM-hits-back-at-Cong-says-no-food-riots-in-Bengal/231498/. For further details, go to http://www.guardian.co.uk/environment/2007/nov/03/food.climatechange.

need to redirect and reformulate national and international plans and policies that the goal of human development and sustainability be commonly achieved. All economic and political decisions must have the bearing of an environmental impact. This would mainly affect the following:

Production patterns Systematic scrutiny of all toxins, gases, and waste

Alternative sources of energy Support to develop alternative sources of energy

Transport Reduction of emissions in transport and promotion of environmentally friendly public transport

Water Concerns of water scarcity to be addressed urgently

Thus, Agenda 21 is a comprehensive programme of action for sustainable development. It defines the rights and responsibilities of the states.

(a) Human beings have a right for development and a healthy and productive life, in harmony with nature.
(b) Scientific debates should not delay measures to prevent irreversible and serious damages to the environment.
(c) States have sovereign rights to utilize their natural resources, without causing negative consequences to the other states.
(d) Eradication of poverty is a reduction in inequalities, which is indispensable for sustainable development.
(e) Full participation of women is essential to attain the goals of sustainable development.
(f) With greater harnessing of the world's resources, the developed countries bear greater responsibility towards the creation of sustainable development.

There must be a concerted effort to green the planet, and all economic and social instruments must be used to make the world green again. The United Nations Commission on Sustainable Development (CSD) proposed to include the Agenda under the Economic and Social Council, which will facilitate all the global stakeholders, governments, businesses and industries, and non-governmental agencies to come together to generate the social and economic changes needed for sustainable development.

Symbiosis of Multi-stakeholders

Indian polity is a highly informed society in matters of politics and economics. Very often, some general remarks are made about illiteracy and ignorance. These may be true in the domain of sciences. However, in so far as social ground realities are concerned, people have strong opinions. This became clear during the anti-SEZ movements and food riots. The problem lies with the government and corporations who appear to have alienated themselves from the people, who in fact are their customers. Both the government and corporations want to impose their will and their methods of development. People oppose because it is against their interest.

People, corporations, and governments are all stakeholders in sustainable development. A symbiotic relationship already exists due to the nature of society. Any differences must be overcome, but not from the powerful position of the government or the resourcefulness of corporations. A relationship needs to be built on trust.

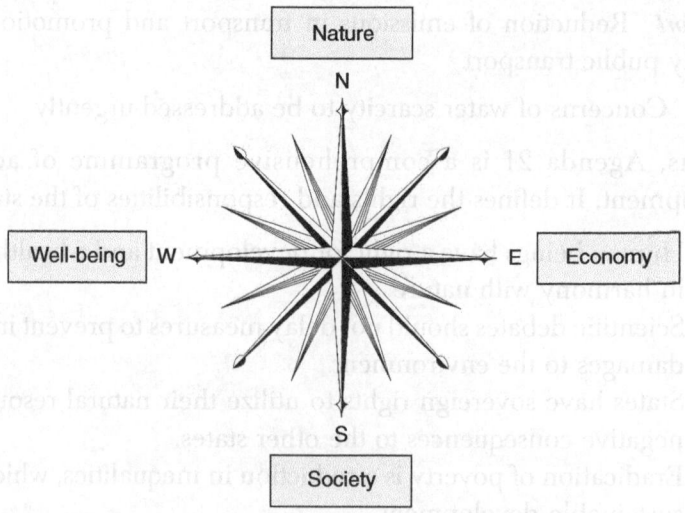

Fig. 17.1 Symbiotic relationship of stakeholders

Source: The Natural Advantage of Nations, pp. 448–49.

The symbiotic relationship between the above three main stakeholders and their subdivisions would have to come together to form a compass of sustainability, as shown in Figure 17.1.

All the stakeholders have to travel to the north, the nature's way, to attain sustainability. It is an all-embracing concept, which includes the issues of human development like economic growth, healthcare, education, housing, cities and towns, industries, and leisure. We would have to combine the moral principles of development and scientific work, which include research work, performing empirical analysis, and providing solutions to attain our goal.

We can define sustainability as 'meeting the needs of the present without compromising the ability of future generations to meet their own needs.'[4]

Nothing but the Truth

Truth about climate change

It may be providential that Al Gore lost the most controversial US presidential election and took up the cause of climate change[a] due to global warming and went around the world with a simple but telling presentation about the health of planet Earth. A documentary film *An Inconvenient Truth* was also produced by Davis Guggenheim, where Al Gore was again the protagonist of the story on global warming. It was a simple lecture with a slide presentation. It told the simple truth that the Earth was having high fever, the ice was melting, and the climate was changing. We are at an alarming stage. A catastrophe may strike at any time.

Contd

---

4 Brundtland Commission, http://www.un.org/documents/ga/res/42/ares42-187.htm.

Box Contd

Not one but several catastrophes struck. The tsunami in South East Asia, Hurricane Katrina in the US, earthquakes in Pakistan and China, floods in India, storms and floods in Europe, famines in Africa, and even South America—no continent upon the Earth was left unaffected. Gore's message sank deep into the consciousness of people. Governments got worried, and the United Nations got on to its feet in haste.

The truth is that global warming is real. It is catastrophic and is caused by humans. The slide show has quantitative data. Curved lines and dots on the Keeling curve showed a pattern of the steadily increasing carbon dioxide in the atmosphere. Scientists got the handle on this and frantically got down to research. All worked in tandem. It is not as if there was no controversy. There were perhaps an equal number of experts who decried the doomsday prophesized by

Al Gore, and supported by R.K. Pachauri, the head of the UN scientific research team, Intergovernmental Panel on Climate Change (IPCC), with scientific evidence. But the messenger (Gore) and the scientist (Pachauri) insisted, 'It was not what the people wanted, but it is what they brought upon themselves. The very development on which people hinged their hopes was the source of despair and destruction of the only home known to mankind. This, then is nothing but the truth: an inconvenient truth.'

Questions

(a) What is the role of the multi-stakeholders in climate change?

(b) Why did the message of *An Inconvenient Truth* make an impact?

(c) How important is the communication between the various stakeholders in a sustainable world?

 ª See http://www.algore.com/.

SUMMARY

- Environmental problems arise due to human exploitation of nature, which is too quick and damaging for nature to repair.

- Environmental protection is needed for our survival.

- The principle of survival is apt with natural justice, not only for human beings, but also for all living as well as non-living earth systems.

- Humans are a part of the ecological system and sustaining the system is a moral duty.

- All sentient beings have the value of life, and so have a right to live.

- Environmental ethics analyses the moral rights and duties of human beings in relationship to other living beings and nature as a whole.

- Nature in itself is a moral value.

- Deep ecology, eco-feminism, and the like are moral reflections to highlight the value of nature in itself, without being useful or valuable to others.

- The greatest wrong perpetrated by human beings is the mindless extraction and exploitation of natural resources and their unsustainable use.

- There should be sustainability in the use of resources, without harming the future use of such resources.

- Environmental management is to conserve and sustain natural resources.

- Business opportunity lies in finding technological means to promote human development that is supported by natural sustainability.

- Sustainability gives a competent edge to business.

- The government is duty bound to enact laws and draw up policies in accordance with the sustainability principles.

- The world bodies must also organize and conduct programmes that exceed all the national and cultural limits and boundaries to save the earth and save life.

- The concept of multi-stakeholdership must become the cornerstone of a civilized and an economically developed society.

KEY TERMS

Environment   The surroundings in which an entity finds itself.

Environmental ethics   Moral behaviour of humans towards the environment.

Environmental sustainability   To maintain and preserve nature during and after the use of its resources.

Extending ethics   Going beyond the confines of the relationship between humans and nature, and recognizing the other systems in nature that have their own moral value over which human beings have no right. Animals, organisms, and the earth have their own inalienable right to exist and live.

Multi-stakeholdership   Those who have an interest in an idea or state of affairs.

Natural environment   The physical world.

Sustain   To maintain.

CONCEPT REVIEW QUESTIONS

1. What are the main issues that are involved in environmental ethics?

2. How can corporations meet the challenges of environmental degradation?

3. Do businesses have an advantage if they adopt the sustainability principle?

4. Why should the government have a role to play in matters of the environment?

5. How does multi-stakeholdership work? Does it have any moral value?

CRITICAL THINKING QUESTIONS

1. Develop the concept of right to life.

2. Would there be morality without human beings upon the earth? Explain.

3. How can the environment be the responsibility of corporations?

4. Illustrate whether the environmental laws are consistent with the moral laws?

5. Is multi-stakeholdership a kind of multi-tasking? Is there a multi-tasking morality too?

FURTHER READING

Report of the World Commission on Environment and Development: Our Common Future. It is available at http://www.un-documents.net/wced-ocf.htm.

'Charlie' Karlson Hargroves and Michael H. Smith (eds), *The Natural Advantage of Nations, Business Opportunities, Innovation and Governance,* Earthscan, London (2005).

CASE STUDY

Goa 2100

Sustainability Model

Introduction

Goa 2100 is a project for transition from the present economic, social, and governance forms to a sustainable one.[a] The State of Goa and its capital city, Panaji, are the project's laboratory. Goa 2100 started as an international competition, to develop

[a] The entire case is courtesy Goa 2100, and the author of this book is also one of the leaders who are taking forward the project; he has crystallized the concepts and has also used the pictures and exhibits from the project.

a vision for the transition to a sustainable future for the town of Panjim. The Indian team selected Goa, after analysing forty cities and regions, as the site for a possible transition to a sustainable future. This was presented to a distinguished audience in Tokyo in 2003 and won a special prize. It has been presented, written, and spoken about as an idea in many locations across the world, where it has been hailed as a path-breaking vision for a new twenty-first century India.

In the course of time, I interacted with several of the international teams that participated in the Tokyo Competition, which was organized by the International Gas Union, and came together in Goa not for competition but to team up for research and seek avenues of implementation in different parts of the world. We organized the first international conference in 2004 in Goa. Ever since, it has been an annual event, where in addition to the international teams, we have people from multi-disciplinary areas like political leaders and bureaucrats representing various government departments and non-governmental agencies that share their research work and experiences on one single subject: sustainable development. The following is a mere glimpse of project Goa 2100. We will not deal with research per se, which involves very complex designs, scientific tools, and enormous empirical data, but only with the principles of the project. You may access the Goa 2100 project, as well as the international teams and the research work, at http://www.bridgingtothefuture.org.

Part I

Historical Background

About 500 years ago when the Portuguese came to Goa, it lay at the crossroads of trade between the Vijaynagar kingdom and Arabia. Within a hundred years, the city that they rebuilt—Old Goa, became one of the great world cities of the sixteenth century, an international centre of commerce, education, healthcare, and culture. Old Goa (Fig. 17.2) was a city larger than Lisbon, the largest arsenal and shipyard outside Venice, the location from where the Black Ships sailed to China, Japan, and Lisbon. This was a rich and prosperous land that drew people from all parts of India and the world. Great edifices were built in the following decades and fortunes were made in months.

Fig. 17.2   A portion of the city of Old Goa, circa seventeenth century

But this development was unsustainable, a bubble that burst in less than 150 years, as it was based on the colonial culture of extraction, cruelty and trade, exploitation of local resources and people, and a limited understanding of the challenges and fragility of the Goan environment. Plague and pestilence bedevilled the city and it collapsed. Old Goa became a forgotten vestige of a once grand imperial dream. Its grand houses and markets were mined for stone, to build village houses, and a more down-to-earth new capital at Panjim (now Panaji). Goa's citizens were largely forgotten by a power more concerned with the revolutions sweeping continental Europe, but tenaciously unwilling to let go, to enable the rightful self-determination, development, and freedom of the people in its far away colonies. The best and the brightest Goans migrated across the world to seek their fortune. Many stayed and turned inwards to a more simple life, as the world changed and moved on.

Goa in Independent India and the Price of Development

Goa became a part of independent India in 1961, a small drop in the ocean of millions suffering from poverty and illiteracy. But in the past five decades, Goa has done well. Today it is considered an economically forward state with the following indicators:

(a) Highest per capita income
(b) Two-digit growth rate

(c) Negligible poverty levels

(d) Highest levels of literacy and health

(e) Urbanization

(f) Higher economic and social infrastructure

(g) A moderately good system of governance and citizen participation

But Goa has paid a very high price for its development:

(a) High levels of underdevelopment and unemployment, especially in the rural areas, certain *talukas*, and among the educated youth

(b) High-levels of in-migration, especially of poor wage labourers from the neighbouring states, leading to a wide range of potential conflicts

(c) Massive changes in the environment, devastating critical ecosystems that not only provide essential ecosystem services but threaten the identity of Goa, its residents, and high-value tourism

(d) Mal-development of cities and under-development of rural areas threatening the rural-urban fabric of Goa—the balance between the countryside and the city

(e) Overload on the existing infrastructure leading to shortages of water, land, power, and road space

(f) A growing culture of waste and consumption, with little concern for equity or the environment

(g) A wide range of institutional conflicts and challenges such as the balance of public and private roles, the facilitation of real devolution and de-centralisation and the balancing of various ethnic and community interests

(h) An insular and short-sighted political culture

The question before us then is whether Goa's recent spurt of development is yet another fifty-year miracle, like the bubble that was Old Goa, or is it something that will last, that will be sustainable in the long run? Moreover, will this sustainability be based on the Goan values of equity and sharing, honesty and simplicity, respect for nature and plurality, and a balance of modernity and traditional close knit community? Other concerns are

(a) What kind of economic development do we want and how can we attain it?

(b) How can we improve the quality of life of our people in all its aspects like livelihood, health, education, housing, and water?

(c) What kind of a Goa would we like to live in? How can we enable this?

(d) What are the kinds of institutions, laws, incentives, and civic culture that can enable this?

Part II

Goa 2100: Model for Sustainable Development

The following is the skeleton of the project.

RUrbanism   It is a hybrid concept to metabolize the village and sustainable city development. This is the cornerstone of Goa 2100 (see Fig. 17.3).

- RUrbanism is balancing the urban with the rural—co-evolution of the countryside and its embedded city.

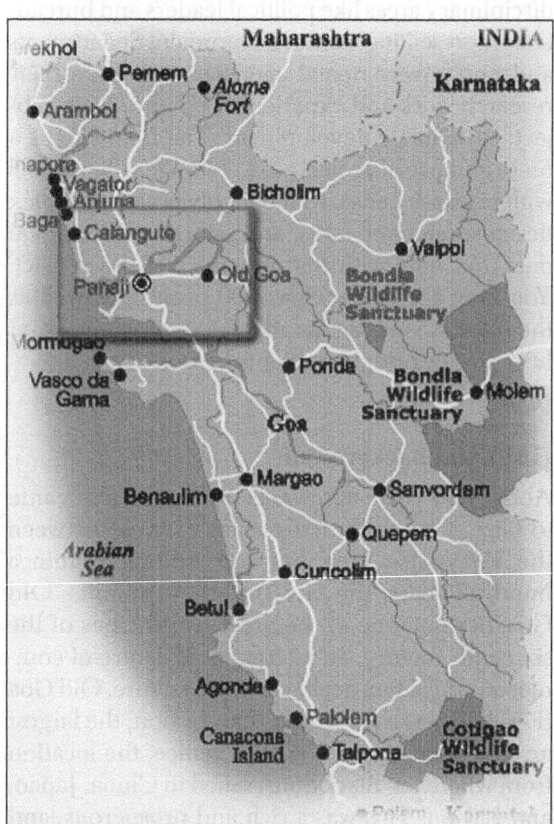

Fig. 17.3   Map of present-day Goa; the squared area is the Goa 2100 project area

- This approach by 2050 could allow 120 million Indians to meet their basic needs without endangering the bio-diversity of India's fragile western coast.

To attain RUrbanism, it is imperative to set a goal.

Three goals for the sustainability transition are

(a) *Sufficiency and equity* well-being of all people, communities, and ecosystems

(b) *Efficiency* minimal through-put of matter-energy-information

(c) *Sustainability* least impact on nature, society, and future generations

Seven organizing principles for sustainability

(a) Satisfying the basic human needs of all people and providing them an equal opportunity to realize their human potential.

(b) Material needs should be met materially and non-material needs non-materially.

(c) Renewable resources should not be used faster than their regeneration rates.

(d) Non-renewable resources should not be used faster than their substitution rates by renewable resources.

(e) Pollution and waste should not be produced faster than the rate of absorption, recycling, or transformation.

(f) The precautionary principle should be applied where the 'response' time is potentially less than the 'respite' time.

(g) 'Free-energy' and resources should be available to enable redundancy, resilience, and reproduction.

Five strategies for land-use management

All strategies are directed towards achieving biodiversity (see Fig. 17.4). An organic model is used for the human footprint in the surrounding ecological system as an organism that grows and consolidates itself as a part of the system.

(a) Enable a long-term ecological succession from forest to cropland, to city, to forest.

(b) Design the landscape first. Situate the city in the interstitial niches.

Fig. 17.4   Growth of dense urban islands (white) in the sea of biodiversity

(c) Land-use transitions governed by the demand for ecosystem services, resource potential, natural ecological succession, and contiguity.

(d) Identify static and dynamic elements in the city, design the former, and provide a dynamic vocabulary for the latter to co-evolve with the landscape.

(e) Devolve governance and taxation to the lowest viable level.

Six tactics to manage physical stocks and flows

(a) Use less with Factor 4 technologies for supply and social limits of sufficiency and equity on demand.

(b) Grow your own, tapping harvestable yields as autonomously as possible.

(c) Build two-way networks for security. Every consumer is also a producer.

(d) Store a lot because renewable resource yields are often diurnal and seasonal

(e) Transport less over shorter distances using least life-cycle cost technologies.

(f) Exchange using intelligent wireless networks, to enable real-time trade and delivery of goods.

Dynamic fractal morphology

A new design of the human settlement as a part and parcel of the larger organism that does not exploit but becomes the link in the ecological system had to be invented. The model was found in the cell of our organism (see Fig. 17.5), which would structure human activity within the ecosystem.

(a) Cellular structure—nuclei, cores, spines, and skins

(b) Hierarchical networks adapting to topography

(c) Optimal densities, settlement structure, and heights enabling security

(d) Contiguous and hyper-linked with interpenetration of living net

(e) Dynamic consolidation and nucleation around fractal boundaries and surfaces

Attaining Goals

From where will the money come to attain such utopian goals? This was the crux of the problem for those people who attended our workshops and seminars. We told them that this programme is designed to deliver from the existing allocations that the government makes to public works (see Fig. 17.6). We also told them that the dynamics of the project are such that the participation of the citizens, businesses, and corporations are

incorporated. It is a common development that is shared and profited by the people. Sustainability allows for a harmonious working as in an organic system.

In this manner, we would be able to achieve our goals, which we set in the beginning, in a realistic way.

- First Indian state to cross the upper middle-income country barrier, that is, a per capita income in excess of $3,265 per capita, or Rs 1.5 lakh per capita by 2020

- First Indian state to have no poor citizens by 2010

- First Indian state to achieve the core UN Millennium Development Goals by 2015

- First Indian state to significantly improve environmental quality by 2015

We must find new ways and examine innovative solutions that try to address the roots of our basic challenges. This is what the Goa 2100 project represents.

Part III

Conclusion

Goa 2100 may sound like a utopian idea, but in practice it is nothing but the application of a

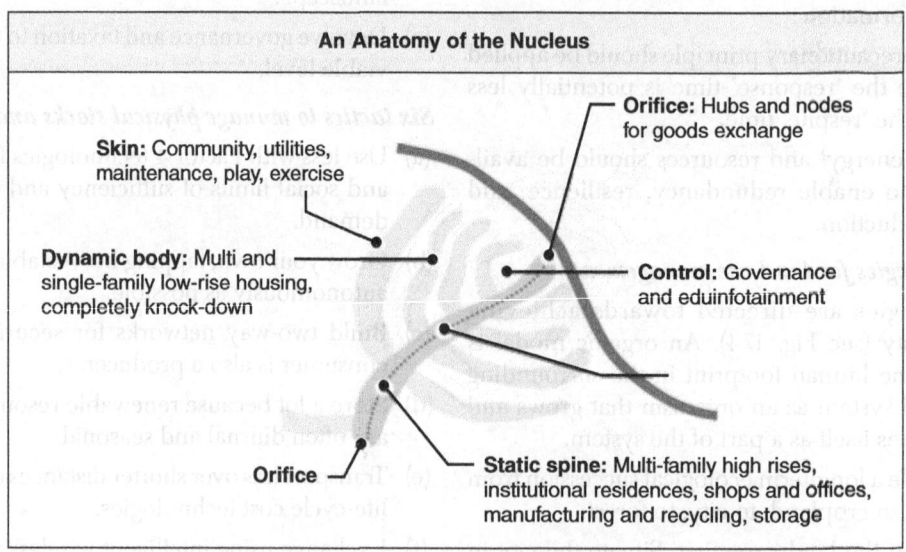

Fig. 17.5   Fractal morphology

Investment structure by end-use for the Sustainability Transition (2003–2030)

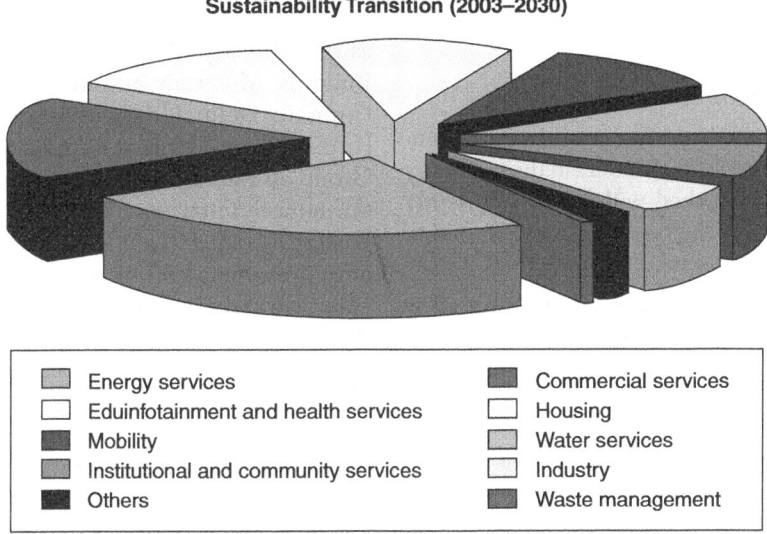

▨ Energy services	▨ Commercial services
☐ Eduinfotainment and health services	☐ Housing
▨ Mobility	▨ Water services
▨ Institutional and community services	☐ Industry
▨ Others	▨ Waste management

Fig. 17.6   Division of finances

number of simple common-sense principles to all spheres of development in a systematic manner. By breaking down the process of long-term change into a set of achievable goals and processes, we can, for example, examine whether we can integrate this into our Eleventh Plan framework. This would help Goa attract a new set of private and public investments, agencies, and institutions, hastening the process of change and adaptation to a new world. Any town or any city in India, or elsewhere in the world, can adopt this project without having a special outlay of budget other than the one that is normally allocated for development work. So, why not adopt a sustainable development?

Discussion Questions

1. What is the business of ethics in drawing a development plan for the future?

2. Why environmental sustainability is an ethical principle?

3. Is it necessary for human beings to exist to sustain the world?

4. What moral reasons can you give to see the shortcomings in the present human development policies of the government?

5. Are the methods of science compatible to ethical principles?

6. What ethical principles does Goa 2100 follow?

7. What is the ethics of nature?

8. Why it is important for Goa 2100?

9. Does our economic development, policies, and planning clash with ethical principles?

10. How can we be sure that sustainability is the right principle?

Going Further . . .

Workshop

- Give each group themes from Part II of the case study.

- As a background for arguments, study the interview in the following section.

ETHICAL DEVELOPMENT PROGRAMME

Management Training

Multi-stakeholdership Workshop

(a) Conduct a workshop after considering a comprehensive list of stakeholders in the company that you have worked with, or are presently working with, or the one where you intend to work.

(b) The MBA students may co-ordinate their workshop and integrate it in one of the conferences that are organized by the institute.

Background

Sanjay Prakash is one of the architects of Goa 2100 and is actively involved in the project. This interview was conducted over a period of time through e-mail correspondence. Hence, the answers are a deep reflection of our group's research work. This interview must be read in tandem with the case study in this chapter. Having worked on both these, you would be able to conceive and form some project on the same principles of Goa 2100, for the sustainable development of your city, town, or village.

Sanjay Prakash, aged 50, is a Delhi-based international architect and heads his own firm Sanjay Prakash & Associates. He is an alumnus of All India Institute of Architecture (A.I.I.A) and is a practising architect with a commitment to energy-conscious architecture, eco-friendly design, people's participation in planning, music, and production design. His areas of practice and research over the past 25 years include passive and low-energy architecture, hybrid air-conditioning, autonomous energy and water systems, earth construction, community-based design of common property, and computer-aided design. Under his guidance, many persons have developed capabilities in performing design and conceptual or management work in the above areas. He is a life member of Sri Aurobindo Ashram and is on the managing committee of its Mirambika Free Progress School. He is the team director of a progressive school, Shikshantar, in Gurgaon. In an honorary capacity, he has been an advisor or member of various public and international bodies, such

as the Ministry of New and Renewable Energy, Building Materials and Technology Promotion Council, Delhi Urban Art Commission, UIA (International Union of Architects) Working Group on Energy and Architecture. He is a part of the international environmental think tank, the Balaton Group. His name and work are mentioned in the twentieth edition of one of the main reference works in architectural history, *A History of Architecture* by Sir Bannister Fletcher.

Interview

Question: Protection of the environment has become the most important moral issue in our society. The problem, however, is how to express this new value? Should we express it in terms of usefulness of environment for our lives or does it have an independent value apart from our existence?

Sanjay Prakash: The environment doesn't have an advocate. So even before we express the value of protecting the environment, we need to have a representative. Since human beings are creatures evolved with a natural sense of survival, I think the most remembered arguments in favour of Gaia are often those that are utilitarian—from the point of view of humans. Therefore, the expressions of the value of environment work best when we talk about

(a) The necessity of having essential biological processes that make all plant growth (and therefore agriculture) possible, or

(b) The fairly established outcome of space exploration—that there is no 'final frontier', no real likelihood of being able to colonize and exploit the moon, Mars, or outer space, and extend our free lunch, or

(c) Negative environmental outcomes like global warming or water pollution, which are undesirable for human societies because they reduce long-term productivity, or

(d) Tiger conservation being essential as it is an indicator of biodiversity, which in turn is necessary to maintain water balance, or

(e) Nature being simply beautiful, relaxing, rejuvenating, etc.

But does the environment have a value independent of human utility? Clearly, this is a non-question, since when asked in the context of the human-environment relationship, it leads to the equivalent of the metaphysical question of quantum physics—what is reality, except that which is observed? This also has the corollary that the observer-observed components of a system influence each other and, in fact, change each other.

However, there is the danger that in looking at utility alone to engender environmental values, we may disregard nature out of ignorance. After all, we are a part of nature, so in preserving her, we preserve ourselves. This is not just utilitarian. It is a simple practical approach and finds an expression in most Eastern religions that stress the oneness of all life. It is especially evident in Buddhism. If we become too utilitarian, we run the risk of ending up committing the equivalent of suicide by, for example, sending our parents for euthanasia as soon as their use to us is over. From an ethical standpoint, therefore, we should be giving the benefit of the doubt to environmental values, understanding that were it even to cease to be useful to us, it would not be reason enough to decimate it, as we may run the risk of missing something we required from it, but were unable to see.

So, should we express environmental values in terms of the usefulness of the environment? Yes, certainly, to get the right action from human beings.

Does it have independent value? Yes, but does it matter?

Question: Let us look at it this way. According to you, we are the product of our natural environment. We have been evolved in a natural process. Now we, who are the products of this environment, are destroying it, and thereby effectively cancelling our own existence. This is suicidal. Environmental protection thus, immediately becomes our inclusive and inseparable value. Most of the blame for environmental destruction is laid squarely at the doorstep of the industry. Is the industry to be blamed?

Sanjay Prakash: As a part of the creation, we may be acting in a self-defeating way, yes, but not in a conscious way, so not suicidal. Suicide is more deliberate and negative. A lot of what is happening is due to the exploitative nature of the human existence on earth. All living species exploit the environment as well as contribute to it. Only, humans have done it too efficiently, and so have overshot the limits. To adapt from Aro's[5] formulation on cities, human societies have exploited an internal proletariat (slavery), an external proletariat (colonialism), or nature (fossil-fuel based industry). Since indefinite exploitation is unsustainable, one has to look at

(a) New exploitable frontiers, such as outer space (scientists have seriously looked at these possibilities to tap inexhaustible resources from outer space for many decades now, though with an increasing sense of failure—it seems we are doomed to live on our one and only Mother Earth), or

(b) New exploitable eras of time, such as the future (which is what we are currently doing by causing global warming, taking our grandchildren's resources like the fabled man who killed the goose that laid the golden eggs), or

(c) Create a new society based on not exploiting anything, a technically, hugely challenging task.

Our genetic make up has evolved us into becoming social animals that have a vested interest in propagating our species, but there is not enough time for nature to mutate the 'global-sustainability-principle' genes into us. So it is not the industry that is to blame. The industry is only a natural outcome of a series of movements caused by our evolutionary make up that makes us instinctively fatten ourselves up for improving our chances of

---

[5] Aromar Revi, the founder of the Delhi headquartered TARU, the environmental management consulting firm, is doing in-depth environmental research. He is an expert on disaster management. Sanjay Prakash is closely associated with Revi on several projects.

survival. Agriculture too was an outcome of environmental stress caused by overpopulation, and bought us a lease of life of about eight millennia. Colonialism lasted five centuries, and the industry, about three centuries. Each phase caused irreversible changes in Gaia.

However, the foundations of our contemporary commerce have a flaw. They were designed around the 1930s, to inject all market economies with a growth serum, and we all know from biology that this is nothing more, nothing less, than causing cancer. It has to be stopped with a suitable antidote. Will we invent our way out of trouble this time, too? Probably, we know that this is a global crisis and is a first step towards going faster. But this time, we cannot depend upon our nature changing, cannot wait for us to become different animals.

Question: Your analysis that we have exploited our natural resources for such a long time that we couldn't care less for the sustainability principle, and that we have not used our imagination to undo our business, as usual behaviour with the exploitation of our resources is quite acceptable. Let us begin then with what we need most. Energy is the sole resource for our development. The trend is to tap in non-conventional energy resources. Quite an admirable quantity of technology is already being developed. What policies need to be implemented to make these non-conventional energy resources conventional?

Sanjay Prakash: Yes, the issue of energy is central, although it is not the only issue of sustainable development. Water is probably more critical, while food and minerals are not negligible issues.

Despite the global increases in the harnessing of renewable energies, the world today largely runs on coal and oil. Sometime in the late eighteenth century, in response to the resource crisis of depleting forests and rising population, Europe saw a dramatic increase in the use of fossil fuels, mainly coal, at a non-renewable rate. The consequent prosperity in turn seeded the environmental crises that came two centuries later. Industrial economy has gone global in the late twentieth century, with oil moving people and goods and largely, coal-dependent electricity grids carrying energy conveniently into buildings.

I am not including numbers in my answers, but oil and coal really run the world, accounting for nearly three-fourths of the energy we use.

There are many features of renewable energies that need to be understood to develop policies to support transitions towards their adoption as discussed here.

Infirmity Many renewable technologies are infirm, that is, they cannot be stored in a tank or shed like fuel, so their deployment leads to complex engineering, which cannot assure temporal coordination of demand with supply. In this category we have solar, thermal, photovoltaic, and wind power. These technologies have low-load factor. The actual production to peak power installed is low and dependent on weather factors, such as 20 per cent maximum for wind and photovoltaic, which makes their investment per peak unit an incorrect measure of capital efficiency, and are therefore slated to meet 'base' loads, meaning the first preference for production for loads that conveniently match the energy availability. Wind and photovoltaic power used during windy or sunny seasons, respectively, fall in this category.

Storage Alternatively, if affordable energy storage is developed, which is possible for heat but not yet for electricity, then infirm technologies can be used more easily. Solar thermal is therefore already a viable technology, with the potential to reduce space and water heating demand globally. Similarly, chilled water or ice storage is on the margins of being viable and can reduce peak cooling demands. Affordable electrical storage too is a potentially disruptive technology. This is the reason that development of ultra-capacitors is being carefully watched by the renewable energy world.

Poor load factor In a sense, hydro-electricity is its own storage, and so is a firm and renewable technology, whose potential was therefore developed early, at a large scale, in the middle part of the twentieth century. But once you store the water and let it cascade over a turbine, it's gone for the year, especially in monsoon countries, so the annual load factors are low. That is why, for instance, while India has 25 per cent power capacity available as hydro, the actual energy produced by this capacity is 6 per cent. In this sense, hydro is infirm.

Environmentally difficult zero-carbon technologies Large hydro has its share of energy problems, but nuclear energy, not strictly renewable, which offers a hope to produce large quantities of electricity without emissions, has even greater challenges of radiation leakage and ultimate storage of spent fuel. Since photovoltaic is infirm, and biomass gasification (see below) is too diffuse, it may be necessary to include nuclear in a final list of production technologies if we need to meet the very large power demands that modern industry places on the grid.

Firm but too low density Biomass gasification or biodiesel are poorly understood in terms of their production economics. Many of these may compete for food and fodder production, and nations like India and China cannot afford to take their agricultural outputs for granted, thereby imposing a limit on biomass development. Even if large tracts of land were made available, the output density of biomass is ultimately quite low. In order of magnitude, one could expect to get 20 tons of biomass per hectare per year, but this translates, at best, only to a continuous power output of 2kW/hectare! This is definitely a rural demand mitigation technology, but cannot allow us to remain *homo mobili*; I cannot imagine a world full of cars and planes running on biodiesel, without causing civil strife in Brazil.

Producing 'Negawatts' Conservation is also a type of infirm renewable energy and I personally consider it an extremely important source, especially when it can reduce peaking by demand management, technical efficiency-based suppression of demand, efficiency by mitigating the emissions of supply through sequestration, temporal adjustment of demand, or by ethical restriction of wasteful demand. But ultimately, even conservation doesn't stand alone, because it only allows us to consume less of a bad thing, much like Diet Coke may drastically reduce the ill effects of Coke, but is it good for one's health?

Renewable energy potentials of each group of sources therefore, remain in the single digits in terms of percentage. In a world of renewable energy, gas will be a dominant transition fuel, ultimately leading to a combination of production technologies (wind, solar, nuclear, biomass, and geothermal) and carriers (electricity, hydrogen, heat pipes) combined with storage (ultra-capacitors, earth). We will not be able to conveniently supply just oil on tankers and electricity through a grid to do everything. This is all right, as no-one expects a single coal-fusion or clean-fission 'magic' technology to allow us to continue behaving as industrial man did, just burning away available capital. This means a systemic dismantling of the large energy utilities that have matured with the age of fossil fuel use, to a multiple-energy-stream neighbourhood utility model, for which the pilot is likely to be energy-starved Japan.

So now we can address the question of policy. The world of renewable energy will probably have a different economic model. For a start, it would have to treat investments over life cycles, rather than discount them and expect them all to attract the same rate of return, which the medium of money standing in for capital allows us to do. The world will also have to integrate an economics, where it would not be possible to externalize negative consequences of technology, which is done by the oil industry by not having to pay for diseases caused by tailpipe emissions, for instance. The new economics would have to deal with de-centralization and user-generation of resources. Every consumer can also be a producer, something the ICT industry already understands well.

The policy therefore would allow banks and investments to achieve the following:

- Encourage rapid innovation in renewable energy. There was a banking problem in India in the late nineties: wind generators were facing such a rapid technical advance that banks were unwilling to fund them unless they showed profits within three years, something not possible for wind mills, which will freely produce energy for at least twenty years, because according to the banks, the plants had very little resale value, as better technology became available every year!

• Subsidize and tax logically and not under pressure of lobby groups. The Reva car remained expensive till 2007 due to excise rules erected under pressures from the car lobby. Insulation was under a tariff barrier because it was considered a 'luxury' good, since air-conditioning was a luxury. There's a move in the US Senate to bail out dinosaur-like Detroit jobs, even as GM refuses to design fuel-efficient cars on the plea that this is not their business strength.

• Promote R&D investment and energy services companies (ESCOs) to realize their potential. ESCOs are not developing in India, as they have no security of contract, and so their investment in energy efficiency can get locked behind the property owner's lock, even as the user defaults in paying up the energy tariff agreed upon.

• Eliminate split incentives, as between a landlord who needs to recover his investment from a tenant in eleven months due to a legal environment that makes it insecure for him to have a longer lease.

This list is too short to be comprehensive; I have tried to describe the foundations on which these new policies need to be built, but it is too time consuming to actually list a possible set of policies, though these are being developed in India by the group working on the National Action Plan on Climate Change.

Question: You have been one of the protagonists of the Goa 2100 project that won the award for Sustainable Urban Systems Design at the World Gas Congress 2003 in Tokyo, Japan. The principles of that project have been incorporated in this chapter, because they have very strong social and ethical foundations. What was your experience throughout this project that could motivate my students as well as readers to create and implement similar projects?

Sanjay Prakash: Well, firstly, the process of evolving the design itself was highly widely consultative. The Indian team was assembled from various design and consulting firms located in Mumbai, Delhi, Hyderabad, and Goa, stressing on gathering the most competent team of young designers, sustainability specialists, and development professionals in India that could work collaboratively on this challenging task. They were supported by eminent sector advisors from India, Europe, and the US. Some of the team never met face to face, and electronic collaboration allowed this to become productive for almost three years.

Then, the 'product', or outcome, was multi-disciplinary, something that we tend to forget is essential in a multi-dimensional world. There are no simple solutions in our complex world. There are no one-size-fits-all. Hence, engineers must collaborate with demographers, policy must be attuned to architectural possibility, and transport planning must interface with sociology to create possible pathways to the future.

Look at the multi-disciplinary flavour of the following five-point agenda that was about the economic outcomes.

(a) Exporting 1 MW wind turbine from Ella to Japan each month

(b) Stem cell therapy from the high-value medical biotechnology unit at Chorao Island

(c) A daily web-cast by the world-famous Panjim Music Conservatory with its conductor, who works from Berlin

(d) Twenty-year long conservation effort at the Old Goa world heritage site and the pre-colonial temple tanks on Diwar

(e) A ten-minute long trip to watch birds fishing as the tide goes down in the mid-town Salim Ali bird sanctuary

But due to the extremely limited experience of such trans-disciplinary work and its relatively recent dialectic, it was also necessary to work in fairly abstract terms, as the reader can see in one of the concluding list of organizing principles that came out:

(a) Seven organizing principles for sustainability.

(b) Satisfying the basic human needs of all people and providing them an equal opportunity to realize their human potential.

(c) Material needs should be met materially, and non-material needs non-materially.

(d) Renewable resources should not be used faster than their regeneration rates.

(e) Non-renewable resources should not be used faster than their substitution rates by renewable resources.

(f) Pollution and waste should not be produced faster than the rate of absorption, recycling, or transformation.

(g) The precautionary principle should be applied where the 'response' time is potentially less than the 'respite' time.

(h) 'Free-energy' and resources should be available to enable redundancy, resilience, and reproduction.

What can I say to motivate students?

Firstly, look at the environment as something part of, not opposed to, society and economics.

Secondly, do not take demand or consumption as a given. Question its quality and quantity.

Thirdly, try to internalize negative externalities of a project and avoid or pay for exploiting the commons, watching which resources you use, as you can't get something from nothing.

Finally, understand that a sustainable world begins with a sustainable lifestyle and that it implies starting with you, here and now. We can all do our bit without waiting for some magic technology to do it for us.

Afterword

Outside of project design, lifestyle changes have to become (and are becoming) the cornerstone of environmental change driven by society. For an urban middle-class Indian family, the most important lifestyle changes are

(a) Not driving when you can cycle or walk

(b) Getting a good cycle with a basket, to be able to do all local work

(c) Sharing car trips or using public transport for commuting

(d) Not flying or driving when you can go by train or bus

(e) Keeping enough reusable bags in your vehicles so that you never have to get anything you buy in plastic bags

(f) Separating your waste into organic and inorganic

(g) Composting the organics, even if it is in a window box

(h) Managing with natural ventilation whenever the weather or your state of mind allows this

(i) Reducing air-conditioning to the minimum

(j) Getting air-conditioners with good temperature controls

(k) Setting these air-conditioners as high as possible (28 °C)

(l) Using ceiling fans in combination with air conditioners

(m) Drinking lots of water

(n) Wearing appropriate clothes (loose cotton clothes in the summer)

(o) Keeping cool

(p) Reducing or eliminating food, high-water content in your diet, like coffee, refined sugar, red meats, white meat—this is healthy for you, too

(q) Keeping faucets closed while brushing, shaving, soaping yourself, etc.

(r) Reducing the flow volume and duration of your shower

(t) Installing a flush cock and reducing the flushed water quantities

(u) Installing a solar water heater (it even pays back for itself within two years)

(v) Organically growing your own food, even if it is 1 per cent of your total demands at home, even if it is in a window box, because it is chemical free

As you can guess, I follow most of these in my own life and that difference is probably more benign for the Earth than my entire green project career taken together.

Management Mantra

Lone Ranger–The Tale of Two Rangers

Here is an adaptation of Jean Giovo's 'The Man Who Planted Trees', originally titled *L'homme qui plantait des arbres.*

Fictional Lone Ranger	Real Unofficial Rangers
Elzéard Bouffier was a shepherd who lived at the foothills of Provence in France, at the beginning of the last century. For some odd reason, this valley region had hardly any trees or vegetation. The place was eerily desolate and there was not even a bit of water for a thirsty hiker. Bouffier had an idea. He would go to the surrounding places and collect acorn seeds and come back and sow them into the earth using his staff. Slowly but surely, a huge forest started growing here. Bouffier gave up his flock so that it may not graze in the forest.	Kendupatti is a small village in Tamil Nadu. Around it, there was this government land that was once a forest. In the early 1980s, the villagers decided that something must be done about this ruined forest. They started reviving it by planting trees and guarding it against intrusion. The trees grew steadily over a stretch of 140 acres of land. The villagers decided that the forest will not be used for their needs. They wanted it to grow as nature allowed it. Left to itself with no human interference, it grew so well that it was incredible.
A hiker who had discovered Bouffier when he was sowing acorns returned to the valley to find a forest that did not exist previously. He wrote that this forest cured him of his stress and ailments, which he suffered during the war. Hundreds and thousands of people came to the forest. The authorities declared it as a reserved forest sanctuary. The hiker, of course, told the authorities about the shepherd who had planted the forest. The shepherd was honoured and recognized, and lived a simple and long life, doing what he always did—letting the forest grow.	But the success of their efforts was short-lived. The forest department woke up to the reality of a forest that territorially belonged to it. The local authorities and other vested interest groups soon joined them. To carry on their activities unhindered, the forest department appointed guards! Naturally, the villagers objected to the official intrusion and took measures to protect the forest. The forest department took legal action against the villagers!

> **MANTRA**   *Credit or discredit, plant trees anyway.*

18

Challenges of Cyber Age

Twenty years ago no one could have imagined the effects the Internet would have—entire relationships flourish, friendships prosper on the e-mail screen, there's a vast new intimacy and accidental poetry (from the osprey-tracking site to tours round old nuclear silos and the extraordinary aerial trip down the California coastline and a thousand others), not to mention the weirdest porn. The entire human experience seems to unveil itself like the surface of a new planet.[1]

—J.G. Ballard

Computers are logically malleable in that they can be shaped and moulded to do any activity that can be characterized in terms of inputs, outputs, and connecting logical operations. Because logic applies everywhere, the potential applications of computer technology appear limitless. The computer is the nearest thing we have to a universal tool. Indeed, the limits of computers are largely the limits of our own creativity.

—J. Moor

LEARNING OBJECTIVES

After studying this chapter, you will be able to

> Understand information technology and its moral significance to business
> Define data identity and security
> Determine Internet crime and punishment
> State the intellectual property rights

INTRODUCTION

Our objectives in this chapter will be to discuss the serious problems that affect the business world in cyber age. We may not find easy solutions, but just like Narad Muni of the ancient Indian scriptures, who travelled with ease between heaven and earth, we would have to exercise agility between the physical world and the cyber world

---

[1] J.G. Ballard, the futuristic novelist, in an interview to the *Guardian*. For more details, see http://www.guardian.co.uk/books/2004/jun/22/sciencefictionfantasyandhorror.jgballard.

and relate to them morally. Prudence is the moral standard that we will have to apply, because much of this is uncharted territory for ethical analysis.

That the Chinese government is wary of the Internet and clamps down even that which it remotely suspects is against the communist ideology or the government is a huge understatement. The Chinese authorities are vehemently against dissent and they censor all forms of public communications. The Internet is very difficult to censor, but they have succeeded so far by forcing individuals as well as multinationals to do their bidding. Most of the multinationals and Internet companies such as Microsoft, Google, and Yahoo do oblige to the wishes of the government, so that they may not lose official favour to run their businesses. Google has even gone overboard by creating a separate search engine for the Chinese. One day, when China becomes a democracy, the international businesses will have nothing to show but culpable complicity with the communist regime.

However, centuries of civilization and tempered wisdom have actually helped the people of China to overcome the vagaries of dynasties and despots in the past, and the communists are not an exception. Songs and stories, the medium of the Internet, and lately, even *Falun Gong*—smooth-flowing exercises—have been ingeniously used to criticize the government and its leaders.

A report in *Time*[2] describes the ingenuity of certain Internet sites that get away with the worst behaviour possible against the government. The humble alpaca is used for the purpose and it is everywhere on the Internet, sold as toys, videos, or other merchandise such as a mythical horse made of mud and grass (*Cao Ni Ma*), but in a derived sense, horribly vulgar and lewd. The authorities are in a dilemma as to how to get rid of the real and living alpacas, toys, videos, paintings, sketches, books, and the virtual ones that millions of people have downloaded on their computers and mobiles. The question is to ban or not to ban, to censor or not to censor.

The Chinese government uses censorship strictly. Ironically, thanks to Western technologies such as the firewall, the authorities can nanny people's moral and political Internet behaviour. The Western countries which have been trying to introduce democracy and free-speech in China are in a way helping, through their technology that they sell to them, to subvert it. Despite the direct and indirect help of the multinationals, the people do find a way to express their fundamental rights as human beings. In this case, they just sing a 'Song of the Grass Mud Horse!'

The challenges of the cyber age facing modern corporations are many and complex. The fundamental question is, can they claim moral leadership in the cyber age?

Cyber is a prefix to everything that transports us instantly into the virtual world. The Internet is the vehicle to the cyber world, and cybernetics is the complex technology that governs it. The moral law that governs the relationships of people in the physically interactive world, also governs the virtual world relationships. From

---

[2] Randy James in 'Chinese Internet Censorship'. For further details, see http://www.time.com/time/world/article/0,8599,1885961,00.html (18 March 2009).

cyber birth to cyber suicide, from cyber games to cyber business, the world is small enough to be placed on a pin top, or as large as the universe itself. In the cyber world, things move at the speed of thought. The cyber community is so large, and mostly anonymous, except for the virtual faces and names, that it makes the relationships even more complex.

As in the above case of the *Cao Ni Ma*, the entire physical world and the cyber world is involved. The interaction between the subjects of these two worlds is complex, dynamic, and fast. Just as authorities have problems in deciding what is right and wrong, and how to grapple with the problems, businesses also find themselves between deep moral chasms and virtual thunderbolts. Morality has become very difficult and very complex. In the above case, when people direct filthy abuse against the authority, the authority, as a social responsibility, crushes dissent and destroys the basic human right. Businesses abdicate their moral responsibility towards people in order to please the authorities—nothing seems to go right either in the real world or in the virtual world. One wonders what choice one has to make a moral decision.

INFORMATION TECHNOLOGY AND ITS MORAL SIGNIFICANCE TO BUSINESS

Information technology (IT) that operates through the applied technologies of computer science and the new medium of electronic communications, such as the television, telephone, and the Internet, is of moral significance because they are our actions for which we are responsible, their virtue or vice is applicable to us, and their consequences of right and wrong can be attributed to us.

The use of knowledge as a commodity was not in such sharp focus as it is now in the cyber age. Humans took a very long time to develop the information they gathered into knowledge, and from knowledge they developed tools that they perfected into technology. (Figure 18.1 shows an example of information developed into knowledge.)

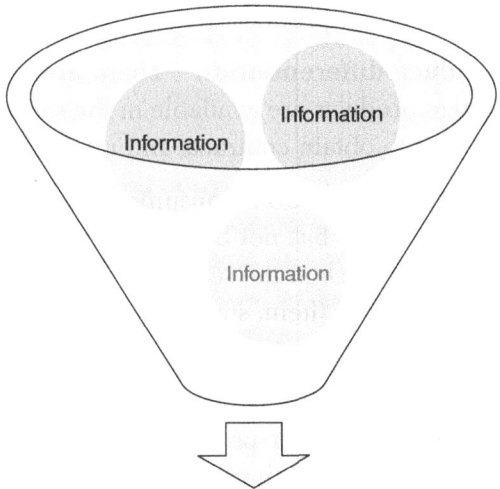

Fig. 18.1   Product knowledge is a result of processed information

With the coming of the era of cyber technology, information was used as raw material to generate intellectual and technological tools, and put them to use.

The issues involved are about personal identity, intellectual property, software ownership, sexuality, privacy, etc. Today, no part of our life remains untouched by the knowledge economy, and business corporations are the reason for it. Moral significance has become greater and not lesser. As long as any human action is wilful and affects people individually and collectively, the moral significance is essentially bound to it.

Understanding Information Technology vis-à-vis Business and Morality

IT is the new economy, the knowledge economy. India is in the forefront in this new business. In fact, no old economy functions without the new economy—the knowledge economy. Manufacturing, marketing, advertising, distribution and logistics, organizing human capital, trade and commerce, governance, transport, engineering, communications, entertainment, and leisure are all managed by the new economy, the IT. Some salient features of the knowledge economy are discussed below.

Knowledge is a product   The knowledge product is an intangible asset. However, its excellence is measured by the quality of its performance, what the software programs can deliver, and with what efficiency they can perform the tasks which they purport to perform.

Production through skilled minds   Land and labour of the old economy has been sidelined. Skilled people who are skilled in computation, programming, and analysis work in teams to design solutions for managing the business world.

Targeted product   There are particular solutions to particular problems. Banks, capital markets, air traffic, governance, education, libraries, entertainment, and the media, all need IT and these products are customized as per the needs of the customers.

Knowledge product differentiation   There are competitors in the market, and different knowledge products are available in the same requisite area; companies are in fierce competition to obtain contracts and retain their clients.

Knowledge consumers   The IT consumer market is as large as the globe itself; today, there is no one who has not been influenced by it in some way or the other. Even birds, animals, and fish in the seas have a small chip inserted into them, so that it may help experts to track them, study them, and thus create programmes for their preservation and protection.

Creative product   Knowledge products are created by people and they rightfully belong to them. The creators or producers have their rights over them, which are both moral and legal. We call them intellectual property rights, just as musicians, painters, and authors have right over their creations. Those who infringe the creative rights, cheat. They are like pirates; they are thieves. Software piracy causes the biggest losses for the IT companies.

Data ownership   Data is the stored information that rightfully belongs to an owner. The data generated by the IT are exclusive property. Just as one's house and property documents, shares, bonds, debentures, cash, personal information, and the rest are exclusive property, so also the IT data. Those who find a way to steal the data or hack it are as bad as the burglars who break into houses and rob.

The cyber age, powered by IT, has revolutionized the lives of the people around the world. It has significantly altered all the aspects of life, from commerce, employment, security, transportation, to health and entertainment. The information and communication technologies which define cyber age, have a good as well as a bad impact on the family and community life, human relationships, education, careers, freedom, democracy, and other aspects of human existence. Thus, cyber ethics may be defined as that branch of applied ethics, which studies and analyses human behaviour that is related to information and communication technology.

IT Code of Conduct

In 1992, the Computer Ethics Institute, a non-governmental organization with an objective to bring ethical responsibility in technology, formulated a code of conduct that closely resembled the literary method of the biblical Ten Commandments[3]:

(i) Thou shalt not use a computer to harm other people.

(ii) Thou shalt not interfere with other people's computer work.

(iii) Thou shalt not snoop around in other people's computer files.

(iv) Thou shalt not use a computer to steal.

(v) Thou shalt not use a computer to bear false witness.

(vi) Thou shalt not copy or use proprietary software for which you have not paid.

(vii) Thou shalt not use other people's computer resources without authorization or proper compensation.

(viii) Thou shalt not appropriate other people's intellectual output.

(ix) Thou shalt think about the social consequences of the program thou art writing or the system thou art designing.

(x) Thou shalt always use a computer in ways that ensure consideration and respect for thine fellow humans.

These are simple basic rules. If these are followed, the virtual world would be a great joy and happiness for mankind. But human nature is such that it chooses to act in ways which are contrary to the above codes. Hence, the authorities and governments are forced to introduce laws. Laws are nothing but forced morality, and today we have laws that apply to the cyber world also.

---

[3] See http://www.computerethicsinstitute.org/images/TheTenCommandmentsOfComputerEthics.pdf.

Gold Farming

World of warcraft

The days when one could sit quietly on a weekend afternoon and play a game of chess or dominos or Chinese checkers, and reap pure joy may still be around for the older generation; but the new generation is a gaming generation that helps to create a very large virtual economy. A case study reported in the UK daily *Guardian*[a] reveals that the virtual gaming industry employs an estimated 4 lakh workers from Asia; for a change, the Chinese are in the virtual sweat shops and not the Indians. The consumer base consists of those who are gaming, and it is increasing everyday, and is presently estimated at 10 million.

The most popular game is World of Warcraft (WoW).[b] It was started by Blizzard Entertainment in 2001, and is one of the most popular games on the Internet. It is growing, without dampening the spirits, even during the financial crisis. WoW7 Gold is a sophisticated gold farming company that employs just over a hundred people, and is well organized into production, sales, advertising, and research. It makes close to $2 million. The company supplies in-game advantages to WoW players, who generally belong to developed countries. They may ask for new *avatars*, increased skill levels, magic swords, or precious ore to be obtained. In other words, the players pay money to obtain skills rather than work for the same. The work is done by 'playbourers'.

Playbourers are people who sweat away in very meagre conditions in China, and earn about $200 a month. They work or do gold farming for their clients, who pay money to enjoy their game with the various levels of tools and weapons to be supplied by the playbourers. This exotic-sounding game seems like a dream job. It comes at a cost of being away from home,

working in shifts for more than ten hours, gulping down company-supplied food, and sleeping on bunker beds.

Youngsters who are just out of college slog away hours after hours to earn their living and, as researchers found out, the people who have money to pay, of the same age group, do not even think twice that those who give them the pleasure at gaming are actually slaving away—digging gold farms for them, and earning only a pittance.[c] The research was conducted by Prof. Richard Heeks of Manchester University, who found out there are scammers, hackers, and pornographers, thus creating a virtual underworld around gaming. There are also other gangsters who take money but do not supply the services, falsify or hack credit cards, and spam or fill websites hawking gold.

Ever since the case was published in the *Guardian*, it has evoked a great debate among youngsters, the clients of the game on the Internet.[d] Although some would not care less, many do believe that this is a serious issue in business morality, just as poignant as carpets being woven by child labour. But then, gaming involves much more than mere sweatshop jobs for the young. It is outright criminal and even dangerous.

Questions

(a) Is it prudent to believe that change in human activity, from the physical to the virtual, does not cause a change in the fundamental principles of ethics?

(b) What is the economic principle of fixing just wages?

(c) In what way has the virtual economics widened the gap between the haves and the have-nots?

[a] Visit the gaming site at www.worldofwarcraft.com.

[b] Look up 'Welcome to the new gold mines' by Rowenna Davis at http://www.guardian.co.uk/technology/2009/mar/05/virtual-world-china, accessed on 5 March 2009.

[c] See http://news.bbc.co.uk/2/hi/technology/7575902.stm.

[d] See http://www.escapistmagazine.com/forums/read/9.94313.

DATA IDENTITY AND SECURITY

Imagine you are travelling in a foreign country; when you need some money, you go to an ATM to withdraw it. There is no money in your account. You are worried; you think you have made a mistake and you repeat the process; you insert the card, punch the password, and draw a blank. It dawns on you that someone has laid hands on your ID number and password, and used it to withdraw all your money. How did you lose these things? Someone asks you whether you had done some transaction on the Internet, where you paid with your card. You say that you do that all the time, from buying tickets to a cinema, or air and rail tickets, to paying your bills and taxes. Then the person concludes that someone has stolen your identity and your money. Sometimes, virtual reality leaves you to fend for yourself in the cold.

Data security is of enormous importance because these are information assets, which are of monetary value and must be protected; it is also a fact that the data is meant for further wealth generation. There are three important values that need protection—confidentiality, integrity, and availability. Data security problems are fundamentally ethical problems, which also take a legal turn when ethics fails to motivate moral character.

Ethical Issues in Data or Information Security

Information has always been a very sensitive issue. In ancient times, rulers and kings developed their own secret code so that the documents they sent to their counterparts or to their generals, would not be deciphered even if these were lost or snatched away from the messengers. During the two world wars, information technology developed rapidly, and they grappled with the problems of espionage and the infiltration into information of the enemy strategies on either side of the warring alliances. The key to win the war was information that was collected through a network of highly intelligent and smart spy network.

Today, human life is unthinkable without IT. From running a household to running a government, from managing corporations to running hospitals and for education, we depend on IT. This raises the stakes in its security. It consists of protecting information and its technology from unauthorized access, use, disruption, modification, or destruction. The respective ethical values are confidentiality, integrity, and availability, and these are paramount. Following are the basic principles governing security.

Confidentiality   Prevention of disclosure of information to unauthorized persons. In the case of the card identity theft mentioned above, somewhere in the process between the customer and the authorized person (seller), there must have been a breach such non encryption and faults in databases, log files, backups, printed receipts, etc. Thus, when an unauthorized person accesses that credit card number and uses it to his benefit, confidentiality is breached and a theft takes place. Breach of confidentiality can take place very easily at work places, where someone is able to look over the computer screen and get a key word, a password, or some other authorizing key.

Integrity In Mumbai, someone got access to a school database and changed the grades. Everything in the issued certificate was right except the grades, which no one could detect, until the teacher found the discrepancy. The volume of the violation of data integrity is enormous, from employees modifying their payrolls, to the vandalization of the data through hacking. Imagine the catastrophe caused when the diagnosis of a patient is altered by some enemy of the patient.

Availability It is very annoying when you visit your bank and the employee tells you blandly that the 'system is down or the power is out'. If the requisite data is unavailable when needed, it is not only a big disappointment, but also a breach of trust. Non-availability of data has caused enormous inconvenience and loss to the customers.

One may also further add some measure of commonsense to the three basic ethical values, to safeguard the data. Thus, always verify the authenticity of the data when receiving or dispatching it. Honesty also demands that one should not deny having sent or received the data. It is also an ethical responsibility to bear the risk in data protection. The business corporations have a special responsibility to manage their data risk. Laxity in risk management will cause loss to business, and perhaps in extreme case, total bankruptcy.

Risk Management

To secure risk management,[4] business corporations have to take the path of creating a new corporate culture that is conscious of information security. Following features may help in risk management.

Awareness Information security awareness programmes within the corporation are the beginning to develop a culture of information security. The human resource department should take up the responsibility initially to acquaint the employees with the importance of the information security.

Cross-functional teams Risk councils, security steering committees, and the like have to get their act together in their information security objective. This increases communication, encourages the coordinated effort, and reduces duplication and costs.

Management commitment The culture of an organization depicts the reasoning behind its activities and its goals. When it is the culture of an organization to be assertive on information security, it filters from the top authorities, down to the last employee.

---

[4] For complete information, see *Security Management: An Introduction to the Business Model for Information Security* at http://www.isaca.org/.

Approach   An assessment of the actual risks and their constant review helps to know and understand the real risks rather than follow a system blindly. An intentional approach to security can help select appropriate controls and mitigate risk.

Balance between organization, people, processes, and technology   The core of risk management is organizational support, competent people, efficient processes, and appropriate technology. Each of these has their impact on risk management.

Thus, business corporations taking initiatives in information security risk management not only put the firm on a good business model, but also a trustworthy ethical model.

Processes

The centre of IT lies in its processes. The companies bear responsibility towards themselves and their stakeholders. Today, companies function depending on the information processes in every field of business management. It calls for serious accountability, one that is similar to the financial accountability. The concepts used in accounting would also be useful for the IT processes.

Prudence   The people responsible for running the IT systems must possess prudence apart from competence. They must be endowed with commonsense to manage the affairs of information. Anything contrary will result in losing information to unwanted and unauthorized persons.

Due care   Due care should be taken to safeguard the interests of the stakeholders so that they can entrust their most treasured information and reputation in the hands of able managers, who do not vacillate in their integrity.

Due diligence   Due diligence is the foremost virtue in the eyes of the law. Legal processes are very important to run a company. Today due diligence in the matter of information security plays a very big role in areas such as in the capital market. The entire gamut of corporate governance depends on this concept of due diligence, where disclosures and declarations are true to the information that the company possesses. Falsifying data could lead to serious problems.

Seen in a broad spectrum of modern human life, IT is a common good for the benefit of all. Hence, the professionals of IT have a special responsibility to be the stewards of this technology which is growing rapidly. Their professional duty also demands that competent services are offered and the people's privacy and property are protected. It is for the IT professionals to improve and advance in their chosen occupation, to excel through further research and development. Above all, to remain above conflicts of interest and uphold the trust that others have placed on one's professional competencies. The above mentioned information security processes presuppose the existence of laws, to govern information security. All countries have enacted laws with the objective of safeguarding the integrity of the data, the privacy

Dance Like a Butterfly, Sting Like a Bee

Credit card ID theft

On 20 March 2009, BBC[a] broke the story of a sting operation that had a broker in its net selling credit card details of UK customers, for as little as $10 per card. While the morality of sting operations is still debated upon, their operations may well be described with the old song dedicated to Mohammad Ali, the boxer, 'Dance like a butterfly, Sting like bee...' That is exactly what these purportedly covert operations of filming do, while decoying like a butterfly.

After learning from some sources about the malpractices of the employees and their cohorts (the brokers) of the Delhi-based Indian call centre Symantec, BBC set up a sting operation. The deal was struck while sitting in an up-market coffee shop. The broker flaunted his goods, which were a list of the credit card details of certain UK customers. The sting operators, posing as fraudsters, struck a deal with the broker. The broker was brimming with business success on the TV screen. He said that he had a large stock of information on cards. The stingers agreed to buy fifty, but he gave them only fourteen; he promised to send the rest by email. He even divulged that his sources were the call centres that handled mobile phone sales or phone bill payments.

The epilogue to the above story was rather comical. All the details that the broker gave were right, including the names, addresses, and pin codes; but the numbers fell short of a digit!

The Financial Time brought out a story that Symantec had immediately launched an internal investigation.[b] The company offered credit card monitoring services to its allegedly cheated customers. In the various foray on the Internet, many vented their feelings against the sting operation by saying that they were after the Indian call centre industry to destroy it. The fact is that data theft has become a global phenomena; no amount of regulation is going to control it. However, through a well-grounded ethics programme, the companies can save themselves from much ignominy and loss of business.

Questions

(a) Why is data integrity such a critical issue in business?

(b) Do sting operations belong to the cyber world ethics?

(c) Does commonsense help to overcome the problems of data security?

[a] Look up the BBC website at http://news.bbc.co.uk/2/hi/south_asia/7954139.stm.

[b] See http://www.financialexpress.com/news/Credit-card-details-on-sale-in-India-Report/436927/.

of the individuals, and the protection of businesses; but these serve neither adequately nor efficiently.

CRIME AND PUNISHMENT

In 2004, there was a case of two highschool students, both minors, from a reputed school in Delhi, who had recorded their own sexual act and sent it around through MMS. Another enterprising student from an IIT made its CDs, and put them for sale on Baazee.com, an online auction portal.[5] But the law came hunting for the CEO of the Internet auctioneer, and arrested him with the charge under the IT Act 2000 that

---

[5] For a very interesting discussion on the subject, see http://in.rediff.com/money/2004/dec/21binter.htm.

stated that any such pornographic commerce was illegal, it warranted an arrest, and was punishable.

Information Act 2000

The Indian Parliament enacted the Information Technology Act 2000.[6] It was amended in 2006. It replaced the old laws that regulated posts and telegraphs, and now reflects the new realities of the new information communication technology.

Protection by the law   We need such laws that people can do transactions over the Net through credit cards. The Act offers the much-needed legal framework, so that information is not denied legal effect, validity, or enforceability, solely on the ground that it is in the form of electronic records. It provides ways to deal with cyber crimes. In view of the growth in transactions and communications carried out through electronic records, the Act seeks to empower government departments to accept filing, creating, and retention of official documents in the digital format. The Act has also proposed a legal framework for the authentication and origin of electronic records communications through digital signature.

E-commerce   The provisions of the Act contain many positive aspects. The implications of these provisions for the e-businesses would be that email would now be a valid and legal form of communication in our country that can be duly produced and approved in a court of law. Companies shall now be able to carry out electronic commerce using the legal infrastructure provided by the Act.

Digital signatures   Digital signatures have been given legal validity and sanction in the Act. The Act throws open the doors for the entry of corporate companies in the business of being certifying authorities for issuing digital signatures certificates.

Notification   The Act now allows the government to issue notification on the web, thus heralding e-governance.

Official communication   The Act enables the companies to file any form, application, or any other document with any office, authority, body, or agency owned or controlled by the appropriate government in electronic form, by means of such electronic form as may be prescribed by the appropriate government.

Information security   The IT Act also addresses the important issues of security, which are very critical to the success of electronic transactions. The Act has given a legal definition to the concept of secure digital signatures that would be required to have been passed through a system of a security procedure, as stipulated by the government at a later date.

---

[6] A study of the Act is strongly recommended; see https://nicca.nic.in/pdf/itact2000.pdf.

Data protection Under the IT Act 2000, it shall now be possible for corporations to have a statutory remedy, in case anyone breaks into their computer systems or network and causes damages or copies data. The remedy provided by the Act is in the form of monetary damages, not exceeding Rs 1 crore.

However, many feel that the law is not comprehensive. We have related two cases that deal with data theft and the sale of pornography, on the *Baazee* portal. In the first case, no action has been taken so far, since the offender who sold the stolen information could not be pinned down; there was also an issue about the legality of an evidence of a sting operation. In the second case, the arrest of the CEO of the auction portal was bizarre, because the guilt appeared to be far fetched. This was so because the auction portal functions free from interferences between the buyers and the sellers. The arrest of the CEO had caused widespread consternation in the IT industry.

Internet Censorship

The constitution grants the freedom of speech as a fundamental right. The Internet is a new and powerful tool of communication to exercise such a right. Internet censorship, however, is the control and suppression of select information with the objectives of protecting morality, preventing religious and social sentiments from being thrust, stopping the propagation of hateful ideologies, etc. The censorship is also used by totalitarian states to control all information against their policies. IT companies have very often crumbled under the pressure of government censorships as China has demonstrated. Even in India, there is heavy censorship and many have questioned and even sought information of the banned or censored sites under the Right to Information Act (RTI). The debate for and against censorship has been very fierce.

According to Vint Cerf, who has been considered the Father of Internet, censoring it would become impossible. The tools of the Internet can overcome any form of surveillance and banning of access.

No territorial borders Censorships imposed on books, papers, films, CDs, and DVDs can be controlled within the borders of a country, with physical checks and balances. The Internet has no national borders, except where its facility itself is banned, such as in North Korea. With more and more convergent technologies in communication, the mobile phone has taken over the medium of the computer, and the Internet has moved into the pockets of the people.

Smart censorship Censorship employs more intelligent software programmes to sensor. SmartFilter is one such software whose customers are ironically those who smother democracy by limiting the freedom of speech. The irony of IT is that, just like the weapons of destruction, this tool could also be used for suppressing the very freedom of speech, which the technology proposes to advocate. Some of the countries who use this technology are Saudi Arabia, to safeguard its Islamic culture, Sudan, to protect dictatorship, and surprisingly, even the US and UK, to restrict certain sites. Figure 18.2 shows the world Internet censorship map.

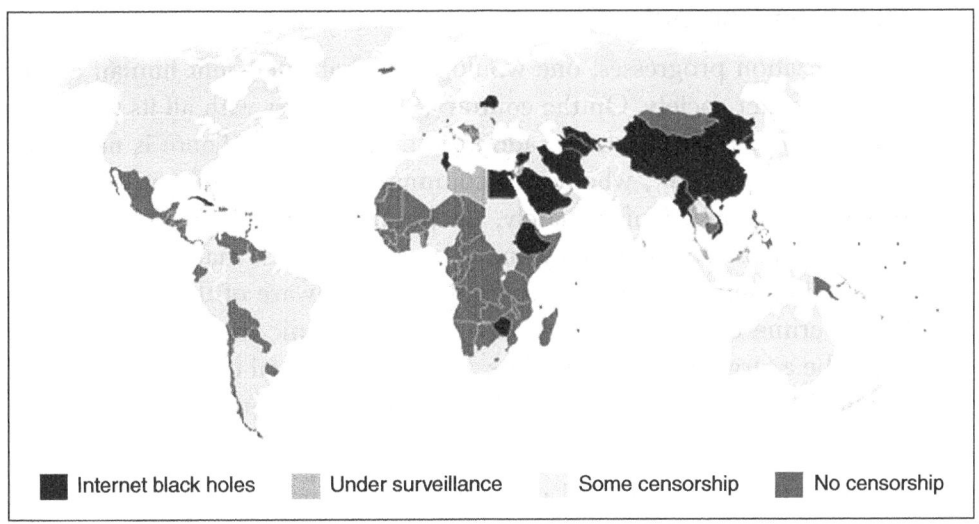

Fig. 18.2 The world Internet censorship map

Source: http://en.wikipedia.org/wiki/Internet_censorship.

Unintended censorship There are several software programmes that work as Net-nannies in educational institutions, workplaces, and households. These case sensitive programmes block even the most innocent words, as some of their spellings may match pornographic slang.

Circumvention of censorship There is software available today to circumvent the net nannies, government bans, and site blocking technology. Proxy servers are virtual private networks which can be subscribed to. For example, *Psiphon* allows Internet access even where there is censorship, *Tor*, bypasses all Internet censorship.

Sneakernet When everyone got caught on the cyberspace and censors were busy roaming the virtual world in order to suppress, there emerged a new strategy which took the Internet to the basics of communication—carrying the physical data from one place to the other and distributing it. This needed no network at all.

Censorship can be justified on several moral grounds, but prudence is called for, so that the people's basic rights to communication and freedom of expression are not violated. Pornography, when seen from its production aspect, is a violation of human dignity because it uses persons as sexual objects. Seen from its consequences, it is a cultural and religious degradation; but when the minors view these sites and interact through them, its social repercussions are obviously undesirable. The dilemma is that all sexual or adult material works against the traditionally held moral values, but is legally protected and is a hugely growing industry. The people who work in this industry live in self-doubt. They feel morally more guilty than the customers. It is natural to lose one's self-worth by merely being an object of sexual pleasure for millions of anonymous people.

Common Computer Crimes

As civilization progresses, one would think that intelligent human evolution would create a better society. On the contrary, the progress with all its technology has also caused undesirable results, in addition to the desired. There is no doubt about the benefits of computer, whether in communication, business, governance, and even distant healthcare. Unfortunately, people misuse the technology and cause untold misery and also loss of money and property. Business managers, to save themselves from being duped or face losses, must be well aware of the common cyber crimes. Cyber crime consists of the abuse of the electronic media, where a computer can either be a target or a tool of crime, or even incidental to crime. The profile of cyber criminals is no different from that of traditional criminals. The difference is only in the tool of crime.

Hacking   Illegal intrusion of a computer system without authorization of the owner or user.

Spam   Flooding of the victim's computer with spam to affect the bandwidth, whereby the user is unable to access and work on the computer.

Virus dissemination   Malicious software that attaches itself to other software and destroys the programmes and data on the victim's computer. Trojan Horse, Time Bomb, Logic Bomb, Rabbit, etc., are some of the common viruses.

Software piracy   Software theft through illegal copying of genuine programs for the purpose of selling and distribution. It causes loss to the lawful owners and vendors of the software.

Pornography   Exploiting human sexuality to generate revenue. They also use deceptive marketing strategies such as mouse trapping. Publishing and transmitting of such material is illegal under IT Act 2000.

Paedophilia   Similar to pornography, but involves children as objects of sex.

IRC or Internet relay chat   These social sites are used by the criminals for their own ends; they even stalk their victims by keeping track of them on the net.

Credit card theft   This may be done through hacking, keeping a surveillance device at ATMs, or any of such devices as skimmer, etc.

Net extortion   After getting the data, there is an illegal threat for a ransom.

Phishing   Hacking and taking out confidential information such as from banks; they even supply counterfeited bank web pages, where gullible customers key in their financial details.

Spoofing   One computer on a network pretending to have the identity of another computer; it is a kind of impersonation in order to get access to other computers.

Brothers SMS

SMS scam of Mumbai

The Nadar brothers, thirty-year-old Jayanand and Jayaraj, lived in the posh locality of Juhu. They made a name for themselves as young entrepreneurs, and no one grudged them their lifestyle and the finest cars that they drove. They had another associate called Ramesh Gala, who was a proficient accountant belonging to their age group.

In August 2006, the Nadar brothers and their friend Gala set out with a business plan.[a] To begin with, they started a publicity blitz with a tempting slogan, 'Nothing is impossible: The word itself is: I M Possible. Earn Rs 10,000 monthly.' Then they changed the campaign to SMS mode and sent SMSs to numbers at random. The plan was simple to understand. They told the world to subscribe to a scheme that they represented through an American company called Aropis Advertising, which wanted to market its products through SMS. The subscribers to the scheme had to deposit Rs 500. The subscribers would then receive several messages of various products. Further, the subscribers would receive a handsome commission if they supplied more subscribers to the scheme. The business grew and more agents were roped in from among the subscribers to get even more subscribers. A website named getpaid4sms.com made the scheme spread nationwide.

In the beginning, the cheques that the subscribers received were in small amounts. This firmed up the faith of the subscribers in the scheme. However, as the commission amount grew to several thousands, the cheques bounced. The number of SMSs reduced and then stopped completely. The anxious and agitated customers had no other course of action left, but to take the help of the law. The complaints increased from a trickle to a torrent. There were 50,000 subscribers to the scheme in Mumbai alone. The police transferred the cases to the Economic Offences Wing (EOW). The investigation found that thousands of subscribers were cheated and the estimated amount was more than Rs 40 crore. The Nadar brothers and their friend Gala are cooling off their heels behind bars.

Questions

(a) What is the law worth if only a few are caught and punished for their crimes, while innocent people lose their money?

(b) How can censorship help to deter fraudsters?

(c) Does the Internet need laws or ethics? Either way, how would you enforce good behaviour?

[a] See http://cybercrime.planetindia.net/conmen_in_rs400m_sms_scam_arrested.htm and http://www.funonthenet.in/component/option,com_smf/Itemid,36/topic,35554.0/wap2,wap2.

Cyber defamation After obtaining damaging information, the criminal disseminates the information to defame you and take revenge on you, or cause loss.

Threatening Just as in a traditional crime, threats are generally anonymous; hate mail is also another form of harassment.

Salami attack After getting the required information, for example, financial information from a bank, the criminal transfers a very insignificant amount such as Rs 2, from other people's accounts, into his account. But by transferring it from several thousand people's accounts, he makes a large amount for himself, while the victims never bother with the loss of a mere Rs 2.

Thus, cyber crimes in many ways show the darker side of society. These also show, in the same social proportion, the economic crime rate. The criminals have just switched to a different tool. What is most unfortunate for society is that the new brood of criminals are young and educated; hence, the anxiety of civil society for the future is real and worrisome.

INTELLECTUAL PROPERTY RIGHTS

The intellectual property right issue is a burning issue in today's world of knowledge economy. There are substantial ethical, economic, and legal concerns surrounding this issue. The problem may be stated simply as that an individual product in this realm is extremely costly to produce, such as complex software programmes; but once it is done, it is child's play to copy it, just as good as the original, and use it with childish abandon.

Perspectives on Intellectual Property

Let us have a glimpse of three different perspectives.[7]

Moral perspective   The inherent quality of a property is to be owned. Thus, we own our name or identity, our belongings, our skills, and all that we make for ourselves. When we write a book or compose a piece of music, it bears our authorship. It makes no logical sense to say that it is authored by all. Its source is a person and that person owns it. If he/she could make money out of it that only adds to his/her physical property. Only he/she has the right over it, and no one else. He/she may give it up freely, but that is according to his/her will. This is a moral point of view.

Legal perspective   Intellectual property (IPR) right is an issue of right. Justice demands that a right ought to be honoured, be it a physical property, or an intellectual property; the ownership is legally bestowed on the particular person. This is a legal point of view.

Business perspective   The question of IPR must be understood in terms of business. In other words, there are trademarks, trade secrets, and patents which have been developed by highly skilled people in specially built environments. These have nothing against the morals or the law; in fact, they depend on them for their existence. The products of intellectual skills call for large and very complex investments. People dedicate their lives to the research and development of such products. The cyber age is a direct result of these developments. Intellectual property right is a *sine qua non* for business. This is the business view.

---

[7] See http://www.britannica.com/EBchecked/topic/911774/intellectual-property-law/231532/Economic-and-ethical-issues.

Intellectual Property Implications
Case

Shawn Fanning of California, who was nicknamed Napster, was just eighteen years old when he developed a programme that enabled people to access MP3 music files from each other's computers. When he posted his program for a free download on a website by the same name, there were 300,000 who took hold of it. It became the enviable download of the week. A venture company offered $15 million as a start-up for the new company, Napster Inc. that has become well known both for its earnings as well as for controversy. The controversy was that as a result of the mass copying, the companies lost business and the music artists were robbed of their earnings.[8]

Arguments for preservation of intellectual rights

The ethical and economic issue of the case is that if software copying is ethical and economically legal, the people in the knowledge business would be robbed of their property and their creative skills through which they earn their living. The authors will not get any royalty, the artists and musicians will have no earnings, and the businesses connected with all electronic programmes and software will come to a standstill. Eventually, everything will come to a standstill—technology, governance, education, industry, business, and so on without end.

Those who argue against this issue by saying that it is only restricted to music, and just as books are lent and shared among friends, so also such software as music and images should not come under the purview of ownership as in the case of copyrights, trade secrets, and patents. However, this is countered by the weight of the sheer quantitative argument that a circulation of the book through lending by friends is restricted to very few people. The software copying and that too, direct downloading is of global proportions which will, to begin with, hit the music industry. It will then spread to every software based product, which will eventually destroy itself.

Arguments against intellectual rights

There are an equal number of people opposed to any intellectual property ownership of software products. Linux is one of the best examples, as its software of operating system (OS) for computers is freely available and is continuously upgraded. People do not have to buy OS that can get out-dated quickly. Today, individuals as well as large corporations use this software successfully and no one has seen the businesses of Microsoft or Apple, who come in the protected category of IPRs, going down. There are thousands of other downloadable programmes freely available on the Internet. All the results show that their free distribution has been a platform for bigger and larger businesses, to conduct their business in the ever-expanding Internet market.

[8] See Intellectual Property Rights, http://plato.stanford.edu/.

The present trend of free software clearly demonstrates that no business or industry is coming to a standstill.

Intellectual Property Rights and International Law

In International Law, the issue of IPRs has taken precedence over all the other major issues. The agreement on Trade-related Aspects of Intellectual Property Rights (TRIPS) has contributed to the consciousness and expansion of the issues. It obligates the World Trade Organization (WTO) to establish and enforce minimum levels of copyright, patent, and trademark protection. The countries that do not comply with these provisions are subject to WTO administered penalties and sanctions.

The developing countries have been slow in implementing the provisions of TRIPS. These countries argue that the regulations are biased against the developed countries, and are formulated to protect the interests of the developed countries.

TRIPS

Trade-related intellectual property rights

The Preamble[a]:

Desiring to reduce distortions and impediments to international trade, and taking into account the need to promote effective and adequate protection of intellectual property rights, and to ensure that measures and procedures to enforce intellectual property rights do not themselves become barriers to legitimate trade.

Recognizing, to this end, the need for new rules and disciplines concerning:

(a) the applicability of the basic principles of GATT 1994 and of relevant international intellectual property agreements or conventions;

(b) the provision of adequate standards and principles concerning the availability, scope, and use of trade-related intellectual property rights;

(c) the provision of effective and appropriate means for the enforcement of trade-related intellectual property rights, taking into account differences in national legal systems;

(d) the provision of effective and expeditious procedures for the multilateral prevention and settlement of disputes between governments; and

(e) transitional arrangements aiming at the fullest participation in the results of the negotiations.

Recognizing the need for a multilateral framework of principles, rules, and disciplines dealing with international trade in counterfeit goods;

Recognizing that intellectual property rights are private rights;

Recognizing the underlying public policy objectives of national systems for the protection of intellectual property, including developmental and technological objectives;

Recognizing also the special needs of the least-developed country members in respect of maximum flexibility in the domestic implementation of laws and regulations in order to enable them to create a sound and viable technological base;

Emphasizing the importance of reducing tensions by reaching strengthened commitments to resolve disputes on trade-related intellectual property issues through multilateral procedures;

Desiring to establish a mutually supportive relationship between the WTO and the World Intellectual Property Organization (referred to in this Agreement as 'WIPO'), as well as other relevant international organizations.

[a] See http://www.wto.org/english/docs_e/legal_e/27-trips_02_e.htm.

Our Moral Imperatives

Any new phenomenon introduced in society has its fledgling time. When we look into the history of technological development such as the discovery of motor engines, it first used simple energy and later progressed to fossil, electric, and nuclear energy. We find that even these have their problems in view of the environment. So we make efforts to find better and cleaner sources of energy. The Internet is a new phenomenon that is just lifting itself up on the horizon, and there is an entire future ahead for this technology, where it will lead man into greater realms of space, as well as the inner realms of our own being. The starry heavens above will not be accessible, if the moral law within does not evolve to meet the challenges. Only adherence to the moral law will ensure common good of mankind. Following are some of the most important moral imperatives:

(a) Recognize and enhance the dignity of man by giving each his due, both physical and spiritual rights.
(b) Raise the social contract to protect privacy, property, and accessibility of the individual.
(c) Information technology must help fulfil these goals and not diminish them.

We must make sure that we do not have to fight a losing battle with IT, as we are doing presently with our environment and economy.

Chain Reaction

Burn a CD for me

Prakash is a college-going student. He is a great movie buff. He noted that a movie would be telecast on TV when he would be at college. So, he simply programmed the TV to record it for him. As he was watching the movie later that night, he got an SMS on his mobile from his friend Rahul. It read that Rahul had programmed his TV to record the same movie, but since there was an electricity failure at the time of its TV broadcast, it could not be recorded. Prakash sent Rahul an SMS telling him not to worry, and that he had a copy of the movie and would hand it over to Rahul the next day at college.

The following day, Prakash handed over the CD to his friend at college. He also gave a couple more to his other friends, saying, 'I just copied it for you, too.' His friends were happy that he had thought about them, and thanked him. Very soon, the entire class gathered in the canteen and the requests poured in to 'Burn a CD for me.' Promises were made to make further copies of the movie and hand them out.

Questions

(a) Would you, as a movie producer, approve of the behaviour of the people in the above case?
(b) Why is it legal to record a TV programme for personal viewing?
(c) How much replication makes multiplication of the programme for distribution among friends illegal?

Note: The case is fictional and has been narrated to bring out the complex moral issues in simple everyday behaviour.

SUMMARY

- Cyber technology is a computer-assisted information and communication system and is a vehicle of information gathering, storing, analysing, and creating new knowledge, and disseminating it.

- These intelligent systems have a direct relationship to moral actions, since these are directly connected to making decisions and choices, which affect being right or wrong in relation to people.

- A code of conduct is therefore called for, so that the people's identity, rights, privacy, intellectual property, and economic, social, political, and the other aspects of life are protected.

- The moral crux depends on confidentiality, integrity, and the availability of the information.

- It is incumbent on the businesses that all information and processes of information are safeguarded with due care, due diligence, and prudence.

- The greatest responsibility of the businesses is risk management.

- When moral law is not able to necessitate a better behaviour, then legal laws are enacted to enforce a minimum ethical balance.

- As ethical limits are crossed increasingly, there is a plethora of laws, both national and international, to govern the cyber world so that identity, signature encryptions, information security, data protection, etc., are taken care of, and severe punishments are delivered for infringements.

- Censorship has tried to reduce the various crimes on the Internet.

- One of the complex and critical problems of cyber technology is the protection of intellectual property rights.

- The moral imperative for the protection of intellectual property rights is to recognize and enhance the dignity of man.

KEY TERMS

Censor   To edit, cut, or repress images or written words to protect the moral and social sensibilities.

Confidential   Private, undisclosed information.

Cyber age   Era of technology dealing with virtual reality.

Data   Any kind of information in cyber technology.

Data integrity   The complete, total, unaltered, and non-interfered data.

Identity   A mark or sign indicating one's individuality.

Information   Facts, statistics, figures, numbers, etc., of computer data.

Intellectual property   One's ideas, knowledge products.

Intellectual property right   Knowledge products which, like private property, are recognized by moral law and have legal bindings.

Internet   International computer network.

Privacy   Personal matters, all those states of affairs which one would not like to disclose; the breach will result in its violation, which breaks both moral and criminal law.

Prudence   Caution and care exercised in our actions lest hasty decisions impair moral, social, business, etc., responsibilities.

Risk management   The way companies use and protect the data.

Risk   The possibility of loss of data, misuse by criminals.

Software   Computer programmes that power the functioning of cyber technology.

CONCEPT REVIEW QUESTIONS

1. Why is cyber technology a moral issue?
2. Of what benefit will a code of conduct be in information technology?
3. Why should the virtual actions in cyber space affect moral behaviour?
4. Why is confidentiality as important as it is made out to be?
5. What relevance does data privacy have?
6. What constitutes the intellectual property rights?

CRITICAL THINKING QUESTIONS

1. Is there a morality for the use of free software?
2. If a Linux programme is for free, then why are its copies and books based on it, produced and sold?
3. Can we not hack ethically?
4. How can one control intellectual property rights?
5. Is it fair for IT companies to patent their products, when they could help the world with the free availability of the software, which would help economic development?

FURTHER READING

Tom Forester and Perry Morrison, *Cautionary Tales and Ethical Dilemmas in Computing,* The MIT Press (1993).

CASE STUDY

Indernet

The Story of Indian Village IT

Achieving sustainable human security is a priority task. This will call for harmony with nature and with each other. Knowledge connectivity within and among countries will help to achieve this goal. This is why we should make 'Mission 2007: Every Village Knowledge Centre' a success.[a]

—National e-Governance Plan, Mission

Introduction

In the 1990s, the world suddenly woke up to a new reality that India was the only IT developed country in the world. Several other titles came its way, namely, Computer Country, Asian Giant, World's BPO, IT Superpower, and more. It was an amazing experience for me, as I was in a German University at that time, and people would ask me about computers, the IT education, and

English language education in India, instead of the usual questions on poverty, cows roaming on the streets, and naked *sadhus*. It was a leapfrog as far as the image change was concerned. The German media was full of the success stories of the Indian IT industry. The German government announced an immigration policy alteration to get the Indian IT experts, and offered them documents that were equivalent to the US Green Cards. There was so

---

[a] See http://www.it.iitb.ac.in/~prathabk/egovernance/egov.html.

much hype about the Indian IT industry that the media at times termed it as INDERNET, in place of Internet. *Inder* in German stands for Indian (masculine).

Objectives

The main objectives of the case are

- To see the positive side of IT
- To know IT as a good tool
- To understand what helps the poorest of the Indians as a moral talisman

E-Governance

E-Governance is the mantra that the Government of India wants to follow, and has successfully established in every state of the country. There is a National e-Governance Plan 2003–2007, which seeks to lay the foundation and provide the impetus for a long-term growth in the country.[b] Today, e-governance is available in the following areas:

(a) Income tax

(b) Passport and visa service

(c) Company affairs

(d) Central excise

(e) Pensions

(f) Land records

(g) Road transport

(h) Property registration

(i) Agriculture

(j) Municipalities

(k) Gram panchayats (Rural)

(l) Police

(m) Employment exchange

(n) E-courts

The state governments all over the country now find it easier to manage services to the people in the above fields. They recognize the advantages of the IT-enabled working environment.

Bureaucrats now find it easier to do people's business, and deal with their bitter complaints and unhappy situations. People have liked the plan, as it is easily accessible. There is now less opportunity for corruption. Efficiency has reduced the grievances of the people. A lot needs to be done to bridge the digital divide between the urban and the rural. But initiatives taken by some IT companies in partnership with the government have helped in bringing governance to the folks in the villages.

Karnataka   In Karnataka, for instance, there is a project called *Bhoomi*[c] which has computerized all the land records. This has solved to curb disputes, litigation, and corruption. Earlier, the villagers had to bribe the village accountants. All such inconveniences and problems have been solved. The impact has been phenomenal. Seventy lakh villagers in 30,000 villages have benefited from one such project.

Gujarat   In Gujarat, there are websites where citizens log in and get access to the concerned government department on issues such as land, water, and taxes.

Andhra Pradesh   In Andhra Pradesh, through *e-Seva*, citizens can view and pay bills for water, electricity, and telephones, besides municipal taxes. They can also avail the birth and death registration certificates, passport applications, permits and licences, transport department services, reservations, and the Internet and B2C services, among other things.

Contrary to old prejudices, even in the remotest corners of the country, people realize the all-round benefits of computer technology. Until now, people extracted promises of electricity, road, and water from their political leaders; but now they are demanding mobile phones, computers, and Information Technology Enabled Services (ITES). The political leaders have also become extremely savvy and use SMSs extensively in their campaigns.

---

[b] See http://india.gov.in/govt/national_egov_plan.php.

[c] See http://www.expresscomputeronline.com/20050131/egovernance01.shtml.

The National e-Governance Vision Statement says, 'All government services accessible to the common man in his locality through a one-stop-shop (integrated service delivery) ensuring convenience, efficiency, transparency and reliability.'[d]

I-Farmer

Over 80 per cent of the population of India is agrarian. It is an economy that has steadied pitfalls in the Indian economy. It may also be well said, in times of the great financial meltdown around the world, that the steady agriculture has saved the country. The business corporations have realized the potential of the Indian farmer and they are approaching the farmers with technology. E-Chaupal, ITCs trading programming for farmers has become known around the globe; it has helped the farmers to not only get rid of the middlemen and get a fair price for their produce, but it was a strategic shift that helped the company to procure its raw materials and build a rural friendly brand name.

Farmer's new tool: Mobile phone

Most of the farmers are not educated. Tata Consultancy Services (TCS) has now developed a new utility called *m-Krishi.* It allows farmers to send queries to agricultural experts in their own language and receive advice in voice SMS. This innovation of the TCS has thus helped the farmers in Tamil Nadu on a personalized basis, and being illiterate is not an impediment.

The Mumbai based TCS Mobile Agro Advisory System has evolved from the efforts of TCS Innovation Labs. It researches into sensor as well as speech recognition. The company has also used an internally developed IVR (interactive voice response) type platform—packet interactive multimedia response (PIM2R)—which uses the inexpensive data channel for transferring rich content.

Farmers would have to use CDMA mobile phones[e]. Along with their queries, they can also send a photograph of the crop through a camera phone. The information related to crop, soil, and micro-environment, that is gathered by sensors is sent to experts through an automatic weather station using the cellular network. Farmers receive responses to their queries through the same channel.

The programme has won several national and international awards. TCS has also won the patent for this innovation.

M-Marketer

It is true that when ITC came to the villages, it chased out the middleman. The other big players with a heart for the villages, such as the Future Group and Reliance, also came to the villages, and even lobbied with the government to get rid of the much vilified middleman.

But there are some big corporations who think that the middlemen are actually the farmers' angels.[f] Multi Commodities Exchange of India and Reuters Plc, the world's renowned information provider have come together to organize wholesale *mandis* with the help of the middlemen. According to them, the middleman is a key player who is too precious to lose, for he has comprehensive information, and hence, they make him a part of the plan. The companies, with the help of middlemen, disseminate information through SMS and help farmers pledge their produce to electronic *mandis* across the entire country. The middlemen are the vital link. The farmers may then choose to sell in whichever market that is agreeable to them. The combined companies, who are in their initial stages, already have twenty-five *mandis* in Maharashtra alone.

Twenty-first Century Student from Village

The National Mission on Education, through the Information Communication Technology (ICT) is

---

[d] See http://www.it.iitb.ac.in/~prathabk/egovernance/national_egov_plan.html.

[e] Shanti Kannan, 'Harnessing technology for farmers' in *Hindu.* See http://www.hindu.com/2009/03/15/stories/2009031555101000.htm.

[f] Vishal Krishna, 'Farmers Angels' in *Businessworld.* For more details, see http://www.businessworld.in/index.php/Information-Technology/Farmers-Angels.html.

the focused plan of the Eleventh Five-year Plan of the country. The target of the mission is to train 550 million people by 2022. Following are the objectives:

(a) Building connectivity and knowledge network among and within institutions of higher learning in the country, with a view to achieving a critical mass of researchers in any given field

(b) Spreading digital literacy for teacher empowerment

(c) Development of knowledge modules having the right content to take care of the aspirations of the academic community, and to address the personalized needs of the learners

(d) Standardization and quality assurance of e-contents, to make them world class

(e) Research in the field of pedagogy for the development of efficient learning modules for disparate groups of learners

(f) Making the e-knowledge contents available free of cost, to Indians

(g) Experimentation and field trial in the area of performance, and optimization of low cost access devices for the use of ICT in education

(h) Providing support for the creation of a Virtual Technological University

(i) Identification and nurturing of talent

(j) Certification of competencies of the human resources, acquired either through formal or non-formal means, and the evolution of a legal framework for it

(k) Developing and maintaining the database with the profiles of our human resources.

The above objectives are to be obtained by providing connectivity and creating content. An amount of Rs 4612 crore has been allocated by the Planning Commission during the Eleventh Five-year Plan for the National Mission on Education through ICT. There is a budget provision of Rs 502 crore during the current financial year,

2008–09. The *Sarva Siksha Abhiyan* is the government's massive movement for elementary education.

CPU—Computer, New Teacher in Village

The consciousness that education is the only key to India's development has been well propagated by the non-governmental organizations (NGOs). Corporations too are spending large funds for education in rural India and they are doing it in partnership with the NGOs and the government. The Government of India has established a Council for Advancement of People's Action and Rural Technology (CAPART) that facilitates a coordinated effort in rural education.[g]

There is a great want for schools and teachers in the villages. Well trained teachers do not want to go to the village schools, due to backwardness of the villages. Those teachers who go to the villages, do so because of the government scale of salary; they only register their attendance and do not teach. This dismal situation has now brightened up with the arrival of the new and effective instructor in the village—the Computer.

CAPART has massive programmes in advancing education in the villages through computers. The government is also aiding projects which may develop laptops for educational purposes, with minimum but effective technology, for connectivity and imparting of education. Distance education, adult education, technical education, etc., are catching up with increasing speed. These are going to bridge the gap between the cities and the villages.

The content is made available directly to the computers through the information grids which have been established. The teachers do not have to depend on textbooks. The lessons are available online, and are understandable due to the images and visible teaching methods, even without an instructor. The animation technology is also used in the lessons to not only make the children learn better, but to keep them glued to the screens as

---

[g] See http://capart.nic.in/.

well. Following are some of the advantages that a traditional school may not have:

(a) Computers used for networking

(b) Better option in comparison to postal distance learning

(c) Flexible learning

(d) Lessons can be repeated with the same intensity

(e) Medium of language is not a problem, since options are available to select the lessons in a language of one's choice

(f) A computer costs much less than the salary paid to the teachers

CAPART has generated big opportunities for employment for technicians, teachers, village schools, and all the infrastructure needed for education. Hundreds of NGOs have been sponsored by the Council.

I-Doctor

Infosys, India's leading IT firm has developed a patient management tool. It is a web application that facilitates real-time flow and access of interoperable clinical data among health providers. It will be a part of a healthcare programme called Extension for Community Healthcare Outcomes (ECHO).[h] It was developed in collaboration with the University of Mexico. It has an intuitive web interface that efficiently and securely integrates patient data in real-time, from all the participating health providers. Consequently, the doctors are able to co-manage patients, based on a more accurate exchange of data. It will help in taking correct medical decisions and provide a continuous training of medical personnel working in the rural and remote areas. This is another addition to the already existing teleconferences and telemedicine, which will strengthen a comprehensive healthcare programme. The programme has been successfully functioning since 2004. Project ECHO has helped overcome the barriers of distance, money, and specialized medical care. It helps to deal with

multiple chronic diseases and health conditions such as HIV, cardiac conditions, mental health disorders, diabetes, autism, and substance-abuse disorders, among others. The system is delivered via a software-as-a-service (SaaS) model; it reduces potential technology barriers which existed in the rural health clinics.

The Ministry of Health and Family Welfare has prioritized its healthcare under its spotlight programme, National Rural Health Mission (NHRM).[i] Primary healthcare is one of the main instruments of action. It recognizes the importance of health in the process of economic and social development, and improving the quality of the life of our citizens. The mission adopts a synergistic approach by relating health to the determinants of good health, such as segments of nutrition, sanitation, hygiene, and safe drinking water. It also aims at mainstreaming the Indian systems of medicine, to facilitate healthcare.

The success of rural health depends on the technology vehicle, which is indigenously developed. We also have a huge army of NGOs and corporations, who want to combine their efforts in bringing healthcare to the villages of India. With IT, we could become a self-sufficient and healthy nation.

B2C—Village Mall

Satyan Mishra earned his MBA from Delhi University and worked as an entrepreneur for eleven years. Those days of the 1990s were the heady days of dot coms. But his heart lay in the village. He thought that he must take the ICT to where his heart belonged. He had a vision of a robust village economy, and so, along with a few others, he founded a company solely with a rural mission, and named it *Drishtee* or Vision, appropriately. He thought that education was the first priority, and started a programme called *Gyandoot* (The Messenger of Wisdom). Soon, he ventured into other fields like computer education, micro-finance, healthcare, and women's

---

[h] See http://www.digi-help.com/it-booster-shot-for-rural-healthcare-courtesy-infy/.
[i] See http://india.gov.in/spotlight/spotlight_archive.php?id=15.

empowerment activities, all with an entrepreneurial edge.

The approach to this rural entrepreneurship was simple. Most of India lives in its villages. The customer target is over 80 per cent of the billion people or more, who have little or no access to trade, governance, business, education, and health. ICT is a vehicle which can help deliver these services. Even if a small fee is charged, the volume of business would be in billions.

It has adopted a tiered franchise and partnership model. *Drishtee* facilitates the establishment of ICT nodes, enabling access to information as well as local services to the rural community, at a nominal fee. A village franchisee owns the village node to operate a self-sustaining, profitable kiosk. It provides access to information like government records, agricultural data, health insurance, commodity product rates in different markets, and education like computer courses; it helps in the filing of applications for licences, certificates, compensations, and benefits. It also offers programmes like spoken English. *Drishtee* has a fixed sharing with the franchisee, and a variable revenue sharing with the service providers.

Mishra has it well calculated in his mind. For every 50 rupees of social cost incurred, a social benefit which is twenty times more, is generated. Each kiosk can serve 1200 households, which have an income of about Rs 100. Mishra has set his sight—Drishtee—on 600,000 villages of India. So far, the figure reached is over 4000 villages. There is a long way to go before all the villages become Drishtee malls. Its motto is, 'Connecting Communities Village by Village'. Its philosophy is, 'Enhancing access and empowering communities by supporting rural entrepreneurship'.[j]

New Indian Village

Mahatma Gandhi dreamed of a village that was educated and industrious, but not industrialized to

exploit nature, be self-sufficient, environmentally sustainable and socially and politically conscious, enjoying true democracy and freedom. He may not have even dreamt that the whole world can come to the village through the ICT. He would not have imagined that such a communication technology could deliver education, health, business management, and even leisure. When the IT was discovered, people had thought it is meant for the developed world. But India has shown it to the world that it is a vehicle of true development and freedom for the poorest of the poor. IT is changing the image of the Indian village. Internet is, indeed, home grown *Indernet.*

Discussion Questions

1. What is the new Indian village?
2. What are the basic rural issues in India?
3. Why is economic development an ethical issue?
4. There is apparently no proportional development through the money that is allotted to rural programmes. Is it morally right to spend the tax payers' money on such rural nonproductivity?

Going Further . . .

A *gram sabha* or *panchayat* style discussion:

You may role play, or if there is a live project going on, then conduct a real meeting with

- The *panchas*
- IT kiosk owners
- Representatives of corporations
- Media
- NGOs and SHGs

---

[j] See http://www.drishtee.com.

ETHICAL DEVELOPMENT PROGRAMME

Management Training

A. Company Initiative

Develop a time bound, specific Information Communication Technology program as an initiative from your company/institute, for a single village in your area.

B. Arguments and Counter Arguments

Give counter arguments for the following arguments.

Objectives:

(a) To seek the other perspective

(b) To differentiate between moral and legal

(c) To develop sound moral reasoning of complex issues and personal beliefs.

(a) I am a college student. I have large posters of my favourite singers and film stars in my room. I also have the posters of my favourite sports stars. I love music and I download lots of songs from the net. Recently, I started my own webpage, where you will find my favourite singers and sports stars and also my favourite music. Some people were telling me that it is not the right thing to do. But I feel that if I can have all those things in my room, then why not on my website as well? Just as my friends would visit my room, they now visit my website.

(b) I am employed in an office where Internet is available. The work is not much, and I like to visit chat rooms and take part in discussions in some forums. However, over a period of time, I came across a couple of interesting people, and I like to be a part of their chatting sessions. Some people tell me that following people on the net like I do is not correct. But I am not harming them in any way. I like their company; they may not even realize it, because I am quite discreet.

(c) After practicing it for such a long time, I have finally found some skills and tools to hack. I know that hacking is wrong, but I just do it for the thrill of it, and do not intend to harm anyone. It is as though I pass by your house and find your garden very nice. I walk in, have a good look, and then, I am on my way.

(d) I am an MBA student and I have been hearing a lot of pro and contra arguments about copyrights in my class. Now if I copy music or some other data from the net for my future use, nobody will grudge me. If I copy to make money out of it that may not be unethical. Or is it? I am not sure. Anyway, what is important is that I should not break the law. But it is my frank opinion that copyright is a business strategy. It creates a competitive edge, for instance, in the music market, it may not have anything to do with the law either. In business, only strategy matters.

(e) I am a retired person and my hobby is reading. One of the things that often happens in our country is that some book or some movie gets banned on a regular scale. I am absolutely certain that those who burn copies of such books in protest have not even read a single page of it. But what is banned is freely available on the net. So how can something be banned and illegal on the ground, while it is accessible on the net? Further, I find that even if a book is banned and declared illegal, I do not find anything morally wrong in reading its hard copy or soft copy.

(f) We are a group of six girls studying in high school. Our common hobby is music. We spend all our free time trying to form an all girls' band. That is our dream anyway. We do not have much pocket money to spend on music CDs and DVDs. We copy them from the net. Secondly, it is not worth buying recorded music, because out of the many songs, only one or two are good ones. We also find that some songs are available only on the net. We do not think anyone is going to lose money just because a small group like ours makes copies of the music from the net. Actually, we have an idea to pick the best songs from the net and burn them into CDs and sell them at a very reasonable rate in our school. After all, other students also do not have much pocket money to buy music CDs from the market.

Management Mantra

Fathering Internet: Vinton Gray Cerf

The world knows him as Vint Cerf and not as Vinton Gray Cerf. The world calls him the 'father of the Internet', but he honestly feels that it is unfair because there is a large background with many people involved in the development of the computer in general and the Internet in particular. Indeed, it is quite natural that when awards are given out, both he and his colleague Robert E. Kahn receive it together. They conducted research on packet network interconnection protocols and co-designed the DoD TCP/IP protocol suite, from 1972–76, at Stanford University. In plain language, they designed the net's basic protocols that ensure that all those packets of data reach their intended destination.

In an interview with BBC in 2004, Dr Cerf said, 'When we were doing the original TCP/IP specifications, my sense was we were just getting all the networks to work together. It was just an engineering problem.' He said that he did realize its potential in a commercial venture much earlier, but it was stranded by the fact that the Internet was available for only academic and military research. This prompted him to move to MCI, the phone company, and set up a mail service, which was supported by legislation. The rest is history, and it is very close to two decades now. He believes that the next decade will belong to the net, and it will completely replace the telephone, which is at present the vehicle for the Internet. It would be impossible to stop the proliferation of the Internet and the advance of its technology into space and even to other planets.

Cerf believes that the Internet belongs to the people and it reflects society. It is like a mirror that reflects society. 'If we do not like what we see in that mirror, the problem is not to fix the mirror. We have to fix society.'

MANTRA   *Fix the problem before the problem fixes you.*

19

Challenges of Violence

Never before have so many people had so much in common, but never before have the things that divide them been so obvious.[1]

—Shridath Ramphal

Every gun that is made, every warship launched, every rocket fired signifies, in the final sense, a theft from those who hunger and are not fed, those who are cold and are not clothed. The world in arms is not spending money alone. It is spending the sweat of its laborers, the genius of its scientists, the hopes of its children... This is not a way of life at all, in any true sense. Under the cloud of threatening war, it is humanity hanging from a cross of iron.[2]

—Dwight D. Eisenhower

LEARNING OBJECTIVES

After studying this chapter, you will be able to

> Understand global business
> Distinguish between multinationals and militaries
> Differentiate between business and terrorism
> Describe multinational corporations and multinational responsibilities

INTRODUCTION

The objective of this chapter is to deal with the wide-ranging global challenges of violence, war, and terrorism, from which businesses cannot remain unaffected. In fact, a business has the most essential part to play, which is often negative and destructive to humanity. Arms, at least some of them, are essential for use by the police forces. However, an arms race among nations is destructive and a waste of the world's wealth. The ethical dilemma is that we must have arms for self-defence, but at

---

[1] Sir Shridath Ramphal, *The Commission on Global Governance*, http://www.cgg.ch.
[2] Former US President Dwight D. Eisenhower's speech made on 16 April 1953.

the same time, we must not have arms because they are destructive. The fundamental moral standard to be applied is justice. Injustice is the cause of violence. Without justice there cannot be peace. We will attempt to achieve an understanding of the above subject in this chapter.

In early April 2009, the group of twenty developed and developing nations of the world (G-20), met in London. It was like the allies coming together after World War II to form a new world order. The big difference was that the allies of the war were all victors. The G-20 consisted of losers of an economic war, a financial crisis of approximately three years, which was a result of two decades of financial profligacy of the developed countries within the G-20. They wanted to establish a new world order—government responsibility, corporate governance, and fiscal discipline—in short, business ethics.

The banks, the large multinational companies, the smart CEOs who travelled the world in private jets, the scamsters, who during the years of imaginary plenty made loads of money, were castigated as villains of the lost war on world economy. It was agreed that international financial institutions like the World Trade Organization (WTO), the World Bank (WB), and the International Monetary Fund (IMF) will be funded and reformed. The G-20 worked out a stimulus plan for the world economy, amounting to $1.1 trillion. One wondered, from where such funds would be collected, except by banishing fiscal discipline.

The largest economy in the world, the US, is also the largest debtor. Although the US owes billions of dollars to most of the countries that do business with it (China has almost $2 trillion trade surplus), yet the complexities of the economics are such that China and the others cannot pull the rug from under the US's feet and demand their dues. It is simply because the moment the creditors encash their government treasury bonds, effectively selling all the dollars, the money markets will fall with the dollar and its value. The money received by the creditors will be worth little.[3] The challenge for today's corporations is global and they cannot act as individual corporations; their fate is inextricably bound with the fate of the nations. Individuals are nationals, but corporations are multinationals. Even when they have no financial interests abroad, they are somehow connected to the global economy.

When Alexander the Great marched with his armies and conquered lands, people resigned and surrendered easily. The reason being, in those days it really did not matter who the ruler was because no matter who ruled, there would be taxes and levies to be paid. Tribes fought against tribes and rulers against rulers. They amassed armies, paid their soldiers, and granted them plunder rights. As history progressed, the wars became more sophisticated and were fought over land and water. No matter for what reason they were fought, people had to bear their costs. Governments would press the patriotism button and people would pay.

---

[3] For a well-illustrated point, see Marcus Gee, 'Beijing isn't Washington's banker. Try its grocer', in http://www.theglobeandmail.com/servlet/story/RTGAM.20090312.wcogee13/BNStory/specialComment (13 March 2009).

History students realize that human history is a record of wars. The interval between two wars was used in the preparation for the next war. This involved massive investments for which the rulers, kings, or heads levied heavy taxes on the people. The military economics created jobs. But in the end, the final result of the wars was destruction. Neither the victors, nor the losers had any trophies. In the final analysis, everyone was a loser from the point of view of economics.

Wars have stopped being exclusively territorial; they have become technological. Presently, every country is vying for military superiority through the acquisition of nuclear technology, the ultimate deterrent against attack by an enemy. It is also a bargaining chip, since it puts any country on equal footing with the strongest. To achieve superiority and maintain it with newer and more sophisticated technology, people are made to pay more money. The money goes into creating ever more complex and complicated machinery. Military is the largest industry in the world. However, there is no question of going to war in a big way on a battlefield, as in the last two world wars. But there is a continuous war going on in the military factories of the world, claiming superiority over others at each stage. The money utilized for this purpose comes from the people. The great military technological wonders come out as exhibits in military parades, a posturing of strength to other nations. Then they go back to the barracks and contemplate even further developments. People lose even more money, which they would have otherwise spent on their children's education, training, career, health, and their own standard of living. Human beings pay a very heavy price for their insecurity and lack of trust. Military and military commerce is a very complex issue between nations, and corporations are a part and parcel of supporting and advancing the military commerce with its arsenal and logistics. The combination of economics and the military account for a very dangerous world.

Just when one thought that war deterrents had been finally achieved, and people could think of better things, there appeared unwanted, senseless terror outfits across the world, irrespective of class, creed, race, and nationality. Although these are purportedly being cited as reasons, yet they have only causes to kill, and not a single cause worth dying for. They are the terrorists; they strike at innocent people anywhere, anytime, with impunity. This is a rare phenomenon; it is violence with no purpose. It is perpetration of evil.

Business corporations have been adversely affected by terrorism. At the same time, fingers are pointed at corporations, from whom the terrorists benefit. There is also a so called, state sponsored terrorism, where a nation supports and promotes terrorist activities against another state, with the purpose of undermining its enemy or wage a proxy war, which is cost effective and revengeful. India has accused Pakistan of such subversive support to terrorism; the US and its allies have called Iran, Libya, Cuba, and North Korea as rogue states that export terrorism. Conventional arms, which have been developed by well known corporations, conduct very lucrative business in the arms market and arms trade is a big business.

UNDERSTANDING GLOBAL BUSINESS

When heads of states or governments visit other countries, they travel with a planeload of business persons. It is a symbol of how governments and corporations have become partners in managing international relations. A study conducted for Corporate Watch 2000 has very interesting facts. Of the top 100 economies in the world, fifty-one are multinational corporations; only forty-nine are nation-states. If the economies of the G-8 countries are excluded, then the 2000 corporations have a combined wealth of the 182 countries of the world. The top 200 corporations in the world control a quarter of the global economy. All this wealth unfortunately is shared by only a third of the world, while the remaining two-thirds of the world eke out an existence of the infamous dollar a day. In such a situation, we do not have to seek reasons for the causes of violence in the world. However, the irony is that two-thirds of the world are not causing the violence which, if they had, would have been justifiable. The causes of violence lie with the rich and the corporations that serve them.

Global Economic Interdependence

'Make trade not war', seems to be the contemporary slogan. Today, we consider ourselves a thorough Global Community, an International Community, a Global Family and several other such epithets. Nations are increasingly being linked to each other, even in simple day-to-day matters. Although India is self-sufficient in grains and pulses, yet it imports a considerable quantity of these food stuffs from as far as Australia. India's political relations with China are at best tense but muted; but the trade between the two countries is becoming highly significant. Most of the poor people in India, who could not afford their own products, are happy to buy cheap clothes and electronic gadgets which have flooded even the remote markets of India. The greater the interdependence, the greater is the depth of a relationship, which is the foundation ethics, one that forms an ethos of relationships. There are several factors which facilitate economic interdependence in the international community.

Falling trade barriers It has become necessary to cut trade barriers, form regional and global economic blocs, and form international institutions for the purpose. World Trade Organization is the largest international trading bloc. The regional trade blocs are the European Union, ASEAN among the South East Asian Nations, and SAARC among the South Asian Region including the entire Indian subcontinent, NAFTA among the North American nations for free trade, etc.

Opening up of the political frontiers Economic need has driven political establishments to seek avenues to give up protectionism and open trade. The economic reasons actually caused the downfall of communism, which has redrawn the political boundaries in Eastern Europe and there is a strong movement for the unification of the entire European continent. Despite the political rivalry and enmity, trade has opened gates of commerce between the South East Asian Nations and Japan. Sworn political enemies such as China and Taiwan, India and Pakistan, despite problems, are seeking to open up their hardened positions.

Information technology   The technological advances in communication have changed not only those who do business, but also the nature of business. It is this single factor that has revolutionized international commerce; now international business can be transacted instantly in real time, across the globe, round the clock. Technology has even negated the need to travel, as business meetings can be held through video-conferencing.

Capital   Until recently, the capital for the industry used to be indigenous; today, very few corporations can do without foreign capital. Free flow of capital between countries has changed the status of the law, thus breaking not only financial barriers between the countries, but also the legal barriers.

Production   Today, the management of production and services can be universally performed. Different countries, due to their comparative advantage in raw materials, develop a related industry, e.g., production of auto spare parts, or computer and TV screens is done in one country; some other countries produce machines and tools. All these are then assembled and put together in another country for proximity of marketing. This kind of global management allows the industries to produce economically and supply the products and services efficiently.

These raise serious issues of managing relations. For instance, Coca-Cola is a company which does business even in countries with whom its country of origin, the US, may not have good political relations. McDonald's, the fast food chain, which is popular around the globe, does not always have smooth relations with the local interest groups, and their businesses face several challenges, including violence. The acceptance or rejection of a relationship of a multinational company creates ethical problems; the phenomenon reflects globalization, whether one likes it or not, and the local reactions to it are now a reality, and must find ways and means of living together.

International Business Issues

From what we have noted above about the phenomenon of the international business, it would seem that we may have arrived at an enlightened stage in our understanding of international relations through trade and commerce. The truth about this is that we are still quite far away from those goals. The biggest dilemma in international trade issues is how to promote and protect the domestic industry while embracing the multinational business economy? This issue came to a boiling point during the financial crisis of 2008. As the developed economies felt the brunt of the crisis, they took measures by imposing tariffs on imports, restrictions on outsourcing to the developing countries, and withdrew or sold their investments abroad. The crisis not only showed how interdependent we are globally, but it also exposed the dangers of multi-nationalism in running international trade and commerce.

Risks International trade is a highly risky business due to specific national issues of culture, of gender inequality and unequal salary, labour laws, industrial policies, tax regime, dispute settlement and other legal aids, culture of bribery, etc. In addition to local issues in international business, the global financial issues are even more risky. The global financial situation is not something any multinational can control. Thus, companies in international business find it very hard to formulate long-term policies. The managers of these companies are goaded on by the shareholders to make maximum short-term profits. This was one of the reasons why the financial crisis occurred; the managers tried to do the bidding of the senior management, and the shareholders heated up the capital market that ballooned and burst. This created a backlash against the managers by the shareholders, for being irresponsible. The top executives who were looked upon with great awe and respect—CEOs of Ford, Diamla Chrysler, the chairmen and managing directors of the insurance companies, hedge funds, and mutual funds—became the whipping boys of public anger and government censure.

Political environment Multi-national corporations (MNCs) have to live in a very volatile political atmosphere. Not only do regimes change around the world, but the ideologies of governance also change. The North Korean regime has isolated itself behind the communist ideology, and is relentlessly pursuing nuclear military goals. Japan, the highly developed economy of Asia lives in the mortal fear of this weak economic country lest it uses its nuclear arsenal against it. Iran and Iraq possess a significant percentage of oil reserves, the energy resources of the global industry. While Iran is both a military and economic challenge, Iraq's repercussions on world economy are highly political and military in nature, and since the invasion of Iraq by the US, the global political situation is fragile. The US and its allies in Iraq, that is, the developed countries, are suffering the worstever recession in eighty years, since the depression of the 1930s. Their economies are shrinking; most MNCs which originate in these countries are closing down. This has made millions of well-to-do employees jobless. The vast sprawl of their sister companies, subsidiaries, and collaborations in the developing countries are suffering and are orphaned.

Economic scenario Trade disputes are the bane of international business. Various international organizations such as the WTO, GATT, CRT (Caux Round Table) agreements between the member states have not eliminated the disputes. Nations would not like to follow what they have agreed to, due to the changes taking place, which adversely affect the concerned nations. There was a time when the developing nations like India and China were protective of their industry; however, once they started making their mark, they found that protectionism was counterproductive. The developed countries in recession which were always against protectionism, suddenly adopted protectionism to prevent their industries from going bankrupt. Now, India and China are in the forefront demanding cancellation of protectionism, to allow their products and services to penetrate the developed markets unhindered.

Thus, such an economic see-saw is one of the greatest challenges in pursuing stable international policies.

Global social consciousness Today's technological progress in transport and communication has changed the way people look at the world. People are instantaneously aware of the important events that are taking place around the globe through live news telecasts. Billions of people watch world events such as the swearing-in ceremony of the US President, the funeral of a famous public personality, or just a good game of football or cricket. People's mentalities are taking global dimensions. However, there are also other challenges that are quite daunting, like employment-oriented migration, violence against migrants, and economic and political refugees. Today, all these issues assume global dimensions. Globalization and free movement of goods and people, instead of solving the challenges of poverty, population, politics, and economics, appear to have only compounded the challenges, from local confinements to global proportions. Thus, in a global world, the business challenges have also become global.

The solutions to the above were sought at the CRT conference. The reason for this new consciousness was that although the technological global reach was evidently very efficient, the human dissent, disagreement, opposition, reaction, retaliation, trade conflicts, and even violence and war were putting the world asunder.

Caux Round Table Principles

The CRT is an international network of business leaders that came into existence in 1986. Frits Philips Sr, former president of the renowned Philips Electronics, Oliver Giscard d'Estaing, former Vice-Chairman of INSEAD, and Ryuzaburo Kaku, the then Chairman of Canon, Inc., came together in Caux, Switzerland and founded an organization that has come to be popularly known as the CRT. The mission was to promote a moral and sustainable way of doing business. In 1994, it formed the CRT principles[4] around three ethical values—stewardship, protection of human dignity, and *Kyosei*, which stands for living and working for mutual advantage. In the following year, the CRT presented its proceedings to the United Nations World Summit on Social Development. CRT works in association with global business leaders, international institutions, and policy makers to improve business environments. The CRT Principles for Business articulate a comprehensive framework of moral grounding for MNCs across the globe. The principles for responsible business published by CRT in March 2009, at the height of the global financial crisis, are given in Table 19.1.

---

[4] For a detailed study on the Caux Round Table, see http://www.cauxroundtable.org.

Table 19.1 CRT principles of responsible business

Principle	Particulars
1. Respect stakeholders beyond shareholders	■ Contribute value to society through wealth ■ Economic viability not just for shareholders, but also for stakeholders ■ Act with honesty and fairness towards customers, employees, suppliers, competitions, and the community
2. Contribution to economic, social, and environmental development	■ Prosperity is possible through economic development ■ Contribute to economic, social, and environmental development of the communities ■ Effective and prudent use of resources ■ Innovation in technology and business practices
3. Respect the letter and the spirit of the law	■ Some legal businesses can have adverse consequences for the stakeholders ■ Adhere to the spirit of the law, not merely its literal meaning, but a conduct beyond the minimum legal obligations ■ Truthfulness, transparency in business ■ Keep the promise
4. Respect rules and conventions	■ Respect local cultural traditions in the communities, where business is being conducted ■ Practice fairness and equality ■ Respect all applicable national and international laws and conventions ■ Trade fairly and competitively
5. Support responsible globalization	■ Support open and fair multilateral trade ■ Support reform of domestic rules and regulations which hinder global commerce
6. Respect the environment	■ Protect and improve the environment ■ Avoid wastage of resources ■ Follow the best environmental practices ■ Practice sustainable environmental management
7. Avoid illicit activities	■ Do not participate or condone corrupt practices like bribery, money laundering, and other illicit activities ■ Do not participate or facilitate transactions that are linked to support terrorist activities, drug trafficking, etc.

Stakeholder Management Guidelines

The seven CRT principles were followed by a clear set of guidelines for stakeholder management. There are more specific standards for the benefit of the key stakeholders in the community (see Table 19.2). The stakeholder communities are those who contribute to the success and sustainability of business. They are customers who buy goods and services and provide cash flow. They are employees who produce goods and services. They are also the owners and shareholders, who provide capital and operational security. The stakeholder is also the environment that supplies and regenerates resources.

Table 19.2   Stakeholder management guidelines

Stakeholders	Guidelines
1. Customers	▪ Provide highest quality goods and services consistent with their requirements ▪ Customer satisfaction—both services and remedies ▪ Ensure health and safety norms ▪ Protection from harmful environmental consequences ▪ Respect human rights and dignity
2. Employees	▪ Provide compensation that improves standards of living ▪ Ensure safe and healthy workplace conditions ▪ Share relevant information transparently ▪ Attend to employee grievances ▪ Avoid discriminatory practices, ensure equal treatment, opportunity, and pay ▪ Support employment of differently abled persons in fields where they are most productive ▪ Upgrade employee skills ▪ Be sensitive to employee dislocations ▪ Responsible executive payment, reward those with prudent risk management, increase wealth, discourage excessive risk ▪ Ban illicit and abusive child labour
3. Shareholders	▪ Apply professional and diligent management to secure fair, sustainable, and competitive returns ▪ Transparent disclosure relevant to shareholders ▪ Respect shareholder views, complaints, and formal resolutions
4. Suppliers	▪ Ensure fairness in supplier and subcontractor relationships, including pricing, licensing, and payment in accordance with agreed terms of trade ▪ Make sure all concerned activities are free from coercion and threats ▪ Take suppliers into confidence about business planning and integrate them ▪ Foster long-term relationships in return for value, quality, competitiveness, and reliability ▪ Respect human dignity ▪ Prefer suppliers with good environmental records
5. Competitors	▪ Foster open markets ▪ Promote competition to favour environmentally responsible business ▪ Avoid malpractices to gain competitive edge ▪ Respect tangible and intangible (intellectual property) rights ▪ Desist industrial espionage or obtain commercial information illegally
6. Communities	▪ Respect human rights and promote democratic institutions ▪ Support policies to promote human resource development ▪ Work for good relations between corporations and communities ▪ Support rule of law ▪ Adopt sustainable development ▪ Perform duties of a good corporate citizen

The importance of CRT lies in the fact that it is an organization by the business leaders of the world for global business practice. The necessity of CRT will become clear in the following sections that deal with corporations and the arms race and the contemporary dangers of terrorism. In the face of these two burning issues, the CRT is a simple, clear, and significant manual or guide for international business.

Fight over Bananas

Trade that threatened to disintegrate world order

If someone had prophesized that NATO would split over an issue of bananas,[a] and there would be a new world order before entering the new millennium, people would have definitely ridiculed such a silly prophecy. All the progressive and not-so-progressive economists, politicians, and business corporations believed that after the fall of communism, and as the world came closer to the new millennium, trade barriers would fall and there would be free trade all around the globe. All were wrong. A trade war broke out in a very old-fashioned way and threatened the NATO alliance.

The issue was the protection and favoured treatment between the two blocs of banana traders. The EU gave favoured treatment to the banana producers from the former African, Caribbean, and Pacific colonies, over and above the Latin American countries of Ecuador, Guatemala, Honduras, and Mexico, where large US corporations such as Chiquita, Dole, and Del Monte were involved. These corporations ran to their government with complaints, and Uncle Sam took up their cause in earnest.

In 1993, the EU introduced a new banana import policy that protected and encouraged banana trade from their above mentioned former colonies by abolishing trade tariff. Further, the policy even granted them guaranteed quotas. Thus, the EU tried to save the collapsing market of the suppliers, to save the farmers from abject poverty, while the Latin American growers faced stiff tariffs. In other words, the American companies who were in business found it extremely discriminating.

The US protested this EU policy with dire consequences. The US threatened the EU with 100 per cent taxes on their products. The EU attacked the US, acting on pressure from the corporations and domestic politics. The rivals produced a list of items they would blacklist. The tension across the Atlantic was so palpable that some even speculated that it would end the strategic military treaty. NATO, which successfully functioned all through the cold war era, now due to the banana trade, merely hung there by a tenuous link.

The US pressurized WTO and got the ruling in its favour. The EU played the moral card saying that their clients served only a small percentage and that without the European markets, the Caribbean would be plunged into poverty. Some cosmetic changes were made as per the WTO ruling. However, there is no guarantee that a war of attrition may start in the future, because banana wars have been erupting for over a century now.

Questions

(a) What moral arguments can you make in favour of the EU?

(b) Was the stand taken by the US ethical? Give reasons.

(c) Why are trade relationships so fragile?

[a] Anup Shah, 'The Banana Trade War' in http://www.globalissues.org/print/article/63 (May, 2002); also see T.B. Simi and Atul Kaushik, 'The Banana War at the GATT?WTO' in http://www.cuts-citee.org/pdf/TLB08-01.pdf.

MULTINATIONALS AND MILITARIES

Military spending is the biggest business in the world. It is well over $1 trillion, which amounts to 2 per cent of the world's GDP. Most leading military enterprises belong to the developed countries. The buyers are the developing nations, and India is the biggest arms customer of these companies. Corporations and national governments work closely together while dealing with the sale and purchase of arms. This is because the complexities of geopolitical logic demand certain coordinated efforts, to maintain a semblance of balance of military power. In fact, international relations are dictated by customer relations among the trading and purchasing nations. Relations may be bilateral, where government to government commerce takes place, or multilateral, where governments and their business enterprises do business with the customer countries. When it comes to arms trade, it appears that nations practice the old dictum, 'Everything is fair in love and war'. For, if some good reason was applied, then one would certainly consider the present state of arms race as nothing but irrational and destructive. For a trillion dollars a year, the world could have wiped out poverty, educated the young, saved the newborns, eradicated diseases, raised the standard of living of two billion people, and saved another two billion people from sheer poverty of living on a dollar a day.

Military Machine

The phrase military industrial complex was articulated by Dwight D. Eisenhower, to describe the entire gamut of the economy of the military enterprise. The enterprise is called the defence industry. The armed forces, politics, and commerce come to form a powerful triad to develop this industry. There are government owned as well as private industries that participate in obtaining contracts and producing arms.[5]

Conventional arms arsenal

During the Cold War era, the era of the two superpowers, the US and the USSR, there began an unprecedented arms race which resulted in a stockpile of nuclear arsenal that could annihilate the world scores of times, and yet there was no end to building more and more sophisticated arms. Ronald Regan, the US President of the 1980s started the missile defence programme, popularly known as Star Wars, during his tenure. The USSR finally buckled under the pressure of military spending, and it resulted in the collapse of its communist ideology; and with it, the Soviet Bloc countries redrew their maps. The Cold War ended, and new democracies in Eastern Europe were born. The arms race too came down to a trot. However, the new world order, with its new tensions, separatist activities, regional conflicts as in Africa, steadily increased the military spending.

---

[5] For details of conventional arms, see http://www.fas.org/programs/ssp/asmp/factsandfigures/government_data/2008/RL34723.pdf.

There is a parallel illegal arms production economy that deals with the production of small arms, bombs, grenades, guns, and small missiles. This is mainly prevalent in the civil strife torn countries of Africa, some Latin American countries, the terrorist promotion areas of Chechnya, Afghanistan, Pakistan, Iraq, and Sri Lanka (see Fig. 19.1).

There is also a significant size of clandestine arms trade which involves arms smuggling. There is corruption in the regular defence industry, where a large cache of arms are pilfered, and the covert supply of arms by the countries supporting proxy wars or sharing ideological missions are the sources of illegal selling and buying of arms. The customers of this illegal trade are the terrorists, the separatists, the insurgents, the liberation organizations, etc. The market is world wide and it consists of the separatists of Chechnya, the European RAF organizations, the Spanish Catalonian separatists, the Irish Republicans, the white racist organization, the Ku Klux Klan of the US, the various insurgent outfits of North-East India, the liberation and separatist organization of Kashmir, the Tamil Tigers of Sri Lanka, and the Maoists of Nepal, and hundreds others around the world, practically from every country.

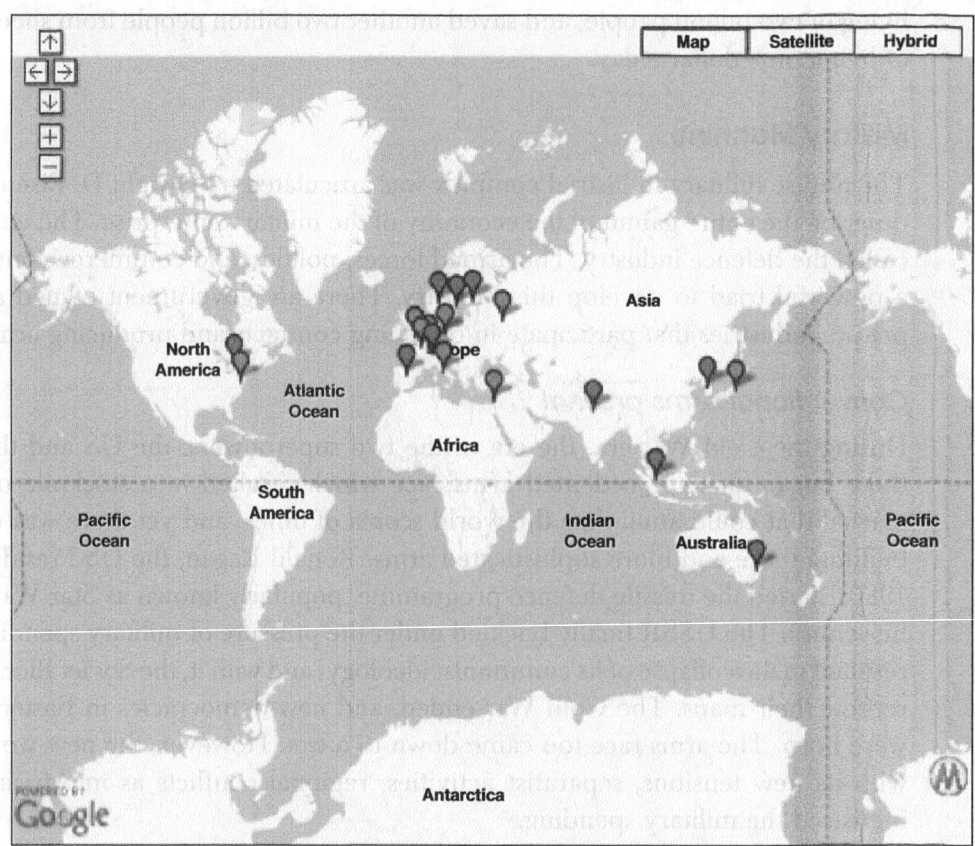

Fig. 19.1   Google map showing arms producing countries

Source: http://www.sipri.org/googlemaps/aprod_country_map_2006.html.

Major Companies in Military Industry

The military arms and services is in itself a very large industry. It gives employment to a sizeable number of people, and not just the armed forces. Stockholm International Peace Research Institute (SIPRI) is one of the watchdog organizations in arms trade. Some of the major companies involved in arms production and trade are listed by the organization. The organization admits that the available data is very constricted due to the non-availability of such data, for obvious reasons of exposure feared by the concerned companies and countries of their origin.[6]

The sales consist of both military goods and services to the military customers. These goods and services are specially designed for military purposes. The military goods are military-specific equipments such as the conventional arms list shown in Table 19.3.

Table 19.3 Conventional arms arsenal

Category	Armoury
Tanks and self-propelled guns	Light, medium, and heavy tanks; self-propelled artillery; self-propelled assault guns
Artillery	Field and air defence artillery, mortars, rocket launchers, and recoilless rifles—100 mm and over; FROG launchers—100 mm and over
Armoured Personnel Carriers (APCs) and Armoured cars	Personnel carriers, armoured and amphibious; armoured infantry fighting vehicles; armoured reconnaissance and command vehicles
Major surface combatants	Aircraft carriers, cruisers, destroyers, frigates
Minor surface combatants	Minesweepers, sub chasers, motor torpedo boats, patrol craft, motor gunboats
Submarines	All submarines, including midget submarines
Guided missile patrol boats	All boats in this class
Supersonic combat aircraft	All fighter and bomber aircraft designed to function operationally at speeds above Mach 1
Subsonic combat aircraft	All fighter and bomber aircraft designed to function operationally at speeds below Mach 1
Other aircraft	All other fixed-wing aircraft, including trainers, transports, reconnaissance aircraft, and communications/utility aircraft
Helicopters	All helicopters, including combat and transport
Surface-to-air missiles	Ground based air defence missiles
Surface-to-surface missiles	All surface to surface missiles without regard to range, such as Scuds and CSS-2s; it excludes all anti-tank missiles. It also excludes all anti-ship missiles, which are counted in a separate listing
Anti-ship missiles	All missiles in this class such as the Harpoon, Silkworm, Styx, and Exocet

---

[6] See SIPRI 100 at http://www.sipri.org/contents/milap/milex/aprod/sipridata.html. For the latest on SIPRI, see the *SIPRI Yearbook 2008: Armaments, Disarmament and International Security*, Oxford University Press, Oxford (2008).

Table 19.4 lists the major arms producing companies of the world; the government ordnance factories are also included. These deliver military hardware, which are sold to 187 countries in the world. The list of the companies given below is indicative of the arms industry around the world; only major companies are listed. The US has forty-one companies and supplies more than 50 per cent of the total arms to the world. The Western European countries have thirty-seven companies, and India has three companies, with the earnings amounting to under $4 billion. China is growing at a very high rate and its arms sales has become a pricking geopolitical issue for the developed countries.

Table 19.4 World's arms producing companies

Countries	Companies
Argentina	■ Fábrica Militar Fábrica Militar de Aviones
Austria	■ Glock ■ Steyr Mannlicher
Australia	■ Tenix ■ Australian Defence Industries ■ Australian Submarine Corporation ■ Commonwealth Aircraft Corporation
Belgium	■ Fabrique Nationale de Herstal
Bosnia and Herzegovina	■ Zrak dd
Brazil	■ Ares Aeroespacial e Defesa ■ Avibras ■ CBC—Companhia Brasileira de Cartuchos ■ Embraer ■ Helibras ■ IMBEL—Indústria Brasileira de Material Bélico, belonging to the Brazilian Army, Taurus
Canada	■ Colt Canada
China	■ Norinco ■ AVIC I ■ AVIC II ■ Chengdu Aircraft Industry Group ■ China Nanchang Aircraft Manufacturing Corporation ■ Changhe Aircraft Industries Corporation ■ China State Shipbuilding Corporation (CSSC) ■ China National Nuclear Corporation ■ China Aerospace Science & Technology Corporation (CASC)
Denmark	■ Hydrema ■ Terma
Egypt	■ AOI

Contd

Table 19.4 Contd

Countries	Companies
France	■ EADS ■ Dassault Aviation ■ DCN ■ Thales Group ■ GIAT Industries
Germany	■ Carl Walther GmbH Sportwaffen ■ Diehl BGT Defence ■ EADS ■ Heckler & Koch ■ Krauss-Maffei ■ Rheinmetall ■ Mauser ■ Luerssen ■ Thyssenkrupp ■ MBDA
Greece	■ EAS ■ HAI
India	■ DRDO ■ Hindustan Aeronautics Limited ■ Ordnance Factory Board of India
Indonesia	■ PT Pindad ■ Periindustrian Angkatan Darat
Israel	■ Israel Aerospace Industries ■ Israel Weapon Industries ■ RAFAEL Armament Development Authority ■ Elbit
Italy	■ Beretta ■ Finmeccanica ■ Fincantieri ■ Avio ■ AgustaWestland ■ Benelli (firearms)
Mexico	■ ALFA ■ DGIM ■ Hydra Technologies of Mexico ■ Mabe ■ Mendoza ■ Mondgran ■ San Luis Rassini ■ SEDENA ■ SEMAR ■ Valdez Industria ■ Xiuhcoatl
Myanmar	■ Reliable Technology Ltd.

Contd

Table 19.4 Contd

Countries	Companies
Norway	▪ Kongsberg Defence & Aerospace ▪ Nordic Ammunition Group
Poland	▪ Bumar ▪ PZL
Pakistan	▪ Pakistan Aeronautical Complex ▪ Heavy Industries Taxila ▪ Pakistan Ordnance Factories
Portugal	▪ INDP
Russia	▪ Sukhoi ▪ Mikoyan ▪ Mil Moscow Helicopter Plant ▪ Tupolev ▪ Ilyushin ▪ Yakovlev ▪ Tikhomirov Scientific Research Institute of Instrument Design ▪ Moscow Institute of Thermal Technology ▪ IZH ▪ Kartsev-Venediktov Design Bureau ▪ Almaz Scientific Industrial Corporation ▪ Vympel NPO ▪ Beriev
Serbia	▪ Zastava Arms ▪ Yugoimport
South Africa	▪ Denel
South Korea	▪ Hyundai Rotem ▪ Samsung Techwin
Spain	▪ EADS-CASA ▪ Nvantia ▪ Santa Barabara (General Dynamics)
Sweden	▪ BAE System Bofors ▪ Kockums ▪ Saab
Switzerland	▪ SIGARMS ▪ RUAG ▪ Pilatus Aircraft ▪ Armasuisse ▪ MOWAG (General Dynamics)
Turkey	▪ MKEK ▪ TAI ▪ Aselsan

Contd

Table 19.4 Contd

Countries	Companies
Ukraine	■ Antonov ■ KMDB ■ Malyshev Factory ■ RPC Fort ■ Yuzhmash ■ Yuzhnoye Design Bureau
UK	■ BAE Systems ■ Cobham plc ■ MBDA ■ Rolls-Royce
US	■ AAI Corporation ■ BAE Systems Inc. ■ Boeing ■ Carlyle Group ■ Colt's Manufacturing Company ■ General Atomics ■ General Electric (through GEAE) ■ General Dynamics ■ Honeywell ■ Lockheed Martin ■ Northrop Grumman Corporation ■ United Technologies

The military services are also specific, which include information technology, maintenance and repair, and operational and logistic support.

SIPRI catalogues some of the military services provided by the private companies as given in Table 19.5.

Table 19.5 Military services provided by private companies

Service	Description	Companies
Research and development, analysis, and planning	Basic research and technology, strategic research and consulting, threat analysis, war-gaming, etc.	ASIC, CACI, Battellle, Mitre, SAIC, Booz Allen Hamilton
Technical services	Software development, IT systems support, infrastructure development simulation, supporting operations of military equipments and systems	EDS, Computer Sciences Corp.
Equipment maintenance, repair and overhaul, etc.	Military bases	Babcock, Serco, Northrop, Grumman, Chugach, Alaska Corp
Operational support— Logistics, training	Combat forces, simulation, managing firing ranges, weapons system training	Halliburton, L-3 Communications, Northrop, Lockheed Martin, DynCorp, etc.
Armed security	Protection of diplomats and civilian convoys in conflict zones	Blackwater, DynCorp, Armour Group, etc.

The developing countries are the primary focus of arms sales, and India is the biggest buyer followed by Saudi Arabia. The share of arms purchase for the developing countries is three-fifths of the total arms production. The purchases, in percentage are as follows:

1. India   13%
2. Saudi Arabia   11%
3. China   7%
4. UAE   6%
5. Pakistan   6%
6. Egypt   5%
7. Israel   4%
8. South Korea   4%
9. Syria   3%
10. Venezuela   2%
11. All the other 39%

Even a country known otherwise for its natural beauty, tourism, and political neutrality earns over $200 million a year[7] (2007) from its arms sales. It is also interesting to see that as an individual country, Brazil netted over $7219 million in 2007, compared to $3814 million in 2000. It only goes to show the lucrative nature of the arms trade.

Arms Trade and Geopolitical Economic Agenda

The management of relations between nations in terms of their military and economic strengths is a very complex issue;[8] it involves the relationship of all the nations in the world. Each and every country seeks its own interests. There are, however, only five countries in the world that produce enough weapons to destroy several worlds. The club of five consists of the US, the UK, Russia, France, and China. They are the permanent members of the United Nations, and hold veto powers. They possess the key to global decisions, particularly, on war and peace (Fig. 19.2).

Balance of power   Geopolitics is about the balance of power on two levels—first, within the club of five, the inner circle of the United Nations, and second, on how it influences and has repercussions around the globe and plays on the fate of nations and their people. The geopolitics of the world may be compared to the turf management in a city's underworld. The territories are mutually divided, based on the strength of the operations, but they constantly try to outdo each other. The nations around the world, in their turn, try to jockey around the big five powers in a secondary level, to exercise power over their regional turfs. The regional bosses then try to subjugate the

---

[7] See the SIPRI report at http://www.sipri.org/contents/milap/milex/aprod/sipridata.html.
[8] For an extensive treatment, see http://www.globalissues.org.

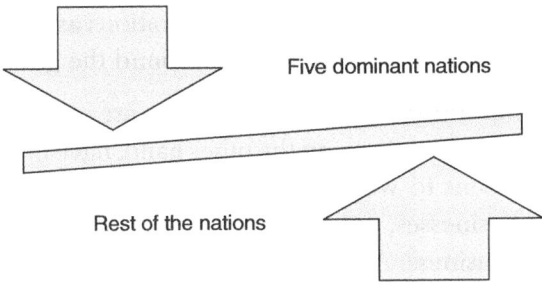

Fig. 19.2   Balance of power

local turfs and buy their allegiance. The big bosses employ people to do their job, and pay them a part of their booty. In the geopolitical world, these employees are the corporations that work for their governments in the arms trade.

Strategic bargains   United Arab Emirates (UAE) is one of the big purchasers of arms. Its supplier is the US. A few years back, when the US government agreed to sell eighty F16 fighter planes for an estimated $15 billion, it made sure that it got a naval base with deep-water capability, for its carriers in the Persian Gulf. This led to an arms race not only in the Gulf region, but in the entire sub-continent. The French and the British supplied to their allies; the Russians and the Europeans supplied to India. Pakistan became a strategic partner of the US for its Gulf interests, by using it in the Afghan problems against the USSR, and then by supporting the warlords. The attack by the US on Al Qaida for its suspected role on 11 September 2001, further destabilized the old balance. The growth in arms now became a reason to counter the new common enemy.

Bilateral business   Only governments have the monopoly to conduct business in arms trade. The arms producing nations market their products through ingenious diplomacy and real or propagated threat perceptions from third parties, which are mostly the neighbouring countries. Arms trade has a twin purpose—political and economic. Political power is important to exercise the will, and effectively maintain the dominant position in the world. The greater the political power, the greater is the presence in the world market. Once a dominant country is able to supply enough arms to depend on it, it will further tighten its stranglehold through the grant of economic aid. Thus, a country is strategically bound by the dominant country. The dilemma of the customer country is that if it refuses to buy arms, it will also forego the aid. The aid given by the dominant country is indirectly a subsidy to the subject country, which deviates from the money to buy arms.

Cooperation of corporations   The above delineation of the world situation, where nations are in dire situations, calls for the demand in arms and its trade. The greater is the conflict, or even its perception, the greater is the opportunity for arms producing corporations to bag contracts from the affected governments. While the governments in the arms-producing countries hire corporations as contractors to supply arms, they also work as marketing agents for them around the globe.

Managing competition   Governments, who are patrons of corporations, have politics as their priority. Corporations, on the other hand, have business priorities. It is important for the government to whom the arms are sold to maintain political dominance. However, for businesses, only doing business matters. It really does not matter with whom they do business. All their customers are kings. So, corporations clandestinely approach the governments of the buyer countries to curry favour, so that their company may get the contract. The Bofors gun scandal in India that rocked the country and sullied the reputation of the Swedish company is a classic landmark case in defence deals kickbacks. Another case was that of BAE, the British arms manufacturer, who approached Saudi Arabian officials to buy their fighter planes. The British government promptly stopped the deal and investigated the matter. The papers reported that the Saudi Prince was offered a $150-million airliner as a gift. For manufacturers to offer such a gift or a bribe is an insignificant matter, compared to the billions of dollars made in the trade. In the heavily militarized regions, such as the Middle East, arms manufacturing companies have to compete and bribe governments to net deals. Since the Middle East does not boast of any democratic state of relevance,

---

Détente

Checks and Balances

The Cold War, the military rivalry between the two superpowers, the US and the USSR, reached its apex during the 1970s, as Leonid Brezhnev strode the world with the ever-expanding communist countries. However, concentration on military power eroded the economic development of the USSR; but the US leaped ahead in political manoeuvring, robust economic growth, military build-up, and highly successful global culture. The USSR could not cope with it, and hence sought to change tracks and offered friendly relations. This eased the tensions and led to negotiations, particularly in the field of defence. This new phenomena of softening of relations was called as *détente*.

Détente helped reduce military tensions and increased trade. In 1972, the Soviets and the Americans signed treaties to reduce nuclear arms. The negotiations were called Strategic Arms Limitation Talks (SALT). In 1975, the Soviets and several others were ready to talk about human rights, freedom of expression, and religion, and the Helsinki Accord was

signed. Thus, there followed Western goods, technology, and cultural exchange. As the ideas of freedom of expression gained in strength, the communists found it too difficult to deal with it. Intellectuals, scientists, and political liberals ended being rounded up and sent to the labour camps of Siberia. Alexander Solzhenitsyn was one of them, whose writings attracted the Western world and he was conferred the Nobel Prize for Peace; he was deported to the West. Later, in the 1970s, détente took a severe setback under the Carter administration. At the fag end of 1979, the Soviet Union invaded Afghanistan, thus closing a unique chapter in international relations.

Questions

(a) What makes international relations balanced?

(b) Why did détente fail?

(c) What can businesses learn from the détente relationships?

the companies find it easier to negotiate with authoritarian governments, military rulers, or dictators.

Wages of peace   Peace in the world presents great problems, both for governments as well as corporations. Peace will spell doom for military business. It is a business, which towards the end of the first decade in the twenty-first century is aiming at a $2-trillion market. Peace will shatter this economy!

Once caught in the vortex of the arms race, the countries have to update their military hardware and technical know-how, and the arms producing countries spur that demand by ever improved technology and new modes of weapons. For instance, in the wake of a new enemy, terrorism, the geopolitical situation in Kashmir has taken a new turn. India now spends more on arms purchases, and so does Pakistan. The arms manufacturers are only too happy to oblige. Overtly, there is a great deal of voicing of concern and advice to exercise restrain by the US and the UK. In reality, both the countries are vying for a bigger share in the defence budget pie of both the countries. It has been stated that two nuclear powers at loggerheads, create a unique selling opportunity.[9]

BUSINESS AND TERRORISM

It would be terribly naïve to believe that business is a victim of terrorism. Here we will delineate in very general terms, the relationship that exists between business enterprises and terrorism in the global context. When we consider terrorism in a particular context such as tourism, it immediately becomes clear to us that terrorism causes a great loss for business. It is obvious that people avoid touring the places of leisure, where terror prevails. On the other hand, when we observe terrorism in a historical and political perspective with global dimensions, there clearly emerges an economic and political pattern, which is very disconcerting and at times frightening. For instance, the Palestine Liberation Organization (PLO) was the dreaded terrorist organization for decades; but it ended up being highly respectable, and its leader, Yasser Arafat became one of the world's most respected leaders. However, what happened to the life of the people in the entire Middle East? How did it affect the countries of the East and West? What would have been the world's history, without the violence in the Middle East? Several conjectures are possible, most of them being positive, like peace and development. Violence has its determining values politically, economically, and culturally; business is not an exception. Does terrorism impact business more than business helps terrorism? A debate is called for.

---

[9] Edna Fernandes, 'Arms dealers see bonanza in stand-off: Foreign companies hope tension on the Indo-Pakistan border will boost sales', *Financial Times*, 27 February 2002; For further details, go to http://globalarchive.ft.com/globalarchive/article.html?id=020227001489.

WTO Meeting in Doha in the Aftermath of 9/11

The World Trade Organization (WTO) met for its fourth Ministerial Conference in Qatar's capital Doha, from 9 to 13 November 2001.[10] The Ministerial Conference of the WTO is its highest decision-making body. It takes comprehensive decisions in matters of multilateral trade agreements. It met at Doha amid a highly charged global background—the aftermath of the terrorist attacks on the US on 11 September 2001. The 9/11 attack led to the 'war on terror' declared by President George Bush of the US, the burst of the IT bubble in the Silicon Valley, and the recessional trends around the globe that increased the misery of the poor countries and the fears of the developing countries. There were protests around the globe about the agenda and the intentions of the Doha Round. There was more opposition in the developed countries, from activist groups against the pro-Western stance of the WTO. In the developing and poor countries, there were protests against the WTO, for its policies would further worsen their situation. The Doha Round gives us a glimpse into the intricacies of global business, terrorism, freedom, and democracy.

Philosophy of the Doha agenda The Doha Ministerial Conference adopted the so-called Bush Doctrine, which stated that 'the free world is defined by free trade. Free trade defines democracy. Those who are against freedom and democracy are terrorists.' With such support from the only superpower in the world, the WTO had what in business jargon is known as 'the clear goal', and in its attitude showed that it could not care less about its espousal of free trade, without looking at the consequences in the developing countries. It was clear to the common folk that such a simplistic doctrine of trade would completely destroy the fragile economies of the developing world, which would be colonized by the commerce of the developed world.

Arm-twisting the developed countries Economists, critics, and other experts immediately voiced that there was a hidden agenda in the WTO to push past the economic agenda under the blanket of fear of terrorism. Only trade would promote freedom and defeat terrorism. The leaders of the developed nations tried to convince people of the veracity and reliability of WHO by explaining how trade would irradiate poverty. When this did not work, the developed nations withdrew into the green room. In other words, they had their own private meeting, excluding others, and worked out strategies to fight the objections and push through their own agenda by employing their bigger delegate power, economic, military, and aid clout over the opposing countries.

Logic of the under-trodden The developing nations and their supporters said that they are not against freedom, development, and free trade. They said that they are equally or more against terrorism than the wealthier nations. However, they said that the current WTO policies were not creating conditions for a fair trade. The draft

---

[10] For a detailed analysis, see http://www.globalissues.org/article/296/wto-meeting-in-doha-qatar-2001.

declaration was unbalanced and ignored the concerns of the developing countries. Most of the African countries opposed the recommendations tooth and nail. India led the opposition brigade. The developed countries tried to put the opposing countries in a negative light and threatened not to cooperate, and hinted at aid cuts.

New issues and their consequences   There were three new issues—investment, competition, and transparency in government procurement and trade facilitation—meant to open up the domestic markets of a country to foreign firms, with minimal government regulation. The consequences were that the local manufacturers who were not being able to compete with the international firms would be wiped out. The ensuing job losses would be catastrophic. In addition, governments would also lose their right to regulate domestic markets. This would result in their loss of power to socially sensitive subjects, such as the public distribution system in India (ration card provisions for the poor). In fact, eventually, even the national sovereignty would be a mere hollow. To sum it up succinctly, it would be the East India Company revisiting.

The idea of WTO as a trade organization of the world is a good one. Economics in general and trade in particular are fundamental human issues and there must be place in the WTO for serious social problems, to fight poverty and disease, and promote health and education. With these purposes, trade and commerce would make the WTO a truly human organization, and not a profit generating machine, meant only for the developed countries. The philosophy that free trade, as advocated by the developed countries, is freedom is far from the truth. It will actually lead to a new twenty-first century colonialism.

Business of Terrorism

Common folks always wonder where the terrorists get funds to finance their destructive activities. No armed conflict is productive, except for those who manufacture them. So who supplies arms to the Sri Lankan rebels, the warring groups in Africa, the RAF in Europe, the various separatist and insurgent groups in India, the Taliban in Pakistan and Afghanistan, and above all, al-Qaeda? For some people somewhere, the business is booming in the supply of arms, ammunition, vehicles, training, logistics, intelligence gathering, consulting, strategizing to keep a step ahead of the enemy, engineering, governance, food procurements, combat gear, clothing, communication, transport, spare parts, maintenance, information technology, travel, housing, highly motivated human resource management, and the rest of the businesses, which have given rise to illicit economies. This goes to prove that the terrorist organizations are also organizations and they transact business[11] in the very same world as the others do.

Sources of funds   Terrorist organizations need huge amounts of funds due to the high price of arms and ammunitions. They also need double the funds to run their

---

[11] 'Business of Terrorism' by W.A. Tupman discusses IRA and al-Qaeda. See http://www.freerepublic.com/focus/f-news/1404919/posts.

clandestine organizations, than a normal organization does. They also need to infiltrate into the legal organizations to build their network. The following sources of funding have been identified—drug trafficking, extortion and kidnapping, robbery, fraud, gambling, smuggling and trafficking in counterfeit goods, state sponsorships, contributions, and donations, sale of legal and illegal publications, and legitimate business activities.

New roles   There are several terrorist organizations that have transformed themselves and have donned legitimate and political roles. The Maoists of Nepal which began as a terrorist organization, systematically captured territories, and ran a parallel government, and thereby enjoyed revenues by taxing the people. Eventually, the organization was able to rope the people of the country into their philosophy, and the Maoists successfully took over the government. The organization had by this time transformed itself into a political party and even contested the elections and won. As promised, they threw out the monarchy, and one of the oldest kingdoms on earth became a republic. Similar is the story of the PLO. IRA has obtained legitimacy and is a political party after the successful peace negotiations regarding Northern Ireland, with the UK. The Tamil Tigers in Sri Lanka are fighting for such legitimacy in their determined area, but have been unsuccessful so far. The Tigers have a large constituency of sympathizers in Tamil Nadu, India, and are a sensitive political plank for all the political parties. The dilemma for the Indian political establishment is that if they do not support the Sri Lankan Tamil cause, they would displease their vote segments, but if they do, then the whole world will brand them as supporting, recognizing, and funding terrorists, which may result in losing Sri Lanka, which is a strategic partner and neighbouring country. In Spain, ETA has been terrorizing to gain control over the Basque country, but so far without success. Similar is the position of FARC in Columbia. However, all of these have been able to fund their organizations very well and the concerned governments have not been able to disconnect their sources of money.

The above demonstrates, albeit very roughly, the complexity in the relationship between business and terrorism. We see how the terrorist organizations finally capture political power and legitimacy. After the Soviet retreat, the Taliban took over Afghanistan and showed to the world how the change of roles did not change them. They remained terrorists and, in the name of religion, set up a regime of crime and oppression, with scant respect for human dignity, decency, and development. They destroyed everything that came across their path. The war on terror that followed destabilized the whole region and renewed the arms race, particularly between India and Pakistan.

It is really difficult to say what impact terrorism has had on business while the terrorists used business for their purpose. While they have increased the businesses that we have stated earlier, the business of the people has certainly suffered. People have also been used by the terrorist organizations, who spread a wide net of sympathizers, fund raisers, and even unsuspecting individuals, who may have had a

---

Terror in Tea Cup

TATA–ULFA controversy

In August 1997, a good Samaritan helped a young woman with a baby, who had medical complications. The benefactor was so good that he did not mind paying for her air ticket from her home state, Assam, to Mumbai and got her treated at Jaslok Hospital, which is one of the best hospitals in Mumbai. He also made arrangements for her to stay in a very good hotel before she was admitted to the hospital, and once the treatment was over, arrangements were made for her to return by air.

When she was about to board the aircraft, the police put a spanner in the Samaritan's deed. The Director General of Police called a press conference in Guwahati in early September and blew the lid off.[a] The explosion was so loud that it stunned not only the Indian industry, but also the common man of India.

The young woman was the secretary of the United Liberation Front of Asom (ULFA), the dreaded terrorist organization leading the separatist movement in the North East of the country. There was an escort who accompanied her, who was on the terrorist list. The role of the good Samaritan was played by Tata Tea Ltd (TTL).

Out of the over forty tea gardens that the Tatas own, more than half of them are in Assam. Most of the well known tea companies have their gardens in Assam. It is an open secret that all the companies buy peace from ULFA and the Bodo militants. They pay both in money and in kind. Paying hospital bills is one of the ways of supporting the terrorists.

Tata officials denied that they paid money or helped the ULFA in anyway. To support their arguments, they cited examples of their officials being threatened and harassed by the terrorists and of one of their executives being captured and was held hostage for eleven months.

The police, however, had more evidence under its belt. Not only the Tatas, but several other tea companies were also involved in paying extortion money to the terrorists. They arrested an official of another company on similar charges. The tea industry came out of the denial mode and agreed for a meeting with the government. A meeting was held on 28 September 1997 by the Consultative Committee of Plantation Associations with the government of Assam. They convinced the chief minister that they would act and would avoid all such instances of support to the terrorist organization. They pleaded with the chief minister not to take such a hard-line view of the tea industry in the state so as to brand them anti-national.

Questions

(a) What is the legal and ethical problem of buying peace from the terrorists?

(b) Can paying in kind be a strategy to make the terrorists realize their wrong ways?

(c) In the above case what would you do as a manager of Tata Tea Ltd?

[a] For a detailed treatment, see *India Today*, http://indiatodaygroup.com/itoday/20101997/cov2.html; http://en.wikipedia.org/wiki/Tata_Tapes_controversy.

---

part in their designs. For example, communications networks are used by the terrorists. Politics, economics, business, culture, and religion are all intricately bound with terrorism.[12] The case study in this chapter about the terrorist attack on the twin towers by the al-Qaeda shows the complexity of business and terror, and also the complicity of the victim in the act.

---

[12] For a very interesting article on this concept, see Noam Chomsky's, 'Who Are the Global Terrorists'; link: http://www.zmag.org/content/ForeignPolicy/chomskyglobeterr.cfm.

MULTINATIONAL CORPORATIONS AND MULTINATIONAL RESPONSIBILITIES

The quotation at the beginning of this chapter by Dwight D. Eisenhower describes succinctly the future that man has created for himself. The military machine that man has created deprives humanity of even the basic needs of food and clothing. It is also a great waste of man's scientific achievement, human labour, and the future of children. Humanity has caused its own destruction and death, done systematically by governments by spending more on arms than on social development, education, health, infrastructure, and good governance. Thus, arms are the cause of human suffering. There are various organizations around the world that have for several decades advocated disarmament movements. The pertinent question to ask is, 'Can multi-nationals fulfil their responsibilities?'

Development of Multinational Business Philosophy

In our contemporary world of militarization, there is a need to use human intelligence for better purposes than the artificial creation of fear and distrust and proliferation of weapons of mass destruction. We have seen above the waste of human intelligence and wealth in the pursuit of armaments. There are some fundamental assumptions through which we can reverse the violent trend that the human civilization is taking and turn it into an opportunity to build a better world. Some of the following assumptions could be the starting point of a new thinking.

Common good Human nature is oriented towards the good. The good will, as Immanuel Kant advocated, can only will what is good. The contemporary world needs to have a new social contract to make this good productive. The goal of humanity is to aim for the common good. The Earth's goods are to be shared and sustainably increased to produce wealth for all.

Disarmament People cannot work intelligently when a gun is pointed at them. The change in thinking demands action on the ground. The perception of the common good is possible when the threats to security are removed. When there is no threat, there is no reason for the existence of arms.

World citizenship World citizenship is possible. War divides and erects boundaries. With the threat of war completely eliminated, a total disarmament of nuclear weapons, and other weapons of mass destruction such as biological and chemical being removed, humanity can look forward to a world without national boundaries. Business, which has helped cross over the national boundaries, can now prosper in a truly global world, without the fear of war and division.

World government When humanity puts its will collectively on a goal, nothing is impossible to achieve. The concept of world government is over a century old. The idea has to some extent been made real in the existence of the United Nations. Some decisive decisions of intervention in the national affairs of a country have been beneficial against hunger, disease, genocide, civil war, and several other issues, although the results remain largely unsatisfactory due to the narrow interests and the lack of will among the powerful nations of the UN.

Universal franchise   The present limited concept of universal franchise is to be extended to include the world community. A world government was thus far not possible, not because it had not been thought about, but because of lack of consensus. Emperors, kings, despots, hegemonistic countries, and the others who wanted to dominate and rule the world have existed since ancient times. Their purpose was to impose their will and not to seek the will of the people. Their ideas have only succeeded in dividing the world, rather than unifying it. Unification of the world is possible with a new tool—the universal franchise, which is the key to a world democratic government.

Make trade not war   This idea too is not a new one. Rightly understood, it will involve practically every other trade that benefits humanity, except the arms trade. We only have to use a little bit of common sense to make this possible. A simple salesman understands the logic of making friends to run the business. The global business too can put into use the same logic to enamour the world, to do business and not war.

Institutions for World Governance

If we make ourselves conscious about world affairs by reading the newspapers or watching the daily news on TV, we will realize how the world, despite all the problems, is evolving towards a world government. The necessary institutions for such a government are already working.

United Nations   It is a global parliament of all the nations of the Earth who sit in dialogue about the world affairs. It has various departments of governance, economics, health, aid, and even military peace corps.

Regional parliaments   The European Parliament, the Arab Parliament, the Pan-African Parliament, the Latin American Parliament, the South American Parliament, the Mercosur Parliament, the Central American Parliament, and the Inter-Parliamentary Union.

Regional bodies   The European Union, the Latin Union, and the Arab League, the African Union, Union of South American Nations, Association of South East Asian Nations, Association of Caribbean Nations, Commonwealth of Independent States, Organization of American States, South Asian Association for Regional Cooperation, and the Pacific Islands Forum.

Banks   There are very potent global financial institutions like the World Bank, the International Monetary Fund, the World Trade Organization, and the Commonwealth of Nations.

Interpol   Interpol is a body that unites the police forces across the globe, to deal with international crime. When alerts are sounded, the police forces in the concerned nations join forces in a concerted effort to solve a crisis. Interpol is a help even among those countries that do not have a bilateral extradition treaty.

International courts   The International Criminal Court, the International Court of Justice, and several regional courts of justice such as the European Court of Human Rights, the Central American Court of Justice, etc.

Law and treaties   The United Nations Charter, the international law, the Geneva Conventions, the Rome Statute, the Kyoto Protocol, and several other treaties and agreements.

We have to be optimistic if we have to obtain a secure future. Some would say that it would be difficult to change the belligerent nature of man. Optimists would, however, argue that humanity has come a long way to build civilization by making intelligent and moral choices. There is no reason why we collectively cannot make a moral decision to desist from war and to conduct human affairs with a worthy human mind and heart. The poet Lord Tennyson says in Locksley Hall.

For I dipt into the future, far as human eye could see,
Saw the Vision of the world, and all the wonders that would be;
Till the war-drum throbb'd no longer, and the battle-flags were furl'd
In the Parliament of man, the Federation of the world.
There the common sense of most shall hold a fretful realm in awe,
And the kindly earth shall slumber, lapt in universal law. *

Multi-national Arms Trade Code of Conduct

The arms selling countries and the arms purchasing countries have developed a code of conduct in arms trade.[13] Although the intentions of the codes may be admirable in themselves, their drafting and application is done so strategically that there are sufficient loopholes to continue trading. The global organizations engaged in humanitarian work do keep a close watch and work for arms control and disarmament. The Council of European Union recognized the special responsibility of the arms exporting states and declared several measures following two meetings, in 1991 and 1992. We will very briefly outline the European Code of Conduct on Arms Exports.[14]

(a) Set high common standards for conventional arms transfer and exchange relevant information among arms exporting countries for greater transparency.

(b) Prevent the export of arms, which may be used for internal repression or international offensive or regional instability.

(c) Stop illicit transfers of arms and prevent illicit arms trafficking.

(d) Recognize self-defence right of the states as recognized by the UN Charter.

---

[13] For a detailed treatment, see http://www.cafi-online.org/arms-trade-treaty.php.
[14] See http://www.fas.org/asmp/campaigns/code/eucodetext.htm.
* Alfred Lord Tennyson, 'Locksley Hall Sixty Years After' 1886; see http://home.att.net/tinnysonpoetry/ei.htm.

(e) Refuse exports under the following conditions:
- Violation of UN commitments
- Violation of nuclear non-proliferation treaty
- Violation of human rights

(f) Ensure that the internal situation in the country of destination must not be such that provoke conflict against its own people or others.

(g) Help preservation of peace, security, and stability.

(h) Take into account the situation in the purchasing country when exporting arms:
- That the arms are not used for terrorist purposes
- That the arms would not be diverted to third-party countries
- That the recipient country has complete control over the weaponry

(i) The compatibility of the arms exports with the technical and economic capacity of the recipient country must be assessed, based on reports from the UNDP, the World Bank, OECD, and the like. The assessment must be done on a case-by-case basis.

Only a responsible form of transfer of arms must be conducted in this manner, so that the genuine defence needs of the importing countries may be met. But the above code has been considered as too general and its application has been a problem. The reason is that the code is only political in nature and is not legally binding. Several Nobel Peace Prize winners, like Amnesty International, Oxfam, and others, have been campaigning for arms control. The following measures have been suggested to correct the anomalies and include them in international law.

(a) All international transfers of arms shall be authorized by a recognized state and carried out in accordance with national laws and procedures, which reflect, as a minimum, the states' obligations under international law.

(b) States shall not authorize international transfers of arms that would violate their expressed obligations regarding arms under international law.

(c) States shall not authorize international transfers of arms where they will be used or are likely to be used for violations of international law.

(d) States shall take into account other factors, including the likely use of the arms, before authorizing an arms transfer.

(e) States shall submit to an international registry, comprehensive national annual reports on international arms transfers, and the registry shall publish a compiled, comprehensive, international annual report.

(f) States shall establish common standards for specific mechanisms to control all aspects of arms transfers, including brokering, licensed production, etc., as well as operative provisions to strengthen implementation.[15]

---

[15] Oxfam and Control of Arms, July 2005, p.17; see http://www.oxfam.org.uk/what_we_do/issues/conflict_disasters/arms_trade_treaty.htm.

Only if the treaties are legally binding will they have an effect on the sale of arms. Governments will be bound to obey the law. The watchdogs of arms trade that we have discussed would be able to question governments and take legal action. The peace organizations argue that since 2006–08, nearly 7,00,000 people have become the victims of the arms trade. The tackling of poverty, education, and health has been hampered, making an arms trade treaty an urgent need for the international community.

Multi-national Corporate Social Responsibility

At the turn of the new millennium, the United Nations adopted a few goals called the Millennium Development Goals (MDGs).[16] In addition to the already delineated corporate social responsibility in the earlier chapters, multinationals are repeatedly urged by humanitarian agencies to adopt these goals, which have been listed below, and thus economically empower two-thirds of the world population and respect their human dignity.

1. Eradicate extreme poverty and hunger
   (a) Reduce by half the proportion of people living on less than a dollar a day.
   (b) Reduce by half the proportion of people who suffer from hunger.
2. Achieve universal primary education
   (a) Ensure that all boys and girls complete a full course of primary schooling.
3. Promote gender equality and empower women
   (a) Eliminate gender disparity in primary and secondary education preferably by 2005, and at all levels by 2015.
4. Reduce child mortality
   (a) Reduce by two-thirds the mortality rate among children under five.
5. Improve maternal health
   (a) Reduce by three-quarters the maternal mortality ratio.
6. Combat HIV/AIDS, malaria, and other diseases
   (a) Halt and begin to reverse the spread of HIV/AIDS.
   (b) Halt and begin to reverse the incidence of malaria and other major diseases.
7. Ensure environmental sustainability
   (a) Integrate the principles of sustainable development into country policies and programmes; reverse loss of environmental resources.
   (b) Reduce by half, the proportion of the people who are without sustainable access to safe drinking water.
   (c) Achieve significant improvement in the lives of at least 100 million slum dwellers by 2020.
8. Develop a global partnership for development
   (a) Develop further, an open trading and financial system that is rule-based, predictable, and non-discriminatory. Includes a commitment to good

---

[16] See http://www.un.org/millenniumgoals/.

governance, development, and poverty reduction—nationally and internationally.

(b) Address the least developed countries' special needs. This includes tariff-free and quota-free access for their exports, enhanced debt relief for heavily indebted poor countries, cancellation of official bilateral debt, and more generous official development assistance for countries committed to poverty reduction.

(c) Address the special needs of the landlocked and small island developing states.

(d) Deal comprehensively with the developing countries' debt problems through national and international measures to make debt sustainable in the long term.

The Minefield

Least cost business at the price of most lives

Landmines are little hidden bombs or explosives that are detonated by the inadvertent exertion of pressure by a human being or an animal walking over it. The mines may be as simple and as small as firecrackers, when compared to the sophisticated tanks or ships and the submarines in the sea. The menace of landmines was highlighted by the glamorous British Royal, the late Princess Diana. It is only when she visited civil war-torn Africa and cuddled the maimed children and limbless youngsters that the shocking pictures stunned the world and urged the world leaders to take effective action. The following statistics will shed light on the dangers of these deadly mines. The International Campaign to 'Ban Landmines' is one of the organizations that works to eliminate landmines in the world.[a]

Kinds of landmines	350
Estimated landmines under the ground	110 million
Clearance cost	$33 billion
Number of years required to clear	1,100
The present stockpile in warehouses	250 million
Annual deaths	26, 000
One person dies every	15 minutes
In the past three decades, the number of people who died	1 million

Disabled children	300,000
Cost of a single land mine	$3
Cost of clearing a single mine	$1,000
Time required to plant a mine	Less than one hour
Time to clear a mine	More than 100 hours

Landmine is the cheapest weapon which works unmanned; it is used along international borders, militarily sensitive areas, against infiltration, and also by the terrorists. Their proliferation in conflict zones and the former conflicts zones have become killing fields of the innocent. Under the pressure of various international social and human rights groups, a treaty was finally signed—the Ottawa Treaty 1999. The US, China, and Russia, the countries with the most proliferations of the landmines, have not signed it. India is a signatory to the treaty.

Questions

(a) Why the big military powers do not want to ban landmines?

(b) What kind of punishment may be imposed on those who promote proliferation landmines?

(c) What persuasive moral arguments—political, economic, and social—can you give against the landmines?

[a] For these and other details, see: http://www.icbl.org/.

(e) In cooperation with the developing countries, develop decent and productive work for the youth.

(f) In cooperation with pharmaceutical companies, provide access to affordable essential drugs in the developing countries.

(g) In cooperation with the private sector, make available the benefits of new technologies, especially information and communications technologies.

Arms trade fuels conflicts and undermines human rights, thus hitting at the root of MDGs.[17] These issues have been summarized in Table 19.6.

Table 19.6   Efficacy of the MDGs

MDGs	How arms trade fuels conflict	How arms trade undermines human rights	How arms trade undermines MDGs
Eradication of extreme poverty and hunger	Loss of livelihood, unemployment, disruptions in service provision, international trade, and markets	Extra-judicial killings of family bread winners; displacement of people, lack of food, amenities, jobs, and trade	Diversion of funds from social and economic development; increase in debt
Universal primary education	Shut-down of schools, recruitment of teachers and pupils as soldiers, and complete loss of educational opportunity for girls	Displacement, refugees, absence of education	No priority for education in shattered in economies
Gender equality and promotion of empowerment of women	Imbalance in demography due to wars and conflicts; increase in gender violence; women and girls not spared from contribution to war	In the absence of men, brunt of caring for the families on women; women forced into flesh trade	MDGs remain a dream
Reduction in child mortality Maternal care	Medical facilities destroyed by war, infant mortality high in the absence of care for pregnant women and newborns	Heavy toll on humanity by war	MDGs lose meaning
Eradication of HIV/AIDS, malaria and other diseases and epidemics	Health service wiped away by wars and conflicts; sexual violence, spread of HIV/AIDS due to prostitution	Displaced people, refugees, victims of sexual abuse	No MDGs exist
Sustainable environment	Destruction of infrastructure, migration of poor to cities, urban life collapse, exploitation of natural resources	Destruction of natural resources in armed conflict; basic energy needs met unsustainably	No concept of MDGs

[17] For further reading and links, go to http://www.globalissues.org/article/80/a-code-of-conduct-for-arms-sales.

Stand Up—Take Action[18] is a campaign in support of the MDGs, which started in mid-October 2008 and mobilized over a 100 million people around the world. The purpose of the campaign has been to keep the torch of the MDGs burning and not allow nations to slip away under the excuse of a global financial crisis. It is imperative on multinational companies to see the logic of the empowerment of people for their own sake.

SUMMARY

- The world is full of strife. There is a violent evolution.
- The means to inflict violence has progressed even to space through technology, since man has failed to overcome his violent nature.
- The people of the world divided themselves into nations, and are ambitious to dominate each other.
- Business has gone global and has created a complex network of geopolitical relations, by indulging in power games with the nation-states.

- Arms trade is the biggest trade. Governments have become agents of the arms producing multinational corporations.
- Terror acts are perpetrated by non-state players, who have become a dominant force.
- Terrorists have been manipulated by nation-states. They thrive by causing divisions in the will of the international community.
- Multinational corporations have grave responsibilities for the safety of the citizens and long-term business interests.

KEY TERMS

Arms trade code of conduct   A tool to prohibit the world's arms producers, virtually all developed countries, from providing military assistance and conventional arms transfers to foreign governments that do not meet certain requirements.

Balance of power   Maintenance of military equilibrium of international defence systems.

Common good   A specific 'good' that is shared and beneficial for all (or most) members of a given community.

Geopolitics   Dynamics of international relations.

Millennium Development Goals (MDGs)   The eight UN goals to be achieved by 2015 to respond to the world's main development challenges.

CONCEPT REVIEW QUESTIONS

1. How do global businesses influence people's lives?

2. What is wrong with the arms trade if it helps a country defend itself?

3. How does terrorism affect business?

4. Is punishment not violence? From where does the state get its power to punish people?

5. What responsibilities do corporations have in a global business?

6. Explain the significance of the Caux Round Table.

---

[18] See http://www.standagainstpoverty.org/en/.

CRITICAL THINKING QUESTIONS

1. Why is the human society violent?
2. How does one solve the dilemma of trade and war? If you trade arms there is war; but if there is no war, then there is no trade.

3. Is it terrorism when a state wages war? How do we use violence for different purposes?
4. Can multinationals not regulate and censor themselves, rather than wait for costly and complicated state interventions?

FURTHER READING

A.M. Rugman and T.L. Brewer, *Oxford Handbook of International Business*, Oxford University Press (2003).

CASE STUDY

The Game
al-Qaeda

Our war on terror begins with al-Qaeda, but it does not end there. It will not end until every terrorist group of global reach has been found, stopped, and defeated.[a]

—George W. Bush

The Player

Usāmah bin Muḥammad bin 'Awaḍ bin Lāden, born in 1957, has a towering height of 6′6″ and belongs to a rich family from Saudi Arabia. He is a qualified engineer, accomplished businessman, and millionaire, and has been the acclaimed American hero against the Soviet occupation of Afghanistan. He possesses an incredible talent of leadership, to inspire young men and women to sacrifice themselves for the cause of his mission, offers death as a reward for his willing and inspired employees, is a master of planning and execution of strategies, and keeps miles ahead of his rivals and enemies, is a financial wizard who manages easy cash flow from business to run a war under the very noses of his detractors and enemies. He achieves goals with minimum cost and a total success rate. All this and more is spelt in the name of Osama bin Laden. Anyone who gives information about his whereabouts will be richer by $250 million.

Big Chess Game

1980s: Jimmy Carter in the White House and Leonid Brezhnev in Kremlin ruled a polarized twin superpower world. Afghanistan became the chess-board of geopolitical games, arms trade, proxy war, heady religious and cultural brews, and a queer new world order.[b] The Soviets had established their puppet government in Afghanistan and smelled the oil fields of the Gulf. Not that they were interested in oil—they had had enough of those natural resources—but the Gulf would be the last bastion of global power to claim the singular honour of the superpower of the world.

The threat to US interests was too hard to ignore. The peace-loving Jimmy Carter, who had made human rights the core of his well-publicized foreign policy, had to make an uncharacteristic decision. He decided to support the Afghan resistant groups clubbed as Mujahidin. The two intelligence agencies—CIA of the US and ISI of Pakistan—would work together to supply the

---

[a] US President George W. Bush's 20 September 2001 address to the Joint Session of Congress.
[b] Steve Coll, *Washington Post*, 19 July 1992. See http://www.globalissues.org/article/258/anatomy-of-a-victory-cias-covert-afghan-war.

Mujahidin with arms, ammunition, and training. Not to be left behind in helping her fellow Muslim country, now occupied by the infidels, Saudi Arabia agreed to equally participate and finance the cause. It suited the Carter administration not to sully its hands as brazenly as it had been doing in its operations against the Soviet-supported forces in Nicaragua and Angola. Carter sanctioned $2 billion worth of small-scale conventional arms to the Mujahidin in Afghanistan.

Soon, Ronald Reagan took over the reigns in the White House, and the Afghan mission intensified. The CIA found it more efficient to supply arms to the Mujahidin by purchasing them from the Chinese. The merchandise consisted of assault rifles, grenade launchers, mines, and SA-7 light antiaircraft weapons. All this had to be transported through Pakistan. The Mujahidin, with their religious enthusiasm, coupled with the power of the increasingly sophisticated armoury, had successes, which the US, Saudi Arabia, and Pakistan initially could not believe was possible. Nervousness crept into Kremlin as the troops got bogged down and the body bags of the dead soldiers arriving in Moscow increased.

In 1985, Mikhail Gorbachev was busy trying to take over in Kremlin. The KGB, the Soviet intelligence agency, was able to convince its bosses for better military supplies and highly trained troops. This again tilted the balance in favour of the Soviets. To thwart this escalation, the Pentagon, the defense ministry of the US, sought out a different approach. Guerrilla training, sophisticated satellite communications, and more specialized arms were supplied to the Mujahidin. The Reagan administration squarely met the escalated war with so much military hardware as never used since World War II. Islamabad played the decisive role of a perfect partner, and the Saudi princes were the perfect patrons.

Sophisticated arms needed sophisticated handling, logistics, and overall management of war machinery and personnel. The CIA and the ISI laid the groundwork for training the Mujahidin in modern warfare by opening training centres or

madrasas. The Mujahidin were taught to handle weapons like the Swiss-made Oerlikon heavy gun, the British-made Blowpipe missile, and the Stingers of the US. First, the Pakistani officers got their training in the US. They then returned to the camp and educated and trained the Mujahidin. The training was comprehensive, with sophisticated simulators to combat airborne targets.

Game Surrender

Mikhail Gorbachev inherited a bankrupt federation of countries called the Soviet Union, held together by an ideology that the people hated because it only brought misery and war. Due to the unprecedented arms race started by the US and its allies, and due to its commitments around the world to fight the capitalists, the Soviets had drained themselves out. There was a huge food crisis. People were standing in serpentine lines for meagre bread and essential items, which were heavily rationed. The military was beyond the means of maintenance, the industry was a paper tiger, and the economic management needed for a competitive superpower had no worth. The economy collapsed, and so did the military, and the faith in the ideology crashed. The game in Afghanistan was given up, and the soldiers came home as losers.

The Union broke up. From 1989 to 1991, the entire map of Eastern Europe was redrawn and the mighty union was now only a part that remained as Russia. The new hero, Boris Yeltsin, denounced his red religion, drummed up Russian patriotism, insulted his one-time colleague Gorbachev, embraced Western capitalism, and got elected as President and entered the White House, the presidential palace by the Moscow River.

Knight of Game

The name of the knight of the game is Osama bin Laden.[c] Son of a very wealthy businessman, Osama, while studying at the King Abdel Aziz University in Jeddah, was greatly influenced by the teachings of his mentor, Abdullah Azzam, in the puritanical beliefs of the orthodox Islamic Wahhabi sect, the strictest and the narrowest of Sunni Islam.

---

[c] Lisa Beyer, 'The Most Wanted Man in the World', *Time.* See http://www.time.com/time/covers/1101010924/wosama.html.

He resolved that he would be the one to lead the one billion Muslims around the globe in a Jihad against all the infidels, and restore Islam to its purity from the land of its origin, his motherland, Saudi Arabia.

At the age of 22, although he was the inheritor of a large business empire, he did not hesitate to volunteer to go to Afghanistan as the infidel Soviets invaded a Muslim country. He diverted his own business funds, and influenced many rich Saudis to contribute to the cause in Afghanistan. An organization eventually came into existence, which after being named in several phrases finally settled to al-Qaeda (the Base). Along with his mentor, recruited followers from all the Arab countries and other Muslim nations around the world. The CIA, the US intelligence operator in Afghanistan, recognized his ability. Unconfirmed reports believe that it is their active support, both financially and through military and training, that helped al-Qaeda become a formidable and reliable ally against the Soviets. After a decade of fighting, the depleted, distressed, and de-motivated Soviets left Afghanistan in 1989 to fend for itself.

Having accomplished the mission, Osama returned to his home. To his utter shock, he realized that the rulers of his country had become extremely corrupt and could not care less for the religious sites and the welfare of the Muslims. In 1990, when Saddam Hussein invaded Kuwait and even threatened Saudi Arabia, Osama approached the Saudi rulers and told them that he and his organization can fight Hussein and his army. The rulers, however, had a different world view and called in for the US troops. Osama felt betrayed and totally outraged. For the first time in history, foreign troops consisting of Christians and Jews, with their women in pants and rock music blaring, were romping around the sacred land of Islam. He strongly felt that this was a sacrilege against the holy places of Mecca and Medina. When he wrote and objected, the rulers confined him, but he escaped and fled to Sudan, whose ruler had the same puritanical views as Osama. Here, he was able to establish a sprawling business empire and finance his organization, al-Qaeda.

Knight Is King

al-Qaeda is a different game of chess. There is no superpower. There is only God and his servant, al-Qaeda. The enemies are infidels and they will do everything to survive, because they are afraid to die, but the al-Qaeda believers live to die. Osama promises them the crown of martyrdom. It is a religious war, or jihad. Everything is fair in such a war. All targets are legitimate. There are no innocent people. They are all beneficiaries of the great Satan. They must die, too. Osama uses his enemies' most potent weapon, business. He establishes multi-million dollar businesses, and channelizes funds to procure arms. Several sympathetic regimes to his cause also join forces with him, and through him, take revenge against the arrogant self-proclaimed superpower, the US. Osama has effectively taken over the world. The proof is that the superpower and its allies are fighting a losing battle with his intelligent, low-cost, fear-inspiring, and effective conquest. His strategy has put fear in people, and people have surrendered their will to his power. Some of the major attacks by al-Qaeda are

1992: Hotel bombing, Aden, Yemen—killed Australian tourist

1993: Bombings in Mogadishu on US troops

Bombing of World Trade Center on 26 February, 6 dead and over a 1000 injured

1995: Bombing in Riyadh, Saudi Arabia

1996: Bombing of Khobar Towers, Saudi Arabia

1998: Bombing of US embassies in Kenya and Tanzania

2000: Bombing of ship, USS Cole, in Yemen

In the mid-1990s, Osama moved with his three or four wives and ten children back to the mountains of Afghanistan bordering Pakistan. Here he turned his al-Qaeda into a pan-Islamic organization, networking with likeminded ideologists and supplying them with financial and human resource help. For the first time, he could send his well-trained foot soldiers into the camps in the mountains to spread terror. Immediate effect was felt in Egypt, Algeria, the Palestinian territories, Kashmir, Philippines, Eritrea, Libya, Jordan, Tajikistan,

Bosnia, Chechnya, Somalia, Sudan, Yemen, and other countries. It is said that Osama has a direct control over 5000 al-Qaeda members, who network in the countries that they are sent to on mission to network with similar groups. He has built his organization along business lines: he franchises terror to other groups around the world, and supports them with training and also some money.

B-to-B Game

Osama bin Laden owns legitimate businesses mostly in countries sympathetic to his mission, which in turn are the sources for his Jihadist business. Some of his businesses have been identified as

- A construction company, el-Hijrah for Construction and Development Ltd
- Wadi al-Aqiq Co., an export-import company
- Taba Investment Co. Ltd, which dealt in global stock markets
- Part-ownership of the el-Shamal Islamic Bank
- Several farms, raising peanuts, sunflowers, etc., which were also used as training camps for terrorists.
- Laden International Import-Export Company
- Bakery, furniture company
- Bank of Zoological Resource cattle-breeding programme
- International al-Ikhlar Co., making honey and other sweets

Osama also has a $150 million-worth construction company in Sudan, farming projects in several countries, and even forests in Turkey. He also claims to have Ostrich farms and a shrimp boats business in Kenya, diamond mining in Africa, and agricultural projects in Tajikistan. It is also said that Osama has covertly invested very large shares in the Silicon Valley companies. In short, the enemy of the free world is moving freely through the institutions of the open market, beating them at their own game. The State Department of the US has estimated the financing by al-Qaeda at $300 million.

Checkmate

Osama made his checkmate move on the morning of 11 September 2001. That fateful morning, nineteen al-Qaeda Jihadists hijacked four commercial passenger jets. Two of these crashed intentionally, with all the passengers aboard, into the Twin Towers of the World Trade Center in New York City. The third hit the Pentagon, the defence department of the US in Arlington County, Virginia, and the fourth crashed into a field in Shanksville, Pennsylvania. The death toll was 2998, excluding the nineteen hijackers, who were presumed dead. Over 6291 people were injured. An unprecedented history was made, which barely resembled Pearl Harbour that dragged the US into World War II. The citizens of several countries, who were doing business at the World Trade Center, as well as in other places of the attack, died. The outrage was unspeakable. People were shell shocked. Billions watched on TV the World Trade Center tumble down into a dreadful, dusty heap, taking down with it all the victims, in a pitiless act. The superpower of the world appeared to be on its knees, clueless, stunned, and traumatized, smitten to smithereens. The player who checkmated was far away in some cave of the Afghan mountains, but his presence seemed to overpower everything else upon the Earth.

War Game

The entire country backed President George W. Bush when he ordered Operation Enduring Freedom, hitting both Taliban, the fundamentalist government of Afghanistan, and al-Qaeda, where it had taken refuge. The United Nations, in its resolution 1373, made it obligatory for all member states to criminalize any assistance for terrorist activities, deny financial support, and stop giving safe haven to terrorists. In 2003, protocols were designed, and these became the international laws against terrorism.

The phrase 'war on terrorism' was coined by the Western press, and eventually by the US and other governments. The Bush administration developed a systematic programme to counter terror and defend their national interests abroad and at home. The entire presidency of George Bush was spent on fighting terror activities and conducting two wars simultaneously, in Afghanistan and Iraq.

Costly Game

The people's economy is the first to get hit by a war, although the economy of war may script its own story of war as business. Productivity gets the first blow. Energy resources become scarce and costly. Economists try hard to measure the impact of the terror attacks in countries like India, Israel, and Spain, where terrorism has become a part and parcel of life. However, it is the 11 September 2001 attacks that highlighted the costs of countering terrorism on a global level. The US is the largest economy in the world, and when it is made unsure by a terrorist attack, there are global repercussions.

What is incalculable, however, is the human cost. People who could have created enormous wealth, jobs, and better conditions for life simply lost their lives or have been discouraged from pursuing business.

Those industries involved in the war economy, such as the military hardware, the armed forces, the logistics and information systems, may find an opportunity to do more defence-oriented business. Apart from these, insurance companies too see huge opportunities, since the terror risks to business are estimably quite high.[d]

The direct cost of 11 September 2001 has been roughly estimated at $20 billion. The Comptroller of the City of New York has estimated the property loss to be $21.8 billion. The mere clean up operation was estimated at $11 billion. The capital market loss has been estimated at a quarter of a per cent of the US annual GDP. The 9/11 attacks prompted a new secretariat for Homeland Security. The defence and homeland security departments cost the US approximately $500 billion, 20 per cent of the federal budget and an increase equivalent to 0.7 per cent of the GDP, annually.

It has hit the common man squarely. The supply chain costs of transports and logistics have gone up. This has impacted not only the developed countries, but also the emerging economies. It has significantly affected the poverty alleviation programmes also.

Indian Game

On 26 November 2008, Mumbai, which has been a target for terrorists over the past two decades, was shocked and stunned, when over ten coordinated attacks sent similar shock waves as those in New York on 9/11. The railway station, two five-star hotels, a Jewish synagogue, a famous café, a cinema house, the docks, and even a taxi were attacked. After three days of unending terror and gore, the body count was 173, with over 300 injured. The terrorists, originating from Pakistan, had hit the finance capital of India.

India played a different game, and clearly showed to the world that terrorism need not affect the economy adversely. The very day after the end of the attacks, Mumbai was back in business. It was the spirit of Mumbai. In fact, business never stopped. More and more people came out to show their spirit of resilience and to give a fitting positive reply to the attacks. In the months that followed, the economy has taken a turn for the better. The two-digit inflation deflated to almost a zero, raising fears of deflation and stagflation. The capital market rebounded and recovered steadily, and by April 2009, the Sensex crossed the 10,000 mark.

Pakistan, which has been a haven for terrorists and their training camps from the days of the Afghan–Soviet confrontation, has further degenerated into chaos. The Taliban have systematically occupied the mountain territories and established their rule in the Swat valley. The military dictatorship has given place to a discordant democracy. The economy is destroyed and now depends on the aid of the arms supplying countries such as the US and the UK.

---

[d] For a very extensive treatment, see http://www.oecd.org/dataoecd/11/60/1935314.pdf.

Endgame

The above case has highlighted the hypocrisy of the arms trading countries. It has exposed how their strategies have backfired on them and their interests at home. Their minds have become numb with violence, and they can think of no other way than to end terror with more violence. Their citizens are living in perpetual fear. India, on the other hand, has been a victim of terror and has steadily dealt with terrorism on its own, without the help of the developed countries, through its resilient spirit. From the separatists' movements in Punjab to the insurgencies in the North East, and from the Naxalite menace in several states to the Jihadist movements in Kashmir, India has persistently dealt with terrorism. The terrorists have not succeeded in destroying the political integrity, a booming economy, and the harmonious social fabric of the Indian society.

Discussion Questions

1. What are the international issues in the above case?

2. Can we apply an international ethical code for this case?

3. Is violence wrong if it has a just cause? Is there a just war?

4. What is the difference between violence exercised by the state on its citizens or on the other states and the violence inflicted by individuals or groups on other individuals or groups?

5. If some terrorist groups can eventually be recognized as legitimate groups, such as the PLO and the Maoists of Nepal, why did the state oppose them in the beginning?

6. Is there a violence that can be justified as morally right?

7. What is the role of religion in terrorism?

Going Further . . .

Conduct a panel discussion on the following:

- Do terrorists have human rights?

- Can terrorists be detained and punished without out trial?

- Should lawyers represent terrorists in a state trial?

- When states commit violent crimes against humanity, who punishes them?

- Is the sovereignty of a state inviolable in all instances?

- Can morality help overcome terrorism? What are the moral principles that help us to deal with terrorism?

ETHICAL DEVELOPMENT PROGRAMME

Management Training

A. Game: Reality Chess

Objective: To understand the political and business relationships.

Method:

(a) Get two groups of sixteen people each to represent sixteen pawns on the chess board.

(b) Give each person the name of an MNC or Government, depending upon their importance to your world order.

(c) Play the game in a park or a playground, with well-marked chess squares. You may also organize to play on a projected image.

B. Research Project

Themes: Pick one of them

(a) The impact of multinationals on my state.

(b) The impact of terrorism on the industries in my state.

The research may be done with sponsors such as the Chambers of Commerce, business associations, etc.

Management Mantra

Axis of Evil: Mind Game

In the aftermath of 11 September 2001, President George W. Bush enjoyed an unprecedented approval rating of 86 per cent of the Americans, and practically the whole of the Congress, for the swift decision he took to declare war on terrorism. In his State of the Union address in early 2002, he dwelt extensively on the problem of terrorism and coined the phrase 'axis of evil' to describe the safe havens of state-sponsored terror—Iran, Iraq, and North Korea. Bush's speechwriter, David Frum, is the actual author of the phrase. The brief given to the author was to prepare for the offensive against terrorism in the countries of their origin, and thus prevent future attacks on the US and its allies. The phrase had its desired effect. Iran shouted loud slogans against the 'Great Satan', the US. The entire Middle East and North Korea joined in. The media, especially stand-up comedies, documentaries, films, and Internet gaming, picked up the phrase and transformed it to suit their own interests.

> MANTRA   *A word in the mind is worth two in the bush.*

Challenges of Unsolved Problems

All human beings are born free and equal in dignity and rights. They are endowed with reason and conscience and should act towards one another in a spirit of brotherhood.[1]

—United Nations' Universal Declaration of Human Rights

Respect for all living beings is non-violence.[2]

—Lord Mahavira

LEARNING OBJECTIVES

After studying this chapter, you will be able to

➢ Define the food, shelter, and clothing rights
➢ State the gender rights
➢ Understand the human rights
➢ List the animal rights

INTRODUCTION

Our objectives in this chapter are to discuss the four areas where business has not made any significant contribution, but is expected to do so. The first objective focuses on the right to a decent life. The second on the rightful place women must have in society. The third on the advocacy and protection of fundamental human rights. The fourth objective focuses on the other sentient beings, the animals who share this earth with us. Why should business corporations adopt and promote these objectives? The answer to this is a counter question—with whom and where else would they like to do business?

Lord Mahavira, the twenty-fourth Jain Tirthankara saw how people had created many problems for themselves due to restlessness, discontent, greed, stealing, and

---

[1] United Nations' Declaration of Human Rights; see http://www.un.org/Overview/rights.html.
[2] A Lord Mahavira quote; see http://quotequotez.blogspot.com/search/label/jain%20qoutes.

above all, strife and violence. To him, the world that man had created for himself appeared like a man who was seated on top of a tree in a forest that was being consumed by fire, and soon his fate would also be the same.

Oddly enough, that foolish man's world is what we have created for ourselves—a world of poverty, quarrel among the genders, and cruelty to our fellow human beings and animals as well. If we do not use our intelligence, we will end up destroying ourselves. We have to resolve our seemingly unsolvable challenges.

Experience is the foundation of the formation, association, and development of ideas. The themes in this chapter can be termed as 'challenges of unsolved problems'. The problems of poverty, gender bias, human rights, and animal rights are very sensitive moral problems. They are highly explosive political problems with wide geopolitical ramifications. They are basic economic problems, challenging business problems, and endemic social problems. These problems cry out for justice.

For an important emerging economy like India poverty is not just a stigma, it is an insurmountable problem. All the government schemes and programmes for over half a century have not significantly improved the conditions of the poor. India has a whopping 400 million population that is struggling to eke out an existence. All the progress that the country makes, even that which is close to a two-digit economic growth, is lost in the desert of poverty. Deaths by starvation are reported from Orissa, West Bengal, Andhra Pradesh, and even in the most developed state, Maharashtra.

Gender bias is a global issue. Half the population of the world are women, and yet they have to fight for their rights. In some regions and countries of the world, they do not have the right to free movement, speech, and even clothing of their choice. Some religions discriminate them by barring entries to prayer halls and temples. Businesses are not far behind; for even the most advanced corporations have shown discrimination in payment, not abiding by equal opportunity employment, particularly in the developed countries.

Human rights in business is becoming controversial. Supporting despotic regimes, causing direct and indirect harm to people, aggravating human trafficking problems, letting employees live in sub-human conditions, protecting and proliferating sweat shops, etc., have sullied the image of corporations.

The wonderful products of personal hygiene, cosmetics, perfumes, etc., have the painful stories of animal experimentation, suffering, and death behind them. Fashion accessories such as bags, belts, valets, coats, shawls, etc., use animal product. Humans also consume an unbelievable amount of flesh, of even endangered species such as the whales, tigers, deer, etc.

FOOD, SHELTER, AND CLOTHING RIGHTS

Absolute poverty is privation from food and shelter; anything more than this is relative poverty. Thus, the poor people of the developed countries could be relatively well-to-do in the subcontinent.

Getting Used to Poverty

If one mentions poverty, it may strike a moral chord because we are all familiar with poverty. But if one insists on the right to food, shelter, and clothing, it would make its point legally, and our business managers and corporations may realize that where they do business, the first priority of the people is the right to food and shelter. Further, one would insist that they have no right to do business for profit, where people are starving and have no roof over their heads.

You may be ridiculed if you were to say that it is very difficult to tell Indians what poverty is. There is a story about Satyajit Ray, the world-renowned film-maker from Bengal, whose films depicted with poignancy, the varied miseries and privations wrought by poverty. Once, a well-known foreign film-maker visited him. Both waded through the crowded streets of Calcutta (now Kolkata) where they had to jostle with the beggars, bullock carts, homeless people living on the pavements, the rickshaw pullers, street urchins, and dirt. The visitor was shocked by the sprawling poverty, but it seemed to him that his host Ray seemed quite unmindful of it. When the visitor questioned him on the matter, Ray replied, 'Human beings get used to anything.'

All our big cities are crowded with the urban poor. It does not shock us when we routinely say that 65 per cent of the people in Mumbai live in the slums. Similarly, in the rural areas where poverty is abject and at every election the politicians drive through the dusty roads promising alleviation of poverty, nothing ever changes. It is amazing how even the poor are used to their poverty and the well-to-do are used to living among the poor, without making a difference to each other. Has our sense of morality numbed? Can business corporations bring a change to empower the poor and turn them into their customers?

Poverty Statistics to Stimulate Conscience

More than half the world, that is, three billion people, lives in poverty on about Rs 100 a day; some live on just Rs 50 a day. India has the largest number of the poverty stricken population, which is close to 400 million.[3]

- The poorest 40 per cent of the world's population accounts for 5 per cent of the global income.
- The richest 20 per cent gobble up more than 75 per cent of the global income.
- 25,000 children die every day out of sheer poverty.
- 1.8 million people die of diarrhoea.
- 72 million children in the developing countries do not go to school.
- One billion people in the world are illiterate.
- 40 million people suffer from HIV/AIDS, 3 million of them die annually.
- 1.1 billion people in the world do not have safe drinking water.

---

[3] WDR (World Development Report) by The World Bank, 2008.

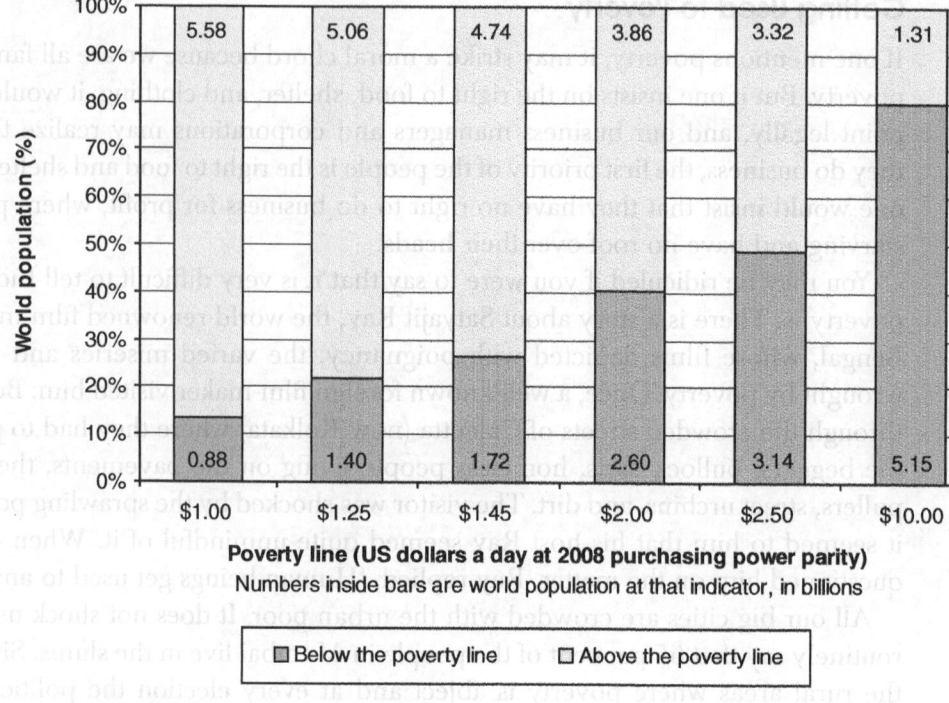

Source: World Bank Development Indicators, 2008.

Fig. 20.1 Percentage of people in the world at different poverty levels, 2008[4]

- In developing countries, 2.6 billion people lack basic sanitation.
- The wealthy, who consist of 20 per cent of the population, use 85 per cent of the piped water.

Poverty is the deprivation of resources to keep the body and soul together. The above statistics show some indicators of the poverty and their magnitude in numbers that are incredibly high. Figure 20.1 clearly shows that the policy makers who set up economic drivers, the social leaders who motivate people and business entrepreneurs to create wealth, have failed miserably. The poor are poor due to certain circumstances. The business enterprises must provide opportunities to the poor and gain in business.

Right of Roof over One's Head

Birds have nests, animals have their burrows, dens, and caves but millions of people have no roof over their heads. The 2001 census of India says that there are two million homeless people in the country. As per the official definition, homeless means those who have no roof over their heads, except for the sky. In other words, slum dwellers,

---

[4] This chart is as per the figures of 2005.

Death by Dearth

Starvation in Orissa

This is one of the stories of the fate of a tribal man and his family.[a] In 1998, the government of Orissa banned bamboo cutting from forests. Earlier on, in the 1970s, the government had taken over *kendu* leaf and later, *Sal*. With the ban on bamboo cutting, the government took complete control over the forests and started to harvest and market these products. This was done to save the forests and, at the same time, to use the non-timber goods as a source for state revenues.

Santara and his wife Sajani, like their tribal ancestors, depended solely on the forest for their livelihood. They were artisans who weaved baskets made from bamboo and sold these in the local market and eked out an existence. They had two daughters, who helped them in their work.

When the bamboo ban came into effect, the family had no source of livelihood. Basket weaving had been the family trade for generations. Santara could do no other work as he belonged to a low caste called *dom*, and the other villagers who had fields would not employ him. It was not a city where he could go begging; but he tried to solicit food from the villagers. Since the other villagers were also poor, he could not approach them always.

Now, Santara possessed a Below-the-Poverty-Line (BPL) card and also the much touted, National Rural Employment Guarantee Scheme (NREGS) card. NREGS is a multi-crore national programme that gives employment for at least 100 days. Santara could not purchase grains and pulses with his BPL card, because he had no money. He went with his NRGES card to the local *panchayat* and said that he was actually starving. They gave him Rs 50 and told him to go to the district collector, who in turn sent him to the Block Development Officer (BDO). The BDO could do nothing because there was no employment available under NREGS. The *sarpanch* of his *panchayat* doled out 10 kg of rice to him a couple of times; sometimes, the family was given some rice from the mid-day meal of the local school. Finally, hunger took hold of Santara and he got ill; Sajani ran from pillar to post asking for help, but to no avail. Santara breathed his last, or in other words, was starved to death.

It is a year now since he died of starvation. The district collector promptly denies that starvation was the cause of Santata's death. There were dozens of such deaths in the state, which the state government denies. The irony is that when people die of starvation, they die by contracting some illness, which is the final cause of death; that is the cause of death acceptable to the government and not starvation per se. Hence, no one dies of starvation as per the government.

Santara's wife and children are totally emaciated and still live by begging for food. They want to work but no one hires them for the very same reason their father was not hired. They are resigned to their oncoming death when they say, 'How long can we beg? We will also soon die of starvation.'

Questions

(a) Orissa is a state known for its natural resources and minerals. Find out the industrial strength of the state of Orissa. Find out how many companies are involved in mining. Do you not think that these industries, apart from the government, have a moral duty to be conscious about the subhuman conditions of the inhabitants of the forests?

(b) From time immemorial, tribals of Orissa and other states have lived as people of the forest. If their lifestyle were to destroy the forest, then the forests would have vanished several centuries ago. These people have been part and parcel of the forest life and its food cycle. Is it not a deprivation of their fundamental right to ban them from the forest?

(c) What are the moral implications of starvation?

[a] Arpan Tulsyan, 'Starvation persists in Orissa' report in http://www.indiatogether.org/2008/jul/pov-starve.htm.

shanty dwellers, those living in makeshift tents, plastic sheet covers, etc. are those who own homes.

One per cent of Delhi's population, that is, 1,40,000 people live under the canopy of the sky. Researchers and the census department merely make a quantitative estimation (guess), because how would these agencies get hold of the people who have no holding?

The majority of people think that homeless people are homeless because of their own fault; they are lazy to work; they are responsible for their poverty. The homeless face a lot of problems, such as when VIPs visit the city, the homeless are hunted out and driven away.

Homeless are seen as criminals; they are rounded up periodically and herded into government asylums built for them. There are frequent reports of homeless people being run over by drunken drivers. In addition, they are frequenty victims of extortion, abuse, and sexual assaults.

Right to Clothing

In his autobiography, *My Experiments with Truth*, Mahatma Gandhi describes the evolution of his attire, which was just one piece of loin cloth. After he returned from South Africa, and before he plunged into domestic politics, he wanted to see and experience the Indian reality for himself. He travelled across India by train in a third class compartment. When he returned from South Africa, he realized that most of the people in India were just half clad. So he gave up his Western clothing, which in itself was a protest against the Western goods, and adapted to wearing the simple Indian loin cloth and a piece of cloth across his shoulders. He wore the clothes that he himself had spun on his *charkha*. The self-woven clothing and the *charkha* became the symbol of resistance against the colonialists.

When the train approached Allahabad, it halted near the Naini bridge over the Jamuna River. Not very far away down the river is its confluence with the Ganga. All went down to the river to pay respects to the sacred river and refresh themselves. Gandhiji also went along and as he was washing himself, he saw a woman, who wore a threadbare sari and was trying to wash one end of it. It dawned on him that she had just one sari to wear, and that perhaps, she was washing a part of it every day. He took off the cloth that covered his torso, and let it float on the water towards her. From that day on, Gandhiji's clothing consisted of just one piece of loin cloth. The British derided him as a half-naked fakir; but he used it to symbolize the nakedness of India, to show the British how they had denuded the country.

After sixty years of independence, and emerging as the second fastest growing economy in the world, and being a world leader in textile production and export, a quarter of India's population is still half clad.

Homeless in Capital City

Ramavatar and his street family

Ramavatar, who was in his mid-40s, landed in Delhi along with several others like him, in a general compartment of a train, from Saharsa, a district in Bihar.[a] For the first time in his life, he had travelled such a long distance without a ticket. He arrived in the early hours of the morning at the Old Delhi Railway station. He carried a small plastic bag in which he had his loin cloth and an old shirt. In the crowd, he somehow escaped from being checked for ticket at the exit. As he came out, he saw a big line of tea shops. His hungry stomach churned, but he had no money, not even a single rupee for half a cup of tea. He went near a tea shop and sat on his haunches at a distance. The person manning the tea kiosk observed him for a long time and finally signalled him to come closer. He asked him whether he had come from Bihar. Ramavatar nodded to say yes and wondered aloud how he knew. The man at the tea kiosk said, 'Thousands like you come everyday. So, what is your story?'

Ramavatar told him that due to floods, he had lost his entire household—his wife, his three children, and his old parents. The three acres of land that he possessed was also washed away when the Kosi river changed its course. Hence, he decided to come to Delhi along with a few other villagers, and start a new life here. The tea shop owner said that he too was from Saharsa, and had landed in Delhi many years ago. His parents were shot dead by dacoits, but he had managed to run away. The tea shop did not belong to him. He was only doing the night shift. He introduced himself as Shekar.

When his boss arrived the following morning to take over from him, Shekar spoke to him. The latter agreed to hire Ramavatar as a dishwasher, and to supply tea to the various shopkeepers and vendors around the place. Shekar slept in the park during the day and worked at the tea shop at night. Ramavatar worked at the shop the whole day and tried to be with Shekar as late as possible. He would then go to sleep in the lobby of the railway station, at night. He could also use the railway toilet. He paid a weekly sum (*hafta*) of Rs 50 to the police for this favour.

One day, the police told him that he should look for another place to sleep for the next four days, since there was a high profile VIP movement at the railway station. That night, Ramavatar settled himself at the doorstep of a shop not very far away from his tea kiosk. Suddenly, there was commotion in the middle of the night. Four men were trying to drag away two young women, and the third was pleading with them to let them go. Ramavatar jumped to his feet and was by their side in a jiffy. One of them hit him in the stomach and demanded to know who he was. He replied that he is the uncle of the mother of these young children, and begged the men to let them go. They demanded whether he had any money with him. He reached into his shirt pocket, took out all the money he had, and showed it to them; it was Rs 200 and some change. They took the currency notes and returned the coins to him. They passed some lewd remarks and rode away on their two wheelers.

Ramavatar did not go back to sleep; he went to the tea kiosk and narrated the event to Shekar. Both, resigned to their fate of poverty and homelessness, laughed with disdain and said, 'Welcome to Delhi, the capital of India', as they saw more and more people like them pouring out of the railway station.

Questions

(a) What principles do destitution and homelessness work against?

(b) Whose moral responsibility is it, if some starve and others have no homes?

(c) What is the role of the business corporations, real estate industry, and the housing schemes in India, for the homeless?

---

[a] The literary form is fictitious and is written to highlight the real facts.

GENDER RIGHTS

Do women play second fiddle to men? The question is futile, because the answer has always been in the positive. Business is no exception. A female employee of the world-renowned retailer Wal-Mart, along with six other female colleagues, has filed a law suit for not getting paid at par with their male counterparts, for the same amount of work done, and for being denied promotions. The repercussions of such a case can ruin the supermarket chain, with over 3000 branches. The plaintiffs have pleaded that all the female employees, whether present or former, be compensated

---

Echoes of Freedom

Goonj—cloths distribution system

The CNN-IBN television channel highlighted the efforts of social leaders and their unusual programmes. One of them was Anshu Gupta. In 1998, he started an organization called Goonj[a]—meaning echo. He collected old clothes, to distribute among the poor during the winter season. What began as a small initiative, today distributes 20,000 kg of clothes. It has a volunteer strength of 300, and 150 grassroot organizations working in 20 states of the country. The following programmes are currently being undertaken by Goonj.

Vastra-daan It collects old clothes from urban centres, modifies them, cleans them, and then distributes them among the needy.

Cloth for work The village communities are motivated to work for their own communities. They repair roads, build school boundaries, plant trees, and help in cleanliness drives. They are paid in clothes for this work.

S2S It is a school to school programme, in which the waste of the urban school is remodelled or recycled, such as old books, uniforms, shoes, school bags. It has brought a great sense of awareness among the city school children about their counterparts in the villages. It has also been able to build bridges between the rural and urban children.

Not just a piece of cloth There is no concept of personal hygiene among the village women. Goonj

educates the rural women in personal hygiene, and distributes simple cloth napkins to them. It has saved thousands of women from contracting various infections. So far, this issue was taboo in the villages, but Goonj has now raised the consciousness of the women to personal hygiene. This initiative won an award for the organization by the World Bank.

Rahat It is to give need-based systematic relief during the disasters such as floods and tsunami. The organization's work in Assam, Bihar, and West Bengal has won the Changemakers' Award.

Anshu Gupta, the founder of Goonj (http://www.goonj.info) is a graduate from Indian Institute of Mass Communication. He was inspired by a little girl, who was shivering in the cold. He resigned from his communications manager job in a reputed corporation, and dedicated himself completely to the cause of clothing those in need. Goonj is a self-sufficient organization and has also won the NGO of the year award for innovative practices.

Questions

(a) Why is clothing a moral issue?
(b) If you are the manager responsible for CSR arm of your company, what reasonable strategies would you frame for a similar project as the above?
(c) What is the moral strength needed to look at the poor differently?

[a] See http://www.goonj.info.

for their lost salaries and promotions since 1998. Wal-Mart is trying its best to fight this lawsuit.[5]

Gender, Law, and Living

Traditionally in India, women are likened to goddesses. Women are considered to possess the virtues of goddesses such as Durga, Laxmi, Saraswati, Parvati, etc. However, practically, women are downtrodden, ill-treated, vilified, given limited opportunities for education, burnt for dowry, and sexually abused. Female foeticide, prevalent even today, is an extreme form of violence against women. From cradle to grave, females are social, economic, political, cultural, and religious pariahs.

The constitution of the country, the civil code, the criminal code, various Acts of the parliament, and the precedents of the court judgements, all stand in support of gender equality. It is the moral behaviour of one half of the humanity against the other that is corrupt, and that needs to be changed. The law provides:

- The Workmen Compensation Act 1921
- Payment of Wages Act 1936
- Factories Act 1948
- Maternity Benefit Act 1961
- Minimum Wages Act 1948
- Employees State Insurance Act 1948
- Pensions Act 1987

In addition to this, the Constitution of India, which is regarded as the supreme law of the land, gives special protection to women.

Gender Equality and CSR

There is one common experience that women face when direct sales people, the door-to-door sales campaigners come selling their goods. When the woman of the house faces them and refuses to buy, they insist on seeing the man of the house, who can decide better. The companies seem to promote gender discrimination[6] rather than diminish it. In what way can corporations fulfil their responsibility towards gender justice? While it is unfair not to offer equal opportunity and benefits to females, it would be extremely foolish for the companies to ignore the other half of their customers. Further, there are other stakeholders such as the suppliers, shareholders, etc., who are women.

---

[5] See http://in.reuters.com/article/governmentFilingsNews/idINN1835622520090325 (25 March 2009).
[6] See: Gender and Sustainability Reporting, at http://www.ifc.org/ifcext/sustainability.nsf/AttachmentsByTitle/web_GenderReporting_index/$FILE/index.html.

Discrimination in Air

Air India hostesses demand equality

Air India is a public sector unit air carrier. In its wisdom, it lowered the retirement age of its female flying crew from fifty-eight to fifty, while males retirement age was left untouched. The Supreme Court of India, which has been a harbinger to uphold the rights of the female gender, failed exceptionally to uphold its noble tradition, and in its review, supported the carrier's decision to lower the age of its women flight crew to fifty, without revising that of males. Some of the following facts will illustrate the state employer's discriminatory policies:[a]

(a) Air hostesses are considered junior to all male crew members on board, irrespective of age and service.

(b) Even women executives are subordinate to males, aboard a flight.

(c) Women are not eligible for supervisory positions on board.

(d) All crew undergo a weight check before boarding; women crew is either grounded or penalized for overweight. Males are never grounded.

(e) Women above the age of thirty-five have to undergo gynaecological tests; males are free from any medical examination.

(f) Women are allowed to have only two children; there is no such policy for the males.

(g) Until recently, women crew members with spectacles were not allowed on board.

(h) In the 1960s, they had to retire at the age of thirty, or as soon as they got married. Over the years, the age limit was raised gradually.

(i) Pregnancy was not allowed until the Air India versus Nargesh Mirza case came to the Supreme Court, which declared that the employer's stand was arbitrary and abhorrent to society.

If a prestigious employer such as this government run international carrier can treat its own women employees, the real face and identity of the carrier, the way it is prevalent now, what will the fate of the other women employees be, in other enterprises?

Questions

(a) What is the characteristic in human nature that deliberately suppresses the female gender?

(b) What ethical principle is at stake in women seeking equality of opportunity at the workplace?

(c) What specific measures can companies take to ensure gender equality?

[a] Anupam Katakam, 'A case of discrimination' in http://www.hinduonnet.com/fline/fl2021/stories/20031024005413000.htm.

External: Impact study

The companies will do well to seriously consider the gender impact.

(a) Consider the gender impacts of products and services
(b) Adopt proper gender information for innovative product development
(c) Reconsider gender issues in supply chain labour practices
(d) Study gender impacts on the community
(e) Take feedback and inputs from women customers, to meet gender specific needs

Internal: Gender reporting

We have seen disclosures as one of the best practices of corporate governance. It has been suggested that gender reporting must be more than mere outlining of gender policies, and giving programme information. Thus, reporting should involve monitoring and evaluation efforts, identification of opportunities for continuous improvement, and show overall transparency. This will accrue several benefits to the company.

(a) Optimization of human resource—recruiting, retaining, and motivating female employees

(b) Strengthen the company's image as an equal opportunity employer, 'women friendly' and without gender bias

(c) Improve brand differentiation, the customers (half of whom are females) expect the companies whose products they patronize, to act ethically towards women

Gender Challenges and Future Opportunities

Many companies are actually quite wary of gender reporting, because such revelation may expose the company as gender biased. Yet, other companies may be too small or the nature of work, such as mining, may not show the actual image of the company in its true light. We must also admit the fact that corporate governance practices have not evolved enough, to set up standards for gender reporting. To overcome the challenges, the following recommendations may be considered:

(a) Multi-stakeholder workshops

(b) Formation of advisory groups

(c) Gender reporting practitioners' network

Corporations have yet to learn gender incorporation. But they have an example to follow. The non-governmental organizations (NGOs) and self-help groups (SHGs) are very successful in this field. In fact, the success stories of NGOs and SHGs depend on the women. Some of the well-known organizations are Grameen Bank, Microfinance ventures, Grain banks, Food for work, Cloths bank, etc.

HUMAN RIGHTS

When something is as magnificent, as sacred, as wonderful, as beautiful, and as unique as life, everything else in the world and beyond seems inconsequential. Human life is incomparable to any other form of life. Humans can want, decide, think, choose, speak, sing, read, write, gather knowledge, and build a civilization. Humans are superior to all creatures, but their worst enemy is none but themselves, because one human will not let the other survive.

Definition of Human Rights

The Universal Declaration of Human Rights, defines human rights as, 'All human beings are born free and equal in dignity and rights. They are endowed with reason and conscience and should act towards one another in a spirit of brotherhood.' In our day-to-day dealings with human rights, we may quite simply assert the much-used cliché that human right is to live and let live.

Lessons from Lakshadweep

Haseena and Tajunnisa

Haseena and Tajunnisa are two young Muslim women[a] in their twenties, who teach at a local school in Agatti, one of the small islands of Lakshadweep, the union territory off the Western Coast of India, about 250 km from the coast of Kerala. The islanders are orthodox Muslims. This is the story of how these two young ladies put their so far unknown speck of island, on the global map.

In 2004, the Darwin Initiative of UK granted funds to the Bombay Natural History Society (BNHS) for a project named International Marine Protected Area. BNHS proposed Agatti, a small island, just seven km long, and highly vulnerable to ecological change. The people live by fishing tuna fish and giant clams. The researchers had found that the larger tuna had mercury toxins, and the giant clams which were used for food, as well as to carve curios for the tourists were becoming endangered. The livelihood of the islanders was at stake.

BNHS found two willing volunteers in Haseena and Tajunnisa, who took it upon themselves, the task of the facilitators. The first step was to educate the community about the problem. They conducted programmes and presentations which educated the local people about ecology, biodiversity, and marine life. The people could relate the scientific explanations to their daily experiences. This brought the community together and aided greater participation to undertake appropriate action. The islanders being literate made the task easier as many more joined as facilitators. From the collection of data to processing and implementation was done entirely by the local people, under the leadership of Haseena and Tajunnisa. The entire community is working on the project and is reaping huge benefits from sustainable fishing, coconut growing, and tourism. The group facilitators get trained periodically in the UK, Belgium, and Australia. The group of facilitators have an equal ratio of males and females.

When the Royal Bank of Scotland awarded its prestigious prize, Earth Heroes 2008 to Haseena and Tajunnisa, it was not a surprise to the islanders.

Questions

(a) What is the difference in the functioning of an NGO and a business corporation?
(b) What prevents companies from adopting similar gender equality practices of the NGOs?
(c) Are community developments, environmental sustainability, education, gender equality, and ensured livelihoods inconsistent with company policies?

[a] Papri Sri Raman; for further details, see http://www.indiatogether.org.

In the business world, the above definition has enormous legal and moral implications. All that we have said in this book is an elaboration of this point. The preamble to the Universal Declaration states that 'every individual and every organ of society, keeping this Declaration constantly in mind, shall strive by teaching and education to promote respect for these rights and freedoms'.[7] Every organization and individual has a legitimate right to be concerned about and the responsibility to promote human rights. Business corporations bear great responsibility towards the people who depend on them for their livelihoods. There are laws and regulations enacted by every country, region, and the United Nations; there are conventions, traditions,

---

[7] The Preamble can be accessed at http://www.un.org/Overview/rights.html.

councils, and conferences on human rights. Yet we see that their violation is gross, and business corporations are one of the worst violators. Those who are supposed to take care, end up harming the very people they serve. Only moral consciousness can help overcome these problems.

Reasons for Corporations to Respect Human Rights

Returning to the Universal Declaration on Human Rights, the following arguments are some of the reasons as to why business corporations must respect and promote human rights.

Article 7   This article states that all are equal before the law and are entitled to equal protection of the law. How would you like to propose that you and your company are not equal before the law, or that you do not need its protection; or would you propose that you are above the law when you like it, but would seek the protection of the law when you are in trouble?

Article 9   The article states that no one shall be subjected to arbitrary arrest, detention, exile, etc. As a business organization, would you venture where there is always a risk of being arrested and harassed for apparently no good reason? What would you do as a manager, if your staff has been harassed and threatened by the state and non-state players, given short notice to leave the country, or unceremoniously deported? When a government changes suddenly, it brings in drastic policies against your company which is a multinational and nationalizes it. What would you do then?

Article 17   The article confers the right to own property individually, as well as in association with others. What would you do if your company is suddenly confiscated, your bank accounts frozen, and the employees charged with unlawful activities and even treason? Would you not fight, as much for your life, as to protect your business?

Articles 18 and 19   These articles refer to the freedom of thought and expression. If these freedoms are suppressed, how are you going to run an organization which needs sharing of honest opinions? How would creativity, innovation, and progress take place, which will give a competitive advantage to your business, if no one is allowed to express their thoughts?

Article 26   This article grants the right to education. Is it possible today, to do business where there is no education? Will you be able to run your company with uneducated and unskilled people?

Article 27   This article grants the right to intellectual property rights and insists that these moral and material interests need to be protected. How would you run your manufacturing company without the protection of patent rights? How would you survive if people cheat you and make money for themselves out of your products?

These are merely a few examples from which you may well be able to deduce that modern corporations cannot run for long without mutually respecting human rights. It is becoming a greater universal imperative, as business becomes increasingly global. As political boundaries are crossed and the cultural milieu is widened, the above reasons sufficiently indicate why corporations have the biggest stake in human rights, globally.

Corporations with Worst Human Rights Violations

We have already considered how in the geopolitical scenario, corporations play a willing negative role such as in arms trade, political funding, illegal lobbying, and corruption.[8] Colluding with despotic regimes, supporting military juntas, supporting subversive activities, and helping the terrorists are some of the serious transgressions by the multinational corporations. Table 20.1 lists the human rights violations by some of the well-known brands.

Table 20.1   Corporations with the worst human rights violations

Company	Human rights abuses	Case
Caterpillar	Business with known human rights violations, house demolitions, equipment that killed Palestinians and peace activists	▪ Caterpillar supplies bulldozers to the Israeli military, specifically used for demolition of Palestinian houses. ▪ Palestinians as well as others have been killed. In 2003, Rachel Corrie, a peace activist was crushed under the bulldozer. A court case is going on against the company.
Chevron	Environmental destruction, health violations, and violent killings	▪ The petrochemical company unleashed toxins by leaving more than 600 unlined oil pits in the Amazon rainforest, causing immeasurable chemical disaster. ▪ It dumped 18 billion gallons of toxic waste in the river; people use the river water for drinking and bathing. ▪ The company destroyed freshwater and farmlands. ▪ People suffered from skin problems, birth defects, miscarriages, and cancer. ▪ People had to migrate; it caused large displacement of people. ▪ The Nigerian army supported the company and opened fire on its own people.
Coca-Cola	Violent killings, kidnap and torture, water privatization, discriminatory practices	▪ The leading global company is also a leader in human rights abuses. ▪ In Columbia, several labour union leaders were killed. The Columbian labour union SINALTRAUNAL members have been kidnapped, tortured, and killed. ▪ In Turkey, the drivers who were hired by Coca-Cola have been beaten and tortured by the police, along with their families.

Contd

---

[8] See http://www.globalexchange.org.

Table 20.1 Contd

Company	Human rights abuses	Case
		■ In Placimada, Kerala, India, the company depleted the water resources completely, thus forcing thousands of farmers to abandon their fields; whatever water was available got contaminated, causing innumerable skin, eye, and digestion problems; similar is the situation in cities like Varanasi and Thane. ■ In the US, the African–American employees have sued the company for racial discrimination in pay and promotions.
DOW Chemical	Chemical weapons, poisonous chemicals, dumping of toxins, environmental problems, and health problems causing death	■ The company caused a chemical disaster in Vietnam through Agent Orange, causing suffering to both the Vietnamese and US soldiers, animals, and the environment. ■ It provided pesticides to Saddam Hussein in 1998, ignoring warnings of its being used as a chemical weapon. ■ In 2001, the company took over the Union Carbide Factory that killed thousands of people in the heinous Bhopal Gas Tragedy in 1984, and tens of thousands of people still continue to suffer. ■ It has not honoured Union Carbide's undertakings and the settlement of the liabilities.
Lockheed Martin	War profiteering, war mongering	■ It is the world's largest military contractor. The company earned $21.9 billion in Pentagon contracts in Iraq, in the 2003 invasion. ■ Profits have been tripling ever since. The company is very efficient in marketing war. ■ It works behind the scenes to influence public policy and US decision-making in foreign affairs, particularly in the areas of defence.
Nestle	Abusive child labour, repression of workers' rights, aggressive marketing of harmful products, violation of health and environmental laws	■ The raw cocoa for the chocolate comes from the labour of children, bonded labourers, and slaves. ■ Hundreds of thousands of children under the age of 12 work over-time to supply the raw material. ■ Aggressive marketing done in developing and poor countries, to replace breastfeeding has caused disastrous consequences concerning both the health and economy. ■ Its infant formula contained the chemical Isopropylithioxanthone (ITX)—packaging ink— and the company knowingly sold the product. ■ The company is most unpopular with its workers; it is the most boycotted company in the world.

The above is a tiny tip of a very large iceberg. One would have thought that with greater globalization and interdependence, greater responsibility will be shown. It appears that the multinationals have lost their mission. The moral leadership is perhaps a non-existent commodity in the globalized market. Should corporations not become more conscious about their global role and own responsibility for human rights? Can they not influence human rights in a positive way?

Common people are creating movements around the world and are trying to bring corporations to the book and face the law. It is a shame that corporations with so much knowledge capital fail to perceive the rights of their customers.

From Ogoniland to Agonyland

Ken Saro-Wiwa versus Shell

Ken Saro-Wiwa was a Nigerian author, who led a movement to save the River Niger Delta, where the Ogoni people live. The region is also known as Ogoniland. The Royal Dutch Shell plc was causing environmental destruction due to its extensive oil drilling and mindless spread of effluents and toxins, both on the land and in water.[a] Shell has been extracting oil from the delta region since 1958. It ran its business unhindered, by suppressing the public complaints about environment damage through its very cosy relationship with the ruling military regime of Abacha. With so much oil available, any other country would have an economic boom like the Middle Eastern oil producing countries; but Shell and the Nigerian government succeeded in reducing 70 per cent of Nigeria's population to live in abject poverty, on less than a dollar a day. Oil spills, gas fares, effluents, and toxins have destroyed farming, fishing, and drinking water sources, and caused widespread deforestation and soil contamination, rendering the Ogoni people to indescribable poverty and agony.

The Movement for the Survival of the Ogoni People (MOSOP) was founded in 1990. Within a couple of years, a majority of the Ogoni people started supporting the movement that was committed to a non-violent struggle. Ken Saro-Wiwa, the founder of the movement, through his charismatic leadership and writing, attracted the world's attention to the suffering of the Ogoni people. Shell did not want to lose easy business and the military ruler did not want to lose power. So they banded together against Saro-Wiwa and his movement. There was open violence against the farmers, who were shot dead in their farms, or arrested, tortured, and then jailed. The women were raped, and terror was unleashed by the military ruler, through his soldiers and the support of Shell.

Saro-Wiwa and his colleagues were arrested and beaten up several times. The more they were tortured, the more the world came to know about it. Shell would call upon the Nigerian police whenever they needed to encroach upon the farming land or forests to sink oil rigs or when the activists opposed the company's work. They called these security operations. Shell wanted an end solution to their problems. Saro-Wiwa was their biggest hurdle. It developed a strategy, which the Nigerian government willingly followed. Saro-Wiwa, along with eight more of his colleagues, was arrested on the charges of killing four Ogoni elders. The false witnesses that were collected recanted. But the summary trial proceeded. Shell's lawyer was granted the privilege by the Nigerian government, to watch the trial. The director of Shell's subsidiary gave Saro-Wiwa's younger brother the option to arrange for amnesty of his brother and his friends, if they categorically gave up their movement. He refused.

The especially instituted tribunal declared Saro-Wiwa and his eight colleagues guilty. Saro-Wiwa made the following statement before the tribunal, 'I repeat that we all stand before history. I and my colleagues are not the only ones on trial. Shell is here on trial and it is as well that it is represented by a counsel said to be holding a watching brief. The Company has, indeed, ducked this particular trial, but its day will surely come and the lessons learnt here may prove useful to it for there is no doubt in my mind that the ecological war that the Company has waged in the Delta will be called to question sooner than later and the crimes of that war be duly punished. The crime of the Company's

Contd

Box Contd

dirty wars against the Ogoni people will also be punished.'

'In my innocence of the false charges I face here, in my utter conviction, I call upon the Ogoni people, the peoples of the Niger delta, and the oppressed ethnic minorities of Nigeria to stand up now and fight fearlessly and peacefully for their rights. History is on their side. God is on their side. For the Holy Quran says in Sura 42, verse 41: "All those that fight when oppressed incur no guilt, but Allah shall punish the oppressor. Come the day."[b]

Saro-Wiwa and his eight colleagues were hanged. It is said that Saro-Wiwa was hanged last because he was forced to see the execution of his eight colleagues. It is also said that they had to take a couple of takes to hang him. These were his last words, 'Lord take my soul, but the struggle continues.' Ken Saro-Wiwa (10 October 1941–10 November 1995).

There are several cases filed against Shell by human rights organizations around the world. The most significant ones are the cases in the US Supreme Court, by Centre for Constitutional Rights and Earth Rights International, charging Shell of human rights violations in Nigeria, summary executions, crimes against humanity, torture, inhuman treatment, and arbitrary arrest and detention. The trial date was set for 26 May 2009.

Questions

(a) What would you say and do, if you were one of the managers of Shell in Nigeria?

(b) Does not the principle of Utilitarianism—greatest good of the greatest number—apply to Shell, which makes a few people suffer in Nigeria, so that people around the globe can be served with oil supplies at a lower price?

(c) Where do justice and ethics meet in the above case?

[a] See http://wiwavshell.org/the-case-against-shell/.

[b] As quoted on the Greenpeace site at http://archive.greenpeace.org/comms/ken/murder.html.

ANIMAL RIGHTS

Millions of web pages, thousands of books, hundreds of animal activist organizations, and dozens of theories for and against animal protection, all come to a standstill when I see a *Jain Muni*—the bare bodied Jain monk—plodding his path surrounded by his disciples. He is *digamber*, implying that he is sky-clad, and has renounced all worldly goods, including a stitch of cloth to cover his nakedness. He does not consider himself naked, because he is adorned with true wisdom. His disciples encircle him to protect him from the vulgar gaze of the passersby. He knows that when they see him bare, they see their own moral nakedness; but he does not express it. He is too humble to do it; he does not need to do it because the beholder will realize it. Wherever he goes, the *muni* teaches that the meaning of life is *karuna*, or compassion. Compassion to all sentient beings is the cornerstone of morality; right living is a derivative of *ahimsa*, or non-violence towards all the living beings.

Problem

Animals and animal products are a part and parcel of our daily living. Animal products are used mindlessly in food, clothing, footwear, accessories, and a myriad other uses.

The animals have been exploited as beasts of burden, travel, sports, recreation, and as exhibits in zoos.[9] Animal husbandry is one of the largest industries, where the farming of animals is prevalent; this in turn gives rise to a very lucrative fodder industry. The industry is worth hundreds of billions of dollars. The pharmaceuticals, cosmetics, and scientific research industries use animals for experimenting and testing. There thrives a very profitable industry of pet, manufacture of pet foods, its advertising and marketing; pets trafficking (mostly illegal) is a booming business, particularly while dealing with exotic animals, reptiles, birds, and fish. Following are some of the ethical problems associated with the animal industry.

Farmed animals It is estimated that approximately 50 billion animals are raised and killed for food annually. Out of the six billion people on the earth, two billion are very poor and they can ill-afford meat in their daily diet; another three billion people live on modest means; it appears that most animals are eaten by the rest one billion people. The farmed animals live in crammed conditions, they are transported pitilessly, and slaughtered on a large scale, often without the stipulated practices to mitigate pain. Chickens and pigs are thrown into scalding water even while they are still in the throes of death, after being decapitated; bigger animals such as calves, cows, horses, etc., are hung from hooks, with life still twitching in them, and are skinned and disjointed. Most companies defend their position by saying that they follow strict legal norms, and weakly admit that the outsourced products cannot be equally accounted for.

Animals for research Medical research, medicines, cosmetics, pesticides, etc., need repeated and excessive experimentation and tests to find out the effects of the products on human beings. Rats, mice, rabbits, dogs, cats, apes, monkeys, frogs, etc., are used for such experimentation. These are injected with the lethal viruses, acids, chemicals, and pesticides and their limbs and internal organs are dissected. The research supporters say that there is no other alternative.

Animals for entertainment Bulls, buffaloes, horses, camels, snakes, dogs, cocks, eagles, hawks, pigeons, and parrots are used in sports. Their training involves pain, as sticks, electric shocks, etc., are used. The training and practice sessions in circuses are cruel; the animals constantly live in crammed conditions; they perform acts and tricks unnatural to them; it causes them extreme strain and pain. If there is a perverted image of morality, then circus is one of them, which is branded as a form of family entertainment.

Environmental disaster Mindless game hunting has depleted the wildlife population, thus causing huge gaps in the food chain. The near extinction of tigers around the globe tells the sorry tale of the diminished and decimated wildlife and the green cover of the planet.

---

[9] Stephanie Ernst, 'Major animal rights issues and controversies', in http://animalrights.change.org/blog/view/major_animal_rights_issues_and_controversies.

With groups arrayed on two sides of the spectrum of protection of animals and animal rights, the problem is far from finding a solution. The animal rights activists ridicule the idea of the humane killing of animals. The animal industry accuses the activists for unleashing violence on humans, to protect the animals. The industry is of the view that without animal products, not only food, but all the other by-products without which life would be unthinkable, would make people go without jobs and food. They advocate that the activists must realize the greater good of the humans. The human rights activists say that all that have life, consciousness of pain and pleasure are no different than human beings, who are also primarily animals. Therefore, the very same right to life must be granted to them.

Animals for Human Benefit

Morality is a code of conduct that human beings have created for themselves; thereby, they have assumed all the rights to themselves. We have been putting animals to use for our own benefit, ever since our existence. Since there is an increased consciousness about the rights being extended to animals, the following question resurfaces. Should animals be used for human benefit?[10]

Livestock   Imagine India without domestic animals like cows, buffaloes, oxen, sheep, donkeys, horses, mules, camels, and yaks. The economy of a billion people depends on our animals. India has the highest per capita animals in the world, and we depend on them for work, nutritious milk, transport, manure for the fields, and so on. Without our domestic animals, life would be impossible.

Animal rights or animal welfare   In the emotive hype of animal rights, we may lose the much pragmatic virtue of animal welfare. Animal rights activists advocate an evocative argument about the torture and death of animals; they showcase humans as insensitive. It may raise our consciousness and help us become sympathetic to the physical sufferings of the animals. At the same time, we may argue that the use of animals has been an obvious fact. No one accuses us of stealing the milk from the young of the animals, or of other malpractices for getting milk from the animals for our food. We are also not blamed for using them to plough our fields or pull our carts. In other words, there is a place for the responsible use of animals.

Questionable uses   We have seen above that uses of animals for research in labs, slaughtering them for food, and obtaining other by-products from the animals has been controversial. We have to admit that organizations like People for Ethical Treatment of Animals (PETA) have valid arguments to support their case. However, it must also be admitted that there are adequate laws to safeguard these activities. The business corporations and other institutions would have to make conscientious decisions

---

[10] Ashley Brander, 'Should animals be used for human benefit' in https://www.msu.edu/~brandera/portfolio/Should%20Animals%20be%20used%20for%20Human%20Benefit.pdf.

Nature Worshippers

Bishnois of Rajasthan

While the rest of the world only waxes eloquent about the environmental protection and liberation of animals, the Bishnois of Rajasthan[a] and its surrounding areas live what others preach, and do not talk. The Bishnois are a reformed Hindu sect, who worship nature and live their lives in its harmony. In the mid-fifteenth century, Guru Jambeshwar, fed up with the Hindu–Muslim communal conflicts and having suffered paucity of water in the desert of Rajasthan, founded a religious sect with twenty-nine principles.

The name Bishnoi is derived from the number of principles—*bis* means twenty and *nav* means nine. Together, they form the word, *bisnavi*, which is commonly pronounced as Bishnoi. The principles were all about truth and honesty, non-violence, and reverence to all forms of life—humans, animals, or trees. They believed that one should be ready to sacrifice one's life for the sake of the animals or trees. The Guru also taught that the black buck needs special protection, since it is so delicate that it can die of fright. The dead should not be cremated, lest trees be cut for the purpose, but buried and become one with the earth. This principle even attracted the Muslims, and thus, the communal conflict was resolved.

In 1730, the Maharaja of Jodhpur was building a palace and men were sent to cut trees for timber. A Bishnoi woman, who came to realize that someone was cutting trees, ran to protest, accompanied by her two young daughters. The men said that she had a choice between paying them money or her life. She refused to give money, and willingly offered her life. Her daughters followed her similarly. By this time, the news spread in the surrounding villages and villagers rushed to save the trees. The king's men said, 'One life for one tree.' The men, women, and children offered themselves to be felled by the axes, and did not allow the trees to be cut. When the king's men had beheaded

363 people and more people were not afraid to die, the killers panicked. But the people kept embracing the trees. (This became the inspiration for the Chipko Movement of our times.) When the king came to know about the massacre, he was full of remorse. He passed a decree that prohibited the killing of animals and the cutting of trees. Violation of the decree would entail severe punishment; no one would be spared, including the rulers. The decree has been followed ever since, by all the rulers, colonialists, and the modern government. Some celebrities who recently violated this statute are undergoing prosecution.

The life of the Bishnois is very simple, but environmentally sustainable. Their villages are an oasis of biodiversity and plentiful water, in the midst of the harsh desert. There is no modern equipment, but there are plenty of natural practices that preserve water in aquifers, irrigate the fields, and care for the domestic as well as the wild animals. Indeed, the wild animals such as deer, antelope, the black buck, and the ubiquitous peahens and peacocks are a part and parcel of their community life. It is not a rare sight when the young fawns are equally cared for like one's own offspring. The dogs are trained not to attack the wildlife. Cats have a pride of place for catching rodents and snakes, and are fed with yogurt and milk. This sounds straight out of fiction, but it cannot be anything but the truth.

Questions

(a) What is the moral value of living in harmony with nature?

(b) What inspiration can managers derive from the Bishnois, and design future models of human habitats?

(c) What new business models can be created for the use of animals with a purpose?

[a] Aunpama Bhattacharya, 'Bishnois: Fierce Custodians of Nature' in http://www.lifepositive.com/spirit/traditional-paths/tribal-faiths/bishnoi.asp; also see: http://www.rajasthanunlimited.com/folk/bishnoi.html.

to seek ethical ways, and alternative methods to achieve their goals. To begin with, abiding by the existing laws is the best way to begin.

Fundamental freedoms of animals   In order to treat animals ethically, we must follow five fundamental ways:

(a) Freedom from thirst, hunger, and malnutrition
(b) Freedom from discomfort
(c) Freedom from pain, injury, and disease
(d) Freedom to express natural/normal behaviour
(e) Freedom from fear and distress

We do not live in a perfect world; but as intelligent human beings, we are evolving and developing. Maybe, one day human beings will raise their consciousness to the one like that of Lord Mahavira and the other sages and seers, and grant complete freedom to the animals. Maybe, science will advance so much that we will stop using animals for food or any of its by-products.

SUMMARY

- All living beings have a right to live; this is the foundation of morality.

- Animal rights concern our reverence to life, the respect we must have for all life that has the will to live.

- Animals are a part of the people's economy; we are known by the way we treat them.

- Corporations are a part of the social contract; they have no right to do business without respecting the fundamental rights of the people.

- Corporations can help eradicate this problem by making it a part of their disclosure responsibilities.

- For businesses, animals are a capital, an indispensable resource, which if used well, pays dividends; hence, their welfare is the businesses' welfare.

- Gender inequality is one of the unjustifiable features of modern businesses.

- Human rights are the essence of a social contract; society exists because of it.

- Poverty is the largest negative economic phenomena of the world; businesses can devise strategies to overcome it.

- Problems are challenges to overcome; some of them seem unsolvable because of our lack of will to solve them.

- The problems of poverty, gender bias, human rights, and animal rights are actually easily solvable, only if we have the moral courage to refuse to have them, by not being greedy, acknowledging that all are equal, and always having reverence for life.

KEY TERMS

Animal   Living beings, mammals, reptiles, etc.

Clothing   That which covers and protects a bare body.

Equality   Parity, equal opportunity.

Food   Stuff that sustains life.

Gender   Sexual characteristics—masculinity and femininity.

Life   Existence between birth and death.

Poverty   Privation of resources.

Reverence to life   Respecting the will to live.

Rights   Claims—natural, legal, economic, political, etc.

Shelter   That protects from the vagaries of environment.

Starvation   Death due to lack of food.

CONCEPT REVIEW QUESTIONS

1. How would you describe an acceptable human existence?

2. What responsibilities do corporations have towards the poor?

3. Why is it important to maintain gender equality in business corporations?

4. What is the meaning of human rights for the people working in corporations?

5. Why should corporations respect the human rights?

6. Can human rights create geopolitical problems? Explain with cases.

7. How are animals a resource for business enterprises?

CRITICAL THINKING QUESTIONS

1. Are there any poor corporations? Is it important to help them?

2. Do corporations respect human rights? Explain with examples, when they have these rights, and when they forfeit it.

3. How corporations are found guilty of human rights abuses?

4. How far does the international law succeed in keeping in check the corporations that violate human rights?

5. Can animals claim a legal redress?

FURTHER READING

Malcolm MacIntosh, *Visions of Ethical Business*, Financial Times Prentice Hall, London (2002).

Paul Gordon Lauren, *The Evolution of International Human Rights: Visions Seen*, University of Pennsylvania Press (2003).

Norman Stockman, Norman Bonney, and Xuewen Sheng, "Women's Work in East and West", M.E. Sharpe (1995).

Peter Singer, 'Animal Liberation', HarperCollins (2001).

CASE STUDY

Fowl Industry

Solution against Poverty

Poultry farming in India was mostly a backyard venture till 1960s. Indigenous chicken constituted the major share. Their productivity was around 60–70 eggs per bird per year. During the past three decades, the poultry scenario in the country has changed dramatically. Today poultry farming has transformed itself into an organized industry. It plays a major role in the fight against malnutrition and poverty among the rural masses of our country. The importance of poultry sector in solving the problems of unemployment and under-employment is well-conceived by planners and personnel in the developmental programmes. Among the livestock vocations, poultry farming requires only less capital investment and it has at the same time added advantage of ensuring quick returns.[a]

—National Open School

Introduction: Poultry Business

It is said that Indians domesticated the fowl more than 3,000 years ago, and used it to obtain eggs and meat. Today, it is one of the very important contributors to the economy of rural India and semi-urban India. It contributes close to $300 million to the GDP. Despite the drawbacks of the recent years due to avian flu and culling of millions of birds, poultry products are popular and there are trends of a steady growth. However, India merely ranks seventeenth among the poultry production index; it is the fifth largest producer of eggs, with a production of over 34 billion eggs, and ranks ninth in the poultry meat production, with six lakh tons. This growth is expected to triple before 2020. The Southern states of India—Andhra Pradesh, Karnataka, Kerala, and Tamil Nadu account for 45 per cent of India's egg production; the Eastern states, for 20 per cent. The egg consumption rate is growing faster than that of meat. The four Southern states have a per capita consumption of 57 eggs and 0.5 kg of meat, while the Central and Eastern states have a per capita consumption of 18 eggs and 0.13 kg of meat.[b]

There are small scale and large scale producers; the bulk of the production is accounted for by the small scale producers. The poultry business employs approximately 1.6 million people; 80 per cent of them are directly employed, while the rest 20 per cent are in allied areas such as feed, equipment, medicines, etc. There are an equal number of people, that is, 1.6 million involved in the business of marketing and sales of poultry products. India's production consists of table eggs, meat, live birds, egg powder, and frozen yolk, amounting to Rs 5 billion.

The industry is promising, but suffers from several drawbacks.

(a) Lack of basic infrastructure such as storage facility, transport, chain of cold storages

(b) This lack of storage causes price fluctuations of this perishable commodity

(c) Marketing is still unorganized and inefficient

(d) There are too many agents and intermediaries

(e) Non-availability of nutritious food

(f) Lack of right medical knowledge and its administration

Part I

Factory Farming

Factory farming may be on a large scale or a small scale. It involves land, labour, buildings, equipment, poultry food, and medicines. It is capital intensive, but with expectations of high returns. Factory farming is highly organized and functions according to the managerial standards. Modernized hatcheries, systematic confining and growing plan for the fowls, scientific feeding and tending help efficient industrial management. Further, marketing and sales too are a highly specialized business. Factory farming looks beyond the domestic markets and pitches for exports. It also efficiently manages its other by-products such as feathers, for high-end use in upholstery, pillows, and quilts. The bird droppings are processed into organic manure; bones too are put to appropriate use. Thus, the modern poultry industry, like any other, must adopt up-to-date machinery and management practices.

Suguna's case

Welcome to Coimbatore, or rather, it would be presently more appropriate to say, welcome to Suguna. Indeed, the little poultry farm with just 200 fowls that B. Soundarajan started in 1986 is the leader of poultry farms and poultry products in the country. It is ranked among the top ten poultry companies in the world. It operates in eleven states of India, and runs fully integrated operations, which consist of broiler and layer farming, hatcheries, feed mills, processing plants, vaccines, and

---

[a] Introduction to the Poultry Farming Course of the National Open School; the minimum qualification required to enrol for the Self-Employment Course is a Class X pass certificate. See http://www.nos.org/poultry.htm.
[b] All statistics are as per 2004. For further details, see http://business.mapsofindia.com/rural-economy/industries/poultry.html.

export facilities. Suguna has a successful chain of modern retail outlets. The ISO certified company has a wide range of products and is well stocked across the country, whether in supermarkets or small retail shops. The following is a fact sheet of Suguna[c]:

- No. 1 in Indian broiler production
- 10th largest poultry enterprise in the world
- Rs 2030 crore turnover
- Presence in 11 states
- 4,800 strong workforce
- More than 15,000 farmers
- 25,000 channel partners
- 500,000 people benefit from indirect employment
- 395 million chickens produced per annum
- 36 hatcheries
- 50 feed mills
- 1.56 million tons feed production per annum
- 10,000 tons of processed chicken meat per annum
- First company in the poultry industry to implement Oracle E Business Suite Integrated ERP System
- Commissioned India's largest Automated Feed Mill in Hoskote near Bangalore
- First poultry company to obtain the direct soya procurement licence from the Government of Maharashtra in India, to purchase directly from the *mandi*
- Successfully implemented NEFT and RTGS payment systems for farmers that will benefit the farmer society
- Continuously working to protect and preserve environment by distributing over 25 lakh saplings

Suguna has succeeded in establishing a large scale industry with wide operations and product differentiation. It has also created subsidiary industries and has given value to both the shareholders and the stakeholders. It even boasts of a tree plantation campaign of planting over twenty-five lakh trees. However, this model of poultry has not succeeded in realizing our objective of making a difference to the poor.

There are several other farmers in this country who have turned entrepreneurs, not on an industrial scale like Suguna, but quite admirably, whose examples can be imitated.

Sidhu's case

Ranjit Singh Sidhu[d] comes from the heart of Punjab, and is a farmer to the core. He inherited thirty-two acres of land from his father, who was a World War II veteran. Despite being a science graduate, Sidhu wanted to pursue his heart's desire; he became a farmer. Very soon, he realized that the rice and wheat cycle were not yielding much, and so he turned to cultivating potato and seasonal fruits such as melons and mush melons. He loved to do his own marketing and sales, and thus was rewarded with better returns. But even this eventually gave diminishing marginal returns. It is then that Sidhu thought of going into the poultry business. He built a large shed that was good enough for 50,000 fowls, but his relatives, friends, and others in the poultry business dissuaded him by citing innumerable problems associated with the birds, their feed, and the diseases they suffered from. Sidhu accepted the challenge and cautiously started his business with just 500 fowls, in 1981.

Today, Sidhu boasts of a business, with close to four lakh birds producing a phenomenal nine crore eggs, and the turnover is a hefty Rs 14 crore plus. Sidhu has managed his farm well, with his own innovations to equip his farm, rather than investing in costly machinery. He keeps visiting the best farms in the country and abroad, and comes back and designs structures, equipment, and techniques to suit his needs. Presently, his son who is computer savvy has designed a monitoring system and this saves the Sidhus an enormous amount of money. The mere management of monitoring eggs from breakage, saves over Rs 8 lakh a year. Due to the father and son's personal interests, constant

[c] The statistics as per the Suguna website can be accessed at http://www.sugunapoultry.com/about_suguna/overview/factsheet.asp.
[d] Ramesh Vinayak, 'Enterprise—It is a Coop', in http://indiatoday.intoday.in/index.php?option=com_content&task=view&issueid=79&id=2973&sectionid=20&secid=33&Itemid=1.

vigilance and care, the birds have been free from diseases and have kept the fears of avian flu successfully at bay. The Sidhus are among the 2000 small scale poultry farmers in Punjab, and have received the chief minister's award for excellence in that category.

No doubt that such a success story as that of the Sidhus is worth emulating. It has all the rural ingredients—low investment, small land holding, quick returns which can be ploughed back into the enterprise, etc. Despite the success story, it does not appear that a model such as this is going to help attain our stated goals. There are some serious problems that are ethical in nature, which plague the poultry industry. All these problems may be avoided in a new business model that we are going to propose as a new paradigm to attain our objectives.

Part II

Poultry Ethics

One sight at the way how the fowls are transported in our cities and towns, should give us goose bumps in utter disgust at the appalling cruelty, but it does not. We are used to it. Sometimes, since we think that we are helpless to do anything, we just harden our hearts and look the other way. The birds are hung upside down, with their legs fastened together onto a cycle that might carry a couple of dozen birds. They are crammed in small wired cages, stacked upon each other like soft drink crates, and transported openly in the hot sun. No one hears their cry, although they shriek, are frightened, and smeared in their own excreta. They are slaughtered in the live selling chicken shops, in the crudest possible way. Following are some of the serious ethical problems we will face if we go into large industrial poultry farming.

Battery farming Battery farming consists of putting the egg laying fowls in small wire-mesh cages, and allowing no space for movement. This prevents the eggs from getting damaged, otherwise they would have been laid on the poultry floor and could be trampled upon. The birds consume less feed, since less appetite is created due to lack of

movement. The layers lay more eggs than those on the shed floor. Studies have revealed the obvious torture that a living being suffers due to lack of movement. The calcium demand for these birds is high, and with total lack of exercise, they suffer from osteoporosis. The hens also break their beaks and bones in the battery cages. This has led to an outcry from the experts as well as the animal welfare organizations. Several European countries have banned the use of battery farming; by 2012 battery farming will be illegal in all the EU countries.

Cruelty Apart from confinement, there are other atrocities perpetrated on the birds. Drugging and performing surgery is quite common. The beaks of the chicks are trimmed so that they do not peck others and harm them by causing infection and disease. The birds are in constant stress due to lack of space and over-crowding; they express their boredom and frustration by pecking other birds.

Food In industrial farming, it was thought that the food would be standardized, and as a result, poultry food would be well regulated. However, in order to induce a high growth in the shortest possible time, the manufacturers use a combination of grains, several fish, and animal by-products to feed the birds. The dangers emanating from such food are obvious. The most feared one is the dreaded salmonella infection. In recent years, the poultry industry has lost millions of dollars after the detection of this infection.

Health Large farms have the advantage of giving better healthcare[e] through systematized, well attended, and professional personnel. However, ever since the pandemic of avian flu (H5N1 type), the poultry industry, both big and small, is worried. The avian flu is classified as pandemic because it has spread to all the continents, and humans are the likely victims of it. Millions of fowls have been culled and are still being culled around the globe. Health experts fear that human flu viruses and bird flu viruses could unleash a new virulent virus if their genetic material is exchanged. Such a possibility is looming large. Hence, looking

---

[e] See http://www.who.int/csr/disease/avian_influenza/en/.

after the health of poultry farms and the birds should be of utmost priority. It all depends on the food and medicines that are administered to poultry birds. Governments are discovering the unethical practices in food preparation and drug administration, and are taking steps against such practices. In the smaller towns and villages of India, people do not heed to the government's order to cull the birds. They clandestinely eat them or sell them at lower rates.

Environment Every poultry bird drops about 100 grams of excrement a day; this multiplied by billions of birds is millions of tons of excrement alone. Huge quantities of hot water for scalding and cold water for rinsing are used in the processing plants. The place where all the waste and effluents end up will have an environmental impact.[f] Processing of excrement into manure and recycling the water are recommended. Due to the legal requirements, large plants abide by these norms to some extent. Small scale and household farms do no such thing. It is a profitable business if it is done; it can be hazardous if the effluents and chicken waste end up in lakes, seas, water bodies, etc. They can also severely pollute the groundwater. One environmental problem leads to another; it will affect the biodiversity and will cause great damage to the environment, animals, and human beings.

Genetic engineering Poultry has been one of the first subjects in genetic engineering.[g] If we could create a scientifically modified species that could increase production efficiently, and reduce diseases considerably, we could have a booming poultry industry. These assumptions and experiments have serious ethical problems. The genetically modified foods and cotton have already caused disaster. Avian flu almost shut down poultry farming. Now, genetic modification with no surety for its success is not something to be risked.

Is there a way out of the above problems?

Part III
Laying Golden Eggs

Indeed, if we adopt a smart, simple, and intelligent model for our poultry, the result will be nothing short of our happy hens laying the proverbial golden eggs. We will not have to kill the hen; we can have the hen and eat the egg too. In our new model, we will be able to overcome all the above ethical problems. In addition, we can have really happy hens running free in their own environment. It would generate employment, nutrition, raise the standards of living, and create peace and harmony in society. Yes, the hens can do it!

Back to village with Gandhi

The new poultry model is based on Gandhiji's paradigm of a self-sufficient village. Gandhiji wanted the village to be self-sufficient in clothing. So he advocated the use of *Khadi*, hand-woven using a *Charkha*. We could have several other village occupations, and poultry could be one of them. A concerted effort by the villagers in every village of India could generate enough meat and eggs to feed the entire world. According to the 2001 census, India has 6,38,365 villages, where 80 per cent of the over one billion population lives. Even if a household in the village maintains just about a dozen birds, the production thereof is going to swamp the earth with food.

Small poultry holding (SPH)

Each household can begin a very small poultry holding. All it needs is an unsophisticated coop, some grains and a small existing yard with some green grass, where the birds can move around and forage through the yard for food.

(a) Little flocks of poultry need no industrial feed

(b) The birds are domestic and have freedom

(c) Neither much time nor effort is needed to take special care of them

---

[f] See http://www.innovations-report.com/html/reports/agricultural_sciences/report-48133.html; http://www.wattpoultry.com/poultryinternational/article.aspx?id=12698.

[g] Karen Davis, 'The Ethics of Genetic Engineering and the Futuristic Fate of Domestic Fowl', the alliance for Animals Conference, University of Wisconsin-Madison (12 October 1996); see http://www.upc-online.org/genetic.html for more details.

(d) If the flocks are very small, say about a dozen, they supplement the home income and food needs

(e) If the flocks are about fifty in number, they could sustain the families on their own; if they are over a hundred, it would liken to a handsome cottage industry and fetch much more than what village artisans and farmers could earn

SPH co-operative

Despite the highest per capita animal ratio, India was struggling for milk and milk products, until one man, P.J. Kurien, saw that cooperatives could solve the milk problem. Thus, the white revolution began in Anand, Gujarat, which empowered the village folks in the surrounding villages. Today, its brand Amul is a global competitor, whose legs are firmly planted in the villages of Anand.

Marketing Poultry cooperatives can solve the problems of marketing; the villagers will bring in the birds—layers or broilers—as per the determined categories, and they will be collected as per age and weight. Likewise, the eggs—white and brown—will be collected and the cooperatives will take up their distribution and sale.

Disposable income This will ensure a steady income for the villagers, which can be used to supplement their domestic needs, their health, and education for their children, and even make a saving.

Micro-credit The villagers can take small loans individually or through cooperatives, to start or expand their poultries. National Bank of Agriculture and Rural Development (NABARD) are already giving loans for various programmes in the rural areas. It could include poultry on its list.

NREGS Instead of hunting for some un-gainful employment for the unemployed, the National Rural Employment Guarantee Scheme could give the scheme money, which is the wages for 100 days, to start a household poultry.

Provision of hatcheries The cooperatives can supply hatchery services and medicines to make the SPHs more efficient. Thus, these costly equipment need not be owned by individuals.

Organic poultry

Organic farming is not new to India; it is the country's traditional farming and the chickens on the farm too are a natural heritage. Indian villages were natural depositories of organic farming, until the industrially produced fertilizer came into use. The cow dung, along with dry leaves, crops waste, and other natural biodegradable wastes used to be the natural fertilizers for the fields. The grain that grew was the food for both man and beast, and poultry was no exception. The chicken were fed with the grain that remained after chaffing and sieving the harvested crops. The little, broken corns of grain were adequate, as the fowls were set free to forage in the fields and orchards. Thus, there were no chemicals used, directly or indirectly. These birds were usually quite healthy and robust because a major portion of their food came from the plants. Nature had taught them to look after themselves. It was men who crammed them up in battery cages, gave them hybrid food, injected antibiotics, grew them in record time to make quick money, and those who ate it became a part of the harmful chemical cycle.

Small flocks Poultry should be a small flock reared on a farm; this will ensure space and natural surroundings for them.

Food The poultry will depend on what is available on the farm; in some parts of the country, small farmers are feeding them with termites. It is very easy to provide termites. In a pot, place some cow dung, some leaves and a bit of moisture if the matter is dry. The pot will be full of termites in a day or two. Studies have proved that this is a healthy food for the fowls.

Cooperative To speed up production, consult the cooperatives and the agricultural departments.

The demand for organic products is abounding and there is a premium on these products; at times, the prices are more than double that of the usually marketed goods. Supermarkets have special sections reserved for organic products, including chickens and eggs. To the disappointment of many, a lot of establishments sell organic products which are really not what they claim to be. How can one distinguish an organic farm egg from a non-organic egg? Only integrity and honesty will help organic farming in the long run. With the training available, one is eligible to get employment in a poultry factory, or start one's own business in a scientific way.

Careers in poultry

Today, secondary school education is freely available in the villages. Those who pass this school can get industrially trained. Education and training in poultry farming is available in various educational institutions and colleges. Generally, it is a one-year course, which deals with poultry production, breeding, the varieties of birds and their needs, diseases, the equipment, and the general management of a poultry farm. Extensive knowledge and skills on breeding farms, broiler farms, and layer farms are imparted in these institutions.

For those seeking higher careers, there are advanced studies in agriculture, and specialization courses in animal husbandry and poultry. Research and development in poultry is highly in demand. The Institute of Poultry Management (IPM) in Pune offers a full-fledged programme in poultry related disciplines. There are other such institutes in the country.

Part IV

Conclusion

The above has been an unusual case, where a case is created. It is because the present scenario in India does not offer encouraging signs of any policy or government initiative that is going to solve the basic needs of its most poor populace, namely food, shelter, and clothing. Just as Gandhiji saw a glimmer of hope in a piece of thread, or there was some hope in the above case or in one that has been created especially to highlight an unsolvable problem, there is hope in this simple, domesticated bird.

for the poorest of the poor. It will help produce food, shelter, clothing, employment, education, self-sufficiency, and economic growth. When poverty is wiped out from the six and a half lakh villages of India, the global implications of it will be enormous. There could be hundreds of thousands of Soundarajans and Sidhus spread all over the length and breadth of India.

Discussion Questions

1. Has poverty any moral value?
2. Should the poor blame themselves for their fate?
3. Do you think that the *khadi* suggested by Gandhiji, or the poultry farming suggested in the last case is more of a symbolic gesture than real?
4. Are not the poor people of this country a big liability?
5. What prevents India from adopting the most successful Western economy?
6. Do our villages help sustain the environment?
7. The government has not succeeded in educating our villagers, or providing them with sustainable economic programmes, and taking care of their health in the past sixty years. Can you suggest a better plan?
8. What are the ethical standards by which you can analyse this case?

Going Further . . .

- Get a social scientist to address the issue of the vicious circle of poverty, to help you to reflect over it.
- Express only your views and perspectives on poverty, the environment, employment, rural problems, the economy, and the global impact of Indian villages, etc.

ETHICAL DEVELOPMENT PROGRAMME

Management Training

Four Projects

In accordance with the objectives of this chapter, the following four projects are suggested. Choose

any one of them. These projects are for people who would like to make sacrifices for the sake of the community. These go beyond submitting a project report to your instructor or superior. This project is for real. Like several cases in this chapter, you are challenged to take up one of the projects as an individual or as a group. Your test is whether you are able to challenge yourself to make a difference to the community.

A. Poverty alleviation

(a) Create a poverty alleviation project and implement it.

(b) Submit your academic report after six weeks.

(c) Would you like to give up your intended career and dedicate your life to your project?

B. Fighting for gender equality

(a) Select an ongoing gender discrimination case that has taken place in your community.

(b) Help the victim with legal aid and team up to fight the case.

(c) Mobilize public opinion and create a movement.

(d) Manage the people and the media.

(e) File your report after six weeks.

(f) Would you like to continue fighting for this cause?

C. Protection of human rights

Select a human rights case. The rest of the task is similar to that mentioned in section (B) above.

D. Animal rights

(a) Conceive and organize a project for the protection of animal rights.

(b) Find the economic perspective to create a business opportunity.

(c) File a report after six weeks.

(d) Would you like to continue the business?

Management Mantra

Babe: Pig and Farmer

Babe is an Australian film, directed by Chris Noonan and written by Dick King-Smith and others, that won the Academy Award in 1995. It is a modern parable that teaches us several lessons through the verbal communication between humans and animals. The protagonist of the film is a piglet called 'Pig' by its master. The piglet does not want to accept its obvious destiny of ending up as a sumptuous dish on its master's table. He would like to be the farmer's sheepdog instead, but not the usual one that herds the sheep into the pen by force. He would like to rather talk to the sheep and explain why they should voluntarily get into the pen. Despite the ridicule of all, the piglet succeeds. The farmer wins a prize for the efforts of the pig. The farmer and the pig exchange glances. They understand each other.

> MANTRA *Dialogue is the strategy; understanding brings happiness.*

Select References

The list below includes all the referred sources as well as others whose study has helped in the association of ideas. For researchers, students, and executives, it is ideal to pick one thinker or author whose work closely represents their perspective and pursue their research, study, or work, respectively. The following are ready-to-use resources and links for the purpose.

BOOKS

AIMA (1997). *Corporate Governance and Business Ethics*. New Delhi: Excel Books.

Albuquerque, Daniel (1998). *Freedom and Future*. Pondicherry: Sri Aurobindo Ashram.

_____ (2004). *Master's Mind, Manifestations of Consciousness*. Delhi: Originals.

Aurobindo, Sri (1910). *The Supramental Manifestation and Other Writings*. SABCL, Vol. 16, p. 164, Pondicherry: Sri Aurobindo Ashram.

_____ (1970–1973). Sri Aurobindo Birth Centenary Library (27 Volumes). Pondicherry: Sri Aurobindo Ashram.

Aurobindo, Sri and Mother (1995). *A New Education for a New Consciousness*. Pondicherry: Sri Aurobindo Ashram Trust.

Bandyopadhyaya, Anu (2004). *Learning from Gandhi*. New Delhi: Teri Press.

Bhatia, Tej K. (2000). *Advertising in Rural India: Language, Marketing Communication, and Consumerism*. Institute for the Study of Languages and Cultures of Asia and Africa, Tokyo University of Foreign Studies, Tokyo: Tokyo Press.

Brown, Lestor R. (1992). *Zur Rettung des Planeten Erde: Strategien fuer eine oekologish nachhaltige Weltwirtschaft*. Frankfurt am Main, Germany: S. Fischer.

Buckingham, David (2003). *Media Education: Literacy, Learning and Contemporary Culture*. Cambridge, UK: Polity Press.

Burns, James McGregor (1978). *Leadership*. New York: Harper Torchbooks.

Capra, Fritjof (1976). *The Tao of Physics*. Toronto: Bentam Books.

_____ (1992). *The Turning Point*. New York: Simon & Schuster.

Chakraborty, D. and S.K. Chakraborty (2004). *Leadership and Motivation: Cultural Comparisons*. New Delhi: Rupa and Co.

Chakraborty, S.K. (1991). *Management by Values: Towards Cultural Congruence*. New Delhi: Oxford University Press.

_____ (1998). *Value and Ethics for Organizations, Theory and Practice*. New Delhi: Oxford University Press.

_____ (2002). *The Management and Ethics Omnibus*. New Delhi: Oxford University Press.

Chawla, Navin (2003). *Mother Teresa: A Biography.* New Delhi: Penguin Paperbacks.

Chomsky, Noam (1996). *Powers and Prospects.* London: Pluto Press.

Davar, Rustom S. (1997). *The Human Side of Management.* New Delhi: Universal Bookstall.

Dawkins, Richard (2006). *The God Delusion.* Boston: Houghton Mifflin Company.

Debroy, Bibek (ed.) (1998). *Challenges of Globalization.* Delhi: Konark Publishers.

Donaldson, Thomas (1989). *The Ethics of International Business.* New York: Oxford University Press.

Drèze, Jean and Amartya Sen (1989). *Hunger and Public Action.* Oxford: Clarendon Press.

Drucker, Peter F. (1992). *Managing the Non-profit Organization: Practice and Principles.* New York: Harper-Business.

———— (1993). *Post-capitalist Society.* Oxford: Butterworth Heinemann.

———— (2001). *The Essential Drucker: Selections from the Management Works.* New York: Harper-Business.

Fernando, A.C. (2008). *Corporate Governance, Principles, Policies and Practices* (2nd edn). Delhi: Pearson Education.

Fletcher, Alan (2001). *The Art of Looking Sideways.* London: Phaidon Press.

Forester, Tom and Perry Morrison (1993). *Cautionary Tales and Ethical Dilemmas in Computing.* Cambridge, MA: The MIT Press.

Friedman, Thomas L. (2008). *Hot, Flat and Crowded: Why the World Needs a Green Revolution—and How We Can Renew Our Global Future.* London: Penguin.

Freeman, Lee and A. Graham Peace (eds) (2005). *Information Ethics: Privacy and Intellectual Property.* Hershey, PA: Information Science Publishing.

Freeman, R.E. (1984). *Strategic Management: A Stakeholder Approach.* Boston: Pitman.

———— (1984). *Strategic Management: A Stakeholder Approach.* Boston: Pitman.

Friedman, Milton (1962). *Capitalism and Freedom.* Chicago: University of Chicago Press.

Friedman, Thomas (2008). *Hot, Flat and Crowded: Why the World Needs a Green Revolution—and How We Can Renew Our Global Future.* London: Allen Lane.

Fukuyama, F. (2002). *Our Postmodern Future: Consequences of the Biotechnology Revolution.* New York: FSG.

Galbraith, John K. (1978). *The New Industrial State.* Boston: Houghton Mifflin.

———— (1991). *The Affluent Society.* London: Penguin.

———— (2001). *The Essential Galbraith.* Boston: Houghton Mifflin.

Gandhi, M.K. (1948). *Non-violence in Peace and War.* Ahmedabad: Navajivan Publishing House.

Giraudoux, Jean (1945). *The Madwoman of Chaillot.* Evanston, IL: Northwestern University Press.

Goethe, J. (1809). *Elective Affinities.* New York: Penguin (1978).

Greenspan, Alan (2007). *The Age of Turbulence: Adventures in a New World.* New York: Penguin Press.

Hale, Angela and Jane Wills (2007). *Women Working Worldwide: Transnational Networks, Corporate Social Responsibility and Action Research.* University of London: Blackwell Publishing.

Hamilton, Carl (2002). *Absolut: The Biography of a Bottle.* Texere.

Hamish McDonald (1999). *The Polyester Prince, The Rise of Dhirubhai Ambani.* Sydney: Allen & Unwin.

Hargroves, Karlson and Michael H. Smith (eds) (2005). *The Natural Advantage of Nations, Business Opportunities, Innovations and Governance in 21st Century.* London: Earthscan.

Harris, Ian (2000). *Buddhism and Ecology. Contemporary Buddhist Ethics,* ed. Damien Keown. Surrey, UK: Curzon Press.

Hartman, Laura P. and Abha Chatterjee (2007). *Perspectives in Business Ethics.* New Delhi: Tata McGraw-Hill Publishing Co. Ltd.

Hill, Alexander (1998). *Just Business.* Madison, WI: Paternoster Press.

Hofstede, G. (1980). *Cultures Consequences: International Differences in Work-related Values.* Beverly Hills, CA: Sage.

———— (1991). Cultures and Organizations: *Software of the Mind.* New York: McGraw-Hill.

Iyengar, Srinivasa K.R. (1972). *Sri Aurobindo: A Biography and a History.* Pondichery: Sri Aurobindo International Centre of Education.

Johnson, Craig E. (2007). *Ethics in the Workplace.* Delhi: Sage Publications.

Kalam, Abdul A.P.J. (2001). *Wings of Fire.* Hyderabad: University Press.

Kant, Immanuel (1786). *Grundlegung zur Metaphysik der Sitten.* Stuttgart (1998): Philipp Reclam.

———— (1878). *The Critique of Practical Reason,* translation, The Project Gutenberg, e-Book at http://www.gutenberg.org/eteat/5683.

Kapoor, G.K. (2004). *Business and Corporate Laws* (4th edn). Delhi: Sultan Chand & Sons.

Koerner, S. (1955). *Kant.* London: Penguin.

Kotler, Philip (1967). *Marketing Management: Analysis, Planning, and Control* (2003 edn). Englewood Cliffs, NJ: Prentice-Hall.

————. *Strategic Marketing for Nonprofit Organizations* (2009 edn). Upper Saddle River, NJ: Prentice-Hall.

Kotler, Philip and Lee Nancy (2005). *Corporate Social Responsibility.* Hoboken, NJ: John Wiley.

Krishnamurthy, Bala (2005). *Environmental Management.* New Delhi: Prentice-Hall of India.

Kumar, Surender (2002). *Corporate Governance: A Matter of Ethics.* New Delhi: Galgotia Publishers.

Küng, Hans (1990). *Projekt Weltethos.* Muenchen, Germany: Piper.

Lauren, Paul Gordon (2003). *The Evolution of International Human Rights: Visions Seen.* Philadelphia: University of Pennsylvania Press.

Leeson, Nick and Edward Whitley (1996). *Rogue Trader: How I Brought Down Barings Bank and Shook the Financial World.* New York: Little Brown and Company.

Malhotra, N.K. and D.F. Birks (2006). *Marketing Research: An Applied Approach.* Harlow, UK: Prentice-Hall.

Mead, George Herbert (1934). *Mind, Self, and Society,* ed. Charles W. Morris. Chicago: University of Chicago Press.

Milgrom, Paul and John Roberts (1992). *Economics, Organization and Management.* London: Prentice-Hall.

Miller, Arthur (1976). *Death of a Salesman.* New Jersey: Penguin.

Morita Akio, Edwin Reingold, and Mitsuko Shimomura (1986). *Made in Japan.* New York: Dutton.

Nicholls, A. (2006). *Social Entrepreneurship: New Models of Sustainable Social Change.* Oxford: Oxford University Press.

Nietzsche, Friedrich (1886). *Beyond Good and Evil,* p. 108, (tr) Walter Kaufmann. New York: Vintage Books.

Obama, Barack (2007). *Audacity of Hope: Thoughts on Reclaiming the American Dream.* New York: Three Rivers Press.

Pascal, Blaise (1670). *Pensees,* p. 67, (tr) W.F. Trotter. New York: Random House (1941).

Peirce, C.S. (1879). *How to Make Our Ideas Clear.* Bloomington, IN: Indiana University Press (1992).

Peterson, Robert A. and Oc Ferrell (2005). *Business Ethics, New Challenges for Business Schools and Corporate Leaders.* New Delhi: Printice-Hall of India.

Pfeffer, J. (1998). *The Human Equation: Building Profits by Putting People First.* Boston, MA: Harvard Business School Press.

Pollard, C.W. (1996). *The Soul of the Firm.* Grand Rapids, MI: Harper Business and Zondervan Publishing House.

Prahalad, C.K. (2005). *The Fortune at the Bottom of the Pyramid: Eradicating Poverty through Profits*. Wharton: Wharton School of Publishing.

Prahalad, C.K. and M.S. Krishnan (2008). *The New Age of Innovation*. New Delhi: Tata McGraw-Hill Publishing.

Rajagopalan, R. (2003). *Directors and Corporate Governance*. Chennai: Company Law Institute of India Pvt. Ltd.

_____ (2005). *Environmental Studies: From Crisis to Cure* (4th edn). Delhi: Oxford University Press.

Rangarajan, L.N. (tr) (1987). *Kautilya: The Arthashastra*. London: Penguin.

Rawls, John (1971). *A Theory of Justice*. Cambridge, MA: Belknap.

Regan, T. (1983). *The Case for Animal Rights*. Berkeley: University of California.

Roberts, J. (2004). *The Modern Firm: Organization Design for Performance and Growth*. New York: Oxford University Press.

Rugman, A.M and T.L. Brewer (2003). *Oxford Handbook of International Business*. Oxford: Oxford University Press.

Sen, Amartya (1982). *Choice, Welfare and Measurement*. Oxford: Basil Blackwell.

_____ (1990). *On Ethics and Economics*. New Delhi: Oxford University Press.

_____ (1992). *Inequality Reexamined*. Oxford: Oxford University Press.

_____ (1999). *Development as Freedom*. Oxford: Oxford University Press.

Senge, Peter (1990). *The Fifth Discipline: The Art and Practice of Learning Organizations*. New York: Doubleday.

Sharma, Subhash (2006). *Management in New Age, Western Windows Eastern Doors* (2nd edn). New Delhi: New Age International Publishers.

_____ (2007). *New Mantras in Corporate Corridors, From Ancient Roots to Global Routes*. New Delhi: New Age International Publishers.

Shekar, R.C. (2002). *Ethical Choices in Business* (2nd edn). Delhi: Response Books.

Shultz, Uwe (1990). *Kant*. Hamburg: Rowohlt.

Singer, Peter (1979). *Practical Ethics* (reprint 1990). New York: Cambridge University Press.

Singh, M.F. (2001). *Honest Living* (4th edn). Delhi: Radha Swaami Satsang Beas.

SIPRI Yearbook (2008). *Armaments, Disarmament and International Security*. Oxford: Oxford University Press.

Smith, Adam (1759). *The Theory Of Moral Sentiments*. Oxford: Oxford University Press.

_____ (1776). *Wealth of Nations*. London: W. Strahan and T. Cadell.

Smith J.W. (2003). *Cooperative Capitalism: A Blueprint for Global Peace and Prosperity*. Quality Books Inc.

Solomon, R.C. (2003). *Ethics and Excellence*. Oxford: Oxford University Press.

Sternberg, R.J. (1997). *Thinking Styles*. New York: Cambridge University Press.

Sundaram, P.S. (tr) (1990). *Thiruvalluvar: The Kural*. London: Penguin.

Suppes, Patrick (1967). 'Decision Theory,' in *Encyclopedia of Philosophy*, pp. 310–14, ed. P. Edwards, Vol. 1, Macmillan Publishing, London, reprint 1972.

Tagore, Rabindranath (1916). *Stray Birds*. Gloucestershire, UK: Dodo Press.

Tennyson, Alfred Lord (1837). *Locksley Hall*. http://home.att.net/~tennysonpoetry/ci.htm.

_____ (1859). 'Guinevere', *Idylls of the King*. http://www.enotes.com/nineteenth-century-criticism/idylls-king-alfred-lord-tennyson.

The Institute of Company Secretaries of India (2003). *Corporate Governance* (6th edn). Delhi: Taxmann.

Valesquez, Manuel G. (1997). *Business Ethics: Concepts and Cases*. New Jersey: Printice Hall.

William, James (1896). *The Will to Believe and Other Essays in Popular Philosophy*. New York: Longmans 2006.

Zimbardo, Philip F. (2007). *Lucifer Effect: Understanding How Good People Turn Evil.* New York: Random House.

COMPENDIA

Flew, Anthony (1979). *A Dictionary of Philosophy.* London: McMillan Press.

Picktall, Mohammed Marmaduke (1994). *The Meaning of the Glorious Qur'an* (trasl). Delhi: Madhur Sandesh Sangam.

The New Jerusalem Bible. Darton Longman & Todd, London, pocket edn, 1990.

The Oxford Dictionary of Quotations. Oxford: Oxford University Press, 1985.

Tripp, Rhoda Thomas (compiler) (1972). *The International Thesaurus of Quotations.* London: Penguin.

Walker, Benjamin (1983). *Hindu World: An Encyclopedic Survey of Hinduism* (2 vol.). London: Allen & Unwin.

JOURNALS AND ARTICLES

Abdolmohammadi, M. and J. Sultan (2002). 'Ethical reasoning and the use of insider information in stock trading', *Journal of Business Ethics* 37(2):165–173.

Armstrong, R.W. (1996). 'The relationship between culture and perception of ethical problems in international marketing', *Journal of Business Ethics* 15(11):1199–1208.

Ashley, Caroline and Gareth Haysom (2006). 'From philanthropy to a different way of doing business: Strategies and challenges in integrating pro-poor approaches into tourism business', *Development Southern Africa* 23(2).

Bahujan Students (2007). 'Premier institute or the hub of caste discrimination', *Network (BSN)* (this report is prepared by Network (BSN) with the help of students of IISc Banglore September 2007).

Bamett, T. (2001). 'Dimensions of moral intensity and ethical decision making: An empirical study', *Journal of Applied Social Psychology* 31(5):1038–1057.

Baucus, Melissa S., William I. Norton, Jr., David A., and Sherrie Baucus E. (2008). 'Human fostering creativity and innovation without encouraging unethical behavior', *Journal of Business Ethics* 81:97–115.

Beauchamp, Tom L. (1992). 'The moral standing of animals in medical research', *The Journal of Law, Medicine & Health Care* 20(1–2), Spring–Summer, 7–16.

Bluhm Louis H. (1987). 'Trust, terrorism, and technology', *Journal of Business Ethics* 6:333–341.

Borkowski, S.C. and T.J. Ugras (1998). 'Business students and ethics: A meta-analysis', *Journal of Business Ethics* 17(11):1117–1127.

Burger, Kenneth R., 'A brief history of packaging', University of Florida. See http://edis.ifas.ufl.edu/pdffiles/AE/AE20600.pdf.

Carroll, A.B. (1979). 'A three-dimensional conceptual model of corporate social performance', *Academy of Management Review* 4(4):497–505.

Chatzidakis, Andreas, Sally Hibbert, Darryn Mittusis, and Andrew Smith (2004). 'Virtue in consumption?', *Journal of Marketing Management* 20:527–544.

Chaves, Jorge Arturo (2002). 'Economic democracy, social dialogue, and ethical analysis: Theory and practice', *Journal of Business Ethics* 39:153–159.

Chiu, Hung-Chang, Yi-Ching Hsieh, and Mei-Chien Wang (2008). 'How to encourage customers to use legal software', *Journal of Business Ethics* 80:583–595.

Chun, Liu (2008). 'How does morality evaluate public works? Justifications in a community-based environmental dispute in Shenzhen', *Chinese Sociology and Anthropology* 40(2):(Winter 2007–8) 35–64.

Chung, Grace and Sara M. Grimes (2005). 'Data mining the kids: Surveillance and market research strategies in children's online games', *Canadian Journal of Communication* 30:527–548.

Conn, Cynthia E. (2008). 'Integrating writing skills and ethics training in business communication pedagogy: A résumé case study exemplar', *Business Communication Quarterly* 71(2):138–151.

Cullinan, C. Dennis Bline et al. (2008). 'Organization-harm vs organization-gain ethical issues: An exploratory examination of the effects of organizational commitment', *Journal of Business Ethics* 80:225–235.

Dabholkar, P.A. and J.J. Kellaris (1992). 'Toward understanding marketing students' ethical judgment of controversial personal selling practices', *Journal of Business Research* 24:313–329.

Das, Sandip (15 June 2007). 'Caste discrimination at workplace', *Down to Earth*, http://www.downtoearth. org.in.

Dawson, L.M. (1969). 'The human concept: New philosophy for business', *Business Horizons*.

———— (1992). 'Will feminization change the ethics of the sales profession?', *Journal of Personal Selling and Sales Management* 13:21–32.

Donaldson, T. and W.T. Dunfee (1994). 'Towards a unified conception of business ethics: Integrative social contracts theory', *Academy of Management Review* 19(2):252–284.

Doran, Caroline Josephine (2009). 'The role of personal values in fair trade consumption', *Journal of Business Ethics* 84:549–563.

Drucker, Peter F. (1981). 'What is "business ethics"?', *The Public Interest* 63:18–36.

Everett, Jeff Dean Neu Abu Shiraz Rahaman (2006). 'The global fight against corruption: A Foucaultian, virtues-ethics framing', *Journal of Business Ethics* 65:1–12.

Ferrell, O.C. and L.G. Gresham (1985). 'A contingency framework for understanding ethical decision making in marketing', *Journal of Marketing* 49 (Summer):87–96.

Forsyth, D.R. (1980). 'A taxonomy of ethical ideologies', *Journal of Personality and Social Psychology* 38(1): 175–184.

———— (1992). 'Judging the morality of business practices: The influence of personal moral philosophies', *Journal of Business Ethics* 11(May):461–470.

Frederick, W.C. (1991). 'The moral authority of transnational corporate codes', *Journal of Business Ethics* 10:165–177.

Freestone, Oliver M. and Peter J. McGoldrick (2008). 'Motivations of the ethical consumer', *Journal of Business Ethics* 79:445–467.

Friedman, Milton (1970). The Counter Revolution in Monetary Theory (lecture at University of London), London: Institute of Economic Affairs.

———— (1970). 'The social responsibility of business is to increase its profits', *The New York Times Magazine* 13 September.

Friedrich, J.P. and O.C. Ferrell (1992). 'The impact of perceived risk and moral philosophy type on ethical decision making in business organizations', *Journal of Business Research* 24(4):283–295.

Ganesh, J., M.J. Arnold, and K.E. Reynolds (2000). 'Understanding the customer base of service providers: An examination of the differences between switchers and stayers', *Journal of Marketing* 64(3):65–87.

Ghoshal, S. (2005). 'Bad management theories are destroying good management practices', *Academy of Management Learning & Education* 4(1):75–91.

Grant, Colin (2002). 'Whistleblowers: Saints of secular culture', *Journal of Business Ethics* 39(4).

Groves, Kevin, Charles Vance, and Yongsun Paik (2008). 'Linking linear/nonlinear thinking style balance and managerial ethical decision-making', *Journal of Business Ethics* 80:305–325.

Handy, Charles (2002). 'What's a business for?', *Harvard Business Review* 80(12):49–55.

Harrington, S.J. (1997). 'A test of a person-issue contingent model of ethical decision making in organizations', *Journal of Business Ethics* 16(4):363–375.

Hofmann, Eva and Erik Hoelzl (2008). 'A comparison of models describing the impact of moral decision making on investment decisions', *Journal of Business Ethics* 82:171–187.

Jamali, Dima J (2008). 'A stakeholder approach to corporate social responsibility: A fresh perspective into theory and practice', *Journal of Business Ethics* 82:213–231.

Jenkins, Gregory J., Donald R. Deis, Jean C. Bedard, and Mary B. Curtis (2008). 'Accounting firm culture and goverannce: A research synthesis', *Behavioral Research Accounting* 20(1):45–74.

Johnson, Samuel (1759). *The Idler, Weekly Gazette,* no. 40, 20 January.

Jose, San Leire and José Luis Retolaza (2008). 'Information transparency as a differentiation factor of ethical banking in Europe: A radical affinity index approach', *The ICFAI University Journal of Bank Management,* Vol. VII, No. 3.

Karen Lightstone and Cathy Driscoll (2008). 'Disclosing elements of disclosure: A test of legitimacy theory and company ethics', *Canadian Journal of Administrative Sciences (Revue canadienne des sciences de l'administration)* 25:7–21.

Kashyap, R., R. Mir, and E. Iyer (2006). 'Toward responsive pedagogy: Linking social responsibility to firm performance issues in the classroom', *Academy of Management Learning & Education* 5(3): 366–376.

Katz, A. (2005). 'A network effects perspective on software piracy', *University of Toronto Law Journal* 55(2):155–216.

Khera, I.P. (2001). 'Business ethics east vs. west: Myths and realities', *Journal of Business Ethics* 30:29–39.

Koenig, Philip C. and Robert C. Waters (2002). 'Adam Smith on management', *Business and Society Review* 107(2):241–253.

Krishnan, Gopal V. and Linda M. Parsons (2008). 'Getting to the bottom line: An exploration of gender and earnings quality', *Journal of Business Ethics* 78:65–76.

Kulshrestha, P. (2007). 'Economics, ethics and business ethics: A critique of interrelationships', *International Journal of Business Governance and Ethics* 3(1):33–41.

Lim, Suk-Jun and Joe PhillipsEmbedding (2008). 'CSR Values: The global footwear industry's evolving governance structure', *Journal of Business Ethics* 81:143–156.

Livingston, J.S. (1971). 'Myth of the well-educated manager', *Harvard Business Review* 49(1):79–89.

Martin, K. and R.E. Freeman: (2003). 'Some problems with employee monitoring', *Journal of Business Ethics* 43:353–361.

McCoy, Bowen H. (1983). 'The parable of the sadhu', *Corporate Ethics, Harvard Business Review,* Sept–Oct.

Millington, Andrew and Markus Eberhardt and Barry Wilkinson (2005). 'Gift giving, *quanxi* and illicit payments in buyer–supplier relations in China: Analysing the experience of UK companies', *Journal of Business Ethics* 57:255–268.

Milton-Smith John (2002). 'Ethics, the Olympics and the search for global values', *Journal of Business Ethics* 35:13–42.

Moor, J. (1985). 'What is computer ethics?', *Metaphilosophy* 16(4), pp. 266–75, 269. Malden, MA: Wiley and Blackwell.

Myring, Mark J. and Robert Bloom (2007). 'International transfer pricing and intellectual property: The Prime Co Case', *Issues in Accounting Education* 22(4):769–774.

Nyberg, Daniel (2008). 'The morality of everyday activities: Not the right, but the good thing to do', *Journal of Business Ethics* 81:587–598.

O'Higgins, Eleanor R.E. (2006). 'Corruption, underdevelopment, and extractive resource industries: Addressing the vicious cycle', *Business Ethics Quarterly* 16(2).

Oliver, M. and Peter J. McGoldrick (2008). 'Freestone motivations of the ethical consumer', *Journal of Business Ethics* 79:445–467.

Parboteeah, K. Praveen and Edward Andrew Kapp (2008). 'Ethical climates and workplace safety behaviors: An empirical investigation', *Journal of Business Ethics* 80:515–529.

Parrett, William G. (2004). 'Globalization's next frontier–Principled codes of conduct that bolster the rule of law', *Business and Society Review* 109(4):577–582.

Pelletier, Kathie, L. Michelle, and C. Bligh (2008). 'The aftermath of organizational corruption: Employee attributions and emotional reactions', *Journal of Business Ethics* 80:823–844.

Roberts, Mason (1974). 'What's a PR director for anyway?', *Harvard Busienss Review*, Sept–Oct.

Robin, S. Snell and Neil C. Herndon, Jr. (2004). 'Hong Kong's code of ethics initiative: Some differences between theory and practice', *Journal of Business Ethics* 51:75–89.

Roehling, M.V., M.A. Cavanaugh, L.M. Moynihan, and W.R. Boswell: (2000). 'The nature of the new employment relationship: A content analysis of the practitioner and academic literatures', *Human Resource Management* 39(4):305–320.

Sachitanand, Rahul (2007). 'Get a privacy shield', *Business Today*, 17 August.

Shaw, William H. (2009). 'Marxism, business ethics, and corporate social responsibility', *Journal of Business Ethics* 84:565–576.

Shrivastava, P. (1995). 'The role of corporations in achieving ecological sustainability', *Academy of Management Review* 20:936–960.

Singer, P. (1979). 'Not for humans only: The Place of non-humans in environmental issues', *Ethics and Problems of the 21st Century*, eds K. Goodpaster and K. Sayre, 191–206,. Notre Dame: University of Notre Dame Press.

Sloane, Stephen Burton (2008). 'Creative rebellion and moral efficiency as elements of managerial ideology', *Journal of Business Ethics* 81:609–622.

Soares, Conceicaçõ (2007). 'Corporate legal responsibility: A Levinasian perspective', *Journal of Business Ethics* 81:545–553.

Steenhaut, Sarah and Patrick Van Kenhove (2005). 'Relationship commitment and ethical consumer behavior in a retail setting: The case of receiving too much change at the checkout', *Journal of Business Ethics* 56:335–353.

Steinberg, R. (2006). 'Economic theories of nonprofit organizations', eds W.W. Powell and R. Steinberg, *The Nonprofit Sector: A Research Handbook* 13–31. New Haven: Yale University Press.

Steven D. Jamar (2007). 'Resolving intellectual property license disputes out of court', *The Computer & Internet Lawyer* 24(9):24–32.

Stratton, W.E., W.R. Flynn, and G.A. Johnson: (1981). 'Moral development and decision making: A study of student ethics', *Journal of Enterprise Management* 3:35–41.

Surie, Gita and Allan Ashley (2008). 'Integrating pragmatism and ethics in entrepreneurial leadership for sustainable value creation', *Journal of Business Ethics* 81:235–246.

Thomas, Shibu (2008). 'Allergy not occupational hazard: HC', *Times of India*, 30 April, p. 6.

Tian, Qing (2008). 'Perception of business bribery in China: The impact of moral philosophy', *Journal of Business Ethics* 80:437–445.

Tian, Zhilong, Haitao Gao, and Malcolm Cone (2008). 'A study of the ethical issues of private entrepreneurs participating in politics in China', *Journal of Business Ethics* 80:627–642.

Vignon, Jerome (1989). 'Economic constraints and ethical decisions in the context of European ventures', *Journal of Business Ethics* 8:663–666.

Vitell, S.J., A. Singhapakdi, and J. Thomas (2001). 'Consumer ethics: An application and empirical testing of the Hunt–Vitell Theory of ethics', *Journal of Consumer Marketing* 18(2):153–178.

Vitell, S.J., and A. Singhapakdi (1993). 'Ethical ideology and its influence on the norms and judgments of marketing practitioners', *Journal of Marketing Management* 3(Spring/Summer):1–11.

Vitell, S.J., K. Rallapalli, and A. Singhapakdi (1993). 'Marketing Norms: The influences of personal moral philosophies and organizational ethical culture', *Journal of the Academy of Marketing Science* 21(Fall):331–337.

Vitell, Scott J., Joseph G.P. PaoUllo, and Jatinder J. Singh (2005). 'Religiosity and consumer ethics', *Journal of Business Ethics* 57:175–181.

Waddock, Sandra (2004). 'Creating corporate accountability: Foundational principles to make corporate citizenship real', *Journal of Business Ethics* 50:313–327.

Weller, Steven (1988). 'The elffectiveness of corporate codes of ethics', *Journal of Business Ethics* 7:389–395.

West, Andrew (2008). 'Sartrean existentialism and ethical decision-making in business', *Journal of Business Ethics* 81:15–25.

Yu, Xiaomin (2008). 'Impacts of corporate code of conduct on labor standards: A case study of Reebok's athletic footwear supplier factory in China', *Journal of Business Ethics* 81:513–529.

WEBLINKS

E-Encyclopedia and Compendia

Business Ethics: http://www.fact-archive.com/encyclopedia/Business_ethics.
Catholic Encyclopedia: www.newadvent.org.
Encyclopedia and Dictionary: http://www.answers.com/library.
http://www.britannica.com/Encyclopedia Britannica: www.eb.com.
Encyclopedia of Ethics: http://www.routledge-philosophy.com.
Glossary: www.glossarist.com/glossaries/business/management.
Internet Encyclopedia of Philosophy: http://www.iep.utm.edu.
Investor online: http://www.investopedia.com.
Online Encyclopedia: http://en.wikipedia.org/.
Online Guide to Ethics and Moral Philosophy: http://caae.phil.cmu.edu.
Routledge Guide: www.routledgestudents.com.
Stanford Encyclopedia: lato.stanford.edu.
World Fact Book: http://www.cia.gov/cia/publications/factbook.

E-Books and Links on Thinkers and Leaders

For the following authors: Aristotle, Plato, Immanuel Kant, Friedrich Nietzsche, Marx Karl and Frederick Engel, James William, Robert Frost, C.S. Peirce, Thomas Aquinas, Thiruvelluvar,

Chanakya, Bertrand Russell, Mao Tse-tung, Adam Smith, John Maynard Keynes, David Recardo, William Stanley Jevons, etc.

http://www.gutenberg.org/browse/authors.
Bhagvad Gita: www.gita-society.com.
Mahatma Gandhi: http://www.mkgandhi.org Comprehensive link on Thinkers: www.epistemelinks.com.
B.R. Ambedkar: http://www.ambedkar.org/.
Karl Marx: http://www.marxists.org/archive/marx/works/1867-c1/ch06.htm.
http://www.narmada.org/resources/books/.
Albert Gore: http://www.algore.com/.
Trial of Warren Hastings, Edmund Burke: http://www.bartleby.com.
http://www.ourcivilisation.com.
Indian business leaders: http://www.indiaprofile.com.
http://www.funonthenet.in/forums/index.

E-News Papers, Magazines, and Portals
International

http://topics.developmentgateway.org.
http://www.thaindian.com/newsportal.
http://www.reuters.com/.
http://www.time.com.
Wall Street Journal: http://online.wsj.com.
http://www.cnn.com.
http://www.washingtonpost.com.
http://www.guardian.co.uk.

National

http://timesofindia.indiatimes.com.
http://www.rediff.com/money/.
http://www.asianage.com.
http://www.indianexpress.com.
http://www.blonnet.com.
http://newsblaze.com.
http://www.tehelka.com.
http://www.zeenews.com.
http://infochangeindia.org.
http://indiatodaygroup.com.
www.mapsofindia.com.

International Organizations

Basel Accord: http://www.nationmaster.com/encyclopedia/Basel-Accord.
Brundtland Commission: http://www.un.org/documents/ga/res/42/ares42-187.htm.
GAAP: www.gaap.com.
ILO: www.ilo.org.

International Monetary Fund: http://www.imf.org.

OECD: http://www.oecd.org.

The Commission on Global Governance: see: http://www.cgg.ch.

The World Development Report 2001/2: http://www.worldbank.org/poverty/wdrpoverty/report/index.htm.

United Nations Organization: http://www.un.org.

WHO: http://www.who.int/en/.

World Bank Development Report, 2003: http://econ.worldbank.org/wdr/.

World Bank: www.worldbank.org.

World Trade Organization: www.wto.org/english/docs_e/legal_e/27-trips_02_e.htm.

WTO: www.wto.org.

National Organizations

Transparency International India: www.transparencyindia.org.

Indian GAAP: http://rbidocs.rbi.org.in/rdocs/PublicationReport/Pdfs/18354.pdf.

http://ncw.nic.in/pdfreports/Sexual%20Harassment%20at%20Workplace%20(English).pdf.

Dalit: http://www.pucl.org/from-archives/Dalit-tribal/mandal-2.htm.

http://www.cmsindia.org/cms/highlights.pdf.

http://www.combatlaw.org/information.php?article_id=277&issue_id=11.

ASCI: http://www.ascionline.org.

Banking: http://www.banknetindia.com/board/817.html.

National for Laboratory Animal Research: http://icmr.nic.in/nclas.htm.

http://www4.nationalacademies.org.

Indian Statistics: www.indiastat.com.

Ethics

Comprehensive links: http://www.ethicsandbusiness.org/links/.

www.business-ethics.com.

http://www.computerethicsinstitute.org.

http://www.ethicsweb.ca.

www.questia.com.

www.societyforbusinessethics.org.

www.web-miner.com.

Sample: code of conduct P&G: http://www.pghhcl.in/download/codeofconduct.pdf.

Government of India

http://cyberjournalist.org.in/links.html.

Capital Market Regulatory Authority: http://www.sebi.gov.in.

National Highway Authority of India: www.nhai.org.

Ministry of Corporate Governance: http://www.mca.gov.in.

SEZ: http://sezindia.nic.in.

CBI: http://www.cbi.gov.in.

Law

Constitution of India: http://india.gov.in/govt/documents/english/coi_part_full.pdf.
Supreme Court Cause List: http://causelists.nic.in/scnew/index1.html.
The Gazette of India: http://gazetteofindia.org.
Texts: http://www.laws4india.com/acts/labourlaws.
Labour: http://labourbureau.nic.in/reports.htm.
Wages: http://labour.nic.in/wagecell.
Court Case Discussion: http://www.combatlaw.org.
General: http://www.elaw.org.
Women: http://ncw.nic.in/Amendments%20to%20laws%20relating%20to%20women.pdf.

Business

Government portal: http://www.business.gov.in.
http://www.business-standard.com.
www.financialexpress.com.
www.globalbusinessinsights.com.
http://economictimes.indiatimes.com.
http://www.rediff.com/money.
http://www.usatoday.com/money.
http://www.ciadvertising.org/studies/student/98_fall/theory/weirtz/classic.htm.
http://sify.com/finance.
http://www.guardian.co.uk/business.
http://www.crowdedsite.com.
www.thehindubusinessline.com.
www.business-standard.com.

Management

http://harvardbusiness.org.
http://www.managementparadise.com.
http://www.mindtools.com.
http://www.sevenpillers.com.

Human Resource

Sexual harassment: http://www.epw.org.in/epw/uploads/articles/8254.pdf.
http://www.sambhavindia.org/PDF/Sexual%20Harrassment%20at%20.
Workplace: http://www.pluggd.in/indian-it-industry/workplace-ethics-indian-companies-teamlease-survey-2373/.
International Labour Organization: http://www.ilo.org.
www.managementhelp.org/ethics.
www.allbusiness.com/human-resources/...ethics.
www.humanresources.about.com.
Trade Union: rajyasabha.nic.in/book2/reports/ethics/3rdreport.htm.

http://www.vakilno1.com/bareacts/tradeunionact/tradeunionact.htm.
www.tradeunionindia.org.
http://labourbureau.nic.in/TU%202k2%20Chapter%201.htm.

Economy

http://www.economist.com/.
http://www.econlib.org.
http://www.econlib.org.
http://www.freemaninstitute.com.
http://papers.ssrn.com.

Finance

The Institute of Chartered Accountant of India: http://www.icai.org.
Finance and accounting: http://www.iasplus.com/index.htm.
Articles and finance problems: http://www.articlesbase.com/finance-articles.
Code for accountants: www.cvc.nic.in/codeethics.pdf.
Managerial accounts: www.managementaccountant.in.
http://www.investopedia.com/terms/g/gaap.asp.
Accounting standards of the world: http://www.iasplus.com.

Consumer Rights

Ministry of consumer affairs and food and distribution: http://fcamin.nic.in/.
http://fcamin.nic.in/Events/EventListing.asp?Section=Consumer%20Rights&ID_PK=18&ParentID=0
    Consumer Unity and Trust Society: http://www.cuts-international.org.
Consumer grievance: http://www.direct.gov.uk/en/Governmentcitizensandrights/Yourrightsand
    responsibilities/DG_10015892www.settlement.org.
Consumer education: www.consumer-voice.org/consumerrights.

Scams and Whistleblowing

Scams: http://www.ivarta.com.
Bofors: http://www.indianexpress.com/oldstory.php?storyid=86371.
http://www.nytimes.com/2008/12/09/world/asia/09china.html?ref=todayspaper.
Conflict of interest: http://greatbong.net/2005/08/29/conflict-of-interest/.
http://www.marketoracle.co.uk/Article11965.html.
http://www.basel-ii-risk.com/Investors/Infamous-and-worst-Investors/Financial-Scams.htm.
Indian scams: http://www.suchetadalal.com/?id=baebd5a4-0b2c-eda7-492e8a70763c&base=
    sub_sections_content&f&t=10+years+of+financial+scams.
Business scams: http://www.quatloos.com.
Business fraud: http://www.fraudaid.com.
Whistleblowing: http://whistleblowing.org.
http://www.theglobalfund.org/documents/oig/Whistle-blowing_Policy_for_the_ secretariat.pdf.
http://indiblog.com/88/whistleblowing-is-a-deadly-affair.

Corporate Governance and CSR

General: www.academyofcg.org.

General aspects of corporate governance or Cadbury Report: http://www.ecgi.org/codes/documents/cadbury.pdf.

Corporate governance: http://www.corpgov.net/library/olarticles.html.

National Foundation for Corporate Governance: http://www.nfcgindia.org.

Sarbanes–Oxley: http://www.soxlaw.com.

CSR example: http://www.infosys.com/infosys_foundation.

Stakeholder: http://www.stakeholderforum.org/.

Corporate initiative: http://www.businessroundtable.org/initiatives/leadership/governance.

Caux: Caux Round Table: www.cauxroundtable.org.

Best practices: http://rru.worldbank.org/PapersLinks/Codes-Best-Practice.

OECD: http://www.oecd.org/dataoecd/20/60/40809412.pdf.

Compliance: http://www.corporatecomplianceinsights.com.

http://www.hp.com/hpinfo/globalcitizenship/csr.

IT and IPR

Standards for Internet security: www.cisecurity.org.

Gaming: www.worldofwarcraft.com.

Crime: http://cybercrime.planetindia.net/conmen_in_rs400m_sms_scam_arrested.htm.

E-governance: http://www.it.iitb.ac.in/~prathabk/egovernance/egov.html.

Computer fraud and abuse statute: http://cio.doe.gov/Documents.

Copyrights: http://www.lib.ncsu.edu/scc.

Information security: http://www.isaca.org.

IPR: http://www.digital-law.net/IJCLP.

http://plato.stanford.edu.

http://www.eff.org/Intellectual_property.

http://chortle.ccsu.ctstateu.edu/law_ethics/index.html.

http://www.linuxinsider.com/story/63421.html.

http://www.technewsworld.com.

Fair use: http://fairuse.stanford.edu.

http://www.britannica.com/EBchecked/topic/911774/intellectual-property-law/231532/Economic-and-ethica.

Privacy: http://www.privacyinternational.org.

Industry

http://www.forbes.com.

SEZ: http://in.diarealestate.com/2008/07/india-sez-statewise-statistics.html.

Websites for company profile, mission, codes, HR policies, etc.

Tata Motors: http://tatamotors.com.

Hindustan Unilever Limited: http://www.hul.co.in.

History of packaging: http://edis.ifas.ufl.edu/pdffiles/AE/AE20600.pdf.

Dabur India: http://www.dabur.com.
Amul: http://www.amul.com.
Satyam: http://www.satyam.com.
Airlines: http://www.indianairlinesblog.com/.
http://www.hindustan.org/forum.
ITC: http://www.itcportal.com.
Inforsys: http://www.infosys.com.
Suzlon: http://www.suzlon.com.
Reliance: http://www.ril.com.
State Bank of India: http://www.sbi.co.in.
Oil and Gas Corporation: http://www.ongcindia.com.
Larsen and Toubro: http://www.lntecc.com.
Housing Development Finance Corporation: http://www.hdfc.com.
Tata Consultancy Services: http://www.tcs.com.

Environment

United Nations Environment Programme: www.unep.org.
Water: www.worldwatercouncil.org.
Fossil fuel energy: www.wsscc.org.
Renewable energy and sustainability: http://solstice.crest.org.
http://www.ifc.org/ifcext/sustainability.nsf.
Climate change: www.climatechange.org.
Environmental law: www.enn.com.
Energy Resource Institute: www.teriin.org.
Magazine: http://www.downtoearth.org.in.
Report of the World Commission: http://www.un-documents.net/wced-ocf.htm.
Greenpeace site: http://archive.greenpeace.org.
Biodiversity: www.biodiversity.org.
UN world conservation monitoring: www.unep-wcmc.org.

Global Affairs and Human Development and Rights

UN Millennium Goals: http://www.un.org/millenniumgoals.
War and peace: http://www.warandpeace.ru/en/commentaries.
Arms trade: http://www.cafi-online.org/arms-trade-treaty.php.
Animal rights: http://animalrights.change.org.
Chomsky: http://www.zmag.org/content/ForeignPolicy/chomskyglobeterr.cfm.
http://www.freerepublic.com.
Global issues: http://www.globalissues.org.
SIPRI 100: http://www.sipri.org/contents/milap/milex/aprod/sipridata.html.
http://www.theglobeandmail.com.
http://www.globalexchange.org.
Council on foreign relations: www.cfr.org.
World Audit of Democracy and Human Rights: www.worldaudit.org.

http://www.globalexchange.org.
Amnesty International: www.amnesty.org.
UN Children's Fund: www.unicef.org.
UN Development Programme: www.ndp.
UN Human Rights: www.un.org/en/rights/.
National Human Rights Commission: www nhrc.nic.in.

NGO/NPO

Socio-economic, political, environmental, and global issues: http://www.indiatogether.org.
Global food and refuge crisis: http://www.oxfam.org.uk/press/releases/target.htm.
Ken Sarowiwa: http://wiwavshell.org/the-case-against-shell/.
Narmada Bachao Andolan: http://www.narmada.org.
Centre for Social Research and Empowerment: www.csrindia.org.
Social markets: www.csmworld.org.
Centre for Science and Environment: www.cseindia.org.
Rural health: http://www.digi-help.com.
Governance: http://www.it.iitb.ac.in/~prathabk/egovernance/egov.html.
Poverty: http://www.standagainstpoverty.org/en.

Research Agencies and Expert Blogs

Erst and Young: www.ey.com/india.
McKinsey: www.mckinseyquarterly.com.
http://www.mckinsey.com/locations/india/mckinseyonindia/.
Council on Foreign Relations: http://www.cfr.org/index.html.
Sucheta Dalal, capital market specialist: http://www.suchetadalal.com.
Lauren Bloom: http://www.thebusinessethicsblog.com.
Chris McDonald: http://www.businessethicsblog.com.
New York Times: http://boss.blogs.nytimes.com.
Indian current affairs: http://indiancurrentaffairs.blogspot.com.
Current finance and accounting practices: http://www.deloitte.com/.
http://harvardbusiness.org.
Leadership: www.ethicalleadershipgroup.com/blog.

Index